Five Months in Berlin

Publication Series of the Landesarchiv Berlin

Edited by Uwe Schaper

Volume 21

Five Months in Berlin

Letters of Edgar N. Johnson from Occupied Germany

Edited by
Werner Breunig and Jürgen Wetzel

DE GRUYTER
OLDENBOURG

The German edition was published in 2014 with the title "Fünf Monate in Berlin. Briefe von Edgar N. Johnson aus dem Jahre 1946."
All translations from German into English: Sage Anderson, PhD.

MIX
Papier aus verantwortungsvollen Quellen
FSC® C016439
www.fsc.org

ISBN 978-3-11-064681-8
e-ISBN (PDF) 978-3-11-065105-8
e-ISBN (EPUB) 978-3-11-064693-1
Library of Congress Control Number: 2019944878

Bibliographic information published by the Deutsche Nationalbibliothek
The Deutsche Nationalbibliothek lists this publication in the Deutsche Nationalbibliografie; detailed bibliographic data are available on the Internet at http://dnb.dnb.de.

Cover illustration: Edgar N. Johnson (right) and his Executive Officer Elliott W. Schryver, Munich, July 1945 (The University of Chicago Library, Special Collections Research Center, Chicago, Illinois, USA, Edgar N. Johnson Papers).
Printing and binding: Hubert & Co. GmbH & Co. KG, Göttingen

www.degruyter.com

Contents

Preface to the German Edition

Edgar N. Johnson, Professor of European History at the University of Nebraska, came to the four-power city of Berlin at the beginning of March 1946 to take on important assignments for the American military government. Appointed as Special Assistant by General Lucius D. Clay, Deputy Military Governor, he was simultaneously assigned to act as Political Adviser to the American Commandant of Berlin. Johnson's letters to his wife, Emily, along with a report written after his stay in Germany, give a detailed account of his five months in the former Reich capital, his encounters with political actors of the occupation and German political and cultural figures, as well as his observations, thoughts, and insights. These records open up a multifaceted panorama of everyday life during occupation and the political reconstruction of Berlin in 1946.

This volume contains not only the letters written from Berlin between March 7 and July 15, 1946 (Docs. 15–75), which constitute the majority of the documents, but also those written on the way to Berlin between February 12 and March 5, 1946, in Washington, D. C., and New York, on board the *George W. Goethals*, and in Le Havre and Paris (Docs. 1–14). It further includes the letters that Johnson wrote during his trip through the American occupation zone between July 21 and August 1, 1946, in Butzbach, Stuttgart, and Munich (Docs. 76–79), and at the end of his stay in Germany, on August 7 and August 9, 1946, in Bremerhaven (Docs. 80–82). Except for the lines addressed to his two small sons and to his father (Doc. 60 and Doc. 69), all of the messages went to his wife in Lincoln, Nebraska. The concluding document is the undated report "Five Months in Berlin" (Doc. 83), apparently written by Johnson shortly after his homecoming, looking back on his experiences. It is possible that he had recourse to the letters he had written to his wife while composing the report, which he may have started to work on during his return voyage by sea. The possibility that he may have originally intended to publish the report cannot be ruled out.

In the autumn of 1946 Johnson also gave several lectures under the title "Five Months in Berlin," among others for members of the Lincoln chapter of the American Library Association and for the University of Nebraska Faculty Women's Club.

Johnson's records were found in an old trunk in his "study cabin" on the vacation property that he acquired in 1951, in the Rocky Mountains in Allenspark, Colorado. "I had never expected to see these published when I found them,"[1] writes Johnson's daughter-in-law, Candice E. Johnson. "The trunk had been used by Edgar in Austria and Berlin and contained the letters all inside the original envelopes, tied in bundles with string."[2]

In 2005 the letters were transferred to the University of Chicago Library, Special Collections Research Center, where they form part of the Edgar N.

1 Candice E. Johnson in an email to Werner Breunig from May 4, 2007.
2 Candice E. Johnson in an email to Werner Breunig from May 24, 2010.

Johnson Papers.[3] The report "Five Months in Berlin" also belongs to the collection maintained in Chicago.[4]

While the report was typewritten, the letters were written by hand. Although it cost a great deal of effort "to read his terrible handwriting,"[5] the editors have succeeded in providing a complete transcription.

The texts reproduced here are for the most part unaltered and unabridged. In two exceptional cases, minor omissions are made out of consideration for privacy; these are marked [...] and explained in footnotes. Incorrect spelling of proper names (for example, "Drum" instead of "Glum," or "Ullbrecht" instead of "Ulbricht") has not been corrected; the correct spelling can be found in footnotes. Abbreviations such as "Em." for "Emily" are spelled out in brackets. Underlined words are reproduced in italics.

The commentary on documents included in this volume is based on analysis of privately owned materials (primarily documents from Edgar N. Johnson's estate that are not part of the University of Chicago Library collection, belonging to Johnson's son, Thomas R. Johnson, and his daughter-in-law, Candice E. Johnson, in Denver, Colorado, USA), as well as numerous holdings from domestic and foreign archives, in addition to conversations with contemporary witnesses and information from institutions and individuals. The letters written to Edgar N. Johnson by his wife, Emily, preserved by Candice E. and Thomas R. Johnson, were also taken into account. Additionally helpful for the commentary were the microfiche holdings of the OMGUS files (OMGUS = Office of Military Government for Germany [US]) at the archives of the Institut für Zeitgeschichte in Munich and the Bundesarchiv in Koblenz, along with the microfiche holdings of the OMGBS files (OMGBS = Office of Military Government, Berlin Sector) at the Landesarchiv Berlin. Protocols from OMGUS staff conferences were analyzed as well, using protocol copies held at the archive of the Institut für Zeitgeschichte in Munich, along with protocols from meetings of the Local Government Committee, Allied Kommandatura Berlin, which were found in The National Archives, Kew, Richmond, Surrey, Great Britain, in the holdings "Allied Kommandatura: Directives, Minutes and Papers." Finally, it is worth mentioning the documents from the estate of Louis Glaser, property of Anthony J. Glaser, Bethesda, Maryland, USA, and the Lieutenant Colonel Harold Hays MBE Collection in the Imperial War Museum Duxford, Cambridgeshire, Great Britain. Glaser led the Civil Administration Branch of the American military government in Berlin and served as the American representative on the Local Government Committee, Allied Kommandatura Berlin, while Hays served as the British representative. Johnson worked with both of them.

Alongside members of the occupation forces and German political and cultural figures, the letters mention many friends and acquaintances from time shared in the Office of Strategic Services (OSS), the intelligence service where Johnson worked from 1943 to 1945 in Washington, D. C., and in Europe, as well as colleagues from the University of Nebraska and relatives at home. The footnotes offer biographical information on all individuals named in the records.

3 See University of Chicago Library, Guide to the Edgar N. Johnson Papers 1930–1966, https://www.lib.uchicago.edu/e/scrc/findingaids/view.php?eadid=ICU.SPCL.ENJOHNSON (accessed June 3, 2018). Letters: Box 1, Folder 8–10; Box 2, Folder 1.

4 Box 2, Folder 13.

5 Candice E. Johnson in an email to Werner Breunig from May 4, 2007.

Until now, no attention has been paid to Johnson in the literature on Berlin. In the source edition published in 1990, *Die Entstehung der Verfassung von Berlin*, his name appears in six documents from the Allied forces that relate to two topics: the search for a date for the first postwar elections in Berlin, and the creation of a provisional Berlin constitution.[6] Published in 1987, the 1945 to 1948 diaries of the District President of Darmstadt, Ludwig Bergsträsser, chronicle a meeting between Bergsträsser and Johnson on July 26, 1946, in Darmstadt.[7] On July 12, 1946, the weekly newspaper *OMGUS Observer* reports in detail on a lecture that Edgar N. Johnson gave for the American Women's Club of Berlin.[8] While in Berlin Johnson wrote the foreword for a German edition of Benjamin Franklin's autobiography, published in 1946 by Karl H. Henssel Verlag, Berlin.[9] Excerpts of Johnson's foreword were printed in the American-licensed Berlin journal *Horizont. Halbmonatsschrift für junge Menschen*.[10]

After working for the American military government, Johnson did not publish any of the impressions and insights he had gained, whereas after his OSS-deployment in Austria he had published an essay titled "The American Occupation of Austria."[11]

We would like to sincerely thank all of the individuals and institutions that helped us in the search for sources and with particular questions for the commentary. Above all, our thanks go to Edgar N. Johnson's son, Thomas R. Johnson, PhD, Senior Research Associate, and daughter-in-law, Candice E. Johnson, MD, PhD, Professor of Pediatrics, from Denver, Colorado. Their consent made this publication possible, and they obligingly provided information and material time and time again. We also thank them for an inspiring conversation in Berlin. We would like to thank Professor DDr. Oliver Rathkolb from the Institut für Zeitgeschichte of the University of Vienna for drawing our attention to Edgar N. Johnson's work for the American military government in Germany, and for making Johnson's Berlin letters available to us at a time when they had not yet been transferred to the University of Chicago Library. Our thanks also go to Professor Dr. Uwe Schaper, Director of the Landesarchiv Berlin, who patiently supported us and facilitated the inclusion of this edition in the Publication Series of the Landesarchiv Berlin.

Berlin, March 2014 Werner Breunig and Jürgen Wetzel

6 See *Die Entstehung der Verfassung von Berlin. Eine Dokumentation*, on behalf of the President of the Abgeordnetenhaus of Berlin, ed. Hans J. Reichhardt in collaboration with Werner Breunig/Josephine Gabler, 2 vols., Berlin and New York 1990, pp. 296f., 299, 301, 308, and 336.

7 See Ludwig Bergsträsser, *Befreiung, Besatzung, Neubeginn. Tagebuch des Darmstädter Regierungspräsidenten 1945–1948*, ed. Walter Mühlhausen (= Biographische Quellen zur deutschen Geschichte nach 1945, vol. 5), Munich 1987, pp. 149f.

8 See "'Shun Nazis', Wives Told At Women's Club Meeting," in: *OMGUS Observer* from July 12, 1946, p. 2.

9 See *Benjamin Franklin. Sein Leben von ihm selbst erzählt*, Berlin 1946.

10 See "Benjamin Franklin und die deutsche Jugend," in: *Horizont*, vol. 1, no. 20 (September 1, 1946), p. 19.

11 In: *Nebraska History*, vol. 26 (1945), pp. 201–210.

Preface to the English Edition

The 2014 edition *Fünf Monate in Berlin. Briefe von Edgar N. Johnson aus dem Jahre 1946* has been well received among experts in both German and English contexts.[1] We are happy to fulfill the request for a fully English-Language edition that will increase access to Johnson's letters.[2]

Our thanks go to Sage Anderson, PhD, who completed all translations from German into English with great care. We would also like to thank Professor Dr. Uwe Schaper, Director of the Landesarchiv Berlin, for his support in the preparation and publication of this edition.

Berlin, August 2019 Werner Breunig and Jürgen Wetzel

1 See E. N. Anderson, "Letters from a Vanished World" (review from October 27, 2014, of: *Fünf Monate in Berlin. Briefe von Edgar N. Johnson aus dem Jahre 1946*, eds. Werner Breunig/Jürgen Wetzel [= Schriftenreihe des Landesarchivs Berlin, vol. 18], Munich 2014), https://www.amazon.com/gp/customer-reviews/RC115REABPFUX/ref=cm_cr_arp_d_rvw_ttl?ie=UTF8&ASIN=3486735667 (accessed March 15, 2018); Frank Biess, review of: *Fünf Monate in Berlin. Briefe von Edgar N. Johnson aus dem Jahre 1946*, eds. Werner Breunig/Jürgen Wetzel (= Schriftenreihe des Landesarchivs Berlin, vol. 18), Munich 2014, in: *The Journal of Modern History*, vol. 88, no. 4 (December 2016), pp. 983f.; Jost Dülffer, review of: *Fünf Monate in Berlin. Briefe von Edgar N. Johnson aus dem Jahre 1946*, eds. Werner Breunig/Jürgen Wetzel (= Schriftenreihe des Landesarchivs Berlin, vol. 18), Munich 2014, in: *Zeitschrift für Geschichtswissenschaft*, vol. 63, no. 7/8 (July/August 2015), pp. 709f.; Björn Grötzner, review of: *Fünf Monate in Berlin. Briefe von Edgar N. Johnson aus dem Jahre 1946*, eds. Werner Breunig/Jürgen Wetzel (= Schriftenreihe des Landesarchivs Berlin, vol. 18), Munich 2014, in: *sehepunkte*, vol. 15, no. 7/8 (July 15, 2015), http://www.sehepunkte.de/2015/07/26908.html (accessed March 15, 2018); Henning Köhler, "Der Beginn des Kalten Krieges. Fünf Monate wohnte der Geschichtsprofessor Edgar N. Johnson 1946 im 'Wannsee-Hotel.' Er schrieb seiner Frau Briefe nach Nebraska. Die sind jetzt aufgetaucht. Ein Dokument der Nachkriegszeit," in: *Berliner Illustrirte Zeitung. Das Wochenend-Magazin der Berliner Morgenpost* from June 28, 2015, p. 3; Scott Krause, review of: *Fünf Monate in Berlin. Briefe von Edgar N. Johnson aus dem Jahre 1946*, eds. Werner Breunig/Jürgen Wetzel (= Schriftenreihe des Landesarchivs Berlin, vol. 18), Munich 2014, in: *H-Soz-Kult*, July 9, 2015, https://www.hsozkult.de/publicationreview/id/rezbuecher-24187 (accessed March 15, 2018); Lars Lüdicke, "Vom Brennpunkt der Welt. Briefe von Edgar N. Johnson über Berlin im Jahr 1946" (review of: *Fünf Monate in Berlin. Briefe von Edgar N. Johnson aus dem Jahre 1946*, eds. Werner Breunig/Jürgen Wetzel [= Schriftenreihe des Landesarchivs Berlin, vol. 18], Munich 2014), in: *Frankfurter Allgemeine Zeitung* from May 5, 2015, p. 6; Paul Steege, review of: *Fünf Monate in Berlin. Briefe von Edgar N. Johnson aus dem Jahre 1946*, eds. Werner Breunig/Jürgen Wetzel (= Schriftenreihe des Landesarchivs Berlin, vol. 18), Munich 2014, in: *The English Historical Review*, vol. 131, no. 551 (August 2016), pp. 959–961; Manfred Uhlitz, review of: *Fünf Monate in Berlin. Briefe von Edgar N. Johnson aus dem Jahre 1946*, eds. Werner Breunig/Jürgen Wetzel (= Schriftenreihe des Landesarchivs Berlin, vol. 18), Munich 2014, in: *Mitteilungen des Vereins für die Geschichte Berlins*, vol. 114, no. 4 (October 2018), pp. 359f.; Alexander Vazansky, review of: *Fünf Monate in Berlin. Briefe von Edgar N. Johnson aus dem Jahre 1946*, eds. Werner Breunig/Jürgen Wetzel (= Schriftenreihe des Landesarchivs Berlin, vol. 18), Munich 2014, in: *Jahrbuch für die Geschichte Mittel- und Ostdeutschlands*, vol. 61 (2015), pp. 468–471.

2 In the 2014 edition, the documents – letters as well as the report "Five Months in Berlin" – are left in the original English; all other parts, such as notes and introductory essays, are in German. For the English edition, only minor additions have been made to the notes in the document section and to the bibliography.

Werner Breunig

Edgar N. Johnson: A Biographical Sketch

Edgar Nathaniel Johnson arrived in a bombed-out Berlin in March 1946. Who was this serious and tense American about to take on important responsibilities in postwar Germany as an assistant to General Lucius D. Clay? What lay behind him, what lay ahead of him? The following pages outline the course of his life, which began in 1901 and ended in 1969, while also chronicling his time in the four-power city of Berlin.

Edgar N. Johnson was born on April 4, 1901, as the son of parents of Swedish origin in Chicago, Illinois. His father, Frank E. Johnson (originally Johanson), grew up in Sweden with eleven siblings and left as a young man due to material hardship. He became a US citizen in 1898. Edgar's mother, Mabel A. Johnson, née Walstrom, was born in Chicago as the daughter of parents who had emigrated from Sweden. Edgar had one older brother who died as a child. Two younger siblings, a brother and a sister, were born in 1904 and 1911. The family moved away from the great metropolis of immigrants on Lake Michigan when the father found work as a piano-maker in Holly, Michigan, and later in La Porte, Indiana. Edgar's parents spent a large part of their lives in the small town of La Porte, not far from Chicago.

Edgar went to elementary school first in Holly and then in La Porte, graduated from the public La Porte High School and began his studies in the autumn of 1918 in his city of birth, Chicago. He majored in history at the private University of Chicago, with minors in political science, economics, and French. To earn money for his studies, he played the piano for silent film screenings. Like his father, he was an accomplished piano player, and the love of music accompanied him throughout his life. "Loved music, and relaxed by playing the piano, which he did very well – mostly 19th century classical music, often Baroque."[1]

In 1922 Johnson completed his undergraduate studies at the University of Chicago and earned a Bachelor of Philosophy (PhB), "with honorable mention and special honors for work in history."[2] Afterwards, from September 1922 to June 1924, he gained his first professional experience: he taught European history at the prestigious Culver Military Academy[3], a private school in Culver, Indiana, about an hour by car from his hometown of La Porte. During the summer he taught at a school camp.

Culver was only a short stopover for Johnson. In the autumn of 1924 he returned to the University of Chicago to begin graduate studies in medieval and

1 Eugene N. Anderson Jr. in an email to Werner Breunig from July 17, 2007.

2 Letter from Edgar N. Johnson to Charles Henry Oldfather, Chairman of the Department of History at the University of Nebraska in Lincoln, Nebraska, from May 13, 1931, in: University of Nebraska-Lincoln (UNL) Libraries, Archives & Special Collections, Lincoln, Nebraska, USA, Biographical File of Edgar N. Johnson, RG/52-01, Box 134.

3 Founded in 1894 by Henry H. Culver. See https://www.culver.org/about/the-culver-story/our-foundation (accessed May 15, 2018).

European history. His main interest was in the Middle Ages, which had captivated him ever since he had read Henry Adams's fascinating work *Mont-Saint-Michel and Chartres*. He spent three academic years as a graduate student at the University of Chicago. Scholarships helped him to finance his studies: "During the last two of these years I held fellowships from the department."[4] Among his teachers were Godfrey Davies, Walter L. Dorn, Carl F. Huth Jr., Einar Joranson, Ferdinand Schevill, Bernadotte E. Schmitt and James W. Thompson. His most important teacher was Thompson, an expert in medieval and early modern history (particularly the Holy Roman Empire and France). As of 1932, Thompson taught at the University of California, Berkeley, and in 1937 he and Johnson jointly published a voluminous work: James Westfall Thompson/Edgar Nathaniel Johnson, *An Introduction to Medieval Europe, 300–1500*, New York 1937. This was Johnson's complete revision of an earlier book by Thompson.

In the summer of 1927, Johnson left Chicago "for a fourteen months stay of travel and study in Europe,"[5] supported by a scholarship from the Berlin-based Alexander von Humboldt Foundation[6]. In the winter semester of 1927/1928, he studied medieval history at the Ludwig-Maximilians-Universität Munich[7] – "to which I did not become wholly attached."[8] His travels carried him all throughout Europe: "Time away from Munich I spent in travel in England, France, Germany, Czecho-Slovakia, Austria, Hungary, Italy and Switzerland."[9]

He was accompanied by his friend John D. Bickford, who held a PhD in classics from Princeton; Bickford had been teaching since 1920 at Culver Military Academy, where Johnson had also taught.[10] Their co-authored essay, "The Contemplated Anglo-German Alliance: 1890–1901,"[11] was published in March 1927.

4 Letter from Edgar N. Johnson to Charles Henry Oldfather, Chairman of the Department of History at the University of Nebraska in Lincoln, Nebraska, from May 13, 1931, in: UNL Libraries, Archives & Special Collections, Biographical File of Edgar N. Johnson, RG/52-01, Box 134.

5 Ibid.

6 On the Humboldt Foundation, founded in 1925, see Holger Impekoven, *Die Alexander von Humboldt-Stiftung und das Ausländerstudium in Deutschland 1925–1945. Von der "geräuschlosen Propaganda" zur Ausbildung der "geistigen Wehr" des "Neuen Europa"* (= Internationale Beziehungen. Theorie und Geschichte, vol. 9), Göttingen 2013.

7 According to a telephone conversation with Holger Impekoven (see note 6) on October 16, 2013, Johnson was one of four American students to study in Germany with financial support from the Humboldt Foundation in the winter semester of 1927/1928.

8 Edgar N. Johnson in a letter written to his wife, Emily, from Salzburg on July 8, 1945, in: The University of Chicago (UChicago) Library, Special Collections Research Center, Chicago, Illinois, USA, Edgar N. Johnson Papers.

9 Edgar N. Johnson, Curriculum Vitae, undated [ca. 1963], p. 1, in: UChicago Library, Special Collections Research Center, Edgar N. Johnson Papers.

10 According to a telephone conversation with Holger Impekoven (see note 6) on October 16, 2013, Bickford did not hold a Humboldt scholarship.

11 In: *Political Science Quarterly*, vol. 42, no. 1 (March 1927), pp. 1–57.

Johnson described it as "the offshoot of one of Professor Schmitt's seminars, which I worked out with a friend of mine."[12] After returning from Europe, Bickford taught German as well as Latin at the prestigious and exclusive Hotchkiss School in Lakeville, Connecticut. In 1934 he married the sister of his friend Edgar N. Johnson, Mildred H. Johnson, who was around 20 years younger than him. Bickford died two years later at the age of only 45, a painful loss for his wife and for his brother-in-law. "Mildred left to spend a year at the Sorbonne in Paris to study French and became profoundly depressed, losing 20 pounds weight before she returned."[13]

In Munich Johnson attended lectures or tutorials by Professors Heinrich Günter, Paul Joachimsen, Paul Lehmann, Hermann Oncken, and others. Courses such as "The German Imperial Period: The Middle Ages," by Günter, "Luther, Zwingli, Calvin," by Joachimsen, "Introduction to Latin Philology of the Middle Ages," or "Critical Tutorial for the Seminar on Latin Philology of the Middle Ages" by the classicist Lehmann would have attracted his interest.[14]

During his academic stay in Munich, Johnson lived at Hohenstaufenstraße 10/II,[15] in a boarding house not far from the university. It was run by Anna Engelhorn, a woman from Strasbourg, Alsace, who was educated as a painter. Her father, August Winnecke, had been Professor of Astronomy at the University of Strasbourg. Her husband, Kommerzienrat Karl Engelhorn, a former bank director, had just died in August 1927. She is described by her grandson Wolfgang Oppenheimer as "always jovial, hospitable, closely connected to her relatives – but also to politics."[16] Johnson and Bickford actively exchanged letters with this warm, cheerful, life-affirming, and witty woman[17] for years to

12 Letter from Edgar N. Johnson to Charles Henry Oldfather, Chairman of the Department of History at the University of Nebraska in Lincoln, Nebraska, from May 13, 1931, in: UNL Libraries, Archives & Special Collections, Biographical File of Edgar N. Johnson, RG/52-01, Box 134.

13 Candice E. Johnson in an email to Werner Breunig from June 1, 2010.

14 ("Die deutsche Kaiserzeit. Das Mittelalter," "Luther, Zwingli, Calvin," "Einleitung in die lateinische Philologie des Mittelalters," "Kritische Übungen des Seminars für lateinische Philologie des Mittelalters") See *Ludwig-Maximilians-Universität München. Verzeichnis der Vorlesungen Winter-Halbjahr 1927/28*, Munich 1927, pp. 26 and 29.

15 See *Personenstand der Ludwig-Maximilians-Universität München. Winter-Halbjahr 1927/28*, Munich 1928, p. 116.

16 ("immer jovial, menschenfreundlich, stark verbunden mit ihrer Verwandtschaft – aber auch mit der Politik") Letter from Wolfgang Oppenheimer to Werner Breunig from January 10, 2012.

17 "Behind her cheerfulness, tolerance, and affirmation of life there stood a tested, steady inner faith. If I judge correctly, her happy disposition allowed her to always recognize the positive in life and draw attention to it." ("Hinter ihrer Heiterkeit, Toleranz und Lebensbejahung stand ein geprüfter, innerlich gefestigter Glaube. Ihr glückliches Naturell erlaubte es ihr, wenn ich recht urteile, immer das Positive im Leben zu erkennen und darauf hinzuweisen.") Memoirs of Marcus Löw-Suter, p. 61, private collection of Dieter Loew, Basel, Switzerland.

come; even during the Nazi period there was continued contact with Anna Engelhorn,[18] a firm opponent of the National Socialist regime.[19]

In the autumn of 1928 Johnson returned to the University of Chicago and taught as an instructor in the Department of History until June 1931, simultaneously working on his dissertation. According to Johnson in 1931, "My work here has been with the freshmen survey course in the history of civilization. For two years the instructors gave this course individually. For this year we have been working with Professor Arthur P. Scott. I have also given two courses in the Down Town College for Professor Huth, one on the Middle Ages, and the other on the Absolute Monarchy in the seventeenth and eighteenth centuries."[20]

18 In October 1933 she reported in a letter to her "dear good friends" ("lieben guten Freunde") that she had "escaped our German prison and madhouse for 3 weeks" ("unserem deutschen Gefängnis u. Narrenhaus einmal für 3 Wochen entronnen"), and she was staying in Switzerland at Lago Maggiore where her stepdaughter Clara, who was married to the German-Jewish industrialist Clemens Oppenheimer, lived with her family, who had relocated from Germany. Letter from Ascona from October 27, 1933, in: Documents from the estate of Edgar N. Johnson, private collection of Candice E. and Thomas R. Johnson, Denver, Colorado, USA. Engelhorn writes, "Do you know what we say in G[ermany] as a joke? There are only 2 kinds of Germans anymore, 1. those who hold office and 2. those who hold their tongues, and Goebbels, the head of propaganda, the one who shoots his mouth off, we call him 'Wotan's Mickey Mouse' or the darkened shrinking Teuton. We release tension by relaying bon mots so as not to burst from gathered up vexation." ("Wissen Sie, was wir zum Scherz in D[eutschland] sagen? Es gibt nur noch 2 Sorten Deutsche 1. Statthalter u. 2. Maulhalter u. den Maulaufreisser u. Propagandachef Goebbels nennen wir 'Wotans Mickymaus' od. den nachgedunkelten Schrumpfgermanen. So entlasten wir uns durch weitergegebene 'Bon mots' um nicht an aufgesammeltem Verdruss zu zerplatzen.") Ibid. Regarding her grandson Wolfgang Oppenheimer, who later made a name for himself as an academic, historian, and author, she writes: "What an enchanting, gifted child, and he is supposed to be unworthy of German citizenship, they want to stamp him as unworthy!" ("Welch ein bezauberndes hochbegabtes Kind, das nicht wert sein soll deutscher Staatsbürger zu sein, dem man den Stempel der Minderwertigkeit aufprägen will!") Ibid. In January 1935 she writes that she has "suffered immensely under the upheaval of the past 2½ years." ("ungemein gelitten unter den Umwälzungen der letzten 2½ Jahre") Letter from Basel from January 5, 1935, in: Documents from the estate of Edgar N. Johnson, private collection of Candice E. and Thomas R. Johnson, Denver, Colorado, USA. "The interferences in the universities, education, and the churches are of the dark Middle Ages, the actions against the Jews are a shame on our culture. Not easy to have to be so bitterly ashamed of one's own people." ("Die Eingriffe in die Universitäten, die Erziehung, die Kirchen sind finsteres Mittelalter, das Vorgehen gegen die Juden eine Kulturschande. Nicht leicht sich seines eigenen Volkes so bitter schämen zu müssen.") Ibid.

19 "As an adherent of Anthroposophy, but also by character, Aunt Aenne opposed National Socialism as it approached and supported all efforts to save the victims of this movement." ("Schon als Anhängerin der Anthroposophie, aber auch nach ihrer Eigenart lehnte Tante Aenne den aufkommenden Nationalsozialismus ab und unterstützte alle Bemühungen, um die Opfer dieser Bewegung zu retten.") Memoirs of Marcus Löw-Suter, p. 61, private collection of Dieter Loew, Basel, Switzerland.

20 Letter from Edgar N. Johnson to Charles Henry Oldfather, Chairman of the Department of History at the University of Nebraska in Lincoln, Nebraska, from May 13, 1931, in: UNL Libraries, Archives & Special Collections, Biographical File of Edgar N. Johnson, RG/52-01, Box 134.

At the end of 1931 Johnson earned the title Doctor of Philosophy (PhD) from the University of Chicago with his dissertation "The Secular Activities of the German Episcopate, 919–1024." Historian Karl Jordan, who worked for the Monumenta Germaniae Historica in Berlin, discussed this work in the *Deutsche Literaturzeitung*. It "is of the school of I. W. Thompson, who has brought medieval German history to the particular attention of American historians through various works in recent years,"[21] Jordan writes. "From the larger set of questions that Thompson dealt with in his 1928 book *Feudal Germany*, J[ohnson] singles out a specific problem, the role of the episcopate in the Othonian state, and aims to provide a multifaceted presentation."[22] The "generally clearly and coherently written"[23] work would offer "the American reader a comprehensive and essentially accurate picture of the unique role of the German episcopate in the times of the Saxon emperors."[24]

"I had meanwhile been invited to join the staff of the University of Nebraska beginning with the fall semester of 1931."[25] In May 1931 Johnson wrote to Professor Charles Henry Oldfather, Chairman of the Department of History at the public University of Nebraska in Lincoln, the capital of Nebraska: "I need not say, perhaps, that I am very happy over the opportunity of coming to Lincoln, and that I anticipate eagerly my work there, and look forward to becoming acquainted."[26] He thanked Oldfather "for your offer to keep an eye open for a place for me to live. I am obliged to live quite modestly – a place to sleep, to work and for books is about all that I need."[27]

Johnson was 30 years old when he left Chicago, a city of millions, for the comparatively small Lincoln, Nebraska, which at that point had fewer than 80,000 inhabitants. His job at the local university began in September 1931. Initially he was an instructor, then as of 1932 assistant professor. In 1935 he was promoted to associate professor, and in 1942 he achieved the rank of full professor. In 1943 he describes his tasks as follows: "Teaching classes, both under-

21 ("ist aus der Schule von I. W. Thompson hervorgegangen, der durch seine verschiedenen Arbeiten der letzten Jahre die amerikanischen Historiker in besonderem Maße auf die mittelalterliche deutsche Geschichte hingewiesen hat") Karl Jordan, review of: Edgar Nathaniel Johnson, *The Secular Activities of the German Episcopate, 919–1024*, Lincoln, Nebraska, 1932, in: *Deutsche Literaturzeitung*, 1933, no. 50, cols. 2378–2380, here col. 2378.

22 ("Aus dem großen Fragenkreis, den Thompson in seinem 1928 erschienenen Buche Feudal Germany behandelt hat, greift J[ohnson] ein einzelnes Problem, die Stellung des Episkopats im Staate der Ottonen, heraus und ist bestrebt, ihm eine vielseitige Darstellung zu widmen.") Ibid.

23 ("im allgemeinen klar und übersichtlich geschriebene") Ibid., here col. 2380.

24 ("dem amerikanischen Leser ein umfassendes und im wesentlichen zutreffendes Bild von der eigenartigen Stellung des deutschen Episkopats zur Zeit der sächsischen Kaiser") Ibid.

25 Edgar N. Johnson, Curriculum Vitae, undated [ca. 1963], p. 1, in: UChicago Library, Special Collections Research Center, Edgar N. Johnson Papers.

26 Letter from Edgar N. Johnson to Charles Henry Oldfather, Chairman of the Department of History at the University of Nebraska in Lincoln, Nebraska, from May 13, 1931, in: UNL Libraries, Archives & Special Collections, Biographical File of Edgar N. Johnson, RG/52-01, Box 134.

27 Ibid.

graduate and graduate in European History, supervising graduate research in mediaeval History and serving on University Committees."[28] He describes his activity at the University of Nebraska in detail in a later resume: "During these years I always taught in the elementary course in European history, and in fact, always enjoyed working with good freshmen. In addition I always taught regularly a year's course in mediaeval history and irregularly a similar course in Reformation. But under the stimulus of Ferdinand Schevill's emphasis at Chicago I early substituted for the course on the Reformation, first, a year's course for advanced undergraduates and graduates on mediaeval civilization, and then a two years' course which I labelled, perhaps rather ambitiously, the History of Western Culture. This course spends the first year on the ancient and medieval periods (including the Renaissance) and its second year on the period from about 1600 to date. It aims to be what it is called, a history of western culture, culture being defined in historical rather than anthropological terms as the discipline of thought and the arts. As World War II approached the course developed into a history of the western tradition. […] I have found the course on the History of Western Culture to be, perhaps my most useful teaching, for it has served to aid advanced undergraduate and graduate students to integrate their historical and other studies."[29]

Johnson belonged to the American Historical Association, founded in 1884. Additionally, he was an early member of the Mediaeval Academy of America, "one of the first members of the Academy, which was founded in 1925,"[30] and he served as Councillor from 1946 to 1949.[31] Later he also belonged to the Renaissance Society of America, initiated in 1954.

Around 1934 he met his future wife, Emily L. Floyd, from Beatrice, Nebraska. She studied at the University of Nebraska beginning in 1931 and attended his classes. In June 1935 she graduated with a Bachelor of Arts (AB) in English and history. She was born on November 20, 1910, on a farm in Goodland, Kansas, as the oldest of eleven children.

The two were married on July 14, 1936, in La Porte, Indiana, where Edgar N. Johnson's parents lived. Exactly ten years later, on July 14, 1946, Johnson writes from Berlin: "This is the day 10 years ago. 10 full and precious years."[32] These words from Emily also indicate that theirs was a happy marriage: "I wish we

28 Application for Federal Employment from January 30, 1943, p. 2, in: National Archives and Records Administration (NARA), College Park, Maryland, USA, Record Group 226 (Records of the Office of Strategic Services), personnel file Dr. Edgar N. Johnson.

29 Edgar N. Johnson, Curriculum Vitae, undated [ca. 1963], pp. 1f., in: UChicago Library, Special Collections Research Center, Edgar N. Johnson Papers.

30 Lisa F. Davis, Acting Executive Director, Medieval Academy of America, in an email to Werner Breunig from May 29, 2013.

31 Johnson was elected as a member of the Council in April 1946. See "Historical News," in: *The American Historical Review*, vol. 51, no. 4 (July 1946), pp. 788–804, here pp. 794f.; "The Mediaeval Academy of America. Proceedings of the Twenty-first Annual Meeting of the Corporation 1946," in: *Speculum*, vol. 21, no. 3 (July 1946), pp. 362–375, here p. 362.

32 Doc. 74.

had met and been married long before we did."[33] A friend of the family writes: "He [Edgar N. Johnson] had a close and wonderful marriage. His wife Emily was a really intelligent and totally delightful and charming lady. In those days, women stayed home and raised kids, and she put up with that pretty well. She was an outstanding cook."[34]

The marriage resulted in two sons. John F. Johnson was born in September 1939 in Lincoln, and Thomas R. Johnson in July 1944 in Washington, D. C.

For one semester, from September 1939 to February 1940, Johnson taught as a visiting professor at the public University of Wisconsin, Madison, filling in for the historian Gaines Post, who was on leave. His task: "Teaching classes in European History, both graduate and undergraduate."[35]

As of February 20, 1943, Johnson was released from the university "for duration of war,"[36] in order to work for the Office of Strategic Services (OSS) in Washington, D. C., an American intelligence service established in 1942 and disbanded in 1945. By far the largest department in this agency was the Research and Analysis Branch, primarily devoted to the preparation of interdisciplinary regional studies for observation of the enemy and occupation planning. Johnson was to work as a Research Analyst in the Central European Section of this research department. There was good reason for his employment in this section: "Dr. Edgar Johnson, Professor of History at the University of Nebraska, is one of the ablest students of German affairs among the members of the American Historical Association. Although he acquired his present reputation largely through his scholarly publications in medieval German history, he is without doubt one of the best-informed students of contemporary Germany in the Middle West. [...] Dr. Johnson is without doubt one of the ablest American students in the field of Medieval German history. He has published a number of brilliant monographs in this field, all of which were reviewed with warm enthusiasm. Notwithstanding his reputation as a medievalist, his keen interest in the internal development of Germany under the Nazi regime has borne fruit in a number of excellent articles. In addition to his training in historical method, Dr. Johnson is a close student of the social sciences. He is a reflective, thorough scholar with an unusual capacity for work. His scholarly background and present equipment offer the promise that he will become one of the most useful members of the Central European Section."[37]

33 Emily L. Johnson in a letter to her husband, Edgar, from May 15, 1946, in: Documents from the estate of Edgar N. Johnson, private collection of Candice E. and Thomas R. Johnson, Denver, Colorado, USA.

34 Eugene N. Anderson Jr. in an email to Werner Breunig from July 17, 2007.

35 Application for Federal Employment from January 30, 1943, p. 3, in: NARA, Record Group 226 (Records of the Office of Strategic Services), personnel file Dr. Edgar N. Johnson.

36 Bulletin of the University of Nebraska, August 31, 1945, p. 42, in: UNL Libraries, Archives & Special Collections, Bulletins & Catalogs (University, General), RG/00-07.

37 Robert H. Alcorn, Office of Strategic Services, in a note from December 21, 1942, Subject: Dr. Edgar Johnson and Miss Ethel P. Ross, attachment, in: NARA, Record Group 226 (Records of the Office of Strategic Services), personnel file Dr. Edgar N. Johnson.

This established scholar, who had a command of the German language and sound knowledge of Germany and Germans,[38] was employed in the Central European Section of the Research and Analysis Branch in Washington, D. C., as of February 22, 1943. Franz L. Neumann, a German lawyer and political scientist who had emigrated to the US, started in the Central European Section on the same day. He had made a name for himself as a sharp analyst of National Socialism with his book *Behemoth*, a structural analysis of the "Third Reich." Johnson tells his wife, "A refugee by the name of Franz Neumann (he has written a book on Germany called Behemoth – considered the best) came in on the same day with me."[39]

In the Central European Section, where American academics worked together with academics in exile, Johnson belonged to an intellectual elite of experts on German history and politics, along with Franz L. Neumann and the emigrants Felix Gilbert, Hajo Holborn, and Herbert Marcuse. The section was under the direction of Walter L. Dorn, expert in 18th-century Prussian history, son of a German-American pastor's family from the Midwest, whom Johnson already knew from the University of Chicago. Dorn proved not equal to his organizational task as section leader.[40] "Dorn is a washout as an administrator, and as long as he is chief nothing serious will be done,"[41] Johnson quickly realized. "[…] I shall get a desk in the Congressional Library. You can't work in the Office with Dorn around."[42] Dorn was finally moved to Great Britain and replaced by his former deputy, the historian Eugene N. Anderson, likewise a specialist in German history. Like Dorn, Anderson had done research in Germany, and he and Johnson were close friends.

"It was tentatively decided today that I shall specialize on the German Church and Churches, which would be up my alley a bit and would interest me,"[43] Johnson tells his wife at the beginning of his deployment as Research Analyst. "In OSS I was associated, first, with the work on Germany and then on Austria. In the former capacity I was responsible for the final edition of the *Handbook on the German Church* and the *Military Government Guide on the*

38 Johnson had language skills in German, French, Italian, and Latin. By his own account, he could read German and French very well, speak sufficiently, and understand well; he could also read Italian sufficiently and Latin well. See Application for Federal Employment from January 30, 1943, p. 2, in: NARA, Record Group 226 (Records of the Office of Strategic Services), personnel file Dr. Edgar N. Johnson.

39 Letter from Edgar N. Johnson from Washington, D. C., to his wife, Emily, from February 24, 1943, in: Documents from the estate of Edgar N. Johnson, private collection of Candice E. and Thomas R. Johnson, Denver, Colorado, USA.

40 See Walter L. Dorn, *Inspektionsreisen in der US-Zone. Notizen, Denkschriften und Erinnerungen aus dem Nachlaß*, trans. and ed. Lutz Niethammer (= Schriftenreihe der Vierteljahrshefte für Zeitgeschichte, no. 26), Stuttgart 1973, p. 11; Ernst C. Stiefel/ Frank Mecklenburg, *Deutsche Juristen im amerikanischen Exil (1933–1950)*, Tübingen 1991, p. 152.

41 Letter from Edgar N. Johnson from Washington, D. C., to his wife, Emily, from February 24, 1943, in: Documents from the estate of Edgar N. Johnson, private collection of Candice E. and Thomas R. Johnson, Denver, Colorado, USA.

42 Ibid.

43 Ibid.

German Church."[44] Until the Moscow Declaration of November 1, 1943, when the Allies first presented the prospect of re-establishing an independent Austria with pre-1938 borders, there was only an "Austria problem" within the general association of the German Reich; until that point, there were no separate plans for Austria.[45]

In an evaluation from November 1943, it was certified that he was one of the most competent members of the Central European Section: "Mr. Johnson has proved to be one of the ablest members of the Section and has written some of our most important reports. He is a mature scholar, the author of several books and has more than carried his share of the intellectual leadership of the Section. He is responsible for the coverage of Church questions and is serving as the general director of the studies on Austria. In this capacity he assists in planning and in criticising the work of a number of other persons in the Section."[46]

Lorenz Eitner, an Austrian who joined the Central European Section in 1944, describes Edgar N. Johnson as a "nearsighted, very serious man with hunched shoulders, who had attained his knowledge of Austria at second hand, through diligent study."[47] Eitner's comment that Johnson "quite obviously did not feel comfortable among the Neumanns & Marcuses (and probably was not taken very seriously),"[48] might be a false impression based on Johnson's unobtrusive, reserved, modest manner; never one to force his way into the spotlight, Johnson was no prima donna.

After his departure from Lincoln and the beginning of his work for the OSS, Johnson did not stay separated from his family for long. In March 1943 his wife, Emily, and son John came to live with him in Washington, D. C. The house they had purchased in Lincoln in 1941 was rented out. Their son Thomas, also called Timmy or Tim, was born in the American capital in July 1944. However, by this time Johnson was no longer active in the OSS headquarters, but rather in the London office of the Research and Analysis Branch as head of the Austria section: "In June 1944 I went to London as the Chief of the Austrian Section of the

44 Edgar N. Johnson, Curriculum Vitae, undated [ca. 1963], p. 2, in: UChicago Library, Special Collections Research Center, Edgar N. Johnson Papers.

45 See Oliver Rathkolb, "Professorenpläne für Österreichs Zukunft. Nachkriegsfragen im Diskurs der Forschungsabteilung Research and Analysis," in: *Geheimdienstkrieg gegen Deutschland. Subversion, Propaganda und politische Planungen des amerikanischen Geheimdienstes im Zweiten Weltkrieg*, eds. Jürgen Heideking/Christof Mauch (Sammlung Vandenhoeck), Göttingen 1993, pp. 166–181, here pp. 167 and 169.

46 Personnel Action Request from November 24, 1943, in: NARA, Record Group 226 (Records of the Office of Strategic Services), personnel file Dr. Edgar N. Johnson.

47 ("kurzsichtigen, sehr ernsten Mann mit vornübergebeugten Schultern, der sich sein Wissen über Österreich aus zweiter Hand angeeignet hatte, durch fleißiges Studieren") Letter from Lorenz Eitner to Oliver Rathkolb from June 14, 1985, quoted in Oliver Rathkolb, "Professorenpläne für Österreichs Zukunft. Nachkriegsfragen im Diskurs der Forschungsabteilung Research and Analysis," in: *Geheimdienstkrieg gegen Deutschland. Subversion, Propaganda und politische Planungen des amerikanischen Geheimdienstes im Zweiten Weltkrieg*, eds. Jürgen Heideking/Christof Mauch (Sammlung Vandenhoeck), Göttingen 1993, pp. 166–181, here p. 168.

48 ("sich ganz offensichtlich unter den Neumanns & Marcuses nicht wohl fühlte [und wahrscheinlich auch nicht sonderlich ernst genommen wurde]") Ibid.

Research and Analysis Branch and was there until the spring of 1945 working closely with military government and state department officials who were preparing to go to Austria. In the spring of 1945, before leaving for Italy, I worked at the American Embassy preparing material for Mr. Philip [E.] Mosely to use in some of his negotiations with Mr. [Fedor Tarasovič] Gusev over the division of Vienna among the Allies."[49] Johnson "appeared to have been the main contact in London for questions about Austria."[50]

Johnson returned to the US for two months at the beginning of 1945 after the death of his 68-year-old mother.

In April 1945 he went from London to Caserta in Southern Italy, "where various task forces for Austria were located."[51] A year later, Johnson remembers May 8, 1945, "Victory-in-Europe day," as follows: "A year ago – on the first V-E day I was in Caserta. I still of course remember the great relief of that day. It was finally over. I remember the delicious quality of the Italian spring day. OSS gave a party in the garden of the hunting lodge belonging to the present crown prince of Italy."[52]

After the end of the war, in May 1945, Johnson went to Austria, where he remained until November 1945. "In Austria, after the cessation of hostilities, as the chief still of the Austrian section of the Research and Analysis Branch of OSS, I was associated with the restoration of governments in the Länder of Salzburg and Linz, and in Vienna got to know the members of the [Karl] Renner government fairly well and helped American officials in their contacts with this government. At this period also I worked closely with Ambassador [John G.] Erhardt and was privileged to help rectify mistakes of military government in Linz."[53]

In July 1945 Johnson took the opportunity to travel from Salzburg to Munich, in the American zone of Germany, to see with his own eyes what had become of the city where he had spent time as a student. "Munich is only the empty shell of a dead city,"[54] he finds. "That is a slight exaggeration, of course, there

49 Edgar N. Johnson, Curriculum Vitae, undated [ca. 1963], p. 2, in: UChicago Library, Special Collections Research Center, Edgar N. Johnson Papers.

50 ("schien in London der Hauptansprechpartner in Österreichfragen gewesen zu sein") Oliver Rathkolb, "Professorenpläne für Österreichs Zukunft. Nachkriegsfragen im Diskurs der Forschungsabteilung Research and Analysis," in: *Geheimdienstkrieg gegen Deutschland. Subversion, Propaganda und politische Planungen des amerikanischen Geheimdienstes im Zweiten Weltkrieg*, eds. Jürgen Heideking/Christof Mauch (Sammlung Vandenhoeck), Göttingen 1993, pp. 166–181, here p. 169; see Oliver Rathkolb (ed.), *Gesellschaft und Politik am Beginn der Zweiten Republik. Vertrauliche Berichte der US-Militäradministration aus Österreich 1945 in englischer Originalfassung*, Vienna, Cologne, and Graz 1985, pp. 13f.

51 Edgar N. Johnson, Curriculum Vitae, undated [ca. 1963], p. 2, in: UChicago Library, Special Collections Research Center, Edgar N. Johnson Papers.

52 Doc. 45.

53 Edgar N. Johnson, Curriculum Vitae, undated [ca. 1963], pp. 2f., in: UChicago Library, Special Collections Research Center, Edgar N. Johnson Papers.

54 Edgar N. Johnson in a letter from Salzburg to his wife, Emily, from July 8, 1945, in: UChicago Library, Special Collections Research Center, Edgar N. Johnson Papers.

are people about."[55] The destruction of German cities through aerial warfare, "no matter what the justification, is hard to take."[56]

While in Munich, Johnson also visited Hohenstaufenstraße 10. The building where he had lodged on the second floor with Anna Engelhorn was bombed out, presenting itself as a shell without content. "I was a bit sobered – after all this was home for about six months and home with a very sweet and liberal person."[57] "And here many evenings were spent listening to Lieder by Germany's Brahms and Schubert, Strauss and Wolff,"[58] he reminisces. Now he was provided with a very peculiar musical experience, as the sound of Ludwig van Beethoven's *Moonlight* Sonata resonated in the middle of the silent ruins: "The whole area, except for one house is a shell. In that house someone was playing a piano – the Moonlight Sonata, a little uncanny."[59]

When Johnson toured Germany in November 1945, after completing his assignments in Austria, his route initially took him back to Munich. From there he traveled all the way across the American zone, from Augsburg, Ulm, Nuremberg, Schweinfurt, Bamberg, Würzburg, and Aschaffenburg – his medievalist's gaze also fell on more or less severely damaged historical structures such as the Fuggerei in Augsburg, the Ulm Minster, or the Nuremberg Castle – to Wiesbaden, where the OSS Germany had its headquarters. From Wiesbaden, he had the opportunity to make the short trip across the Rhine to Mainz, in the French zone. Visiting the Mainz Cathedral, "one of my favorite churches in Germany,"[60] which had been struck by bombs during World War II, memories were awakened: "When I last saw it, it was a warm sunny day, not the cold grey day it has been today and for some days. And I saw the church, built in red sandstone glow with a late afternoon light. I tried to capture that experience in a passage in the book. It wouldn't have been right today to have had that effect. For a glowing cathedral would have been out of place in desolate Mainz."[61]

In Frankfurt am Main there was a reunion with Walter L. Dorn. "He has had the opportunity to play much the same rôle in the American zone in Germany as we played in Austria."[62] "The professors (Drs. as they are known to the military) have not done so bad in this war,"[63] Johnson notes.

Berlin, former Reich capital now occupied by the four Allied powers, was a further destination. The sight of the severely war-marked city on the Spree must have shaken Johnson as much as the image of other destroyed Germany cities. This may have been his first time in Berlin. There is a detailed diary from Ed-

55 Ibid.

56 Ibid.

57 Ibid.

58 Ibid.

59 Ibid.

60 Edgar N. Johnson in a letter from Wiesbaden to his wife, Emily, from November 7, 1945, in: UChicago Library, Special Collections Research Center, Edgar N. Johnson Papers.

61 Ibid.

62 Edgar N. Johnson in a letter from Berlin to his wife, Emily, from November 10, 1945, in: UChicago Library, Special Collections Research Center, Edgar N. Johnson Papers.

63 Ibid.

gar's student days in Germany in 1927/1928, and from the return trip he made in the summer of 1932. According to Thomas R. Johnson, "There is no mention of visiting Berlin on either trip."[64]

After his tour of Germany – in many ways "a dreary trip," "dreary because of the devastation, dreary because of the general hopelessness, and dreary because of the rainy weather"[65] – Johnson flew back to the US and was able to spend Christmas with his beloved family.

He published the impressions and insights he had gained in Austria in the quarterly journal *Nebraska History*.[66]

Johnson later received the high civilian honor "Medal of Freedom" for his work at OSS in Europe, "for services from June 1944 to September 1945."[67]

In February 1946 he headed back to Europe to work for the American military government, Office of Military Government for Germany (US), OMGUS for short. As one of four occupation forces in Germany, the United States endeavored "to honestly help the German people find their way back into the international community."[68] Johnson was among the civilians "who are going over to help solve the German problem."[69] After his successful deployment in Austria, which was also occupied and controlled by the four Allied powers, Johnson was to work as a War Department employee on the staff of General Lucius D. Clay, Deputy Military Governor and Commanding General of OMGUS. He was also meant to act as head of the important Regional Government Coordinating Office (RGCO) in Stuttgart. James K. Pollock, Professor of Political Science at the University of Michigan, had begun setting up this office in October 1945;[70] it served as a coordinating body between the American military government and the German Länderrat of the US zone.[71] It was one of the most important agencies within the occupation mechanism, providing direct access to Clay, his assistants, and the directors of the state military governments.[72]

64 Thomas R. Johnson in an email to Werner Breunig from May 31, 2017.

65 Edgar N. Johnson in a letter from Berlin to his wife, Emily, from November 10, 1945, in: UChicago Library, Special Collections Research Center, Edgar N. Johnson Papers.

66 See Edgar N. Johnson, "The American Occupation of Austria," in: *Nebraska History*, vol. 26 (1945), pp. 201–210.

67 Notice of the Adjutant General, Department of War, to the Director, Strategic Services Unit, from July 31, 1946, in: Documents from the estate of Edgar N. Johnson, private collection of Candice E. and Thomas R. Johnson, Denver, Colorado, USA.

68 ("ehrlich dem deutschen Volk zu helfen, seinen Weg in die internationale Gemeinschaft zurückzufinden") Edgar N. Johnson, "Vorwort," in: *Benjamin Franklin. Sein Leben von ihm selbst erzählt*, Berlin 1946, pp. 5–10, here p. 6.

69 Doc. 9.

70 See James K. Pollock, *Besatzung und Staatsaufbau nach 1945. Occupation Diary and Private Correspondence 1945–1948*, ed. Ingrid Krüger-Bulcke (= Biographische Quellen zur deutschen Geschichte nach 1945, vol. 14), Munich 1994.

71 See Josef Henke/Klaus Oldenhage, "Office of Military Government for Germany (U. S.)," in: *OMGUS-Handbuch. Die amerikanische Militärregierung in Deutschland 1945–1949*, ed. Christoph Weisz (= Quellen und Darstellungen zur Zeitgeschichte, vol. 35), Munich 1994, pp. 1–142, here pp. 122f.

72 Cf. Conrad F. Latour/Thilo Vogelsang, *Okkupation und Wiederaufbau. Die Tätigkeit der Militärregierung in der amerikanischen Besatzungszone Deutschlands 1944–1947*

From the beginning of his trip in February 1946 until the end of his work in Germany in August 1946, Johnson wrote long, diary-like letters to his wife, who was thus able to witness and relive everything. Extensively, directly, bluntly, and in detail, he reported on his daily experiences, tasks, everyday life, conversations, meetings, and encounters with political actors from the occupation and German political and cultural figures. Particular attention is due to his assessment of individuals, his critical remarks on occupation policies, and his opinions, views, and comments on Germany, Germans, the Allies, living conditions, as well as the mood and atmosphere in Germany. His descriptions of people testify to a distinct gift of observation. As he did not keep a diary, his experiences are recorded exclusively in these letters. On the one hand his aim was to keep his wife and partner posted, letting her know as much as possible about everything that was happening, allowing her take part, and keeping up an intellectual exchange. On the other hand he wanted to hold onto his experiences, observations, thoughts, and insights, so that later he would have the foundation for publications or lectures. Written under the impression of immediate experience and not intended for the public, these letters afford us new, profound insights into occupation and political reconstruction in the four-power city of Berlin in 1946.

At the beginning of his trip, Johnson was reminded of his semester as a visiting professor at the University of Wisconsin in 1939/1940, when he had struggled with depression: "Generally speaking I am still low and begin to wonder if perhaps what I am doing now is not going to be something like another Wisconsin semester."[73] He was troubled by a certain psychological lability from the start, questioning the meaning of his endeavors, and feeling the burden of his separation from Emily and the "sweet boys."

Johnson could not be dispatched to Europe by plane as originally planned, and departure on the US Army transport ship *George W. Goethals* was only possible some days later. He thus arrived in Berlin behind schedule, on March 7, 1946. At first he stayed in the former official villa of the General Director of the Kaiser Wilhelm Society for the Advancement of Science, at Ihnestraße 14 (today Brümmerstraße 74) in Dahlem, a district that had been largely spared from bombing. "[...] they treated me as a VIP and put me, not in the ordinary hotel but in a room in a very nice house reserved for special guests."[74]

Located in the middle of the Soviet zone, the Allied four-sector city was home to the OMGUS headquarters. This was meant to be only a short stopover for Johnson on the way to Stuttgart, where RGCO was located. In Berlin, however, it soon became clear to him that Pollock might continue to lead RGCO until his return to the US in the summer of 1946, not coming to the Spree as Clay's Political Adviser as originally planned. Johnson was naturally very disap-

(Studien zur Zeitgeschichte), Stuttgart 1973, pp. 123f.; Josef Henke/Klaus Oldenhage, "Office of Military Government for Germany (U. S.)," in: *OMGUS-Handbuch. Die amerikanische Militärregierung in Deutschland 1945–1949*, ed. Christoph Weisz (= Quellen und Darstellungen zur Zeitgeschichte, vol. 35), Munich 1994, pp. 1–142, here p. 43.

73 Doc. 1.

74 Doc. 15.

pointed; in their first conversation, Clay suggested to him "that for the next few weeks I should spend my time getting acquainted with the international and military government set-up here in Berlin and in the zone preparatory to whatever I shall be doing after that date."[75] "What would be Pollock's fate he had not yet decided, i. e., whether he was to be permanently here or remain in Stuttgart and I was led to believe that if it were Stuttgart I could be here in some advisory capacity to him, and if Pollock were to come here then I should be in Stuttgart."[76]

Johnson was to orient himself for a start ("along the highways and by-ways of OMGUS"[77]), getting acquainted with the military government as well as the four-power committees, and preparing himself for future tasks in Berlin and in the US zone. He was assigned to the Civil Administration Branch of the Internal Affairs and Communications Division, OMGUS,[78] and personally supervised by General Charles K. Gailey, head of this branch. From then on, he took part in meetings and discussions, also on the four-power level. As of March 9, 1946, Johnson participated in regular OMGUS staff conferences, which served the purpose of information exchange between Clay and his team of advisers.[79] "After the various people had reported Clay made a very nice introductory speech concerning me, referring to my previous acquaintance with Germany and my experience with OSS and then asked all those present to extend to me every courtesy possible in order to aid me in getting acquainted with the set-up here in Berlin. He then asked me to stand up. This certainly was extremely decent and helpful of him to do."[80] "I must say he makes a good impression, conducting the meeting with good sense, efficiency, authority and good humor and breaking into the reports with sharp questions, and rigorous comments."[81] Later, after a conversation at a party with the three-star general about the KPD and America's future in Germany, Johnson notes: "He has a terribly good head."[82]

75 Doc. 16.

76 Ibid.

77 Doc. 83.

78 The Civil Administration Branch had the following responsibilities: "settlement of four-power agreements on the decentralization of political structures in Germany, re-establishment of democratic conditions in local self-government, monitoring of political parties, preparation of central administrative institutions, alignment and coordination of policies and administration on the state level, as well as monitoring of the reform of civil service." ("Vereinbarung von Vier-Mächte-Abkommen zur Dezentralisierung der politischen Strukturen in Deutschland, Wiedererrichtung demokratischer Verhältnisse in der kommunalen Selbstverwaltung, Überwachung der politischen Parteien, Vorbereitung zentraler Verwaltungseinrichtungen, Angleichung und Koordinierung der Politik und Verwaltung auf Länderebene sowie Überwachung der Reform des Öffentlichen Dienstes") Josef Henke/Klaus Oldenhage, "Office of Military Government for Germany (U. S.)," in: *OMGUS-Handbuch. Die amerikanische Militärregierung in Deutschland 1945–1949*, ed. Christoph Weisz (= Quellen und Darstellungen zur Zeitgeschichte, vol. 35), Munich 1994, pp. 1–142, here p. 110.

79 See Bernd Steger, "General Clays Stabskonferenzen und die Organisation der amerikanischen Militärregierung in Deutschland. Die 'Clay-Minutes' als historische Quelle," in: *Vierteljahrshefte für Zeitgeschichte*, vol. 27 (1979), pp. 113–130.

80 Doc. 17.

81 Ibid.

82 Doc. 55.

When it was definite that Pollock would stay in Stuttgart until his return to the United States, Clay appointed the professor from Nebraska as his Special Assistant, and provided him with an office at the OMGUS headquarters in Berlin-Dahlem. "I am to spend some time each week in this office keeping acquainted with the affairs of Omgus and I am to be permitted to see necessary documents to keep me in touch."[83] Additionally, Johnson was "lent out" "on a temporary basis"[84] to General Ray W. Barker, Commanding General, US Headquarters Berlin District, American Commandant of Berlin, in order to act as his Political Adviser (Special Assistant for Political Affairs). Walter L. Dorn had also shown interest in this assignment, but he was appointed as Clay's Special Adviser for relations between military government detachments and German regional offices; a short time later, he was appointed as Clay's Personal Adviser on denazification, retaining his previous duties. Johnson was also considered for these jobs. Baker was skeptical of Dorn's "red leanings,"[85] and as a result he was happy to have gained Johnson, who would become his valued counselor.

A political thinker, Barker did not agree with Clay on all questions. He was also in poor health due to back problems.[86] At the end of April/beginning of May 1946, he was replaced by General Frank A. Keating, a relatively politically disinterested organization man. Johnson experienced Barker's departure as a loss. "It will be a worthy task to do what I can to help the new general,"[87] he writes to his wife. "But somehow or another I have become personally devoted to Barker in the little time that I have been permitted to work for him, and I don't like to see him go. He is one of the few in high places here who does have any principles."[88] With respect to Keating, Johnson writes: "The new general is quite unpolitical, though not, I take it, without intelligence. I am told he is something of a hot headed Irishman."[89] These assessments and fears did not prevent Johnson from doing his job in Berlin, however, including acting as an adviser to Barker's successor. Keating built his career under Clay; when Clay became Military Governor in March 1947, Keating took over the function of Deputy Military Governor and Commanding General, OMGUS.

Johnson found the Berlin job interesting and important. After all, under the sovereignty of the four Allies, the former Reich capital was "a center of importance, what is done here has significance for all of Germany and certainly it is an indication of what we stand for to all the world."[90] As adviser to the American Commandant, he had an office at the headquarters of the American military government for Berlin (Office of Military Government, Berlin District [OMGBD]) in Berlin-Steglitz. Initially he was occupied with the de-

83 Doc. 25.
84 Doc. 41.
85 Doc. 33.
86 "Because of a bad back, he sat at meetings in a padded chair, with a big green pillow behind him, but always started to squirm in acute discomfort after the first half hour." Frank Howley, *Berlin Command*, New York 1950, p. 109.
87 Doc. 39.
88 Ibid.
89 Doc. 41.
90 Doc. 34.

velopment of a new Civil Administration Branch, OMGBD,[91] to which he was assigned.

Against the background of the unification of the KPD and SPD into a Sozialistische Einheitspartei (Socialist Unity Party), driven by Soviet occupation forces, Johnson supported the development of a new Berlin SPD by those Social Democrats who resisted the forced party fusion in Berlin.[92] In the Soviet zone it was not possible to make free decisions about the future of Social Democratic party organization, and the majority of the SPD Central Committee bent to pressure and went the way of merger with the KPD. In the four-power city, however, opponents of the merger could push through a membership vote within the party on the planned unification. However, this member survey could only be conducted in the American, British, and French sectors; there, 82.6 percent of SPD members who cast votes were against "the immediate merger of both labor parties."[93]

Johnson was convinced that the merger was not voluntary, and that the Communists – "whom I am coming to hate here, not because of their program, but because of their dirty, tricky, methods"[94] – would set the tone in the new party. The oppositional Social Democrats opposed the KPD's unity slogans. After the Berlin membership vote, they built their own party organization. Johnson's sympathy went out to them, and to politicians like Otto Suhr, "a very able fellow,"[95] who became Acting Secretary General of the new SPD. Johnson wished that the American military government would break through the distance to meet these forces with understanding and actively support them. "These are the people we ought to be supporting because they stand for the kind of democratic decency which we stand for. But we are doing nothing to support them. We won't even let them have a newspaper yet."[96] He sharply criticized the neutral,

91 "On the 25th of January a Civil Administration Branch was organized and started operations. On the 4th of April it was officially activated with terms of reference approved by the Commanding General." "Civil Administration. Six Months Report, 4 January–3 July 1946," in: Office of Military Government U. S. Berlin District (ed.), *Six Months Report, 4 January–3 July 1946*, Berlin 1946, pp. 40–43, here p. 41. "Matters which have been of primary interest to the Civil Administration Branch and which it has handled or helped to handle are: (a) the SPD referendum of 31 March, (b) establishment of civil rights free from political interference in U. S. Sector, (c) recognition of the SPD, (e) a new constitution for Berlin, (f) plans for city-wide elections." "Digest of Reports, 4 January–3 July 1946," in: ibid., pp. 17–22, here p. 19.

92 On the merger of the SPD and KPD into the SED, and on the construction of a Social Democratic party organization by opponents of the unification, see Werner Breunig, "Berlin 1945/46. Vom Kriegsende bis zum parlamentarischen Neubeginn," in: *"Berlin kommt wieder." Die Nachkriegsjahre 1945/46* (= Ausstellungskataloge des Landesarchivs Berlin, 16), Berlin 2005, pp. 7–43, here pp. 24–26.

93 ("den sofortigen Zusammenschluß beider Arbeiterparteien") Ballot for the internal party membership vote on the question of unity on March 31, 1946, in: Landesarchiv Berlin (LAB), Germany, F Rep. 280 (Quellensammlung zur Berliner Zeitgeschichte [LAZ-Sammlung]), no. 1226.

94 Doc. 39.

95 Doc. 56.

96 Doc. 39. The newspaper *Der Sozialdemokrat. Organ der Sozialdemokratie Groß-Berlin* was published beginning on June 3, 1946, under British license.

passive stance adopted by the American military government; by not energetically countering Soviet dominance, the Soviets would be encouraged in their belief that they could act in Berlin as they did in their zone, thwarting the special development of the four-power city: "Don't we care whether the real democrats have a chance here or not? Why did we fight this war? As I remember it was for the American way of life or at least it had something to do about democracy? If we don't care about democracy in Europe then we'd better get the hell out of here and turn the place over to the Communists and the Soviets, and if we do we had better organize ourselves in some positive way and make a display, and a protest. As it is we are permitting Russia to run away with the game here."[97] Johnson had justified concerns and he was of the opinion that "it might be best for not only Germany but for our relations with the Russians if we come out for a policy of straight democratic socialism, supporting the Social Democrats."[98]

Clay, on the other hand, insisted on absolute political neutrality;[99] he refused to support the rebellious Social Democrats.[100] At a staff conference on the day before the membership vote, encouraged by his liaison to the State Department (Robert D. Murphy, Political Adviser for Germany), he had presented the view that the SPD Central Committee "was within its rights in urging a sabotage of the referendum"[101] – an unacceptable position for Johnson. "Later I learned," he tells his wife, "that Clay would have been ready to forbid the referendum which would have raised an uproar at home. If Clay is supposed to be kept politically wise by Murphy then Murphy has failed in his job so far. I intend, pardon the presumption, to take upon myself, with a little help, the job of making Clay politically informed."[102]

After the merger of the KPD and SPD, the SED in Berlin was initially only recognized in the Soviet-occupied Eastern sector, while the SPD newly constituted by opponents of the unification was only recognized in the Western sectors. It was only at the end of May 1946 that the Commandants allowed the SED as well as the SPD in all four sectors – "upon my initiative,"[103] according to Johnson, who had campaigned for this compromise solution. For him it was crucial that the SPD resulting from the membership vote could operate in the whole city in the future, as a political counterforce to the SED.

Johnson took on further important tasks with the Local Government Committee, a panel of experts for the Allied Kommandatura, which acted as the highest political organ of the city.[104] He took part as an additional American

97 Doc. 39.

98 Doc. 36.

99 Cf. John H. Backer, *Die deutschen Jahre des Generals Clay. Der Weg zur Bundesrepublik 1945–1949*, Munich 1983, pp. 174f.

100 Cf. Harold Hurwitz, *Die Eintracht der Siegermächte und die Orientierungsnot der Deutschen 1945–1946* (= Demokratie und Antikommunismus in Berlin nach 1945, vol. III), Cologne 1984, p. 117.

101 Doc. 30.

102 Ibid.

103 Doc. 55.

104 The Local Government Committee dealt with "all governmental affairs and enterprises (such as the constitution of Berlin and the census of Berlin), all political mat-

member, alongside Lieutenant Colonel Louis Glaser, who led the Civil Administration Branch of the OMGBD.[105] The Local Government Committee was occupied with the question of the first postwar municipal elections in Berlin. In the American zone, elections had already taken place in the smaller municipalities in January 1946, and the Americans vehemently insisted that the Berlin elections be held soon. The Soviets initially opposed setting an election date; only after the merger of the KPD and SPD into the SED, and the settlement authorizing the SED and new SPD as parties in all of Berlin, did they agree on the level of the Control Council that the Berlin elections could be held soon, in October 1946. Their expectation was that the majority of the electoral base of the SPD would shift to the SED.[106] Taking German templates into consideration, the Local Government Committee prepared a provisional Berlin constitution, on the basis of which the elections were to be held. The committee thus functioned as a constituent body. Johnson tackled the constitutional work with enthusiasm and interest, and because he spoke German, he could work with the German constitutional text provided by the municipal government (Magistrat). Colonel Glaser, on the other hand, "knows no word of German, and the draft of the Constitution as submitted by the City Government is of course not in English. There is an English translation but it is pretty frightful and no one could make much sense of it. This is a good example of what could happen if there were no-one around who could handle the German in some fashion."[107]

The British representative on the Local Government Committee, Major Harold Hays, later remembers his colleague Johnson as "a most charming man."[108] During discussions of the four-power committee, Hays reports, Johnson argued

ters, and the broad list which would be included under the term 'local government.'" "Civil Administration. Six Months Report, 4 January–3 July 1946," in: Office of Military Government U. S. Berlin District (ed.), *Six Months Report, 4 January–3 July 1946*, Berlin 1946, pp. 40–43, here p. 41.

105 The cooperation between Johnson and Glaser in the Civil Administration Branch was not without friction. "I think," Johnson writes, "that Col. Glaser would be only too glad to get rid of me, since my position as political advisor to the Commanding General sort of cramps his style. He is moreover a jealous and ambitious person, an advertising man, who takes, I think a certain amount of pleasure in shoving people about." Doc. 47.

106 On confrontations regarding the date of the first elections, see Werner Breunig, *Verfassunggebung in Berlin 1945–1950* (= Beiträge zur Politischen Wissenschaft, vol. 58), Berlin 1990, pp. 174–183.

107 Doc. 64. Later, when the final text of the constitution was available, OMGBD Director Frank L. Howley noted: "The official language of the constitution is German and I am informed that the German is much more accurate and correct than either the English or Russian translations; much of the work of the Committee having been done in the original German because of the reference material being in German, the recommendations of the Magistrat being in German and the need for speed." OMGBD, Interoffice Memo Slip, August 20, 1946, Subject: Constitution for Greater Berlin, in: LAB, B Rep. 036-01 (Office of Military Government, Berlin Sector [OMGBS]), 4/136-1/9.

108 Memoirs of Harold Hays, chapter 10: Berlin Constitution 1946, p. 148, in: Imperial War Museum (IWM) Duxford, Cambridgeshire, Great Britain, Lieutenant Colonel Harold Hays MBE Collection.

to define not only the number of Magistrat departments in the constitution, "but the type and functions of each. He did in fact produce a list of 18 Departments, fully named, and he only withdrew it on the urgent representation of the British and Soviet Representatives, who claimed that such was an infringement of the democratic rights of the elected Assembly, and that any alteration proposed in future would bring in its train an amendment to the Constitution itself!"[109] The final constitution text solely states that the number of departments should not exceed 18. While the suggestion to name Magistrat departments was not successful, this example clearly shows Johnson's committed participation in the formulation of a Berlin constitution.

Johnson exchanged ideas with German constitutional experts including the former Secretary General/General Director of the Kaiser Wilhelm Society for the Advancement of Science, Friedrich Glum, at that time adviser to the American military government in constitutional and administrative issues. Above all, Johnson was in contact with the Acting City Treasurer, Friedrich Haas. An administrative and constitutional expert, Haas belonged to the CDU and was significantly involved in creating the Magistrat's draft constitution.

Working on the constitution, the Local Government Committee was under enormous time pressure; the date set for the elections was not to be endangered, and there was to be no delay in going to the polls. The Americans in particular, out of concern about holding the October elections, were interested in finishing the work quickly and delivering a constitution to the German side in a timely fashion – "a valid instrument under which elections could be held."[110] In spite of the different conceptions with which the four powers approached their common task,[111] and not least of all due to the time pressure and the resulting willingness to compromise and atmosphere of "good will," they managed to agree on a constitutional text. Regarding successful Allied cooperation on the Local Government Committee, Johnson later writes: "The necessity for meeting in long sessions at frequent intervals soon broke down whatever official character there was to these meetings. The members of the Committee became friends. As meeting after meeting passed and every difficulty was settled, it became clear that no difficulty was to be too great; the Committee would come out with an agreed report."[112]

Nowhere else in Germany was a constitution jointly created by all four occupation forces, an unparalleled constitution-making process. The agreement reached shows that in 1946, there was still cooperative behavior, which stood in opposition to the signs of an incipient East-West confrontation.

In a letter of thanks from the Commandants to members of the Local Government Committee – Johnson is also named in the letterhead – it says among other things: "The Commandants of the Allied Kommandatura Berlin are

109 Ibid.

110 "Civil Administration. Six Months Report, 4 January–3 July 1946," in: Office of Military Government U. S. Berlin District (ed.), *Six Months Report, 4 January–3 July 1946*, Berlin 1946, pp. 40–43, here p. 41.

111 See Werner Breunig, *Verfassunggebung in Berlin 1945–1950* (= Beiträge zur Politischen Wissenschaft, vol. 58), Berlin 1990, pp. 186–189.

112 Doc. 83.

aware of the long, arduous hours that the Local Government Committee has labored in formulating and drafting the Constitution of the City of Berlin and the instructions to the Magistrat concerning the 'Electoral Procedure of Berlin'. The members of the Local Government Committee have given unstintingly of their time, and have drawn deeply upon their professional knowledge and experience to complete this important and difficult task assigned them by the Commandants."[113]

The Provisional Constitution of Greater Berlin[114] – teamwork of the Americans, British, French, and Soviets – facilitated the election of council members (Stadtverordneten) in October 1946, and the formation of a new, democratically legitimate Magistrat. This municipal authority replaced the city government put in place by Soviet occupation forces in May 1945,[115] thus breaking through the SED dominance that stemmed from the brief period of Soviet absolute power in Berlin.[116]

From the time that he took over advisory service for General Barker, Johnson lived in the Wannsee Hotel/Wannsee Officers' Club, Am Sandwerder 17/19, where he had a magnificent lake view of Großer Wannsee. "[…] there may be a good chance here to sit quietly once in awhile, and reflect about the meaning of what is going on here,"[117] writes Johnson at the end of March 1946 when he moved in under Barker's orders. "I need lots of time to think. Now I have a good place to do it."[118] The old villa on the eastern shore of the lake, where Johnson had a nice apartment at his disposal, was only a few minutes by foot from Barker's residence at Am Sandwerder 27, "only a few steps from General Barker and he has asked me to drop down in the evenings whenever I please."[119]

Gardener Albert Redmann had been tending the large gardens of the estate at Am Sandwerder 17/19 for 25 years, and Johnson learned about the history of the house from him. Redmann had known it since the days when the Belgian-British botanist and geographer Marcel Hardy had lived there after the

113 Letter from August 31, 1946, in: Documents from the estate of Louis Glaser, private collection of Anthony J. Glaser, Bethesda, Maryland, USA.

114 The constitution made Groß-Berlin (Greater Berlin) the official designation for Berlin.

115 On the appointed Magistrat, see *Die Sitzungsprotokolle des Magistrats der Stadt Berlin 1945/46*, part I, *1945*, edited and introduced by Dieter Hanauske (= Schriftenreihe des Landesarchivs Berlin, vol. 2/I), Berlin 1995; *Die Sitzungsprotokolle des Magistrats der Stadt Berlin 1945/46*, part II, *1946*, edited and introduced by Dieter Hanauske (= Schriftenreihe des Landesarchivs Berlin, vol. 2/II), Berlin 1999.

116 For a detailed account of the creation of the Provisional Constitution of Greater Berlin, see Werner Breunig, *Verfassunggebung in Berlin 1945–1950* (= Beiträge zur Politischen Wissenschaft, vol. 58), Berlin 1990, pp. 154–235. See also the report of the Soviet Lieutenant Colonel Alexander Mikhailovich Zozulya from June 18, 1946, on the preparation of the Berlin municipal elections and the question of the constitution, in: *Die UdSSR und die deutsche Frage 1941–1948. Dokumente aus dem Archiv für Außenpolitik der Russischen Föderation*, eds. Jochen P. Laufer/Georgij P. Kynin in collaboration with Viktor Knoll, vol. 2, *9. Mai 1945 bis 3. Oktober 1946*, Berlin 2004, Doc. 142.

117 Doc. 31.

118 Doc. 32.

119 Doc. 33.

First World War, as a member of the Allied Reparations Commission. Later the Jewish banker Hans Arnhold moved in; he had to emigrate in 1938. After that it was NS politician Walther Funk, Reich Economics Minister and President of the Reichsbank, "who now" – Johnson writes – "occupies quarters of an entirely different character at Nürnberg."[120] After the Second World War, the estate was requisitioned by the Americans. Redmann outlasted all of this change: "His gardening has brought him through the crises all right – Englishman – Jew – Nazi – Americans, and he goes on growing his flowers and his vegetables."[121] One might say that "gardeners like bureaucrats have a nice ability to survive all regimes."[122]

Since 1998 the villa on Wannsee has been home to the American Academy in Berlin, Hans Arnhold Center, a cultural institute serving communication and intellectual exchange between Germany and the USA.

Despite his full calendar, Johnson still found time to write the foreword for a German edition of Benjamin Franklin's autobiography, solicited by the young Berlin publisher Karl Heinz Henssel. When the text was finished, Johnson was highly satisfied with the results of his work: "If you will pardon, I shall say that I don't think it's bad,"[123] he writes to his wife. "Indeed I think that it is perhaps the best thing I have ever written. Properly understood there is much of myself in it, the meaning of the war for me, the experience in Austria, and especially the experience here, which I think, the intelligent German can catch, all these things rising up through Franklin's text and catching hold of certain phrases and sentences which seem to have particular meaning for this sad Berlin of June 1946."[124] The book with Johnson's foreword came out in 1946 with Karl H. Henssel Verlag, Berlin.[125] A review states: "The foreword by Edgar N. Johnson establishes the connection between this work from a past century and our world of today. Humanely above any bias or pharisaic desire to educate, it assumes a German task between East and West as immanent, seeing Franklin's ethos as a matter of importance for all of today's humanity."[126] Excerpts of the foreword were published in the American-licensed Berlin journal *Horizont. Halbmonatsschrift für junge Menschen*, under the heading "Benjamin Franklin and German Youth."[127]

120 Doc. 83.
121 Doc. 47.
122 Doc. 83.
123 Doc. 64.
124 Ibid.
125 See *Benjamin Franklin. Sein Leben von ihm selbst erzählt*, Berlin 1946.
126 ("Das Vorwort von Edgar N. Johnson stellt die Verbindung zwischen diesem Dokument eines vergangenen Jahrhunderts und unserer heutigen Welt her, indem es, menschenwürdig erhaben über jegliche Parteilichkeit oder pharisäisches Erziehenwollen, eine deutsche Aufgabe zwischen Ost und West als immanent annimmt und das Franklin'sche Ethos als Anliegen der ganzen heutigen Menschheit sieht.") Ursula Seyffarth, review of: *Benjamin Franklin. Sein Leben von ihm selbst erzählt*, Berlin 1946, in: *Welt und Wort. Literarische Monatsschrift*, November 1946, p. 188.
127 ("Benjamin Franklin und die deutsche Jugend") See *Horizont*, vol. 1, no. 20 (September 1, 1946), p. 19.

Johnson also made time for a lecture on July 9, 1946, at Harnack House, for the American Women's Club of Berlin, to whom he offered valuable advice and ideas for their stay in Berlin. "The ladies seemed to like the speech and asked for copies. I referred to you at the beginning and at the end,"[128] he tells his wife. The weekly newspaper *OMGUS Observer* reports in detail, under the headline "'Shun Nazis', Wives Told At Women's Club Meeting": "American families should have no toleration for Nazi-Germans, no matter how cultured or charming they seem to be, stated Dr. E. N. Johnson, Special Assistant to the Commanding General, Headquarters, B[erlin] D[istrict] at the second meeting of the American Women's Club of Berlin, Tuesday, when he discussed the responsibilities of American women in occupation. 'But Germans who conspicuously fought and resisted the influence of distorted Nazi minds should be fought and resisted the influence of [sic!] build their country along democratic lines,' he pointed out. 'The American women should reach out to German women like Helen Weber who are now trying to organize healthy political parties in a wholesome German government, or to persons like Gunther Weisenborn, who after imprisonment in concentration camps for underground activities against the Nazis, is still trying to direct the people away from the hypnotic influence of Nazism.' As Berlin is the nerve center of the world, Dr. Johnson said that what happened here would have lasting influence on the world of tomorrow. Therefore it is up to American women, who other women of the world are closely watching, to study international situations and keep abreast of world problems, particularly those to which they are so close. As the American families are apt to lose their sense of value and timing because of their comfortable communities, he advised them not to isolate themselves from the German people and their problems. 'The coming of American wives and families to Europe,' Dr. Johnson said, 'is but a further extension of America into Europe, a further representation of the best that America stands for in a Germany which has sore need for it. Your coming, in fact, amounts to the introduction into Germany of another American institution, the American home.'"[129] Johnson's speech was the first in a series of lectures "on occupation problems."[130]

Johnson found relaxation and distraction in evening gatherings ("just a drink, a smoke, and some salted nuts"[131]), parties at the exclusive Lakeside Club for high-ranking officers ("the top personnel in Omgus"[132]), sailing on Wannsee, and above all in the music that meant so much to him. In his letters he reports on musical experiences at the German State Opera in the Admiralspalast or unforgettable evenings with "my cellist friend"[133] Max Baldner, who played in the Zernick Quartet and taught cello at the Berlin Hochschule für Musik.

128 Doc. 72.

129 "'Shun Nazis', Wives Told At Women's Club Meeting," in: *OMGUS Observer* from July 12, 1946, p. 2.

130 Ibid.

131 Invitation to a gathering on July 5, 1946, in: Documents from the estate of Edgar N. Johnson, private collection of Candice E. and Thomas R. Johnson, Denver, Colorado, USA.

132 Doc. 17.

133 Doc. 55.

An ongoing theme in the letters is Emily's tedious search for a new piano for their musically talented son John, in whom his father saw a piano wunderkind. In a letter to her husband, Emily writes: "My hunting for pianos is even more amusing than your working on a constitution for Berlin!"[134] A statement from John and Thomas's babysitter also demonstrates the great value that music held for the family: "They [the Johnsons] had a nice record player and an interesting collection of records. I discovered a taste for Schubert's string quintets there (after putting the kids to bed)."[135]

In a letter to his father from June 29, 1946, Johnson gives a concise, vivid summary of his experiences and activities: "I have been a little disappointed in coming back here. As Norman [Edgar N. Johnson's brother] may have told you, the job I thought I was going to get wasn't ready for me when I came because of the long time it took for me to get back here. Consequently I was sent down to Berlin to become the political adviser of the Commanding General of the troops in the Berlin area. This work has been interesting and important enough, and I have not felt that my time was wasted. During the first part of it there was a nasty political fight going on here between the Communists and the Socialists. The Communists, with the support of Russia, wanted the Socialists to join with them in a united workers' party, and the Socialists wanted to retain their independence. The Socialists lost out in the Russian zone, but in Berlin, with the help of the British, French, and ourselves they managed to preserve their independence. I had something to do with this and for this I am glad. Since that time we have been busy trying to get ready for elections in Berlin in October. This has meant preparing a constitution for the city and preparing for the machinery of elections. In another week or so this work should be done."[136]

General Clay assumed that Johnson would take over the Stuttgart job after Pollock's departure in August 1946. Things turned out differently, however. The separation from his family was extremely difficult for Johnson.[137] He could have had his loved ones join him, but his wife could not bring herself to come to Europe with the children. Thus, Johnson was resolutely determined to conclude his work for the American military government and return to his family and his alma mater. A colleague told him "that he thought it very strange and absurd that I should be abandoning my position here, which was of considerable importance, to return to the academic life of Nebraska. Here I would be associated with the making of history rather than the teaching of it. He insisted that if I stayed on here for a few more years, I could accumulate enough money to carry us over an interim period until I could get an academic position which would be worthy of my experience in the past few years."[138] Johnson was un-

134 Emily L. Johnson in a letter to her husband, Edgar, from June 26, 1946, in: Documents from the estate of Edgar N. Johnson, private collection of Candice E. and Thomas R. Johnson, Denver, Colorado, USA.

135 Alison E. Gass in an email to Werner Breunig from January 10, 2010.

136 Doc. 69.

137 "I was so lonesome yesterday I could have wept, and I am almost in the same state today – a lovely Easter Sunday. Lonesome of course for my sweet wife and for my boys," Johnson writes in a letter to his wife. Doc. 39.

138 Doc. 67.

doubtedly tempted by the possibility of devoting himself to the reconstruction of Germany and helping to shape the course of history; yet this tempting offer receded into the background, eclipsed by the need to be with his family, who stood above everything else for him as an indispensable support in life. The opportunity to take on a prominent, lucrative position in the American military government was never realized. "It is something of a temptation to stay on here," he writes to his father, "but Emily does not want to come over with the children, and I am not sure that I want to abandon the university for work of this kind inasmuch as there is really no guarantee of how long it will last. I shall have to take a huge salary cut, which, with the inflation imminent in America will make things a bit difficult but I have made up my mind. I couldn't stay over here another year in any case without my family."[139]

It was not easy for Johnson to let Clay know about his plans to withdraw; after all, for Clay this meant losing one of his "chief professional assistants."[140] At the beginning of July 1946, he told the General about his decision in a letter. He simultaneously informed General Keating, who answered with a friendly letter of thanks. "I do not know what I would have done without your help,"[141] writes the Commandant. "That is saying too much," Johnson opines in a letter to his wife, "but I am glad he feels that I have not been utterly useless."[142]

On July 20, 1946, before his return to the United States, Johnson set out on a trip through the American zone with his chauffeur, Artur Sanow. The trip, authorized by Clay and very well prepared, took him to Greater Hesse, Württemberg-Baden, and Bavaria "to study political conditions in the zone."[143] A dense program was meant to convey interesting insights, but he soon began to doubt the sense in his tour of the zone, which had originally been meant to serve as orientation before the start of his actual work for the military government: "My work is really over and the uncertainty of our future in Germany makes it seems pointless to consider how much positive good we can do here. The Germans, I am sure, are itching for us to leave in order to get control themselves."[144]

Via Kassel and Butzbach, he headed first to Wiesbaden, where he was hosted by the head of the military government for Greater Hesse, Colonel James R. Newman, who had a PhD in education. In Darmstadt Johnson visited an American internment camp, CI Camp 91, a tent city surrounded by barbed-wire fencing and watchtowers, "where 17,000 Nazis considered dangerous enough to be put away are kept."[145] He reports on the efforts to maintain humane living con-

139 Doc. 69.

140 Doc. 71.

141 Letter from General Frank A. Keating to Edgar N. Johnson from July 5, 1946, in: Documents from the estate of Edgar N. Johnson, private collection of Candice E. and Thomas R. Johnson, Denver, Colorado, USA.

142 Doc. 72.

143 OMGUS, Office of the Commanding General, Subject: Orders, July 18, 1946, in: Documents from the estate of Edgar N. Johnson, private collection of Candice E. and Thomas R. Johnson, Denver, Colorado, USA.

144 Doc. 77.

145 Ibid.

ditions in the camp: "They have organized a university within the camp and there are all sorts of workshops, and artists' ateliers busy doing things, I am afraid, for American officers. There is a theatre and an orchestra. Indeed they played the Egmont Overture for me. But I hardly know what to think,"[146] because: "I learned that these people were being fed 1700 calories a day which is a good deal more than the average German gets. And one man at a machine who was doing especially hard work was getting a ration of 2500 calories which is more than the heavy workers ration in Germany."[147] This also caused resentment among the population.[148] However, there were to be no emaciated camp inmates who would be a reminder of concentration camp prisoners.

In his notes Johnson does not mention his visit on July 26, 1946, to the District President in Darmstadt, Ludwig Bergsträsser, a Social Democratic member of the Verfassungberatende Landesversammlung (constitutional advisory state assembly) of Greater Hesse.[149] Bergsträsser writes in his diary: "Around noon [Major William R.] Sheehan came with Professor Edgar N. Johnson, who will soon return to the States to work there, also in the public, against the illusionists and for the development of German conditions. For three weeks now he is visiting the American zone to inform himself about the particulars. Long, very interesting conversation. He asked all kinds of questions and was amazed when I said to him that it is a great stupidity that books cannot be sent to us from over there. Ultimately I don't see the reason why we are only allowed to send letters with private content. If, for example, I wish to write about political things to send over there, I have to ask Sheehan to pass it along, I can't do it directly. He also asked about the possibility of further democratic development and many other things. I emphasized economic necessity, also resources coming in for our export, and pointed to Offenbach industry."[150] Johnson informed Berg-

146 Ibid.

147 Ibid. Johnson had already been concerned with this issue at an earlier point; after the OMGUS staff conference on May 25, 1946, he writes to his wife: "It came out in Clay's meeting this morning that the camps for civilian internees (these are mostly Nazis put away for safe keeping) are much better fed than the ordinary German civilian. So if you don't mind your loss of freedom you can be better fed." Doc. 52.

148 See http://www.fr.de/politik/zeitgeschichte/zeitgeschichte/internierungslager-mit-eigener-zeitung-und-universitaet-a-1199998 (accessed May 15, 2018).

149 A visiting card given by the District President to his American guest is evidence of the meeting between Johnson and Bergsträsser. Found in: Documents from the estate of Edgar N. Johnson, private collection of Candice E. and Thomas R. Johnson, Denver, Colorado, USA.

150 ("Gegen Mittag kam [Major William R.] Sheehan mit Professor Edgar N. Johnson, der bald in die Staaten zurückkehrt und dort gegen die Illusionisten und für die Entwicklung der deutschen Zustände auch in der Öffentlichkeit wirken will. Er besucht jetzt drei Wochen die amerikanische Zone, um sich im einzelnen zu informieren. Langes, sehr interessantes Gespräch. Er stellte vielerlei Fragen und war erstaunt, wie ich ihm sagte, es sei doch eine Dummheit, daß uns nicht von drüben Bücher geschickt werden dürften. Schließlich sähe ich den Grund nicht ein, warum wir nur Briefe privaten Inhalts hinüberschicken dürften. Wenn ich z. B. über politische Dinge nach drüben schreiben wolle, müsse ich Sheehan bitten, diese weiterzugeben, und könne das nicht direkt tun. Er fragte auch nach den Möglichkeiten der demokratischen Weiterentwicklung und vielen anderen Dingen. Ich betonte die

strässer about teamwork in the Allied Kommandatura: "He worked in the International Kommandatura in Berlin and talked about how laborious it is, because of the language alone. They argued for two hours just about the question of the oath and the word 'unparteiisch' [impartial], which the Russians desperately wanted to construe as 'unpolitical.'"[151] Further Bergsträsser notes: "He very much agreed with my opinion that there should be large-scale exchange of professors and students, and also teachers. When I said during our conversation that I have never been in the States, he said it must be arranged for me to come over someday soon. He strongly emphasized the significance of denazification for public opinion in the USA."[152]

In Stuttgart, capital of the state of Württemberg-Baden, Johnson was the guest of the head of the military government for Württemberg-Baden, Colonel William W. Dawson, a law professor in civilian life. Dawson was soon to become James K. Pollock's successor as Director of RGCO, thus taking over the office that Johnson could have held.[153]

"This is a lovely spot, and it would have been pleasant to be here,"[154] Johnson notes in Stuttgart. To get a fleeting "glimpse of the job I was to have,"[155] he visited Pollock in the Villa Reitzenstein, former seat of the Württemberg Minister-President, where RGCO and the Länderrat were housed. "I can see that he is a very difficult person – capable, to be sure, but a little of a stuffed shirt. At least he treated me rather coldly and off-hand, leaving me to be impressed with his importance. Yet at the same time he was polite, has invited me to dinner today,"[156] Johnson writes of the outgoing RGCO Director.

Johnson was able to revive memories of his former travels when he visited the Bebenhausen Monastery near Tübingen in the French zone, one of the most beautiful and best-preserved monasteries in Germany, "a wonderful Cistercian abbey."[157]

Johnson's travel list also included the university city of Heidelberg, which had been spared from the destruction of the Second World War, "to see some of the

wirtschaftliche Notwendigkeit, auch das Hereinkommen von Rohstoffen für unseren Export, verwies auf die Offenbacher Industrie.") Ludwig Bergsträsser, *Befreiung, Besatzung, Neubeginn. Tagebuch des Darmstädter Regierungspräsidenten 1945–1948*, ed. Walter Mühlhausen (= Biographische Quellen zur deutschen Geschichte nach 1945, vol. 5), Munich 1987, pp. 149f.

151 ("Er hat in der Internationalen Kommandantur in Berlin gearbeitet und erzählte, wie umständlich es sei, schon der Sprache wegen. Sie hätten allein über die Frage des Eides und das Wort 'unparteiisch', das die Russen krampfhaft als 'unpolitisch' auffassen wollten, zwei Stunden diskutiert.") Ibid., p. 150.

152 ("Meiner Meinung, daß Austausch von Professoren und Studenten, auch Lehrern im großen Maßstab geschehen müsse, stimmte er sehr zu. Als ich im Gespräch sagte, ich wäre noch nie in den Staaten gewesen, sagte er, das müsse arrangiert werden, daß ich bald einmal hinüberkomme. Er betonte sehr stark die Bedeutung der Denazifizierung für die öffentliche Meinung in USA.") Ibid.

153 Dawson died in February 1947, a few months after taking office. Colonel Charles D. Winning was then Director of RGCO until the dissolution of RGCO in 1948.

154 Doc. 78.

155 Doc. 73.

156 Doc. 78.

157 Ibid.

professors there."[158] Among his documents[159] is a list with the names of some professors he could have visited, representatives of intellectual life: Fritz Ernst, historian and Pro-rector of the University of Heidelberg, Adolf Rausch, trade unionist and SPD Stadtrat, Dolf Sternberger, editor of the monthly journal *Die Wandlung*, Alfred Weber, economist and sociologist, as well as the latter's sister-in-law, Marianne Weber, widow of Max Weber, economist and sociologist.

In Nuremberg, former "City of Nazi Party Rallies," Johnson was present as an observer at the trial of the major war criminals before the International Military Tribunal. He describes the men in the dock as "a horrible looking bunch."[160] "Except for a few they seemed to be all in a fairly cheerful state of mind, and munched bread during the hearing."[161]

His travel route finally took him to Munich, where he was able to speak with the Minister-President of Bavaria, SPD politician Wilhelm Hoegner, and the Chairman of the CSU, Josef Müller, among others. Additionally, he visited his former boarding-house hostess Anna Engelhorn, whom he had last seen in November 1945. "The nicest thing about the trip was, I guess, the couple visits to Frau Engelhorn."[162] "[...] she still has sharp intelligence, good humor, and is certainly one of the best if not really the best German, I have ever met."[163] Her house and its furnishings had been requisitioned by the Americans, "as part of the so-called American Military Communities which are established here in the zone: blocks of barbed-wire surrounded houses. The Germans don't react well to this separation."[164] Johnson was very concerned about this issue. In one OMGUS staff meeting he had heard about protests in Stuttgart, where residents of the Sonnenberg district were meant to evacuate their homes for the families of members of the occupation forces. "We have never tried to distinguish between Nazis and non-Nazis in the requisition of dwelling space, a hot issue in this country where rooms are at premium."[165] Regarding the housing situation for Americans in Berlin, he later writes: "Nobody from the lowliest to the high could complain about quarters. We had simply taken over the best available, and could not be bothered much about the political histories of those we obliged to get out."[166]

Johnson's travel plans also included seeing "some of the so-called church heroes,"[167] whom he had written about as a Research Analyst at OSS, and visiting the Archbishop of Munich, Cardinal Michael von Faulhaber. The letters do not indicate whether a meeting with this prominent representative of the German episcopate actually took place. It is clear that Johnson was disappointed by the

158 Ibid.
159 Documents from the estate of Edgar N. Johnson, private collection of Candice E. and Thomas R. Johnson, Denver, Colorado, USA.
160 Doc. 79.
161 Ibid.
162 Doc. 80.
163 Ibid.
164 Doc. 79.
165 Doc. 26.
166 Doc. 83.
167 Doc. 75.

church, "that church which I once thought was going to be such a great help in bringing back Germany to its feet"[168] – a church "which doesn't want to get rid of its Nazi clergy,"[169] and whose "heroes" "do not happen to be at the moment, the heroes I thought they were going to be."[170]

General Walter J. Muller, head of the military government for Bavaria, "paid no attention to me, nor any of his henchmen, and the people on his M[ilitary] G[overnment] staff whom I could find in their offices were a little condescending or else a little dead."[171]

A side trip led Johnson to picturesque Oberammergau, famous for its Passion Play, where he stayed in the guesthouse of the European Theater Intelligence School[172]. "I have thought how nice it would be to come here some summer, perhaps, when the Passion Play is on, which it will certainly be again, and spend part of the summer here, and part in Austria."[173]

When his travels were being planned, Johnson had also considered a trip to Vienna: "I suppose I ought to try to go to Vienna again, and catch up with the situation there."[174] This side trip fell victim to a lack of time, however.

Upon completion of his approximately two-week tour through the zone, Johnson returned to Berlin on August 4, 1946. Two days later he left the city for good. He traveled by train to Bremerhaven, and after a few days he was able to head home by ship across the Atlantic. He joyfully anticipated a restorative vacation with his family in the mountains of Colorado before once again taking up his work at the university. Arriving home in Lincoln at the end of August, he could finally embrace his loved ones, without whom he had not wanted to remain in Germany any longer.

Johnson never returned to Germany. He probably could have worked for OMGUS again, since qualified personnel were rare. Prior to his departure from Germany, Donald R. Heath, the Director of Political Affairs who had worked in diplomacy, had suggested to him, "that if I found the life of the University to be a little too much to take, I should write him here at Berlin with the idea of coming into the service of the State Department here. I think he meant it."[175] People from the Education and Religious Affairs Branch had also expressed their interest in him: "[…] the Education people would be glad to take me on for an important job if I wished to come back here."[176] A letter to his wife, Emily, un-

168 Doc. 74.

169 Doc. 52.

170 Doc. 75.

171 Doc. 80.

172 Among the faculty was Henry Kissinger, later US Secretary of State and winner of the Nobel Peace Prize. Born in 1923 in Franconian Fürth, Kissinger emigrated to the USA in 1938 with his family; the Second World War had brought him back to Germany.

173 Letter from Oberammergau to his wife, Emily, from August 1, 1946, in: Documents from the estate of Edgar N. Johnson, private collection of Candice E. and Thomas R. Johnson, Denver, Colorado, USA. The unsigned letter was misplaced by Johnson and never sent.

174 Doc. 72.

175 Doc. 75.

176 Ibid.

equivocally demonstrates that his work at the university and above all his family were more important to him. Contemplating the time after return to his home in Lincoln, he writes: "I think when I get there I shall want, despite all my talk about trying to get into politics to do nothing much more than stay at home and tend to my classes. Staying at home will mean cultivating you, cultivating the boys, and I suppose the garden. We have lost over two years, and you are always rightly reminding me of how really little time there is left. It is rather futile to think that I shall ever be able to do anything much outside of the rôle of teacher, and there is much still that I have to make up for. May be the time is coming with the boys getting a little older when you will get a better break, and when we can share more fully than we have ever shared, and cultivate more than we have ever cultivated a larger intellectual life. I have always in mind too being adequate for the boys. All this is enough without worrying about others promotions and salaries."[177]

It seems that Johnson only briefly felt the bite of the political bug mentioned here ("trying to get into politics"). The idea of going into politics to oppose isolationist tendencies and to convince his fellow citizens of the necessity of American engagement and active shaping of postwar Germany and Europe, and of the idea "that the peace, having not yet been won, was as vital to win as the war,"[178] came to him in June 1946. At this time in Nebraska, the Republican senator and isolationist Hugh A. Butler was able to succeed against Dwight P. Griswold, who belonged to the internationalist wing of the Republican Party, to be nominated once again as the candidate for US senate. "I wonder if the Nebraskans realize the extent to which this is world news, and how much the Europeans will seek in it a confirmation of their notion that we are certain to abandon them again,"[179] Johnson writes regarding this decision in Nebraska. "I propose to offer my services to the Democratic Party of Nebraska to campaign against Butler for as much as they want to use me."[180] Would Johnson have been well suited as a politician? "[...] sometimes I think I could let go my academic reserve and get down to basic sentiments which might have a popular emotional appeal."[181] Yet Johnson could not bring himself to get into politics. "To my knowledge," Thomas R. Johnson shares, "he never tried to get into politics, although, as you might imagine, he voted for Democrats most of the time and was most likely a registered Democrat although I have no proof of that. The closest he came I think was helping to put together and contributing to the essay collection 'Freedom and the University', from the Cornell University Press, which was a response to the Joseph McCarthy-inspired investigations into liberal/left academicians."[182]

In the few months that he spent in occupied postwar Berlin, it is certain that this university professor from Nebraska, a highly intelligent, versatile, capable man, made a small but significant contribution to political reconstruction and

177 Doc. 65.
178 Doc. 83.
179 Doc. 62.
180 Doc. 64.
181 Ibid.
182 Email from Thomas R. Johnson to Werner Breunig from October 18, 2013.

the establishment of democratic foundations. Among other things, he was involved with the vote among Berlin SPD members on the question of the unification of Communists and Social Democrats, the recognition in all four sectors of the SPD newly constituted by opponents of the merger, the planning of the first postwar municipal elections, and the Provisional Constitution of Greater Berlin. His active participation in the consultations of the Local Government Committee of the Allied Kommandatura makes him one of the fathers of this constitution.

Qualified Germany experts from the American academic world were indispensable for OMGUS. Johnson was one of them, along with others such as Richard T. Alexander and John W. Taylor, who worked in the Education and Religious Affairs Branch, Internal Affairs and Communications Division. Taylor, an English teacher at the Kaiser-Friedrich-Realgymnasium in Berlin-Neukölln in 1930/1931, had written a dissertation on "Youth Welfare in Germany." After 1945 Taylor had asked his former teacher Alexander – Professor of Education in the Teachers College at Columbia University in New York City, and recognized expert on the German educational system – to come to Germany as an employee of the military government. Johnson met both of them in Berlin, and for a while he also considered working for the Education and Religious Affairs Branch. There were many demanding jobs for which there were not enough suitable people. Franz L. Neumann rightly recognized "that there ought to be more Edgar Johnsons in Germany."[183]

Johnson earned gratitude and praise for the work he had done. According to the OMGBD Director, Colonel Frank L. Howley, Dr. Johnson had done "great work for the Berlin District."[184] Unlike Glaser, Johnson did not receive the commendation ribbon or a similar decoration for his meritorious service to the military government, because the period of five months was too short; instead, General Lucius D. Clay was meant to write a letter of commendation to the Chancellor of the University of Nebraska, with particular emphasis on Johnson's participation in drafting a constitution for Berlin: "During the past five months he has been my personal advisor on political matters in Berlin and has been largely responsible for the temporary constitution for the City of Berlin which has just been approved by the Allied Control Authority for Germany and which previously had been approved by the Berlin Allied Kommandatura. The preparation of this constitution called for a most thorough knowledge of German political history and a deep knowledge of practical constitutional law. In order to draw up the constitution with the unanimous approval and assistance of his Russian, British and French colleagues, Doctor Johnson displayed extraordinary tact and persuasion."[185]

183 Letter from Franz L. Neumann to Edgar N. Johnson from May 17, 1946, in: UChicago Library, Special Collections Research Center, Edgar N. Johnson Papers.

184 OMGBD, Interoffice Memo Slip, August 7, 1946, Subject: Commendation for Dr. Edgar N. Johnson, in: LAB, B Rep. 036-01 (Office of Military Government, Berlin Sector [OMGBS]), 4/135-2/14.

185 Letter to the Chancellor of the University of Nebraska, Reuben G. Gustavson, from August 8, 1946, suggested for General Lucius D. Clay's signature, in: LAB, B Rep. 036-01 (Office of Military Government, Berlin Sector [OMGBS]), 4/135-2/14.

To Johnson, Clay writes: "It was unfortunate that delays over which we had no control brought you back to Germany too late for the assignment with the Landerrat. However, it did make you available as the adviser to Berlin Military Government at a time when the political structure of the city was in grave difficulty. Your contribution can be measured by the fact that prior to your departure, the four Allied Governments had agreed on a democratic city charter and a free election. I shall ever be grateful to you for the spirit in which you undertook a changed assignment and to your insistence on a liberal and democratic philosophy of city government which will mean even more to Berlin and Germany in the future."[186] Further in the letter he adds: "We miss you at our staff meetings. However, we also hope you will have an occasional pang of regret that you are not still with us. In any event, if liberalism can become a reality in Germany, it will grow from the foundation which you helped so much to place."[187]

Upon completion of his work for the American military government, Johnson processed what he had experienced in a report about his time in Berlin: "Five Months in Berlin."[188] He also held several lectures with this title in the autumn of 1946, for example on November 8 for members of the Lincoln chapter of the American Library Association.[189] In this way, he brought the significance of the American presence in Berlin and Germany home to his fellow citizens.

On October 20, 1946, the election of Stadtverordneten was held in all of Berlin. The SPD emerged as clear winner, while the SED, favored by Soviet occupation forces, had to accept a heavy defeat. On the same day, the Provisional Constitution of Greater Berlin took effect. Around five weeks later, on November 26, 1946, the Stadtverordneten, elected for two years, opened a new chapter in Berlin's postwar history and began with parliamentary work.[190] Johnson had been substantially involved in the preparation of these remarkable events in the political life of Berlin. When they took place, he had long since returned to the United States. "All the excitement without waiting for the event."[191]

Johnson had friendly contact with Acting City Treasurer Friedrich Haas in Berlin.[192] "[…] he is the kind of German upon whom Germany will have to rebuild."[193] They discussed questions of constitutional law together. At the end of December 1946, Haas – by then head of the Finance Department of the new Magistrat – thanked Johnson in writing: "for your valued note, which I received

186 Letter from General Lucius D. Clay to Edgar N. Johnson from September 12, 1946, in: UChicago Library, Special Collections Research Center, Edgar N. Johnson Papers.

187 Ibid.

188 Doc. 83.

189 See *Lincoln Nebraska State Journal* from November 9, 1946, p. 2.

190 See Werner Breunig, "Der parlamentarische Neubeginn. Die Konstituierung der Stadtverordnetenversammlung von Groß-Berlin am 26. November 1946," in: *Berlin in Geschichte und Gegenwart. Jahrbuch des Landesarchivs Berlin 2011*, pp. 213–235.

191 Doc. 54.

192 It is worth mentioning that Johnson invited Haas and his wife, Charlotte, to a meal at the Wannsee Officers' Club after they had been to the opera together: "I brought them out here for dinner and they stayed until after twelve – the first Germans, I imagine, who have been entertained in this expensive club." Doc. 74.

193 Ibid.

in October."[194] He told the professor in far-off Nebraska about further developments in Berlin, which were likely of burning interest to Johnson: "The provisional constitution, in which you had such a great part, was published on August 13, 1946, and it took effect on the day of the election, October 20. Meanwhile the new Magistrat has been elected and has for the most part started activity. The change from the old, put in place by occupation forces, to the new, elected by citizens, was not easy. At present we find ourselves still in the transition stage."[195] The following lines demonstrate how closely and amicably Haas and Johnson had worked together during the Berlin days: "Currently I am using the days around Christmas and New Year's to write the commentary to the provisional constitution that I told you about. I hope to be finished with the draft by the middle of January. As soon as it is printed, I will send you a copy. I need not emphasize that I think about our friendly and open discussion with nearly every word of commentary on the provisional constitution. I shall not forget the hours and days of our acquaintance and collaboration for a greater, future-oriented common cause."[196]

Johnson also maintained contact with his former chauffeur, Artur Sanow, sending CARE packages to the Berliner during bleak times.[197]

War and occupation had led Johnson beyond his tasks as an historian. After three and a half years of absence and activity on the international stage, he returned to the University of Nebraska in the autumn of 1946, re-entering the small, narrow world of the Department of History. Was this the right domain for him? He had his doubts. "I shall not be perfectly happy in University work again, at least to begin with,"[198] he writes in one of his letters from Berlin.

The Department of History was in search of a new chairman after Charles Henry Oldfather had asked to be released from his position. In Berlin, Johnson had given the succession some thought. "I am not anxious for it since it would be only extra administrative and personal problems pain, having to do with

[194] ("für Ihre werten Zeilen, die ich im Oktober erhalten habe") Letter from Friedrich Haas to Edgar N. Johnson from December 30, 1946, in: UChicago Library, Special Collections Research Center, Edgar N. Johnson Papers.

[195] ("Die vorläufige Verfassung, an der Sie so großen Anteil hatten, ist am 13. August 1946 veröffentlicht und am Wahltag, am 20. Oktober, in Kraft getreten. Inzwischen ist der neue Magistrat gewählt und hat zum größten Teil seine Tätigkeit aufgenommen. Der Wechsel vom alten, von den Besatzungsmächten eingesetzten, zum neuen, von den Bürgern gewählten, war nicht einfach. Wir befinden uns zur Zeit noch im Übergangsstadium.") Ibid.

[196] ("Augenblicklich benutze ich die Tage um Weihnachten und Neujahr, um den Ihnen angekündigten Kommentar zur vorläufigen Verfassung zu schreiben. Ich hoffe, mit dem Entwurf Mitte Januar fertig zu sein. Sobald er gedruckt ist, werde ich Ihnen ein Stück zugehen lassen. Daß ich bei der Erläuterung der vorläufigen Verfassung beinahe bei jedem Wort an unsere freundliche und offene Aussprache denke, brauche ich wohl nicht besonders zu betonen. Die Stunden und Tage unseres Kennenlernens und Zusammenarbeitens für eine größere, in die Zukunft weisende gemeinsame Sache bleiben mir unvergessen.") Ibid.

[197] See confirmation of receipt of a CARE package from January 10, 1948, in: Documents from the estate of Edgar N. Johnson, private collection of Candice E. and Thomas R. Johnson, Denver, Colorado, USA.

[198] Doc. 39.

raises and promotions. […] But should I refuse it, if it comes my way? Ben Franklin said he would never ask for, never refuse, and never resign from an office."[199] Following this advice from Benjamin Franklin, Johnson took over the position of temporary chairman in the autumn of 1946. He probably held the post for only a year.

Johnson knew how to put the knowledge and experiences that he had gained in the war years to use in his teaching and publications. "My experience in the war years has colored a good deal of my subsequent teaching and writing. How it has colored a mediaeval theme could be seen in my essay, *The Background of the University Tradition* in 'Freedom and the University' (Cornell University Press, 1950)."[200]

It was a great joy for Johnson that he could bring his good friend, the historian Eugene N. Anderson, to the University of Nebraska. Anderson had been working for the State Department since the dissolution of OSS; he was not comfortable there, and he was very happy to turn his back on the State Department to once again take up a university position and devote himself to scholarship. "I wanted to be independent, not to be at anyone's service,"[201] he later comments. He did not really like the people at the State Department, "they were too bureaucratic for me, too oriented towards hierarchy."[202] "He left in 1947 with infinite relief and delight to go to U[niversity] [of] N[ebraska],"[203] recalls his son, Eugene N. Anderson Jr.

As an historian, Anderson primarily dealt with 19th- and 20th-century German history. He had studied at the University of Berlin in 1924/1925 and received his PhD from the University of Chicago. After a research stay in Germany, he was Professor of Modern European History at the University of Chicago, then worked at the American University, and taught as a visiting professor at the University of Nebraska. As of 1943, he led the Central European Section of the Research and Analysis Branch at OSS, where he was Johnson's boss. Eugene N. Anderson Jr. remembers his father and Edgar N. Johnson: "He [Johnson] was my father's lifelong best friend, and our families were very close."[204] Johnson and Anderson "could talk shop for hours and hours, and my father," writes Eugene N. Anderson Jr., "got a lot of stimulation – my father was also tense and bright but more quiet, less adventurous – he needed Edgar and Edgar's strong

199 Doc. 65. The passage in question reads: "[…] I had read or heard of some Public Man, who made it a Rule never to ask for an Office, and never to refuse one when offer'd to him. I approve, says I, of his Rule, and will practise it with a small Addition; I shall never *ask*, never *refuse*, nor ever *resign* an Office." Benjamin Franklin, *The Autobiography*, with an introduction by Daniel Aaron, New York 1990, p. 109.

200 Edgar N. Johnson, Curriculum Vitae, undated [ca. 1963], p. 3, in: UChicago Library, Special Collections Research Center, Edgar N. Johnson Papers.

201 ("Ich wollte unabhängig sein, wollte niemandem zu Diensten sein") "Interview mit Prof. Eugene N. Anderson am 10. Dezember 1983 in Santa Barbara/Californien," in: *Zur Archäologie der Demokratie in Deutschland*, vol. 2, *Analysen von politischen Emigranten im amerikanischen Außenministerium 1946–1949*, ed. Alfons Söllner, Frankfurt am Main 1986, pp. 22–34, here p. 32.

202 ("sie waren zu bürokratisch für mich, zu Hierarchie-orientiert") Ibid., here pp. 31f.

203 Eugene N. Anderson Jr. in an email to Werner Breunig from July 30, 2007.

204 Eugene N. Anderson Jr. in an email to Werner Breunig from June 23, 2007.

opinions and mercilessly sharp mind to get him going. Edgar I think got some benefit from my father's quietness and philosophical attitude toward the world. Edgar kept up on current events and the world in general more than my father did, and was always great to talk to about most anything. Both of them were compulsive workers, though, so finding a chance to talk with them was always pretty difficult."[205]

In 1955, after accusations made by the American Legion during the McCarthy era, Anderson moved to the University of California, Los Angeles. Johnson stayed in Lincoln until 1958. In his book *Prairie University: A History of the University of Nebraska*, Robert E. Knoll describes Johnson's work: "In the Department of History, Edgar N. Johnson attracted a circle of admirers almost in spite of himself. Concerned with the largest intellectual questions, he offered a two-year course in the history of Western civilization in which he asked students to ponder the rise of rational liberalism from ancient times through the Enlightenment down to modern 'scientism,' one of his words. He did not pretend to be unbiased and thought that history revealed the eternal truths of civil rights. Cultural relativism was not for him. After Harley Burr Alexander left the campus, Johnson was sometimes referred to as the intellectual conscience of the University. A very intense man, rather indifferent to his appearance, he talked to freshmen as though they were his intellectual equals and to advanced students as though they were as passionately committed to the intellectual life as he was. In devoting himself to his grand ideas, he did not always seem aware of the individual students to whom he lectured, but they did not mind. He opened doors to worlds they had not known existed, and he changed the lives of some. Edgar Johnson was a synthesizer, a writer of textbooks, and a generalist."[206] He clearly enjoyed the particular esteem of his students. In the foreword to *Prelude to Democracy: A Study of Proportional Representation and the Heritage of Weimar Germany, 1871–1920*, a study based on his dissertation and published in 1958, Donald J. Ziegler writes that he owed his thanks to Johnson "for an approach to history which emphasizes the goodness and the rationality of man."[207]

Johnson spent the academic year of 1956/1957 as a visiting professor at Washington Square College, part of the private New York University, where he covered for the medievalist Wallace K. Ferguson. Emily and the children had already moved to New York in 1953 so that John could attend the prestigious Juilliard School of Music. Emily studied at a teacher's college in the East Coast city, and then taught at the Barnard School for Boys.

In New York there may have been a reunion with an old acquaintance from the Berlin days: Frank L. Howley, in 1946 OMGBD Director and Deputy Commandant of Berlin, was now serving as Vice Chancellor for University Develop-

205 Eugene N. Anderson Jr. in an email to Werner Breunig from July 17, 2007.

206 Robert E. Knoll, *Prairie University. A History of the University of Nebraska*, Lincoln, Nebraska, 1995, p. 87.

207 Donald J. Ziegler, *Prelude to Democracy. A Study of Proportional Representation and the Heritage of Weimar Germany, 1871–1920* (= University of Nebraska Studies, New Series no. 20), Lincoln, Nebraska, 1958, p. VII.

ment at New York University. Johnson had counted him among those occupiers "who are out to make this show a pleasure and an adventure for themselves."[208]

Edgar N. and Emily L. Johnson might have been glad to remain in cosmopolitan New York. Thomas R. Johnson writes: "I don't know whether they wished to move to N[ew] Y[ork] C[ity] permanently or not, though I am sure they felt much more culturally attuned to that city than to Lincoln Nebraska. I suspect, but do not know for sure, that Edgar was negotiating for a new job in several places at that time; perhaps New York University was one."[209]

A continuation of his activity at New York University was not possible, however, as there was no need for another medievalist in addition to Wallace K. Ferguson. Bayrd Still, head of the History Department, writes in a letter to Edgar N. Johnson from June 18, 1957: "You fitted into the Department with remarkable ease and unobtrusiveness and helped us admirably in filling the gap left by Wally Ferguson's departure. I know that a number of us enjoyed you and your wife so much as to wish we had a place for another medievalist at N[ew] Y[ork] U[niversity]. Unfortunately, our needs do not seem to point in that direction at the moment."[210]

After the academic year of 1956/1957, the Johnsons returned to Lincoln, in rural, conservative Nebraska. Their son John, who turned 18 in September 1957, continued his training at the Juilliard School in New York; in 1957/1958 he was a student of the Russian-American pianist Rosina Lhévinne. The hoped-for great career as a pianist did not materialize, however.

For whatever reasons, Edgar N. Johnson had repeatedly turned down offers from other universities in the past. "I remained in Lincoln, thinking it wise to decline invitations to come to Scripps College, the University of Southern California, and Ohio State University (chairmanship)."[211] However, after the departure of his close friend and colleague Eugene N. Anderson, and the time in New York with its cultural and intellectual offerings, it seemed that there was nothing more keeping him in the prairie city named for Abraham Lincoln. In 1958 he left the University of Nebraska, where he had taught for almost three decades. He moved to Brandeis University in Waltham, outside of Boston, capital of Massachusetts – "wanted to be back in a city with a lot of intellectual activity, as well as a more professionally good placement."[212] At this small, private university, founded in 1948 by Jewish immigrants, he would be Chairman of the Department of History for a number of years, until April 1963. One of his colleagues was Herbert Marcuse, Professor of Politics and Philosophy; Johnson already knew Marcuse from his time at OSS, and at Brandeis they worked together in the History of Ideas Program. For this program, Johnson taught

208 Doc. 46.

209 Thomas R. Johnson in an email to Werner Breunig from April 24, 2013.

210 Quoted according to Claire A. Wolford, Graduate Assistant, New York University Archives, in an email to Werner Breunig from April 11, 2013.

211 Edgar N. Johnson, Curriculum Vitae, undated [ca. 1963], p. 1, in: UChicago Library, Special Collections Research Center, Edgar N. Johnson Papers.

212 Eugene N. Anderson Jr. in an email to Werner Breunig from July 3, 2007.

courses such as “Intellectual History of the Twelfth and Thirteenth Centuries,”[213] or “The Thought of the Latin Fathers of the Church.”[214]

Among his students at Brandeis was Angeliki Laiou from Greece. In 1961/1962 she lived with the Johnsons in Newton, outside of Boston, and Thomas R. Johnson lived with the Laious in Athens. Through this family exchange, Edgar N. Johnson returned to Europe in 1962 for the first time since 1946, travelling to Greece with his wife, Emily, and Angeliki Laiou. Thomas R. Johnson recalls: “I stayed with Angeliki’s family (parents, brother and grandmother) from September, 1961 until about June, 1962 in Athens. Angeliki stayed with my parents in Newton, Massachusetts for the same period. Edgar, Emily and Angeliki came to Greece at the end of my stay and Emily, Edgar and I traveled around a bit after that.”[215] It would be Edgar N. Johnson’s last stay in Europe. He did not make a side trip to Germany.

As of 1981, Angeliki Laiou was Professor of Byzantine History at Harvard University, and she was considered “one of the world’s leading historians of the Byzantine empire – the successor of the Roman empire in the Middle East – and of the Crusades.”[216] At different points she was head of the History Department at Harvard University, member of the Greek parliament, and Deputy Secretary of Foreign Affairs in Greece.

Emily L. Johnson continued the educational work that she had begun in New York, directing the Charles River School in Dover, outside of Boston.

Brandeis was not Edgar N. Johnson’s last professional station. At the end of his career, he held a professorship at the public University of Massachusetts, Amherst, in western Massachusetts. His work at this university began in September 1965. In 1968/1969 he held a “Colloquium in Intellectual History”[217] at Regis College, a private Roman Catholic women’s college in Weston, Massachusetts. He retired in the spring of 1969.

Emily L. Johnson, “an innovative and progressive educator,”[218] founded The Common School in Amherst in 1967, “an independent elementary school that inculcated a love of learning and a respect for different cultures and learning styles among its students.”[219] This school “became a vibrant community of learners that thrives today. Over 100 students from ages 3 to 12, take part in joyful learning, based on Emily Johnson’s earliest ideas about educating children.”[220]

A few months after his retirement, on New Year’s Eve, 1969, Edgar N. Johnson died of a heart attack at the age of 68 in the Cooley Dickinson Hospital in Amherst’s neighboring town of Northampton. His ashes were spread at the

213 Brandeis University Bulletin, 1958–1959, p. 129.
214 Brandeis University Bulletin, 1963–1964, p. 132.
215 Thomas R. Johnson in an email to Werner Breunig from April 24, 2013.
216 https://news.harvard.edu/gazette/story/2010/09/angeliki-e-laiou/ (accessed May 15, 2018).
217 Email from Sister Mary Rita Grady, Archivist, Regis College Archives, to Werner Breunig from April 25, 2013.
218 https://vimeo.com/12266425 (accessed May 15, 2018).
219 Ibid. (accessed May 15, 2018).
220 Ibid. (accessed May 15, 2018).

family's vacation property, acquired in 1951, on the edge of Rocky Mountain National Park in Allenspark, Colorado. He had enjoyed visiting this place whenever possible. The "study cabin" where the scholar had often retreated to work still stands today; it was here that the letters addressed to his beloved and revered wife were later found in an old trunk.

Emily L. Johnson directed the school that she had founded in Amherst until 1975. She moved to Allenspark permanently in 1981, remaining in contact with The Common School. She died in Boulder, Colorado, on September 10, 1985, at the age of 74.

In 2005 Thomas R. Johnson transferred his father's written documents, including the letters written in Berlin in 1946, to the University of Chicago, where Edgar N. Johnson had studied, commenced his teaching activity, and received his doctorate.

Jürgen Wetzel

"Winning the Peace"

At the beginning of March 1946, Edgar N. Johnson arrived in a city of ruins and human misery. Poorly dressed, starving people were dwelling in bombed-out buildings, fighting for their very survival. The dead buried along roadsides had not even been reinterred at this point. After these first impressions, Johnson had his doubts as to whether or not Germany could ever again rise from the ruins.

The contrast to the well-fed American occupiers, living in shielded residential quarters, could not have been greater. These contrasts and palpable political tensions in the city moved Johnson so much that he confided his impressions and observations in long letters to his wife, Emily, nearly every day. With no time for detailed notes, he wrote these letters like a diary, analyzing and commenting. "I am sorry to omit details because if I don't write them to you they will escape me forever,"[1] he writes apologetically to his wife. "[…] I am keeping no journal, no diary. Only my letters to you contain a chronicle of what is happening to me."[2] It is possible that he intended to use the letters later as a basis for historical discussion, as he had already done with his Austrian experiences in "The American Occupation of Austria."[3] Aware of the explosive nature of his messages, he asked for discretion, and hoped that his letters would not be censored. The confidential information was not to be shared in their circle of acquaintances: "Please do not use these details in conversation,"[4] so that they would not find a way to the press. This could have meant losing his job in Berlin, he feared, and he did not want to disappoint his superiors: "I must be absolutely loyal."[5]

Johnson was originally slated to manage the liaison office between the Länderrat and the American military government in Stuttgart, as "Regional Military Governor."[6] James K. Pollock, head of the office at that time, was to come to Berlin as political adviser to the military government in exchange. Johnson wanted to stay in Germany until the autumn of 1947, potentially; he was considering having his family – his wife and two small sons, from whom he was reluctantly separated – join him in Europe, possibly in Switzerland due to the precarious situation in Germany.[7] His encounter with Pollock at the beginning of March in Berlin was quite chilly, however, and soon it became clear that Pollock would not leave the position before the end of the summer. At first

1 Doc. 28.
2 Doc. 67.
3 In: *Nebraska History*, vol. 26 (1945), pp. 201–210.
4 Doc. 27.
5 Doc. 26.
6 Doc. 41.
7 See Doc. 23 and Doc. 43.

Johnson was not informed of these reorganization measures.[8] He did not want to play "second fiddle" in Stuttgart, and he did not want to wait in Berlin until August, because his wife, Emily, also showed no willingness to come to Europe with their sons.[9] This was a bitter disappointment for him, especially as a lengthy impasse followed regarding his assignment in Berlin: "[...] it is a little hard on me. If I had known that I wasn't going to have the Stuttgart job, then I shouldn't have returned here."[10] The Deputy Military Governor, General Lucius D. Clay, advised him to start by looking around and informing himself about the structure of the military government.[11] It took some time until the clumsy military administration, with which Johnson had already had bad experiences before his departure from America, finally assigned him a position as "Special Assistant to the Deputy Military Governor," and an office near Clay and across from Ambassador Robert D. Murphy, Political Adviser for Germany.[12] In this position he took part in the staff conferences led by Clay, department discussions, and four-power meetings of the Allied Control Authority. Among the items on the agenda were demilitarization, dismantling of industry, the food situation, denazification measures, police reform, the forced unification of the KPD and SPD into the SED, and elections in Berlin.[13]

Johnson initially found the atmosphere in the OMGUS headquarters to be very hectic and confusing. Quickly learning how the occupation regime functioned, he recognized that people often enough acted against "principles of American democracy."[14] "I am just a little bit dizzy. I have attended so many meetings today; met and seen so many generals that I'm not quite sure where I am what I am or who I am,"[15] he writes to his wife. Yet not free of vanity, he felt flattered when he was treated as a VIP, moving among high military officers and diplomats. In spite of his unsatisfying position, he developed a trusting relationship with General Clay. Johnson admired Clay, and their relationship was marked by mutual respect. Since Clay shared the view that the position would not be fulfilling for Johnson, the latter was "lent out" to the military government responsible for Berlin, upon request of the American Commandant, General Ray W. Barker.[16]

As "Political Adviser to the Commanding General," Johnson was assigned to the Civil Administration Branch. He was impressed by General Barker, "an altogether decent and interesting fellow."[17] The feeling was mutual. Barker appreciated Johnson's advice just as Clay did, and the two of them also devel-

8 See Doc. 15, Doc. 16, Doc. 24, Doc. 43, Doc. 47, and Doc. 78.
9 See Doc. 49 and Doc. 69.
10 Doc. 24.
11 See Doc. 16 and Doc. 17.
12 See Doc. 25 and Doc. 74.
13 See Doc. 16, Doc. 17, Doc. 19, Doc. 27, Doc. 50, Doc. 52, Doc. 54, Doc. 55, Doc. 67, and Doc. 74.
14 Doc. 17.
15 Ibid.
16 See Doc. 24.
17 Doc. 25.

oped a close, trusting relationship: "My early impressions of him are confirmed. He is a man definitely worth working for,"[18] Johnson writes. In contrast, his relationship to the head of the branch, Lieutenant Colonel Louis Glaser, and the Director of the Berlin military government, Colonel Frank L. Howley, remained distantly chilly, although Johnson accompanied Glaser to meetings of the Local Government Committee of the Allied Kommandatura and represented him there several times. Both men were arrogant and ambitious, in Johnson's opinion. They only saw pleasure and adventure in their job, and Johnson had the feeling that Glaser wanted to get rid of him as quickly as possible.[19]

Johnson had the best qualifications to act as an adviser. Unlike Glaser and Howley, he had very good knowledge of German and Germany. In 1927/1928 he had studied in Munich with a scholarship from the Alexander von Humboldt Foundation under the renowned professors Paul Lehmann and Hermann Oncken, and he himself had been Professor of European History at the University of Nebraska in Lincoln since the 30s. As an historian, he possessed a well-trained eye for the political upheavals in Europe after the Second World War, which were concentrated in Berlin. He had gained practical experience for his job in Berlin by working since 1943 as a Research Analyst in the Office of Strategic Services in Washington, D. C., London, Caserta, and also in Austria immediately after the war.

In Berlin Johnson initially stayed in a house on Ihnestraße. At the end of March, General Barker arranged for him to move to the so-called Wannsee Hotel/Wannsee Officers' Club, Am Sandwerder, in the prestigious villa of the former Nazi Reich Economics Minister, Walther Funk. The house was directly on the lake shore of Großer Wannsee; Johnson enjoyed the wonderful view, budding spring, and sporting opportunities, particularly sailing. At the Wannsee Hotel, high-ranking Americans lived in elegant, comfortable quarters.[20]

For work he moved into a "splendiferous"[21] office in the headquarters of the Berlin District in Steglitz. He had a German secretary as well as a car with a German chauffeur. By order of Barker, Johnson was to establish a "political reporting office."[22] Even though Clay saw this as "small potatoes,"[23] Johnson's mood lifted after the disappointments of the past weeks. "Actually I think the job is going to be an interesting one,"[24] he writes to his wife in relief. During his initiation, Barker told him that the work of the military government in Berlin was "politics and education." Finally he could do important work, making contact with Germans – this was very close to his heart – and supporting them on the way back to democracy.

18 Doc. 28; see also Doc. 33.
19 See Doc. 40, Doc. 46, Doc. 47, Doc. 52, Doc. 53, Doc. 64, Doc. 67, Doc. 71, and Doc. 80.
20 See Doc. 31, Doc. 33, Doc. 36, Doc. 37, Doc. 41, Doc. 45, and Doc. 56.
21 Doc. 25 and Doc. 28.
22 Doc. 20.
23 Ibid.
24 Doc. 25.

At first he was assigned by the General to prepare for discussions of the Kommandatura. Barker took Johnson along to the meetings, which fascinated him. The explosive negotiations and observation of the actors gave him the feeling that he had arrived at the center of political happenings in Berlin. He learned how the "international machinery" functioned: "These international meetings are fun"[25] and "highly exciting,"[26] he writes enthusiastically. Given the babel of the many participants, various secretaries, and clumsy translation into two different languages, it astonished him that it was possible to communicate at all, and even to reach some agreements. He was particularly fascinated by the banquets with "lots of liquor, lots of food."[27]

The East-West conflict in the Allied city experienced its first big endurance test shortly after Johnson's arrival. The situation in Berlin was "particularly hot,"[28] as he writes to his wife. In the spring of 1946, the Soviet-influenced Communists in the Soviet zone and in Berlin forced a merger "with the Social Democrats into a new left-wing, workers' Unity Party (Einheitspartei)."[29] Johnson believed that if this fusion succeeded, it might have great political repercussions for Germany's future. The Soviets expected to gain greater influence on all of Berlin with this measure; they hoped to get closer to their goal of pushing the Western Allies out of Berlin and incorporating the city into their sphere of control. Many Social Democrats resisted the unification and the dominance of the Communists. They had suffered greatly under the Nazi regime, and they did not want to be forced from one dictatorship into the next. Johnson saw the resolution of this conflict as a central task of American politics; he conveyed information, analyses, and suggestions to General Barker, which the Commandant used in Kommandatura negotiations and in his addresses. When the Central Committee of the SPD wanted to sabotage a free vote on the unification, Johnson directly intervened: "This made me mad," he writes, "and I went to Barker with the suggestion that he write a letter to the Central Committee reminding them that he wanted a free expression of opinion on the matter to be held and that he also release a statement to the press expressing his point of view. He agreed (he is a man of principle) and let me write the letter and the release."[30] Indeed, the press release drafted by Johnson appeared on March 30 in the Berlin newspapers, and the membership vote took place on March 31, albeit only in the Western sectors, where the large majority of SPD members rejected the unification.[31] In long negotiations of the Allied committees, which Johnson actively experienced, the occupation forces finally agreed upon a compromise that Johnson had suggested: "I had

25 Doc. 28.

26 Doc. 25.

27 Ibid.

28 Doc. 20.

29 Ibid.

30 Doc. 30; see also Doc. 69.

31 See *Berlin. Kampf um Freiheit und Selbstverwaltung 1945–1946*, edited on behalf of the Senate of Berlin (= Schriftenreihe zur Berliner Zeitgeschichte, vol. 1), revised and supplemented second edition, Berlin 1961, p. 401, no. 97, and p. 404, no. 105.

written out a statement of our policy for the last meeting which was circulated among all the Commandants. It proposed simply that both parties be recognized."[32] Both parties, SED and SPD, were to be allowed to operate with equal rights in all of Berlin; in the Soviet zone, however, the Einheitspartei alone prevailed. In the run-up to these confrontations, Johnson visited party events and spoke with German politicians. He met the Social Democrat Otto Grotewohl, who thwarted the will of his party and opportunistically offered his services to the Communists. "I didn't like the look in his eye," Johnson writes after an encounter in May, adding: "But he was hardly a man in whom you could really put your trust."[33]

Johnson found that American politics lacked positive approaches in opposition to Soviet initiatives. He got the feeling that the American authorities in Washington were not developing a forward-looking strategy to counter Soviet aggression. In his view, they clearly had no proper sense of the help that was urgently needed in Germany to protect the country from Communist influence, and to secure peace. It seemed to Johnson that even "the best Americans [...] were not that interested in winning the peace."[34]

Johnson's most important responsibility was his work on the Local Government Committee of the Allied Kommandatura. He helped to install a parliamentary regime in Berlin. This meant drawing up a constitution and preparing municipal elections, in order to ultimately establish a democratically legitimized Magistrat. Through their trusting collaboration, Johnson had the opportunity to intensively advise General Barker before meetings of the Commandants in all matters related to Berlin. On April 27 he writes, "I think I reported on the last meeting when I had carefully prepared statements for General Barker to present at the previous meeting on such important subjects as elections in Berlin, the recognition of the anti-merger Social Democrats, and the supervision of political activities in the city of Berlin."[35] Elsewhere in the letter it says: "I had briefed him."[36]

At the beginning of May 1946, General Barker quit the service, perhaps for health reasons, but probably because he pursued "a line somewhat different from Clay."[37] "There is also the fact that he and Clay do not see eye to eye on all matters,"[38] as Johnson explains the difference between Clay and Barker. He deeply regrets the departure of the Commandant, writing: "He has been a fine person to come to know, and I regret very much his going."[39] Barker was replaced by General Frank A. Keating, who had no knowledge of the circum-

32 Doc. 40; see also Doc. 31, Doc. 32, Doc. 33, Doc. 37, Doc. 38, Doc. 55, Doc. 71, and Doc. 83.
33 Doc. 52.
34 Doc. 83; see also Doc. 39.
35 Doc. 40.
36 Ibid.; see also Doc. 29, Doc. 49, Doc. 55, Doc. 67, and Doc. 83.
37 Doc. 28.
38 Doc. 33.
39 Doc. 41.

stances in Berlin; in Johnson's opinion, Keating was "quite unpolitical"[40] and "quite innocent of politics."[41] Johnson did not develop a close adviser relationship to him, and this was a further disappointment for him. Also because his wife did not want to come to Europe with the children, he strengthened his resolve not to wait until the position in Stuttgart became available, but rather to return to Lincoln in August as originally planned. "If you don't want to come here, I shall be in Lincoln in the Fall."[42] There were patriotic reasons to stay in Berlin, he said, but on the other hand it was a complete waste of tax money for him to remain even longer in Berlin without fulfilling tasks.[43] For all of his career hopes in the military government, family always stood at the center of his emotional world. He felt lonely. Again and again, he was overcome by longing for his wife and his sons in far-away Nebraska. "I can't stand being alone. It is not good for me."[44] For them, he sacrificed the prospect of a prominent position in the military government with a light heart. However, it was difficult for him to inform General Clay of his intentions. He put off the conversation time and again, because Clay was counting on Johnson to take over from Pollock in the summer.[45] The Stuttgart job had originally attracted him based on the possibility of shaping policy, and the pay; with the money he could have improved his living standards and professional status in America. Yet he did not want to stay in Germany for another year without his family, and he also feared that he would thus cut off his roots in Lincoln. On the other hand he dreaded returning to the university's tangle of intrigue. With resignation, he noted that the prospect of teaching in Lincoln was just as unsatisfying as staying in Berlin: "In some ways I hate to enter this small world again, and I think perhaps I shouldn't,"[46] he remarks indecisively. Johnson writes to his wife that a colleague in Berlin found it absurd that he would decide to give up his position in Germany and return to academic life: "Here I would be associated with the making of history rather than the teaching of it."[47]

However, his disappointments and plans for return did not mean that he did not continue to observe and analyze American and Allied politics in Berlin with an alert mind. He was particularly engaged in the drawing up of a provisional constitution for Berlin in the Local Government Committee of the Allied Kommandatura. Regarding the problems in Berlin, he remarks: "The important decisions depend upon so many factors that the historian cannot ever hope to get at from the documents."[48] In addition to their reports about political developments in Berlin, which are mostly well known, his letters thus have

40 Ibid.
41 Doc. 53.
42 Doc. 47.
43 See Doc. 44, Doc. 56, Doc. 59, and Doc. 63.
44 Doc. 47; see also Doc. 42 and Doc. 69.
45 See Doc. 41, Doc. 43, Doc. 44, Doc. 53, Doc. 58, and Doc. 63.
46 Doc. 65; see also Doc. 41, Doc. 42, Doc. 43, Doc. 44, Doc. 53, Doc. 63, and Doc. 67.
47 Doc. 67.
48 Doc. 40.

particular value as sources because they capture the atmosphere in the city and shed light on the behavior of people and political actors.

Johnson felt that American occupation policies were too severe towards Germans who had not been found guilty. Most Americans were uneducated and unprepared for their assignments. Due to insufficient language skills they had no contact with Germans, and no understanding at all of their situation. Johnson deplored many injustices in the rigorous American politics of denazification; even in Clay's staff conference he had to note that Nazi detainees in the camps were better nourished than unencumbered Germans.[49] Germans needed assurance: "These Germans need some ray of hope,"[50] because their situation at the time was hopeless. They were undernourished and shabbily dressed, they seemed psychologically exhausted, and begging children wandered the ruin-lined streets. "But politics must have a future."[51] "Did we really, under the circumstances, have anything positive to offer this people?"[52], Johnson asks.

In contrast to most Americans, he sought out contact with the people. He took extra courses to improve his German.[53] It was necessary to speak German with the Germans in order to be able to better communicate with them. Yet in his encounters, people lamented their misery, and he experienced a lot of self-pity. Germans ignored the fact that they were responsible for their own situation. Many acted as though there had been no Nazi regime. Johnson regretted the absence of acknowledgment that the Germans had started the war, and that the world tragedy had sprung from Berlin. None of the people he talked to felt shame that the Germans were responsible for indescribable crimes. Many, Johnson found, would prefer to flee the consequences: "A great majority of Germans, I think, would now like to emigrate, if only they had some place to go. Having ruined their own country they would now like to escape the consequences of that ruin."[54] After these experiences, he feared a long occupation: "I am afraid this has to be a very long occupation, and that we have to make very long range plans. These people have literally to be re-educated over a long period by themselves but under our direction."[55]

Johnson was just as critical of American politics and the American occupation, however. On the ground he saw the American military government hindered by the worst bureaucracy. The chain of command from the top down to the occupying soldiers was too long and thus ineffective.[56] Many Americans in Berlin were acting without the requisite experience and necessary intelligence. He saw opportunists and adventurers at work, among them "hus-

49 See Doc. 52 and Doc. 77.
50 Doc. 21.
51 Ibid.
52 Doc. 83; see also Doc. 21, Doc. 36, and Doc. 42.
53 See Doc. 40 and Doc. 49.
54 Doc. 66; see also Doc. 18, Doc. 22, Doc. 50, and Doc. 76.
55 Doc. 49.
56 See Doc. 56.

ky-throated, hard-faced women,"[57] who shamelessly made money for themselves with cigarette currency in black-market transactions. At home many occupying soldiers were nothing, but in Berlin they were kings, and they wanted to hold on to their privileged position in Germany for as long as possible: "I believe the atmosphere is becoming more corrupt – corrupt in the sense of creating a privileged conqueror-class which is interested in nothing much more than what they can get out of it."[58] He condemned with particular severity American GIs' abuses of the German population, atrocities that were not reported in the press and not prosecuted. "I don't suppose," he comments on these occurrences, "that any historian, or other person can quite comprehend it all."[59] Far from the ruins in which Berliners seemed to be gradually adjusting to life in the broken city, the occupiers lived in an unnatural atmosphere in elegant villas in Dahlem, Wannsee, and Zehlendorf. In Frankfurt am Main, he reports, people referred to the shielded American living quarters as the "Ghetto of the Pharisees."[60] The Americans allowed themselves to be served by German domestic servants, gardeners, and chauffeurs. Contact with Germans took place solely on this level. Many Americans seemed only to pursue their own pleasure; one party followed the next, and they were always carrying a bottle of brandy. Indeed, spoiled by the luxury that surrounded them, Johnson saw some of the occupiers as "a new group of American colonial governors."[61] Above all, he found the waste of food particularly despicable; Germans did not even get the crumbs from the masters' tables. The Americans were also not willing to share their surplus with orphans or sick people.[62] He also sharply criticized the reduction of calories by British and French occupation forces: "You can't preach democracy on empty stomachs."[63] He hoped that the Americans would not follow this example, because: "It would be disastrous for the slow progress we have made here, and fatal to whatever trust the Germans put in us."[64]

An encounter in the house of Dr. Max Rheinstein, a German-American lawyer in the Legal Division of the military government, affected him deeply. The Americans had seized the prestigious villa in Dahlem, while the owner, cellist Max Baldner, had to live in a bombed-out house nearby with his four children and his wife. The whole family had suffered under the Nazis because of the wife's Jewish heritage. Baldner gave a solo cello concert for the occupiers: "How would you like to be a guest of your conquerors in your own house,"[65] Johnson asks his wife, ashamed. He was appalled that even former concentration camp prisoners were driven out of their houses by the American military

57 Doc. 83; see also Doc. 49.
58 Doc. 51; see also Doc. 21, Doc. 49, and Doc. 67.
59 Doc. 56; see also Doc. 67.
60 Doc. 79 and Doc. 83.
61 Doc. 83; see also Doc. 49.
62 See Doc. 27, Doc. 33, Doc. 56, and Doc. 83.
63 Doc. 23.
64 Ibid.; see also Doc. 26.
65 Doc. 25; see also Doc. 21, Doc. 34, Doc. 55, and Doc. 83.

government: "It is true that concentration camp people have had to get out to make room for the conquerors."[66]

Johnson, who came from a musical family, took advantage of every opportunity to see concerts and opera performances in Berlin. Accounts of the performances take up a lot of space in his reporting, along with great interest in the musical education of his son John.[67]

Despite the destruction, Johnson saw Berlin as not only the most important city in Germany, but also in Europe: "There could be no doubt that this city was still the most important in Germany […]. From the point of view of what was going on here, it was even the most important city in Europe. From the point of view of the struggle between East and West it was one of the most fascinating, if discouraging, focal points in the world."[68] He foresaw that it was here that the fate of the continent would be decided. Euphoria among the Allies over shared victory against the NS regime had long since evaporated, yet the Americans still held fast to the close brotherhood in arms with the Soviets. Whereas the military leadership continued to believe in partner-like cooperation with the Soviets to handle Germans and Germany, Johnson already saw many signs that pointed to tensions among the Allies, and to the incipient Cold War. "You remember when I came here I said that our relations with the Soviets were gradually getting worse. They have continued to go in that direction,"[69] he notes in June. The Soviets would do anything to make American politics appear in a bad light. He heard a rumor of "five Russian armies being concentrated in the Russian zone from the Czech border to Stettin, so powerful that, if anything were to happen they could sweep the rest of the western powers out of Germany and not be stopped until they reached the Atlantic and the Spanish border."[70] As early as April he writes: "I find myself taking on an ever stronger anti-Russian stand here."[71] He already refers to Berlin as "an international island in the Russian sea."[72] On the one hand he lamented the lack of orientation in American politics. On the other hand he saw how, as a consequence, the Soviets were working towards driving the Western powers out of the city in order to be able to incorporate all of Berlin into their occupation zone.

The Soviets in Berlin had already set the course for this aim: a Magistrat dominated by Communists, a police administration that received its instructions from Moscow, and parties, unions, youth and women's organizations in which "Russian trained Communists"[73] pulled the strings. Johnson met some of these people, among others Walter Ulbricht, whom he saw as "agents of Rus-

66 Doc. 52.
67 See Doc. 36, Doc. 38, Doc. 59, Doc. 66, Doc. 71, and Doc. 72.
68 Doc. 83.
69 Doc. 58; see also Doc. 44 and Doc. 61.
70 Doc. 63; see also Doc. 52.
71 Doc. 38.
72 Doc. 83.
73 Doc. 58.

sian policy."[74] In his opinion, Karl Maron was the real leader of Magistrat politics. He characterized Wilhelm Pieck as an "empty-headed Communist leader," and Ulbricht was for him "an unscrupulous and clever demagogue"[75]: "They are like the Nazis now and want to forget the past."[76] Added to this was the Communist control of most of the press and broadcasting. Whether voluntarily or by force, all efforts of the parties and organizations had only one aim: to gain influence and power. There were privileges for those who went along with it, and deportations or even death penalties for those who opposed such politics. "This was the system that was crowding in on quadripartite Berlin from the Russian zone and the Russian sector. Could it be stopped? Could it be modified? Could East and West really come together in the city?"[77], Johnson asks in doubt.

At first the Western powers did not see through this Soviet strategy; rather, with Order No. 1 in the first meeting of the Allied Kommandatura on July 11, 1945, they had approved all of the orders issued by the Soviets after surrender. In the course of further meetings of the Kommandatura, the American military government also went a long way to accommodate Soviet wishes in order to maintain a climate of friendly cooperation, and to demonstrate solidarity vis-à-vis the German population. Thus the Soviets could expand their position step by step. In Johnson's opinion, under these circumstances, should it not have been the task of the Americans to take countermeasures? Instead, they reduced their personnel in the military government so drastically "that it was neither possible to keep close watch on the *Magistrat*, or to keep in close enough contact with what was going on in the American sector of Berlin."[78]

Despite the Soviet politics of aggression, strict neutrality was still the official line of the United States in all internal German matters. Johnson is extremely angry about this, asking: "And where do we stand in this fight? Neutral! What does the liberal tradition of American democracy mean to these people? Nothing. [...] What are we doing to present the American picture in a positive light? Nothing. Don't we care whether the real democrats have a chance here or not? Why did we fight this war? As I remember it was for the American way of life or at least it had something to do about democracy? If we don't care about democracy in Europe then we'd better get the hell out of here and turn the place over to the Communists and the Soviets."[79] In Johnson's view, these politics were "political indifference,"[80] shortsighted and dangerous. The Americans had to give up their neutrality and promote and support politicians like the Acting Secretary General of the Berlin Sozialdemokratische Partei, Otto Suhr, and the Acting City Treasurer, Friedrich Haas, with whom Johnson also associated pri-

74 Doc. 83.
75 Ibid.
76 Doc. 58; see also Doc. 61 and Doc. 83.
77 Doc. 83; see also Doc. 61, Doc. 62, and Doc. 71.
78 Doc. 83.
79 Doc. 39.
80 Doc. 83.

vately. They had opposed Soviet pressure; with people like Haas and Suhr, the Americans could shape a democratic Germany. "These were the kind of Germans we wanted to support, the kind in whose hands a future Germany ought to be."[81]

In the free municipal elections promoted by the American side, Johnson saw a prospect for the city to do away with the Communist dominance of the Magistrat put in place by the Soviets. The preparation of a provisional constitution was the precondition for free elections. He took part in these preparations on the Local Government Committee of the Allied Kommandatura. After lengthy negotiations, the Soviets agreed for elections to be carried out in hope of having gained a favorable position for the Communists through the unification of KPD and SPD: "They know what Berlin means to Germany, and they want a victory of the new Communist dominated SED when elections are held in Berlin."[82] In contrast, the Americans hoped to be able to force back Soviet influence on the Magistrat with the elections, reducing Soviet pressure and facilitating democratic development in Berlin. Johnson saw in Berlin the future center of Germany's democratic renewal. He hoped for the support of the churches to help Germans get back on their feet, morally speaking.[83]

Aside from setting a political course, it seemed very important to him to convince Berliners of the "American way of life" in the ideological confrontation with the Soviets: "We need books about America, and people who can speak to Germans in German about America. We need to introduce into the educational system a breath of the fresh air present in our schools and universities, into the German press some of the virtues of our press (and there are some) and into German political life some of the tolerance, the give and take which we do have. This it seems to me is what the Germans need now. They don't need Communism at the moment, certainly, if they need it at all,"[84] he writes to his wife.

Johnson, who saw himself as one of Clay's "chief professional assistants,"[85] was disappointed about his assignment in the American military government, and he did not feel fulfilled. He would have been glad to experience "the rebirth of Germany,"[86] yet he notes: "I shall leave here with regret because there is much to do but I have never thought that my decision to leave is unwise."[87] Beginning in May he was increasingly occupied with his future life in Lincoln. In his correspondence he discusses detailed vacation plans with his family as well as personnel policies and his role at the University of Nebraska.[88] Yet he was still putting off the official notification of his decision to return. At the be-

81 Ibid.; see also Doc. 40, Doc. 56, and Doc. 74.
82 Doc. 40; see also Doc. 64, Doc. 68, Doc. 69, Doc. 70, Doc. 74, and Doc. 83.
83 See Doc. 74 and Doc. 68.
84 Doc. 40.
85 Doc. 71.
86 Doc. 74.
87 Doc. 73.
88 See Doc. 49, Doc. 52, Doc. 60, and Doc. 62.

ginning of July, he finally managed to inform Clay and Keating of his plans, and he asked Clay for the privilege to conclude his stay in Germany with a trip through the American zone. Unhappy to see Johnson go, Clay granted him this request.[89]

During his 16-day trip in a chauffeured staff car through Greater Hesse, Württemberg-Baden, and Bavaria, he met high-ranking officers of the regional military governments. In his report on the visit to Villa Reitzenstein in Stuttgart there is a sense of regret at not residing there as originally planned. Correspondingly, his judgment of Pollock was quite negative: "He has the most palatial and colonial office I have yet seen in Germany."[90] A short stay in Nuremberg made it possible for him to attend proceedings of the Nuremberg War Crimes Tribunal; this reinforced his loathing for Nazi leaders.[91] In Munich, the last station of his travels through the American zone, he also met German bigwigs, among others Minister-President Wilhelm Hoegner and some ministers of his government, and gained interesting insight into the situation in the American zone. Before his departure from Bremerhaven, he once again had a bad experience with military bureaucracy in the organization of his return trip, and ultimately he left Germany with relief.

Some weeks after his deployment, Johnson took stock of American occupation policies and the situation in the four-power city of Berlin in the report "Five Months in Berlin." He was convinced that the occupation of Germany was the most important enterprise that the United States had ever undertaken beyond its borders. The Americans ought to maintain control over Germany for at least ten more years, not pulling out prematurely as they had after the First World War. However, he sums up, "we can do a still better job in Germany."[92] In his opinion, Germans had to be won over for "American capitalism and English socialism, both associated with certain democratic liberties."[93] As early as April he writes: "[…] we need here a positive policy which will go as far as is possible to the left but still proclaims and implements the few things we are able to stand for."[94] Johnson saw denazification and re-education as positive approaches in American politics, along with the carrying out of free elections and increasing involvement of unencumbered Germans in political organization in the American zone: "In our own sphere of action, that is in our zones, I think much more could have been done if we had begun to collaborate immediately with those Germans and Austrians whom we could trust. […] In Berlin we have not really done it yet in our sector."[95] The establishment of the Länderrat in Stuttgart seemed to him to be the right path towards Germany's democratic renewal. On the other hand, however, American policies seemed to

89 See Doc. 70.
90 Doc. 78.
91 See Doc. 79.
92 Doc. 83.
93 Ibid.
94 Doc. 40.
95 Doc. 45.

him still too unfinished, without future-oriented perspectives, and above all too acquiescent vis-à-vis the Soviet challenge in Berlin and Germany. The Americans had won the war, and he had come to Germany "to assist in winning the peace."[96] However, he had his concerns as to whether peace could actually be won in Germany and Europe under the current conditions.

96 Doc. 83.

List of Documents

Documents

Doc. 1
Letter to His Wife
Washington, D. C., Gene's[1] office[2], February 12, 1946

Dear Sweetheart and the boys:

I am going down to a store or two to get some things that I couldn't get yesterday in the officers' shop at the Pentagon[3]. Gene tells me that they don't open until about 9:30 and accordingly I am up here in his office awaiting their opening time.

Nothing much happened yesterday. The lady whom I was supposed to see was surprised and somewhat annoyed that I had arrived a day early but I explained that they don't work in Omaha[4] on Saturday and Sunday and accordingly could not get me here on time with a departure on Monday[5]. Then she gave me my passport with visas for Britain and France. The passport is valid until May only which strikes me as strange – this suspicious state department. Then with instructions on how to get my picture taken for a new AGO[6] card she bade me make an appearance on Wednesday[7] morning before 9:30. At this

1 Eugene N. Anderson (1900–1984), American historian, 1924/1925 study at the University of Berlin, 1928 PhD, University of Chicago, 1930/1931 research stay in Germany (Social Sciences Research Fellowship), 1932–1936 Professor of Modern European History, University of Chicago, 1936–1941 American University, 1941/1942 Research Assistant, Office of Coordinator of Information, 1942–1945 Assistant Chief/Chief, Central European Section, Research and Analysis Branch, OSS, 1945–1947 Department of State, 1947–1955 University of Nebraska, accusations by the American Legion during the McCarthy era, 1955–1968 University of California, Los Angeles, subsequently until 1970 University of California, Santa Barbara. Edgar N. Johnson was friends with Eugene N. Anderson all his life. Anderson's son, Eugene N. Anderson Jr. (see Doc. 4, fn. 30), writes in an email to Werner Breunig from July 17, 2007: "He [Johnson] and my father could talk shop for hours and hours, and my father got a lot of stimulation – my father was also tense and bright but more quiet, less adventurous – he needed Edgar and Edgar's strong opinions and mercilessly sharp mind to get him going. Edgar I think got some benefit from my father's quietness and philosophical attitude toward the world. Edgar kept up on current events and the world in general more than my father did, and was always great to talk to about most anything. Both of them were compulsive workers, though, so finding a chance to talk with them was always pretty difficult."

2 In the Department of State, where Anderson was working as Acting Assistant Chief, Area Division V – Occupied Areas.

3 The building of the Department of War in Arlington, Virginia, on the border of Washington, D. C., erected on a pentagonal ground plan.

4 City in the US state of Nebraska, northeast of Johnson's home in Lincoln.

5 February 11, 1946.

6 Adjutant General's Office.

7 February 13, 1946.

time I shall get my AGO card and my orders. Then I think everything will be done except going to airport headquarters. And how long after this before getting away I don't know.

After this exciting experience I went to the Officers' Uniform store and bought instead of another coat such as I have, a short dress battle jacket as the one I left at home but made of the same material as my present coat. For an overcoat I bought one of the combination affairs – combination topcoat, raincoat and overcoat somewhat like the beltless one I have at present only with a belt and all wool. The lining snaps instead of buttons in. Then a pair of trousers. I need now only some gloves and a scarf and some insignia. The overcoat will be very useful after this is all over.

I had lunch with Franz[8] who had nothing much to say and went over to the old headquarters in OSS[9] to see if my things had come from Vienna[10]. As a mat-

8 Franz L. Neumann (1900–1954), German-American lawyer and political scientist, born in Kattowitz, Germany, 1923 Dr. jur., University of Frankfurt am Main, until 1933 lawyer specializing in labor law in partnership with Ernst Fraenkel (1898–1975) in Berlin and Lecturer at the Deutsche Hochschule für Politik, 1932/1933 legal adviser for the SPD, 1933 emigration to England, 1936 PhD, London School of Economics and Political Science, 1936 move to the USA, until 1942 employee of the Institute for Social Research, Columbia University, 1942/1943 Consultant, Board of Economic Warfare, 1943 US citizenship, 1943–1945 Research Analyst, Research and Analysis Branch, OSS, 1946 Chief, German Research Section, Office of Research and Intelligence, Department of State, as of 1948 Professor of Government, Columbia University, 1952 honorary doctorate from the Freie Universität Berlin. Franz L. Neumann and Edgar N. Johnson had gotten to know each other in the Central European Section, Research and Analysis Branch, OSS.

9 Office of Strategic Services, the American intelligence service established in 1942 and disbanded in 1945, headquarters located at 25th and E Streets, N. W., Washington, D. C. By far the largest department in this agency was the Research and Analysis Branch, primarily devoted to the preparation of interdisciplinary regional studies for observation of the enemy and occupation planning. After the disbanding of OSS, the operational departments were incorporated into the Department of War as precursors to the Central Intelligence Agency (CIA), and the Research and Analysis Branch was incorporated into the Department of State. Edgar N. Johnson had worked as a Research Analyst for the Central European Section, Research and Analysis Branch, OSS, from 1943–1945. "There were several highly qualified academics and officials who had emigrated from Germany and other countries in Central Europe working in this section, among them Franz Leopold Neumann [see fn. 8], Herbert Marcuse, Otto Kirchheimer, and Oscar Weigert, former Ministerialdirektor in the Reich Labor Ministry. Louis Wiesner [see Doc. 8, fn. 11], who came from the Council on Foreign Relations to the Central European Section in November 1943, charged with the collection and evaluation of information about Social Democratic and union exile and resistance groups, remembers this section as '*strongly* pro-social democratic, which you might expect from Franz Neumann, Herbert Marcuse, and so on.'" ("In dieser Sektion arbeiteten mehrere hochqualifizierte, aus Deutschland und anderen Ländern Mitteleuropas emigrierte Akademiker und Beamte, darunter Franz Leopold Neumann, Herbert Marcuse, Otto Kirchheimer und Oscar Weigert, ein früherer Ministerialdirektor aus dem Reichsarbeitsministerium. Louis Wiesner, der im November 1943 vom Council on Foreign Relations zur Central European Section kam und mit der Sammlung und Auswertung von Informationen über sozialdemokratische und gewerkschaftliche Exil- und Widerstandsgruppen beauftragt wurde, erinnert sich an diese Sektion als '*strongly* pro-social democratic, which you

ter of fact they have but how to get them home is a question. The section is over-crowded with Germans home from the wars – I mean people like Felix[11] and Len[12] for example who are going through much the same experience as I have being going through with respect to their colleagues and reaction to the present scene. They do not seem to have much to do and the great source of the bureaucracy – the New York Times[13] was much in evidence. I'll write more about this later. And more about the other things that have happened since I left you.[14]

Generally speaking I am still low and begin to wonder if perhaps what I am doing now is not going to be something like another Wisconsin semester.[15] Not

might expect from Franz Neumann, Herbert Marcuse, and so on.'") Michael Fichter, *Besatzungsmacht und Gewerkschaften. Zur Entwicklung und Anwendung der US-Gewerkschaftspolitik in Deutschland 1944–1948* (= Schriften des Zentralinstituts für sozialwissenschaftliche Forschung der Freien Universität Berlin, vol. 40), Opladen 1982, p. 61. On OSS, see *Zur Archäologie der Demokratie in Deutschland. Analysen politischer Emigranten im amerikanischen Geheimdienst*, vol. 1, *1943–1945*, ed. Alfons Söllner, Frankfurt am Main 1982; Bradley F. Smith, *The Shadow Warriors. O. S. S. and the Origins of the C. I. A.*, New York 1983; *Zur Archäologie der Demokratie in Deutschland*, vol. 2, *Analysen von politischen Emigranten im amerikanischen Außenministerium 1946–1949*, ed. Alfons Söllner, Frankfurt am Main 1986; Robin W. Winks, *Cloak & Gown. Scholars in the Secret War, 1939–1961*, New York 1987; Barry M. Katz, *Foreign Intelligence. Research and Analysis in the Office of Strategic Services, 1942–1945*, Cambridge, Massachusetts, and London 1989; George C. Chalou (ed.), *The Secrets War. The Office of Strategic Services in World War II*, Washington, D. C., 1992; Petra Marquardt-Bigman, *Amerikanische Geheimdienstanalysen über Deutschland 1942–1949* (= Studien zur Zeitgeschichte, vol. 45), Munich 1995; Christof Mauch, *Schattenkrieg gegen Hitler. Das Dritte Reich im Visier der amerikanischen Geheimdienste 1941–1945*, Stuttgart 1999.

10 Johnson returned to the USA at the end of 1945, "when OSS in Austria disbanded." Edgar N. Johnson, Curriculum Vitae, undated [ca. 1963], p. 3, in: The University of Chicago (UChicago) Library, Special Collections Research Center, Chicago, Illinois, USA, Edgar N. Johnson Papers.

11 Felix Gilbert (1905–1991), German-American historian, born in Baden-Baden, Germany, student of Friedrich Meinecke (1862–1954), 1930 Dr. phil., University of Berlin, 1936 emigration to the USA, 1939–1943 Institute for Advanced Study, 1943 US citizenship, 1943–1946 Research Analyst, Central European Section, Research and Analysis Branch, OSS, and Department of State, 1946–1962 Bryn Mawr College (Professor as of 1947), 1962–1975 Institute for Advanced Study, 1980 honorary doctorate from the Freie Universität Berlin, 1981 induction into the Order Pour le Mérite for Sciences and Arts. Photo with Gilbert in Appendix of Illustrations, ill. 10.

12 May refer to Leonard Krieger (1918–1990), American historian, 1942 MA and 1949 PhD, Yale University, Research Analyst, Central European Section, Research and Analysis Branch, OSS, taught from 1946–1962 at Yale University (first as Instructor, as of 1950 Professor), 1962–1969 University of Chicago, 1969–1972 Columbia University, as of 1972 University of Chicago. Felix Gilbert and Leonard Krieger had conducted field research in occupied Germany in 1945. See Tim B. Müller, "Die gelehrten Krieger und die Rockefeller-Revolution. Intellektuelle zwischen Geheimdienst, Neuer Linken und dem Entwurf einer neuen Ideengeschichte," in: *Geschichte und Gesellschaft*, 2007/33,2, pp. 198–227, here p. 220. See also Felix Gilbert, *Lehrjahre im alten Europa. Erinnerungen 1905–1945*, Berlin 1989, pp. 205–230.

13 American daily newspaper.

14 Johnson had parted from his wife on February 8, 1946. See Doc. 2, fn. 33.

15 Johnson was reminded of the depression he had suffered when he was a visiting professor at the University of Wisconsin in Madison, capital of the US state of Wiscon-

in detail I mean but only bad judgement. I send my love, and all of it to my sweet Emily and to the boys.[16] Edgar

Doc. 2
Letter to His Wife
Washington, D. C., The Roger Smith[1], Pennsylvania Avenue at 18th Street, N. W., February 13, 1946

Dearest Emily and my boys:

This is the hotel in which the War Department reserved a room for me. I cancelled it last night inasmuch as I went out to Polly's[2] last night. I shall cancel it again tonight for I shall return there for what is I hope my last night in Washington. It has, however, been a discouraging morning. I went to my Mrs. Chatham in the Overseas Branch of the War Department hoping to get final papers and to be sent to the Air Transport Command. I got my orders and this completed all my papers but I got the news also that there were no planes available, and that I should have to go by boat – a liberty ship[3]. I did not want to let this go without further protest and so I went up to General Hilldring's[4] office, to the Colonel Chard[5] who got results before, and wrote me the decent letter. There was nothing he could do but turn me over to Major Smith, General Clay's[6] liaison officer with whom I talked over the phone from Lincoln[7], a boy-

sin, from September 1939–February 1940, filling in for the historian Gaines Post (1902–1987) while Post was on leave. On the visiting professorship, see University of Wisconsin/Madison (UW-Madison) Archives, Madison, Wisconsin, USA, Department of History, Faculty Personnel Files, Series 7/16/3/1 Box 10.

16 Eugene N. Anderson Jr. (see Doc. 4, fn. 30) writes in an email to Werner Breunig from July 17, 2007: "He [Johnson] had a close and wonderful marriage. His wife Emily was a really intelligent and totally delightful and charming lady. In those days, women stayed home and raised kids, and she put up with that pretty well. She was an outstanding cook. Edgar was pretty strict with his sons."

1 Hotel, opened in 1912 as Hotel Powhatan, torn down in 1975.

2 Pauline R. Anderson, née Relyea (1903–1985), wife of Eugene N. Anderson (see Doc. 1, fn. 1), whom she had met while studying in Germany, American historian, 1937 PhD, Bryn Mawr College. The couple lived in Washington, D. C.

3 A type of cargo ship.

4 John H. Hilldring (1895–1974), Major General, 1943–1946 Director, Civil Affairs Division, Department of War, 1945 member of US Delegation, Berlin Conference, April 1946–1947 Assistant Secretary of State for Occupied Areas.

5 Robert H. Chard (1906–1958), Colonel, 1929 graduate of the United States Military Academy, 1945 Personnel Officer, USGCC, 1945–1947 Executive Officer, Civil Affairs Division, Department of War.

6 Lucius D. Clay (1897–1978), Lieutenant General, 1918 graduate of the United States Military Academy, 1945–1947 Deputy Military Governor, Germany (US), Commanding General, USGCC/OMGUS, 1947–1949 Military Governor, Germany (US), Commander-in-Chief, European Command, 1953 honorary doctorate from the Freie Universität Berlin, 1961/1962 Special Representative of US President John F. Kennedy (1917–1963) in Berlin, 1962 appointed as Honorary Citizen of Berlin. Photos with Clay in Appendix of Illustrations, ill. 21 and ill. 24.

ish blond major whose present position is understandable. As I came into his office there were people – one described to me as an adviser to General Clay – whose flight had been cancelled yesterday. There was nothing to do. Various explanations were offered. Planes had been taken off. There was a back-log of three or four hundred people waiting to get out of Washington, and they just had to stop taking on more until they could up. The Mamas had been so anxious to have their boys out of the army that, while there were plenty of planes and crews there were not sufficient ground crews to take care of them. Not much point in trying to find out the reason. Certainly it can't be for lack of planes. About the only people who can get away are those with a 1 priority – and this is, I suppose reserved for generals. A colonel in Col. Chard's office said he was trying to get back to Germany. He had a 3 priority which is my priority and said he didn't expect to get away until the 25th. Major Smith said the air delay would take months to clear up. All 2-3-4 priorities have been cancelled. The Colonel in Col. Chard's office said you had to be a cabinet member in order to get a 2. So there you are. My orders are being amended. I get the amended orders tomorrow at 1 or 1:30 pm. I go to New York tomorrow afternoon or evening. I go to Captain Rosenzweig to make arrangements to get a boat.[8] He was on this job when I left in June 1944[9]. When a boat will take me I haven't the slightest idea. I am discouraged. It is hard to get to work. I suppose I ought to cable Walter Dorn[10]. It would be amusing if the job[11] were already filled when I got there.

7 Capital of the US state of Nebraska, where Johnson lived with his family and taught at the university.

8 In order to travel to Europe by ship, Johnson was to proceed to the US Army's New York Port of Embarkation, which he already knew from his crossing to Europe in 1944.

9 "In June 1944 I went to London as the Chief of the Austrian Section of the Research and Analysis Branch [see Doc. 1, fn. 9] and was there until the spring of 1945 working closely with military government and state department officials who were preparing to go to Austria." Edgar N. Johnson, Curriculum Vitae, undated [ca. 1963], p. 2, in: UChicago Library, Special Collections Research Center, Edgar N. Johnson Papers.

10 Walter L. Dorn (1894–1961), American historian, son of a German-American pastor's family in Illinois, 1917 BD, Concordia Seminary, as of 1923 Instructor, University of Chicago, 1925 PhD, University of Chicago, as of 1927 two-year scholarship, research stays in London and Berlin, subsequently Professor, University of Wisconsin, as of 1931 Ohio State University, 1942/1943 Chief, Central European Section, Research and Analysis Branch, OSS, training instructor at the schools for military government officers in Shrivenham and Manchester, Great Britain, 1945 adviser to the military governments in Rhineland, Saxony, and Bremen, 1945/1946 Personal Adviser to Clarence L. Adcock (see Doc. 14, fn. 9), as of April 1946 Special Adviser for German Civil Administration and as of June 1946 also Personal Adviser on Denazification to Lucius D. Clay (see fn. 6), as of 1947 again at Ohio State University, 1957–1961 Columbia University. Dorn had been a teacher of Johnson's in the 1920s at the University of Chicago. Additionally, they knew each other from their time together at OSS. Photo of Dorn in Appendix of Illustrations, ill. 23.

11 Johnson assumed that he would take over leadership of the Regional Government Coordinating Office (RGCO), OMGUS, in Stuttgart. James K. Pollock (see Doc. 15, fn. 6) had started to set up RGCO in October 1945. The office served the American military government as a coordinating agency in all questions that concerned more

I went to Harold's[12] and Marguerite's[13] last night for dinner and stayed on into the evening. Marguerite's Mother[14] is there. Harold and I got there first after shopping for some meat. Marguerite came later, tired after a hard day's work but with a new and to her unsatisfactory hair-do. She is much grayer. I find her magnificent. After much conversation about you and John[15] and Timmy[16], and they are much devoted to you all, we got on to the prospects of peace and had a very gloomy conversation. I was astounded to find that she assures, as you assure, that there is going to be war, and that it will be the horrible end of everything. She has a new job in the Navy[17] and is working harder than ever and very tired and anxious to get out. We finally got on to the topic of Harold's return.[18] You must not repeat anything I say about this. Harold asked me not to say anything. He is writing Henry[19] over the weekend, and after you have heard

than one German state in the US zone. It advised and supervised the Länderrat of the American zone, in which the heads of state government worked together to ensure a degree of uniformity in German administrative operations beyond the state level. See Josef Henke/Klaus Oldenhage, "Office of Military Government for Germany (U. S.)," in: *OMGUS-Handbuch. Die amerikanische Militärregierung in Deutschland 1945–1949*, ed. Christoph Weisz (= Quellen und Darstellungen zur Zeitgeschichte, vol. 35), Munich 1994, pp. 1–142, here pp. 122f.

12 Harold C. Vedeler (1903–2007), godfather of Thomas R. Johnson (see fn. 16), American historian, 1933 PhD, University of Wisconsin, 1934–1941 Professor, University of Idaho, Southern Branch (today Idaho State University), 1941–1943 University of Nebraska, 1943–1965 Department of State, lastly Director, Office of Eastern European Affairs.

13 Marguerite D. Vedeler, née Drew (1898–1988), wife of Harold C. Vedeler, godmother of Thomas R. Johnson (see fn. 16), 1920 BA (English and political science), Swarthmore College, 1922/1923 study of political science at Stanford University, 1935/1936 Dean of Women, University of Idaho, Southern Branch (today Idaho State University), 1943–1946 Navy WAVES, Washington, D. C.

14 Marian P. Drew, née Pendleton (born 1872), "who worked in 'textile crafts.'" Email from Will Treece, Friends Historical Library Intern, Swarthmore College, to Werner Breunig from July 6, 2009.

15 Johnson's son John F. Johnson (born 1939), who later became a musician. See Appendix of Illustrations, ill. 3 and ill. 4.

16 Johnson's son Thomas R. Johnson (born 1944), who later became a molecular biologist. See Appendix of Illustrations, ill. 3.

17 "Mrs. Vedeler, a Nebraskan, served during World War II as officer in charge of the first Waves' barracks in Washington and later as women's representative at the Washington Navy Yard." Dorothea Pattee, "Mrs. Floberg's at the Helm for Navy Ball," in: *The Washington Post* from April 13, 1952, p. 5S. "In 1943, Mrs. Vedeler came to Washington as an officer in the Navy WAVES. She was the women's representative at the Naval Gun Factory. She left the service in 1946 as a lieutenant commander." "Marguerite Drew Vedeler. Teacher and Navy Veteran," in: *The Washington Post* from September 7, 1988, p. B7 (Obituaries).

18 Refers to return to the University of Nebraska, where Vedeler had taught until his leave in 1943.

19 Charles Henry Oldfather (1887–1954), American historian, studied among other places at the University of Munich (1911/1912), 1922 PhD, University of Wisconsin, 1912–1914 teacher, Syrian Protestant College, Beirut, 1914–1916 Professor of Classics, Hanover College, 1916–1926 Professor of Greek and Ancient History, Wabash

that he has written you can talk. The upshot of the matter is that he isn't going to return. Henry offered him the same financial inducements as he did to me, i. e., his raise of last year plus yearly raises since his departure. No increase in rank. But he doesn't ask for anything. He said to me that to take an increase in rank would be to violate University standards for such promotions. He was not entitled to it and would not have it. He said it was simply the importance of the work he was now doing. It is also I imagine partly Rudy's[20] return.[21] It is just possible that this return will always keep the department from getting good people. I had an explanation of why perhaps Rudy is returning from Francis Williamson[22] in the State Department. When it came time to appoint a chief army historian, the job was offered to someone else in Rudy's group (one Greenfield[23] from the U. of C.[24]) and not to Rudy. I thought this would be Harold's decision. For he is doing very important work. When I came into the State Department yesterday he was working on the preliminary draft of a treaty of peace with a country in which I recently spent a considerable amount of time.[25] Nothing could be more important than this. He will take over the Austrian desk when Francis Williamson journeys soon to the Continent.[26] He has already done very important work. His chief thinks very highly of him. He will be con-

College, as of 1926 Professor of Ancient History, University of Nebraska, 1929–1946 Chairman, Department of History, 1932–1952 Dean, College of Arts and Sciences.

20 Rudolph A. Winnacker (1904–1985), American historian, born in Germany, came to the USA in 1919, 1933 PhD, Harvard University, 1936–1941 Professor, University of Nebraska, 1941/1942 Office of Coordinator of Information, 1942–1945 Research Analyst, OSS, 1945–1949 Historical Division, Department of War (as of 1947 Department of the Army), 1949–1973 Chief Historian, Office of the Secretary of Defense.

21 Rudolph A. Winnacker was granted leave from the University of Nebraska in 1941 "for service to the government in Washington," and Harold C. Vedeler took his place as Visiting Professor of European History. "Historical News," in: *The American Historical Review*, vol. 47, no. 2 (January 1942), pp. 442–458, here p. 457.

22 Francis T. Williamson (1907–1964), American historian, 1935 PhD, Johns Hopkins University, 1930–1937 Instructor, Johns Hopkins University, 1937–1943 College of the City of New York, 1943/1944 Research Analyst, OSS, as of 1944 Department of State.

23 Kent R. Greenfield (1893–1967), American historian, 1915 PhD, Johns Hopkins University, 1920–1930 Professor of History, Yale University, as of 1930 Professor of Modern European History and Chairman, History Department, Johns Hopkins University, as of 1942 Assistant to the Historical Officer in the Army Ground Forces, 1946–1958 Chief Historian of the Department of War/Department of the Army. "Kent Roberts Greenfield, formerly of Johns Hopkins University, has been made chief historian of the War Department. He will direct the writing of the Army's 120-volume history of World War II and on September 1 will become professional adviser to a special staff section which, with the aid of teams of officers and men working in actual battle zones, has been collecting material for the work since early in the war." "Historical News," in: *The American Historical Review*, vol. 51, no. 4 (July 1946), pp. 788–804, here p. 799.

24 University of Chicago. Greenfield came from Johns Hopkins University.

25 Refers to the draft of a peace treaty with Austria. Vedeler worked for the Department of State as Country Specialist, Division of Territorial Studies.

26 Williamson went to Vienna in 1947 as US delegate, Four Power Commission.

stantly promoted and become more and more important. They would as a matter of fact have to come back to Lincoln. But they worry about finding a place to live among other things. In any case they won't be there and it is a very great loss. Now we know one person who is coming back and one person who is not coming back. I have mentioned the matter to Gene[27] but I don't think he will be much interested, and I shall mention it to Paul Sweet[28], who may be interested, though I wonder how he will care to contend with the boy who always intended to come back to the department.

I'll write about my own feelings about coming back later since I must rush off to an appointment. I will only say that after talking with the Vedelers[29] last night I think I ought to try, what with this new job, to make myself eligible for a job as important as Harold's.

Your lovely letter of Sunday[30] and John's Valentine[31] arrived yesterday.[32] Tell John I have bought him a big balloon for a valentine. I bought it from a man on the street. It is supposed to be an army weather balloon and the man I bought it from (a street vendor) suggested that to fill it one could use the exhaust of the vacuum cleaner. I'll send it when I get the time. I'm sorry you didn't get a cab home.[33] I don't yet feel equal to writing about the beautiful stay at home but I shall get over my depression at leaving, a depression that has stayed with me. Your very wonderful last paragraph is a start at recovery.[34] I will only say now that I love you and love you, that in the months to come I shall exert myself to the utmost to be worthy of what you write me, and to make possible a future for us that may be better than what we have had. I shall write John about the Valentine. Kiss him for me and tell him his Father loves him. Kiss the baby[35] for me too. And my darling beloved, let me kiss you too. Edgar

27 Eugene N. Anderson. See Doc. 1, fn. 1. Anderson had taught at the University of Nebraska as a visiting professor in the summer of 1939.

28 Paul R. Sweet (1907–2003), American historian, studies among other places at the University of Göttingen (1929/1930) and University of Munich (1930), 1934 PhD, University of Wisconsin, taught from 1934–1936 at Birmingham-Southern College, 1936–1943 Bates College, Professor, 1943–1945 Research and Analysis Branch, OSS (as of April 1945 Edgar N. Johnson's deputy on the team responsible for Austria), temporarily (May 1944–March 1945) Intelligence Officer, Psychological Warfare Division, 12th Army Group, 1946/1947 University of Chicago, 1947 Colby College, as of 1948 Department of State, 1959–1963 US Embassy in Bonn, 1963–1967 Consul General in Stuttgart, subsequently taught at Michigan State University.

29 Harold C. Vedeler and Marguerite D. Vedeler, née Drew. See fn. 12 and 13.

30 February 10, 1946.

31 John F. Johnson's valentine to his father for Valentine's Day on February 14, 1946, letter with postmark from February 10, 1946.

32 The letters, addressed to Eugene N. Anderson's address in Washington, D. C., are part of the documents from the estate of Edgar N. Johnson, private collection of Candice E. and Thomas R. Johnson, Denver, Colorado, USA.

33 Johnson's wife had written: "There was no cab when I got out of the station Friday." On February 8, 1946, she had parted from Edgar N. Johnson at the train station in Lincoln, Nebraska.

34 Among other things, she had written: "I want to tell you I love you above all else in this world or any world."

35 Son Thomas. See fn. 16.

Doc. 3
Letter to His Wife
Washington, D. C., February 15, 1946 (morning)

Dearest Sweetheart and my boys –

I am afraid I am getting even more unmilitary for my job. I seem to have lost the green fountain pen, trying to put it into the shirt behind a military blouse was too much. I don't like to lose it for it has written many *important* things – important at least to me. I find now that one shoe has one kind of a lace and the other another and this is rather conspicuous. And I notice that my glasses are beginning to droop. The other of the pieces that goes over the ear is wobbly.

If I have to wait much longer for transportation I shall be completely demilitarized – the way a good German is now supposed to be. When I went yesterday for my *amended* orders – amended to send me by water[1] I waited for hours (1:30 to 4:30) and when a batch came up mine was not among them. So they will perhaps be ready today. If so I shall go on to New York today and try to arrange to see Sin[2] and Hajo[3] over the week-end[4]. I have been summoned to the POE (Port of Embarkation)[5] for Monday[6]. It will perhaps be just as inexpensive to go to the Armstrongs[7] at Providence[8] and drop off at New Haven[9] as it would be to stay in New York. Besides it seems unreasonable to ask them to come to New York if I am free. But how long after being summoned to the POE does one have to wait before venturing out on the wide, deep and I suppose strong Atlantic?

I did change my reservation in Chicago on Saturday[10] morning, until 10 in the evening and left for Milwaukee[11] on a 9:15 train. I went straight to Dad's[12] room

1 See Doc. 2.
2 Sinclair W. Armstrong (1897–1959), American historian, taught from 1923–1928 at St. George's School, Newport, Rhode Island, came to Brown University as a Lecturer in 1930, 1935 PhD, University of Wisconsin, as of 1935 Professor, Brown University, 1941/1942 Office of Coordinator of Information, 1942–1945 OSS/Office of Military Government in Washington, D. C., London, and Germany.
3 Hajo Holborn (1902–1969), German-American historian, born in Charlottenburg, Germany, student of Friedrich Meinecke (see Doc. 1, fn. 11), 1924 Dr. phil., University of Berlin, 1926–1931 Privatdozent, University of Heidelberg, 1931–1933 Professor, Deutsche Hochschule für Politik, 1933 Privatdozent, University of Berlin, 1933 emigration to England, 1934 to the USA, 1934–1943 Professor, Yale University, 1940 US citizenship, 1943–1945 Research and Analysis Branch, OSS, 1945–1969 Yale University, 1947–1949 Consultant, Department of State, 1967 honorary doctorate from the Freie Universität Berlin, as of 1967 President, American Historical Association.
4 February 16/17, 1946.
5 US Army's New York Port of Embarkation.
6 February 18, 1946.
7 Sinclair W. Armstrong and his wife, Mary H. Armstrong, née Hallock (1898–1958).
8 Capital of the US state of Rhode Island, where Sinclair W. Armstrong taught as Professor of History at Brown University.
9 Seaport city in the US state of Connecticut.
10 February 9, 1946.
11 City in the US state of Wisconsin.
12 Frank E. Johnson, originally Johanson (1872–1949), Edgar N. Johnson's father, piano maker, born in Varola Sköfde, Sweden, 1891 immigrated to the USA, 1898 US citi-

after not finding him at the music store and found him there. I think he looked somewhat better than in December but he has been the victim of a series of colds and complains about burning sensations in two fingers of his right hand and up his right arm. He has been looking for work but has found nothing that he thought he could do and has therefore remained unemployed. He has tried to spend his time writing these marches. Norman[13] says there has been no difficulty of any kind because at least in part there is no opportunity. Norman keeps the money on a weekly ration. He goes to Norman's on Sundays when he wishes. He did not come to Lincoln[14] because he hoped to get a job, was doing some negotiating over unemployment insurance, and I think, under prompting by Norman, did not want to disturb things while I was at home[15]. But he wanted to come and still would like to come. I brought up the question of their being difficulties over his weakness and this, he assured me would not arise. He looks forward to the possibility of being useful especially with the yard and garden and with the kids. He said he would write you. I said I would write you about the whole matter, and that if we agreed again that he should come you would write and set a date for his arrival and he would arrive on that date. Norman spoke of taking him to Billings[16] for a complete check-over, and this could be done, either before he came to Lincoln or en route. Lucille[17], of course, urges you to think the matter over very carefully before you decide to let him come and urges it in a very unpleasant manner. In general I think I should like to try it. He may prove to be of considerable help to you in taking care of the yard and garden, in staying with Timmy[18] while you are out on errands, and in general making it possible for you to get out while he stays with the children. Certainly his life in Milwaukee is desolate at present. Maybe you should wait before actually deciding until I have word about the possibility of your coming to Germany. For if you are to come it would be complicating for you to have to set up arrangements in Lincoln for him while you are away. But if you do not come maybe we could try having him there and see how it works. If not then something else has to be tried. It might be a good idea, until I am back, for Norman

zenship, lived in Chicago, Illinois, worked in a piano factory in Holly, Michigan, and lastly in La Porte, Indiana, an accomplished piano player. "He lived most of his life in La Porte, Indiana as an 'action finisher in a piano factory' and was an accomplished pianist, as was Edgar. He never attended college and could barely write in English." Candice E. Johnson in an email to Werner Breunig from June 1, 2010.

13 Norman D. Johnson (1904–1964), Edgar N. Johnson's brother, first worked in Kansas City, Missouri, as a manager of bonds, then as a businessman at Allis-Chalmers Manufacturing Company, Milwaukee, Wisconsin.

14 Capital of the US state of Nebraska, where Johnson lived with his family and taught at the university.

15 Johnson had been with his family in Lincoln at the end of 1945/beginning of 1946, after his return from Europe.

16 May refer to the Billings Hospital of the University of Chicago.

17 Lucille Johnson, Norman D. Johnson's wife.

18 Son Thomas. See Doc. 2, fn. 16.

to continue to manage his finances from Milwaukee. But I'm sure he is a dear sweet person and by no means hopeless or useless and we should be glad I think for having tried a solution.

I stayed with him until after lunch and then went over to Norman's for a call with him. I found that I had very little to say to Norman and Lucille, I don't believe that relationship can ever improve. On the contrary it will grow worse. I left on a 4 o'clock train for Chicago, and this I will tell you about in my next.

Good-bye to my sweet beloved. I dare not think too much or in too vivid detail about you and John[19] and Timmy. I must try to postpone my yearning for you. I have already had twinges of it. But I love you, love you and send you all a sweet kiss – my sweetest. Edgar

Doc. 4
Letter to His Wife
Washington (16), D. C., 412 Baltimore Avenue[1], February 15, 1946

Dearest Emily –

I'll try to catch up a little with the news while remaining in the clutches of the bureaucracy. I learn now that the difficulty is that the amended orders (to enable travel by sea) have been so amended that payment could not be made (per diems) for the delay in Washington. I did not notice this but someone else did. The result has been a conflict between overseas branch and the Finance branch of the war department as to how the orders are to be ordered in order to make payment possible. This conflict was not resolved until today, the result being (I have just learned by telephone) that the orders won't be ready until Monday[2] morning at 11 o'clock and I am to pick them up by 12. I should have been willing to risk the non-payment in order to avoid this further delay since by imposing upon Polly[3] the way I am. I am not spending much money. But there was not much I could do about it, and of course they don't work on Saturday here either. I wish I were back in Lincoln[4] teaching rather than doing this waiting around. There is no good reason why I shouldn't have been in Lincoln all this time. I suppose now that because of this delay I shall miss the appointment at the POE[5] and have to take the following ship. I wonder what delays are to be met in Europe. I have already thought that it would be best to go from Le Havre[6] to

19 Son John. See Doc. 2, fn. 15.

1 Home of Eugene N. Anderson (see Doc. 1, fn. 1), his wife, Pauline R. Anderson, née Relyea (see Doc. 2, fn. 2), and son, Eugene N. Anderson Jr. (see fn. 30).
2 February 18, 1946.
3 Pauline R. Anderson, née Relyea. See Doc. 2, fn. 2.
4 Capital of the US state of Nebraska, where Johnson lived with his family and taught at the university.
5 US Army's New York Port of Embarkation.
6 French seaport city on the Atlantic coast.

Paris to Frankfurt[7] to Walter Dorn[8] in order to get at the heart of the matter. Maybe they can get me transportation to Berlin. Perhaps one can become hardened to this kind of thing.

I think I abandoned Milwaukee[9] at 4:00 pm on last Saturday[10] for Chicago.[11] I finally got a taxi out to Mildred's[12] traveling with a noisy GI[13] just returned from Germany and a blind man who was trying to get vicarious war experiences. Mildred had had Aunt Hannah[14] come out to help her with the supper. She spoke appreciatively of the dress and Mildred did likewise about their Christmas box from us. Mildred looks well and not too tired. She is still a bit large from the pregnancy. William Williams[15] is a charming baby. He was sleeping most of the time I was there but Mildred took him up and laid him on the bed and he awoke and smiled and kicked ingratiatingly. David Henry[16] is also a beautiful and smart and apparently healthy child. He does not walk yet but crawls all over and stands and will walk at almost any time. I did not hear him talk. He made friends with me. David[17] is devoted to him and David Jr.[18] is undoubtedly very very affectionate, the result they think of the terrible things he has been through. […][19] Kirsten[20] is still very active, very independent and certainly clever. Her dress fitted. She paid little attention to me.

David is not going to teach during the Spring Quarter (April May June) but will teach during the Summer Quarter.[21] If by any chance you are to come over to Germany during April they might want to have our house for that period. I mentioned this but I did not talk about it. I suppose they would not feel free to leave their Chicago doctor unless it could be assured that Hancock[22] could han-

7 Frankfurt am Main, city in the state of Greater Hesse in the American zone of Germany.

8 See Doc. 2, fn. 10.

9 City in the US state of Wisconsin.

10 February 9, 1946.

11 See Doc. 3.

12 Mildred H. Williams, née Johnson, widowed Bickford (1911–2009), Edgar N. Johnson's sister, teacher of Latin and French.

13 Government Issue, slang for American soldier.

14 Hannah Walstrom (1870–1959), sister of Edgar N. Johnson's mother (see Doc. 46, fn. 13), lived in Chicago, Illinois.

15 William G. Williams (born 1945), son of David G. Williams (see fn. 17) and Mildred H. Williams.

16 David H. Williams (born 1944), son of David G. Williams (see fn. 17) and Mildred H. Williams.

17 David G. Williams (1907–1987), husband of Mildred H. Williams, American philologist, taught from 1945–1973 at the University of Chicago, Department of English Language and Literature, Professor, 1957–1960 Chairman, Division of the Humanities, 1977–1981 Assistant Dean of Students in the College.

18 David H. Williams.

19 Johnson's remarks about the medical history of David H. Williams have been omitted.

20 Kirsten D. Williams, later married Kaiser (1942–1994), daughter of David G. Williams and Mildred H. Williams.

21 David G. Williams taught at the University of Chicago, Department of English Language and Literature. See fn. 17.

22 Probably Dr. Ernest W. Hancock (1894–1954), pediatrician in Lincoln, Nebraska.

dle the case. We talked about the piano some. It is clear that we owe them 20 dollars for storage on the piano, and that all further storage until they bring it to Chicago, if they do, must be paid by us. This I said. They are a little uncertain about bringing it to Chicago since David has a piano at his home which he thinks is better although it would cost more to bring it to Chicago. They are also uncertain about bringing Dad's[23] piano to Chicago because of the cost of moving it about in case they move. There are too many pianos between us. But I think we should offer to pay the storage until they decide which if any piano they want to bring to Chicago. If they decide none for the present, we ought to stop paying storage on the piano in La Porte[24] and have it brought to Lincoln where we can also store it or use it. I am not sure but that if Dad fixed the touch it would be in better shape than the Steinway[25], which is no great improvement over what we had. I perhaps get a little more friendly with David Sr.[26] who took me to the Englewood station[27] for the 10:15 Pennsylvania[28]. David and Mildred have stopped smoking. It was a dreary ride to Washington. I went first to the Vedelers[29] and was given dinner, whereupon I went, before Gene[30] got to bed to the Andersons[31]. About the reactions to Washington I shall have to write later.

Dearest I hope that this venture is not going to turn out as it has begun, as it is so far I would be much better teaching in Lincoln and home with you and the boys. There I would have some meaning and use. Here I have none and what I am to have is doubtful. I cannot write easily about the stay at home. It had a dream-like quality even more intensified than that which we ordinarily comment on. It seems that everything I read mentions this quality about existence. I was aware too many times, although I believe I did not comment on it, about this danger of taking this beautiful family for granted. I hope I did not seem to do so. I sometimes feel I am not adequate enough for this richness it contains of course I have always felt this about you, that I could not match your spirit, your quick intelligence, your lovely humanity, your sweet sensitivity and your gaiety. I know the ways in which I was really inadequate. You are always I think too good to me. No matter how beautiful and lovely the boys, and who can say that there are better boys, the times when we were alone were best, whether at the

23 Frank E. Johnson. See Doc. 3, fn. 12.

24 City in the US state of Indiana, where Edgar N. Johnson went to high school and where his parents spent a large part of their lives.

25 Refers to a piano from Steinway & Sons. The company was founded in 1853 in New York by Heinrich Engelhard Steinweg, as of 1854 Henry E. Steinway (1797–1871), born in Wolfshagen in the Harz region of Germany, and his sons.

26 David G. Williams.

27 Train station in Chicago.

28 Pennsylvania Railroad.

29 Harold C. Vedeler and Marguerite D. Vedeler, née Drew. See Doc. 2, fn. 12 and 13.

30 Eugene N. Anderson Jr. (born 1941), son of Eugene N. Anderson (see Doc. 1, fn. 1) and Pauline R. Anderson, née Relyea (see Doc. 2, fn. 2), later became Professor of Anthropology, University of California, Riverside.

31 Eugene N. Anderson (see Doc. 1, fn. 1), Pauline R. Anderson, née Relyea (see Doc. 2, fn. 2), and son, Eugene N. Anderson Jr.

breakfast table, or in the living room before a fire, or out together, or in each others arms. At these times I can never exhaust your grace and love and resourcefulness. I guess it all comes down to saying I love you, and worship you, that I am utterly and most willingly dependent upon you and that I can think of nothing better to do than to be at your mercy, to do what you want me to do. It is too good a love that lets us be so easily separated, but if it turns out as we expect, we shall not be sorry. It is only worth it if when we see each other again I shall have earned the right to have been away by the things I have done. I shall try to be worthy of you, try to merit your pride in me, fulfill your hope and increase your joy. Dearest Emily if it is within me I shall not fail you, and may be when I come back I shall be a little bigger and better person and a little more worthy of my precious wife and our children.

I suppose you are not writing here any more on the theory that I have departed. My present orders say that until I have a permanent APO[32] address, I should use as a temporary address

New Arrivals Section
25th Base Post Office
APO 800. c/o PM, NY, NY.

Letters addressed here will be forwarded to my permanent APO when I notify this office.

Bye-bye my sweet one. Kiss the boys for me and have them kiss you for me.
Edgar

Doc. 5
Letter to His Wife
Washington (16), D. C., 412 Baltimore Avenue[1], February 17, 1946

Dearest Em[ily] and the boys –

It is a quiet and warmish afternoon here. Gene[2] is napping. Polly[3] is reading to Genie[4]. I want to catch up on correspondence with you with the new pen[5].

We went for a walk this morning first with Genie (i. e. Gene and I). He fell and cut his hand slightly and set up a terrific yell which he continued until we brought him home. […][6]

Gene and I took a subsequent walk through nice Maryland[7] woods in the neighbourhood. It was rather extensive. He talking for the most part about the evils of the bureaucracy and about his own frustration in not being able to get anything accomplished. He wants to get back to teaching but the right job does

32 Army Post Office.

1 See Doc. 4, fn. 1.
2 Eugene N. Anderson. See Doc. 1, fn. 1.
3 Pauline R. Anderson, née Relyea. See Doc. 2, fn. 2.
4 Eugene N. Anderson Jr. See Doc. 4, fn. 30.
5 See Doc. 3.
6 Johnson's remarks on difficulties in bringing up children have been omitted.
7 US state next to Washington, D. C.

not come along.[8] I'll mention him to Henry[9] for Harold's[10] place[11] but I don't believe he's interested. There would be a big salary cut in his case. He is not interested in Rudy[12] and I don't believe the University interests him much. Polly I think is also a little concerned about being confined so much. She devotes hours and hours to Genie.

When I first came here I was much discouraged with what I saw of the bureaucracy – especially in the successor agency to OSS[13] whose fate is still somewhat in doubt, and the thought of returning to it was repugnant. What I have heard of the administrative chaos in the State Department, from others than Gene, is enough to confirm me in the decision I made before I came back – not to go into it. Harold V[edeler] on the contrary is content because, in some way, he gets assigned important work to do, and what he does filters up to the top and gets initialed and ultimately acted upon. But he himself can be critical enough. No policy seems to be made at high levels in sufficient time ahead to make possible comment at lower levels. Policy is first shaped at lower levels and gets established as it goes the rounds to the top. By that time it is watered down into something that is often unspecific – the expression of an attitude not a policy. I got a good example of it earlier in the week from John Howe[14], whom I knew at the University of Chicago[15] and who has been here since September as an assistant to Benton[16], an assistant secretary of state for informational and

8 In an interview conducted with Anderson in 1983, he said that he did not fit in at the State Department. "I wanted to be independent, not to be at anyone's service." ("Ich wollte unabhängig sein, wollte niemandem zu Diensten sein.") He did not really like the people at the State Department, "they were too bureaucratic for me, too oriented towards hierarchy." "[...] if one wanted to get on with American bureaucracy, one had to be a very particular kind of character, one had to watch out, think carefully about one's words, adapt too quickly. In the State Department it was all about ambition, one wanted to rise to the top quickly." ("sie waren zu bürokratisch für mich, zu Hierarchie-orientiert." "[...] wenn man in der amerikanischen Bürokratie zurecht kommen wollte, dann mußte man ein ganz bestimmter Charakter sein, man mußte aufpassen, mußte seine Worte genau überlegen, mußte sich zu schnell anpassen. Im State Department ging es ehrgeizig zu, man wollte schnell nach oben kommen.") "Interview mit Prof. Eugene N. Anderson am 10. Dezember 1983 in Santa Barbara/Californien," in: *Zur Archäologie der Demokratie in Deutschland*, vol. 2, *Analysen von politischen Emigranten im amerikanischen Außenministerium 1946–1949*, ed. Alfons Söllner, Frankfurt am Main 1986, pp. 22–34, here pp. 31f.

9 Charles Henry Oldfather. See Doc. 2, fn. 19.

10 Harold C. Vedeler. See Doc. 2, fn. 12.

11 Harold C. Vedeler did not want to return to the University of Nebraska. See Doc. 2.

12 Rudolph A. Winnacker. See Doc. 2, fn. 20.

13 Office of Strategic Services. See Doc. 1, fn. 9. OSS was disbanded as of October 1, 1945, and its functions were divided up between the Department of War and the Department of State.

14 John P. Howe (1905–1967), 1927 PhD, University of Chicago, 1927–1938 Press Relations Officer at University, 1938–1945 Assistant to Vice President and Executive Secretary of Radio Office, University of Chicago, as of October 1945 Special Assistant to Assistant Secretary of State for Public Affairs, Department of State.

15 University in Chicago, Illinois, founded in 1890.

16 William B. Benton (1900–1973), 1921 BA, Yale University, 1921–1929 advertising business, 1927–1945 Vice President, University of Chicago, 1929–1936 founder and

cultural affairs. John was attending a meeting with Benton and Byrnes[17] late on Saturday afternoon. At the meeting Byrnes received a memo from the White House[18] asking for a draft on what the president[19] should say in his Navy Day speech[20] on international affairs and the control of atomic energy. After Byrnes read it he passed it on to Benton who read it and passed it on to Howe to prepare without any further instructions. Howe worked all Saturday night on a draft, the atomic energy part of which being based on what he learned from professors at the University of Chicago. Benton saw this draft on Sunday and said it would not do. What the president wanted was some vague and generalized statement for public consumption. John had this ready by Monday and it was actually used by the president, as John said, "who in the hell makes American policy."

One gets no better impression of the president's stature here than in Lincoln[21]. The manner in which he handled the Ickes[22] resignation is pretty terrible. Clearly he should have kept Ickes and dropped Pauley[23] both of which he could have done and not gotten into this mess.

So I must say that my present mood is not to enter this scene. Yet all the reasons for good people going into it are as valid as ever. But good people who do not have infinite patience, and a desire to meet with and manipulate with the people who get things done should not go into the government. I could acquire infinite patience but I am not much of an administrator or a manipulator and I am not very good at making the sounds of the important people. Continued frustration is no mood under which to live a satisfactory life. I am impressed more and more too with the necessity for ceasing to follow the will of the wisps of professional governmental advancement which is involved with continuous uncertainty. Our old plans are very good if they include as they did a piano and the mountains. I shall therefore not think much about or hope for a change

president of advertising agency, 1945–1947 Assistant Secretary of State for Public Affairs, Department of State, 1949–1953 Connecticut Senator.

17 James F. Byrnes (1879–1972), American lawyer and politician (Democratic Party), 1911–1925 member of the House of Representatives, 1930–1941 Senator, 1941/1942 Justice on the US Supreme Court, 1943–1945 Director of the Office of War Mobilization, 1945–1947 US Secretary of State, 1951–1955 Governor of South Carolina.

18 Residence of the US President.

19 Harry S. Truman (1884–1972), 1945–1953 33rd President of the United States.

20 Speech by the US President for American Navy Day on October 27, 1945. See *Keesing's Archiv der Gegenwart*, vol. XV (1945), p. 498 G. Navy Day was the birthday of Theodore Roosevelt (1858–1919), 1901–1909 26th President of the United States.

21 Capital of the US state of Nebraska, where Johnson lived with his family and taught at the university.

22 Harold L. Ickes (1874–1952), as of 1933 US Secretary of the Interior, February 1946 resignation.

23 Edwin W. Pauley (1903–1981), American businessman, 1945–1947 US representative to the Allied Reparations Committee with the rank of Ambassador. US President Truman named him Under Secretary of the Navy. Secretary of the Interior Ickes consequently resigned in February 1946, sharply attacking the President in a press conference and criticizing the appointment of Pauley, whom he accused of privileging private oil interests, as well as the selection of Truman's other advisers. See *Keesing's Archiv der Gegenwart*, vol. XVI (1946), p. 649 G. In March 1946 Truman withdrew Pauley's appointment at the latter's own request. See ibid., p. 679 A.

from the University in general. If something specific comes up we shall have to consider it. But I am not going to court anything at this point at least.

I am enclosing 1, a clipping Marguerite V[edeler][24] gave me. It made her furious and 2, the application sheet for this new insurance policy. The policy is not good after you leave the government service but you may take out its equivalent at regular rates. I think we should take it out while I am away and transfer it when I come back. I haven't enough surplus cash to pay the initial fee here so I am asking you to do it.

It is clear I think that you will have to cash enough bonds not only to pay the 1944 income tax but also to provide yourself with some cash to keep going and possibly to send me some cash. When you will get the check covering my accumulated leave is uncertain. At the War Department they told me that allotments are made by the Personnel Officer in Berlin. Whether the action I took in Omaha[25] on this matter is really enough I don't know, and at the present rate I don't know when I shall get to Berlin. I have actually less cash now than I thought I would have, and how it will be when I am permanently stationed I don't know. I hope to make what I have do until I receive a check but I may have to cable from Germany for money. I won't bother you until I am in desperate circumstances. Also will you send that khaki battle jacket to me as soon as I give you a permanent address. I find it can be worn with these green pants, and I should have brought it along.

Tomorrow I suppose I shall be on my way. I miss your letters. I send to you and John and Timmy all my love and a heap of endearments. Edgar

Doc. 6
Letter to His Wife
New York, Hotel Pennsylvania[1], February 18, 1946

Dearest beloved –

For a good deal of the time on the way from Washington to here[2] my mind has been on you, and on the essential senselessness of my leaving you and the boys. Unlike the trains before Christmas this one (I left Washington at 5 p. m.) had practically no military people on it. Except for my uniform I saw only one other army and one naval uniform, an officer back from Japan who commended on the excellent job MacArthur[3] is doing and on the general subservience of

24 See Doc. 2, fn. 13.
25 City in the US state of Nebraska, northeast of Johnson's home in Lincoln.

1 Hotel in New York City/Manhattan, 7th Avenue, 32nd to 33rd Streets. When it opened in 1919, it was the biggest hotel in the world with 2,200 rooms. See *The New York Times* from January 25, 1919, p. 9.
2 New York City.
3 Douglas MacArthur (1880–1964), General of the Army, 1945–1951 Allied commander of the Japanese occupation.

the Japs. The rest were Washington bureaucrats going up to New York for a day or so. You could tell them and you wondered how the government gets along as well as it does.

My thoughts of you were of an intimate character. I could not help thinking of those times together when we were free to be quite one. I thought of the things we did which we had not done before and I wondered why we had not done them before. I thought of your loving receptivity and of your responses and I wondered if there were men who could have sweeter and more endearing wives than I. I wondered if you thought upon these occasions with the same intense longing as I and with the same joyful satisfaction. Sometimes they are well right perfect; sometimes they are quite perfect and sometimes you are obliged to put up with what you should not have to put up with. At all times you are wonderfully kind and exciting to me even though your return is not equivalent. You never act as if you were censorious no matter what has happened and I never think to wonder if the residue left with you is really as you make it out to be, so genuine and good all your reactions are. This part of our marriage has been less than perfect but in spite of the imperfections the actual desire to be together under these conditions has increased for me, and with it, the desire to try to make more of it than we have ever succeeded in making. And there will be time and occasions. I wish tonight that we were sitting alone together in the living room in front of a fire. I wish that we were about to lose each other in the warmth of emotion that comes with the taste of your soft lips and the feeling of your breast. I wish I were about to take you to the bed-room where I might watch the lovely body emerge from the clothes. I wish that I were to feel that body on my body from head to toe. No years of marriage can ever temper completely or assuage this longing. My darling beloved. I love you, love you deeply, love all of you with all of me.

We are to report to the POE[4] tomorrow morning. It is rumored that we sail tomorrow night, but this seems far too soon. It would be some compensation for all this waiting, though the boy sharing my room has been waiting since January 28th and has been taken off a plane. Polly[5] loaded me up with things to take to hungry Germans – particularly the old mother of a friend[6] who just received notice after years that her mother was alive, ill and very hungry. This woman lost her father on the last day of the war – a Russian bomb.

Good-night my sweet beloved. I shall have to go on thinking about you until I fall asleep. Edgar

4 US Army's New York Port of Embarkation.

5 Pauline R. Anderson, née Relyea. See Doc. 2, fn. 2.

6 Refers to Polly's friend Katharina Posner, née Melchior, divorced Bungert (see Doc. 22, fn. 3), whose mother (see Doc. 22, fn. 9) lived in Berlin. See Doc. 23.

Doc. 7
Letter to His Wife
New York # 19, Hotel Knickerbocker[1], 120 West 45th Street, February 19, 1946

Dearest Sweetheart:

We were thrown out of the Pennsylvania Hotel[2] this morning on the theory that we had promised to stay only for the night. But they did help us to get a room in this place. I am rooming with an innocent young man from South Dakota[3] since no single rooms are available. I ran into him at the Pentagon building[4] as he was getting a railroad ticket. I was relieved to find that he is only a clerk-stenographer, who, having been dismissed from the army in December is now out to see the world. He is amazed to find that the taxi-drivers expect tips. I suppose they don't do that in Fargo[5] or wherever Mr. Case is from.

We went out to the POE[6] this morning. The cab driver was as innocent of New York as I was of Boston[7] when we first hit it. After driving around in all directions, and almost crossing the Queensborough and Brooklyn bridges[8], after questioning many cab and taxi drivers he finally gave up in despair and acknowledged us how we'd better get into another cab. The second driver spent his time berating the first, wondering how a driver could take anyone any place if he didn't know where he was going. It happened to be the same place that I went in June 1944[9] when I went for OSS[10]. The difference in atmosphere is great however and expressive of the changed attitude of the work now to be done. Then of course we were in the midst of war and everything was enveloped with the sense of security. I remember though that I called you from here as I must do before leaving here. We were then taken of well. Now we are left to shift for ourselves. Then the offices at the port were manned by GI's[11]. Now, except for Captain Rosenzweig[12] they are manned by pretty girls, and it is even possible to see why the Captain hasn't moved on or been promoted. Then there was a group of young eager people courting the danger of the submarine. Now, in so far as I can tell, there is a group of people who know little of the world they are going to, do not look eager, on the contrary rather dull. There is one person who seems to be something of a big shot. I saw him in Washington where Major Smith[13]

1 Hotel in New York City/Manhattan, opened in 1925, with 400 rooms.
2 See Doc. 6, fn. 1.
3 US state.
4 See Doc. 1, fn. 3.
5 City in the US state of North Dakota.
6 US Army's New York Port of Embarkation.
7 Capital of the US state of Massachusetts.
8 Bridges that span the East River in New York City. Opened in 1909, the Queensboro Bridge connects the boroughs of Queens and Manhattan. The Brooklyn Bridge, completed in 1883, connects Brooklyn and Manhattan.
9 See Doc. 2, fn. 9.
10 Office of Strategic Services. See Doc. 1, fn. 9.
11 Government Issues, slang for American soldiers.
12 See Doc. 2.
13 See Doc. 2.

told me he was an adviser to Clay[14] who had been pulled off a plane.[15] I noticed he was a CAF 14[16]. We are to sail on Thursday[17], if present plans go through on the Goethals[18], the one ship Major Smith in Washington told me to avoid if possible. May be he doesn't know anything about it. There is accordingly nothing very exciting about it. I filled out blanks, got another typhus inoculation and one for smallpox.[19] So that helps my mood.

I also have contracted a heavy cold which descended on me this morning. But the voyage will clear that up I imagine. There is much to do here. Katharine Cornell[20] opens in Antigone[21] tonight and there are many other interesting plays but my stock of cash is running too low what with New York expenses. I shouldn't go any places tonight in any case. Tomorrow however I may try to get a seat for Evans'[22] version of Hamlet[23]. We call tomorrow at 11 for final instruc-

14 See Doc. 2, fn. 6.

15 See Doc. 2.

16 Class 14 employee of the Clerical, Administrative, and Fiscal Service.

17 February 21, 1946.

18 USAT *George W. Goethals*, US Army transport ship beginning in 1942, named after George W. Goethals (1858–1928), chief engineer of the Panama Canal. According to the *Dictionary of American Naval Fighting Ships*: "During World War II *George W. Goethals* operated as an Army transport out of New York, Boston, and Gulf Coast ports to ports in North Africa, France, and the United Kingdom. After the war, she continued transatlantic runs carrying military dependents between the United States and Europe." https://www.history.navy.mil/research/histories/ship-histories/danfs/g/george-w-goethals.html (accessed February 28, 2018). See Roland W. Charles, *Troopships of World War II*, with a foreword by Major General Edmond H. Leavey, Washington, D. C., 1947, p. 31. Photo of the ship in Appendix of Illustrations, ill. 12.

19 See Immunization Register, 1944–1946, in: Documents from the estate of Edgar N. Johnson, private collection of Candice E. and Thomas R. Johnson, Denver, Colorado, USA; Appendix of Illustrations, ill. 6.

20 Katharine Cornell (1893–1974), American actress, Broadway legend, married to the director Guthrie McClintic (1893–1961).

21 *Antigone*, drama by Jean Anouilh (1910–1987) based on Sophocles (497/496 BC–406/405 BC), translated and adapted by Lewis Galantiere (1893–1977), was performed from February 18–May 4, 1946, in the Cort Theatre in New York City/Manhattan, 48th Street East of Broadway. See Sam Zolotow, "'Antigone' Opens at Cort Tonight. Katharine Cornell, Sir Cedric Hardwicke to Star in Modern Dress Version of Classic," in: *The New York Times* from February 18, 1946, p. 17; Lewis Nichols, "The Play," in: *The New York Times* from February 19, 1946, p. 21; https://www.ibdb.com/broadway-production/antigone-1773 (accessed February 28, 2018).

22 Maurice Evans (1901–1989), British-American actor, born in Dorchester, Dorset, England, 1935 came to the USA, where he became one of the most well-known interpreters of Shakespeare, 1941 US citizenship, responsible for an Army Entertainment Section during the Second World War, also worked in movies and television, appeared in the science fiction film *Planet of the Apes* (1968) and the sequel *Beneath the Planet of the Apes* (1970), among other roles.

23 Refers to a shortened version of the tragedy *Hamlet* by William Shakespeare (1564–1616), also known as *G. I. Hamlet*. It was performed for soldiers during the Second World War, and could be seen from December 13, 1945–April 8, 1946, at the Columbus Circle Theatre in New York City/Manhattan, Broadway at 59th Street. "Some of the members of the company served with Major Evans in the Pacific and over twenty were ex-service men." https://www.ibdb.com/broadway-production/hamlet-1751 (ac-

tions and if I feel up to it I might try to do some aht[24] at the Museum of Modern Art[25] or the Museum of the Pennsylvania Coal baron[26].

I hope it doesn't continue as drab as this or I shall be a very very homesick little boy. The fact that I don't know when I shall be able to get news from you does not help. I love you, my dearest Emily, and that and your love will keep me going. Kiss the boys for me, and I kiss you. Edgar

Doc. 8
Letter to His Wife
New York # 19, Hotel Knickerbocker[1], 120 West 45th Street, February 20, 1946[2]

Dearest Emily and my sweet boys –

I am trying to call you by long distance, but the "toll" line seems to be busy. Evidently the services for this small hotel is unlike that for the Pennsylvania[3] for there when I called you upon my return there was no difficulty. There will be some contrast in the moods of these calls but I am eager to hear your voice.

We are leaving tomorrow. At least we have been given a clearance ship and a customs declaration and told to report at the ship's side tomorrow between 11 and 12 a. m. This means I suppose that the ship will actually get off tomorrow – the first of what Captain Rosenzweig[4] intimated would be from 6 to 10 days, meaning of course ten days. The Goethals[5] is an old, slow, tired ship I am told from which too much cannot be expected.[6] Ten days from tomorrow and it will

cessed February 28, 2018). See Sam Zolotow, "Modern 'Hamlet' Arriving Tonight. Maurice Evans Returning in GI Version of Shakespeare Play – Mike Todd the Producer," in: *The New York Times* from December 13, 1945, p. 33; Lewis Nichols, "The Play," in: *The New York Times* from December 14, 1945, p. 25.

24 Refers to "art." Johnson is apparently making fun of the educated American bourgeoisie who pronounce "art" as "aht."

25 MoMA, Museum in New York City/Manhattan, 11 West 53rd Street, dedicated to art from the 1880s (impressionists) up to the present. Founded in 1929, in 1939 it moved into the new building on 53rd Street, which has been expanded several times since then. See https://www.moma.org/ (accessed February 28, 2018).

26 Refers to coal and steel magnate Henry C. Frick (1849–1919) from Pittsburgh, Pennsylvania. In 1913/1914 Frick had a mansion built on the corner of 5th Avenue and 70th Street, in which he housed his precious art collection. His widow continued to live there after Frick's death, and after her death in 1931 the mansion was converted into a museum that opened in 1935. The Frick Collection offers high-quality European art from the 14th–19th centuries. See https://www.frick.org/ (accessed February 28, 2018).

1 See Doc. 7, fn. 1.

2 See Appendix of Illustrations, ill. 11.

3 Hotel Pennsylvania. See Doc. 6, fn. 1.

4 See Doc. 2 and Doc. 7.

5 USAT *George W. Goethals*. See Doc. 7, fn. 18.

6 Possibly confused with the SS *General G. W. Goethals*/USS *General G. W. Goethals* (1919). "*General G. W. Goethals*, a 4707 gross ton passenger-cargo ship, was built at

be already March, and before I get settled in my job I am sure that a full month will have passed since I left you and the boys. As you know I am to go first to Berlin. How one gets transported there I do not know. It will perhaps be best to go by way of Frankfurt[7]. Gene[8] and Polly[9] gave me the names of people to see in Berlin together with food packages. I shall try to see Marshall Knappen[10] and Louis Wiesner[11]. Jimmy Riddleberger[12] in the State Department wanted me to see Ambassador Murphy[13] and his assistants, Jacob Beam[14] and Donald Health[15]. He promised to write ahead introducing me. But I don't know what

Hamburg, Germany, in 1911 as the German commercial steamer *Grunewald*. Later becoming a U. S. flag merchantman, she was taken over by the Navy in March 1919 and placed in commission as USS *General G. W. Goethals* (ID # 1443). As a troop transport assigned to the Cruiser and Transport Force, she was employed carrying U. S. service personnel home from France and taking cargo to Europe. The ship made three round-trip trans-Atlantic voyages for these purposes between April and August 1919, then carried supplies from the East Coast to the Gulf Coast, Caribbean and Panama. Decommissioned upon her return to New York in mid-September 1919, *General G. W. Goethals* was returned to her owner, the Panama Railroad Steamship Company." http://www.shipscribe.com/usnaux/ww1/ships/gen-goet.htm (accessed February 28, 2018).

7 Frankfurt am Main, city in the state of Greater Hesse in the American zone of Germany.

8 Eugene N. Anderson. See Doc. 1, fn. 1.

9 Pauline R. Anderson, née Relyea. See Doc. 2, fn. 2.

10 Marshall M. Knappen (1901–1966), Major, American theologian, historian, and political scientist, PhD, Cornell University, for a short time Pastor of the First Congregational Church Redfield in the US state of South Dakota, 1931 Professor of History, University of Chicago, 1939–1942 Professor of History and Political Science, Michigan State College, 1945/1946 Chief, Religious Section, Education and Religious Affairs Branch, Internal Affairs and Communications Division, OMGUS, 1947 returned to his work as Professor of History and Political Science at Michigan State College, as of 1948 Professor of Political Science, University of Michigan, as of 1960 University of Delaware.

11 Louis A. Wiesner (1916–2002), American Foreign Service Officer, 1938 MA, Harvard University, 1939–1942 Assistant and Teaching Fellow, Harvard University, 1942/1943 Research Secretary, Council on Foreign Relations, 1943/1944 Research Analyst, OSS, 1944–1975 Department of State, until 1949 Labor Affairs Attaché, Office of Political Affairs, Political Adviser (POLAD).

12 James W. Riddleberger (1904–1982), American diplomat, 1944–1947 Chief, Division of Central European Affairs, Department of State, 1947–1949 Director of Political Affairs, OMGUS, deputy of Ambassador Robert D. Murphy.

13 Robert D. Murphy (1894–1978), American diplomat, 1921–1924 Vice Consul, Munich, 1944–1949 Ambassador, Political Adviser for Germany, 1949–1952 Ambassador, Belgium, 1952/1953 Japan, 1959 Under Secretary of State for Political Affairs. Photo of Murphy in Appendix of Illustrations, ill. 22.

14 Jacob D. Beam (1908–1993), American diplomat, 1929 BA, Princeton University, as of 1931 Foreign Service, 1934–1940 Third Secretary, Berlin, 1944–1947 Foreign Service Officer, Staff of Political Adviser for Germany, 1947–1949 Chief, Division of Central European Affairs, Department of State, 1957–1961 Ambassador, Poland, 1966–1969 Czechoslovakia, 1969–1973 Soviet Union.

15 Donald R. Heath (1894–1981), American diplomat, 1937–1941 First Secretary, Berlin, 1945–1947 Director of Political Affairs, Office of the Deputy Military Governor, OMGUS, 1947–1950 Minister, Bulgaria, 1952 Ambassador, Cambodia, 1952–1955 Vietnam, 1955–1957 Lebanon, 1958–1961 Saudi Arabia.

the transportation situation in Berlin will be, and whether I can see these people.

I am still low. Mrs. Roosevelt's[16] statement in today's paper,[17] after her brief trip to Germany,[18] that there is a dearth of good people for important jobs offers some encouragement but I need more than that at the present moment.[19] I wish I had had more sense about judging what would happen to me when once I got to Washington. Being cut off from you and the children so suddenly with only one letter[20] has become something of a trial. And after tomorrow I shall not be able to write a letter that can be mailed immediately for at least ten days. I shall, however, write a chronicle of the trip on the boat which I do not at all look forward to. But certainly it will be weeks yet before I get a word from you.

I love you my sweet darling, you and our precious sons. I am still determined to make what I can of this assignment but it will be difficult. I love you honey and beg of you to write a few letters to the temporary address I sent since I am sure they will come to me at some time. Here suddenly a whole month has disappeared from our lives. Kiss John and Timmy for me and let me tell you again, I love you and I love you. My lovely and sweetest wife. Edgar

Doc. 9
Letter to His Wife
On board the *George W. Goethals*[1], February 22, 1946

Dearest Sweetheart –

I can begin to give you a chronology of this trip but unless there is more paper about I shall run out before the ten days are over. You will remember this

16 Anna Eleanor Roosevelt (1884–1962), American delegate to the United Nations, widow of Franklin D. Roosevelt (1882–1945), 1933–1945 32nd President of the United States.

17 From 1935 until shortly before her death in 1962, Eleanor Roosevelt wrote the column "My Day," which appeared six times a week in many American daily newspapers.

18 On Eleanor Roosevelt's visit to Germany, see "Eleanor Roosevelts deutsche Impressionen. Tagebuchblätter der Witwe des großen Präsidenten der Vereinigten Staaten," in: *Die Neue Zeitung* from February 18, 1946, p. 2.

19 According to Eleanor Roosevelt's newspaper column "My Day" from February 20, 1946: "[…] we need really able people to take over the key positions as the main military establishment shifts responsibility to a civilian administration. I'm told that these key people are hard to find and I'm not surprised, because it means a real sacrifice for the period of time one gives to this job. Yet the job has to be done for our own as well as the interests of the people of Europe." https://www2.gwu.edu/~erpapers/myday/displaydoc.cfm?_y=1946&_f=md000267 (accessed February 28, 2018).

20 Emily L. Johnson's letter from February 10, 1946, in: Documents from the estate of Edgar N. Johnson, private collection of Candice E. and Thomas R. Johnson, Denver, Colorado, USA.

1 See Doc. 7, fn. 18.

paper. It came from you and it was used for the most part in the place to which I first went when I left you.

The boat is not so bad as it was painted by Major Smith[2] who must be used to great luxury or is not a very responsible reporter. It is about a 13 000 ton ship, and therefore not so large, about the size of the Montnairn[3], a Canadian ship I came back on in the late summer of 1928[4]. It has begun to roll and will continue to roll all the way across but I don't expect it will get me. I did not think we would have state-rooms, but rather all be drawn together in one large room. Instead there is a large roomy cabin with eight bunks in it, four lower and four upper. I have one of the uppers. There are springs, and clean sheets and blankets. I have just discovered a shelf in the dresses to pull out and write on. There are lamps and lockers and two toilet-baths for the 6 of us in the cabin. Everything is kept in marvelous order and cleanliness by the steward. The dining room is unpretentious. It must seat over a hundred people. Meals are served at 7:30, 11:30 and 4:30, and there are not, as on larger liners in peace time in between snacks. A 4:30 dinner is a little early but I imagine union conditions make it necessary. It might work better if you were anyplace except a boat. How would you like to be through dinner at 5:30. It would give you a long evening. The long evenings on this boat would be pretty dull without something to read. The food is excellent. Yesterday (I won't give you the menu every day) there was flounder for lunch, and chicken for supper and this morning there were bacon and eggs. So one will gain weight on the trip.

The ship moves very silently, so silently in fact that I did not know immediately that it was leaving the harbor. Yet I got out in time to see the tip of Manhattan[5] before we slipped into the narrows. There is something to be said for a ship over and against a plane. I went out on deck after breakfast this morning. The sun was shining brightly. The water a deep navy blue with white caps, the air brisk but not too cold and after all here was the marvel of 13 000 tons moving through the water at 18 knots an hour and seeming to go very fast. We have a deck to walk upon but it is cluttered with all kinds of naval equipment. There is no decent lounging room. This 13 000 tons of steel is carrying very few people some 200 crew perhaps and may be a hundred passengers[6] what else it is carrying I do not know. Some say 1000 tons of ballast. I saw partly filling the lounging room a great deal of baby equipment including swell high chairs, toilet seats, playpens, Mennen's oil. I wondered whether these could be meant for European children and then was informed that they were for the British wives of our GI's[7]. This is a sweet thought, however, and I doubt if any other nation would

2 See Doc. 2 and Doc. 7.

3 SS *Montnairn*, a steamship of the Canadian Pacific Line. See http://www.norwayheritage.com/p_ship.asp?sh=mont6 (accessed February 28, 2018).

4 Refers to Johnson's return after studying in Europe in 1927/1928.

5 Borough of New York City.

6 A passenger list is not available. "Passenger lists were not considered permanent historical records," according to a letter from the National Archives and Records Administration (NARA), College Park, Maryland, USA, to Werner Breunig from December 21, 2010.

7 Government Issues, slang for American soldiers.

be foresighted and considerate enough (except it be the English themselves) to do a thing like this.

In the cabin are two people I'll try to describe a little more fully later. A Mr. Anderson[8], a road building expert (WPA[9]) and a Mr. Hoover[10], professor of economics at Mills College, California[11]. There is also a Czech boy from Pilsen[12] and of the others one a southerner and the other as yet without form. At lunch yesterday there sat across from me the wife of the assistant military attaché in Berne[13] who was going to Switzerland to join her husband[14]. She had a child about three[15] along and her Mother[16]. She said they were going to live in a hotel at first. No other wives are aboard I think[17] though I have been told that the highest ranking officers in Germany are already bringing their wives over. There are of course the usual number of coca-cola people[18] on board and a further scattering of professors, some of them refugees, with whom I have not yet become acquainted.

22 February, after dinner.

It must be all of 5:15 p. m. and dinner has been eaten. I don't believe I'll eat lunches. It's too much for this lazy life. There are a few corrections to the above gathered from a member of the crew. The ship is 12 000 instead of 13 000. It is coming back on the diaper run as they call it. It has no supplies of any kind for Europe which amazes me. It is of course a transport ship but why, when there is supposed to be a great shipping shortage, and there are no troops aboard, it can't be used to carry something to needy Europeans, I don't understand. As it

8 William J. Anderson (1887–1958), American civil engineer, 1910 BE, Union College, 1946–1948 Highway Consultant, Road Branch, Transport Division, OMGUS, as of 1950 Consulting Engineer, private engineering practice, West Hartford, Connecticut.

9 Created in 1935 as part of the New Deal, the Works Progress Administration (later Works Projects Administration) was conceived as a job creation administration for unemployed people during the Great Depression.

10 Glenn E. Hoover (1888–1961), American economist, LLD, University of Washington, doctoral studies at the University of Strasbourg, initially Professor of Economics and Political Science, University of Oregon, subsequently until 1953 Mills College, 1946/1947 Finance Division, OMGUS.

11 College in Oakland, California.

12 City in Czechoslovakia (today's Czech Republic).

13 Capital of Switzerland.

14 Probably Davis O. Harrington (1913–1984), Lieutenant Colonel, 1935 BA, Yale University, 1935–1940 banker, 1941–1949 US Army, as of November 1945 Assistant Military Attaché, Bern, married to Margaret M. Harrington, née Mercer (1910–1990).

15 Davis O. and Margaret M. Harrington's child, Nancy L. Harrington (born 1943), was just three years old. See "D. O. Harringtons Have Child," in: *The New York Times* from May 10, 1943, p. 14.

16 Margaret V. Mercer, née McGarr (died 1955), widow of James Sidney (Sid) Mercer (1881–1945), American sportswriter.

17 Mrs. Wynona C. Schuyler was also on board (see Doc. 12, fn. 7).

18 Johnson used the term "coca-cola-people" for racists from the southern states of the USA. According to Candice E. Johnson in an email to Werner Breunig from December 16, 2007: "Edgar hated any person who was prejudiced against other races or religions, and he certainly met plenty of them on the ship."

is this is pretty expensive passage. A whole ship and a crew of 170 to carry something like a hundred civilians to work in Germany. I suppose it's a question of bureaucracy. It is impossible to route goods to this ship since it ordinarily does not carry supplies. It is rolling much more now.

The civilians who are going over to help solve the German problem are not a very encouraging lot. I include myself within this characterization. These are a mild oldish looking lot who, I am sure, will not do better than the military in executing American policy. Indeed I think they will do worse. I haven't come across any yet who pretend to know any German. It has not been set up as a requirement. They are just average, well-meaning, conscientious Americans without any particular knowledge of the German scene, and not knowing, in many cases what they are going to do. They are just going to report to Berlin. I think in most cases they are those who did not get in on the first call of the war agencies and who still feel a sense of responsibility for the American mission abroad and who at least want a little foreign experience. From any acquaintance with them I should not think they were of the stuff to keep the Germans in hand once the military are withdrawn. We just do not have experience of that kind. If once we succeed a setting up a satisfactory German administration it will be necessary to recruit a small body of very well trained controllers who know the German language and who know what to look after, otherwise we may loose our battle again.

These men are very easy to get acquainted with. (It is beginning to roll pretty badly now. I don't know which is worse this or turbulence. This reminds me of your mention of turbulence when I left Lincoln[19], and I knew what you were thinking). In fact getting acquainted is a kind of American rite which when properly initiated you are expected by any other American to go through with almost upon demand. You learn as much about a fellow American in this way as you would from a European in months of acquaintance. Take the Scotchman Mr. W[illia]m Anderson who sleeps in a lower bunk across from me in cabin 113. We got down to business last evening (the first evening out) and there was some continuation today. I know something about his grandfather who settled in northern New York[20], something about a great uncle who moved to Kansas[21], but more about his Father[22] and Mother[23]. His Father was a road contractor who used to bring over Italians from Sicily[24] and Calabria[25], move them to Albany[26] and deal with them, not according to name, but according to the number tied around their necks. They were treated, I gather, much like the Mexican sugar beet workers about whom that article in *Accent*[27] had to do. They were

19 Capital of the US state of Nebraska, where Johnson lived with his family and taught at the university.

20 US state.

21 US state.

22 James Anderson (1858–1941), American road construction entrepreneur.

23 Julia F. Anderson, née Fitzgerald (1860–1931).

24 Italian island in the Mediterranean.

25 The southernmost point of mainland Italy.

26 Probably refers to the capital of the US state of New York.

27 Gilbert Neiman, "Lazarus Laughs," in: *Accent. A Quarterly of New Literature*, vol. 6, no. 1 (Fall 1945), pp. 13–22.

our slave labor at the turn of the century or a little later. The father wanted him soon to be a learned contractor and sent him off to Union College[28] in Schenectady[29] to study civil engineering[30]. There he played Varsity football, and did well in school, being duly impressed with the hero of the Union College faculty at that time, a protégé of General Electric[31] one *Steimetz*[32] of whom you may have heard. Mr. Anderson graduated from college in 1910 and went first into his Father's business[33], helped to build the New York subways after the last war[34], and has now landed in the bureaucracy as an expert on road building[35]. While supervising road-building in Kentucky[36] he found his wife[37] who I gather is about 10 years or so his junior. He married her[38] when she was 23 and they tried for 15 years to have children. Her trouble was fibrous tumors but she was determined to have a child in spite of them and succeeded when she was 38 in giving birth to a fine boy[39] and afterwards had the nasty series of many sized tumors removed. The boy is now seven. I have seen all the pictures. I have heard of a great many of "Jimmy's"[40] virtues. I have even had to assure Mr. Anderson that I didn't think children of 6 or 7 nowadays are any smarter than they were when we were that age. He is inclined to think that his boy proves it. They have built a house in Hartford Connecticut.[41] I know how much it cost and how much the lot cost, and I am led to understand what a superior house it is because Mr. Anderson designed and built it. He wants his boy to go to Union College and to be a contractor or a civil engineer.[42] He teaches him how to play contractor. He is to play on the Varsity and be a thoroughly

28 College founded in 1795.
29 City in the US state of New York.
30 Began his studies in 1906.
31 General Electric Company, founded in 1892, had its headquarters in Schenectady.
32 Charles P. Steinmetz (1865–1923), German-American mathematician and electrical engineer, born in Breslau, Germany, studied at the University of Breslau, 1889 emigration to the USA, worked for General Electric Company and taught electrical engineering at Union College.
33 James Anderson & Sons.
34 Refers to the First World War (1914–1918).
35 Beginning in 1944 Anderson worked for the US Public Roads Administration, Washington, D. C.
36 US state. Anderson worked in Kentucky as a civil engineer in the public sector from 1920–1922.
37 Edith B. Anderson, née Bottorff (1899–1994).
38 On June 12, 1923.
39 James E. Anderson (1938–2016), American chemist, 1960 BS, Union College, 1963 PhD, Princeton University, research chemist, Ford Motor Company. Lived with his parents in Berlin while his father was there working for OMGUS: "My father lived by himself in Berlin for approximately 1 year before my mother & I joined him. The 3 of us lived in Berlin for about 1 year." Email from James E. Anderson to Werner Breunig from February 24, 2013. "I attended the American grade school in Berlin-Dahlem." Email from James E. Anderson to Werner Breunig from May 30, 2008.
40 Refers to Anderson's son, James.
41 Anderson came from West Hartford, a city in Hartford County in the US state of Connecticut, 479 South Main Street.
42 Anderson's son indeed later attended Union College. See fn. 39.

"normal" young boy. Mrs. Anderson is a D. A. R.[43] and the boy attends the activities of the C. A. R. (Children of the American Revolution[44]) a new organization to me.[45]

Doc. 10
Letter to His Wife
On board the *George W. Goethals*[1], February 27, 1946

Dearest Emily –

Dinner is over and it is about 5 o' clock. At the table a southerner (Georgia[2]) remarked: "That's one thing I like about Joe Lewis[3]. He's a nigger; he knows it and doesn't try to get out of his place." There are too many southerners aboard. One, who I understand is cracked since he enjoys nothing more than to repeat over and over again his war experiences, is a cocoa-cola expert. When I first went over in June 1944[4] there were cocoa-cola experts on board. Did I tell you the story told by one of them that the founder of the C-C Company[5] once took aboard his yacht a lady named Dubauchee[6]. In a fit of the grand passion this

43 Daughters of the American Revolution, an association for descendants of veterans of the American Revolutionary War, also known as the American War of Independence (1775–1783), promotes patriotism and historical awareness. "The National Society Daughters of the American Revolution was founded on October 11, 1890, during a time that was marked by a revival in patriotism and intense interest in the beginnings of the United States of America. Women felt the desire to express their patriotic feelings and were frustrated by their exclusion from men's organizations formed to perpetuate the memory of ancestors who fought to make this country free and independent. As a result, a group of pioneering women in the nation's capital formed their own organization and the Daughters of the American Revolution has carried the torch of patriotism ever since." https://www.dar.org/national-society/about-dar/dar-history (accessed February 28, 2018).

44 A patriotic association, started in 1895 by the children's book author Harriet M. Lothrop, née Stone (1844–1924), as the children's and youth organization of the Daughters of the American Revolution.

45 Johnson did not include a sign-off because he wanted to send the letters written on board all together.

1 See Doc. 7, fn. 18.

2 US state.

3 Refers to Joe Louis, originally Joseph Louis Barrow (1914–1981), American professional boxer, 1937–1949 world heavyweight boxing champion, 1942–1945 US Army, built up as a positive counterexample to the first black world heavyweight boxing champion, Jack Johnson (1878–1946), in order to avoid hostility from "white America." "[…] his behavior was dignified and friendly at all times. He thereby avoided antagonizing white people, as the earlier heavyweight champion Jack Johnson had […]." Luckett V. Davis, "Louis, Joe," in: *American National Biography*, vol. 13, New York and Oxford 1999, pp. 942–944, here p. 944.

4 See Doc. 2, fn. 9.

5 The founder of the Coca-Cola Company was Asa G. Candler (1851–1929), 1916–1919 Mayor of Atlanta, Georgia.

president Chandler[7] bit off one of the nipples on Madame Dubauchee's breasts. She sued the old rake in a Georgia court,[8] and to convince the jury she hauled out her breast and exhibited the oral mutilation. There is a conspiracy among the southerners aboard this boat to show that every colored unit in the army disgraced itself. We ought to take a trip through the south some summer. It could give us a better picture of this land of ours. My picture at present is a little jaded.

This morning I got up and closed the door of our cabin to shut out the noise of the radio. This left the cabin quite dark. One of the southerners in our cabin awoke later with a start and a yell. He had been drinking considerably yesterday, and thought for a moment when he could not see anything upon awakening, that he had been blinded by the liquor he had consumed. This in fact was why I didn't write yesterday. Our cabin was the scene of a pretty continuous party from about three o' clock on. The room I usually escape to has been closed in order to prepare it for a nursery on the return trip. The other so-called lounge cannot be used as a writing place. To watch the younger generation amuse itself is very discouraging. One of the ladies at the party yesterday was a young girl from Wisconsin[9] with a husky, whiskey throat who I imagine has drunk more liquor than any of the men in the cabin. She said she was the daughter of a tavern owner in Wisconsin. Her friend at the party was only a little more impressive. What is done is to go up on deck after liquor enough has been consumed for necking. Now from another gentleman in the cabin it was learned that the whiskey belle and her partner suffered from pyrhoea[10] (I can't spell it) and that the gentleman who wished to kiss these girls ought to know what they were about. He wouldn't touch them. And the little Czech boy in the cabin who had kissed one of them last week wondered how long it took for pyrhoea to break out. There must be much that goes on in a boat. We had physical examinations before we left port to check up on shots and contagious diseases. They insisted I have two more shots (the smallpox has taken).[11] But we have to have another physical examination before we get off the boat.

When I tried to escape the party by going upstairs to the so-called lounge I was again discouraged to see how they were amusing themselves. In so far as I could see there were few if any people reading. Nor were there any conversations going on. It was mostly cards. Some adults were playing dominoes. A group were avidly bent on putting together a large jig-saw puzzle. The young

6 Onezima de Bouchel, "member of an old Louisiana family, and New Orleans society leader." *The Atlanta Constitution* from February 18, 1923, p. 1.

7 Asa G. Candler. See fn. 5.

8 De Bouchel took Candler to court for breach of the promise of marriage and claimed financial compensation amounting to 500,000 US dollars. On February 5, 1924, a sentence was passed in favor of Candler. See *The New York Times* from October 11, 1922, pp. 1 and 7, from October 12, 1922, pp. 1f., from October 13, 1922, p. 18, from October 14, 1922, p. 13, from October 15, 1922, p. 25, from October 27, 1922, p. 8, from February 18, 1923, p. 1, from March 13, 1923, p. 3, from June 21, 1923, p. 19, from January 31, 1924, p. 6, from February 1, 1924, p. 3, from February 2, 1924, p. 3, from February 3, 1924, p. 22, from February 5, 1924, p. 11, from February 6, 1924, p. 21. See also Kathryn W. Kemp, *God's Capitalist. Asa Candler of Coca-Cola*, Macon, Georgia, 2002, pp. 253–272.

9 US state.

10 Probably refers to gonorrhea.

people do not seem to talk to each other. They sit, listen to radio, yip through a popular song, pass a wise crack – nothing else. Then they go on deck for a little loving – something like a night-cap. I wonder if they are as empty headed as they seem. Mr. Anderson[12] was also horrified by it all (I learn that he is 58[13]) and said that the cause and remedy for it all was the family. And indeed of these young people are typical it is the obligation of some of us who feel some responsibility in the matter to have more children. I am not trying to engage in propaganda. Yet in addition to the problem of the German youth who are empty-headed and evil by indoctrinated there is also the problem of American youth who are empty-headed and aimless.[14]

Doc. 11
Letter to His Wife
On board the *George W. Goethals*[1], February 28, 1946

My sweet darling –

The end of a month. I did not think I should be returning in three months.[2] I sometimes wonder if you have changed your mind to any degree about my returning. You have never said anything. Tomorrow is the last day of the voyage. The gulls have rejoined us and there are poking schooners in some number. Breton I suppose. We disembark at Le Havre[3] on Saturday[4] morning, I understand. I suppose they will get us off to Paris by Sunday[5] but what happens from then on nobody seems to know.

I wrote a letter to Henry[6] yesterday about a successor to Harold V[edeler][7].[8] I suggested they try to get Gene Anderson[9] or Paul Sweet[10]. I don't think Gene really wants to come out our way but I do think there is a possibility of getting Paul if they act quickly. I also mentioned, without going into any detail that I was not particularly happy about R[udy]'s[11] coming back.[12] I thought I ought to say this much to confirm Henry's suspicions. I took a strong stand, too, against

11 See Doc. 7 and Doc. 7, fn. 19.
12 See Doc. 9, fn. 8.
13 Born on August 14, 1887.
14 Johnson did not include a sign-off. See Doc. 9, fn. 45.

1 See Doc. 7, fn. 18.
2 Johnson had returned to the USA at the end of November 1945, and three months later he came back to Europe.
3 French seaport city on the Atlantic coast.
4 March 2, 1946.
5 March 3, 1946.
6 Charles Henry Oldfather. See Doc. 2, fn. 19.
7 See Doc. 2, fn. 12.
8 Vedeler did not want to return to the University of Nebraska. See Doc. 2.
9 Eugene N. Anderson. See Doc. 1, fn. 1.
10 See Doc. 2, fn. 28.
11 Rudolph A. Winnacker. See Doc. 2, fn. 20.

introducing Ginzburg[13] into the department as a teacher of Russian history, saying that I did not think the history department ought to become the graveyard of a dying classicism. It was a good letter, however, and I don't think Henry will mind my being frank. He has much to answer for as a result of some of the decisions he has made as dean. You know, when I stop to think of it, he has not one outstanding accomplishment to his credit. Oh yes, Senning[14] was demoted and Ray[15] made chairman of the English department.

I finished the desultory Antic Hay[16] and was almost ready to shriek when I finished. There is not one half way decent person in the book except the old father architect who does finally do a good deed at the very end of the novel. Madame Myra Viveash[17] was so thoroughly bored throughout the book that I don't believe I can ever use the word bore again or have any patience with anyone who is bored. There is a riot of fornication and adultery of various kinds and degrees. It is a thoroughly rotten society he depicts, and I hope we are not descending to the same. Huxley wields a clever and sophisticated pen, and from these depths it is not surprising that he has swung to Indian theosophy. I should like now to read Ends and Means[18] (wasn't that the title?) to see how he made the swing. There are some foreshadowings of Point Counter Point[19] in the literary critic Mr. Mercaptan[20], and in the artist Lypiatt[21]. There is one passage of considerable satisfaction on advertising – the American brand. But, on the whole, the book leaves nothing but a bad taste in one's mouth.

This is getting to be a very tedious voyage. Everyone is feeling it and if it lasted much longer there would be an outburst of drunkenness, fornication or simply irritability.

Dr. Rheinstein[22] told me today that American authorities in Berlin had arrested the assistant Bürgermeister[23] and some of his entourage for a minor and

12 Johnson assumed that Winnacker wanted to return to the University of Nebraska. See Doc. 2.

13 Michael S. Ginsburg (1902–1982), American classicist, 1924 LLD, University of Petrograd, 1929 DLitt, University of Paris, as of 1931 taught at the University of Nebraska, 1943–1947 on leave, 1945–1947 Chief, Internal Political Section, USSR Division, Office of Research and Intelligence, Department of State, 1947–1966 Professor, Indiana University, Director, Department of Slavic Studies.

14 John P. Senning (1884–1954), American political scientist, 1924 PhD, University of Illinois, 1916–1952 Professor, University of Nebraska, part of that time Chairman, Department of Political Science.

15 Ray W. Frantz (1898–1976), American modern language philologist, 1930 PhD, University of Chicago, as of 1929 University of Nebraska, Professor of English (Chairman of Department).

16 1923 novel by Aldous Huxley (1894–1963), English writer who lived in the USA from 1937 until his death.

17 Character in *Antic Hay*.

18 Philosophical text by Aldous Huxley from 1937.

19 1928 novel by Aldous Huxley.

20 Character in *Antic Hay*.

21 Casimir Lypiatt, character in *Antic Hay*.

22 Max Rheinstein (1899–1977), German-American lawyer, born in Bad Kreuznach, Germany, 1924 Dr. jur., University of Munich, 1925 second law exam, as of 1926 librarian and research assistant, Kaiser-Wilhelm-Institut für ausländisches und internationales Privatrecht, Berlin, as of 1928 member of the SPD, 1932/1933 Privatdo-

unwarranted offense and actually mistreated them. He referred also to the fact that the M[ilitary] G[overnment] authorities in Bavaria[24] have refused to let the recent pastoral letter of the Catholic bishops of Germany[25] circulate because 1) the bishops demanded the return of their denominational schools when they were in no position to demand anything and 2) the bishops ventured opinions on marriage and divorce which were uncalled for, there being an international rather than a German institution.[26] He also mentioned our M[ilitary] G[overnment] officers summoning Minister President Höggner[27] of Bavaria to their offices five and six times a day and keeping him waiting for long stretches at a time. We don't know how to treat the people whom we have asked to cooperate with us. General Truscott[28], (he has taken Patton's[29] place) has issued an order commanding American troops in his area to respect the German authorities. There seems to be room for Americans with a bit of sense.

I think much of you beloved, much more than you suspect. I send you all my love to you and our sweet boys. Edgar

zent, University of Berlin, came to the USA in 1933 with a scholarship from the Rockefeller Foundation, stayed in 1935 after the scholarship period ended, 1935–1968 Professor, University of Chicago, 1940 US citizenship, 1945–1947 employee of the Legal Division, OMGUS.

23 May refer to a deputy of the Oberbürgermeister or a deputy district mayor.

24 State in the American zone of Germany.

25 Refers to the Fulda pastoral letter from August 23, 1945, the first joint pastoral letter of the German Catholic bishops after the war. Reproduced in: *Hirtenbriefe und Ansprachen zu Gesellschaft und Politik 1945–1949*, ed. Wolfgang Löhr (= Dokumente deutscher Bischöfe, vol. I), Würzburg 1985, pp. 40–45.

26 The Chief Publications Officer in Bavaria had called for revision of three passages in the Fulda pastoral letter. This caused a serious conflict with Cardinal Michael von Faulhaber (1869–1952), Archbishop of Munich and Freising, who insisted on complete, uncensored publication of the pastoral letter. It was only after the intervention of a Religious Affairs Officer from OMGUS that the pastoral letter could be read throughout Bavaria on the Sunday before Christmas. See Bernhard Lehmann, *Katholische Kirche und Besatzungsmacht in Bayern 1945–1949 im Spiegel der OMGUS-Akten* (= Miscellanea Bavarica Monacensia. Dissertationen zur Bayerischen Landes- und Münchner Stadtgeschichte, vol. 153), Munich 1994, p. 166. On the content of the demanded changes to the Fulda pastoral letter, see ibid., p. 419, fn. 67. Marshall Knappen (see Doc. 8, fn. 10) writes in his book *And call it peace*, Chicago 1947, p. 103, of "the unfortunate effort of an information control officer at Munich to censor the pastoral letter adopted by the Fulda Conference."

27 Wilhelm Hoegner (1887–1980), German politician (SPD), 1911 Dr. jur., 1930–1933 member of the Reichstag, 1933 emigration to Austria, 1934 to Switzerland, 1945/1946 and 1954–1957 Minister-President of the state of Bavaria, 1961/1962 member of the Bundestag.

28 Lucian K. Truscott Jr. (1895–1965), Lieutenant General, 1945/1946 Commanding General 3rd Army and Eastern Military District of the US occupation zone of Germany.

29 George S. Patton Jr. (1885–1945), General, 1909 graduate of the United States Military Academy, 1944/1945 Commanding General 3rd Army, 1945 Commanding General, Eastern Military District of the US occupation zone of Germany. Patton was removed from command of the 3rd Army and the Eastern Military District after he had given the impression that he was putting the National Socialists on par with Republicans and Democrats in the USA.

Doc. 12
Letter to His Wife
On board the *George W. Goethals*[1], March 1, 1946

Dearest Emily –

This is the last long evening aboard this ship. Inasmuch as they are painting the exterior of the ship for the benefit of the war brides (who, I understand now) are to be French instead of English, we are practically restricted to these dull cabins where much unwanted conversation is forced on one. The conversation last evening centered around the number of hours that would have to be worked abroad, and the rate of pay for over-time.

I have been thinking the last couple of days, since thinking is so cheap, what are the things we must aim to accomplish, before we reach the stage where it is impossible to accomplish anything. The chief ones seem to me to be:

1. Security for you in case of my death.
2. Proper education for the boys[2] until the time when they are able to take care of themselves.
3. A piano for John[3].
4. A place in the mountains where we can spend our summers.[4]
5. A trip around the world with the boys when they are old enough to profit by it.

4 and 5 are I suppose unnecessary but who will deny that they are very desirable?

If I ask how this is to be accomplished I cannot say whether best in Lincoln[5] or elsewhere but I have the feeling that to get it all it will have to planned for, worked hard for and saved for. With one we have made a beginning with the new additional insurance which we will continue. But it will have to be increased by that much again if you are to be adequately secure for in the normal course of events you will live at least ten more years than I. For 2. I imagine we should already be beginning to build up as much surplus as we can, though there is every reason to believe that the boys can do much to help themselves. We are agreed that 3 should be the result of the surplus which comes out of my being in the government. If I do not go into a job when there is higher remuneration than at Nebraska[6], then at Nebraska I shall have to spend some time in writing some textbooks which will take much time and effort. But it would be nice to plan and achieve 4 and 5. Is there anything wrong with this honey? It

1 See Doc. 7, fn. 18.
2 Refers to his sons John and Thomas. See Doc. 2, fn. 15 and 16.
3 Son John. See Doc. 2, fn. 15.
4 In 1951 the Johnsons purchased a piece of land with a vacation cabin in Allenspark in the US state of Colorado, on the eastern edge of Rocky Mountain National Park and at the foot of Longs Peak (see Doc. 67, fn. 52). They bought it from Ellen D. Raysor, née Koopman (1898–1995), and Thomas M. Raysor (1895–1974), Professor of English at the University of Nebraska.
5 Capital of the US state of Nebraska, where Johnson lived with his family and taught at the university.
6 Refers to the University of Nebraska.

ought to be possible to figure it out in monetary terms and to calculate the amount we shall have to be saving in the coming years.

I love you very much sweetheart and I am very lonesome for you and the boys. I am prepared to be for many months to come. I noticed in the ship's bulletin today that a certain Mrs. Schuyler[7] and her son[8] are on board, bound for Bucharest[9] where General Schuyler[10] is the American member of the control council[11].[12] So the wives and children are beginning to move over. I shall make inquiry as soon as I can. It would be tempting to promise to stay over here just in order to bring you and the children over. Much travel in Europe and German could be learned in this time. But we should have to be certain about what to do afterwards. We shall have to be careful not to be tempted by money alone. Sometimes I think that that is what I am doing. Yet that is not fair.

Goodnight my sweet and lovely Emily and good-night to my boys. I love you all very very much. I shall do my best. Without you this voyage, as indeed all other times would have been much more desultory. When I think of you I am happy. I know what I have to come back to. Edgar

Doc. 13
Letter to His Wife
Le Havre[1], March 5, 1946

Dearest and beloved –

It has been too dispiriting to write the last couple days. Soon after I left I began to get into the attitude of the GI[2] that there is no point in concerning yourself about anything, simply let the army do it. I'm pretty well confirmed in this

7 Wynona C. Schuyler, née Coykendall (1902–1981).

8 Philip V. R. Schuyler (born 1932).

9 Capital of Romania.

10 Cortlandt V. R. Schuyler (1900–1993), Brigadier General, 1922 graduate of the United States Military Academy, 1944–1947 US Military Chief, Allied Control Command Romania, 1953–1959 Chief of Staff, Supreme Headquarters Allied Powers Europe.

11 The Allied Control Commission for Romania, consisting of representatives from the Soviet Union, USA, and Great Britain.

12 Philip V. R. Schuyler, who was 13 years old when he traveled with his mother to Europe for a 15-month stay, writes in an email to Werner Breunig from February 8, 2008: "My mother, Wynona Coykendall Schuyler, and I traveled to Europe aboard the 'George W. Goethals' in the spring of 1946, to join my father in Romania. We were among the first – possibly *the* first – family dependents to join American service personnel in Europe after the war." The sea voyage was of course a great adventure for the 13-year-old boy, "especially as I was the only youngster aboard [...]. I spent much time on the crossing chatting with members of the crew and was able to learn much about the Merchant Marine (the ship was a U. S. Army vessel but it was operated by the U. S. Merchant Marine)." Email from March 6, 2008.

1 French seaport city on the Atlantic coast.

2 Government Issue, slang for American soldier.

attitude now. In its destruction of initiative the Army is really a vicious institution.

We arrived in the bay of Le Havre on Saturday[3] night expecting to disembark on Sunday[4] morning fairly well pleased with the voyage, which, after all, had not been unpleasant if exceeding tedious, days passing out of your life almost unaccounted for. I had begun to read a collection of short stories, "Seven Gothic Tales" by one Sak Dinesèn[5], a pseudonym. It was a stormy day and the sea was rough. Later on in the day we learned that s. e.[6] England and France had had storms more severe than for a long time. We learned after breakfast that we would not disembark that day. The reasons? The same reasons for the cancellation of the flight from Washington. Nobody seemed to know or if they did they didn't inform us. This is bad psychology, keeping people uninformed and leads to the speedy propagation of rumors. It was too rough for the pilot to get on board, there was no space for our ship in the harbor, a tanker was sunk across the harbor's entrance, Le Havre was on fire, since no-body worked on Sunday, we wouldn't be able to get off on Sunday! Monday[7] was a French holiday so we wouldn't get off then. You can imagine the effect of this. We spent a dull and listless day wondering about our fate, rocking up and down, to and fro at anchor.

As a matter of fact we did get off early yesterday afternoon. There was a sunk tanker just outside the harbor, and Le Havre, if not burning was badly destroyed. None of the regular piers was functioning. The center of the town was a waste-land dominated by huge piles of bricks which the French are using for re-building. There is some re-building going on. Everyone expected, of course, that it would be known that we are coming and that ships would be taken to get us on our way quickly.

Instead, after disembarking at a temporary pier, we were taken in trucks to one of these embarkation camps for GI's – Home Run[8], supposedly a camp for

3 March 2, 1946.

4 March 3, 1946.

5 Karen Blixen, née Dinesen, originally Baroness Karen von Blixen-Finecke, pseudonym Isak Dinesen (1885–1962), Danish writer. Became famous all at once with *Seven Gothic Tales*, first published in the USA in 1934.

6 Southeast.

7 March 4, 1946.

8 Named after the American cigarette brand "Home Run" (manufacturer: Liggett & Myers Tobacco Co., Durham, North Carolina). "Once France had been liberated, the U. S. Army established a series of camps just outside of the harbor city of Le Havre. Each was named after a popular American cigarette of the period, primarily for security reasons: Lucky Strike, Old Gold, Philip Morris, Twenty Grand, and Chesterfield, among others. In 1944–45, the camps were essentially depots for new arrivals bound for the front lines bordering the West Wall (the 'Siegfried Line'). These replacements were desperately needed to bring the American divisions being bloodied in places like the Hürtgen Forest, the Saar, and, later, the Bulge. After V-E day, they were transformed into way stations for men returning home. Like the cigarettes they were named after, they were a pleasant diversion from war no matter how short-lived, though the men who spent time there going in either direction certainly cursed them at the time." "The Cigarette Camps. The U. S. Army Camps in the Le Havre Area," http://www.skylighters.org/special/cigcamps/ (accessed March 1, 2018).

élite and top-priority people on the way home. In the harbor as we came away were several ships loaded with GI's and on the way off the pier dozens of trucks drew up carrying hundreds upon hundreds of GI's who rushed for the boats. That there were people coming back to this place after the war, these people could not understand. May be as a GI said in our cell last night it was because "this working for the government is a swell racket." I wondered how they would find the USA they were coming back to, whether they would find jobs, and whether they would be lost.

At the camp we put through the same routine as anyone else. We had first to go for blankets, and then be assigned to a bunk in one of the long cone like cells into which this old fort is divided. The fort I understand was built sometime in the early 19th century. Maybe there were a hundred 2 decker beds in the cell. It was pretty dirty. Latrines and washing facilities were a considerable distance away. It was a return to war conditions and for civilians who had not been through it somewhat discouraging. Indeed I don't think that the Army can attract many first class civilians to its service under these conditions.

I tried to get permission to telephone Frankfurt[9] but couldn't. There was nothing-to-do but sit and wait until we were told to get on a train for Paris. The big shots on board the boat had gotten off to Paris yesterday – the Lt. Cols. and Cols. The Military attaché[10] from Bern[11] had driven up from Switzerland to get his wife but the roads were so bad that he was going back with them by train.[12] Why couldn't we get off too? Why did we have to wait more than 24 hours? Wasn't there more than one train a day from Le Havre to Paris? No one seemed to know or if so there was no one who thought it worthwhile to tell us. It was just that way – thrown again into the huge mill of transporting people. Maybe completely totalitarian society is like this or may be it's only bureaucracy or may be only the army – I don't know.

After fixing my bed for the night, three blankets over 2 straw mattresses, I went out to the ramparts of this port and got a good view of this harbor with the Seine[13] flowing into the Atlantic at one side of it. The Nazis had heavily re-fortified it – concrete pill-boxes and gun emplacements at the corners and concrete passage-ways just beneath the top of the ramparts themselves. After this it was about time to go to eat. We are not allowed in the officers' mess being civilians and obliged to pay for our meals (25 cents). But the food was decent enough. A much dissipated-looking, boggy-eyed WAC[14] (sergeant) sat in front of me and ate in a listless fashion. It was estimated by one lady on the boat that about 30 % of the women on board were pregnant as a result of their experiences on the voyage.

9 Frankfurt am Main, city in the state of Greater Hesse in the American zone of Germany.
10 See Doc. 9, fn. 14.
11 Capital of Switzerland.
12 See Doc. 9.
13 River that flows into the English Channel at Le Havre.
14 Member of the Women's Army Corps (US Army unit created during Second World War to enable women to serve in noncombat positions). See "Wacs Mark Fourth Year," in: *OMGUS Observer* from May 17, 1946, p. 3.

After dinner I retreated to what is called the Day-Room supplied with music by an orchestra of German PW's[15]. The camp is kept up by them. Their barracks are alongside of the camps within a brushed wire enclosure. A watch-tower looks after them. The PW camp is next to the cemetery of Le Havre, perhaps a symbolic place for it. The Day-Room was full of GI's, most of them very pale and dirty who were going to Paris on a night train. They had a radio full blast. The library in the Day-Room was especially good and I pulled out T. H. Benton's[16] Account of America[17], which had not been signed out before and got a few chapters of it read before returning to the cell. Good reading, hard on the "parvenu" spirit of the middle-west which crowds out aesthetic expression. But Benton must be a very difficult man and some of the compromises he made to get along in the world were indeed very shady and he tosses them off very easily. The GI's left for their Paris train and went to the cell.

Sleeping in one of the beds was a thirteen-year old boy – pale-dirty, ragged and with one eye. It was said that he lost his eye on D-day[18]. Nobody seemed to know who his parents were – some said they were Danish; some said the father was English. In any case he did not know anything about his parents. Possibly they were foreign workers brought by the Germans to work in France. He had been with American soldiers since the landing in Normandy and they said had fought the whole war with them. His buddies left by boat yesterday. He was being cared for by a sailor who was going to try to get him aboard a boat today and take him to New York where he is supposed to have an uncle. It is uncertain whether he can get aboard. He seems to live on cookies and candy-bars. Why he isn't in the hands of responsible people and being taken care of, I don't know. The Red Cross evidently doesn't want to take him over. How many of these orphans are astray in Europe!

We were kept from going to sleep by a conversation of GI's which made me pretty sick. It is no longer amusing to hear God-damn, fucking, cock-sucker, and son-of-a-bitch interlarded into a conversation as every other word. There is much for youth-leaders in America to do. Finally I got to sleep on my medieval mattress.

On boat the last day there was a grand half-hour listening to C. Franck's Violin and Piano Sonata[19]. But it was turned off for something else. Later I heard a Bach[20] Prelude and Fugue being played. It was turned off for something else.

In one of the stories in "Seven Gothic Tales" there is the sentence: "I believe that this feeling of safety and perfect freedom must be what happily married people mean when they talk about [the] two being one."[21] I am very grateful in

15 Prisoners of War.

16 Thomas H. Benton (1782–1858), American politician and author.

17 May refer to the 1854–1856 work, *Thirty years' view. Or A history of the working of the American Government for thirty years, from 1820 to 1850.*

18 On June 6, 1944, when the landing of Allied troops in Normandy began.

19 Sonata in A Major for Violin and Piano (1886) by César Franck (1822–1890), French composer and organist of German-Belgian descent.

20 Johann Sebastian Bach (1685–1750), German composer of the Baroque period.

21 "The Old Chevalier," in: Isak Dinesen, *Seven Gothic Tales* (Penguin Modern Classics), London et al. 1988, pp. 52–74, here pp. 67f.

these moments, as at all times, for this feeling of safety and perfect freedom. I know quite what is meant. It keeps me balanced here. But I keep wondering why I left you and the children to come back here. Maybe the GI who shouted to us yesterday as he made for the boat "You're crazy to come back here" was right. I love you, love you my sweet beloved. Kiss the boys for me. Edgar

Doc. 14
Letter to His Wife
Paris, March 5, 1946

Dearest Emily:

I am sitting in compartment 19/20 of car 3782 of the equivalent of a pullman car (Schlafwagon)[1] which is leaving for Frankfurt[2] at 5:32, if these details interest you. It is, as a matter of fact my first experience with a European pullman car. When John[3] and I were in Europe we always planned to get to a town in order to put up for the night.[4] They are not as well planned as ours. The car is divided into compartments for two, although I notice that, in case adjoining compartments should desire to get together there are means to join. You can see how desirable this might be for some persons under some circumstances. The hot water is supplied from a little coal stove for each car at the end. The cars are heated by means of little steam radiators. There are upper and lower bunks and the two occupiers face in the same direction. There is a lavatory, a mirror, a little writing stand and an ashtray. There is plenty of room for baggage in this particular the planning is better than for an ordinary pullman of ours. I am lucky to be in this pullman and on this train. I take it it is because of my rating since there were some of our party who did not get on the train at all and

1 Refers to a railway car manufactured according to the design of the Pullman Palace Car Company.

2 Frankfurt am Main, city in the state of Greater Hesse in the American zone of Germany.

3 John D. Bickford (1890–1936), American classicist and teacher, 1914 MA and 1921 PhD, Princeton University, 1914–1917 Instructor, Phillips Exeter Academy, Exeter, New Hampshire, 1920–1927 Culver Military Academy, Culver, Indiana, as of 1928 The Hotchkiss School, Lakeville, Connecticut. In 1927 Johnson and Bickford had published the co-authored essay "The Contemplated Anglo-German Alliance: 1890–1901," in: *Political Science Quarterly*, vol. 42, no. 1 (March 1927), pp. 1–57. In 1934 Bickford married Johnson's sister, Mildred H. Johnson (see Doc. 4, fn. 12).

4 In 1927/1928 Bickford and Johnson had studied at the University of Munich and traveled around Europe. "Time away from Munich I spent in travel in England, France, Germany, Czecho-Slovakia, Austria, Hungary, Italy and Switzerland." Edgar N. Johnson, Curriculum Vitae, undated [ca. 1963], p. 1, in: UChicago Library, Special Collections Research Center, Edgar N. Johnson Papers. They made a return trip in 1932.

5 Control Council. Probably refers to the American military government in Germany, or otherwise the Allied Control Authority for Germany, the highest four-power occupation authority for all matters relating to Germany as a whole, led by the Control

others, one a new addition to the legal section of the CC[5] (Rosenwald[6]) who had to sit in a chair. (The train is moving now). There were plenty of military about, majors and up, and I heard a major say that he got accommodations only because there was a cancellation. With the human being so rank conscious there are really small chances for real democracy. The man who is in this compartment with me sighed with relief when he entered and remarked "It's certainly good not to be classified with the cattle." He has unfortunately caught a cold in his kidneys, and begged for the lower berth when he entered on account of urination. I found a pot in the compartment which he immediately proceeded to use. But he managed to get some on the floor and some on a piece of his baggage. The offending part of the baggage is now turned to the wall. This reminds me to report, while on the same subject that the cells in which we were billeted in camp Home Run[7] were a long distance from the toilet, so long that a journey outside to a neighboring building was necessary. In order to avoid this one GI[8] or one sailor (I cannot believe it was one of our party) actually defecated in his bed, it was discovered in the morning. This was the thing the Viennese were so furious about concerning the habits of the Russians.

The subject of rank may require new significance in the theatre, I mean military theatre. It is reported by those who come from Germany that the army has just got out an order ordering civilians to take from their clothes all braids and brass buttons that are to be found on a regular officer's uniform. If they try to enter officers' clubs without having done this they are refused entrance. The same is true I suppose for officers' messes also. If this is true I can't imagine it will last. I can't imagine an easier way to wreck an administration than to create a distinction between the officer and civilian class. (6th March – Frankfurt) I'll finish this at length later + mail what I have written, I am leaving for Berlin at 4.35. The people I want to see are there. I had lunch with General Adcock[9] this noon. Among other topics of conversation I learned that the above in re civilian uniform is correct. If I had brought my civilian clothes, I could have worn them.

Council that consisted of four Military Governors who were likewise Commanders-in-Chief of the Allied occupation forces. See Gunther Mai, *Der Alliierte Kontrollrat in Deutschland 1945–1948. Alliierte Einheit – deutsche Teilung?* (= Quellen und Darstellungen zur Zeitgeschichte, vol. 37), Munich 1995; id., "Alliierter Kontrollrat," in: *Deutschland unter alliierter Besatzung 1945–1949/55*, ed. Wolfgang Benz, Berlin 1999, pp. 229–234.

6 Henry (Heinz) M. Rosenwald (1905–1978), German-American lawyer, born in Nuremberg, Germany, 1930 Dr. jur., University of Erlangen, lawyer in Nuremberg, 1933 lost his accreditation granted in 1932, 1934 emigration to Italy, lawyer in Milan after renewed law studies with subsequent doctorate, 1939 USA, there further law studies with degree in 1943, worked at a law firm, 1946/1947 worked for the US military government in Berlin, as of 1948 worked in a US patent attorney's office, in a bank, and in the legal department of a food company.

7 Camp Home Run in Le Havre. See Doc. 13, fn. 8.

8 Government Issue, slang for American soldier.

9 Clarence L. Adcock (1895–1967), Major General, October 1945–March 1946 Chief, OMGUSZ, as of April 1946 Assistant Deputy Military Governor for Operations and Deputy to the Commanding General, OMGUS, 1947–1949 US Chairman, Bipartite Control Office (BICO), Frankfurt am Main.

The General took pains to inform me of the change though I hope he was not embarrassed to take me to lunch with a quasi-military uniform.

I am sort of hoping there will be mail in Berlin in case the 25th Base Post Office[10] is in Berlin.[11] In any case I love you very much – dear Sweetheart. Kiss the boys for me, I'll go over now + write some on the train. Edgar

Doc. 15
Letter to His Wife
Berlin, Ihnestraße 14[1], March 7, 1946

Dearest Emily –

I didn't write on the train last night because I was obliged to talk with a military government officer from Karlsruhe[2] (Borter) who is working in Public Welfare. It was not exciting conversation. The boy grew up in Chicago, has a high school education, went to New York and got into welfare work, and then into the regular army from which he transferred to military government. He had a broad New York accent – dees for this, etc., and he has acquired a violent dislike for the German character mixed with a certain amount of sympathy for the actual sufferings of the German people which he is afraid to show because he thinks the Germans interpret sympathy as a sign of weakness and he doesn't want to be weak. What he really wants to do is to go back to Pensacola[3] Florida, where he was for a couple of years and where people are friendly and there is good fishing. He finds it hard to make friends in New York.

10 See Doc. 4.

11 The 25th Base Post Office was located not in Berlin but in Würzburg, in the state of Bavaria in the American zone of Germany.

1 The former official villa of the General Director of the Kaiser-Wilhelm-Gesellschaft zur Förderung der Wissenschaften at Ihnestraße 14 (today Brümmerstraße 74), Berlin-Dahlem, was Edgar N. Johnson's first residence in Berlin. He had a room there until he moved to the Wannsee Hotel (see Doc. 25, fn. 9) at the end of March 1946. The villa of the General Director was built in the summer of 1925 based on plans by the Munich architect Carl Sattler (1877–1966) and occupied until 1938 by Friedrich Glum (see Doc. 66, fn. 20), who had to leave after the National Socialists forced him to resign from the office of General Director. His successor Ernst Telschow (1889–1988) subsequently moved in and lived there until the relocation of the general administration to Göttingen in 1945. Today the building houses employees from various Max Planck Institutes. See Eckart Henning/Marion Kazemi, *Dahlem – Domäne der Wissenschaft. Ein Spaziergang zu den Berliner Instituten der Kaiser-Wilhelm-/Max-Planck-Gesellschaft im "deutschen Oxford"* (= Veröffentlichungen aus dem Archiv der Max-Planck-Gesellschaft, vol. 16/I), expanded and updated fourth edition, Berlin 2009, pp. 68–70. Photo of the villa in Appendix of Illustrations, ill. 42.

2 City in the state of Württemberg-Baden in the American zone of Germany.

3 City in the US state of Florida.

4 Frankfurt am Main, city in the state of Greater Hesse in the American zone of Germany.

At Frankfurt[4] yesterday I found that Walter Dorn[5] was in Berlin, and that Dr. J. K. Pollock[6] was in Berlin. General Adcock[7] invited me to lunch as I mentioned[8] and there was sherry before lunch. I detected nothing particularly wrong in the atmosphere. The General seemed to assume that I would be going to Stuttgart[9] to take the job that I was offered, spoke of the elegant quarters that Dr. Pollock had set up in Stuttgart and that I would inherit, etc., etc., talked a good deal about the importance of this Länderrat[10] until I was rather perked up.[11] It was going to be as I believed or had been led to believe that it was going to be.

This feeling of coming to do an important job was built up today in the way I was treated by the officials who get you processed. I went to the visitors' bureau for various kinds of cards and passes: I went to the personnel office where I was treated as a VIP (very important person). I learned however that I cannot receive more than 10,000 dollars in government employ. I also learned that the allotment slip I made out in Omaha[12] was inadequately filled out.[13] They cabled from here a cancellation of it and made out a new one. I am alloting to you 600 a month, and keeping $ 116.92 for myself. This is based on the following:

Base pay			673.08	
25 % differential[14]			96.15	(1⁄13 of 10,000 – 8750).
			769.23	You will get your first allotment around April 15th. Thereafter soon after the 1st of the month.
From which is substracted:				
	13.85	Quarters		
	38.46	Retirement		
	$ 52.31			
			52.31	
			$ 716.92	

5 See Doc. 2, fn. 10.

6 James K. Pollock (1898–1968), American political scientist, 1925 PhD, Harvard University, taught as of 1925 at the University of Michigan (Full Professor as of 1934), 1945–January 1946 Chief, Civil Administration Branch, Internal Affairs and Communications Division, OMGUS, 1945–August 1946 head of RGCO, OMGUS, April 1946 formally appointed as Director of RGCO, subsequently taught again at the University of Michigan (until 1968), repeatedly acted as adviser for OMGUS/the United States High Commissioner for Germany, 1955–1958 President, International Political Science Association. See Appendix of Illustrations, ill. 20 and ill. 21.

7 See Doc. 14, fn. 9.

8 See Doc. 14.

9 Capital of the state of Württemberg-Baden in the American zone of Germany.

10 In October 1945 the Länderrat was established in Stuttgart; government leaders of the states in the American zone of Germany worked together to ensure a degree of uniformity in German administrative operations beyond the state level. See Sebastian Lamm, "Länderrat (US-Zone)," in: *Deutschland unter alliierter Besatzung 1945–1949/55*, ed. Wolfgang Benz, Berlin 1999, pp. 281–283.

11 See Doc. 2, fn. 11. Pollock was formally appointed as Director of RGCO in April 1946 and held the office until August 1946.

12 City in the US state of Nebraska, northeast of Johnson's home in Lincoln.

13 See Doc. 5.

14 Expatriation allowance.

When I went to the billeting office they treated me as a VIP and put me, not in the ordinary hotel but in a room in a very nice house[15] reserved for special guests. This was the result of some telephone calls.

I met Walter Dorn and Dr. J. K. Pollock on the way back from lunch at the Harnack House[16]. Walter seemed glad to see me but I thought I detected a bit of coldness in Dr. Pollock. I said I wanted to see them both and Pollock said he was going back to Stuttgart on Saturday[17]. This did not seem too strange to me, although I wondered a bit. Pollock and I in Stuttgart? It could only be that he would be there for a short time until I got initiated into my job.

After going to my billet and getting cleaned up, a bath with plenty of warm water, I set out to find General Clay[18]. I was told to go to a Colonel Heastie[19] who turned out to be General Millburn's[20] (Chief of Staff) secretary. The Colonel was out but the General was in and I asked to see him. He was very friendly and said that General Clay would certainly want to see me but that he was for the moment in a meeting of the Coordination Committee[21]. We went to Clay's office and I got an appointment for 9:30 tomorrow morning. Walter Dorn has an appointment for 9:00 from what Millburn said to me I became a little more worried. Pollock was going back to Stuttgart. He was going home during the summer. Certainly there must be some overlapping of work at Stuttgart. I could

15 Ihnestraße 14. See fn. 1.

16 Ihnestraße 16, Berlin-Dahlem, a few steps away from Edgar N. Johnson's residence at Ihnestraße 14 (see fn. 1). Designed by the Munich architect Carl Sattler (see fn. 1) and dedicated on May 7, 1929, the Harnack House served as a lecture and meeting center for the Kaiser-Wilhelm-Gesellschaft as well as a guesthouse for academics from all over the world. It was named after the Protestant theologian and church historian Adolf von Harnack (1851–1930), first president of the Kaiser-Wilhelm-Gesellschaft zur Förderung der Wissenschaften, founded in Berlin in 1911. After the Second World War the house was requisitioned by the Americans and used as an officers' mess, among other things. On March 8, 1946, Johnson saw the movie *The Story of G. I. Joe* in the building's cinema. See Doc. 16 and Doc. 16, fn. 37. On July 9, 1946, Johnson held a lecture at Harnack House for the American Women's Club of Berlin. See Doc. 72, fn. 2. Today the building is again used as an academic meeting place and international guesthouse by the Max-Planck-Gesellschaft zur Förderung der Wissenschaften. See Eckart Henning/Marion Kazemi, *Dahlem – Domäne der Wissenschaft. Ein Spaziergang zu den Berliner Instituten der Kaiser-Wilhelm-/Max-Planck-Gesellschaft im "deutschen Oxford"* (= Veröffentlichungen aus dem Archiv der Max-Planck-Gesellschaft, vol. 16/I), expanded and updated fourth edition, Berlin 2009, pp. 57–67. Photo of the building in Appendix of Illustrations, ill. 41.

17 March 9, 1946.

18 See Doc. 2, fn. 6.

19 Charles F. Heasty Jr. (1917–2010), Lieutenant Colonel, Executive Officer to the Staff Secretary, Office of the Deputy Military Governor, OMGUS, 1947 Acting Secretary General, OMGUS.

20 Bryan L. Milburn (1896–1991), Brigadier General, 1945/1946 Chief of Staff, OMGUS, then Director, Administrative Services and Headquarters Commandant, OMGUS.

21 The Coordinating Committee of the Allied Control Authority, the highest four-power occupation authority for all matters relating to Germany as a whole (see Doc. 14, fn. 5), consisted of the four Deputy Military Governors.

22 See Doc. 8, fn. 10.

be inducted into the office. But certainly General Clay would be anxious to see me.

I went over to see Marshall Knappen[22], and soon learned the full story and why Dr. Pollock and Dr. Dorn are in Berlin. These people here seem to have been completely mystified about the delay in my coming but they have known that I was coming. Pollock has been running the Stuttgart office and has built up a kind of empire there. His job as political adviser to General Clay has fallen through because of some reorganization and a cut in expenditures: *Nobody here has bothered to inform me of this.* He has been content to take orders from a General Dailey[23] who is now heading the Civil Affairs Division[24] under which the Stuttgart office comes. But a shift is taking place. General Dailey is moving up. He is either taking the place of a General Eccles[25] who is Clay's deputy or going to Washington to take General Hilldring's[26] place (General Hilldring is going to the state department as the head of a division of occupied areas[27] – (more reorganization for Gene[28]). Now Mr. Pollock doesn't want to take orders from the civilian (formerly a General – Parkman[29]) who is taking General

23 Charles K. Gailey Jr. (1901–1966), Brigadier General, 1920 graduate of the United States Military Academy, January–April 1946 Chief, Civil Administration Branch, Internal Affairs and Communications Division, OMGUS, April–October 1946 Director, Public Relations, OMGUS, October 1946–1949 Chief of Staff, OMGUS, 1959–1961 Commanding General, Military District of Washington. See Appendix of Illustrations, ill. 24.

24 Refers to the Civil Administration Branch, Internal Affairs and Communications Division, OMGUS. It had the following responsibilities: "settlement of four-power agreements on the decentralization of political structures in Germany, re-establishment of democratic conditions in local self-government, monitoring of political parties, preparation of central administrative institutions, alignment and coordination of policies and administration on the state level, as well as monitoring of the reform of civil service." ("Vereinbarung von Vier-Mächte-Abkommen zur Dezentralisierung der politischen Strukturen in Deutschland, Wiedererrichtung demokratischer Verhältnisse in der kommunalen Selbstverwaltung, Überwachung der politischen Parteien, Vorbereitung zentraler Verwaltungseinrichtungen, Angleichung und Koordinierung der Politik und Verwaltung auf Länderebene sowie Überwachung der Reform des Öffentlichen Dienstes.") Josef Henke/Klaus Oldenhage, "Office of Military Government for Germany (U. S.)," in: *OMGUS-Handbuch. Die amerikanische Militärregierung in Deutschland 1945–1949*, ed. Christoph Weisz (= Quellen und Darstellungen zur Zeitgeschichte, vol. 35), Munich 1994, pp. 1–142, here p. 110.

25 Oliver P. Echols (1892–1954), Major General, July 1945–April 1946 Assistant Deputy Military Governor, Germany (US), 1946/1947 Director, Civil Affairs Division, Department of War.

26 See Doc. 2, fn. 4.

27 Area Division V – Occupied Areas.

28 Eugene N. Anderson (see Doc. 1, fn. 1) worked as Acting Assistant Chief in Area Division V – Occupied Areas.

29 Henry C. Parkman (1894–1958), American lawyer and politician (Republican Party), 1916 MA, Harvard University, as of 1924 worked as a lawyer, 1926–1929 member of the Boston City Council, 1929–1936 member of the Massachusetts Senate, 1940 candidate for US Senate, 1945 Brigadier General, Civil Affairs Division, War Department, as of April 1946 Director, Civil Administration Division, OMGUS, 1947 Governmental Affairs Adviser to the Commander-in-Chief, European Command, and

Dailey's place[30]. He is up here suggesting to General Clay that he will continue in Stuttgart if he can be responsible to Clay and not to Parkman.[31] Dr. Dorn is in Berlin because General Adcock, who wants to go home he told me is coming to Berlin. They are amalgamating the Frankfurt with the Berlin group[32] and here General Adcock will not play the rôle he has hitherto played[33] and it is questionable whether he needs a political adviser here[34]. General Clay no longer has Pollock but only Murphy[35]. So Walter may be out of a job and looking at Stuttgart.

Where does this leave me? I don't know what Clay will say to me tomorrow. If Pollock is going to stay in Stuttgart then I do not have my job. I doubt very much whether I want to play second fiddle to him in the same office. There cannot be room for two of us there. I haven't thought the matter through and can't because I don't know what Clay's proposition is. There are in any case, many jobs available here. I can get a good one from M[arshall] Knappen (Religion and Education). There are others for which I can shop around. I could even go to Austria, I suppose. Or I could come home. I only know now I shall speak rather strongly tomorrow to Clay about being kept uninformed, left in the lurch. I may have to write an article for the Nation[36] on how the generals treat their civilian appointees. Don't concern yourself until you hear how it comes out. But it looks as if I'm being let down on Stuttgart.

All my love to you and the boys. I should never have left you. Edgar

US Military Governor in Germany, 1949/1950 US delegate on the International Ruhr Authority, subsequently Chief, ECA Mission to France, 1953–1955 Assistant US High Commissioner for Germany.

30 Parkman succeeded Gailey as head of the Civil Administration Branch. In April 1946 Civil Administration obtained the status of a division, and Parkman became Director of the Civil Administration Division.

31 Pollock was officially appointed as Director of RGCO in April 1946 and was directly responsible to the Military Governor and his deputy, Clay.

32 Headed by Adcock, OMGUSZ (Office of Military Government [US Zone]) in Frankfurt am Main had the task of carrying out policies decided upon in Berlin by OMGUS (see Doc. 17, fn. 45) in the American zone of Germany. OMGUSZ was dissolved on April 1, 1946, and, apart from a few minor exceptions, responsibilities were transferred to OMGUS. See Josef Henke/Klaus Oldenhage, "Office of Military Government for Germany (U. S.)," in: *OMGUS-Handbuch. Die amerikanische Militärregierung in Deutschland 1945–1949*, ed. Christoph Weisz (= Quellen und Darstellungen zur Zeitgeschichte, vol. 35), Munich 1994, pp. 1–142, here pp. 28 and 36.

33 As of April 1946 Adcock was Assistant Deputy Military Governor for Operations and Deputy to the Commanding General, OMGUS.

34 Dorn was Adcock's Personal Adviser in Frankfurt am Main. See Walter L. Dorn, *Inspektionsreisen in der US-Zone. Notizen, Denkschriften und Erinnerungen aus dem Nachlaß*, trans. and ed. Lutz Niethammer (= Schriftenreihe der Vierteljahrshefte für Zeitgeschichte, no. 26), Stuttgart 1973, pp. 12f.

35 See Doc. 8, fn. 13.

36 *The Nation*, a weekly magazine from New York founded in 1865, considered left-liberal.

Doc. 16
Letter to His Wife
Berlin, Ihnestraße 14[1], March 8, 1946

Dearest and beloved –

One month ago I left for Omaha[2] and then came back to Lincoln[3] again to be with you a few hours. You came with me to the train.[4] Since that time I have had one letter[5] from you and have heard your sweet voice over the telephone. I heard my dear John's[6] voice too. A month ago you came back and found him tearful, fearful that a car had struck you down. I haven't had time to discover as yet whether the 25th Base Post Office[7] is in Berlin or not.[8] There will be mail for me there. But it looks as if I may miss mail for many months to come according to present plans.

I saw General Clay[9] this morning for a few minutes and I must say he was very nice, very considerate and very kind. He proposed that for the next few weeks I should spend my time getting acquainted with the international and military government set-up here in Berlin and in the zone preparatory to whatever I shall be doing after that date. To that end he proposed that I should attend the meetings of his staff[10] beginning at 11:30 tomorrow at which time I am to meet the directors of the divisions and they are to be told to put myself at my services. He also spoke of my attending some meetings of the Coordinating Committee (the subordinate Committee of the Control Council[11] itself composed of the Deputies of the Commanders-in-Chief)[12] and even of the Control Council itself. After familiarizing myself with the situation here I am to go throughout the zone and become acquainted with set-ups in the Länder, including I take it Stuttgart[13].

1 See Doc. 15, fn. 1.
2 City in the US state of Nebraska, northeast of Johnson's home in Lincoln.
3 Capital of the US state of Nebraska, where Johnson lived with his family and taught at the university.
4 See Doc. 2, fn. 33.
5 Emily L. Johnson's letter from February 10, 1946, in: Documents from the estate of Edgar N. Johnson, private collection of Candice E. and Thomas R. Johnson, Denver, Colorado, USA.
6 Johnson's son John. See Doc. 2, fn. 15.
7 See Doc. 4.
8 See Doc. 14, fn. 11.
9 See Doc. 2, fn. 6.
10 On the OMGUS staff conferences that took place every Saturday at the OMGUS building on Kronprinzenallee (today Clayallee), Berlin-Dahlem, providing for the exchange of information between Clay and his team of advisers, see Bernd Steger, "General Clays Stabskonferenzen und die Organisation der amerikanischen Militärregierung in Deutschland. Die 'Clay-Minutes' als historische Quelle," in: *Vierteljahrshefte für Zeitgeschichte*, vol. 27 (1979), pp. 113–130.
11 The Control Council was the highest organ of the Allied Control Authority and consisted of the four Military Governors. See Doc. 14, fn. 5.
12 See Doc. 15, fn. 21.
13 Capital of the state of Württemberg-Baden in the American zone of Germany.

Frankfurt[14] will soon be almost out of the picture.[15] At the end of that time I am to report to him again and then what my task will be will be made clear. I said I was a little disturbed about the change in the picture but he insisted that there was no fundamental change. What would be Pollock's[16] fate he had not yet decided, i. e., whether he was to be permanently here or remain in Stuttgart and I was led to believe that if it were Stuttgart I could be here in some advisory capacity to him, and if Pollock were to come here then I should be in Stuttgart. I mentioned keeping in mind that I might want to go back in the fall and he said that that would be kept in mind. He spoke of Pollock's first wanting to go home in May and then in the summer. He also spoke of his splendid work in Stuttgart and of how he had worked himself into his job[17], and that there was nothing to be done for the time being but to continue his work there. That is quite understandable. He then called General Milburn[18] and told him to introduce me to General Gailey[19] who is the chief of the Civil Affairs Branch of the Internal Affairs and Communications Division[20] who was then to take care of me. I met General Gailey in General Milburn's Office after lunch (the General comes from Georgia[21])[22]. He then took me over to his building and set me up with an office and a secretary and something to read. It was amusing to see the old bureaucratic procedure in order. An administrative officer (female) cleaned the desk, desk top, blotters, paper, pencils, clips, ink, in basket, out basket and before I left in the afternoon things were going into the in-basket. I don't have much use yet for a secretary. Clay mentioned that I was to have transportation. Milburn came along and gave somebody orders about a car. Gailey mentioned a car. Well I don't see that I need a car but I am supposed to take it while I can get it and before I get swallowed into the huge bureaucracy that is here. I shall only have it in any case for a couple of weeks while I am here.

There was nothing to do of course to consent to General Clay's proposals. I saw Walter Dorn[23] at lunch and Mr. Pollock late in the afternoon. Walter confirmed the picture of flux that Marshal[l] Knappen[24] presented last night.[25] He is being washed out with the closing of the Frankfurt office[26] and doesn't know

[14] Frankfurt am Main, city in the state of Greater Hesse in the American zone of Germany.

[15] Johnson is referring here to the dissolution of OMGUSZ in Frankfurt am Main. See Doc. 15, fn. 32.

[16] See Doc. 15, fn. 6.

[17] As head of RGCO, OMGUS. See Doc. 2, fn. 11.

[18] See Doc. 15, fn. 20.

[19] See Doc. 15, fn. 23.

[20] Refers to the Civil Administration Branch, Internal Affairs and Communications Division, OMGUS. See Doc. 15, fn. 24.

[21] US state.

[22] Gailey was born in Conyers, Georgia, "a small deeply segregated town about 30 miles from Atlanta (now a sizeable 'bedroom' suburb)." Gailey's daughter Christine W. Gailey in an email to Werner Breunig from October 26, 2009.

[23] See Doc. 2, fn. 10.

[24] See Doc. 8, fn. 10.

[25] See Doc. 15.

[26] Johnson is referring here to the dissolution of OMGUSZ in Frankfurt am Main. See Doc. 15, fn. 32.

quite what is going to happen to him. He thinks that may be he will be doing the same thing for Clay as he is now doing for Adcock[27], and he hinted that he may get the present position of Gailey should Gailey move to another position. Walter is much tied up with himself and his future prospects. But he urged me to be patient and to see what comes out after the preliminary period of learning and flux is over. He said that there at the moment only three people with a direct relationship to Clay – Pollock, himself and I and that under no circumstances should I release this position for something that will closet me in a division or branch. I think Pollock is all right. He was a little careful with me, seemed to be suspicious that I had had no actual experiences with military government as such, though I tried to correct him a little on this point. He is extremely proud of his part in the Länderrat[28], and of the manner in which it appreciates his efforts and of course does not intend to let anyone interfere with his part unless he is given definite instructions by Clay. But he said that in the present confusion he did not know whether Clay would want him to come up here or stay down there. In this he confirmed what Clay said. He also welcomed me to Stuttgart when it would be time for me to come and expressed the desire to become better acquainted. It is generally agreed that he is a powerful figure with Clay whom he regards highly and I shall do my best to get along with him.

He made a remark which I think is possibly correct that Clay gives people time to prove themselves and then decides what they shall do. That I take it is the position I now am in, and I shall do my best.

I had dinner with Louis Wiesner[29]. Poor kid. In Washington their first child was born dead.[30] He brought his wife[31] to London[32] but she has now gone home and gone to *Reno*[33].[34] She wants to settle down in a teaching position. He is now in the foreign service and wants to make that his career.[35] He is pretty badly broken up.

27 See Doc. 14, fn. 9.
28 See Doc. 15, fn. 10.
29 See Doc. 8, fn. 11.
30 In 1943/1944 Louis A. Wiesner had worked in Washington for OSS, and before that, in 1942/1943, in New York for the Council on Foreign Relations.
31 Probably Jean H. Wiesner, née Hagen.
32 Louis A. Wiesner had gone to London at the end of 1944 as a Foreign Service Officer, "to join Ambassador Murphy's [see Doc. 8, fn. 13] mission at Bushy Park, England, which was on the grounds of Hampton Court Palace. I was assigned to be the assistant labor attaché in Ambassador Murphy's mission." Interview with Louis A. Wiesner from June 5, 1981, p. 2, in: Landesarchiv Berlin (LAB), Germany, F Rep. 037 (Sammlung Amerikanische Behörden in Berlin), no. 99.
33 City in the US state of Nevada.
34 Apparently the marriage ended in divorce in "divorce paradise" Reno. See the divorce announcements in: *Nevada State Journal* from March 23, 1946, p. 8 ("Jean Wiesner from Louis Wiesner"); *Reno Evening Gazette* from March 25, 1946, p. 11 ("Jean Hagen Wiesner from Louis Arnold Wiesner"). Louis A. Wiesner then married Elizabeth Q. Phenix in 1950.
35 "Now, in September of 1944 while I was still at OSS, I was taken into the Foreign Service of the United States and then became an employee of the State Department." Interview with Louis A. Wiesner from June 5, 1981, p. 2, in: LAB, F Rep. 037 (Sammlung Amerikanische Behörden in Berlin), no. 99.

I saw GI[36] Joe[37] at the movies in Harnackhouse[38] tonight. Very excellent. When the captain died a boy broke out sobbing behind us and had to leave the room.

I love my Sweetheart and my boys. I imagine this is going to be a good challenge here and I shall do my best to meet it. Goodnight dearest one – Edgar

Doc. 17
Letter to His Wife
Berlin, Ihnestraße 14[1], March 9, 1946

Dearest beloved:

I am just a little bit dizzy. I have attended so many meetings today; met and seen so many generals that I'm not quite sure where I am what I am or who I am. I understand now a little more completely what it means to have one's head turned by the prospect of power and influence and association with the right people. But you don't have to worry about me. I think the best qualifications for people who are engaged in this sort of work are those which make it possible to look on the scene quite objectively without being moved at all by stars

36 Government Issue, slang for American soldier.

37 Refers to the American film *The Story of G. I. Joe*, directed by William A. Wellman (1896–1975), from 1945. Burgess Meredith (1908–1997) plays the American war correspondent Ernie Pyle, who tours the battlefields of North Africa and Italy along with an infantry company during the Second World War, and Robert Mitchum (1917–1997) plays Lieutenant/Captain Bill Walker, who is killed during a charge on the German front. "Mud, monotony and the grueling life of the infantryman are well depicted In *The Story of GI Joe* […]. Burgess Meredith, portraying a sincere and unassuming Ernie Pyle, follows C Company of the 18th Infantry through the African and Italian campaigns. The story revolves around the siege and subsequent capitulation of historic Cassino. While Combat Infantry Badges are still to be seen these days in OMGUS, this film should serve to impress on newcomers the loftiness of the ideals for which so much was sacrificed. The captain of C Company says to Ernie, 'I know … I know its not my fault they get killed, but I feel like a murderer. I can't stand to look at them anymore. If only some good could be made to come from all this energy, and all these men.' A bitter sort of humor is injected into the movie with situations similar to those Bill Mauldin illustrated in his 'Up Front' cartoons. No attempt is made to glorify or to glamorize the real heroes of this war. The men fight, freeze, go beserk, die and 'wolf' in an unexalted 'there's a war to be won' manner. If you've never been in combat, *The Story of GI Joe* will undoubtedly give you a truer concept of what it's like than you have received from any previous Hollywood attempt. If you have been in combat, you may feel the film falls short in many of the real and often galling details. Where else but in Hollywood would every Doughboy in the midst of battle wear a raincoat?" "'Life of GI Joe' is Films' Best Tribute to Doughs," in: *The Grooper* from March 2, 1946, p. 2. See *Das Jahr 1945 und das Kino*, Berlin 1995, p. 173.

38 See Doc. 15, fn. 16.

1 See Doc. 15, fn. 1.

on the shoulders, villas on the lakeside or exclusive clubs, and who are capable of asking simply what is being done here for the American people, and for the principles of American democracy.

I have been more or less taken in tow today by General Gailey[2], (I think it's perhaps two stars)[3] who is head of the Civil Administration Branch of the Division of Internal Affairs and Communications[4]. The General is from Georgia[5] (as I learn is General Clay[6])[7] and he is a regular officer, indeed a West Point Graduate[8]. He strikes me as a simple, decent and altogether likeable individual who has no particular pretensions with respect to his own intellectual abilities but who is accustomed to exercise authority. He said rather simply today in re Nebraska – Biff Jones[9] and Dana X Bible[10] (that is how the University of Nebraska[11] is identified) that he just loved football and it turned out as we discussed why he loved football that it was not so much the actual game but the environment of the game. I have always said that football was to be enjoyed because it afforded the spectators the occasion to go on an emotional drunk. And he added after he had enumerated the features outside of the game itself that it gave oldish men a day of escape back into the days when they were kids, well that must be very true and it is human, and I sort of liked the general for the remark.

He invited me to lunch after the meetings of the morning. We were whisked out to his house in his car and with his own driver. It is on the westernest edge of the American zone in Berlin, on an island in the Swansee[12], one of the large lakes on the outskirts of Berlin.[13] It was a swell place. The large living room

2 See Doc. 15, fn. 23.
3 Gailey was a Brigadier General at the time (one star).
4 See Doc. 15, fn. 24.
5 US state. See Doc. 16, fn. 22.
6 See Doc. 2, fn. 6.
7 Clay was from Marietta, Georgia.
8 Gailey had graduated from the United States Military Academy in West Point, New York, in 1920.
9 Lawrence McC. (Biff) Jones (1895–1980), American College Football Head Coach, 1937–1941 University of Nebraska.
10 Dana X. Bible (1891–1980), American College Football Head Coach, 1929–1936 University of Nebraska, predecessor of Lawrence McC. (Biff) Jones.
11 University founded in 1869 in Lincoln, Nebraska.
12 Refers to Großer Wannsee, a bight of the Havel (see Doc. 74, fn. 24) in southwest Berlin.
13 Gailey lived on Schwanenwerder, an island built up with villas located in the Havel at the outlet of Großer Wannsee, belonging to the Berlin administrative district of Zehlendorf, Wannsee area. Later he lived with his family in the same house, according to information from his oldest son, Charles K. Gailey III (see fn. 18), in an email to Werner Breunig from November 2, 2009. In an email from October 26, 2009, Charles K. Gailey III writes: "We lived […] in the house on the west side that had a huge thatched roof. We had a beautiful view of the water." Gailey's daughter Christine W. Gailey, born in 1950, shares in an email from October 25, 2009, that the house had belonged to a "film maker." Apparently it was the thatched country house at Inselstraße 36, built in 1939 (architect: Jürgen Schweitzer [1907–1996], owner: actor and director Carl Ludwig Duisberg, pseudonym Achaz [1889–1958], son of the chem-

(beamed) was covered with oriental rugs (I imagine it was some important Nazis' place and it is OK with me to see these generals occupy houses the Nazis were thrown out of)[14]. Two large plate glass windows looked out over the lake, on one side of which the high British officials live.[15] The room was simply but elegantly furnished. A large fire-place dominated one end and the German servants had a fire crackling when we came in and kept it crackling. There was a piano in the room and books (English, French and classical German authors including Joyce[16] and Proust[17] which I don't believe the General reads). In one corner was a large white vase filled with magnificent branches of pussy willows, four and five feet in length. Smaller vases of the same were on other tables. There was also a small vase of snow-drops, and some tulips. It is tulip time here (re-forced plants). There are in most offices and I asked my secretary (!) who has nothing to do to get some for my office. It was a simple lunch (soup and fresh fruit and coffee) and the general and I got along very well. At least he invited me to come out and stay with him when my tenure at this place is over. He liked to talk, he said, and would like to thresh over some problems. I think I'll do it. I can't imagine a nicer place to stay. There may be a chance for some walks. The General knows everybody around here and can help me to get properly and thoroughly indoctrinated into the place. I think to put it professionally that to have won the General's confidences to this extent is not so bad for a two days' presence. And I mean to make friends with him. His family is coming over in August and he has two boys[18], younger even than ours[19].[20] There are so many people who are old (he must be in his 50's[21]) and who have young children. He laughs easily and heartily and does not appear pretentious. But in meetings with his subordinates he speaks with authority.

ist and industrialist Carl Duisberg [1861–1935]). See Janin Reif/Horst Schumacher/Lothar Uebel, *Schwanenwerder. Ein Inselparadies in Berlin*, Berlin 2000, pp. 234–237. Duisberg and his family were registered on Schwanenwerder as of June 3, 1940. See registration cards Carl Ludwig Duisberg, in: LAB, B Rep. 021 (Einwohnermeldeamt Berlin).

14 After 1933 Joseph Goebbels (1897–1945), Adolf Hitler's (see Doc. 22, fn. 19) personal physician Theodor Morell (1886–1948), and Albert Speer (1905–1981) moved to the island, among others. See Georg Schertz, "Schwanenwerder. Eine Insel im Spiegelbild der Geschichte," in: *Berlin in Geschichte und Gegenwart. Jahrbuch des Landesarchivs Berlin 2005*, pp. 209–223, especially pp. 214f.

15 View of the western shore of Wannsee, and the villas occupied by British occupation officers in Kladow, an area of Berlin in the administrative district of Spandau (British sector).

16 James Joyce (1882–1941), Irish writer.

17 Marcel Proust (1871–1922), French writer.

18 Charles K. Gailey III (1942–2016) and John Bruce Gailey (1943–2017). A third son, Timothy H. Gailey, was born in April 1946.

19 Johnson's sons John and Thomas were born in 1939 and 1944, respectively. See Doc. 2, fn. 15 and 16.

20 Gailey's wife, Margaret A. Gailey, née Pearsall (1913–1981), and their three sons came to Berlin in November or December 1946. Information from Charles K. Gailey III in an email to Werner Breunig from October 26, 2009.

21 Gailey, born on May 14, 1901, was 44 years old.

22 Morrison C. Stayer (1882–1969), Major General, 1945/1946 Chief, Public Health and Welfare Branch, Internal Affairs and Communications Division, OMGUS.

The first meeting I attended was that of the staff of General Stayer[22] (who is a Public Health man and was active in our last occupation of Germany[23]) and who is head of the Division of Internal Affairs and Communications[24]. I found Marshal[l] Knappen[25] and Taylor[26] (Education – whom I have mentioned)[27] attending the meeting and went to sit by them, but General Gailey insisted that I came over to sit by him. I was introduced to most of the colonels who were present and listened to their reports for the week. They were not particularly exciting but it gave you a good idea of how the Divisions work. It was reported that the Religion and Education people are a little perturbed to find GI's[28] and Fräuleins on the davenports in their offices when they come in to work in the evening. The GI's use showers on their floor and run around naked in the evenings to the consternation of the German women who are cleaning up the place.

At 11:30 I went to General Clay's weekly staff meeting[29] with General Gailey. It is held in a big room next to General Clay's office[30]. I have never seen so much brass together in one place. They sat around four huge tables arranged in a square. There must have been from 60 to 75 top ranking officers. On each side of this square were two small tables at one of which sat the members of the secretariat and at the other Mr. Pollock[31], a naval officer of some kind and I. The officers at the main tables were the heads of the offices and the Divisions and some heads of Branches. Clay was flanked by Milburn[32] his Chief of Staff and Echols[33], his Deputy who is supposed to be leaving. Mr. (Ambassador) Murphy[34] sat next to General Echols. Around the table were people I had heard of since OSS[35] days or had just recently met: General Draper[36] (Industry – he is

23 1919–1921 Chief Health Officer, American Occupation Forces Germany.

24 At the time Frank C. Meade was Director of the Internal Affairs and Communications Division, OMGUS (see Doc. 20, fn. 53).

25 See Doc. 8, fn. 10.

26 John W. Taylor (1906–2001), Lieutenant Colonel, American educationalist, 1930/1931 English teacher, Kaiser-Friedrich-Realgymnasium, Berlin-Neukölln, 1936 PhD, Teachers College, Columbia University, 1945/1946 Chief, Education Section, Education and Religious Affairs Branch, Internal Affairs and Communications Division, OMGUS, May 1946–1947 Chief, Education and Religious Affairs Branch, Internal Affairs and Communications Division, OMGUS, 1947–1950 President, University of Louisville, 1952/1953 Acting Director General, UNESCO.

27 See Doc. 15.

28 Government Issues, slang for American soldiers.

29 See minutes of the OMGUS staff conference on March 9, 1946, in: Archiv des Instituts für Zeitgeschichte (IfZ), Munich, Germany, OMGUS – Staff Conferences (copies of minutes), Fg 12/3.

30 On Kronprinzenallee (today Clayallee), Berlin-Dahlem.

31 See Doc. 15, fn. 6.

32 See Doc. 15, fn. 20.

33 See Doc. 15, fn. 25.

34 See Doc. 8, fn. 13.

35 Office of Strategic Services. See Doc. 1, fn. 9.

36 William H. Draper Jr. (1894–1974), Brigadier General, as of 1945 Director, Economics Division, OMGUS, 1947 Economics Adviser, Office of the Commander-in-Chief, European Command, 1947–1949 Under Secretary of the Army, 1952/1953 US member, NATO Council, Paris.

often in the New York Times[37]), General McClure[38] (Information Control – press-films-radio), General Stayer, General McSherry[39] (Manpower), General Conrad[40] (Intelligence) and a host of other officers including some naval people. Clay goes around the table asking for a report, calling some of the people by their first names, including Murphy. I must say he makes a good impression, conducting the meeting with good sense, efficiency, authority and good humor and breaking into the reports with sharp questions, and rigorous comments. When General Conrad reported that the Germans were conducting themselves with more independence, meaning this as something bad, Clay interrupted to suggest that it might on the contrary be something good that we should rejoice that there is evidence that the Germans were discarding their abject submissiveness and conducting themselves like men. He also used the terms "bad Germans" and "good Germans." After the various people had reported Clay made a very nice introductory speech concerning me, referring to my previous acquaintance with Germany and my experience with OSS and then asked all those present to extend to me every courtesy possible in order to aid me in getting acquainted with the set-up here in Berlin. He then asked me to stand up. This certainly was extremely decent and helpful of him to do. After this Pollock made a short report and the meeting was over. This was a new experience to me, to see the results of what I suppose is the work of thousands of people here for a week summarized in the form of short oral reports to McNarney's[41] Deputy. I don't really believe I was at the meeting and was presented to them.

(There was a meeting here with the Civil Administration Branch[42])

I went back to my office after lunch and was called in the afternoon by a Colonel of the Office of Administrative Service[43] asking me if I wanted to join a club[44] of the top personnel in Omgus (Office of Military Government U. S.)[45].

37 See among others Kathleen McLaughlin, "Allies Asked to Pool Food To Avert Crisis in Germany," in: *The New York Times* from March 1, 1946, pp. 1 and 8.

38 Robert A. McClure (1897–1957), Brigadier General, 1944/1945 Director, Psychological Warfare Division, SHAEF, 1945 Director, Office of Information, USGCC, 1945/1946 Director, Office of Information Control Services, Office of the Deputy Military Governor, OMGUS, 1947 Director, Information Control Division, OMGUS.

39 Frank J. McSherry (1892–1977), Brigadier General, 1945/1946 Director, Manpower Division, OMGUS.

40 G. Bryan Conrad (1898–1976), Brigadier General, 1945/1946 Director, Office of the Director of Intelligence, OMGUS.

41 Joseph T. McNarney (1893–1972), General, 1945–1947 Commanding General, US Forces in the European Theater, Commander-in-Chief, US Forces of Occupation in Germany, Military Governor, Germany (US).

42 Civil Administration Branch of the Internal Affairs and Communications Division, OMGUS. See Doc. 15, fn. 24.

43 Refers to the Office of the Director of Administrative Services, Office of the Deputy Military Governor, OMGUS.

44 Refers to the exclusive Lakeside Club for high-ranking officers.

45 OMGUS (Office of Military Government for Germany [US]), established on October 1, 1945, under the control of Lucius D. Clay (see Doc. 2, fn. 6), was the highest political entity in the American-occupied part of Germany. In the Allied Control Authority (see Doc. 14, fn. 5) in Berlin, along with the other three military governments, it constituted the highest four-power authority for all matters relating to Germany as

General Millburn[46] had referred to this previously. I said yes, and the Colonel said he would send over a membership card and literature. In due time a WAC[47] sergeant delivered the stuff. I found out that the initiation fee was twenty-five dollars and the dues 2.50 a month. I found out that the club was limited to 75 of the "top personnel" (the by-laws) of Omgus but I notice that my membership card is 79. The Club house is on the shores of the Wannsee[48] and they are opening formally tomorrow night with a buffet supper and dance. I shall go tomorrow, and attend once in a while thereafter. I can see well enough into the situation here to see that it is important for me to do this.

It is going to be interesting enough for the next five or six weeks, and I am going to make the most of it. There is no doubt of the wisdom of my decision of staying with Clay until I see just exactly what is going to happen to me. By that time if they have not formed an unfavorable impression of me, I ought to be put in a position of some importance and influence where I can make good.

I love you my sweet angel and my boys. I think we'd better use this APO[49] as a permanent address until further notice. I'll cable it and this will be confirmation. I shall be here about two weeks more and then out in the zone for about a month. They can hold mail for me here or else send it out into the zone. Possibly I can get some from the temporary address (I haven't been able to find out where 25th Base Post Office[50] is[51]) before I leave here. The address is:

Office of Military Government for Germany (U. S.)
Internal Affairs and Communications Division
APO # 742[52]
c/o PM, N. Y., N. Y.

I hope it won't continue to be as hectic as this has been but I am sure it is going to be a very very busy time. There is a tremendous shortage of personnel here. But in so far as I can see excellent work is being done in the implementation of the policy so far announced. What I have heard does not lead one to suspect that the Russians are impossible in international negotiations. But they are undoubtedly pulling fast ones in politics.

I love you my sweet one and I shall be so happy when my first word comes from you. Goodnight – beloved. Edgar

a whole. OMGUS had its office on Kronprinzenallee (today Clayallee), Berlin-Dahlem, on the grounds of the NS Luftgaukommando III. See Josef Henke/Klaus Oldenhage, "Office of Military Government for Germany (U. S.)," in: *OMGUS-Handbuch. Die amerikanische Militärregierung in Deutschland 1945–1949*, ed. Christoph Weisz (= Quellen und Darstellungen zur Zeitgeschichte, vol. 35), Munich 1994, pp. 1–142. See photo in Appendix of Illustrations, ill. 39.

46 Bryan L. Milburn. See Doc. 15, fn. 20.
47 Women's Army Corps. See Doc. 13, fn. 14.
48 Refers to Großer Wannsee, a bight of the Havel (see Doc. 74, fn. 24) in southwest Berlin.
49 Army Post Office.
50 See Doc. 4.
51 See Doc. 14, fn. 11.
52 Berlin-Dahlem, Kronprinzenallee (today Clayallee).

Doc. 18
Letter to His Wife
Berlin, Ihnestraße 14[1], March 11, 1946

Dearest and beloved:

I am a little cheerful tonight because I learned that the 25th Base Post Office, APO[2] 800[3] is located at Würzburg[4] and that brings the possibility of my getting a letter from you in a few days. I wrote them yesterday giving them my new APO address. It shouldn't take long for this to get to Würzburg nor for letters to be returned here. Maybe there will be more than one. You should be hearing from me from here about the same time.

I called on some friends of Gene's[5] yesterday afternoon where he stayed in 1930 when he met Polly[6].[7] I was ushered into a bedroom on the top floor of the house which was unheated. One daughter of the family is employed by Omgus (Office of Military Government US)[8] only an office or so from me. Then I was invited by the daughter down to the one heated room in the house for afternoon coffee. There were twelve people in the room. Another daughter and her four children who had fled the Russian zone and were on their way to the British zone to live in the country. 2 of the children had whooping cough. But they and the two others were fat, and even red-cheeked, and the baby, not much younger than Timmy[9] (the sweet kid) was drinking milk from a bottle when I came in. I was surprised at what I was served even as I always am when Germans or Austrians entertain. The coffee was quite potable and there was plenty of it. There was, in some abundance, toasted white bread, good black bread and a tasteless fruit tart. The kids had marmalade and sugar on their bread. I was even offered a glass of schnaps. But I refused and of course did not eat much of their stuff.

The conversation, however, I could not stomach very well. There was much self-pity, much complaint, much of the usual anti-Russian talk, and no admission that Germany had started a war, exploited most of Europe, and lost the war. It was as if there had been no Nazi regime. The old Mother, in good shape indeed, said that the world had suffered some Judgment of God, some stroke of Fate, but not that the German nation had spawned the Nazis. She said no guilt could be assessed and referred somewhat caustically to the repetition of the old dispute after the war of 1918 as to war guilt.

I went to the opening of the Lakeside Club.[10] The motor pool sent over a staff car which is more than OSS[11] ever did, though I must not forget my blue

1 See Doc. 15, fn. 1.
2 Army Post Office.
3 See Doc. 4.
4 City in the state of Bavaria in the American zone of Germany.
5 Eugene N. Anderson. See Doc. 1, fn. 1.
6 Pauline R. Anderson. See Doc. 2, fn. 2.
7 Eugene N. Anderson had gotten to know Pauline during a research stay in Germany in 1930/1931.
8 See Doc. 17, fn. 45.
9 Johnson's son Thomas, who was 20 months old at the time. See Doc. 2, fn. 16.
10 The club was opened on March 10, 1946. See Doc. 17.
11 Office of Strategic Services. See Doc. 1, fn. 9.

Plymouth[12]. The driver was a POW[13] whose home is in Saarbrücken[14], a simple and rather dumb person who was glad to be working for the Americans, and glad an American car ran like a Mercedes[15]. He was also beware of MP's[16]. The place on the shore of Wannsee[17] is a swanky one, the former home, it was said, of Brigitte Helm[18], a movie actress and mistress of a German industrialist[19].[20] General Gailey[21] was there, and took me in hand a bit, General Clay[22] shook hands and introduced me to Ambassador Murphy[23] who remarked that he noticed me at the staff meeting[24]. I met a few others. There was a bar with a plenteous assortment of liquors including whiskies which are not ordinary here. There was a sumptuous buffet dinner – everything. There was entertainment, a ballet dancer, an acrobat, and what was introduced as a "favorite of General

12 Sedan from the American car manufacturer Plymouth, which had been made available to Johnson in Austria in 1945.

13 Prisoner of War.

14 German city in the Saar region, which belonged to the French zone of Germany. In 1947 the Saar region was partitioned, removed from the responsibility of the Allied Control Authority, and economically incorporated into France.

15 German car brand.

16 Military Police officers.

17 Refers to Großer Wannsee, a bight of the Havel (see Doc. 74, fn. 24) in southwest Berlin.

18 Brigitte Helm, originally Schittenhelm, married Kunheim, divorced Weißbach (1908–1996), German movie actress, became famous overnight with the female lead double role of Maria and the robot in the silent film *Metropolis* (1927) by Fritz Lang (1890–1976). She was "for a decade the epitome of an enigmatic screen diva and demonic temptress." ("für ein Jahrzehnt der Inbegriff einer enigmatischen Leinwanddiva und dämonischen Verführerin.") Kay Weniger, *Das große Personenlexikon des Films*, vol. 3, *F–H*, Berlin 2001, p. 628.

19 As of 1935 Brigitte Helm was married to her second husband, the businessman Dr. phil. Hugo Kunheim (1902–1986), who managed the coal wholesale firm Caesar Wollheim.

20 The Lakeside Club was located at Am Großen Wannsee 2/4 in the Berlin administrative district of Zehlendorf, Wannsee area, where Brigitte Helm had lived after her marriage to Dr. Hugo Kunheim. See *Berliner Adreßbuch*, 1936–1943: Dr. phil. Hugo Kunheim; registration card Brigitte Kunheim, née Schittenhelm, in: LAB, B Rep. 021 (Einwohnermeldeamt Berlin). "A house that most Americans know is the very modernistic Lion House, so called because of the almost life-sized bronze lion on the front porch. This house was owned formerly by a famous German movie actress, Brigitte Helm. It was taken over for the Officers Lake-Side Club and is now the home of one of OMGUS General's." Viviane W. Adams, "Wannsee," in: *OMGUS Observer* from June 28, 1946, pp. 4f. and 8, here p. 8. The two-story house with a flat roof was built in 1932/1933 (architect: Moritz Ernst Lesser [1882–1958]). See Ingo Krüger, *Landhäuser und Villen in Berlin & Potsdam*, no. 3, *Großer Wannsee, Colonie Alsen, Villa Liebermann*, Bremen 2005, pp. 14f. According to an interview from 2003 with Brigitte Helm's son Pieter Kunheim (1936–2007), "[…] the house still exists, I have been there. We left it around 1943, the air raids were too heavy, and our father wanted us out of Berlin." ("[…] das Haus existiert noch, da bin ich mal hingefahren. Das haben wir ungefähr 1943 verlassen, da wurden die Bombenangriffe zu heftig, und unser Vater wollte uns aus Berlin raus haben.") Daniel Semler, *Brigitte Helm. Der Vamp des deutschen Films*, Munich 2008, p. 214. Photo of the house in Appendix of Illustrations, ill. 59.

21 See Doc. 15, fn. 23.

22 See Doc. 2, fn. 6.

23 See Doc. 8, fn. 13.

24 Refers to the OMGUS staff conference on March 9, 1946. See Doc. 17.

Eisenhower's[25]" a good looking and competent accordian player. There was also an orchestra and dancing. The officers had their secretaries along for the most part. But I was alone and did not know many people and left early. I don't imagine I shall use the Lakeside Club much.

Goodnight to my sweet Emily and to my sweet boys. I love them intensely. Edgar

Doc. 19
Letter to His Wife
Berlin, Ihnestraße 14[1], March 12, 1946

Dearest, my dearest Emily:

Today has been an interesting day. You have heard me comment on the difficulty of 4 powers speaking three different languages ever getting anything done. Today I had a chance of witnessing the difficulty. General Gailey[2] took me to a meeting of the Allied Commission on Civil Administration[3].[4] This is a quadripartite committee on the Branch level. The branches are sub-divisions of the Divisions. My branch at present is the Civil Administration Branch[5]. My division is the Internal Affairs and Communications Division (IA + C). The quadripartite committee of the corresponding divisions is called a Directorate, and the directorate of my division is accordingly the Directorate of Internal Affairs and Communications (DIAC).[6] The Branch Committees report to the Division Committees. They have, as well, Sub-Committees and so-called working parties under them. The Directorates report to the Coordinating Committee (com-

25 Dwight D. Eisenhower (1890–1969), General of the Army, 1944/1945 Commander-in-Chief, Supreme Headquarters Allied Expeditionary Force, Commanding General, US Forces, European Theater, 1945 Commander-in-Chief, US Forces of Occupation in Germany, Military Governor, Germany (US), 1945–1948 Chief of Staff, US Army, 1949–1952 Supreme Allied Commander Europe (NATO), 1953–1961 34th President of the United States.

1 See Doc. 15, fn. 1.

2 See Doc. 15, fn. 23.

3 Civil Administration Committee, Directorate of Internal Affairs and Communications, Allied Control Authority.

4 See minutes of the 22nd meeting of the Civil Administration Committee, Directorate of Internal Affairs and Communications, Allied Control Authority, on March 12, 1946, DIAC/CAC/M (46) 7, English version, in: Archiv des IfZ, OMGUS-Akten (microfiche reproduction), 2/124-3/2-4.

5 Civil Administration Branch of the Internal Affairs and Communications Division, OMGUS. See Doc. 15, fn. 24.

6 The head of the Internal Affairs and Communications Division, OMGUS, represented the USA in the Directorate of Internal Affairs and Communications, Allied Control Authority. See Josef Henke/Klaus Oldenhage, "Office of Military Government for Germany (U. S.)," in: *OMGUS-Handbuch. Die amerikanische Militärregierung in Deutschland 1945–1949*, ed. Christoph Weisz (= Quellen und Darstellungen zur Zeitgeschichte, vol. 35), Munich 1994, p. 30.

7 See Doc. 15, fn. 21.

posed of the Deputies of the Commanding Generals)[7] and the Coordinating Committee reports to the Control Council[8] itself.

All these meetings are held in the building of the German Supreme Court[9] which is decorated with the four Allied flags, and is about five miles from the Headquarters of Omgus[10]. The meeting was held in a conference room (135)[11] outside of which German workmen were making furious pounding noises. A Russian lieutenant leaned out the windows and shouted at them to stop, and they did of course. The chairmanship of the meetings of the Allied Control Authority (ACA) are this month in the hands of the Russians. They change every month. The Russian presiding officer (Shkvarin)[12] was a Colonel and played a minor part in the discussions. His deputy was a civilian (Soldatin?[13]) who was not too well dressed, had on a dirty collar and an ill-fitting tie. The Colonel picked his teeth with a toothpick after lunch. To the right of Soldatin was the French interpreter of the Soviet Delegation. To the left of Shkvarin was the English interpreter of the Soviet Delegation. But the English interpreter was not up to her job and most of the Russian-English interpretation was made by the American interpreter who did both our Russian and French interpretation and played a good share in the negotiations because the Russians trusted him and were somewhat embarrased by the poor quality of their own English interpreter. There were in addition two Russian secretaries, one a woman, rather shabbily dressed, and the other a rather smart and good looking lieutenant. There was in addition a Russian expert. The French delegation was headed by a

8 See Doc. 16, fn. 11.

9 Building erected in 1913 for the Prussian Kammergericht at Kleistpark in Berlin-Schöneberg, beginning in 1945 office of the Allied Control Authority for Germany (see Doc. 14, fn. 5). After July 20, 1944, the notorious show trials of the resistance fighters who had been part of the failed coup against Adolf Hitler (see Doc. 22, fn. 19) were staged in the plenary meeting room before the so-called Volksgerichtshof and its highest judge, Roland Freisler (1893–1945). On October 18, 1945, the International Military Tribunal was set up here, established for the trial of major war criminals. In this first meeting, the prosecutors presented the indictment. The proceedings continued in Nuremberg. After the activity of the Allied Control Authority came to a standstill in 1948, the building was used by the Allied Air Safety Center. Today the building is again property of the judiciary system. Photo of the building in Appendix of Illustrations, ill. 36.

10 See Doc. 17, fn. 45.

11 Ulrich Wimmer, judge in the Kammergericht, in an email to Werner Breunig from November 6, 2012: "[…] according to the local caretaker, who took over the building from the Allies back then, the numbering of the rooms remained unchanged. Room 135 […] is used today as a courtroom for civil trials. The Allies had used it as the Berlin Air Safety Center (BASC), which controlled air traffic over the city as well as in air corridors." ("[…] nach Auskunft des hiesigen Hausmeisters, der seinerzeit das Gebäude von den Alliierten übernommen hat, ist die Numerierung der Räume unverändert geblieben. Der Saal 135 […] wird heute als Sitzungssaal für Zivilprozesse genutzt. Die Alliierten hatten darin die Luftsicherheitszentrale platziert (Berlin Air Safety Center – BASC), von dem aus der Flugbetrieb über der Stadt sowie in den Luftkorridoren kontrolliert wurde.")

12 Alexei Ivanovich Shkwarin (born 1905), Soviet Major, 1945–1947, Deputy of the Head of Administration of Internal Affairs, SMAG.

13 According to minutes: Soldatov. May refer to the head of the Branch for the Persecution and Detention of War Criminals in the Western Zones of the Administration of Internal Affairs, SMAG (1947).

M[onsieur] Mauleon[14], a bureaucrat, either a prefect or sub-prefect[15]. He had with him a capable Russian interpreter (female), a deputy (M[onsieur] Fontaine), an English interpreter (male) but the French did not bother with secretaries. The English delegation was headed by a fine looking civilian (Mr. Inghram[16]), a deputy (Col. Hall), a capable Russian, and French interpreter (both female) and an officer secretary (male). We had for our chief General Gailey, who was assisted by an acting deputy (Dr. Wells[17]). We had one interpreter, the above-mentioned Russian-French interpreter (Lt. Forrest), a representative of our Secretariat (Col. Rosengren[18]) and a secretary (Miss Kramer). When the Russian chairman spoke, he had to speak sentence by sentence. Each sentence was translated first into English (when the Russian lady could manage it) and then into French. When the French chief spoke, his interpreters translated into Russian and English. When the British and Americans spoke their words, sentence by sentence, were translated into French and Russian. It is incredible that there is any understanding at all.

There were three matters up for discussion: (1) the general conditions under which future elections were to be conducted in Germany; (2) the establishment of a Sub-Committee to settle civil service problems and (3) the resolution of certain questions which had to do with the forthcoming German census.

The first question took about two hours to settle. It was settled not by agreeing on the conditions under which future elections are to be held but by turning over the question to a special working party to write up in detail, the second question was more easily dispatched because there was no substance to discuss, only the formality of a committee. The discussion on point 3 was interesting to me because it shows the great disadvantage of language as a means of understanding. On the census questionnaires which are to be submitted information is wanted on the citizenship of those at present in Germany, and on the nationality of those at present in Germany. Could you explain the differences between citizenship and nationality in English? The Russians are supposed to want information as nationality because they feel there are still here a number of persons whom the Germans deported from Russia. These they want back in Russia. The German word for citizenship is Staatsangehörigkeit. They have essentially two words for nationality. Nationalität and Volkszugehörigkeit. The Russians wanted to use Volkszugehörigkeit for nationality since it is a well established word. But the French, English and Americans did not want to use it because the Nazis gave a definite legal meaning to the word which involved

14 Mauléon, head of the Division des Affaires Intérieures, Groupe Français du Conseil de Contrôle.

15 According to minutes: Prefect.

16 William Harold Ingrams (1897–1973), British colonial civil servant, 1945–1947 Assistant Secretary, Allied Control Commission for Germany (British Element).

17 Roger H. Wells (1894–1994), American political scientist, 1923 PhD, Harvard University, taught from 1923–1963 as Professor at Bryn Mawr College, 1927/1928 Guggenheim Fellow in Germany, 1946/1947 Civil Administration Division, OMGUS, Deputy Director, 1951–1953 Chief, Historical Division, HICOG, 1963–1968 Visiting Professor, Mac Murray College.

18 Roswell P. Rosengren (1902–1988), Lieutenant Colonel, 1927 LLB, University of Buffalo Law School, 1946 Chief, Civil Service Branch, Civil Administration Division, OMGUS.

denying Germans with Jewish grandparents German nationality. Question 7 in the census sheet is to concern citizenship and Question 8 nationality. How make this distinction clear to the person (simple and ignorant) who has to fill out the blank. After prolonged discussion they agreed. The translation of the German equivalent for the French, English and Russian words for nationality was to be left up to German linguistic experts only it was forbidden that they come to the conclusion that Volkszugehörigkeit was to be used. You can get cynical about this dispute over the meaning of words while industry is at a stand-still and people are going hungry and living crowded in ruins. But if there is going to be any community of action in the 4 zones (not that these decisions really secure it) then these questions have to be discussed and agreed upon.

The questions were not of such serious political import that humanity was left out of the meeting. During it all the Russians knew what they wanted but were conciliatory. The French were clear definite and to the point but no less insistent upon their point of view. The British were quite human and civilized perhaps the most well balanced of the lot. We were not too greatly interested, but were not going to let anything be put over on us. But we sort of stole the show with our interpreter upon whom everyone came to rely.

The world could easily be run by simple men of this good will. I was attracted to them all, but especially to the French and the British. But the poor human race, trying to solve its problems by this antiquated method, antiquated in so far as language is concerned. How the world needs a universal language, and how long it will take it to get it. I could have wept at some moments. General Gailey admitted that he was discussing the use of German words, the meaning of which he did not really understand. And so we heard Staatszugehörigkeit and Volksangehörigkeit as well as Volkszugehörigkeit and Staatsangehörigkeit. Every American should understand the difficulty of these negotiations.

I hope it continues as interesting as this for the next four or five weeks. If so it will have been worth returning here.

Goodnight my sweet ones, I love my Em[ily] and John and Tim. Edgar

Doc. 20
Letter to His Wife
Berlin, Ihnestraße 14[1], March 14, 1946

Dearest beloved –

I arrived a week ago today.[2] Five weeks have I been away from you, my darling, and my sweet boys. No letter has come but it won't be long now.

There has been a slight development with respect to what I am going to do. Yesterday morning I set out to make the acquaintance of the State Department people. I went to Mr. Murphy's[3] office, but learned that he was out of town and

1 See Doc. 15, fn. 1.
2 Johnson had arrived in Berlin on March 7, 1946.
3 See Doc. 8, fn. 13.

accordingly made an appointment with his secretary, a Mr. Bush[4], who is going to call me when the ambassador returns. All very elegant in Mr. Murphy's surroundings. A large vase with forsythia in it in the reception room. Then I went down to make an appointment to see Mr. Don Heath[5], the director of the political office, whom Harold Vedeler[6] asked me to see. The appointment was for three in the afternoon. Then I went to see Louis Wiesner[7], whom I have spoken of,[8] and who is a labor officer on the political staff here. Louis asked me my opinion of Walter Dorn[9], and I couldn't do else but speak favorably of Walter Dorn. He asked because the State Department people have been asked by General Barker[10], who is the U. S. representative on the Kommandatura[11] (the quadripartite administration for the city of Berlin) to suggest a person who could act as a political adviser and organize a political reporting office for him. The political situation in Berlin is particularly hot at the moment because the Communists[12] are trying to force an amalgamation with the Social Democrats[13]

4 Henry C. S. Bush (born 1900), as of 1926 Clerk, Department of State, as of 1931 Berlin, as of 1945 Attaché, Office of US Political Adviser on German Affairs, Administrative Officer.

5 Donald R. Heath. See Doc. 8, fn. 15.

6 See Doc. 2, fn. 12.

7 See Doc. 8, fn. 11.

8 See Doc. 16.

9 See Doc. 2, fn. 10.

10 Ray W. Barker (1889–1974), Major General, 1945–May 1946 Commanding General, US Headquarters Berlin District, US Commandant, Allied Kommandatura Berlin, 1947–1960 Superintendent, Manlius School. See Appendix of Illustrations, ill. 25, ill. 26, ill. 29, ill. 30, and ill. 31.

11 After the arrival of the Western powers in Berlin, the Allied Kommandatura Berlin had been constituted as the highest political organ of the city on July 11, 1945, at the headquarters of the Soviet military government (Luisenstraße 56, Berlin-Mitte). At the head of the Kommandatura, which set up its office in the building of the Verband der öffentlichen Feuerversicherungsanstalten in Berlin-Dahlem, Kaiserswerther Straße 16/18 (today office of the president of the Freie Universität Berlin), were the four Commandants, who could confer power to their deputies. The Chiefs of Staff of the Kommandatura, who were provided with a permanent secretariat, prepared the agendas and meetings of the Commandants and their deputies, transferred Allied orders to the Magistrat in the form of commands, and cleared up daily questions. Lastly there were expert committees. On all levels of the Kommandatura, chairmanship rotated in 15-day cycles at first, then monthly. The military governments of the individual sectors were grouped around the Allied Kommandatura, which was subject to the Allied Control Authority for Germany. See Doc. 14, fn. 5. Photo of the Allied Kommandatura building in Appendix of Illustrations, ill. 37.

12 On June 11, 1945, the Kommunistische Partei Deutschlands (KPD) was the first party to go public with a call for (re-)foundation. See *Berlin. Quellen und Dokumente 1945–1951*, edited on behalf of the Senate of Berlin, eds. Hans J. Reichhardt/Hanns U. Treutler/Albrecht Lampe (= Schriftenreihe zur Berliner Zeitgeschichte, vol. 4/half-vol. 1), Berlin 1964, no. 469.

13 The Sozialdemokratische Partei Deutschlands (SPD) had published its call for (re-) foundation on June 15, 1945. See *Berlin. Quellen und Dokumente 1945–1951*, edited on behalf of the Senate of Berlin, eds. Hans J. Reichhardt/Hanns U. Treutler/Albrecht Lampe (= Schriftenreihe zur Berliner Zeitgeschichte, vol. 4/half-vol. 1), Berlin 1964, no. 470.

into a new left-wing, workers' Unity Party (Einheitspartei).[14] The fusion has already been noted in the Soviet Zone[15] and the Communists are now apparently trying to push it for Berlin. If they succeed the fusion has all sorts of political implications for the political future not only of German parties but possibly also of the future German state. We don't at least want the matter to be forced, or to have the resultant fusion party, if it is to be formed, dominated by a minority of Communists. There is a certain tension here between the Russians and us over the administration of the city. The Russians have arrested some judges in our area,[16] and we have just arrested some 12 Communists in the area for putting the interests of the Communists party before the orders of military government[17]. I know Walter Dorn was interested in this job when he was up here last because he stayed with General Barker and Colonel Howley[18] and brought the matter up to Clay[19]. But Clay advised him not to take it saying that in comparison with other things that he might do, it was small potatoes. So Dorn I guess dropped the matter.

Louis Wiesner who is interested in being in the new political office, said that he was about to go into Heath's office and was going to recommend me strongly as the State Department's appointee. When I went to see Mr. Heath, who seems to be a terribly nice guy, smooth and affable and elegant, he called in two other members of it[20] staff to meet me, a Mr. Muccio[21], whom I met at the

14 Since the autumn of 1945 the KPD had been calling for a quick merger with the SPD, which it had initially rejected after the end of the war. Massive pressure was put on the SPD through a massive unity campaign by the KPD and repressive measures by Soviet occupation forces against Social Democratic opponents of the merger, which included arrest.

15 In the Soviet zone Social Democrats could not freely decide on the future of their party organization. On February 11, 1946, the majority of the SPD Central Committee had agreed to the increasingly imposed unification.

16 On the arrest of judges in the American and British sectors of Berlin, see *Berlin. Kampf um Freiheit und Selbstverwaltung 1945–1946*, edited on behalf of the Senate of Berlin (= Schriftenreihe zur Berliner Zeitgeschichte, vol. 1), revised and supplemented second edition, Berlin 1961, pp. 335, no. 69 a, and 371, no. 79.

17 See ibid., p. 380, no. 24 a; *Die Sitzungsprotokolle des Magistrats der Stadt Berlin 1945/46*, part II, *1946,* edited and introduced by Dieter Hanauske (= Schriftenreihe des Landesarchivs Berlin, vol. 2/II), Berlin 1999, Doc. 74, pp. 258–260.

18 Frank L. Howley (1903–1993), Colonel, American advertising expert, 1925 BCS, New York University, 1937–1940 President, Frank Howley Advertising Co., Philadelphia, as of 1940 US Army, 1945–1947 US Deputy Commandant, Allied Kommandatura Berlin, 1945–1949 Director, OMGBD/OMGBS, 1947–1949 US Commandant, Allied Kommandatura Berlin, 1949 promotion to Brigadier General, as of 1952 Vice Chancellor/Vice President for University Development, New York University, 1954 honorary doctorate (Dr. med. h. c.) from the Freie Universität Berlin, as of 1962 Vice President, New York University, 1965–1967 Special Assistant to the President, New York University. Photo in Appendix of Illustrations, ill. 32.

19 See Doc. 2, fn. 6.

20 Correct: his.

21 John J. Muccio (1900–1989), American diplomat, born in Italy, 1921 US citizenship, as of 1921 Department of State, 1924 Vice Consul, Hamburg, 1945/1946 Chief, Political Branch and Denazification Branch, Office of the Director of Political Affairs, Office of the Deputy Military Governor, OMGUS, 1949–1952 Ambassador to South Korea.

Lakeside Club[22], and a Mr. Steere[23], who is responsible, among other things, for Kommandatura matters. Both, I think, have had much experience in Germany. I was flattered by being told that my work in Austria was well known to them and after some discussion the question was put to me of whether I would be interested in this job and would talk with General Barker. I indicated, of course, that my fate was really in General Clay's hands but that I certainly would be interested in meeting Gen. Barker. Accordingly I was asked to come over to Mr. Steere's office this afternoon to meet the General, who put the question directly to me. I repeated that I was obligated for the time being to carry out General Clay's instructions about orienting myself here and in the zone, that I did not know what exactly Clay had in mind for me when this was over. The General decided accordingly that he must go to see Clay immediately and left to do so, after talking about how he was going to meet the problem of the misconduct of American troops stationed here in Berlin. I left Mr. Steeres's office for my own. Mr. Steere called later to say that General Barker had reported that Clay was sympathetic to his request for my service, if only for a short time but that he would have to talk the matter over with me and would give Barker an answer by Monday[24]. I suppose I shall hear from Clay tomorrow. It can do no harm to have Clay asked by another general for my services (there are so many generals). If he really has nothing especial in mind for me, this will force him to make up his mind. If he says that I should go ahead (his hesitation with Barker indicated that he is at present uncertain) I shall know that he is willing that I do a job which he told Walter Dorn was "small potatoes." I should not mind because this would be a good, and interesting and important job and I could watch the intimate workings of international machinery on a small scale where something has to be done and can be done and is, of course, being done. I should like to go on with this orientation that Clay has ordered, particularly in the zone, because I should learn much but it is not necessary to do for this Berlin job. If Clay says go ahead, I think then I should have to decide between this job and one which Taylor[25] and Knappen[26] would like to have me take in their division[27]. I suppose too Gailey[28] would offer me a job. There are evidently many good jobs here and no available good people to take them. And it is

22 See Doc. 17 and Doc. 18.

23 Loyd V. Steere (1898–1985), American agricultural economics expert and diplomat, 1923 MBA, Harvard University, as of 1923 Bureau of Agricultural Economics, Department of Agriculture, as of 1926 Assistant Agricultural Commissioner, Berlin Office of the Department of Agriculture, as of 1929 Agricultural Commissioner/Attaché, Berlin, as of 1939 Agricultural Attaché, London, 1945/1946 Chief, Economics Branch, Office of the Director of Political Affairs, Office of the Deputy Military Governor, OMGUS.

24 March 18, 1946.

25 See Doc. 17, fn. 26.

26 See Doc. 8, fn. 10.

27 Refers to the Education and Religious Affairs Branch, Internal Affairs and Communications Division, OMGUS.

28 See Doc. 15, fn. 23.

29 Employee of the Research and Analysis Branch, Office of Strategic Services. See Doc. 1, fn. 9.

interesting again to find that Gen. Barker needs the services of an R + A-OSS[29] just as Mr. Erhardt[30] needed them, and needs them badly.

I had luncheon yesterday with a Captain Biel[31] who is a German refugee here in the Civil Administration Branch[32], who knows the boys in the Central European Section[33], and who is interested in going into the Berlin show,[34] whether he is the right kind of German refugee, I don't know yet. But I doubt it.

General Gailey had me to dinner at his Villa[35] last night. There were drinks beforehand (a choice of Scotch, Rye or Martinis), champagne with dinner and brandy afterwards. Invited also were Mr. Fahy[36], the head of the Legal Division

30 John G. Erhardt (1889–1951), American diplomat, as of 1919 Department of State, 1933–1937 Consul General, Hamburg, 1939–1941 Consul General and 1st Secretary, London, 1945/1946 Political Adviser to Commanding General, United States Forces Austria (USFA)/High Commissioner, Austria (US), 1946–1950 Envoy to Austria, 1950/1951 Ambassador to South Africa.

31 Ulrich E. Biel, originally Bielschowsky (1907–1996), Captain, German-American lawyer, born in Charlottenburg, Germany, 1933 dismissal from legal internship on grounds of race, 1934 Dr. jur., University of Bonn, 1934 emigration to the USA, 1934–1942 employment in American private sector (in international investment and export financing business). 1940 US citizenship, 1942–1946 US Army, 1945 returned to Germany with the US Army, 1946–1949 Chief, Political Affairs Section, Civil Administration Branch/Civil Administration and Political Affairs Branch, OMGBD/OMGBS, 1946–1952 in American civil service, initially at the Department of War/Department of Defense, as of 1949 in the Foreign Service of the Department of State, 1949–1951 US Land Observer for Lower Saxony, Hannover, subsequently employee of the American High Commissioner for Germany, 1952 assessor exam, as of 1953 lawyer in Berlin, 1954 renewed German citizenship, 1965 CDU, 1967 appointment as notary, 1971–1979 member of the Abgeordnetenhaus of Berlin, as of 1975 president by seniority, 1977 Ernst Reuter Medal, as of 1984 Chairman of the Vereinigung ehemaliger Mitglieder des Abgeordnetenhauses von Berlin e. V., 1987 Knight Commander's Cross of the Order of Merit of the Federal Republic of Germany. Anthony J. Glaser (see Doc. 59, fn. 6), son of Louis Glaser (see Doc. 28, fn. 4), writes of Biel in an email to Werner Breunig from October 23, 2012: "He was a nice man but really tough if you had information that he wanted; he could talk it out of you. Since my father had an 'intelligence' job, in addition to his regular military government job, Dr. Biel was a very important asset."

32 Civil Administration Branch of the Internal Affairs and Communications Division, OMGUS. See Doc. 15, fn. 24.

33 Central European Section, Research and Analysis Branch, OSS.

34 Biel became head of the Political Affairs Section, Civil Administration Branch, OMGBD. He "was supposed to select politicians in Berlin with whom the Americans could cooperate." ("sollte in Berlin Politiker auswählen, mit denen die Amerikaner zusammenarbeiten konnten.") Martin Otto, "Ulrich Biel (1907–1996) – graue Eminenz der (West-)Berliner Politik. Eine erste biografische Annäherung," in: *Berlin in Geschichte und Gegenwart. Jahrbuch des Landesarchivs Berlin 2011*, pp. 285–304, here p. 293.

35 On Schwanenwerder Island, Inselstraße 36. See Doc. 17, fn. 13.

36 Charles H. Fahy (1892–1979), American lawyer, 1914 LLB, Georgetown University Law School, 1941–1945 Solicitor General, Department of Justice, 1945–May 1946 Legal Adviser and Director, Legal Division, OMGUS, 1946/1947 Legal Adviser, State Department, 1949–1967 Judge of the United States Court of Appeals for the District of Columbia Circuit.

and a former Solicitor General of the United States, Judge Madden[37], a former judge of the Washington D. C. court of appeals (the same job, I think, that Thurman Arnold[38] now has. There was much talk of Arnold), Mr. Walter Lichtenstein[39], a former vice-president of the First National Bank of Chicago and a very close friend of James W. Thompson[40] and Carl Frederick Huth[41] and a Col. MacLean[42], a product of the Yale Law School[43] and a special assistant to General Clay. The talk was mostly shop by those who know all of what is going on and it centered about the poor press which military government was getting in the United States. The lady who takes care of General Gailey's house is a Ph. D. from the University of Berlin[44].[45] But it was well to meet these people. They all were good substantial American types who spoke about belonging to the fraternity here.

37 J. Warren Madden (1890–1972), American lawyer, 1941–1945 and 1946–1961 Judge of the United States Court of Claims, 1945–May 1946 Associate Director, Legal Division, OMGUS, May/June 1946 Legal Adviser and Director, Legal Division, OMGUS.

38 Thurman W. Arnold (1891–1969), American lawyer, 1943–1945 Judge of the United States Court of Appeals for the District of Columbia Circuit.

39 Walter Lichtenstein (1880–1964), American historian, born in Brunswick, Germany, came to the USA with his family at the age of two, 1907 PhD, Harvard University, 1908–1918 Head Librarian, Northwestern University Library, 1918–1945 First National Bank of Chicago, Vice President, 1945–1947 Chief, Financial Institutions Branch, Finance Division, OMGUS.

40 James W. Thompson (1869–1941), American historian, 1895 PhD, University of Chicago, Professor, University of Chicago, 1932–1939 University of California, Berkeley. In the 1920s Thompson was Johnson's "principal teacher" (Edgar N. Johnson, Curriculum Vitae, undated [ca. 1963], p. 1, in: UChicago Library, Special Collections Research Center, Edgar N. Johnson Papers) at the University of Chicago. In 1937 he and Johnson published a revised edition of his 1931 book *History of the Middle Ages, 300–1500*: James Westfall Thompson/Edgar Nathaniel Johnson, *An Introduction to Medieval Europe, 300–1500*, New York 1937.

41 Carl F. Huth Jr. (born 1883), American historian, 1905 MA, University of Wisconsin, 1909/1910 Lecturer, Columbia University, 1910–1948 University of Chicago (as of 1914 Professor of Ancient History). In the 1920s Huth was one of Johnson's teachers at the University of Chicago.

42 Donald H. McLean Jr. (1910–1984), Lieutenant Colonel, American lawyer, 1935 LLB, Yale Law School, Civil Affairs Division, Department of War, 1945–1948 Special Assistant to Lucius D. Clay (see Doc. 2, fn. 6), then legal office of Socony-Vacuum Oil.

43 Yale Law School, founded in 1843, is the law faculty at Yale University in New Haven, in the US state of Connecticut.

44 Founded in 1810, the university was ceremoniously reopened on January 29, 1946.

45 Presumably a joke. The woman who took care of the house along with her husband was an impressive personality but did not have a doctorate. This was Helene Heller, née Fischer (1896–1984). Her husband was the gardener Erich Heller (1894–1957). They were registered on Schwanenwerder, Inselstraße 30, beginning in 1923. See registration card Erich Heller, in: LAB, B Rep. 021 (Einwohnermeldeamt Berlin). Timothy H. Gailey (see Doc. 17, fn. 18) writes in an email to Werner Breunig from July 29, 2011: "[...] I clearly recall Frau and Herr Heller who took care of us and the wonderful thatched-roof house." The fact that the Hellers took care of Gailey's house was

I had lunch today with General McClure[46], head of Information Control[47] and some of the members of his staff. McClure formerly had Paul Sweet[48] and Saul Padover[49] working for him,[50] said he had heard of me before and certainly remembered Paul. I learned of the present status of Furtwängler[51] who is now in Berlin, and who certainly was not much of a Nazi and of the possible advantages of having control of the paper supply for the press, periodicals, etc. (of course I learned this in Austria where the Russians controlled it in Vienna, to the advantage, the SD's[52] said of the Communists). The talk was mostly political and some colonel asked if he could come over to see me. General Gailey took me into to see General Meade[53] this afternoon who is the head of the IA + C[54] Division. He proceeded to tell me of some things that I might do for him during my trip through the zone, mostly political and interesting in their way and requiring knowledge that I shall have to get a hold of en passant. I have tried to read much these last few days and prepare to meet the other heads of the divisions.

But there are too many generals and colonels and this life so far is just a little bit hectic. I want it to settle down. And I could take a bit of the quiet and comfort and blessed happiness that exists at 3268[55]. There is enough comfort here (too much) but not enough quiet and happiness. I love you my dearest Emily and my sweetest of all boys. I shall be relieved when news comes. Goodnight my beloved. Edgar

confirmed by their son, Aribert Heller, in a telephone conversation with Werner Breunig on January 5, 2010.

46 See Doc. 17, fn. 38.

47 Office of Information Control Services, Office of the Deputy Military Governor, OMGUS.

48 See Doc. 2, fn. 28.

49 Saul K. Padover (1905–1981), American historian and political scientist, born in Vienna, Austria, came to the USA with his parents in 1920, 1932 PhD, University of Chicago, 1938–1944 Department of the Interior, 1944 Political Analyst, Federal Communications Commission, 1944 Research and Analysis Branch, OSS, 1944–1946 Intelligence Officer, Psychological Warfare Division, 12th Army Group, as of 1949 taught political science at the New School for Social Research.

50 McClure had led the Psychological Warfare Division, SHAEF, when Sweet and Padover were working for the Psychological Warfare Division, 12th Army Group.

51 Wilhelm Furtwängler (1886–1954), German conductor and composer, as of 1922 principal conductor of the Berliner Philharmonisches Orchester, 1945 banned from conducting, only after his denazification in 1947 was he allowed to conduct the Berliner Philharmoniker again, retaking leadership of the orchestra as principal conductor in 1952.

52 Social Democrats.

53 Frank C. Meade (1896–1978), Brigadier General, 1945/1946 Director, Internal Affairs and Communications Division, OMGUS.

54 Internal Affairs and Communications.

55 3268 South 31st Street, Lincoln (2), Nebraska, USA, where the Johnsons had lived since November 1941.

Doc. 21
Letter to His Wife
Berlin, Ihnestraße 14[1], March 16, 1946

Dear Sweetheart –

My second Saturday[2] here gone and five weeks away from you. Nothing has come from the 25th Base Post Office[3] of Wurzburg[4].[5] Certainly something will come next week. I confess to being lonesome. When I came to my room tonight I stopped to play a bit on the piano.[6] But I could only think of John[7], his sweet remark the last lesson[8] I took him to about wanting to do well for me because it was the last time, of the piano we are going to have some time, of our house, of you and so I came upstairs.

I think the second staff meeting[9] I attended this morning has left me a little chilled. There is so little that is happening here that is actually encouraging looked at from the fundamental aspects of the situation. Our GI's[10] are not behaving very well. The ordinary civilian help (US) does not have very high standards – they deal a great deal in the Black Market[11] and are still talking about overtime. Of course there are exceptions. I ran into two very strange creatures at my table last night – ex-munition worker Wacs[12] who are now civilians, who are comparatively ignorant, who find this something of a lark and who are determined to stay here just as long as they can possibly stay.

1 See Doc. 15, fn. 1.
2 March 16, 1946.
3 See Doc. 4.
4 City in the state of Bavaria in the American zone of Germany.
5 See Doc. 18.
6 Eugene N. Anderson Jr. (see Doc. 4, fn. 30) writes of Edgar N. Johnson in an email to Werner Breunig from July 17, 2007, that he: "Loved music, and relaxed by playing the piano, which he did very well – mostly 19th century classical music, often Baroque." Candice E. Johnson writes in an email to Werner Breunig from June 1, 2010: "Edgar did play piano in silent movie theaters, to accompany the movies!!"
7 Johnson's son John. See Doc. 2, fn. 15.
8 John's last piano lesson before his father's departure for Europe.
9 See minutes of the OMGUS staff conference on March 16, 1946, in: Archiv des IfZ, OMGUS – Staff Conferences (copies of minutes), Fg 12/3.
10 Government Issues, slang for American soldiers.
11 An illegal "black market" developed because the supply situation was very bad; groceries and necessities were only available in exchange for food stamps, and in small amounts legally from stores. The "black market" became an important factor of everyday survival, particularly as the allocation of rations designated for ration cards often was not assured. See Werner Bührer, "Schwarzer Markt," in: *Deutschland unter alliierter Besatzung 1945–1949/55*, ed. Wolfgang Benz, Berlin 1999, pp. 365f.
12 Members of the Women's Army Corps. See Doc. 13, fn. 14.
13 See Doc. 11, fn. 22.
14 Refers to USAT *George W. Goethals*, the ship on which Johnson and Rheinstein had come to Europe. See Doc. 7, fn. 18, and Doc. 11.
15 Refers to the Nationalsozialistische Deutsche Arbeiterpartei (NSDAP).
16 Frankfurt am Main, city in the state of Greater Hesse in the American zone of Germany.
17 Podbielskiallee 65, Berlin-Dahlem. Today the building belongs to the Embassy of the Islamic Republic of Iran and houses the Iranian School. Photo in Appendix of Illustrations, ill. 56.

This mind I guess has been growing. Yesterday evening I spent the evening with Dr. Max Rheinstein[13] whom I met on the boat[14]. He says there is no one he has met here who is not working under a complete frustration (except me). When I came in he was talking with a German who in earlier days had been a prominent international lawyer in Berlin with clients such as Standard Oil, etc. He became a party[15] member and is now employed as a badge guard. This is what is known as proletarianization. In Frankfurt[16] the German who drove me to the station complained of what he had lost during the war. Dr. Rheinstein lives in the house[17] of a distinguished German cellist[18] who was a member of the Klinger Quartet[19] – evidently a famous quartet.[20] He has a Jewish Wife[21]. He was outcast by the Nazis though his wife had enough for them to live on.[22] We took over his

18 Refers to Max Baldner (1887–1946), 1945/1946 cello teacher at the Berlin Hochschule für Musik. See Appendix of Illustrations, ill. 57 and ill. 58.

19 The Klingler Quartet, founded in 1905 by the German violin virtuoso Karl Klingler (1879–1971) and dissolved in 1936, was an internationally renowned string quartet, particularly focused on the late string quartets of Ludwig van Beethoven (see Doc. 37, fn. 29) and the work of Arnold Schönberg (1874–1951). According to his own account, Baldner became a member of the quartet in 1914 and belonged to it until 1926/1927. See personal questionnaire Max Baldner, in: LAB, C Rep. 120 (Magistrat von Berlin, Abteilung Volksbildung), no. 88, fols. 23–25, here fol. 24; resume Max Baldner, in: ibid., fols. 21f., here fol. 21.

20 Rheinstein did not live in the house alone. Thomas Baldner (see fn. 24) writes in an email to Werner Breunig from September 20, 2010: "Other officers of the military government also lived in the house at Podbielskiallee 65. But Prof. Rheinstein was the one who made use of the lounges of the house in a major way. He started a meeting of young Americans and Germans on Sunday afternoons, where fundamental aspects of a German intellectual reawakening were discussed very discerningly and sensibly. For us boys those were festive hours. It was there, a stranger in my own home, as it were, that I found my best friends of that exciting time. Still today, my great thanks go to Max Rheinstein for this." ("Da haben noch andere Offiziere der Militärregierung im Hause Podbielskiallee 65 gewohnt. Prof. Rheinstein war aber wohl derjenige, der von den Gesellschaftsräumen des Hauses in größerem Stil Gebrauch gemacht hat. Er erfand ein Zusammentreffen von amerikanischen und deutschen jungen Leuten am Sonntagnachmittag, bei dem sehr anspruchsvoll und sinnvoll über die grundlegenden Aspekte eines geistigen deutschen Wiedererwachens diskutiert wurde. Das waren für uns Jungens Feststunden. Ich habe dort, sozusagen als Fremder im eigenen Haus, meine besten Freunde dieser so aufregenden Zeit gewonnen. Max Rheinstein sei dafür heute noch großer Dank.") Friedrich Glum, *Zwischen Wissenschaft, Wirtschaft und Politik. Erlebtes und Erdachtes in vier Reichen*, Bonn 1964, pp. 571f.: "He [Rheinstein] looked after Germans in an exemplary manner. They had assigned him the villa of the cellist Baldner in Dahlem. There he kept an open house – to a certain extent – for students and other young people, whom he also brought together with Americans." ("Er [Rheinstein] nahm sich in geradezu vorbildlicher Weise der Deutschen an. Man hatte ihm die Villa des Cellisten Baldner in Dahlem zugewiesen. Dort hielt er gewissermaßen offenes Haus für Studenten und Studentinnen und andere junge Leute, die er auch mit Amerikanern zusammenbrachte.")

21 Charlotte Baldner, née Lindemann (1901–1996). Her father, the businessman Leopold Lindemann (1862–1923), had been a board member of Lindemann & Co. AG, Berlin, which merged with Rudolph Karstadt AG, Hamburg, in 1929. See LAB, A Rep. 342-02 (Amtsgericht Charlottenburg – Handelsregister), no. 12170.

22 "Because my wife is Jewish, I was excluded from the 'Reich Chamber of Culture' and banned from absolutely any activity in the cultural sphere. My position as the teacher of an apprenticeship class at the Staatliche Hochschule für Musik, for which I had

house, and then threw them out of the house.[23] They are now living with their children[24] in the cellar of a ruined house[25]. The man has been in a concentration camp.[26] The officer who threw them out came to the ruins some days afterwards and offered to sell the wife 20 cans of powdered milk for the children at the Black Market price of 15 dollars (150 Occupation Marks[27]) a can.[28] One of the

been suggested by Professor Schünemann as a successor to Feuermann, failed for the above reason. A time of suffering without compare began for me and my family. We lost the greater part of our assets, my children were expelled from high school, and in November 1944 I myself was deported as a forced laborer to a camp in Leuna. From there I returned to Berlin seriously damaged in body and soul." ("Da meine Frau Jüdin ist, wurde ich aus der 'Reichskulturkammer' ausgeschlossen und mir überhaupt jedwede Tätigkeit auf kulturellem Gebiete untersagt. Meine Anstellung als Lehrer einer Ausbildungsklasse an der Staatlichen Hochschule für Musik, zu der ich von Herrn Professor Schünemann als Nachfolger Feuermanns vorgeschlagen war, scheiterte aus dem oben angeführten Grunde. Eine Leidenszeit ohne Gleichen begann für mich und meine Familie. Wir verloren den grössten Teil unseres Vermögens, meine Kinder wurden aus dem Gymnasium verwiesen und ich selber noch im November 1944 als Zwangsarbeiter in ein Lager nach Leuna deportiert. Von dort kehrte ich schwer geschädigt an Leib und Seele nach Berlin zurück.") Resume Max Baldner, in: LAB, C Rep. 120 (Magistrat von Berlin, Abteilung Volksbildung), no. 88, fols. 21f.

23 Thomas Baldner (see fn. 24) reports in an email to Werner Breunig from September 21, 2010, that the house was "commandeered by a requisition command," "which, led by a captain, so to speak stormed the house with lightning speed two days after the Americans reached Berlin, instructing us to vacate in two hours. All of the reproaches of my father, who spoke fluent English, regarding NS victims, etc., were of no use. We had to get out. The satyr play to this action followed a few days later when I succeeded in 'stealing' one of the grand pianos from the house with a horse carriage to bring it to our other domicile." ("von einem Requirierungs-Kommando in Beschlag gelegt," "das unter Führung eines Captains zwei Tage nach Eintreffen der Amerikaner in Berlin in Windeseile das Haus sozusagen stürmte und uns anwies, es in zwei Stunden zu räumen. Alle Vorhaltungen meines Vaters, der fließend Englisch sprach, bezüglich NS-Opfer etc. nutzten nichts. Wir mussten heraus. Das Satyrspiel zu dieser Aktion folgte ein paar Tage später, als es mir gelang, einen der Flügel mittels eines Pferdewagens aus dem Hause zu 'klauen' und in unser anderes Domizil zu schaffen.")

24 Twins Monika and Thomas Baldner (born 1928) and twins Angelika and Lutz Baldner (born 1931). Lutz died in 2015 in Argentina, Thomas in 2015 in the USA. Angelika and Monika live in Germany.

25 Podbielskiallee 57, Berlin-Dahlem. See personal questionnaire Max Baldner, in: LAB, C Rep. 120 (Magistrat von Berlin, Abteilung Volksbildung), no. 88, fols. 23–25, here fol. 23. Previously the businessman Ernst von Morgen (1893–1963) had lived in the house with his family. See *Berliner Adreßbuch*, 1938–1943: Podbielskiallee 57; registration card Ernst von Morgen, in: LAB, B Rep. 021 (Einwohnermeldeamt Berlin). In 1943 his wife, Margarethe von Morgen, née Countess von Schlitz gen. von Görtz (1909–1994), left Berlin with the children. See registration card Margarethe von Morgen, geb. Gräfin von Schlitz gen. von Görtz, in: LAB, B Rep. 021 (Einwohnermeldeamt Berlin). As Thomas Baldner recalled in a telephone conversation with Werner Breunig on April 29, 2009, the Baldner family spent the last days of the war in the abandoned house no. 57, which had an air-raid shelter. After their displacement from house no. 65 by the Americans, the family lived permanently in house no. 57. Even Max Baldner's good command of English and evidence of the family's persecution by the National Socialists could not prevent them from being displaced from their own home. In a telephone conversation with Werner Breunig on June 18, 2009, Angela Wepper, daughter of Ernst von Morgen, expressed the conjecture that the use of the empty house had been arranged with her father.

boys who came over on the boat left many of his cigarettes on the Paris Black Market and the day after his arrival here was displaying a diamond ring which he had acquired on the Black Market here. There was nothing strange in his attitude. He just took it for granted that you were a fool if you didn't take advantage of the situation. Rheinstein is going home when his present job is completed. We were lamenting the lack of anything positive in our policy, the lack of anything generous or kindly in our treatment of those Germans who are not in any sense guilty. The kids and the concentration camp victims. The sight of the Germans themselves is depressing. These are an abject, beaten bunch in appearance, sort of slinking and slouching around here at Headquarters carrying their food trays around at noon (they are fed from a central building). The kids are loafing and begging though rather piteously. I must begin to carry things around in my pockets. I was down in the center of town today and streets were empty with only a few shabbily dressed people around and the utterly depressing ruins on every hand which one wonders how they are ever going to rebuild.

I went to a political meeting this afternoon held by delegates of the Berlin section of the Conservative Party (the Christian Democratic Union[29]).[30] This is slightly encouraging. I don't see how they can bear to do much political thinking and organization in view of the very uncertain future. But politics must have a future. I found the speech of the main speaker[31] moving in spots. This party is composed of some remnants of the old Center (Catholic) Party[32] and some

26 Max Baldner, who refused separation from his Jewish wife, was sent by the Gestapo to a camp in Leuna as a forced laborer in November 1944. He was released due to illness in December 1944. See personal questionnaire Max Baldner, in: LAB, C Rep. 120 (Magistrat von Berlin, Abteilung Volksbildung), no. 88, fols. 23–25, here fol. 24. "Particularly in the war years, the pressure and the uncertainty of existence increased to the point of intolerability, culminating in my forcible deportation to a camp in Leuna, where I had to do the most difficult and most base work, leading a kind of concentration camp existence behind barbed wire and under constant surveillance. This was the notorious 'Mitte action' executed by the Gestapo and disguised by the O. T. It included all the men who, despite all threats, remained loyal to their Jewish wives. I fell seriously ill there and had to be released." ("Der Druck und die Unsicherheit des Daseins steigerte sich besonders in den Kriegsjahren bis zur Unerträglichkeit und gipfelte in meiner zwangsweisen Deportierung in ein Lager nach Leuna, wo ich die allerschwerste und niedrigste Arbeit verrichten musste und hinter Stacheldraht und unter ständiger Bewachung eine Art von Konzentrationslagerdasein führte. Dies war die berüchtigte 'Aktion Mitte' veranlasst durch die Gestapo und getarnt durch die O. T. Sie erfasste all die Männer, die allen Drohungen zum Trotz, ihren jüdischen Frauen die Treue gehalten hatten. Ich erkrankte dort schwer und musste entlassen werden.") Ibid., here fol. 25 (enclosure).

27 Mark of the Allied military authorities, also called "Besatzungsmark." See order of the Allied Kommandatura Berlin No. BK/Ord. (45) 2 from August 9, 1945, on the validity of paper money issued by the Allied military authorities as legal currency for all kinds of Mark debts in the city of Berlin, in: LAB, F Rep. 280 (Quellensammlung zur Berliner Zeitgeschichte [LAZ-Sammlung]), no. 1267.

28 Thomas Baldner reports in an email to Werner Breunig from September 20, 2010, of a man who "lived in the middle floor of the house [Podbielskiallee 65]" ("im Mittelstock des Hauses [Podbielskiallee 65] wohnte") and "engaged in black market trade on a large scale. At times the living room was nothing but a warehouse, which little by little made its way to the black market at Tiergarten. Unfortunately the man also stole valuables from the house." ("Schwarzhandel in großem Stil betrieb. Zeitweise war das Wohnzimmer ein reines Warenlager, das nach und nach auf den Schwarzen

evangelical elements. When the speaker referred to the fact that indeed the religious groups were the only ones who really fought the Nazis he got cheers.[33] These Germans were proud that they could cite some resistance. I thought of the "God-damned Luther[34] language" in my guide[35]. The speaker took some cracks also at the Poles who are unable to make usable the waste land now being left by the evacuated Germans of Poland.[36] These Germans need some ray of hope. It is not in their immediate situation. That give it to themselves in trying to hope that Germany will again be a united state, somehow or another a more socialized state, that there will be peace, that Germany will gain the respect again of the world. There was talk about the ten commandments, about the fusion of morals and politics. There is no point in taking this all as insincere. It is pathetic. And sitting up at the front of the meeting was a Russian officer

Markt am Tiergarten wanderte. Leider hat der Mann auch Diebstahl betrieben an Wertgegenständen des Hauses.")

29 The Christlich-Demokratische Union Deutschlands (CDU) went public with a call for foundation on June 26, 1945. See *Berlin. Quellen und Dokumente 1945–1951*, edited on behalf of the Senate of Berlin, eds. Hans J. Reichhardt/Hanns U. Treutler/Albrecht Lampe (= Schriftenreihe zur Berliner Zeitgeschichte, vol. 4/half-vol. 1), Berlin 1964, no. 471.

30 On March 16/17, 1946, the first CDU party conference of the Greater Berlin regional association took place in the party office on Jägerstraße in the Berlin administrative district of Mitte. See *Berlin. Kampf um Freiheit und Selbstverwaltung 1945–1946*, edited on behalf of the Senate of Berlin (= Schriftenreihe zur Berliner Zeitgeschichte, vol. 1), revised and supplemented second edition, Berlin 1961, p. 389, no. 53.

31 The first day of the meeting was centered on a lecture by Ernst Lemmer (1898–1970), second Chairman of the CDU in the Soviet zone.

32 The Deutsche Zentrumspartei, founded in 1870, named after its place in the Reichstag, was the most important representative of political Catholicism in Germany until 1933.

33 Lemmer in his lecture: "During the Nazi period there were few places where resistance against the barbarity of racial fanaticism and National Socialism was offered with so much courage as in the pulpits of the Christian church. (Applause.)" ("[...] dass es wenige Stellen in der Nazizeit gegeben hat, an denen mit so viel Mut gegen die Barbarei des Rassenwahns und des Nationalsozialismus Widerstand geleistet wurde, wie auf den Kanzeln der christlichen Kirche. [Beifall]") Vortrag des Parteivorsitzenden Ernst Lemmer auf dem Landesparteitag am 16. März in Berlin, p. 14, in: Archiv für Christlich-Demokratische Politik (ACDP) der Konrad-Adenauer-Stiftung, Sankt Augustin, Germany, Landesverband Berlin, 03-012-032/1.

34 Martin Luther (1483–1546), German reformer.

35 In Johnon's resume it says: "In 1943 I was granted a leave of absence from the University to join the staff of the Office of Strategic Service (Central European Division of the Research and Analysis Branch). In OSS I was associated, first, with the work on Germany and then on Austria. In the former capacity I was responsible for the final edition of the *Handbook on the German Church* and the *Military Government Guide on the German Church*." Edgar N. Johnson, Curriculum Vitae, undated [ca. 1963], p. 2, in: UChicago Library, Special Collections Research Center, Edgar N. Johnson Papers. Petra Marquardt-Bigman, *Amerikanische Geheimdienstanalysen über Deutschland 1942–1949* (= Studien zur Zeitgeschichte, vol. 45), Munich 1995, p. 288, mentions a Civil Affairs Guide prepared by Johnson, "The Protestant and the Catholic Churches in Germany," War Department Pamphlet No. 31-120.

36 Ernst Lemmer said: "Overcoming nutrition difficulties here and all over the world also requires – and let me say this without being misunderstood – that not only in Germany, but in all of Europe, there can be no zone, no territory, in which there is not a show of human effort to extract everything on the land to ensure people's daily

whom the speaker also was trying to please. One wonders if it isn't worth trying real Christianity on these people or at least tempering our present policy with a little bit of it. Don Heath[37] was also present at the meeting.

Clay[38] has not called me about the Berlin job so I gather he is not seriously interested in my going to General Barker[39].

Tell Wilma Peterson[40] I had lunch with Virginia Pettit[41] yesterday. She is none too happy in her job but is, nonetheless, cheerful about getting something better.

I suppose I'll feel better when I get something specific to do. I shall be leaving for the zone by the end of the week if the Berlin thing doesn't eventuate.

Your love for me and mine for you alone give sense to the word. Goodnight my precious Emily and my boys. Edgar

Doc. 22
Letter to His Wife
Berlin, Ihnestraße 14[1], March 17, 1946

My lovely Sweetheart and my boys:

It has been an interesting day, and from it I have learned, I think, much, much that will be of further use, much that helps one to come to basic points of view.

bread. (Shouts: Silesia!) Here we think of different places on our continent, whoever may manage them at present, however their national future may develop; yet it is unimaginable that there should be fertile land on this continent that lies fallow like a dessert when it is time to extract everything from the strengths of the land. (Loud applause.)" ("Zur Ueberwindung der Ernährungsschwierigkeiten bei uns und in aller Welt gehört freilich auch, und das darf ich ohne missverstanden zu werden, aussprechen, dass es nicht nur in Deutschland, sondern in ganz Europa keine Zone, kein Gebiet geben darf, in dem nicht menschliche Anstrengungen sich zeigen, das Letzte auf dem Boden für die Sicherung des täglichen Brotes der Menschen herauszuholen. [Zurufe: Schlesien!] Da denken wir an verschiedene Räume unseres Kontinents, sie mögen zur Zeit verwaltet werden von wem es auch sei, ihre nationale Zukunft mag sich entwickeln wie es nur sei; aber unvollstellbar ist, dass es fruchtbaren Boden auf diesem Kontinent geben darf, der einer Wüste gleich brach liegt, wenn es gilt, das Letzte auf den Kräften des Bodens herauszuholen. [Starker Beifall]") Vortrag des Parteivorsitzenden Ernst Lemmer auf dem Landesparteitag am 16. März in Berlin, pp. 10f., in: ACDP, Landesverband Berlin, 03-012-032/1.

37 Donald R. Heath. See Doc. 8, fn. 15.

38 See Doc. 2, fn. 6.

39 See Doc. 20, fn. 10.

40 Probably an acquaintance who lived in Lincoln, Nebraska.

41 Virginia M. Pettit, later married Loomis (born 1922), from Lincoln, Nebraska, February 1946–1947 "a stenographer with the State Department attached to the Berlin Office Military Government of the United States (OMGUS)." Email from Kelly Loomis, daughter-in-law of Virginia P. Loomis, to Werner Breunig from June 14, 2012. In November 1946 Virginia M. Pettit married John J. Loomis (1921–1995) in Berlin: "Miss Virginia Pettit of Political Affairs will become the bride of John J. Loomis of the Motor Battalion Saturday, November 16th at 3 p. m., in the Nikolassee church, 1 Kirche Weg, with Chaplain Marvin E. Utter performing the ceremony." "Four Weddings Held At OMGUS This Week," in: *Berlin Observer* from November 15, 1946, p. 2.

1 See Doc. 15, fn. 1.

On the day I left Washington, Polly[2] received a telephone call from a German refugee friend whom she had helped, a certain Frau Posener[3], who is the wife of a distinguished German archivist[4], who was employed by the Government Archives in Washington[5], but who, because of the interference of Congress[6], had to give up his job, and is now the Acting Dean of the Graduate School of American University[7].[8] She has just learned the whereabouts of her Mother in Berlin, and Polly therefore gave me as much foodstuffs as I wanted to carry for this Mother whose name is Frau Melchior[9]. This morning, about ten o'clock, I started out to find her. She lives in Wannsee[10], the westernmost part of our zone of occupation in Berlin. She was living in a house which had been pretty thoroughly ruined by bombs which fell in the neighborhood. I was invited to wait in the dining room for her. At the table was a family who had fled the Russians from the East and were now settled in Berlin. I was interested in what they were eating because I have been told by the Germans here that there were no potatoes to be had. But these people had plenty of potatoes to eat for lunch and along with them they were eating what was in so far as I could see was a meat (hamburger) concoction, which supplied also plenty of gravy. The family I did not like because they started to complain to me about the manner in which they had to live. In fact the lady who dominated the scene struck an elevated tone, referred to the menschenunwürdig (inhumane) character of their dwelling; indeed she compared it with a concentration camp. I was almost moved to a very angry speech. Here was a woman accusing me, an American, of subjecting

2 Pauline R. Anderson. See Doc. 2, fn. 2.

3 Katharina Posner, née Melchior, divorced Bungert (1898–1979), 1918/1919 and 1925–1928 assistant at the Preußisches Geheimes Staatsarchiv, Berlin-Dahlem, 1939 emigration to the USA.

4 Ernst Posner (1892–1980), German-American historian and archivist, born in Berlin, Germany, 1920 Dr. phil., University of Berlin, 1922–1935 Staatsarchivrat at the Preußisches Geheimes Staatsarchiv, Berlin-Dahlem, 1930–1935 Lecturer, Institut für Geschichtswissenschaft und Archivwissenschaftliche Fortbildung, Berlin-Dahlem, 1936 forced retirement, 1939 emigration via Sweden to the USA, 1942–1961 head of archive courses at the National Archives in Washington, D. C., 1944 US citizenship, 1945–1961 Professor of History and Archival Administration, American University, adviser to the American military government in establishing German archives, 1954 founder and head of the Institute of Records Management, 1955/1956 President of the Society of American Archivists.

5 Refers to the National Archives of the United States, established in 1934, based in Washington, D. C.

6 Legislative branch of the USA, made up of the Senate and the House of Representatives.

7 University in Washington, D. C., founded in 1893.

8 Eugene N. Anderson (see Doc. 1, fn. 1) and Pauline R. Anderson had helped Ernst and Katharina Posner with their emigration to the USA and maintained friendly relations. See Wolfgang A. Mommsen, "Ernst Posner, Mittler zwischen deutschem und amerikanischem Archivwesen. Zu seinem 75. Geburtstag," in: *Der Archivar*, vol. 20 (1967), no. 3, cols. 217–230; Eugene N. Anderson Papers, Collection 2074, Box 2, Folder 2–5, in: University of California, Los Angeles (UCLA), Charles E. Young Research Library, Department of Special Collections, Los Angeles, California, USA.

9 Hedwig Melchior, née Krüger (born 1870).

10 Area in the Berlin administrative district of Zehlendorf.

Germans to concentration camp conditions without giving a thought to what the Germans had created for other peoples. I think the Germans are fundamentally hopeless. You can't tell them that they are responsible for anything. Frau Melchior is in fact living in very shabby and unsatisfactory conditions but she is alive, and healthy and cheerful and is now beginning to have the support of Americans who have been set on her trail. There are hundreds of thousands of young Americans who are dead to make this possible for her. I brought her foodstuffs from Washington which Polly had given me, and I added to these some of the supplies which I have accumulated since coming here. But I was given to believe that this was no more than was to be expected. The Americans exist in order to administer unto the Germans who now suffer more than anyone else in this world if we are to believe their story. There are of course fundamentally tragic undertones to this general situation. There were at the table to which I referred above, two children. Their Mother had committed suicide in Posen[11] when the Russians approached, and the father's whereabouts were unknown. They had accordingly been taken over by an aunt. But their future is as secure as, under the circumstances it can be, and we can hardly be responsible for mothers and fathers without courage who have fallen for the Nazi Russian propaganda. Under American auspices Frau Melchior will soon move to better quarters[12] and await her transportation to the United States to join her children[13]. She has it much better than the American soldiers who are buried on German soil. I was much annoyed when a young lady who accompanied Frau Melchior and myself on a visit to the quarters which she will soon occupy (now occupied by American GI's[14] of the 209th Division) suggested that of course the few broken windows in the house would be repaired by us before the old lady moved in. These windows have not been repaired in order to make the occupation of American GI's more comfortable and healthful. I don't see why they should be repaired for an old lady in excellent condition whose daughter abandoned her in order to come to the comfortable United States. This young lady expected as a matter of course that we would do more for Germans than we would do for GI's.

I hope we don't become in the U. S. the victims of another crusade of German self-pity and appeal for sympathy. They have much to learn here in order to become convinced that they are not a people whom it is the privilege of the world to exalt above all others. I saw thousands of Germans today. I could not tell what they were thinking, and indeed it is better for my state of mind that I do not know. But I can tell you how these thousands of Germans were dressed

11 Posen (Poznań), today capital of the Greater Poland Voivodeship in Poland, was captured by Soviet troops on February 23, 1945. In September 1939 the German Wehrmacht had occupied Posen, and the city became capital of the Reichsgau Wartheland.

12 According to her registration card, Hedwig Melchior was registered at Spanische Allee 110 in the Berlin administrative district of Zehlendorf as of April 1, 1946. See registration card Hedwig Melchior, née Krüger, in: LAB, B Rep. 021 (Einwohnermeldeamt Berlin).

13 In February 1947 Hedwig Melchior deregistered her residence. She moved to Arlington in the US state of Virginia. See ibid.

14 Government Issues, slang for American soldiers.

and how they looked. Their clothes are a little bit worn, slightly shabby, but they are good and will be good for years to come. The women have on, for the most party, fur coats or fur-decorated coats and the men have on good substantial warm cloth coats. The women's stockings are silk or rayon and I saw no mended ones. The children are well and warmly dressed. These people are not starving. They must have plenty of reserves. They have none of the ashen look which the Viennese had when I first came to Vienna in August[15]. In fact I took particular note of color in the cheeks, and I'll swear that for the most part, they all, old and young alike, had color in their cheeks, more indeed than you and I have. They were all out hunting wood and bringing it back in wagon loads and on their backs. But they all have at least one warm room, and a stove and wood enough and with this it is possible to get along. Who in the hell are these Germans anyway who have brought untold misery upon the world and murdered many millions of their own compatriots as well who expect that the Allies have come to occupy this land in order to prepare for the criminal Germans a situation which is better than that of anyone else in Europe. I want to be fair but I don't want to be the victim of a sympathy campaign. If the Germans don't suffer a bit they won't know what the last 16 years have been all about. I helped some women onto the subway with their little wagons of wood. But they seemed to think that this was to be expected of me. They didn't say thank you. I opened the door of the subway for another lady. She looked at me with slight contempt and did not deign to say thank you.

I ran into a slightly different atmosphere this afternoon when I went to call on some friends of Franz's[16] for whom I brought a heavy package all the way from Washington. They did not seem to be aware of what I had done. At least they did not go out of their way to say thank-you. But there was one woman present who caught my sympathy. She was a Frau Leber[17]. Her husband[18] was a Social Democrat who was involved in the conspiracy of 20 July against Hitler's[19] life.[20]

15 Johnson had gone to Vienna on August 7, 1945.

16 Franz L. Neumann. See Doc. 1, fn. 8.

17 Annedore Leber, née Rosenthal (1904–1968), German politician (SPD), law studies at the University of Munich, training as a seamstress, 1927 SPD, 1945/1946 member of the women's secretariat in the Central Committee of the SPD, as of 1946 licensee of the *Telegraf*, a British-licensed newspaper linked to the SPD, 1946–1951 member of the Stadtverordnetenversammlung of Greater Berlin, 1963–1967 member of the Abgeordnetenhaus of Berlin.

18 Julius Leber (1891–1945), German politician (SPD), unionist, resistance fighter against National Socialism, 1912 SPD, 1920 Dr. rer. pol., University of Freiburg im Breisgau, 1921–1933 member of the Lübeck Bürgerschaft, 1924–1933 member of the Reichstag, 1944 sentenced to death by the Volksgerichtshof, 1945 execution in Berlin-Plötzensee.

19 Adolf Hitler (1889–1945), NS politician, as of 1921 Chairman of the NSDAP, 1933 appointment as Reich Chancellor, 1934–1945 "Führer und Reichskanzler," established the National Socialist dictatorship in Germany.

20 On July 20, 1944, the attack on Adolf Hitler by German resistance fighters and the attempted coup against the NS regime had failed.

He was caught and brought before the Volksgericht[21] (the people's court) which is now the Control Council's headquarters[22]. Her husband was given an official defender. His defense she said, consisted of one sentence: "I know this man has committed a serious crime, and I hope the court will bring out a verdict corresponding to the seriousness of the crime." The man was sentenced to death and Frau Leber is now a widow, prominent in Social Democratic circles, left with two children[23]. What she could not understand, and I agree with her fully, is that, after happenings like this a man like Göring[24] is permitted to take the stand and spew his rot for days on end, and thus awaken all the dormant sentiments of the Nazis lurking in the German Hintergrund. I too wish that we could shoot these guys and have an end of their criminal and offensive talk.

I shall finish my work here this week and be off to the zone. I think too I shall go out and stay with General Gailey[25] tomorrow night. My best use, here, as I see it, is to deal with Germans for the Americans. They have little contact and little understanding. And I think I prefer to be out in the zone. Berlin is interesting politically, and especially at the present moment, when the Communists are trying to force the Socialists into a United Socialist Workers' Party, but it is an ugly city, and rampant with the essential decadence of the metropolis and I prefer to be out where it is possible to look a peasant in the face, and to walk in the shade of a pleasant forest adjoining a nicer valley. I find, so far, that the Germans are a tremendously uninteresting people, not worth the sacrifice we have made to liberate them. And I don't believe they have much to offer the world. They will return to their old ways quickly, and expect us to help them to them. May be the Communists can cure them of this but I doubt it.

Good-night, my beloved, I am sorry to seem so hard-boiled. But I did fill several children's hands with chocolate today and other people's with food-stuffs and cigarettes. I love you and my boys, above all, humans that I know are to be trusted. Edgar

21 The Volksgerichtshof was set up in 1934 in Berlin as a special court for the sentencing of high treason and treason against the NS state; it became an ordinary court in 1936.

22 The Allied Control Authority for Germany had its office in the building of the former Kammergericht in Berlin-Schöneberg. See Doc. 14, fn. 5.

23 Katharina Leber, as of 1950 married Heinemann, later married Christiansen (1929–2008) and Matthias Leber (1931–1963).

24 Hermann Göring (1893–1946), NS politician, 1932 election as President of the Reichstag, 1933 appointment as Minister-President of Prussia, 1935 takeover of command of the Luftwaffe, 1940 received the military rank created for him, "Reichsmarschall des Großdeutschen Reiches," 1946 sentenced to death as a major war criminal by the International Military Tribunal in Nuremberg, escaped execution of the sentence through suicide.

25 See Doc. 15, fn. 23.

Doc. 23
Letter to His Wife
Berlin, Ihnestraße 14[1], March 18, 1946[2]

Dearest Sweetheart –

No letter, still, today. I sent you a cable with my address and with a little ultimate word. Love. I hope you will feel all that went into the word even though the manner of its transmission is just a bit mechanical. I shall soon have to look up the manner and the circumstances under which one may use the international telephone.

You may have wondered why I have not mentioned the possibility of your coming over here. It is because the situation is as I suspected. No one who does not promise to stay at least one year has a chance of bringing his family over and I am told that even in this the military has the advantage over the civilians. Nor do I think that you would be particularly happy in Berlin. Life here for dependents is going to be something like life in a missionary compound in a foreign land. There will not be, I think, any serious discomforts. The quarters will be adequate. I heard of plans today to move out bachelor officers from apartments and houses to "bachelor quarters," so that these facilities will be available to dependents. There will be plenty of food from the army commissary, good medical care from army doctors, and I read today of plans to bring over American teachers to teach American children in American schools in Berlin. It is permitted also to bring over American cars. I suppose, when I get finally settled that I shall be permitted an army car. In general, however, I think, that we shall be confined, American families, I mean, to the environs of Berlin. There are then the advantages of what is going on in Berlin. There is the musical and artistic life of a large city. There may be some chance to get acquainted with the families of our Allies, though all this depends upon language facilities. I don't believe there is going to be any difficulty about disease or unrest. But, in any case, I am not going to be able to bring you over here if I am to come home in the Fall.

There remains the possibility of bringing you over someplace else. I talked with a man at dinner who has his wife and two children in a small inn in Sussex, England. This costs him about 400 dollars a month and all expenses, of course, he has to bear. He can't get to see them very often. The advantage is chiefly their being able to live in England, though I should think that living in an inn in Sussex for an extended period of time might have its limitation. Then there is Switzerland, which, indeed, could be much more exciting. That would cost, I understand, even less. It might not cost more that it costs for you to live with the kids[3] in Lincoln[4]. Transportation expenses would then amount to a payment for

1 See Doc. 15, fn. 1.

2 In the heading it says: "Monday, 17 March 1946." In 1946 March 18 was a Monday, not March 17.

3 Refers to sons John and Thomas. See Doc. 2, fn. 15 and 16.

4 Capital of the US state of Nebraska, where Johnson lived with his family and taught at the university.

the privilege of living in Switzerland for awhile. Other countries are, I think rather out of the question (I am thinking of Denmark) as the Scandinavian countries, because of the difficulty of making arrangements and of my ever getting there. Until I know where I am to be settled I don't think there is much point in our discussing the question further. But if I land in Stuttgart[5] then I believe it is worth contemplating your coming there. It is possible that one could find a lovely out of the way spot in the mountains where you and the kids would be quite delighted, and I could get there once in a while and we could go home together. I think that you should get something out of this foreign migration of mine by way of European experience. But we can't discuss it very practically until we know what it will cost, and that we can't very well know until, if I get to Stuttgart, I can get to Switzerland and make some inquiries.

I had an interview with Ambassador Murphy[6] at noon. I must say he was very cordial and evidently had received some kind of a letter from Jimmy Riddleberger[7] concerning me, for he professed to know about me and what I had done. The interview was unsatisfactory in so far as it was constantly interrupted by telephone, and then finally General Clay[8] appeared and showed the Ambassador a telegram. I was not made to feel as if I should leave the room. In fact I was drawn a bit into the discussion of the telegram without being shown its contents. I could surmise its contents but I don't believe I am free to reveal my surmise. I'll tell you if I am subsequently confirmed by events. In any event my surmise was not encouraging. The Ambassador indicated that he would wish to see me later at some greater length before I go off on my trip. I have been invited for Wednesday[9] to a dinner at Don Heath's[10] at which Murphy may be present. In any case I seem to have gotten off to a good start in so far as the State Department people are concerned. And I am not sorry if General Clay has appeals for my help now from General Barker[11], and then sees me later in Ambassador Murphy's office.

I also had a good talk today with Mr. Fahy[12], whom, I believe, I have already mentioned,[13] the head of the legal division, a shrewd and genial southerner. It was about the mechanics of the legal division for the most part and therefore not especially revealing. I did learn however that the French opposition to the establishment of a central German administration goes so far that they will not even consent to talking about the setting up of a German Central Patent Office. The practice of the legal division is to bring over special experts (on prisons, patents, e. g.) from the U. S. to head the administrative branches here. Tomorrow I am to see the Head of the Manpower Division and this should prove more interesting.[14] I leave at the end of the week for about a month's trip

5 Capital of the state of Württemberg-Baden in the American zone of Germany.
6 See Doc. 8, fn. 13.
7 James W. Riddleberger. See Doc. 8, fn. 12.
8 See Doc. 2, fn. 6.
9 March 20, 1946.
10 Donald R. Heath. See Doc. 8, fn. 15.
11 See Doc. 20, fn. 10.
12 See Doc. 20, fn. 36.
13 See Doc. 19.

through the zone. It ought to be Spring now in the South. After that I hope to get something definite to do.

I have the feeling now that things are going to turn out all right in so far as the importance of what I am to do is concerned. But the future here of all our work depends upon the uncertainty of the food situation. The British, as you know, have cut their rations to something over a thousand, a virtually starvation ration.[15] I read in a German paper today that the French have cut their ration to well below 1000 calories.[16] This is disastrous. You can't preach democracy on empty stomachs, and you can't exemplify democracy by cutting rations. The Germans won't be much interested in the right to elect their own officials if they are starving while filling in the ballot. I only hope that we don't have to reduce the rations in our zone.[17] It would be disastrous for the slow progress we have made here, and fatal to whatever trust the Germans put in us. I hope you will preach the gospel at home of the necessity of keeping up our present minimum ration here in order to achieve even a minimum political victory. If necessary to heal this spot of Europe we have to feed our former enemies before our friends even if Americans have to tighten their belts slightly to do it. In my report of yesterday[18] I think I exaggerated to the extent that the people whom one sees on the streets are those who are healthy enough to be on the streets. I understand there are plenty of people here who are strong enough only to remain in bed from day to day. How true this actually is I don't know. Perhaps for some old people.

This is not an attractive world over here. As it becomes less attractive more Americans will be going home. Those here now and those who stay are to be given credit for sticking out a pretty hopeless job.

I kiss you my sweet Emily, and my dear John and Thomas. How I long for news. It must come soon. I love you with all of me. Edgar

14 See Doc. 24.

15 In the British zone the rations for normal consumers was reduced to 1,014 calories per day. See *Der Tagesspiegel* from February 28, 1946, p. 2; *Berliner Zeitung* from March 1, 1946, [p. 1].

16 In the French zone the bread ration of 270 grams per day was reduced to 200 grams per day. The total allocation thus amounted to less than 1,000 calories per day, the lowest allocation in the four zones. See *Der Tagesspiegel* from March 16, 1946, p. 2; *Berliner Zeitung* from March 17, 1946, [p. 1].

17 On March 29, 1946, US Deputy Military Governor Lucius D. Clay (see Doc. 2, fn. 6) informed the Minister-Presidents of Bavaria, Greater Hesse, and Württemberg-Baden, "that the present daily scale of 1550 calories for the normal consumer in the American Zone would be cut to 1275 calories, effective April 1." "Food Ration Cut To 1275 Calories," in: *The Grooper* from March 30, 1946, p. 1.

18 See Doc. 22.

Doc. 24
Letter to His Wife
Berlin, Ihnestraße 14[1], March 19, 1946

My sweet beloved one:

I am a little discouraged tonight over the future here – my personal future I mean. I started out the day nicely with a conference with Mr. Werts[2], the head of the Manpower (Labor) Division who appears to be a good American liberal. He let me attend a meeting of Labor officers from the field who were discussing the problem of trade union organization in the zone, and this was interesting, and even moving – good Americans trying to do the best job they know how.

When I got back to the office I was told that General Clay[3] was about to call me. He did and asked me to come right over. We talked generally for about fifteen minutes about the difficulties inherent in the general situation here especially with the threatened reduction in our calorie rations[4]. He even read to me the telegram which McNarney[5] sent to the War Department yesterday about this threat.[6] It was the telegram which he and Murphy[7] discussed yesterday in Murphy's office when I was there.[8] Then finally he came to the main point of what I was going to do.

1 See Doc. 15, fn. 1.

2 Leo R. Werts (1905–1989), 1945/1946 Deputy Director, Manpower Division, OMGUS, June 1946–1949 Director, 1949/1950 Associate Director, Office International Labor Affairs, Department of Labor, 1950–1953 Deputy Executive Director, Defense Manpower Administration.

3 See Doc. 2, fn. 6.

4 See Doc. 23.

5 See Doc. 17, fn. 41.

6 Clay mentions the telegram in his memoirs: "In March the signs of need were unmistakable. I felt compelled to advise General McNarney to send a cable to personally ask General Eisenhower [see Doc. 18, fn. 25] for his support for assistance. We had promised the Germans that we would provide sufficient food to keep up the rations granted to them. In his telegram McNarney pointed out that with the reduced rations, the subsistence level was no longer assured; diseases and malnutrition were inevitable, and the work performance of the population would decline rapidly. We could not expect to develop democracy with starvation rations; we could not even stop diseases and dissatisfaction." ("Im März waren die Anzeichen der Not unverkennbar. Ich fühlte mich veranlaßt, General McNarney nahezulegen, General Eisenhower durch ein Kabel persönlich um seine Unterstützung dafür zu bitten, daß geholfen wurde. Wir hatten den Deutschen versprochen, für genügend Lebensmittel zu sorgen, um die ihnen zugebilligte Ration aufrecht zu erhalten. In seinem Telegramm wies McNarney darauf hin, daß mit der verkürzten Ration das Existenzminimum nicht mehr gesichert sei; Krankheit und Unterernährung seien unvermeidlich, die Arbeitsleistung der Bevölkerung werde rapid absinken. Wir konnten nicht erwarten, Demokratie bei Hungerrationen zu entwickeln; wir konnten nicht einmal Krankheiten und Unzufriedenheit aufhalten.") Lucius D. Clay, *Entscheidung in Deutschland*, Frankfurt am Main 1950, p. 297. See Wolfgang Krieger, *General Lucius D. Clay und die amerikanische Deutschlandpolitik 1945–1949* (= Forschungen und Quellen zur Zeitgeschichte, vol. 10), Stuttgart 1987, p. 169.

7 See Doc. 8, fn. 13.

8 See Doc. 23.

The just of it is that the Stuttgart[9] job[10] is out until Pollock[11] goes home which is I believe towards the end of the summer, and that is when I want to go home. He explained quite decently what I understand perfectly – it is nobody's fault except the bureaucracy's in Washington – that because of the protracted delay in my return here (about which they did nothing) he had to send Pollock down to Stuttgart, and that, because Pollock had built up, and grown into and come to love, the job, he could hardly summon him to Berlin, and send me down there. I can understand this. I shouldn't like to be treated this way either – only it is a little hard on me. If I had known that I wasn't going to have the Stuttgart job, then I shouldn't have returned here. I should be in Lincoln[12] with the people I love best of all. He then went on to bring up the job with Colonel Barker[13] which I have mentioned in a previous letter[14], and asked me what I thought about it. I told him that it was a question of alternatives. He then went on to speak of his plans to use Walter Dorn[15] and myself as special assistants to him for the purpose of constant travelling through the zone, in order to keep an oversight over what is going on both in M[ilitary] G[overnment] and German circles – something like Charlemagne's[16] missi do-

9 Capital of the state of Württemberg-Baden in the American zone of Germany.

10 Leadership of RGCO in Stuttgart. See Doc. 2, fn. 11.

11 See Doc. 15, fn. 6.

12 Capital of the US state of Nebraska, where Johnson lived with his family and taught at the university.

13 See Doc. 20, fn. 10.

14 See Doc. 20.

15 See Doc. 2, fn. 10.

16 Charlemagne or Charles the Great (probably 747–814), descended from the family of the Arnulfingers, later named Carolingians after him, as of 768 King of the Franks, as of 774 also King of the Lombards, as of 800 Roman Emperor.

17 The royal messengers dispatched by Charlemagne to oversee the counts appointed as deputies of the king. See James Westfall Thompson/Edgar Nathaniel Johnson, *An Introduction to Medieval Europe, 300–1500*, New York 1937, chapter 9 ("The Frankish State under the Carolingians"), pp. 251f.: "To supervise the counts and check their frequent abuses of power Charles created a new official, the *missus dominicus*, or royal messenger. The empire was divided into districts, each consisting of a number of counties, over which the *missi*, usually two, a layman and a bishop or abbot, made yearly circuits. They were intended also to serve as a direct link between the people and the emperor, to whom they submitted regular reports. In his *General Capitulary about the Missi*, of 802, Charles ordered them 'to investigate and to report to him any inequality or injustice that might appear in the law as then constituted … to inquire diligently into every case where any man complained that he had been dealt with unjustly by anyone, and in the fear of God to render justice to all, to the holy churches of God, to the poor, to widows and orphans and to the whole people; … they are not to be hindered in the doing of justice by the flattery or bribery of anyone, by their partiality for their own friends or by the fear of powerful men.' The *missi* held their own courts, and supervised the administration of the counts and their subordinates, of the bishops and abbots, and of the officers of the royal domain. They were even given the authority in extreme cases to remove for cause royal officials. They were protected by a triple wergild, and armed resistance to them was punishable by death. When loyal and honest the *missi* were an effective aid to efficient centralized administration. But from the beginning Charles feared that they too might become

minici[17] if you remember.[18] He said he planned to get out an order to this effect and to establish us, as special assistants in offices close to him. He explained that Colonel Barker only wanted to borrow me for a period of six or eight weeks, and that he thought that during this time I should only have to spend about three or four days a week on the Berlin job. Since I am over here there is not much point in my getting on my high horse and deciding to come home immediately. I said I was only interested in my greatest utility and that I thought I could be of most use in dealing with Germans and trying to further our democratic aims. He accordingly asked me to get in touch with General Barker as soon as possible and talk over the job with him. Accordingly I have made arrangements to see him tomorrow, and I shall go over the details of the job with him. The only alternative I have is to go with Taylor[19] and Knappen's[20] crowd.[21] I shall make my real decision tomorrow. The Berlin job, according to those I talk with here is an interesting and relatively important job. It involves setting up a democratic government for Berlin,[22] elections, a constitution for the city, etc. To do this involves quadripartite negotiations which ought to be interesting too. Berlin is a kind of small Germany. It involves also becoming acquainted with the political leaders of Berlin, and Berlin is, at the moment, the political center of this potential democratic state.

The inspection of the zone job is also an interesting one. Somewhat along my OSS[23] line. It is the sort of thing which Walter Dorn is now doing for General Adcock[24], and which he will continue to do for Clay when once he moves up here from Frankfurt[25]. This will involve my working with Walter Dorn. But Walter Dorn, I am afraid, can't be worked with. He is a little of a prima donna. Therefore we should either have to divide the Länder between us or I should have to work for Walter, which I did not come back here to do. This may be reason for my preserving a certain amount of independence by taking up the Berlin job.

I was also planning to leave for the zone on Friday[26]. General Gailey[27] made special arrangements at Frankfurt for me to have a car with which to make the

identified with local interests, and provided that their circuits be changed every year, to prevent collusion between *missi* and counts."

18 In April 1946 Dorn was appointed as Clay's Special Adviser for relations between the military government detachments and the German regional offices. See Josef Henke/Klaus Oldenhage, "Office of Military Government for Germany (U. S.)," in: *OMGUS-Handbuch. Die amerikanische Militärregierung in Deutschland 1945–1949*, ed. Christoph Weisz (= Quellen und Darstellungen zur Zeitgeschichte, vol. 35), Munich 1994, pp. 1–142, here p. 45.

19 See Doc. 17, fn. 26.

20 See Doc. 8, fn. 10.

21 Refers to employment in the Education and Religious Affairs Branch, Internal Affairs and Communications Division, OMGUS. See Doc. 15 and Doc. 20.

22 The first Berlin postwar Magistrat had been installed by Soviet occupation forces and thus had no democratic legitimation.

23 Office of Strategic Services. See Doc. 1, fn. 9.

24 See Doc. 14, fn. 9.

25 Frankfurt am Main, city in the state of Greater Hesse in the American zone of Germany.

26 March 22, 1946.

27 See Doc. 15, fn. 23.

trip. It is now possible that I shall have to give this up, or at least make only a short trip. Anyway I want to go to Frankfurt and talk with Walter Dorn. It will depend upon my interview with Colonel Barker tomorrow.

And so this is an unsatisfactory and shifting world. Clay is all right I think. He is hardly to blame and understands the importance of having some satisfactory civilians around. I shall always be well treated by him. But I didn't come here to be well treated by Clay but to do a job. Yet I can't pick up and go home like a child. I can learn something by staying on the spot.

A letter from you would help. I heard today that there are endless delays in getting mail from one city to another in Germany, and I remember how long it took to get things from Munich[28] to Salzburg[29]. Now that you have my cable I can at least hope for something in ten days or so, provided I am at that time in Berlin. I guess I don't really like change when I personally am involved. It's all right in the past.

I love you, my sweetest, and think of you in many, most intimate ways. I kiss you and the sweet little lads of ours[30]. Edgar

Doc. 25
Letter to His Wife
Berlin, Ihnestraße 14[1], March 22, 1946[2]

Dearest beloved:

I have been kept from writing you for a couple of nights by 2 engagements and the necessity of making arrangements to get settled in my new job. For the Stuttgart job is out for the time being as I learned after another conference with General Clay[3] – as I perhaps told you.[4] He has now made me a Special Assistant of his. I am to have an office near his across from Ambassador Murphy's[5]. I am to spend some time each week in this office keeping acquainted with the affairs of Omgus[6] and I am to be permitted to see necessary documents to keep me in touch. I shall try to insist upon an impressive list. For the next 40 days or as long thereafter as is necessary I am to be loaned to General Barker[7], the Commanding General and Chief of M[ilitary] G[overnment] in the Berlin area. Yesterday I spent mostly with General Barker, an altogether de-

28 City in the American zone of Germany.
29 City in the American zone of Austria.
30 Refers to sons John and Thomas. See Doc. 2, fn. 15 and 16.

1 See Doc. 15, fn. 1.
2 In the heading it says: "21 March 1946 Friday." In 1946 March 22 was a Friday, not March 21.
3 See Doc. 2, fn. 6.
4 See Doc. 24.
5 See Doc. 8, fn. 13.
6 See Doc. 17, fn. 45.
7 See Doc. 20, fn. 10.

cent and interesting fellow, teetotaler and non-smoker who knows what he is about. He told me that M[ilitary] G[overnment] in Berlin consists now of politics and education – the mechanics of sewers, lighting etc. can now be taken care of by the Germans. I am going to live in some quarters on the Wannsee[8] (the big lake bordering on our section). We went out together to see what is now called the Wannsee Hotel[9] (formerly the home of Minister of Economics Funk[10], now a War Criminal in Nuremberg[11]). There are wonderful apartments in it overlooking the lake – where there would be swimming and boat. If I don't live there I shall probably live next door in what General Barker told me are equally fine apartments in a large house.[12] This will be a place where I can entertain Germans or anyone else I please, and I think I might as well take advantage of decent quarters. In general the Americans here of any rank live

8 Refers to Großer Wannsee, a bight of the Havel (see Doc. 74, fn. 24) in southwest Berlin.

9 The Wannsee Hotel/Wannsee Officers' Club was located at Am Sandwerder 17/19 (before 1933: Friedrich-Karl-Straße 24) in the Berlin administrative district of Zehlendorf, Wannsee area, on the eastern shore of Großer Wannsee. In 1886/1887 a country house designed by the architect Johannes Otzen (1839–1911) was built here for the chemist Franz Oppenheim (1852–1929). See *Berlin und seine Bauten*, eds. Architekten-Verein zu Berlin/Vereinigung Berliner Architekten, vol. III, *Privatbauten*, Berlin 1896, pp. 172 and 175. Later the house belonged to the Jewish banker Hans Arnhold (see Doc. 47, fn. 7), who had to emigrate with his family during the Nazi period. Afterwards the NS Reich Economics Minister Walther Funk (see fn. 10) moved in. Rebuilt several times since its construction, after the Second World War the house was used by the Americans. "The two top floors of the Wannsee Officers Club are reserved for VIPs; the spacious rooms on the main floor are for dining, lounging and dancing. From the wide Italian terrace the view of the lake and the wooded surrounding far below is magnificent." Viviane W. Adams, "Wannsee," in: *OMGUS Observer* from June 28, 1946, pp. 4f. and 8, here p. 5. The Americans later called the estate the "Wannsee-Outdoor Rec Center." Since 1998 the American Academy in Berlin, Hans Arnhold Center, is located here. This institution serves to promote communication and intellectual exchange between Germany and the USA. Photos of the building in Appendix of Illustrations, ill. 43 and ill. 46; view of Großer Wannsee from the terrace: ill. 47.

10 Walther Funk (1890–1960), German economic journalist and NS politician, 1932/1933 member of the Reichstag, as of 1938 Reich Economics Minister, as of 1939 likewise President of the Reichsbank, in October 1946 sentenced by the International Military Tribunal in Nuremberg to life imprisonment as a major war criminal, 1957 early release for health reasons.

11 City in the state of Bavaria in the American zone of Germany.

12 Refers to the neighboring estate, Am Sandwerder 21/23, which was supposed to function as an extension of the Wannsee Officers' Club: "Next door to the officers club at 23 Am Sanderwerder Strasse is the home of Heinrich Schicht, who was president of the German Sunlight Soap Co. The beautiful rooms with heavily carved doors imported from Italy, rich colored brocade silk walls, and mirrored Hollywood style, ornate bathrooms are now being renovated to serve as an Annex to the Wannsee Officers Club. This house will be run as billets for transient officers." Viviane W. Adams, "Wannsee," in: *OMGUS Observer* from June 28, 1946, pp. 4f. and 8, here p. 5. The house, in which Johann Heinrich Schicht (1912–1944), Sunlicht Gesellschaft AG, had lived, was built in 1906/1907 according to plans by the architect Friedrich Kristeller (born 1860) for the banker Adolph Schwabacher. See *Gartendenkmale in Berlin: Pri-*

in very elegant and comfortable quarters. I am to have a car at my disposition finally, when I get settled. I am to have what is to be some kind of a splendiferous office in the Berlin District (BD) headquarters of Military Government[13], suitable to one who acts in an advisory capacity to a General, etc. etc. Actually I think the job is going to be an interesting one, and I shall be able to do it well I think and get along with the few people who will be helping with it. The Colonel who is now doing it is a good friend of Walter Dorn[14], and Sinclair Armstrong[15] and I learn, after spending a couple hours with him tonight, a very human, intelligent and earnest fellow. He has a grand Steinway piano[16] in his quarters. General Barker took me to lunch yesterday with his regular military staff in a wonderful house the library of which has some original medieval manuscripts. There I met a former student whose name I have forgotten but who is here the secretary[17] of the Chief of Staff[18] to Barker. I met a sergeant the other day who is a former student also. The general let me attend his briefing for the Kommandatura[19] (the 4 Allied Generals governing Berlin) meeting[20] today. He was bitter about the English into which most of the documents was cast. (Russian English which others hesitate to change because the Russians might fear that something is up). He is now reading Krutch's[21] life of Sam Johnson[22] and is well acquainted with Lords and Ladies, and important Frenchmen. I went to the Kommandatura meeting this morning, and it was for me highly exciting, fascinating, mostful depressing. I wish all Americans could attend a meeting of this kind to see how the international machinery works on a

vatgärten, ed. Katrin Lesser, with an introduction by Klaus-Henning von Krosigk and contributions by Josef Batzhuber et al. (= Beiträge zur Denkmalpflege in Berlin, 21), Petersberg 2005, pp. 206f.

13 Refers to the Office of Military Government, Berlin District (OMGBD), which had its headquarters in the building of the Deutsche Forschungsgemeinschaft at Grunewaldstraße 35 in the Berlin administrative district of Steglitz. Neighboring buildings on Brentano- and Kaiser-Wilhelm-Straße (today: Schmidt-Ott-Straße) were also used by OMGBD. Photo of the building on Grunewaldstraße in Appendix of Illustrations, ill. 40.

14 See Doc. 2, fn. 10.

15 See Doc. 3, fn. 2.

16 See Doc. 4, fn. 25.

17 Robert E. Grovert (1921–2003), 1st Lieutenant, graduate of the University of Nebraska, became an Air Force fighter pilot after his deployment in Berlin, Air Attaché at the US Embassy in the Federal Republic of Germany, Bonn.

18 Elmer E. Barnes (1895–1986), Colonel, 1918 graduate of the United States Military Academy, 1946 Chief of Staff, Headquarters Berlin District, US Army. Photos with Barnes in Appendix of Illustrations, ill. 29 and ill. 30.

19 See Doc. 20, fn. 11.

20 8th meeting of the Commandants on March 22, 1946. See minutes of this meeting, BKC/M (46) 8, English version, in: LAB, B Rep. 036-01 (Office of Military Government, Berlin Sector [OMGBS]), 11/148-1/10.

21 Joseph W. Krutch (1893–1970), American writer.

22 Refers to Krutch's biography of the English scholar, lexicographer, writer, poet, and critic Samuel Johnson (1709–1784), which was published in 1944 in New York.

23 Dmitri Ivanovich Smirnov (1901–1975), Soviet Lieutenant General, as of 1920 in the Red Army, 1936 graduate of the Frunze Military Academy, 1945–April 1946 head of the garrison in the Soviet sector of Berlin and Soviet Commandant, Allied Kommandatura Berlin.

small scale, and how delicate it is, so delicate that a slightly impatient or tactless remark would bring it crashing to the ground. I took elaborate notes on it and will write you a full account the first opportunity I get. The Russians were in the chair (General Smirnov[23]) and taking full advantage of the situation. I imagine I shall be participating in some of the meetings considering political matters in the Kommandatura (participating and not attending). I shall also get in on some social gatherings when our Allies are present. I imagine I shall even have to do some entertaining myself. You could let yourself in for a merry round here.

I went to Don Heath's[24] on Wednesday[25]. He had together what I suppose he regards as relatively less important people. I met Col. Howley[26], Barker's Deputy for Military Government who is my military boss but whom, Barker told me I have the privilege of going over the head of. There was Col. Durand[27] (a mediaeval colleague) who is in charge of the OSS[28] unit here. There was a Mr. King[29], formerly British Consul at Paris whose solution for the GI[30] situation is – give them coffee and sugar and they will sit in cafes and talk about politics without doing anything about it. I protested the simplicity of this. There was Mr. Steere[31], under Don Heath, and his very attractive wife[32] (arrived a month ago), a colonel in the Wacs[33], and who knows Mabel Lee[34] of the U[niversity] of N[ebraska] very very well.[35] There was an attractive young British Major – the political division. Lots of secretaries, lots of liquor, lots of food. Entertainment in the abundant Statement Department manner.

24 Donald R. Heath. See Doc. 8, fn. 15.
25 March 20, 1946.
26 See Doc. 20, fn. 18.
27 Dana B. Durand (1904–1982), Lieutenant Colonel, American historian, 1935 PhD, Harvard University (dissertation: "The Origins of German Cartography in the Fifteenth Century"), Assistant Professor of History and Literature, Harvard University, 1941/1942 Associate Professor, Mount Holyoke College, OSS employee, 1947–1964 CIA employee.
28 Office of Strategic Services. See Doc. 1, fn. 9.
29 Alfred Hazell King (1896–1956), British diplomat, 1944 Consul, Paris, as of 1945 Consul General for British zone of Germany, as of 1948 Counsellor and Consul General, Cairo, as of 1952 Counsellor and Consul General, Buenos Aires.
30 Government Issue, slang for American soldier.
31 See Doc. 20, fn. 23.
32 Anna W. Steere, née Walker, widowed Wilson (1909–1999), Lieutenant Colonel, American teacher, 1938 MA, Claremont Colleges, teacher, Beverly Hills High School, Beverly Hills, California, as of 1942 Women's Army Auxiliary Corps/Women's Army Corps, 1943–1945 Staff Director of the Women's Army Corps in the European Theater of Operations.
33 Women's Army Corps. See Doc. 13, fn. 14.
34 Mabel Lee (1886–1985), American physical education teacher, 1908 BSc, Coe College, 1924–1952 worked at the University of Nebraska, Professor of Physical Education for Women, Chairman of Department, belonged to the civil advisory board of the Women's Army Corps.
35 Loyd V. Steere and Anna W. Wilson had married on January 26, 1946, in a church in Bad Nauheim in the state of Greater Hesse in the American zone of Germany. See "Leader in the Wac Bride in Germany. Lieut. Col. Anna W. Wilson Is Wed to Lloyd V. Steere of Military Government Staff," in: *The New York Times* from January 27, 1946, p. 38.

Yesterday evening was something different. Max Rheinstein[36] had Americans and some Germans together in his house[37]. Among them was a Max Bandler[38], a distinguished German cellist, and a pupil of Casals[39]. He played in a former Klinger Quartet[40] here and was ostracised by the Nazis because of a Jewish wife[41].[42] Now he happens to own the house Rheinstein now occupies. He was thrown out by former American occupants together with his family (wife, 2 pairs of twins[43] and another child[44]) and obliged to move into one room of a bombed house[45] next door. How would you like to be a guest of your conquerors in your own house. He was excellent about it. He complained to me that the hairs of his bow are wearing out and there are no hairs for the bow of a cello here. Would you make a special effort to get from the Lincoln[46] music stores some hairs for the stringing of a cello bow. Get enough for a few stringings and send them to me as soon as possible. I told him about John[47] and he is going to investigate for me the possibilities of getting some music for him here.

I turned down parties at the Lakeside Club[48] for tonight and tomorrow. You can see that it is so far interesting here. I wonder for how long? I love you my dearest, am still craving to hear from you, and send you and my boys sweet kisses and caresses. Edgar

Doc. 26
Letter to His Wife
Berlin, Ihnestraße 14[1], March 23, 1946

Dearest Sweetheart –

I am very lonely and depressed tonight. The basic cause of it is the absence of news from you. It is some six weeks now since I have had any account of what

36 See Doc. 11, fn. 22.
37 Podbielskiallee 65. See Doc. 21, fn. 17.
38 Max Baldner. See Doc. 21, fn. 18.
39 Pablo Casals (1876–1973), Spanish-Catalan cellist. Max Baldner had gone to Paris because he wanted to “profit” (“profitieren”) from Casal’s “incomparable art” (“von der unvergleichlichen Kunst”). “This stay in Paris contributed infinitely to my development.” (“Dieser Aufenthalt in Paris hat unendlich viel zu meiner Entwicklung beigetragen.”) Resume Max Baldner, in: LAB, C Rep. 120 (Magistrat von Berlin, Abteilung Volksbildung), no. 88, fols. 21f., here fol. 21.
40 Klingler Quartet. See Doc. 21, fn. 19.
41 Charlotte Baldner, née Lindemann. See Doc. 21, fn. 21.
42 See Doc. 21, fn. 22.
43 See Doc. 21, fn. 24.
44 Not a member of the family but rather a girl from their circle of acquaintance, according to information from Thomas Baldner (see Doc. 21, fn. 24) in a telephone conversation with Werner Breunig on April 29, 2009.
45 Podbielskiallee 57. See Doc. 21, fn. 25.
46 Capital of the US state of Nebraska, where Johnson lived with his family and taught at the university.
47 Johnson’s son John. See Doc. 2, fn. 15.
48 See Doc. 17 and Doc. 18.

1 See Doc. 15, fn. 1.

is going on at home, and God knows what may have happened in this interval. This situation may end some time but it is not sure when it will end. Oh I resent this cutting off from my beloved ones. To be suddenly transported from the immediate delight of being loved and taken somewhat seriously by you and John (even Thomas was becoming aware of my existence) into a kind of darkness where the former immediacy becomes a memory and one cannot grasp the essential reality of his existence, is more than I can take at the moment. I can exert this memory. I can attempt to recapture all the details which go to make up you, and you and me, and all the combinations that result from our having John and Thomas. But this exertion is no substitute for the detail which comes from letters. The most important things in my life, in our lives, may have happened but I do not know them yet, nor will I ever know them from immediate experience. Darling, we must not prolong this precarious and impossible mode of existence. As I have written it is impossible to bring you over as long as I am unwilling to say that I shall stay here for as long as a year. The Switzerland business which I have spoken of[2] is almost out for at least the time being since for as far as I can see I am going to be in Berlin for most of my stay here, and not in Stuttgart[3] where I should be reasonably close to Switzerland. And I am not so sure that American families are going to be very happy over here.

I am going to interrupt this to ask you to be very careful about repeating things I tell you about 1) happenings in General Clay's[4] weekly staff meetings[5], which I attend and 2) happenings in any quadripartite meeting which I may have attended. In so far as I know these letters are not censored. Nor have I received any instructions here about the present security rules. But from what I know of my experience with OSS[6] I should say that anything I say which reflects *in detail* about our conduct here, or anything which reflects discredit or unusual difficulty with our Allies, should be treated by you with extreme caution. In case of doubt wait to be confirmed by stories in the press. Or confine your comments to general remarks which do not reflect detail. In any case don't risk anything that might get into the press. You know I have gone on the practice on telling you everything and it has worked perfectly. I want to go on with this practice with the same feeling of security. In many instances I am convinced that what I say should be well known and understood by Americans in order that they may understand the difficulties and tragedy of what is going over here. But I do not wish to embarrass my superiors or make anything more difficult for them. I must be absolutely loyal. If I am not they will simply send me home, and I have no desire to be sent home for this kind of cause. For Upper Austria, Yes. For a security violation No. So, if you pass on what I have to say, pass on the import and not the details, and pass on the import as though you gather this from your reading of the press.

2 See Doc. 23.
3 Capital of the state of Württemberg-Baden in the American zone of Germany.
4 See Doc. 2, fn. 6.
5 See Doc. 16, fn. 10.
6 Office of Strategic Services. See Doc. 1, fn. 9.

This interruption I have written because in regard to the happiness of families over here, an incident reported in General Clay's staff meeting[7] this morning is revealing. In Stuttgart, the local M[ilitary] G[overnment] authorities were preparing to receive the April assignment of American wives and their children. Their idea is to put them into a compound. So they roped off an area designated for this American compound, and ordered all the people with the ropes to move out instantly.[8] It is a good example of our unwillingness to act wisely in this matter. We have never tried to distinguish between Nazis and non-Nazis in the requisition of dwelling space, a hot issue in this country where rooms are at premium.

In this instance if we wanted people in a given area to move out we should arrange to have some nice Nazi homes for them to move into. But we don't take this little precaution and simply asked them to get out. Accordingly there was in Stuttgart this morning a public demonstration of some 500 people protesting this move.[9] The demonstrators elected a Committee to deal with the local M[ilitary] G[overnment] authorities who voted without consultation with higher-ups. The results of the negotiations were reported in the meeting as unsatisfactory. You

7 See minutes of the OMGUS staff conference on March 23, 1946, in: Archiv des IfZ, OMGUS – Staff Conferences (copies of minutes), Fg 12/3.

8 Johnson is referring here to the announced (partial) evacuation of the Sonnenberg housing development in the south of Stuttgart. In the minutes of the staff conference, pp. 11f., it says: "Just before the meeting, General McClure [see Doc. 17, fn. 38] received a phone call from Stuttgart to the effect that M[ilitary] G[overnment] authorities had roped off a large area, advising Germans that M[ilitary] G[overnment] would take possession to make room for incoming American personnel. As a result, a demonstration was staged in front of the Buergermeister's office with about 500 people attending. A committee has been apppointed to talk with the Military Government authorities." Regarding the evacuation carried out in the spring and summer of 1946, the Sonnenberg-Verein writes: "Residents of Sonnenberg had hardly survived the war to a certain extent when they were dealt a heavy blow: in the spring and summer of 1946 almost all of Sonnenberg had to be evacuated for the American occupation forces. […] 220 buildings in total were evacuated, and 2,503 Sonnenberg residents had to leave their homes. Sonnenberg became an area with an American imprint. […] After a long battle and tough negotiations, it was finally decided that replacement buildings would be created for the Americans. But it took a full nine years before the residents of Sonnenberg could return to their buildings. In 1955 approximately 100 buildings were released, and in 1957 the release of the last building could finally be celebrated." ("Kaum hatten die Sonnenbergbewohner die Not des Krieges einigermaßen überstanden, als sie von einem schweren Schlag getroffen wurden: Im Frühjahr und Sommer 1946 musste fast der ganze Sonnenberg für die amerikanische Besatzungsmacht geräumt werden. […] Insgesamt mussten 220 Häuser geräumt werden, und 2503 Sonnenberger mussten ihre Wohnungen verlassen. Der Sonnenberg wurde zu einer amerikanisch geprägten Siedlung. […] Nach langem Kampf und zähen Verhandlungen wurde schließlich erreicht, dass Ersatzbauten für die Amerikaner erstellt wurden. Aber es dauerte volle neun Jahre, bis die Sonnenberger in ihre Häuser zurückkehren konnten. 1955 wurden ungefähr 100 Häuser freigegeben, und 1957 konnte man endlich die Freigabe des letzten Hauses feiern.") http://www.sonnenberg-verein.de/ (accessed March 1, 2018).

9 The *Stuttgarter Zeitung* reports: "An estimated 200 to 300 women from the Sonnenberg district, some with their children, gathered on Saturday morning to demonstrate in front of the office of the Oberbürgermeister on Schönleinstraße. A delegation of

can imagine how the American wives and their kids will be greeted by this town. And this I imagine is only the first of incidents of this kind. (I have just decided to write a small memorandum to General Clay on this subject). I just can't imagine that American families are going to feel very comfortable over here. American wives and their kids are going to be sporting around in swell clothes, well fed, and driving the own automobiles around. They are being encouraged to bring their own automobiles and some efforts are being made to have special favors tendered them with respect to the sale of a new American cars to them over here. This only emphasizes the differences between conquerors and conquered. And the mere fact that American families are coming over here is enough to indicate to the Germans that the conquerors are here for some time to come.

I am depressed also by a little incident I witnessed in coming home from the office this afternoon. The MP's (Military Police) inspect closely any packages brought out of Omgus[10] headquarters by Germans in our employ. Today I saw an unnecessarily gruff MP inspect the knapsack of a nice old German who was terrified. He found a piece of card-board which the old man was undoubtedly bringing home to burn (the sight of Berliners dragging home wood on Sundays is pathetic enough). The MP tore the card-board out of his knapsack and threw it on a pile. I found this hard to take. I would be a soft MP and an essentially soft (in some respects) conqueror.

I am also depressed by the food situation here. (Why can't you people at home disgorge a little bit). There are already reports of food riots in the British zone (shots being fired), people collapsing at their work, or serving notice that they can go on for only a little time longer. The coal production in the Ruhr[11] is already declining because of the starvation character of the British ration[12]. You can't teach democracy to people who are starving or threatened with starvation, and you don't help the situation by bringing in more troops.

I'll write an account of the Kommandatura[13] meeting tomorrow.[14] Goodnight my sweet. You can be thankful at least that you are not faced with what the German wives and Mothers and kids are faced with. My sweetest love to Emily and John and Thomas. Edgar

six women presented the Oberbürgermeister with the worries and concerns felt by the population of the affected district. Dr. Klett reaffirmed that the city is trying everything to avoid excessive hardship from the evacuation, and to accommodate the affected families elsewhere." ("Schätzungsweise 200 bis 300 Frauen des Stadtteils Sonnenberg, zum Teil mit ihren Kindern, versammelten sich am Samstagvormittag demonstrativ vor der Amtsstelle des Oberbürgermeisters in der Schönleinstraße. Eine Delegation von sechs Frauen trug dem Oberbürgermeister die Sorgen und Bedenken vor, die von der Bevölkerung des betroffenen Stadtteils empfunden werden. Dr. Klett versicherte bei der Gelegenheit noch einmal, daß von seiten der Stadt alles versucht werde, um allzu große Härten bei der Räumung zu vermeiden und die betroffenen Familien anderweitig unterzubringen.") "Vorläufig zwei Häuser beschlagnahmt," in: *Stuttgarter Zeitung* from March 27, 1946, p. 3.

10 See Doc. 17, fn. 45.

11 Significant industrial region in the British zone of Germany.

12 See Doc. 23, fn. 15.

13 See Doc. 20, fn. 11.

14 See Doc. 27.

Doc. 27
Letter to His Wife
Berlin, Ihnestraße 14[1], March 24, 1946

Dearest Sweetheart –

I had a difficult moment at lunch today. I met this guy Thompson[2] from Colorado[3] whom you have heard me speak of[4] and he had with him at the table his wife and his little boy[5] whom he had just gathered in London. I don't know how long I shall be able to stand seeing these wives and children about. He is doing work for the Embassy in Warsaw[6] and is returning there Tuesday[7]. I suggested my coming there to study the Russians in Poland as a background for my work here. He said he would arrange it in Warsaw if I could arrange it here. I guess I'll try. It would be for only a week. He said that the present government in Poland[8] represents some 15–20 % of the people: that if a free election were to be held Mikolacyk(sp?)[9] the peasant party leader, would win by a 70 % majority, that the Russians have moved in new divisions to control the elections, that Russian officers control the Polish Secret Police and that Russians in Polish Uniforms are way down into the ranks of the Polish army. This is all very ugly.

I wonder if you could spare enough money to get me a wrist watch and send it over to me. The present system does not work. The crystal is always coming out. It is out now and I can't spend the time necessary to go and have it repaired constantly. About all I have had my secretary do recently is to keep me informed of the time so that I wouldn't miss my next appointment. At some moment in the future I am going to be embarrassed. If you ever find time or opportunity to send me anything you'd better send me cigarettes. They are worth their weight in gold here and are indeed to the Germans the preferred

1 See Doc. 15, fn. 1.

2 May refer to Llewellyn E. Thompson Jr. (1904–1972), Diplomat, 1928 BA in Economics, University of Colorado, as of 1929 Department of State, 1944/1945 2nd Secretary and Consul, London, 1945/1946 1st Secretary and Consul, London, 1945 Political Adviser, Berlin Conference, 1946/1947 Chief, Division of Eastern European Affairs, 1952–1955 High Commissioner, Austria, 1955–1957 Ambassador, Austria, 1957–1962 and 1967–1969 Ambassador, Soviet Union.

3 Llewellyn E. Thompson Jr. was born in Las Animas in the US state of Colorado.

4 Thomson had not yet been mentioned in the letters written as of February 12, 1946. Johnson may have met him in 1944/1945 in London.

5 Thompson was not married at this time and did not have any children. It may have been a friend and her son.

6 Capital of Poland.

7 March 26, 1946.

8 Stalin (see Doc. 39, fn. 31) had endorsed a coalition government in liberated Poland. Socialist Edward Osóbka-Morawski (1909–1997) was Prime Minister, the Communist Władysław Gomułka (1905–1982) was his deputy, and second deputy and Minister of Agriculture was Stanisław Mikołajczyk (see fn. 9), whose Polish People's Party opposed the policies of the Communist-dominated government.

9 Stanisław Mikołajczyk (1901–1966), Polish politician, 1943/1944 Prime Minister of the Polish exile government, 1945 revival of the Polish People's Party, 1945–1947 Vice Premier of the Communist-dominated government in Poland, opposed the Communists, 1947 fled to England, subsequently to the USA.

currency.[10] It is not right that I use PX[11] cigarettes for purposes of gratuities but I don't see why I shouldn't use cigarettes from home as long as I don't use them for black market[12] activities. Of course food parcels are a boon to these hungry people. The PX rations are very generous here. I counted them yesterday. 12 packages of cigarettes, 16 pieces of candy (including Smith's Cough drops), 5 cans of salted almonds, 1 can of fruit juice. I gave some things to the lady here who does my laundry. She smiled with delight; said it was very touching, and said "heissen Dank" which you don't hear very often. I have it in mind to suggest to General Clay[13] that an opportunity be given to Americans here to share their PX rations with Berlin orphans, Berlin old people, and Berliners in the hospitals by putting a box in the PX store into which they could drop their surplus. Many of them must feel a little guilty over the great abundance they are supplied. The snack-bars have everything from good pastry, sandwiches, and ice cream sundaes to peach melbas and chocolate milk shakes. The regular meals are, I am glad, not served in over-abundant portions but they are good and adequate. Breakfast is always served with two eggs and bacon or ham. There are oranges and apples about, and plenty of liquor at the bars. At dinner in the Harnack house[14] there is a wonderful orchestra, the first violinist of which I am told is a former symphony orchestra player. I am sending some request slips in case you or your friends want to be kind to hungry Germans. I shall try to get them to the right people.

At breakfast this morning I overheard this. A worker for the United Jewish Relief[15] was speaking. A little German kid (there are plenty of them about begging cigarettes for their papas and candy for their little sisters, 4 years old) approached and asked her if she were a Jew. She said yes and he was impressed because he said he had heard that the Jews were bringing bacon to the Germans and he would be glad to get in on it. Of course Jewish Relief is serving the Jews here. But what a magnificent gesture it would be if the Jews brought food to the Germans. Sometimes I think that is what is needed here – a magnificent display of generosity to the right people. We are so hesitant about tempering our punitive rigor with kindness. American latent generosity must be released at least to the innocent or least guilty of our enemies.

10 Because money in Germany after the war continually lost value through inflation, people increasingly preferred the direct exchange of goods. The value-comparison function of money was also taken over by goods, primarily cigarettes, which introduced themselves as a general measure of value, such that people came to speak of cigarette currency.

11 Post Exchange, retail store on US Army posts.

12 See Doc. 21, fn. 11.

13 See Doc. 2, fn. 6.

14 See Doc. 15, fn. 16.

15 May refer to United Jewish Appeal, whose donation collections financed the work of the American-Jewish charitable organization American Jewish Joint Distribution Committee. See Angelika Königseder, *Flucht nach Berlin. Jüdische Displaced Persons 1945–1948* (= Reihe Dokumente – Texte – Materialien, veröffentlicht vom Zentrum für Antisemitismusforschung der Technischen Universität Berlin, vol. 27), Berlin 1998, p. 88.

I worry sometimes that you are in financial straits. Perhaps by now you have gotten the check from OSS[16] (if not write them again). If not you have had to cash in the bonds or established some kind of credit with the banks or your friends. If I were you I'd write to the civil service commission also and try to speed up the permanent leave check. You can never be sure when you will be getting regular checks from here. These details are of course in your letters if ever I get them here.

Let me now try to give you some account of the Kommandatura[17] meeting which I attended last Friday[18].[19] The meeting was held in Kommandatura Headquarters[20] in a room much larger than that in which the Committee meeting was held about which I wrote earlier[21]. The participants were seated around a huge rectangular table. The 4 Generals sat facing each other at the center. Barker[22] sat next to Smirnov[23], the Russian who was chairman and across from them sat the French General Lanson[24] (his first meeting)[25] and the English General Nairs[26]. They were flanked by their Deputies and secretaries. Behind the Generals sat their interpreters. When the Russian spoke, his interpreters translated into English and French. When the Frenchmen spoke, his interpreters into Russian and English, etc. The interpreters were excellent and the meeting went much more smoothly than the other one I attended. But our interpreters came from Brooklyn[27] or New York and it was amusing to hear all the th's translated into d's – de generals and de words.[28]

The first question on the agenda was the question of reforming the Berlin police set up so that the respective Generals could control the orders given to the police in their sectors by the police president of Berlin[29]. The present Berlin government is the one set up by the Russians when they came in; it is dominated by the Communists who are used by the Russians to effect their general

16 Office of Strategic Services. See Doc. 1, fn. 9.

17 See Doc. 20, fn. 11.

18 March 22, 1946.

19 See minutes of the 8th meeting of the Commandants on March 22, 1946, BKC/M (46) 8, English version, in: LAB, B Rep. 036-01 (Office of Military Government, Berlin Sector [OMGBS]), 11/148-1/10.

20 Kaiserswerther Straße 16/18, Berlin-Dahlem. See Doc. 20, fn. 11.

21 Refers to the meeting of the Civil Administration Committee, Directorate of Internal Affairs and Communications, Allied Control Authority, on March 12, 1946. See Doc. 19.

22 See Doc. 20, fn. 10.

23 See Doc. 25, fn. 23.

24 Charles J. M. Lançon (1890–1956), Général de Brigade, March–October 1946 French Commandant, Allied Kommandatura Berlin. Photo with Lançon in Appendix of Illustrations, ill. 26.

25 Lançon had only held the office of Commandant since March 12, 1946.

26 Eric Paytherus Nares (1892–1947), Major General, 1945–1947 British Commandant, Allied Kommandatura Berlin. Photo with Nares in Appendix of Illustrations, ill. 26.

27 Borough of New York City.

28 Refers to how "th" is pronounced as "de" in Brooklyn English.

29 The Chief of Police was Paul Markgraf (1910–1993), former Wehrmacht regimental commander, member of the National Committee "Freies Deutschland" while in Soviet war captivity.

program.[30] Hence the proposed reform was an attempt to control the influence of Berlin Communists in the respective sectors and thus indirectly to control Russian plans in these sectors. Smirnov began by saying that he could see no reason for the reform, that the new reform would be only an adaptation of the Hitler system, would mean additional expense for new police officials, and that the present system was functioning satisfactorily. Lanson countered by challenging Smirnov's comparison of the proposed reform with the Hitler system. It was actually the reverse. The reform aimed to decentralize the police whereas the Hitler system was completely centralized. (This is correct of course). Nairs joined in by saying that the Fr[ench] Eng[lish] and Americans regarded the present police system as unsatisfactory. The fact that Police H[ead]q[uarter]s were in the Russian Sector[31] meant that the Soviets could easily supervise the police. The other Allies couldn't do this. British want the reform but of course the Russians need not establish new offices in their sector unless they want to. Barker joined in with the Fr[ench] and English. He wanted a better system of police administration. Hitler[32] had nothing to do with it. In fact the present system more closely resembled the Hitlerian system than the proposed reform, if one wanted to go into that. The increase in expense was negligible. Americans too were interested in the welfare of Berliners (Smirnov had remarked something about the welfare of the people). He wanted additional police to act as an agency of his M[ilitary] G[overnment] in his sector. He agreed with Nairs that if the reform adopted the Soviets could do what they pleased in their own zone. It was now Smirnov's turn again. He had stated his own point of view. He objected to a solution by sectors. If the Allies wanted to come into Police Headquarters they were welcome. He had no intention of controlling the Police President. In fact he governed only 8 sectors of the city.[33] He advised that present plan be retained and the reform abandoned, and the question be stricken from the agenda. Barker said No. We can't just strike the question from the agenda. We must improve the present system. "There is nothing sacred about the present organization." We have to continue to study and work out a better arrange-

30 The Magistrat had been installed by the Soviets in May 1945, with the non-party affiliated architect Arthur Werner (1877–1967) as Oberbürgermeister. When the Allied Kommandatura Berlin was established as the highest political organ in the city in July 1945 after the arrival of the Western powers, the three Commandants decided in their first meeting to leave in force all orders that the Soviets had issued during the time of their sole rule, thus also keeping the Magistrat in office. On its composition, see *Die Sitzungsprotokolle des Magistrats der Stadt Berlin 1945/46*, part I, *1945*, edited and introduced by Dieter Hanauske (= Schriftenreihe des Landesarchivs Berlin, vol. 2/I), Berlin 1995, pp. 48–56; Dieter Hanauske, "'… als leuchtendes Signal für ganz Deutschland.' Der Berliner Magistrat von 1945/46 als 'antifaschistisch-demokratisches' Musterbeispiel?", in: *Berlin in Geschichte und Gegenwart. Jahrbuch des Landesarchivs Berlin 1999*, pp. 145–183, here pp. 151–154.

31 Police headquarters were located at Linienstraße 83–85 in the Berlin administrative district of Mitte.

32 See Doc. 22, fn. 19.

33 The Soviet sector of Berlin was composed of eight administrative districts: Friedrichshain, Köpenick, Lichtenberg, Mitte, Pankow, Prenzlauer Berg, Treptow, and Weißensee.

ment. Nairs came to Barker's support. British wanted more control in their own sector. Barker returned to his demand for 2 or 3 officials in his sector with whom he could deal. Then Smirnov said: "I don't think I can change my point of view. I suggest we refer the question indefinitely to the future." Barker: "I suggest we postpone it to the next meeting." Smirnov: "Ok, but remember what I have said." And so it was postponed to the next meeting.

Here is the international situation in a nutshell. I don't think I have to press the analogy. I'll go on with the meeting in another letter. Please do not use these details in conversation until I have learned whether it is proper to do so. They are for your own orientation. The intelligent American public needs to be informed about how these things go or they will never understand the realities of the present situation.

I love you my sweet. (All these experiences increase my stature a little bit, I think). I kiss you and my sweet boys and long so much for you. When will there be word. Bye-bye Sweetheart. Edgar

Doc. 28
Letter to His Wife
Berlin, Ihnestraße 14[1], March 26, 1946

Dearest Sweetheart –

I didn't write last night because I was quite tired and went to bed without even bothering to get fully undressed. And today has been a terribly busy day and my head is in a whirl. Let me give you a brief resumé of it.

I got down to what was supposedly going to be my new office in the Military Government Headquarters of Berlin[2] at 9 o'clock supposedly to see General Barker[3]. But he had not arrived as yet so I went to Col. Glaser's[4] office and worked on a T. O. for this new branch which I am going to set up for Barker.[5] Do you know what a T. O. is. I have heard about it a great deal, end-

1 See Doc. 15, fn. 1.

2 See Doc. 25, fn. 13.

3 See Doc. 20, fn. 10.

4 Louis Glaser (1890–1952), Lieutenant Colonel, American advertising expert, 1908–1911 studies at Georgetown University Law Center, founded the Glaser Advertising Agency, Inc., in 1922 in Boston, Massachusetts, as of 1942 US Army, 1945 Mil. Gov. Intelligence, OMGBD, January 1946–1948 Chief, Civil Administration Branch/Civil Administration and Political Affairs Branch, OMGBD/OMGBS, 1948 return to the USA, then worked for the CIA, as of 1951 Office of Defense Mobilization. Louis Glaser's son Anthony J. Glaser (see Doc. 59, fn. 6) writes in an email to Werner Breunig from August 22, 2009: "[…] my father – in addition to being in military government – was involved with secret intelligence for the US within the Soviet Zone of Germany." And in an email from September 27, 2009, he writes: "The US Army awarded the Bronze Star medal to my father for his work in Military Government in Berlin – particularly, I believe, for the work on the constitution and the first free election (since 1933) in Berlin." See Appendix of Illustrations, ill. 35, ill. 53, ill. 68, and ill. 77.

lessly in fact, but I have never really been concerned much with one. It is Table of Organization. It involves drawing a chart of your organization, deciding upon how many people you are going to need, giving them ratings, etc. and then going out to get them.

At ten o'clock I had to go to a Deputy Meeting of the Kommandatura[6] – that is a meeting of the Deputy Commanders of the Berlin District.[7] Col. Howley[8] for us, Col. Dalada[9] for the Russians, Col. (?) Cherdell[10] for the French, and Brigadier Hinde[11] for the British. The hot question on the agenda was elections for Berlin – the Russians stalling on quick elections, the French rather supporting the Russians, the British interested in elections but not wanting to go too fast with them, and we insisting upon speedy elections.[12] Nothing decided. You can't decide things as quickly as all that. The meeting lasted until about 2 o'clock with Col. Howley representing to be sure the American point of view but talking far too much. The Russian was efficient but none too sympathetic, the Frenchman melancholy and intelligent (I respond instinctively to the individual Frenchman as I respond to Paris even though I don't always respond to their policy). The British, clear and incisive, careful and a little bit petulant. These international meetings are fun.

5 Refers to the Civil Administration Branch, OMGBD. "On the 25th of January a Civil Administration Branch was organized and started operations. On the 4th of April it was officially activated with terms of reference approved by the Commanding General." "Civil Administration. Six Months Report, 4 January–3 July 1946," in: Office of Military Government U. S. Berlin District (ed.), *Six Months Report, 4 January–3 July 1946*, Berlin 1946, pp. 40–43, here p. 41. See Harold Hurwitz, *Die Eintracht der Siegermächte und die Orientierungsnot der Deutschen 1945–1946* (= Demokratie und Antikommunismus in Berlin nach 1945, vol. III), Cologne 1984, p. 43; Jürgen Wetzel, "Office of Military Government for Berlin Sector," in: *OMGUS-Handbuch. Die amerikanische Militärregierung in Deutschland 1945–1949*, ed. Christoph Weisz (= Quellen und Darstellungen zur Zeitgeschichte, vol. 35), Munich 1994, pp. 671–738, here p. 704. Organizational chart of the Civil Administration Branch in Appendix of Illustrations, ill. 33.

6 See Doc. 20, fn. 11.

7 See minutes of the 15th meeting of the Deputy Commandants on March 26, 1946, BKD/M (46) 15, English version, in: LAB, B Rep. 036-01 (Office of Military Government, Berlin Sector [OMGBS]), 11/148-1/12.

8 See Doc. 20, fn. 18.

9 Daniil Sergeyevich Dalada (1900–1975), Soviet Colonel, 1933 graduate of the Frunze Military Academy, 1945/1946 Deputy Soviet Commandant, Allied Kommandatura Berlin.

10 René Cherdel (1900–1968), Capitaine de Vaisseau, as of 1945 Deputy French Commandant, Allied Kommandatura Berlin.

11 William Robert Norris Hinde (1900–1981), Brigadier, 1945–1948 Deputy British Commandant, Allied Kommandatura Berlin.

12 See Stenographic Statement made by DOMG [Colonel Frank L. Howley] on the Deputy Commandants meeting held on 26 March 1946, in: LAB, B Rep. 036-01 (Office of Military Government, Berlin Sector [OMGBS]), 4/135-1/2. Regarding disputes among the Allies regarding the date for first elections, see Werner Breunig, *Verfassunggebung in Berlin 1945–1950* (= Beiträge zur Politischen Wissenschaft, vol. 58), Berlin 1990, pp. 174–183.

Col. Howley, an advertising man,[13] invited me to lunch at his magnificent residence[14]. His Deputy was there, a Colonel Svoboda[15], who had something to do with the military gov[ernmen]t of Aachen[16] about which Saul Padover[17] and Paul Sweet[18] once wrote very unfavorably.[19] A Col. Bond[20] who is liaison with the Berlin municipal government, General or Colonel I don't know which Cherdell (who wants to go home. He has two children[21], a boy of two over which he almost went into ecstasy. He said many of the French want to go home because they are permitted to send only ½ of their salaries home to their families)[22]. There was champagne before lunch, and I had a chance to speak quite a bit of French. It was fun. I could build up my French.

13 Howley had managed an advertising agency in Philadelphia, Pennsylvania.

14 Gelfertstraße 32/34, Berlin-Dahlem. Photo of the house in Appendix of Illustrations, ill. 55.

15 Leo A. Swoboda (1898–1979), Lieutenant Colonel, American lawyer, LLB, Kansas City School of Law, 1946 Deputy Director, OMGBD, 1946–1948 Chief, Military Government Courts Sub-Section, Legal Branch, OMGBD/OMGBS.

16 City in the British zone of Germany, which had initially been occupied by American troops.

17 See Doc. 20, fn. 49.

18 See Doc. 2, fn. 28.

19 Johnson is referring here to a report from occupied Aachen, presented to the Psychological Warfare Division, SHAEF, by Field Intelligence Officers Padover, Sweet, and Lewis F. Gittler (1914–1974). They had caused a stir with this report. See S. K. Padover/L. F. Gittler/P. R. Sweet, "The Political Situation in Aachen," in: *Propaganda in War and Crisis. Materials for American Policy*, edited with an introduction by Daniel Lerner, New York 1951 (Reprint 1972), pp. 434–456. See also Klaus-Dietmar Henke, *Die amerikanische Besetzung Deutschlands* (= Quellen und Darstellungen zur Zeitgeschichte, vol. 27), Munich 1995, pp. 252–297, especially pp. 284–297.

20 Charles C. Bond, Colonel, 1945/1946 Liaison Officer Berlin-Schöneberg, 1946–1949 Chief, Police Section, Public Safety Branch, OMGBD/OMGBS.

21 René Cherdel had three children, two daughters and one son: Françoise Cherdel, later married Haour (born 1936), Marie Cherdel, later married de Goy (born 1938), and Jean-Yves Cherdel (born 1944). Jean-Yves Cherdel writes in an email to Werner Breunig from December 2, 2013: "I was already born in 1946, which makes us 3 children." René Cherdel had his family join him later.

22 Members of the French occupation forces initially were not allowed to have their family members join them. "French families will not be represented with Russian, English, and American dependents in the four-power occupation of Berlin. Wives and children of Russian officers, the only occupation families here now, will be joined by the Americans after April 1 and by English about June. 'We have no wish to bring our dependents into Berlin because of the acute food and housing shortage,' commented Lieutenant Jean Francais of the French Public Relations Office in reply to questions asked by THE GROOPER. Despite the French 'no family' policy here, their dependents are occupying other cities in the French Zone." Lynn Davis, "French Won't Bring Families To Berlin, Russians Here Now," in: *The Grooper* from February 16, 1946, p. 3. In the spring of 1946 the French in Berlin were also allowed to have their family members join them. See Dorothea Führe, *Die französische Besatzungspolitik in Berlin von 1945 bis 1949. Déprussianisation und Décentralisation*, Berlin 2001, pp. 48, fn. 33, and 277.

23 Possibly Frau Donneck. See Doc. 80.

I went back to my headquarters where some kind of an office had been fixed for me (it was severely plain, but is going to be more splendiferous). There was a German secretary[23] and the German driver[24] of my car.

I was soon drawn into discussion by Col. Glaser on the hot political question here at the moment – the union of the Communists with the Social Democrats trying to consider steps as to how to keep the Communist + pro union SPD (Social Democratic Party) from using undemocratic methods to achieve their ends. Then I was summoned to a meeting in Mr. Steere's[25] office to discuss the same question. Then after dinner I went out to see General Barker to discuss the same question. (He lives in a magnificient and modern house overlooking the Wannsee[26]).[27] My early impressions of him are confirmed. He is a man definitely worth working for, takes a line somewhat different from Clay[28], is interested in a positive program here, and I shall get along. Then back to B[erlin] D[istrict] H[ead]q[uarter]s[29] to see Col. Glaser on the matter and then back here.

Tomorrow looks like the same with another quadripartite meeting[30] in the afternoon.

I am sorry to omit details because if I don't write them to you they will escape me forever (stories at lunch for example). But I must get some rest. If I don't get to write every day you will know I am pressed.

Good-night my dearest, sweetest beloved – hug my boys for me, and I wish I could be with you tonight. I love you dearest, and I think there is a chance for a job here. Edgar

24 Possibly Artur Sanow. See Doc. 40, fn. 13.

25 See Doc. 20, fn. 23.

26 Refers to Großer Wannsee, a bight of the Havel (see Doc. 74, fn. 24) in southwest Berlin.

27 Barker lived at Am Sandwerder 27 in the Berlin administrative district of Zehlendorf, Wannsee area, on the eastern shore of Großer Wannsee. The house, designed by architect Fritz August Breuhaus de Groot (1883–1960) in the style of a traditionally distinct modernism, was built in 1934/1935 for the businessman Carl H. Bauer (1881–1941), who managed general distribution for Zipp-Blitzverschluss. Bauer lived here with his wife, Else Bauer, née Gutzeit (1882–1945), and their two daughters. "For those times it was a modern house with a copper roof," ("Für die damalige Zeit war es ein modernes Haus mit einem kupfernen Dach,") writes Bauer's granddaughter Hedda Dutilh-von Schmidt Seidlitz in a letter to Werner Breunig from October 19, 2010. She describes a huge windowpane that could be lowered, "so that one had a superb, open view of the terrace and further of Wannsee." ("so dass man einen herrlichen offnen Blick auf die Terrasse und weiter auf den Wannsee hatte.") Ibid. In 1961/1962 Lucius D. Clay (see Doc. 2, fn. 6), then Special Representative of the US President, lived in the house, which the Americans used as a guest house. See Helmut Engel, *Villen und Landhäuser*, photographed by Wolfgang Reuss (= Meisterwerke Berliner Baukunst, vol. I), Berlin 2001, pp. 81 and 83; *Gartendenkmale in Berlin: Privatgärten*, ed. Katrin Lesser, with an introduction by Klaus-Henning von Krosigk and contributions by Josef Batzhuber et al. (= Beiträge zur Denkmalpflege in Berlin, 21), Petersberg 2005, p. 208. See photos in Appendix of Illustrations, ill. 52, ill. 53, and ill. 54.

28 See Doc. 2, fn. 6.

29 See Doc. 25, fn. 13.

30 Refers to a meeting of the Local Government Committee, Allied Kommandatura Berlin. See Doc. 29.

Doc. 29
Letter to His Wife
Berlin, Ihnestraße 14[1], March 27, 1946

Dearest and my beloved:

The best thing that has happened to me since I left you happened today – a series of letters forwarded from the 25th Base Post Office[2] at Wurzburg[3].[4] There were seven of them dating from 20 February to 12 March.[5] I won't try to describe to you the manner in which I rushed from B[erlin] D[istrict] to Omgus[6] to get them, or the excited manner in which I tore through them. I have been through them now a second time, and I am comforted and a bit relaxed. Your last refers to the fact that you got my boat letters[7] on the Monday[8] before. We are therefore about two weeks apart in time, which is almost what we were when I was in Austria. It will be reduced soon to about 10 days which is about the best that we can hope for.

What you have been through – John's[9] illness, and Timmy's[10] almost departing from our midst and then his second little illness. I was in tears waiting to get through that letter telling me of his going to the hospital but I knew the ending was not his death – I had received no cable. I can imagine what you went through with John sick at home and Timmy's in the hands of fate under a steam tent, and not knowing whether you would have him in the morning. Oh I am grateful to you and to Hancock[11] and to the hospital that we still have him. Thank God you know how to call a doctor on time, and that he knows how to act quickly and properly. Tim's reaction to the hospital and to you when you came to see him; his final breaking down when he saw the train in the nursery all moved me very much. I shall be through the letters many times to catch the details and the nuances of the details which they contain. I feel I know Timmy a little bit after the stay at home, but only you and John know him well. At least now I am to have the opportunity of getting to know him better.

It is the same for John even though his care was not so desperate. Please tell him how much his father loves him and treasures every little detail of his life – the report card (the first report card) – and the first of many excellent report cards that are to come for many many years now: the practice and the regular

1 See Doc. 15, fn. 1.
2 See Doc. 4.
3 City in the state of Bavaria in the American zone of Germany.
4 See Doc. 18.
5 Letters from February 20/21, 24, 27, and 27/28, as well as from March 5, 10, and 12, 1946, in: Documents from the estate of Edgar N. Johnson, private collection of Candice E. and Thomas R. Johnson, Denver, Colorado, USA.
6 See Doc. 17, fn. 45.
7 Refers to the letters that Johnson had written to his wife on board the USAT *George W. Goethals*. See Doc. 9–12.
8 March 11, 1946.
9 Johnson's son John. See Doc. 2, fn. 15.
10 Johnson's son Thomas. See Doc. 2, fn. 16.
11 See Doc. 4, fn. 22.

series of five lessons, Herbert's[12] devotion and excitement, the continuation of the refreshments in accordance with a better system than I used to employ, the PTA[13] meeting with the dance program, the new stories, the teachers – all these fill in a horrible vacuum of these last few weeks.

And my sweet and adorable Emily. You say little about what all this has cost you. If I am devoted to you because of what you are I am no less devoted to you because of the beautiful and delicate understanding which you have of the boys – something which I shall never be able to achieve. I love you my dearest, and I trust that some day I shall be able to merit a little improvement on my "some understanding" of your "various foibles." You haven't any foibles, Sweetheart, anyway I love my dearest and I wish only to be everything to her.

I am depressed by the quadripartite meeting I attended today, the lowest level meeting I have attended – a sub-Committee on Local Government of the Kommandatura[14], discussing the question of an organization which has become Communist ridden, the Victims of Fascism[15].[16] The Russians blocked a compromise offered by the French, and so we and British stuck out against the French for our own point of view. The issues are becoming critical because political. The Russians want the German Communists to get a head start here, and we won't tolerate any strong arm methods. What is needed is little and great statesmen who at all levels are willing to sacrifice a point for the sake of international solidarity. You must urge the people at home to be patient and to insist that we do not push these things too fast. Otherwise things may come to a head sooner than anyone would wish.

12 Herbert Schmidt (1895–1987), American pianist and professor of piano, BMus, 1915 graduated from The University School of Music, Lincoln, Nebraska, 1916 Institute of Musical Art, New York, as of 1917 Instructor in Pianoforte/Professor of Piano, The University School of Music, Lincoln, Nebraska.

13 Parent Teacher Association, organization supporting close cooperation between parents and teachers.

14 The Local Government Committee, Allied Kommandatura Berlin (see Doc. 20, fn. 11), was an expert committee with its personnel structured according to the quadripartite principle; it dealt with "all governmental affairs and enterprises (such as the constitution of Berlin and the census of Berlin), all political matters, and the broad list which would be included under the term 'local government.'" "Civil Administration. Six Months Report, 4 January–3 July 1946," in: Office of Military Government U. S. Berlin District (ed.), *Six Months Report, 4 January–3 July 1946*, Berlin 1946, pp. 40–43, here p. 41. Photo of a meeting of the Local Government Committee in Appendix of Illustrations, ill. 68.

15 On June 3, 1945, Stadtrat Ottomar Geschke (1882–1957) had announced the formation of the Hauptausschuss "Opfer des Faschismus" (main committee "Victims of Fascism") in the Magistrat Department of Social Affairs, which he led. As a division of the Hauptsozialamt (main social welfare office), with support from 20 Bezirksausschüsse (district committees), the secretariat of this Hauptausschuss managed social and cultural support for victims of political persecution by the NS regime in Berlin.

16 See minutes of the 11th meeting of the Local Government Committee, Allied Kommandatura Berlin, on March 27, 1946, LG/M (46) 11, English version, in: The National Archives (TNA), Kew, Richmond, Surrey, Great Britain, Allied Kommandatura: Directives, Minutes and Papers, FO 1112/378.

But your letters came today and they are lovely and helpful. I'll write more about them tomorrow. Until then, my dearest and my boys a sweet kiss and all my love. Edgar

Doc. 30
Letter to His Wife
Berlin, Ihnestraße 14[1], March 30, 1946

Dearest:

I must write you a little account (I wish I had sufficient time to be dictating to a secretary all of the details of what is going on here) of my first little victory here. There appeared in the German licensed press here, (and I imagine there is appearing in the American press, and periodicals as well – I wish you would take note of anything you see) this morning a release of General Barker[2] stating that in the coming referendum of the Social Democratic Party on the question of merger with the Communist Party (referendum to be held tomorrow) General Barker is anxious that a free and complete expression of opinion be had, and that, in the American Sector of Berlin, he intends to guarantee that sufficient protection and supervision be at hand so that people may vote as they please.[3] I made the suggestion to General Barker, and with slight revisions,

1 See Doc. 15, fn. 1.

2 See Doc. 20, fn. 10.

3 The statement can be found in *Der Tagesspiegel* from March 30, 1946, p. 1. See Stiftung Archiv der Parteien und Massenorganisationen der DDR im Bundesarchiv (SAPMO-BArch), Berlin, Germany, Nachlass Otto Grotewohl, NY 4090/278, fol. 110; *Berlin. Kampf um Freiheit und Selbstverwaltung 1945–1946*, edited on behalf of the Senate of Berlin (= Schriftenreihe zur Berliner Zeitgeschichte, vol. 1), revised and supplemented second edition, Berlin 1961, p. 401, no. 97. The English version of the statement read as follows: "The American view regarding the SPD-KPD merger has been made clearly known in the press, namely that no merger can be recognized that is not demanded freely by a majority of the voters but only by a group of party leaders. It is further made clear that any voting conducted in Berlin on this question must be in accordance with the customary democratic principles. It is very important to me that this should be the case with the coming Sunday referendum as it is my conviction that this represents an honest attempt of the party membership to express its standpoint. Events in the past week have shown that efforts have been made to prevent a complete expression of opinion of the members of the SPD. In the American Sector of Berlin measures have been taken so that everyone entitled to vote will be afforded the necessary protection so that he may cast his vote unhindered for or against a merger." Special Report of the Military Governor, US Zone, from May 15, 1946: KPD-SPD Merger in Berlin and the Soviet Zone, p. 8, in: Bundesarchiv (BArch), Koblenz, Germany, Z 45 F, 11/147-2/21-47. The American press also reported on Barker's statement. See "Berlin Poll in Question. Voting Today on Socialist-Red Union Off in Some Soviet Areas," in: *The New York Times* from March 31, 1946, p. 20; J. Emlyn Williams, "Berlin Vote Bars Communist Front," in: *The Christian Science Monitor* from April 2, 1946, p. 7. See also Harold Hurwitz in cooperation with Andreas Büning/Johannes-Berthold Hohmann/Klaus Sühl/Ingolore Mensch-Khan, *Die Anfänge des Widerstands*, part 2, *Zwischen Selbsttäuschung und Zivilcourage: Der Fusionskampf* (= Demokratie und Antikommunismus in Berlin nach 1945, vol. IV), Cologne 1990, p. 1189.

wrote the release. The story is as follows: The Communists here, backed by the Russians are favoring a merger with the Social Democratic party into a new Socialist Unitary Party (SEP). The Central Committee of the SPD (Social Democrats of Germany)[4] is using strong armed and high pressure methods to produce this merger in a hurry, before any elections can be held in Berlin, of any kind. The kind of methods they have been using has produced a revolt among the rank and file members who have demanded, and have been supported in their demand by the City Executive Committee of the Party[5] (not to be confused with the Central Committee), that a referendum on the question be held tomorrow. The Central Committee is not happy about this referendum and has tried to sabotage it by coming out with a statement in the Social Democratic Paper[6] urgently recommending all Social Democratic members of the Party to sabotage the referendum tomorrow by not going to the polls.[7] This made me mad and I went to Barker with the suggestion that he write a letter to the Central Committee reminding them that he wanted a free expression of opinion on the matter to be held and that he also release a statement to the press expressing his point of view. He agreed (he is a man of principle) and let me write the letter and the release. The letter was delivered to the Chairman of the Central Committee (Grotewohl)[8] as he was about to deliver an address (together with Pieck[9], the Communist leader) to a meeting of railroad workers[10].[11] The letter made him more conciliatory on the question of referendum than he has hitherto been. The release this morning encourages all those here who believe we

4 The Central Committee of the SPD was the executive committee of the SPD, de facto only responsible for the Soviet zone and Berlin.

5 District committee of the SPD.

6 Refers to *Das Volk. Tageszeitung der Sozialdemokratischen Partei Deutschlands.*

7 Statement of the Central Committee from March 27, 1946, on the membership vote in Berlin, in: *Das Volk* from March 28, 1946, [p. 1].

8 Otto Grotewohl (1894–1964), German politician (SPD/SED), trained book printer, 1912 SPD, 1918 USPD, 1920–1926 member of the Landtag of Brunswick, 1921/1922 Minister of the Interior and Education and 1923/1924 Minister of the Interior and Justice for the Free State of Brunswick, 1922 once again SPD, 1925–1933 member of the Reichstag, 1945/1946 Chairman of the Central Committee of the SPD, 1946 SED, 1946–1954 one of the two Chairmen of the SED, 1949–1964 Minister-President/ Chairman of the Council of Ministers of the GDR. Photo with Grotewohl in Appendix of Illustrations, ill. 82.

9 Wilhelm Pieck (1876–1960), German politician (KPD/SED), trained carpenter, 1895 SPD, 1916 Spartacus League, 1918 KPD, 1921–1928 and 1932/1933 member of the Prussian Landtag, 1928–1933 member of the Reichstag, 1933–1945 exile in Czechoslovakia, France, and the Soviet Union, as of 1934 in the Soviet Union, 1945/1946 Chairman of the KPD, 1946 SED, 1946–1954 one of the two Chairmen of the SED, 1949–1960 President of the GDR. Photo with Pieck in Appendix of Illustrations, ill. 82.

10 On March 29, 1946, Grotewohl and Pieck had spoken at a demonstration in the Charlottenburg streetcar depot, "convened by the united operational groups of the SPD and KPD for the BVG streetcar, the waterworks, post office I, telegraph and construction authorities, the Technische Hochschule, and the Osram factory." ("von den Vereinigten Betriebsgruppen der SPD und KPD der BVG-Straßenbahn, der Wasserwerke, des Postamts I, des Telegrafen- und Bauamtes, der Technischen Hochschule und der Osramwerke einberufen.") Karl Honer, "Machtvolle Vereinigungs-Kundgebung in Charlottenburg," in: *Tägliche Rundschau* from March 30, 1946, p. 2.

have a positive rather than a negative mission, and I believe will receive a warm welcome by the American press and people.

It was brought up at Clay's[12] staff meeting[13] this morning, and I was humiliated to have Clay, supported by Murphy[14], without knowing any of the facts concerning the matter, say that the Central Committee was within its rights in urging a sabotage of the referendum. It is the old question of leaning so far backwards in the support of democracy that you support those who are willing to destroy it. Later I learned that Clay would have been ready to forbid the referendum which would have raised an uproar at home. If Clay is supposed to be kept politically wise by Murphy then Murphy has failed in his job so far. I intend, pardon the presumption, to take upon myself, with a little help, the job of making Clay politically informed.

I am a little happy over the event. I didn't expect to see my words translated so soon into headlines in the German press (the British did something similar). The issue between Soviet-Communist "democracy" and American "democracy" is becoming concrete here, and I know which side I am on.

I send all my love and many kisses to my sweet wife and my sweet boys. If it were not for them I could not be even a bit determined. I love them very very much. Edgar

11 A German translation of the letter addressed to Max Fechner (see Doc. 39, fn. 29) and Otto Grotewohl from March 29, 1946, can be found in: SAPMO-BArch, Nachlass Otto Grotewohl, NY 4090/278, fol. 109. Translated into English, it reads: "In my capacity as Commanding General of the US Armed Forces and as Military Governor of the American sector, I ask you and your colleagues to take note of the following: 1) Last Saturday General Clay issued an announcement to the press in which he called attention to the American position with regard to the intended merger of the Social Democratic and Communist Parties. In this announcement he clearly expressed that while he does not wish to influence the free choice of the Germans interested in this question, he would not recognize any merger that does not correspond to the free will of the majority of affected party members but rather an action by a group of party leaders. He further stated that he would insist that the vote on this question be held in all of Berlin and in the American zone, in accordance with recognized democratic process. I need not emphasize that this is my view as well. 2) In the *Volk* from March 28, 1946, I read the appeal of your Central Committee urgently recommending to all members of the Social Democratic Party that they not take part in the upcoming vote on Sunday. I find that this contradicts the approval of the vote, which according to my information was granted at a meeting of the Central Committee on March 26, 1946, with leaders of the administrative districts also participating. 3) I can only assume that the members of the Central Committee are aware of the implications arising from their announcement in the *Volk*. In my view, the plans for the upcoming vote are an honest attempt by party members to express their opinion on a vitally important question of the organization of the SPD and the political future of Germany. I am anxious that they should have the opportunity to freely indicate their wishes."

12 See Doc. 2, fn. 6.

13 See minutes of the OMGUS staff conference on March 30, 1946, in: Archiv des IfZ, OMGUS – Staff Conferences (copies of minutes), Fg 12/3.

14 See Doc. 8, fn. 13.

Doc. 31
Letter to His Wife
Berlin, Wannsee Hotel[1], Am Sandwerder 17/19, March 31, 1946

Dear Sweetheart –

I have moved out of my single room in Ihnestrasse[2] and into the quarters which General Barker[3] arranged for me in the Wannsee Hotel, the former house of the Nazi Minister of Economics Funk[4], now a prisoner at Nurnberg[5].[6] I move into my own semi-permanent little apartment tomorrow when the present incumbent, a colonel, moves into his new quarters. There will be a bathroom, a bed-room, a sitting room, and a private dining room where I can entertain when necessary – mostly Germans, I hope. The apartment looks out on the Wannsee[7], a huge lake in Berlin's suburbs. Ultimately, I guess, I am to move into a large house, next door which they are taking over, – not the whole house of course, but an apartment which I can choose.[8] I don't know how wise this is going to be since it gets me away from the center of things. I suppose I could share quarters in a house closer to the center. Yet I should just as soon live alone. I am very very close to the subway station[9]. And here there is every facility for eating (the captain in charge says it is the best mess in Berlin) without having to bother about help and commissary purchases and the like. In any case I shall try it out. The idea of being near the lake is attractive, especially if it is going to be possible to swim and boat, and with spring coming on here now[10] it might to be quite nice. It gets you away too from the very American center of Omgus[11] headquarters and there may be a good chance here to sit quietly once in awhile, and reflect about the meaning of what is going on here.

I mentioned in my letter of yesterday, the vote which is being taken by Social Democrats today on the question of merger with the Communists into a new party.[12] I went out with Brewster Morris[13] (a State Department boy) to visit

1 See Doc. 25, fn. 9.
2 See Doc.15, fn. 1.
3 See Doc. 20, fn. 10.
4 See Doc. 25, fn. 10.
5 Nuremberg, city in the state of Bavaria in the American zone of Germany.
6 See Doc. 25.
7 Refers to Großer Wannsee, a bight of the Havel (see Doc. 74, fn. 24) in southwest Berlin.
8 Refers to the house at Am Sandwerder 21/23. See Doc. 25, fn. 12.
9 Refers to the Wannsee station.
10 The day before, Donald H. McLean Jr. (see Doc. 20, fn. 42) had written in his diary: "What a beautiful spring day this is. For the first morning since fall, we wore no overcoats. I have the window open for the first time in weeks." Email from Jack McLean, who has his father's diary, to Werner Breunig from July 16, 2008.
11 See Doc. 17, fn. 45.
12 See Doc. 30.
13 Brewster H. Morris (1909–1990), American diplomat, as of 1936 Department of State, 1938/1939 Vice Consul, Vienna, 1939/1940 Vice Consul, Dresden, 1940/1941 Vice Consul and 3rd Secretary, Berlin, 1944–1948 Office of US Political Adviser on German Affairs, 1961–1963 Consul General, Bonn, 1963–1967 Ambassador, Chad.

some of the election booths today. It was a good lesson in practical democracy. In the booths in the American and British sectors which we visited everything seemed to be going smoothly and people were turning out to vote. In the Russian sector no vote was being taken. In some districts this was because the local Social Democratic leaders had decided no vote would be taken and in somewhat controlled elections had secured this result. In others where the leaders wanted the voting the Russians had not yet given permission to vote. At one of the former districts a lone voter was asking for the vote and was told by a gruff party leader that there was no vote being taken. In one of the districts of the latter category, two Russians stood away from the booth, there was a group of ten voters about, but the Russian Commandant of the district had not yet given permission for the voting to take place. We brought the lone voter from the first place to the second place where he decided to wait to see if permission would be given or no. In a sense this is all symbolic – a good example in miniature of two different points of view. Careless Americans are often wont to say that political democracy doesn't mean very much. In some cases it means very much, everything, especially in the case of a lone voter who is being denied the vote right in front of you.

We are going out tonight to see if there are any results.

I love you my sweet and my dear boys. I haven't had a chance to get at your letters again, but I am going to try when I get home tonight. Goodnight my lovely and dearest Emily. A kiss from me for you and the boys. Edgar

Doc. 32
Letter to His Wife
Berlin, Wannsee Hotel[1], Am Sandwerder 17/19, April 2, 1946

My sweet Emily + my boys:

Just a note to say that I love you very much, and wish you were here in this new apartment. It is a little large for one person. Any room would be too large for one person for me.

I have worked hard all day and all evening writing a report on Sunday's[2] referendum[3] for General Barker[4]. The whole Berlin situation is a little chaotic and steps have to be taken quickly because political events are happening so fast. And when they have to be taken on a quadripartite basis they have to be so carefully taken. The British, e. g.[5] think Clay[6] is obsessed with the notion of not wanting to play their game and are not waiting for us to take the lead. I am of

1 See Doc. 25, fn. 9.
2 March 31, 1946.
3 Membership vote on the merger of the KPD and SPD by members of the SPD in the Western sectors. See Doc. 31.
4 See Doc. 20, fn. 10.
5 Exempli gratia, for example.
6 See Doc. 2, fn. 6.

course willing to take it. It is clear too that some of the people in the State Department crowd wish to use me to prod General Barker, and Murphy[7] and Clay. Besides all this I am supposed to attend quadripartite meetings, start a new civil administration section[8] and consult about all its problems, and keep in touch with what is going on in Omgus[9]. It is too much. At least it is too much at the moment. Clay is a little exercised over these elections, and needs instructions. There are lots of things I should like to write. I need lots of time to think. Now I have a good place to do it. The sunset was nice over the Wannsee[10] tonight.

Goodnight – my beloved ones – sweet kisses and embraces for you. I love my sweet wife, and my John, and my Thomas. Edgar

Doc. 33
Letter to His Wife
Berlin, Wannsee Hotel[1], Am Sandwerder 17/19, April 6, 1946

My dearest and sweetest beloved Emily –

Last night I read all over again your first and second batch of letters – a grand experience. The letters are coming direct now without going to 25th Base Post Office[2]. I think I'd better change to the B[erlin] D[istrict] APO[3] as soon as this seems to be a more or less permanent job. It seems a good while since I have had a chance to write a decent letter.

I am moved into my new quarters in the Wannsee Hotel which is soon to be transformed into the Wannsee Officers' Country Club for use, also, of wives and children when they arrive.[4] I have a large living room with two windows looking out on the lake[5]. The room is nicely furnished with a couch, easy chairs, miscellaneous tables and a writing desk – glass container combination piece. There are three large oil paintings on the walls (nothing any good) and nice rugs on the floor. There is a telephone. I have also a bed-room with a handsome rug on the floor and built in closet space and a window looking out over the lake. Adjoining this is a large bathroom, with shower and tub (and the usual douche facilities for the ladies). It is done in black marble! which is so highly polished as to serve as a kind of mirror. I think I said this was Funk's[6] house.[7]

7 See Doc. 8, fn. 13.
8 Refers to the Civil Administration Branch, OMGBD. See Doc. 28, fn. 5.
9 See Doc. 17, fn. 45.
10 Refers to Großer Wannsee, a bight of the Havel (see Doc. 74, fn. 24) in southwest Berlin.

1 See Doc. 25, fn. 9.
2 See Doc. 4.
3 Army Post Office 755, Berlin-Lichterfelde, McNair Barracks.
4 The first wives and children of members of the American occupation forces were supposed to arrive in Berlin on April 30, 1946. See Doc. 42, fn. 13.
5 Großer Wannsee, a bight of the Havel (see Doc. 74, fn. 24) in southwest Berlin.
6 See Doc. 25, fn. 10.
7 See Doc. 25 and Doc. 31.

I shall have the use of a private dining room, adjoining my living room whenever I need it. The food is very elegant and served in grand manner – the best mess in Berlin I am told. From the house there is a park – like lawn running down to the lake with a swimming pool and a boat house. Last night before supper a gasoline-engine yacht left the pier with officers on board for a ride. This place is now used for transient guests of General Barker[8]. Oh! The high officers live well in Europe, and I don't see why those of them who have been through battle shouldn't. Walter Dorn[9] is in Berlin now, and tried to get me to move into a huge house on the small Wannsee[10] which adjoins this lake. But I decided not to. General Barker went to a great deal of trouble to get me into this place, and he is, indeed, suspicious of Walter's red leanings: He told me the other day that he was glad he had me instead of Walter because I was not so left of center! I was also told by a Major Dollard[11] that the General had spoken affectionately of me. After being moved into these nice quarters I didn't see how I could immediately move into others with Walter. Besides Walter is leaving at long stretches. I can have peace and quiet here. I can think and work in the evenings without interference. This arrangement is not over-pretentious as the other one is, and it is lighter and brighter and altogether satisfactory. In fact I should like to remain independent of Walter. This place, also, is only a few steps from General Barker and he has asked me to drop down in the evenings whenever I please.[12] Walter is a kind of meddler and I don't want him meddling with me.

I am afraid Barker won't be here long and this I shall regret very very much. He is not well as I have explained, I think. He told me that for months now he has not been able to sleep without sleeping powders. He got up out of the hospital in Washington and left for this job on the next day.[13] There is also the fact that he and Clay[14] do not see eye to eye on all matters. He is suspected of being anti-red and pro-British and likes to run his job independently. I should not like to see him go. You never know what you will get in his place. But I think I'll try to stick in this place.

This is army day[15] here, a holiday, and it has been properly celebrated with appropriate ceremonies. I suppose I should have gone to those at Omgus[16] but

8 See Doc. 20, fn. 10.

9 See Doc. 2, fn. 10.

10 Kleiner Wannsee connects Großer Wannsee (see fn. 5) and Pohlesee. Impressive properties are located along the waterfront.

11 William A. S. Dollard (1901–2000), Major, 1926 MA, Columbia University, as of 1939 Instructor, Hunter College, English Department, 1942–1950 US Army Service, March/April 1946 Chief, Education and Cultural Relations Branch, OMGBD, then Chief, Religious Affairs Section, Civil Affairs Division, Department of War, until 1971 Professor, Lehman College (originally Bronx Campus of Hunter College).

12 Barker lived at Am Sandwerder 27. See Doc. 28, fn. 27.

13 Barker had taken office in Berlin on October 10, 1945. See "Maj. Gen. Barker Assumes Command," in: *The Berlin Sentinel* from October 13, 1945, p. 1.

14 See Doc. 2, fn. 6.

15 "'To give special honor to our courageous soldiers,' April 6th was proclaimed 'Army Day,' a national holiday, on March 16, 1937, commemorating the day upon which the United States joined the Allies in World War I in 1917. The 'best dressed, best fed,

I did not.[17] General Barker invited me to come to those at B[erlin] D[istrict].[18] I was given a card for my car which said "Official Guest," and a seat on the reviewing stand. On the front row were Murphy[19], Clay, Barker and Admiral Glassford[20]. Behind them were the Russian, French, and British Commandants and their Deputies. Behind these various colonels, and Mr. Steere[21], Don Heath[22] (State Department). I was in the back row. Barker made a speech and the parade passed by the review stand. About four companies of infantry, all recruits I was told, cavalry, Wacs[23], MP's[24], tanks, and planes flew overhead. But it rained. The poor Wacs must have been furious – makeup running down their faces and wet hair streaming behind. They looked tough. Afterwards there was a reception. Drinks and the most elaborate set-up of food you can imagine. Colonel Thayer[25] couldn't do better in Vienna. I talked a little with Colonel Nye[26] who is one of Barker's favorites. He agreed that such a display, most of it remaining uneaten should not be made in the midst of a hungry city. The British don't do it. They have cut their rations at the same time that they have cut the Germans' rations.[27] We are very spoiled and luxurious in these matters. I also talked with a Colonel Morgan[28], who is in charge of H[ead]q[uarter]s Command and he referred to the fact that the negro troops in Berlin District were not represented. Supposedly this is because they are raw recruits and would not

best paid army in the world' receives today tribute from its country. Americans throughout the world are observing the first peacetime Army Day since the close of hostilities of World War II." "Army Day at OMGUS," in: *The Grooper* from April 6, 1946, pp. 1 and 6, here p. 1. Army Day was celebrated nationwide for the last time on April 6, 1949. Since 1950 the third Saturday in May is Armed Forces Day in the USA.

16 See Doc. 17, fn. 45.

17 See "Army Day at OMGUS," in: *The Grooper* from April 6, 1946, pp. 1 and 6.

18 In celebration of Army Day, on April 6, 1946, a parade of select units of the different troops stationed in Berlin was held in front of the Telefunken Building in Berlin-Lichterfelde, US Headquarters Berlin District. See *Der Tagesspiegel* from April 2, 1946, p. 6; *Der Tagesspiegel* from April 7, 1946, p. 6; *Der Tagesspiegel* from April 10, 1946, p. 3. Photo in Appendix of Illustrations, ill. 26.

19 See Doc. 8, fn. 13.

20 William A. Glassford (1886–1958), Admiral, 1944 Deputy Commander US Naval Forces in Europe, 1945/1946 Commander US Naval Forces, Germany.

21 See Doc. 20, fn. 23.

22 Donald R. Heath. See Doc. 8, fn. 15.

23 Members of the Women's Army Corps. See Doc. 13, fn. 14.

24 Military Police officers.

25 Charles W. Thayer (1910–1969), Lieutenant Colonel, American diplomat, 1933 graduate of the United States Military Academy, as of 1934 Department of State, 1937/1938 Vice Consul, Berlin, 1939/1940 Vice Consul, Hamburg, 1943/1944 Secretary, European Advisory Commission, London, 1944–1946 US Army, 1944/1945 Chief, US Military Mission in Yugoslavia, 1945/1946 Chief, OSS Mission in Austria, 1950/1951 Political Liaison Officer, Bonn, 1952–1954 Consul General, Munich.

26 Wilbur S. Nye (1898–1970), Colonel, 1920 graduate of the United States Military Academy, 1945/1946 G-3 Berlin District, 1950–1954 Chief Historian, US Army for Europe.

27 See Doc. 23, fn. 15.

28 Albert C. Morgan (1899–1964), Colonel, 1919 graduate of the United States Military Academy, 1946 Headquarters Berlin District, US Army.

make a good impression. But he thought it a mistake, nevertheless. It was my first experience on a reviewing stand. The display of local well-equipped power was somewhat impressive but under these conditions with the war over, the emotional fervor is not there.

I don't know how the week has gone but it certainly has gone. It has been chiefly concerned with the aftermath of the vote which the S[ocial] Democrats took last Sunday[29] on whether to join with the Communists.[30] There was no vote in the Russian sector. In the other sectors the vote went overwhelmingly against a merger.[31] The S[ocial] D[emocrat]'s have now decided to hold a meeting tomorrow to elect a new city Committee and cut loose from the present Central Committee[32], a pro-merger and somewhat tyrannical group. This meeting is to be held in our sector and I shall be going.[33] When we heard of the meeting I thought we ought to let the other Allies know, since we are going to try to get them to agree to treat Berlin politics on a quadripartite basis. General Barker let me write an announcement that was read at the Kommandatura[34].[35] I also wrote a report on last Sunday's referendum for him.[36] There have been many informal conferences during the week. I had lunch one day with Murphy and Brewster Morris[37] (a cousin of Charlie Thayer[38]) and Murphy's secretary[39].

29 March 31, 1946.

30 See Doc. 31.

31 71.8 percent of the party members eligible to vote took part in the internal party membership vote in the Western sectors on the question of unity. 82.6 percent voted against "the immediate merger of both workers' parties." ("den sofortigen Zusammenschluß beider Arbeiterparteien.") See Werner Breunig, "Berlin 1945/46. Vom Kriegsende bis zum parlamentarischen Neubeginn," in: *"Berlin kommt wieder." Die Nachkriegsjahre 1945/46* (= Ausstellungskataloge des Landesarchivs Berlin, 16), Berlin 2005, pp. 7–43, here p. 24.

32 The executive committee of the SPD responsible for the Soviet zone and Berlin.

33 The party conference of the oppositional Social Democrats was supposed to take place on April 7, 1946, in the Zinnowwaldschule in the Berlin administrative district of Zehlendorf.

34 See Doc. 20, fn. 11.

35 The statement, read by the US representative during the 17th meeting of the Deputy Commandants on April 5, 1946, was worded as follows: "General Barker wishes to announce that he has approved for the near future a meeting requested by members of the Social Democratic Party in the American Sector, at which there may be present party members from all the Allied Sectors in Berlin. By informing the Kommandatura of this meeting he wishes to aid the promotion of a common Allied scrutiny and control over the political activities of Berlin." Minutes of the 17th meeting of the Deputy Commandants on April 5, 1946, BKD/M (46) 17-220, English version, in: LAB, B Rep. 036-01 (Office of Military Government, Berlin Sector [OMGBS]), 11/148-1/12.

36 See Doc. 32 and Doc. 32, fn. 3.

37 See Doc. 31, fn. 13.

38 Charles W. Thayer. See fn. 25.

39 Possibly Henry C. S. Bush. See Doc. 20, fn. 4.

40 See minutes of the 17th meeting of the Deputy Commandants on April 5, 1946, BKD/M (46) 17, English version, in: LAB, B Rep. 036-01 (Office of Military Government, Berlin Sector [OMGBS]), 11/148-1/12.

41 Refers to the *Berliner Zeitung*.

There were cocktails before lunch, wine during lunch, and brandy after lunch, and the lunch itself was elegant enough. The Ambassador lives well but not with the greatest of opulence. We talked mostly about the political situation in Berlin and its relation to the over-all picture. I found myself at odds on some matters. Murphy is very pleasant, and well intentioned. He has a good head but he is not what you would call a strong character. There are certain differences between him and the rest of the State Dep[artmen]t crowd.

There is a lack of coordination and measure here, and in this I may be of some use. Yesterday at the meeting of the Deputies[40] the Russians had to take it. There were complaints about the way they permitted one paper[41] to represent itself as an organ of the city government when it wasn't.[42] There were complaints about the arrest and detention for about 45 minutes last Sunday of two Americans (one Kathleen McLaughlin[43] – New York Times)[44] while they were trying to see what was going on in the Russian Sector with respect to the referendum.[45] There was a vigorous protest against the Russians for permitting their paper for the Berliners (Tägliche Rundschau[46]) to printed an unwarranted attack upon Col. Howley[47], who is Barker's Deputy for M[ilitary] G[overnment].[48] Howley himself presided at the meeting and made the protest in per-

42 The *Berliner Zeitung* had lost its status as the official publication medium of the Magistrat of the City of Berlin; the *Verordnungsblatt der Stadt Berlin* functioned as the sole official publication of the Magistrat. See *Die Sitzungsprotokolle des Magistrats der Stadt Berlin 1945/46*, part II, *1946*, edited and introduced by Dieter Hanauske (= Schriftenreihe des Landesarchivs Berlin, vol. 2/II), Berlin 1999, pp. 19f., fn. 101.

43 Kathleen McLaughlin (1898–1990), correspondent for the American daily newspaper *The New York Times*.

44 Also arrested was Peter H. Wyden, originally Weidenreich (1923–1998), head of the Berlin office of *Die Neue Zeitung*, a newspaper published in Munich by the American occupation forces.

45 Kathleen McLaughlin wrote about the incident: "Various Russian observers and newspaper correspondents visited the American and other zones to watch the polling, which was relatively quiet. However, this correspondent and Peter Weidenreich of New York, chief of the Berlin office of the United States Military Government newspaper published in Munich, the Neue Zeitung, ran afoul of Soviet military police while touring that sector and, despite our credentials, were taken into custody by two who climbed on our jeep and directed the German civilian driver to proceed to the Allied Control Council headquarters about a mile distant. Excited comment there over a Rolleiflex camera, which this correspondent was carrying, led to our detention for an hour until three Russian officers arrived to interrogate us. After a long conversation with higher headquarters, during which the phrase 'photo apparat' recurred intermittently, we were abruptly dismissed with the warning not to re-enter the Russian sector without having obtained special credentials for travel and for photography there." Kathleen McLaughlin, "Berlin Socialists Reject Merger; Russians Bar Vote in Their Zone," in: *The New York Times* from April 1, 1946, pp. 1 and 3, here p. 3.

46 *Tägliche Rundschau* had been published since May 15, 1945, by the command of the Red Army as the first German-language daily newspaper after surrender.

47 See Doc. 20, fn. 18.

48 Refers to a report from *Pravda* from March 31, 1946, which was reproduced in the *Tägliche Rundschau* on April 3, 1946, p. 2 ("Der Weltspiegel/Eine internationale Uebersicht"). Among other things, it said in the report: "The US Deputy Comman-

son. There was my and Barker's little job about the lack of common control over politics in Berlin. All this (except my statement – which was written out) in unmeasured language. This protest should be well and finally but carefully made. Then there has been the case of two Communists, this week, sentenced for five years for trying to meddle in the affairs of M[ilitary] G[overnment].[49] The sentence is certainly excessive and I am sure it will be cut down or dismissed altogether. So you see how difficult it is for the powers to live together in the city of Berlin. But it is good that they can sit across the table from each other and discuss it. And they are small matters.

I hope you will try to get some help if Mrs. Brown[50] is not able to come back soon. You can't very well go on this way working yourself to death until the early hours of the morning. At least you should implement your resolve to send the washing out. You ought to get that practice established while I am away. I wish too you would get another pair of glasses, so that when the next lens breaks you won't have to go blind and sick for a few days. I am amazed to think that you have taken up gardening with such vehemence and enthusiasm. This relaxation of a firmer resolve I should never have expected. You will be having dogs and cats next. I wish I were there to see it all, and I can only express my admiration. Dad[51] can take over when he comes. Spring is about to break out here but I must say I am much less interested in it here than I am in Nebraska[52]. I should especially like to see the apple trees in bloom. You will tell me about the other things as they come along.

I am almost inclined to say that you should go ahead with the Steinway[53] in order that John[54] is not deprived of it longer than necessary. If you do not I must

dant in Berlin, Colonel Howley, recently explained to the Berlin correspondent of the Associated Press that *the United States in Germany had to assure more aggressive political leadership for the fight against Communism*." ("Der Stellvertreter des Chefs der Amerikanischen Militärkommandantur von Berlin, Oberst Howley, erklärte kürzlich dem Berliner Korrespondenten der Associated Press, daß *die Vereinigten Staaten in Deutschland eine aggressivere politische Führung für den Kampf gegen den Kommunismus sichern müssen*.")

49 Gerhard Jurr (see Doc. 41, fn. 13), secretary of the Schöneberg district KPD, and Wilhelm Kammermeier (see Doc. 41, fn. 14), head of the KPD Betriebsgruppe in the Schöneberg Bezirksamt, were each sentenced to five years in prison by an American military court. The two had tried to bypass regulations of the military government to bring the district administration under the control of their party. See *Berlin. Kampf um Freiheit und Selbstverwaltung 1945–1946*, edited on behalf of the Senate of Berlin (= Schriftenreihe zur Berliner Zeitgeschichte, vol. 1), revised and supplemented second edition, Berlin 1961, p. 408, no. 11; minutes of the hearing against Gerhard Jurr and Wilhelm Kammermeier before the intermediary American military court for the American sector of Berlin in Lichterfelde-West on April 2 and 3, 1946, in: LAB, C Rep. 900-01 (Kommunistische Partei Deutschlands [KPD] – Bezirksorganisation Groß-Berlin), no. 56.

50 Emily L. Johnson's domestic helper.

51 Frank E. Johnson. See Doc. 3, fn. 12.

52 US state.

53 See Doc. 4, fn. 25.

54 Johnson's son John. See Doc. 2, fn. 15.

choose it when I return. I was sorry that you didn't subscribe to "Retort."[55] You know how I feel about "Politics"[56] but you must not be without something to take its place.[57] What happened to the pictures I took at home.[58] You know I have no pictures except of those Washington ones of Timmy[59], and I don't like this.

I think I'll include some food package requests in case you think the consciences of your friends ought to be pricked. Mrs. Moore[60] of M + P[61] might want one. I haven't been able to deliver her package as yet because I haven't been to Kassel[62].[63] Maybe I'll mail it. I'll give this food to Germans, of course. Yesterday evening I noticed that the waiter in the hotel instead of taking uneaten rolls into the kitchen, stuck them in his pocket. Col. Morgan told me that the German keepers at the messes divide the garbage of uneaten food left on the plates among themselves.

Bye-bye, my sweet-heart. I love you and love you, and await the next letters from you. We are not so far apart temporally now. I send you a sweet kiss and many endearments. And remind the boys about me. Bye-bye my sweet-heart, my dearest. Edgar

Doc. 34
Letter to His Wife
Berlin, Wannsee Hotel[1], Am Sandwerder 17/19, April 8, 1946

Sweet dearest:

Before I forget it can you send me a can-opener? Some of the stuff I get in the PX[2] comes in cans (juice – nuts) and I haven't the slightest way of opening

55 An American magazine published from 1942–1951 in Bearsville, New York.

56 An American magazine published from 1944–1949 in New York City.

57 Emily L. Johnson in her letter from March 10, 1946: "My subscription to *Politics* ran out this month + I *shan't* renew it! However, I got a folder from *Retort*, 'an anarchist quarterly of social philosophy and the arts … is the only political-cultural magazine that maintained an entirely uncompromising opposition to the war.' I'm tempted, dear one, but I guess I'll keep the dollar!" Letter in: Documents from the estate of Edgar N. Johnson, private collection of Candice E. and Thomas R. Johnson, Denver, Colorado, USA.

58 Ill. 2 and ill. 3 in Appendix of Illustrations may be among the photos that Johnson is referring to here.

59 Johnson's son Thomas (see Doc. 2, fn. 16), who was born in Washington, D. C.

60 Hanna E. Moore, née Eberle (1887–1966), German-American art and antiques consultant, born in Vachingen, Germany, art studies in Europe, emigrated to the USA in 1909, widow of Burton E. Moore (1866–1925), Professor of Physics, University of Nebraska, to whom she had been married since 1911.

61 Miller & Paine Department Store, Lincoln, Nebraska. Hanna E. Moore was a department manager at Miller & Paine, responsible for art and antiques.

62 City in the state of Greater Hesse in the American zone of Germany.

63 Hanna E. Moore's sister, Rosalie Eberle (born 1879), lived in Kassel. See Doc. 76.

1 See Doc. 25, fn. 9.

2 Post Exchange, retail store on US Army posts.

them. I am also enclosing the request slips I mentioned in a previous letter.[3] It is not necessary that you concern yourself about these. Cigarettes are handy but not necessary. Food I could distribute to hungry Germans. Last Saturday[4] I went to a Musikabend at which the cellist[5] I mentioned in a previous letter[6] was playing a Dvorak[7] Quintet I had never heard with four other colleagues. I remembered that they had 5 children[8] and were living next door in a bombed out house[9]. I thought some candy and nuts for the kids over which they were quite touched. Mrs. Balder[10] exclaimed that I was ein süsses Mensch and insisted that I come over there tomorrow. I brought along to this occasion a Colonel and a General whom I found here at the Hotel at dinner and who was going out night-clubbing for the evening. I told them what I was going to do and asked them to come along. They decided to come along for a while at least, but stayed all evening having a marvelous time talking with Germans. The General had never been in such a gathering before and he promised to get Balder's[11] cello from Salzburg[12] by plane if necessary. The Colonel found that he and Balder both had 14 year old twins (boy and girl).[13] I was somewhat impressed with the Colonel at dinner because he was saying that we ought to be doing something positive for these people, ought to be standing for something as an example. He told me that he takes a walk every morning before going to work and speaks to every German he meets. And he said if any one has a right to speak this way about doing things for the Germans, I have. They have come very close to killing me many times. During the conversation mention was made of at least helping German kids who have no guilt for this war. The Colonel said his rations go to them, and the General said he would see that a box was put up in his PX where surplus stuff could be dropped. Evidently this conversation was overheard by General Myers[14] (you remember him from E. A. C.[15] days. His name

3 See Doc. 27 and Doc. 33.

4 April 6, 1946.

5 Max Baldner. See Doc. 21, fn. 18.

6 See Doc. 21 and Doc. 25.

7 Antonín Leopold Dvořák (1841–1904), Bohemian composer.

8 Max Baldner and Charlotte Baldner, née Lindemann (see Doc. 21, fn. 21), had four children. See Doc. 21, fn. 24. The fifth child was not a member of the family. See Doc. 25, fn. 44.

9 Podbielskiallee 57. See Doc. 21, fn. 25.

10 Charlotte Baldner, née Lindemann. See Doc. 21, fn. 21.

11 Max Baldner. See Doc. 21, fn. 18.

12 City in the American zone of Austria.

13 Twins Angelika and Lutz Baldner were born in 1931. See Doc. 21, fn. 24.

14 Refers to Vincent Meyer (1889–1974), Brigadier General, 1944/1945 Military Adviser, US Delegation, European Advisory Commission, 1945 Allied Control Council, Berlin, 1946/1947 Deputy Chief Operations, UNRRA, Germany.

15 European Advisory Commission. The EAC, which met in London in 1944/1945, was established by the USA, Great Britain, and the Soviet Union to investigate all problems that emerged in connection with the cessation of hostilities in Europe, and to present jointly developed recommendations to the governments. See Hermann Weiß, "European Advisory Commission (EAC)," in: *Deutschland unter alliierter Besatzung 1945–1949/55*, ed. Wolfgang Benz, Berlin 1999, pp. 256–259.

was the only thing ever censored from my letters). He saw me in the PX today and came up to say that when it came to feeding kids he was for feeding American and English kids first. Of course I agree to this but you can't feed American and British kids from here, and there is enough to go around if only the Americans would insist upon tightening their belts a bit. I can't understand why it is not being done. My driver[16] is suffering from boils. The doctor told him it was a question of food and that many Germans are suffering from them. There are of course insufficient medicaments and a little shortage of doctors, since we won't permit Nazi doctors to practice in our Sector.[17] His doctor gave him a little bit of alcohol to use to cleanse the boil.

A letter from you today written the 29th.[18] I am writing Norman[19] tonight telling him to hurry up Dad[20] to Lincoln[21] if they want him to be of any help to you while it is most needed. Good God what a time you are having. It isn't fair that you should be alone, without help, with everything coming on at once, and with this veritable succession of critical illnesses. You are an admirable creature, my dear, in the way you are managing all this and I love you for all this but I wish you could be spared some of the constant day and night labor and fatigue, after almost losing Tim[22] you now have a serious case of measles, and Timmy's buttocks[23], and Timmy's finger[24], after all these incidental fevers and colds. And there is no help, and the garden needs attention, and there is no Dad in sight, and the weather is as rotten as Spring weather in Nebraska can be. I don't see how you have time for it all, and of course you don't. You are just killing yourself. On top of this constant day and night care of the kids you are going in for gardening with more vengeance than ever I did it seems. I hope it will turn out that we shall have fun doing it together, if once you have the chance you do not relax into the things you would prefer to do. I'd love to see the daffodils. We will get more King Alfredo[25]. But here you are raising your own plants, carrying on extensive spraying, transplanting hedge from rear to front, and even clipping

16 Possibly Artur Sanow. See Doc. 40, fn. 13.

17 On the medical care of the Berlin population after the end of the war, see "Public Health. Six Months Report, 4 January–3 July 1946," in: Office of Military Government U. S. Berlin District (ed.), *Six Months Report, 4 January–3 July 1946*, Berlin 1946, pp. 89–100; Andreas Dinter, *Berlin in Trümmern. Ernährungslage und medizinische Versorgung der Bevölkerung Berlins nach dem II. Weltkrieg* (= Geschichte[n] der Medizin, vol. 1), Berlin 1999, especially pp. 138–159 and 194–217.

18 Letter in: Documents from the estate of Edgar N. Johnson, private collection of Candice E. and Thomas R. Johnson, Denver, Colorado, USA.

19 Norman D. Johnson. See Doc. 3, fn. 13.

20 Frank E. Johnson. See Doc. 3, fn. 12.

21 Capital of the US state of Nebraska, where Johnson lived with his family and taught at the university.

22 Johnson's son Thomas. See Doc. 2, fn. 16.

23 On March 29, 1946, Emily L. Johnson had written: "Timmy had a good big shot of immunized human blood […]. He couldn't sit down, poor kid. (They gave it to him in the buttock.)"

24 Emily L. Johnson: "[…] we had to make a flying visit to the hospital with Timmy, because he hurt his finger in a drawer – flour drawer – and it was a mess."

25 Name of a type of daffodil.

the front hedge. My dear Sweetheart this is too much. Get your old gardener back again until Dad shows up. And please, if you haven't sent the laundry out as yet, send it out. You ask me to be careful. I beg it of you.

You complain about my not being shown sufficient attention here. I have an important job which somebody has to do. I have established myself as a person of some importance with General Barker[26] in a job which somebody with a little sense has to do. Political questions are coming to the fore which have to be decided in a clear cut fashion. They cannot be decided without information. The people who participate in the international machinery have to be briefed. American policy, such as it is, has to be enforced. I am in a position to be of help here. I have easy access to all the people that matter in the determination of these questions, and my position will become stronger as time goes on. Berlin is a center of importance, what is done here has significance for all of Germany and certainly it is an indication of what we stand for to all the world. I am not so sure that it is not perhaps as important as Stuttgart[27] (pardon). But I am not being tempted to stay on here. Except for the fact that they didn't tell me I would be doing this and that accordingly I might still be there with you, I think this is important enough. I only hope I don't lose General Barker.

I'd like to taste the asparagus.

Goodnight to my lovely tired devoted Emily. I love you with all of me. Kiss the sweet kids for me. Goodnight Sweetheart – Edgar

Doc. 35
Letter to His Wife
Berlin, Wannsee Hotel[1], Am Sandwerder 17/19, April 12, 1946

Dearest –

A sweet and comforting letter from you today (3 April) telling me among other things of your wonderful gardening triumphs.[2] I wish I were there (I really mean this) to see "the unbearably beautiful" apple blossoms and the lovely daffodils and the other things that are coming along. You mention my being back in the fall to help. I have begun to think about this lately too – about the necessity for returning there.

I need comfort today and that is why your letter came as a blessing. From 10 o'clock this morning until 4 o'clock this afternoon, without lunch, I sat at a meeting of the Kommandatura[3] (the Commandants), the largest meeting on record, at which very important and touching political problems were being dis-

26 See Doc. 20, fn. 10.

27 Capital of the state of Württemberg-Baden in the American zone of Germany.

1 See Doc. 25, fn. 9.

2 Letter in: Documents from the estate of Edgar N. Johnson, private collection of Candice E. and Thomas R. Johnson, Denver, Colorado, USA.

3 See Doc. 20, fn. 11.

cussed.[4] It was really unpleasant and it was unpleasant because the Russians (there is a new Soviet Commandant – Kotikoff[5]) were so unreasonable, aggressive and at one point impudent. They have been impudent before. It is amazing to see how the western mind works. Most of the basic texts which Barker[6] used to-day were those I had written (that is why I haven't been able to write for the last few days). I have determined not to discuss these texts in advance of a meeting with one Ally, without, at the same time discussing them with all of the Allies, and for this I shall never have time. But it was striking to notice that the lines along which I was thinking were the lines along which the British also were thinking, and that in some instances they were ready to make the same special suggestions as me. And under all circumstances when you make a fair and decent democratic suggestion to the French and British, they accept without much discussion. But the Soviets don't seem to care much about what is fair or decent or democratic. They are only interested in their political aims here in Germany, and in this they won't compromise. Since we have really no basic political aims in Germany we are in a position to compromise. When I stop to think of it, it is amazing what we take from the Russians – we are inclined to forget that the Soviets are a Communist state, and that a Communist state supports Communism. We are inclined to forget that a Communist Party State is a one Party State not interested particularly in other parties or at least try to direct and control them. The Soviets support the Communist Party, we support no Party and in so doing give the impression of supporting all but the Communist Party and being anti-Communist. I'll write you at greater length about this over the weekend. It requires men of great patience, moderation, firmness and moral convictions and courage to survive this game.

How nice it is to be isolationist and to say to hell with it all.

I hope our little Timmy will be spared measles for a while – so soon after the incipient pneumonia. I am worried about you – with so much to do and so exhausted most of the time. I wish I were with you – all 108 pounds of you – my sweet and lovable wife. Oh! honey you are so much to me. I love you. Kiss my fine boys and all I can offer you is my endearment from a distance. Edgar

4 See minutes of the 11th meeting of the Commandants on April 12, 1946, BKC/M (46) 11, English version, in: LAB, B Rep. 036-01 (Office of Military Government, Berlin Sector [OMGBS]), 11/148-1/10.

5 Alexander Georgievich Kotikov (1902–1981), Soviet Major General, 1933 graduate of the Military Political Academy, Leningrad, 1943 graduate of the Frunze Military Academy, 1945–March 1946 head of administration for the Military Administration in the Province of Saxony(-Anhalt) in Halle, April 1946–1950 head of the garrison in the Soviet sector of Berlin and Soviet Commandant, Allied Kommandatura Berlin. Photo with Kotikov in Appendix of Illustrations, ill. 26.

6 See Doc. 20, fn. 10.

Doc. 36
Letter to His Wife
Berlin, Wannsee Hotel[1], Am Sandwerder 17/19, April 14, 1946

Dear sweet Emily and my boys:

I have some idea of how lovely it would be to be at home this morning. It is something like a Spring morning here. The Wannsee[2] is smooth and there are sail boats in it. The trees are beginning to show their first green and red along the shores of the lake, and above them on the top of the ridge is the heavy dark green of the pines. The sun is out and the birds are making merry on the lawn. Two blue ones of a kind we do not have in the states were gaily active a few minutes ago beneath my window. At home there would be Spring in our hearts as there is not here. I can scarcely imagine certainly that there is any Spring in anyone's heart who has any real notion of what is going on here. There cannot be any Spring in any intelligent German's heart, for his future is, at all odds an uncertain one, and the best Spring one can provide is a little more adequate meal from time to time. It is certainly praiseworthy how, under these circumstances, there is as much cultivation of the arts as there happens to be. Of course the artist can get along with little, a musical instrument, some paint, some marble or wood and he can create. At home there would be Spring in our hearts – being together as an altogether happy little crowd, and on this kind of a morning we should be out in the yard. By now I take it the crab apple trees and the daffodils are beyond their best but there must be a few hyacinths about, and perhaps crocuses, and at least signs of much that is to come. But that Spring in the heart is what I should like to feel.

Instead I am going off this morning to a press conference which General Barker[3] is holding for a group of journalists who are making the rounds here.[4] They were introduced at General Clay's[5] staff meeting yesterday.[6] Mr. Adler[7] of

1 See Doc. 25, fn. 10.

2 Refers to Großer Wannsee, a bight of the Havel (see Doc. 74, fn. 24) in southwest Berlin.

3 See Doc. 20, fn. 10.

4 The group consisted of 14 American "newspaper and magazine executives," who were on a three-week trip through Europe, primarily the American zones of Germany and Austria, at the invitation of the War Department, "to see the operations of the American Military Government." "News Executives Fly to Paris Today. 14 in Group Will Visit Austria and Germany to View the Operations of AMG," in: *The New York Times* from April 9, 1946, p. 9; "U. S. News Executives in Paris," in: *The New York Times* from April 12, 1946, p. 16. The group stayed in Berlin from April 12–14, 1946. See "News Execs Arrive Today," in: *OMGUS Observer* from April 12, 1946, p. 1; "Editors Urge U. S. Aid. See Danger of Communist Rise Unless Germans Get Food," in: *The New York Times* from April 14, 1946, p. 25. At the end of the trip, on May 2, 1946, a final press conference took place at the War Department in Washington, D. C. See "Food, Russia Seen as Main Problems. Editors and Publishers Tell of Observations on 3-Week Journey in Europe," in: *The New York Times* from May 3, 1946, p. 9.

5 See Doc. 2, fn. 6.

6 See minutes of the OMGUS staff conference on April 13, 1946, p. 14, in: Archiv des IfZ, OMGUS – Staff Conferences (copies of minutes), Fg 12/4.

7 Julius O. Adler (1892–1955), American publisher, Brigadier General, Vice President and General Manager of *The New York Times*.

the New York Times[8], Mr. Luce[9] of Time[10] and Fortune[11], Mr. Frank Gannet[12] of the Gannet newspapers[13] and others from various parts of the country including Des Moines[14], Kansas City[15] and Los Angeles[16]. Would you know what the SPD was if I mentioned it as such. Yesterday at Clay's conference, General Barker was talking about the split of the SPD in the city[17] and the editor of the New York Mirror[18] leaned over and asked me what the SPD was. He seemed relieved to think it was only the Social Democratic Party. This afternoon I am going to my first music in Berlin. Bach's[19] St. Matthew Passion[20] is being sung in a local church[21]. I haven't found anyone to go with me as yet (I have two tickets) but in a pinch I'll take the driver[22] in. This evening Brewster Morris[23], I think I have mentioned him,[24] is having a group of the anti-merger Social Democrats over to his house for supper and talk and he has invited me to come. That is Sunday in Berlin now. It will be like this on Sundays in Berlin for as long as I stay here. I find it is the same here with trying to get into a healthy frame of mind as it was in Vienna. It is just impossible. In the presence of ruin, in the presence of essential hopelessness, and more than anything else with the present unnatural life that one has to lead – away from those few who give real meaning and stability to one's existence how is it possible to enjoy anything – to wait joyfully for the arrival of Spring or to thrill at the rapture of a bird.
Later:

The conference has been held. General Barker stood up in front of the crowd and answered questions. He intended to give us all a chance to say a word but there was not time. These people are subjected to a high pressure program, which takes them here one moment and there the next according to a rigid schedule.

8 American daily newspaper.
9 Henry R. Luce (1898–1967), American publisher.
10 American news magazine.
11 American business magazine.
12 Frank E. Gannett (1876–1957), American publisher, President of Gannett Newspapers.
13 The holding company consisted of several regional newspapers.
14 Capital of the US state of Iowa.
15 City in the US state of Missouri.
16 City in the US state of California.
17 Refers to the split of the Berlin SPD into a group in favor of unification, who supported merger with the KPD and joined the SED, and a group against unification, who established their own Social Democratic party organization after the membership vote on the question of unity.
18 Executive Editor Glenn T. Neville (1907–1965) was the representative of the *New York Daily Mirror* in the group.
19 See Doc. 13, fn. 20.
20 BWV 244. There is disagreement as to whether the *St. Matthew Passion* dates from 1727 or 1729.
21 The *St. Matthew Passion* was performed on April 14, 1946, at 4:30 p. m., by the Singgemeinschaft Rudolf Lamy and the orchestra of the Drahtfunk im amerikanischen Sektor Berlin in the Marienkirche at Neuer Markt (today Karl-Liebknecht-Straße), Berlin-Mitte. See *Der Tagesspiegel* from April 13, 1946, p. 6 ("Berlin muss wissen").
22 Possibly Artur Sanow. See Doc. 40, fn. 13.
23 See Doc. 31, fn. 13.
24 See Doc. 31 and Doc. 33.

They leave by plane this afternoon for the zone. As General Barker said it would have been better to divide them up into small groups and take them around to see how things are going on from the German point of view. Nothing very exciting happened at the press conference. Barker made a little speech and they then asked questions – not terribly interesting as it seemed to me very significant. I said to one of them as we were going out that I hoped they would be going back home to tell the people what their obligations are over here, and he replied that he thought there would be many missionaries returning home. There was a comparatively modest lunch afterwards, and at it the General sat me down next to Mr. Luce of Time and Fortune, husband of Claire Booth[25] *etc*. He is intelligent and we got to talking about the lack of a definite over-all policy here. I said I thought it might be best for not only Germany but for our relations with the Russians if we come out for a policy of straight democratic socialism, supporting the Social Democrats. He agreed about the need for a straightforward long range policy, agreed that for Europe it might be best for it to be democratic socialism but contested that it would smooth over our relations with Russia. He has a good point here, and we did not get far with our argument but he asked me to pursue it in writing for his benefit and send it on. I don't know whether I shall have time to do this. But in any case this issue may be discussed in the American press, and if you come across any references to it I wish you would note it. I imagine that Luce may try to get an article in Fortune about it.

I found a State Department guy to take over to the Marienkirche[26] to hear the Bach, and it is about time to go.

I send to my dearest Emily and my sweet boys all the love that a lonesome guy like me can send. It is, I suppose, too early for me to say that it has not been worthwhile for me to return here, but despite the interest and temporary excitement, it is going to have to be a lot more worthwhile than it has been up to date before I shall be relieved of my present discontent. I love you all, my dearest Em[ily], and my John and Timmy, very very much: Edgar

Doc. 37
Letter to His Wife
Berlin, Wannsee Hotel[1], Am Sandwerder 17/19, April 15, 1946

Dear Sweetheart, my lovely Em[ily] –

The sun has just descended beneath the ridge on the other side of the Wannsee[2]. It has been a lovely Spring day. This is an especially beautiful and quiet place to return to after a day at the office, and it is going to be possible, by the

25 Clare Boothe Luce, née Boothe (1903–1987), American playwright, politician, and journalist, 1942–1946 member of the US Congress, 1953–1957 Ambassador to Italy, married Henry R. Luce in 1935.

26 At Neuer Markt (today Karl-Liebknecht-Straße), Berlin-Mitte, one of Berlin's oldest churches, probably built in the second half of the 13th century, first mentioned in documents in 1292. Damaged in the Second World War, repair of the church began immediately after the war.

1 See Doc. 25, fn. 9.

first of May, to have one of the Faltboots to go out on the lake after the day's work. The swimming pool has already been filled. But I can't get excited about it all. The sun goes down in the west, and westward from here, it is so happens, is no other place than Nebraska, and what is going on in a certain house in Nebraska I know rather well, only I am not there to check up on the details. I think, my dearest, that this coming over, after my Austrian experiences, will put an end to all speculation, as to what I ought to do from next Fall on. This is not after all what I set out to do. Indeed I thought the other night that like Dad[3] I set out to do the wrong thing. I should have gone in for music no matter on how trivial a level. If it turns out that this is what John[4] ought to do, then by goodness, the mistake is not going to be made in the third generation. The world's affairs are in other hands, and into this circle I am too late to make any kind of intrusion. I had best content myself with trying to make young men and women aware of the world and to urge them to go out and take it over. Since you can't be here, and the boys can't be here (I doubt even that you would like it here) I am lost and will continue to be lost until I am back in your arms again. This is the one big fact. I feel responsible to the world in these moments, and there is undoubtedly a need here for responsible people. But there is a need at home, also, for responsible people, and one cannot properly carry out his responsibilities when he is separated from all that gives real substance to his life. I find myself counting the days that have past, and counting the days that are to come before I leave here. I am not one who is going to decide on what is to be done with Germany, or how we are going to solve our future relationship with the Soviet Union. And my obligations are not really here. I don't think it would have been any different had I gone to Stuttgart[5]. Under the present circumstances it is impossible to do anything very positive here. The basic conditions are all against it. We are engaged in making an essentially positive, and I do not say, unnecessarily positive settlement. The country is prostrate, essentially hopeless (I mean this only literally) and there is nothing that we are going to do for years to come to temper our punishment with generosity to the right people. There is a big job of education to be done here, but at the present moment General Barker[6] can't get anybody to spend any money for the few American books and periodicals that these people would devour if they had them. There is work in religion to be done but at the moment, we haven't yet succeeded in getting the horribly Nazi Protestant Church in Germany, to get rid of the Nazi pastors.[7] It is hard to say that there is much fundamental progress of any kind, and I don't see how there can be much for many years to come. To be sure it is only a year now since the end of the war (a year ago I was in Caserta[8]), but how long is a year, short or long.

2 Refers to Großer Wannsee, a bight of the Havel (see Doc. 74, fn. 24) in southwest Berlin.
3 Frank E. Johnson. See Doc. 3, fn. 12.
4 Johnson's son John. See Doc. 2, fn. 15.
5 Capital of the state of Württemberg-Baden in the American zone of Germany.
6 See Doc. 20, fn. 10.
7 Apparently refers to German Christians closely affiliated with the National Socialists.
8 City in the Italian region of Campania, where Johnson had stayed in the spring of 1945: "In April I moved to Caserta, Italy where various task forces for Austria were

I attended a meeting of the Kommandatura[9] today which was a very discouraging affair. It was a meeting of the Education Committee.[10] I was asked to go by a Major Dollard[11] who teaches English at Hunter College[12], and who has done important work in Italy and Austria. At least he has been awarded the bronze star[13]. The man is overworked, and distraught. He is a bit fussy, possibly because he has taught so long in a women's college. Yet he is a devoted servant to the cause. He has practically no staff to work with to help run the educational system of Berlin. Three of the people – the best people have gone home. He has on his Committee a very stubborn Russian[14], and an utterly frivolous, supposedly brilliant Englishman (Creighton[15]) who looks down on his superiors because they do not come from a good enough family (meaning as good as his family[16]). At a recent luncheon this Creighton drank so much vodka that he started to crawl underneath the table at the subsequent Committee meeting. He is a wild driver and killed the German manager of the opera[17] in an acci-

located." Edgar N. Johnson, Curriculum Vitae, undated [ca. 1963], p. 2, in: UChicago Library, Special Collections Research Center, Edgar N. Johnson Papers.

9 See Doc. 20, fn. 11.

10 See minutes of the meeting of the Education Committee, Allied Kommandatura Berlin, on April 15, 1946, English version, in: LAB, B Rep. 036-01 (Office of Military Government, Berlin Sector [OMGBS]), 4/16-1/9.

11 See Doc. 33, fn. 11. Dollard presided over the meeting.

12 College in New York City, founded in 1870, originally a women's college. Men were first admitted in the 1950s.

13 A distinction of the US Armed Forces for outstanding acheivements in a combat mission or exceptional performance of duty. The medal was first awarded in 1944.

14 Refers to Sudakov, Soviet Lieutenant Colonel, 1945–1949 head of the Department of Education in the Administration of the Commandant of the Soviet sector of Berlin. However, Sudakov did not take part in the meeting of the Education Committee on April 15, 1946; he was represented by Lieutenant Levin.

15 Thomas Richmond Mandell Creighton (1915–1987), British linguist, 1941 MA, Trinity College, Cambridge, Great Britain, worked in Bletchley Park during the Second World War, then head of the Education Branch, Military Government British Troops Berlin (MGBTB), later taught at Makerere College, Uganda, at the Universities of Reading, Leeds, and Edinburgh, Great Britain, and was Professor of English, Fourah Bay College, Sierra Leone. However, Creighton did not take part in the meeting of the Education Committee on April 15, 1946; he was represented by Hubert Stanley Middleton (1890–1959), British organist, as of 1931 Organist of Trinity College, Cambridge, Great Britain, 1937 DMus, University of Oxford, and 1943 MusD, University of Cambridge, as of 1938 Lecturer in Music, University of Cambridge.

16 Creighton's grandfather was the historian Mandell Creighton (1843–1901), 1885–1891 Professor, University of Cambridge, 1897–1901 Bishop of London; his grandmother was the author Louise Creighton, née von Glehn (1850–1936); his father, Rev. Cuthbert Creighton (1876–1963), was Headmaster of King's School, Worcester, from 1919–1936 and Hon. Headmaster from 1940–1942. Thomas Richmond Mandell Creighton was a distant relative of the German historian Leopold von Ranke (1795–1886), who in 1843 had married Helena Clarissa Graves (1808–1871) from an old English family. See Karl-Heinz Füssl, *Die Umerziehung der Deutschen. Jugend und Schule unter den Siegermächten des Zweiten Weltkriegs 1945–1955* (Sammlung Schöningh zur Geschichte und Gegenwart), second edition, Paderborn, Munich, Vienna, and Zurich 1995, p. 325.

dent last Fall. The English interpreter is one of his buddies, a person named Tolstoi[18] (I don't know if there is any connection[19]). This young white Russian (most of the English interpreters are white Russians whom the Soviets suspect)[20] has been well educated in French and English and is an excellent linguist. But he treats his job as one that is beneath him, treats the secretaries with flippant scorn, and does his best to make the meeting utterly frivolous. If I had anything to do about it I'd throw him out on his ear. How can you hope to get anything done under these circumstances. If I were Dollard I should try to get home in a hurry, and indeed back to Hunter and my girls.

Brewster Morris[21] had some of the dissident Social Democrats over to his house last night and invited Don Heath[22] over. He treated them very generous-

17 Refers to Leo Borchard (1899–1945), Russian-German conductor, first Artistic Director of the Berliner Philharmonisches Orchester after the Second World War. On August 23, 1945, Borchard was the victim of a tragic accident when Creighton was driving the conductor home. When crossing the border between the British sector and the American sector at what is today Bundesplatz in Berlin-Wilmersdorf, Creighton did not react to the warning signals of American soldiers and failed to stop. Bullets from American automatic weapons fatally struck Borchard, who was sitting in the car. See Matthias Sträßner, *Der Dirigent, der nicht mitspielte. Leo Borchard 1899–1945* (= Schriften der Gedenkstätte Deutscher Widerstand, Reihe A: Analysen und Darstellungen, vol. 9), Berlin 2017 (pp. 378f.: Creighton's Accident Report from August 31, 1945); id., "Chefdirigent für hundert Tage. Wie das Besatzungslastenamt in Berlin 1952 den Status des erschossenen Philharmoniker-Dirigenten Leo Borchard (1899–1945) zu bewerten versuchte," in: *Berlin in Geschichte und Gegenwart. Jahrbuch des Landesarchivs Berlin 2017*, pp. 211–229 (pp. 226–228: Creighton's Accident Report from August 31, 1945).

18 There was also an interpreter named Tolstoi at the Nuremberg trial of major war criminals. He was part of the French delegation, had previously worked in Paris for the news agency "Agence France-Presse," and he was the great-nephew of the Russian writer Leo Nikolayevich Tolstoy (1828–1910). See Arkadi Poltorak, *Nürnberger Epilog*, fifth edition, Berlin 1988, p. 32; Jesús Baigorri-Jalón, *From Paris to Nuremberg. The Birth of Conference Interpreting*, trans. Holly Mikkelson/Barry Slaughter Olsen (= Benjamins Translation Library, 111), Amsterdam and Philadelphia 2014, pp. 238 and 250. While Baigorri-Jalón gives the first name of the interpreter as Mathias (also at http://campus.usal.es/~alfaqueque/pdf/exponuremberg.pdf [accessed March 1, 2018]), Poltorak refers to Lew Tolstoi. Josef Gofman also writes in his book "'Nuremberg is warning' (in Russian) […] that a grand-nephew of the great writer Leo Tolstoy, the Russian emigrant was an interpreter for the French delegation," according to Elena Alekhina, Leo Tolstoy Yasnaya Polyana museum-estate, in an email to Werner Breunig from January 26, 2018. "He was 30–35 years old, and his name was Leo Tolstoy. I do not exclude that the author could have been mistaken," Alekhina writes. This interpreter is also mentioned by Francesca Gaiba, *The Origins of Simultaneous Interpretation. The Nuremberg Trial* (Perspectives on Translation), Ottawa 1998, p. 152, without a first name but with a military rank: "*Lieutenant Tolstoy*, Russian into French." It is unlikely that this is the interpreter who was working for the British in Berlin at the same time.

19 Refers to a family relationship to the writer Leo Nikolayevich Tolstoy.

20 Russians who had fought against the Bolsheviks and emigrated to Western Europe or the USA after defeat (or their children).

21 See Doc. 31, fn. 13.

22 Donald R. Heath. See Doc. 8, fn. 15.

ly: cocktails, wonderful food, brandy, and thereafter a night-cap. Two of the newly elected members of the anti-merger Berlin Committee[23] were there, one Germer[24] with his wife[25], and one Franz Neumann[26] who spent most of his life under the Nazis in prison and concentration camp. He knows, by the way, our Franz Neumann[27]. It was moving to hear them talk, they are for the most part young idealists and honest too. Good Democrats who are tired of the kind of tyranny the Russians have to offer. It was amusing to hear these simple workers, tell Don Heath, who is a strong supporter of American capitalism at its best, that capitalism was but an intermediary stage, and that it would have to superseded by the kind of socialism that puts the individual first of all. It was more pathetic to watch them eat. They take an occasion like this to fortify themselves for days to come. And it was also typically German to have one of the SPD's play music for everybody, a Brahms[28] intermezzo that I used to play and a Beethoven[29] Sonata. I had the feeling that this was his forte and not Social Democratic politics in a time like this. One has to admire the fortitude of these people – and after a little while what they are talking about seems very very far away from America, and certainly from you. One wonders how long he can stand the diet.

Did I ask you to send me a can-opener-cork-screw combination?[30]

Goodnight my sweet one. It's dark outside now. I'll go on with my evening alone, and try to make some sense out of it. I love you, love you, with all of me. Kiss the sweet boys for me. Edgar

23 Refers to the executive committee of the newly organized Berlin SPD, which had been elected at the party conference of the oppositional Social Democrats on April 7, 1946, at the Zinnowwaldschule in the administrative district of Zehlendorf.

24 Karl J. Germer (1913–1999), German politician (SPD), 1931 SPD, studies in economics, training in publishing, after 1933 resistance against the NS regime, commercial clerk, 1945/1946 member of the Central Committee of the SPD and Committee Secretary of the FDGB, firm opponent of the merger of the SPD and KPD into the SED, April 1946 election as one of three equal Chairmen of the newly organized Berlin SPD, announced his resignation in July 1946, 1947–1951 independent publisher, 1951/1952 Political Adviser at HICOG, Berlin Element, Public Affairs Division, 1952–1955 head of the political department of the Federal Ministry for All-German Affairs, Department II, Berlin, as of 1956 aide to the Governing Mayor of Berlin, as of 1957 aide to the Abgeordnetenhaus of Berlin, as of 1958 aide to the Senator for Work and Social Affairs, 1990 resignation from the SPD.

25 Edith Germer, née Berndt (born 1921).

26 Franz Neumann (1904–1974), German politician (SPD), trained locksmith, 1920 SPD, 1925–1931 Deutsche Hochschule für Politik, Berlin, until 1933 youth social worker, 1934 sentenced to one and a half years in prison for alleged preparation of treason, afterwards placed under police supervision, leading opponent of the merger of the SPD and KPD into the SED, April 1946–1958 Chairman of the Berlin SPD, 1946–1960 member of the Stadtverordnetenversammlung of Greater Berlin/Abgeordnetenhaus of Berlin (1946/1947 and 1949–1958 Chairman of the SPD faction), 1949–1969 member of the Bundestag (Berlin representative), 1971 appointed as Honorary Citizen of Berlin. Photo of Neumann in Appendix of Illustrations, ill. 81.

27 See Doc. 1, fn. 8.

28 Johannes Brahms (1833–1897), German composer of the Romantic period.

29 Ludwig van Beethoven (1770–1827), German composer of the Viennese Classical period.

30 See Doc. 34.

Doc. 38
Letter to His Wife
Berlin, Wannsee Hotel[1], Am Sandwerder 17/19, April 18, 1946

Dearest –

I slipped off to hear the Schubert[2] Quintett tonight played at an exhibition called Religion and Art.[3] Do you remember when we heard the Budapest Quartett[4] do it? It was played in a room filled with paintings by Berlin artists portraying very agonized types supposedly in tune with the Leiden period[5]. There was a large Crucifixion with the hands of Christ ripped loose from the nails and raised heavenward.[6] It was made by a man named Vetter[7] whom I met the other night at Rheinstein's[8].[9] Other water colors were of concentration

1 See Doc. 25, fn. 9.

2 Franz Schubert (1797–1828), German composer.

3 The String Quintet in C Major by Franz Schubert was performed on April 18, 1946, by the Zernick Quartet, founded by the violinist Helmut Zernick (1913–1970), as part of a series of events accompanying the exhibition *Das Religiöse in der Kunst* (The Religious in Art). This was an exhibition of the Minerva Verlag in their offices at Kurfürstenstraße 57, Berlin-Tiergarten, opened on April 7, 1946, and on display until April 24, 1946, with works of modern painting, graphic art, and sculpture. See Friedrich Schwerdfeger, "Das Religiöse in der Kunst. Eine Ausstellung und eine Vortragsreihe," in: *Berliner Zeitung* from April 11, 1946, [p. 3]; LAB, B Rep. 036-01 (Office of Military Government, Berlin Sector [OMGBS]), 4/135-2/9.

4 The Budapest Quartet was an internationally successful string quartet founded in Budapest in 1917, which existed until 1967. In 1938 it moved to the USA because of the tense situation in Europe. The interpretations of the Budapest Quartet ranged from classical to contemporary music such as Zoltán Kodály (1882–1967) and Béla Bartók (1881–1945).

5 Refers to the creative period of the Dutch painter Rembrandt van Rijn (1606–1669) in Leiden from 1625–1631, during which he was primarily focused on historical painting and physiognomic studies.

6 Refers to the painting *Verklärung am Kreuz* (Transfiguration at the Cross). Ill. in: *The Grooper* from March 30, 1946, p. 3 (http://www.theberlinobserver.com/archive/1946V2/V2_N13_Mar_30.pdf [accessed March 2, 2018]).

7 Ewald Vetter (1894–1981), German painter, belonged "to the rear guard of German Expressionism" ("zur Nachhut des deutschen Expressionismus") and was "extremely committed to the shaping of the religious theme and the interpretation of human problems." ("der Gestaltung des religiösen Themas und der Interpretation menschlicher Probleme in höchstem Maße verpflichtet.") Rudolf Pfefferkorn in: *Ausstellung Ewald Vetter, Walther-Rathenau-Saal, Rathaus-Wedding (Altbau), Berlin 65, Müllerstraße 146/147, 7.10.–11.11.75*, exhibition catalog of the Kunstamt Wedding, Berlin 1975, [p. 3]. In an article about Ewald Vetter that appeared at the end of March 1946 in *The Grooper*, it says: "Ewald Vetter was the unique and notable exception of a German artist who for many dark and gloomy years continued to produce works of art which will forever reflect all that was rotten, false and artificial in Hitler's Germany." Harold Kempner, "Ewald Vetter. Anti-Nazi Painter," in: *The Grooper* from March 30, 1946, p. 3 (http://www.theberlinobserver.com/archive/1946V2/V2_N13_Mar_30.pdf [accessed March 2, 2018]). Pictures by Ewald Vetter were to be exhibited in the USA: "About 25 of his paintings will be premiered in Rockefeller Center in New York next month under the sponsorship of Life magazine. They will later be on exhibition in all the prominent art galleries in the United States." Ibid.

8 See Doc. 11, fn. 22.

camp figures and experiences. Baldner[10] was the cellist in the Quartett. His wife[11] and children[12] were there, and when I told him you had purchased the hairs for his bow and had sent them on he beamed, and said we were angels.[13] He showed me his present bow. It is in bad shape. The Quintett I found very moving and of the grand character of the later Beethoven[14] Quartetts. It does have an especially religious character. It turned me inside out in a way that I have not been excited for a very long time. I was sitting close enough to Baldner to be able to read his music. He played his Stradivarius cello[15]. If there had been an especially good preacher about I might have been converted to something. It is so obvious here that there is great need of being converted to something. The Germans were also deeply moved, and applauded long and loudly – I should have gone to the Beethoven 130[16] the other night.

I came back to eat at the Officers' Mess on Kaiserstrasse[17]. For officers of Berlin District. It was rather loud, and some had too many drinks before dinner. It was certainly a far cry from Religion and Art. The conversation settled down to the ominous talk of the war with Russia after it was generally agreed that America at the present moment is hopeless. One officer from Dakota[18], a Colonel with a long time in the officers' reserve, said he wouldn't think of

9 Vetter had "two powerful tableaus" ("zwei mächtige Tafeln") in the exhibition, "*Transfiguration at the Cross* and *Undressing,* as well as an impressive piece *In memoriam Ernst Barlach* and portraits of the poets Hölderlin and Novalis, emerging from spiritual vision and internalization." ("eine 'Verklärung am Kreuz' und eine 'Entkleidung', sowie ein eindrucksvolles Blatt 'In memoriam Ernst Barlach' und die aus geistiger Schau und Verinnerlichung entstandenen Bildnisse der Dichter Hölderlin und Novalis.") Friedrich Schwerdfeger, "Das Religiöse in der Kunst. Eine Ausstellung und eine Vortragsreihe," in: *Berliner Zeitung* from April 11, 1946, [p. 3]. In the *Telegraf* it says: "Ewald Vetter's great art of expression, fraught with the painful truth of eternal secrets of the soul, unsettles once again." ("Ewald Vetters grosse Ausdruckskunst, umwittert von der schmerzlichen Wahrheit ewiger Seelengeheimisse, erschütterte aufs neue.") M. J., "Religion und Kunst," in: *Telegraf* from April 14, 1946, p. 5. On January 6, 1946, an exhibition with works by Ewald Vetter and Käthe Kollwitz (1867–1945) had already opened in the Haus am Waldsee in Berlin-Zehlendorf. See Edwin Redslob, "Zwölf Jahre im Spiegel der Kunst. Zur Eröffnung der Ausstellung im Kulturhaus Zehlendorf," in: *Der Tagesspiegel* from January 6, 1946, p. 5.

10 See Doc. 21, fn. 18.

11 Charlotte Baldner, née Lindemann. See Doc. 21, fn. 21.

12 See Doc. 21, fn. 24.

13 See Doc. 25. On April 2, 1946, Emily L. Johnson had written in a letter to her husband: "Miguel [A. Basoco; see Doc. 72, fn. 5] got your cellists bow hairs today and I'll try to get them off for you. They are expensive: $ 2.40 for two sets, in case you are interested." Letter in: Documents from the estate of Edgar N. Johnson, private collection of Candice E. and Thomas R. Johnson, Denver, Colorado, USA.

14 See Doc. 37, fn. 29.

15 Stringed instrument built by the Italian violin maker Antonio Stradivari (Latinized: Antonius Stradivarius) (around 1644 or 1648–1737).

16 Refers to the String Quartet in B-flat Major, Op. 130, by Ludwig van Beethoven (see Doc. 37, fn. 29).

17 May refer to Kaiserstraße, today Martin-Buber-Straße, in the Berlin administrative district of Zehlendorf.

18 US state.

bringing his family to Berlin. He thought too much of them, and Berlin was too far from our security troops in the zone. Another remarked that he didn't see what was to stop the Russians from moving into all of Europe. This seems to me to be very wild talk. The officer from Dakota felt that people at home were greatly excited over the possibility of war with Russia. Is this so? Sometimes I think that one should hold any expression of views that are anti-Russian or that assume the possibility of war with Russia strictly to oneself. At other times I think that only a fair facing of the issues can ever resolve them.

I find myself taking on an ever stronger anti-Russian stand here. This is not the way actually to put it. I find myself when face to face with Russian methods strongly inclined to assert our own. And this is the way of course to shape up the fundamental issues. But what is one to do. There are fundamental issues, and as it works here in Berlin at the moment if you don't stand up for your own you will get run over. And the Russians don't care much whether they run over you or not in so far as I can see here in Berlin.

I have written about the split in the SPD between those who wish to join up with the Communists in a new Socialist Unity Party and those who wish to maintain the independence of their own party. As it is working itself out here this is a question between our methods and Russian methods. To date, although this a city supposedly governed by a Quadripartite machinery the Russians have paid no attention to our methods and have set out to get what they want in accordance with their own methods, and running over everyone else. You can take so much of this in the hope that eventually you will get a compromise. But when you don't get a compromise then you come to the point when you simply can't take any more without seeming to abandon your principles, everything you and your country stand for, and exhibiting weakness and indecision in the face of strong-armed methods. Weakness and indecision are in themselves demoralizing and only prove the way for the victory of strong-armed methods. Things are at this point here now. We are perfectly willing to recognize a democratic SEP throughout Berlin if at the same time the Russians are willing to recognize an independent SPD throughout Berlin. This as yet they show no intentions of doing. In fact they have blocked every attempt of ours to consider the question and to put the political situation here on a quadripartite basis. We are therefore obliged to show them that we mean what we say. We shall refuse to recognize the SEP in our sector until it has been officially recognized by the Kommandatura[19]. The British and French will probably do likewise. We shall indeed all along the line take similar steps refusing to compromise until we get the fair deal we think we ought to get. But as long as the Russians are unwilling to compromise this doesn't help matters. It simply divides the city into an eastern sector under the Soviets and a western sector under the rest of us. You have heard about the world being divided into two armed camps.

You have probably read in the press of the arrest in our sector of some Communists for interfering with the local government in our sector, and of the

19 See Doc. 20, fn. 11.

sentence of two of them to five years.[20] I think I have been instrumental, if only in a small way, in getting the first officer who is reviewing this case, to recommend suspending the sentences. Now it goes up to General Barker[21] and than to General Clay[22]. General Barker has thrown the whole thing in my lap for an opinion. It is interesting how things like this come ultimately your way when you are on the spot. I have read the trial record and I come to rather devastating conclusions. I think the original arrest was a political mistake. I think that the Court, in spite of desperate efforts to be fair was not quite aware of what they were trying to punish. I don't think for example that they quite understood the nature of the document which constitutes the main evidence upon which the Communists were convicted, not did they really understand the circumstances under which the document was published and circulated. That is I don't think that the Court should have found these men guilty of the offences they were found guilty of. I put these conclusions down in a document which I intend to submit to General Barker, and submit it first to my colleague Colonel Glaser[23] for criticism. Glaser takes exception to my criticizing the conclusions of the Court although he too thinks that the original arrest was a political mistake. The Court has come to a decision. Its decision must be defended to uphold its honor, and while the sentence ought to be suspended, they ought to be suspended out of clemency. One of the convicted has been in a concentration camp for a long time. General Barker will probably agree with Colonel Glaser. In any case my condemnation of the Court is now only a matter of academic interest since the important thing is to get the sentence suspended, no matter for what reason. I therefore revised the document accordingly with what was not a complete whitewash of the Court but only a pretense not to be able to comprehend completely all the legal niceties in the case. I shall however give my private opinion to General Barker and explain to him all the circumstances.

What he wanted from me (since he is inclined to believe that the sentences ought to be suspended) was a statement illustrating the fundamental issues in the case, why it wouldn't be taken lightly even though the sentences were suspended – a kind of justification to General Clay of the original harshness of the sentence. The basic issue is clear. These men were guilty of taking advantage of an unnatural political situation here (the Berlin Government is still the Government the Russians put in when they came in)[24] in order to place the interests of the Communist Party above the interests of the local administration of our sector and accordingly, indirectly, above what might be considered our own interests. It is a straight democratic issue and clear. But by getting at it and publishing it in the press you do not necessarily ease our relations with our Soviet Ally who takes offense at all action against Communists. One has to resort to the hope that by bringing the issues to a head rather than by covering them up,

20 See Doc. 20 and Doc. 33.
21 See Doc. 20, fn. 10.
22 See Doc. 2, fn. 6.
23 See Doc. 28, fn. 4.
24 See Doc. 27, fn. 30.

one enables them to be more easily discussed. But this is essentially a democratic and relativistic hope and there is no guarantee that it is justified. The Russians certainly don't work that way.

Your letter of the 8th came today.[25] I am heartsick about John's[26] eyes. I certainly never suspected they were that weak and I hope Hancock[27] is wrong. I feel guilty that we may have hurt them by putting him to reading regular sheet music without ever implementing our good intentions of getting some device made by which he would not have to strain his eyes to read the music. So he will have glasses when I see him again, poor kid. I resent not being there when the reading suddenly comes. Please tell me more about it. But thank God you are on hand to guide him into this wonderful new world. I hope he will always find it as exciting as he now finds it. Tell him I will write him again soon about his excellent second report from school. Sweet old Timmy[28] – certainly now he has been able to go bye-bye again.[29] How about the sand box?

And my sweet darling Em[ily] – when is she going to get to go bye-bye. It will soon be three months since I left. Three months after that will bring me close to the time when I shall be returning. Our Minister-President in Bavaria[30] told the newspaper men I spoke of recently[31] that we ought to stay here for ten or 15 years if we really wanted to do a good job. Would you like to come over here and stay for 10 or fifteen years.

I got my per diem check the other day and am therefore in no need of money. I wonder if you have gotten a salary check at yet. Please let me know when you do, or if you are running short.

Goodnight my Sweetheart. I love you more than anything else in the world. Kiss the sweet boys for me and many fond endearments for my lovely one. Edgar

Doc. 39
Letter to His Wife
Berlin, Wannsee Hotel[1], Am Sandwerder 17/19, April 21, 1946

Dearest wife and Sweetheart and my boys –

I was so lonesome yesterday I could have wept, and I am almost in the same state today – a lovely Easter Sunday. Lonesome of course for my sweet wife and

25 Letter in: Documents from the estate of Edgar N. Johnson, private collection of Candice E. and Thomas R. Johnson, Denver, Colorado, USA.
26 Johnson's son John. See Doc. 2, fn. 15.
27 See Doc. 4, fn. 22.
28 Johnson's son Thomas. See Doc. 2, fn. 16.
29 Emily L. Johnson had written on April 8, 1946: "Timmy is fine, still coughing, but no fever now for a few days. He does so want to go bye-bye, bless him."
30 Wilhelm Hoegner. See Doc. 11, fn. 27.
31 See Doc. 36.

1 See Doc. 25, fn. 9.

for my boys. This being apart is no good, it is no good for any noble cause, since all noble causes are besmeared with the slimy activities of men who want to push people around. I wonder how you have celebrated Easter today. I wonder if that Easter Rabbit came again, whether John[2] wanted it to come, and whether it worked as successfully as it did the last year I was there, or as successfully as last year – I wonder if at least you have had this day free from worries over the outcome of diseases or the possibility of more. I do not have to say that I want nothing more at this present moment than to be home where I belong and not here, a relatively impotent observer of a tragedy involving some millions of people, not only in Germany but in all Europe. The war has brought more misery that it was possible to foresee. It won't be possible for me to stay over here I think even should you be able to come over with the kids. This is no place for them to be, nor do I think it is any place for you to be. It is too hard on the heart. I shall not be perfectly happy in University work again, at least to begin with, but at least that is where our security for the moment lies. May be you can arrange for some time in the mountains for the later part of the summer, and I can join you there when I come home. You have got to have some relief from this awful pace you have been going. After the frightful heat of the summer may be you will be ready for some escape. May be you will want to go for the whole summer. May be you could rent a car to go out. John too will need the refreshment that the mountains will bring after his pretty terrible siege of illnesses this year, not to mention our sweet Timmy[3] who can then be bye-bye most of the time. I worry a great deal about John's eyes. I keep blaming myself for having pushed the music without being careful enough to check whether it was right to ask him to read small notes at such great distances. We should have consulted an eye-doctor about it. May be it is not quite as bad as Doctor Hancock[4] guessed. Half vision is not very good vision. I love my sweet Em[ily], and my John and my Timmy very much. I want more than anything else to withdraw into the protective isolation of their company and love. I have had enough of the world's problems, or at least of this part of the world's problems for awhile, and I certainly need to escape from it for awhile, to hear nothing about it, to see nothing about it, absolutely to escape. May be we can do that best in the mountains. If you'll arrange for the last month before school opens. I'll do my best to be there for all or most of the time. I don't believe it's going to be good for me here from now on. The beauty of the outside world hurts too much as a cloak for the real picture and of what is Germany today and the beauty of the outside world is no satisfaction when the heart demands the beauty – the internal beauty – which only you and the kids give to my world.

I am low, I guess, because for one thing General Barker[5] is going and in his place comes a new general, a General Keating[6], who has no experience in this kind of work and who, I understand, has no other desire but to go home himself.[7] General Barker has principles, experience, and is himself a fighter. It will

2 Johnson's son John. See Doc. 2, fn. 15.

3 Johnson's son Thomas. See Doc. 2, fn. 16.

4 See Doc. 4, fn. 22.

5 See Doc. 20, fn. 10.

6 Frank A. Keating (1895–1973), Major General, May–October 1946 Commanding General, US Headquarters Berlin District, US Commandant, Allied Kommandatura Berlin, October 1946–1947 Assistant Deputy Military Governor for Operations and

be a worthy task to do what I can to help the new general. But somehow or another I have become personally devoted to Barker in the little time that I have been permitted to work for him, and I don't like to see him go. He is one of the few in high places here who does have any principles. The enclosed photograph is taken at the entrance of his house[8].[9] You can see through to the big plate glass window in his living room and through it to the Wannsee[10]. I have under my arm the documents on the trial of the Communists.[11] The Colonel is Glaser[12], the head of the Civil Administration Section in B[erlin] D[istrict][13]. I have the same view of the lake from my window.[14]

I am low too, I guess, because of two political meetings I have attended yesterday and today. Yesterday it was a meeting of the anti-merger Social Democrats who gathered, to the number of some two thousand to listen to a Dr. Schumacher[15], the leader of the Social Democrats in the western and southern parts of Germany.[16] A gang of 20 to 30 pro-merger Social Democrats tried to

Deputy Commanding General, OMGUS, US Commandant, Allied Kommandatura Berlin, 1947 Deputy Military Governor, Germany (US), Commanding General, OMGUS, 1950 Chief US Military Adviser to Korea. See Appendix of Illustrations, ill. 27 and ill. 28.

7 Harold Hurwitz writes: "Barker was relieved at the beginning of May by General Frank Keating, a politically disinterested organization man who was making a career for himself under Clay." ("Barker wurde Anfang Mai von General Frank Keating abgelöst, einem politisch desinteressierten Organisationsmenschen, der unter Clay Karriere machte.") Harold Hurwitz in collaboration with Andreas Büning/Johannes-Berthold Hohmann/Klaus Sühl/Ingolore Mensch-Khan, *Die Anfänge des Widerstands*, part 2, *Zwischen Selbsttäuschung und Zivilcourage: Der Fusionskampf* (= Demokratie und Antikommunismus in Berlin nach 1945, vol. IV), Cologne 1990, p. 1257.

8 Barker lived at Am Sandwerder 27. See Doc. 28, fn. 27.

9 Photo in Appendix of Illustrations, ill. 53.

10 Refers to Großer Wannsee, a bight of the Havel (see Doc. 74, fn. 24) in southwest Berlin.

11 See Doc. 38.

12 See Doc. 28, fn. 4.

13 Civil Administration Branch, OMGBD. See Doc. 28, fn. 5.

14 View of Großer Wannsee from the terrace of the former Wannsee Hotel in Appendix of Illustrations, ill. 47.

15 Kurt Schumacher (1895–1952), German politician (SPD), 1926 Dr. rer. pol., University of Münster, 1930–1933 member of the Reichstag, 1933–1944 imprisonment in a concentration camp, 1945 establishment of the so-called Büro Dr. Schumacher, Hannover, which became the "Büro der Westzonen" (Office of the Western Zones) in February 1946, 1945–May 1946 authorized representative of the Sozialdemokratische Partei for the Western zones, May 1946–1952 Chairman of the SPD, 1949–1952 member of the Bundestag, Chairman of the SPD faction.

16 On the event with Schumacher at the Mercedes-Palast in the Berlin administrative district of Wedding, see verbatim minutes of the functionary conference of the SPD opposition on April 20, 1946, in: LAB, C Rep. 900-02 (Sozialdemokratische Partei Deutschlands [SPD] – Bezirksorganisation Berlin [1945/46]), no. 12; "Sozialismus und Demokratie untrennbar. Dr. Schumacher auf der Funktionärversammlung der SPD," in: *Der Tagesspiegel* from April 21, 1946, p. 2; "SPD will sozialistischen Neubau Deutschlands. Programmatische Erklärungen Dr. Schumachers," in: *Telegraf* from April 21, 1946, pp. 1f.; "Organisierte Versammlungs-Störung," in: *Telegraf* from April 28, 1946, p. 3.

break up the meeting in good Nazi fashion but the ring leaders were thrown out of the meeting and it then went on peacefully.[17] These are the people we ought to be supporting because they stand for the kind of democratic decency which we stand for. But we are doing nothing to support them. We won't even let them have a newspaper yet.[18]

This morning I went to a meeting where the union between the Social Democrats and the Communists of the Russian Zone and of Berlin was noted – that is the formation of the SEP which we, the Allies in Berlin, have not yet recognized![19] It was well prepared for – ran off as smoothly as a Nazi meeting, though I had the impression that the audience were a little sick of the enforced enthusiasm. In the royal box sat General Kotikoff[20] and all the speakers addressed him first. He is the Russian Commandant who at the last Kommandatura[21] meeting[22], had the effrontery to state, that he could not talk about Berlin politics because he was so newly arrived on the scene. Alongside of him sat the Communist major of Berlin, Dr. Werner[23]. On the platform sat the leader of the

17 Schumacher reacted to the disturbance during his presentation with these words, among others: "I noticed with pleasure that there is a group of democracy apprentices in the room." ("Ich habe mit Vergnügen festgestellt, dass ein Trupp von Lehrlingen der Demokratie im Saal ist.") Verbatim minutes of the functionary conference of the SPD opposition on April 20, 1946, in: LAB, C Rep. 900-02 (Sozialdemokratische Partei Deutschlands [SPD] – Bezirksorganisation Berlin [1945/46]), no. 12. As the *Telegraf* later reported, "the troublemakers [got into] the meeting with reprinted, *forged admission tickets*." ("[fand] der Störtrupp mit nachgedruckten, also *gefälschten Eintrittskarten* Einlass in die Versammlung.") "Organisierte Versammlungs-Störung," in: *Telegraf* from April 28, 1946, p. 3.

18 The newspaper *Der Sozialdemokrat. Organ der Sozialdemokratie Groß-Berlin* was published beginning on June 3, 1946, with a British license. The licensing of the SPD organ "was part of a media policy package of the CCG (BE) to support Social Democratic forces in Berlin." ("gehörte zu einem pressepolitischen Paket der CCG (BE), die sozialdemokratischen Kräfte in Berlin zu unterstützen.") Susanne Grebner, *Der Telegraf. Entstehung einer SPD-nahen Lizenzzeitung in Berlin 1946 bis 1950* (= Kommunikationsgeschichte, vol. 13), Münster, Hamburg, and London 2002, p. 180. *Vorwärts. Berliner Volksblatt*, had already been published since April 9, 1946, with a Soviet license, initially edited by the Greater Berlin organizational committee of the SPD and KPD for the merger of the two parties, and then by the Berlin district committee of the SED.

19 On April 21/22, 1946, the party unification conference of the KPD and SPD took place in the former venue of the Deutsche Staatsoper, at the Admiralspalast in the Berlin administrative district of Mitte, Friedrichstraße 101/102. See *Protokoll des Vereinigungsparteitages der Sozialdemokratischen Partei Deutschlands (SPD) und der Kommunistischen Partei Deutschlands (KPD) am 21. und 22. April 1946 in der Staatsoper "Admiralspalast" in Berlin*, Berlin 1946. Photo of the party unification conference in Appendix of Illustrations, ill. 82.

20 Alexander Georgievich Kotikov. See Doc. 35, fn. 5.

21 See Doc. 20, fn. 11.

22 See minutes of the 11th meeting of the Commandants on April 12, 1946, BKC/M (46) 11, English version, in: LAB, B Rep. 036-01 (Office of Military Government, Berlin Sector [OMGBS]), 11/148-1/10.

23 Oberbürgermeister Dr. Arthur Werner (see Doc. 27, fn. 30) did not belong to any political party. He saw himself in the role of a neutral and all-around loyal "city president of Berlin" and essentially limited himself to the functions of a civic repre-

Communist Party here, Ullbrecht[24], who with his goatee looks nothing so much as like Lenin[25].[26] Other Communist leaders were there, including Pieck[27]. Ullbrecht and Pieck are Moscow trained. And alongside of them the Social Democratic leaders (Grotewohl[28], Fechner[29], etc.) who have been whipped and forced into the union, in large part, I think, by Russian methods and aid, and have tried thus to sell away their party. It was clear to see that henceforth they would be at the mercy of the Communists, whom I am coming to hate here, not because of their program, but because of their dirty, tricky, methods. I couldn't stand it, and left after a couple hours. As I went out, I noticed a book stall of the press of the Red Army[30] in Germany, at which was for sale a marvelous collection of books and pamphlets about Russia, Stalin[31] and Communism.

sentative of the Magistrat. Actual leadership of the city government was in the hands of the Communists, which Werner never called into question. See Dieter Hanauske, "'Ein ehrlicher Mann, aber etwas naiv.' Arthur Werner – Berliner Oberbürgermeister von 1945/46," in: *Der Bär von Berlin. Jahrbuch 2002 des Vereins für die Geschichte Berlins*, pp. 131–160.

24 Walter Ulbricht (1893–1973), German politician (KPD/SED), 1912 SPD, 1917 USPD, 1919 KPD, 1928–1933 member of the Reichstag, 1929–1946 member of the Politburo of the Central Committee of the KPD, 1933–1945 emigration, returned to Berlin from Soviet exile in 1945 as head of the "Ulbricht Group" of German Communists, organized the rebuilding of the KPD, 1946 SED, 1946–1971 Deputy Chairman, Secretary General and First Secretary of the Central Committee of the SED, 1949–1960 Deputy Minister-President of the GDR, 1960–1973 Chairman of the State Council of the GDR. Photo with Ulbricht in Appendix of Illustrations, ill. 82.

25 Vladimir Ilyich Lenin, originally Ulyanov (1870–1924), Russian revolutionary, leader of the 1917 October Revolution in Russia, Chairman of the Council of People's Commissars, founder of the Soviet Union and its first head of government.

26 Ulbricht apparently wanted to copy Lenin with his beard style.

27 See Doc. 30, fn. 9.

28 See Doc. 30, fn. 8.

29 Max Fechner (1892–1973), German politician (SPD/SED), trained toolmaker, 1911 SPD, 1917 USPD, 1922 once again SPD, 1925–1928 Stadtverordneter in Berlin, 1928–1933 member of the Prussian Landtag, 1933/34 Oranienburg concentration camp, 1934–1945 independent grocer in Berlin-Neukölln, 1944 Sachsenhausen concentration camp, 1945 cosigner of the call to found the SPD, 1945–April 1946 Cochairman of the Central Committee of the SPD for the Soviet zone, advocate of the merger of the KPD and SPD into the SED, 1946 SED, April 1946–1953 member of the central SED Executive Committee/Central Committee of the SED, October 1946–1948 member of the Stadtverordnetenversammlung of Greater Berlin, 1949–1953 Minister of Justice of the GDR, removal from office after the uprising on June 17, 1953, arrest, expulsion from the SED, detention pending trial at Berlin-Hohenschönhausen, sentenced by the Supreme Court of the GDR to eight years in prison, 1956 early release from prison, 1958 readmission into the SED. Photo with Fechner in Appendix of Illustrations, ill. 82.

30 Until 1946 the official designation for the armed forces of the Soviet Union, founded in 1918, subsequently renamed "Soviet Army."

31 Joseph Vissarionovich Stalin, originally Dzhugashvili (1879–1953), Soviet politician, 1922–1953 Secretary General of the Central Committee of the Communist Party of the Soviet Union, as of 1941 Chairman of the Council of People's Commissars and as of 1946 of the Council of Ministers of the Soviet Union, 1943 Marshal and 1945 Generalissimus of the Soviet Union.

And where do we stand in this fight? Neutral! What does the liberal tradition of American democracy mean to these people? Nothing. They get up on the platform and damn the western powers (particularly the British today) as they please. What are we doing to present the American picture in a positive light? Nothing. Don't we care whether the real democrats have a chance here or not? Why did we fight this war? As I remember it was for the American way of life or at least it had something to do about democracy? If we don't care about democracy in Europe then we'd better get the hell out of here and turn the place over to the Communists and the Soviets, and if we do we had better organize ourselves in some positive way and make a display, and a protest. As it is we are permitting Russia to run away with the game here. There will be a reaction I'm sure but at the moment it is not encouraging. And if the leaders here don't want to fight there is not much the rest of us can do? What do the American people want to do.

I'm sick of it. May a democracy that is so spineless deserves to die.

I went sailing on the lake[32] yesterday afternoon to cure myself but it only helped for a while. I love you very much, you and my boys. Edgar

Doc. 40
Letter to His Wife
Berlin, Wannsee Hotel[1], Am Sandwerder 17/19, April 27, 1946

Dear Sweetheart –

I have 3 wonderful letters before me which I have read many times but have not answered.[2] In fact I have not written, I believe, since last Sunday[3]. Not because I have not wanted to write. I want to write every night, but, for some reason it has been an especially hectic week. 3 of the five evenings were taken upon with engagements, one with work, and last night I was so discouraged and tired by a long all day session at the Kommandatura[4] that I couldn't do much else but go to bed after looking at a few German papers. I shall do better henceforth. By not giving you an account of each day, I not only keep you uninformed but I do not keep up the record for whatever use that might be. I ought to be writing some kind of a journal of goings on here because they all have some slight significance, and the details when not put down are lost. Since I don't

32 Refers to Großer Wannsee, a bight of the Havel (see Doc. 74, fn. 24) in southwest Berlin.

1 See Doc. 25, fn. 9.
2 Emily L. Johnson's letters from April 10, 14, and 17, 1946, in: Documents from the estate of Edgar N. Johnson, private collection of Candice E. and Thomas R. Johnson, Denver, Colorado, USA.
3 April 21, 1946. See Doc. 39.
4 See Doc. 20, fn. 11; minutes of the 12th meeting of the Commandants on April 26, 1946, BKC/M (46) 12, English version, in: LAB, B Rep. 036-01 (Office of Military Government, Berlin Sector [OMGBS]), 11/148-1/10.
5 April 22, 1946.
6 Franz L. Neumann. See Doc. 1, fn. 8.

write a journal letters to you fulfill somewhat that function, and I fancy that you do not mind having a journal written to you as long as it has some interest.

Monday[5] I went to call on Franz's[6] friends the Suhr's[7] who, in fact, asked me to call.[8] There were 2 others there[9], an editor of a Berlin paper, British licensed, The Telegraph[10] and his rather wild-eyed wife[11]. Somehow or another the eve-

7 Otto and Susanne Suhr, who had been married in 1921; Otto Suhr (1894–1957), German politician (SPD), 1914–1920 studies in history, economics, and journalism at the University of Leipzig (interrupted by military service during the war), 1919 SPD, 1923 Dr. phil., University of Leipzig, 1925–1933 head of the economic policy department of the Allgemeiner Freier Angestelltenbund, Berlin, 1926–1933 Lecturer at the Deutsche Hochschule für Politik, 1933–1935 unemployed, afterwards worked as a freelance writer and expert in questions of packaging for the Reich Board for Economic Efficiency, 1945 head of the Referat Druck und Papier, Magistrat of the City of Berlin, Department of Economics, 1945–March 1946 senior department head in the German Central Administration of Industry in the Soviet zone, August 1946–1947 Secretary General (previously Acting Secretary General) of the newly organized Berlin SPD, November 1946–1955 head of the Stadtverordnetenversammlung of Greater Berlin/President of the Abgeordnetenhaus of Berlin, 1948/1949 Berlin representative in the Parlamentarischer Rat (parliamentary council) in Bonn, 1948–1955 Director of the Deutsche Hochschule für Politik, 1949–1952 member of the Bundestag (Berlin representative), as of 1952 Honorary Professor of Political Theory at the Freie Universität Berlin, 1955–1957 Governing Mayor of Berlin; Susanne Suhr, née Pawel (1893–1989), German librarian, journalist, 1917–1921 studies in history and German at the University of Munich and University of Leipzig, 1922 SPD, 1946–1950 *Telegraf* editor, 1948–1954 member of the Bezirksverordnetenversammlung Berlin-Wilmersdorf, 1958–1963 member of the Abgeordnetenhaus of Berlin. Photo of Otto Suhr in Appendix of Illustrations, ill. 80.

8 Franz L. Neumann had already been part of Otto and Susanne Suhr's circle of friends in the 1920s. See Susanne Suhr, "Biographische Einleitung," in: *Otto Suhr. Eine Auswahl aus Reden und Schriften*, with a biographical introduction by Susanne Suhr, preface by Ernst Fraenkel, Tübingen 1967, pp. 3–50, here p. 15; Henrike Hülsbergen, "Otto Suhr," in: *Stadtoberhäupter. Biographien Berliner Bürgermeister im 19. und 20. Jahrhundert*, ed. Wolfgang Ribbe (= Berlinische Lebensbilder, vol. 7), Berlin 1992, pp. 465–483, here p. 471; Gunter Lange, *Otto Suhr. Im Schatten von Ernst Reuter und Willy Brandt. Eine Biographie* (Reihe Praktische Demokratie), Bonn 1994, pp. 71f.

9 The gathering probably took place at the home of Otto and Susanne Suhr at Sodener Straße 36 in the Berlin administrative district of Wilmersdorf (see registration with police authorities, October 26, 1945, in: LAB, E Rep. 200-17 [Nachlass Otto Suhr], no. 528; registration card Otto Suhr, in: LAB, B Rep. 021 [Einwohnermeldeamt Berlin]).

10 The *Telegraf*, a newspaper linked to the SPD, published by the journalist Arno Scholz (1904–1971). Scholz received the British license on March 15, 1946. See "Britische Lizenz für neue Zeitung. Berlin erhält einen 'Telegraf,'" in: *Der Berliner* from March 16, 1946, p. 2. Otto Suhr was supposed to write articles about current economic problems for the *Telegraf*. See letter from Arno Scholz to Otto Suhr from April 9, 1946, in: LAB, E Rep. 200-17 (Nachlass Otto Suhr), no. 662; Gunter Lange, *Otto Suhr. Im Schatten von Ernst Reuter und Willy Brandt. Eine Biographie* (Reihe Praktische Demokratie), Bonn 1994, p. 125. Susanne Suhr became an editor for *Telegraf*. See Susanne Grebner, *Der Telegraf. Entstehung einer SPD-nahen Lizenzzeitung in Berlin 1946 bis 1950* (= Kommunikationsgeschichte, vol. 13), Münster, Hamburg, and London 2002, p. 143.

11 Probably Arno Scholz's partner at the time, Meta Strauß (1904–1959), whom he married in 1952.

ning left a bad taste in my mouth. I had in my brief case a bottle of Canadian Club Whiskey which I had purchased as a part of my ration at Harnack House[12]. It occurred to me that it might be nice to offer these people a drink. So I did but evidently they thought I was offering them the whole bottle for they didn't offer to give it to me as I left. Then of course I had to offer to take the editor and his wife home, and this was somewhat out of the way. Meanwhile my driver, a good-natured, some-what absent-minded Berliner by the name of Sanow[13], had had little to eat and when I arrived here at the hotel I had to get him some chocolate. So I was furnishing to Germans food, drink, and transportation. This I would not have minded if I had had the feeling that it was somehow given to people who understood the American point of view, or were trying to understand it, and were willing to make some sacrifice to avail themselves of its privileges. But I came home with the feeling that I had simply been exploited, that feeling while so many Americans have with respect to what we do over here, that I had been soft when I should have told these people off in some way or another.

Suhr is a left-wing Social Democrat who has recently given up a job with the Russians because he couldn't withstand the pressure and wanted to go along with the anti-merger Social Democrats.[14] He, and I get the impression, many like-minded Germans, want all that we have to give them by way of freedom – and therefore they don't like Communist-Russian methods, but at the same time they want all that is to be had from the Russians by way of a radical social policy. Suhr was quite critical of our policy in general, and I go along with him to some extent. We are not offering to German workers a radical land reform program, a speedy program of nationalization and socialization, and a thoroughgoing program of workers' participation in the management of industry. But I told him that we were doing pretty well considering the fact that we had no Socialists in America. There is some kind of a compromise between these two but it is not to be had here under present circumstances, nor has the compromise been yet worked out anywhere, not even in England as yet. What disturbed me was that these Germans, I felt, would in the last analysis prefer what the Russians had to offer rather than what we had to offer – that is, they would prefer to give up their freedom again. After 12 years of the Nazis I should expect them to want to learn in the other direction if a choice is to be made.

The fact is, I guess, and I have often said it to you, that we can't expect to make much of our impression upon the German worker as long as we are in the state of economic development that we happen to be in at home. There is no longer any room in Europe for the kind of monopoly capitalism which we still have. So, and it is often said in the German press, they equate our freedom, which is genuine and real here under the circumstances, with freedom for reactionaries, (this is the Communist-Russian slogan), and our democracy, with the opportunity for the boys who ran Germany into the ground in 1914 and 1933

12 See Doc. 15, fn. 16.

13 Artur Sanow (1910–1984), chauffeur. See Appendix of Illustrations, ill. 44, ill. 45, and ill. 49.

14 Suhr had been a senior department head in the German Central Administration of Industry in the Soviet zone.

and 1939 to come to the front again and run it into the ground again. That is why we need here a positive policy which will go as far as is possible to the left but still proclaims and implements the few things we are able to stand for. We need books about America, and people who can speak to Germans in German about America. We need to introduce into the educational system a breath of the fresh air present in our schools and universities, into the German press some of the virtues of our press (and there are some) and into German political life some of the tolerance, the give and take which we do have. This it seems to me is what the Germans need now. They don't need Communism at the moment, certainly, if they need it at all.

On Tuesday[15] I went to a dinner given by Col. Glaser[16] at Col. Howley's[17] house[18] for the Local Government Committee of B[erlin] D[istrict][19]. It was accordingly to be an international meeting. But the Russians, although invited, and having accepted, did not show up. (They often do this) So it was only tripartite. I sat next to an English girl interpreter at dinner, whose Mother was Swiss, and who does the French interpreting, and she was quiet, modest and intelligent. Cocktails were served before dinner, champagne at dinner and Benedictine[20] afterwards. On the table at dinner were lovely cherry blossoms or a kind of flowering almond, I do not know which. I spent the evening talking to Americans, unfortunately, about recent developments here and did not see much of the British or the French, who were not, under any circumstances, particularly distinguished representatives. This may be only self defense. In any case I don't like the tone Glaser sets at his parties. He is an advertising man,[21] as I may have told you, and rather proud of it. Yet it seems he doesn't want to go back to advertising and will stay here on a kind of vacationing lark. Besides he has said some not very nice things about his wife[22] who is, however, coming over here. He is the head of the Civil Administration Branch in B[erlin] D[istrict][23].

Thursday[24] I had what I thought was going to be my prospective German teacher out here to dinner in return for a similar favor. She is a middle aged woman who has been doing Russian interpretation for the English, and is in fact an English citizen. But she is Russian born (white Russian) and has studied a lot in Germany. But now I learn that she has been given work with my opposite number, if one may so speak, in the British Office of Political Affairs, a certain Major Spencer[25] who is the political advisor to the British Commanding

15 April 23, 1946.
16 See Doc. 28, fn. 4.
17 See Doc. 20, fn. 18.
18 See Doc. 28, fn. 14.
19 Refers to the Local Government Committee, Allied Kommandatura Berlin. See Doc. 29, fn. 14.
20 A kind of liqueur.
21 Glaser had worked in Boston, Massachusetts, for the George Zain advertising firm, and in 1922 he founded Glaser Advertising Agency, Inc.
22 Marguerite K. Glaser, née Kaufman (1891–1985).
23 Civil Administration Branch, OMGBD. See Doc. 28, fn. 5.
24 April 25, 1946.
25 Kenneth Angus Spencer (1916–2002), Major, 1937 BA (German, French), University College, London, as of 1939 British Army, 1945–1947 British Military Government,

General of B[erlin] D[istrict] – General Nares[26]. This I think is a little embarrassing since the British may think I am trying to get information. This Mrs. Delahaye[27], moreover, (I think her husband is dead) is a little bit boring, although quite nice, and her idea of German lessons is to spend an evening together. I only want an hour or so, once or twice a week, and not an evening. I tried it out first and she invited me to a British Club. The second time we met she had guests and it was at the same British Club. Not much German spoken and certainly none learned. I then had to return the favor. I now think I'll tell her that work has so piled up that I must discontinue German for the time being. Then I'll get a hold of a German who will come here for an evening or so for some methodical work in German. German and society don't really mix, or at least they haven't so far.

The week led up to what I thought was a disastrous climax on yesterday, the meeting of the Kommandatura. I think I reported on the last meeting[28] when I had carefully prepared statements for General Barker[29] to present at the previous meeting on such important subjects as elections in Berlin, the recognition of the anti-merger Social Democrats, and the supervision of political activities in the city of Berlin.[30] I thought we were getting somewhere at the last meeting. Everybody agreed, according to our proposal, that they would come to this meeting with the earliest possible date on which elections could be held, the Russians promised to telephone on the question of recognition of the anti-merger SPD's, and it was agreed that the Local Government Committee[31] would be permitted to discuss methods of bringing political activities in Berlin, under Allied Control. That seemed to be getting ahead, and I was congratulated by State Department people on the progress which had been made. But yesterday was a come-down. You have heard remarks from me to the effect that Kommandatura machinery may break down. That prediction may have been a little premature but nothing that has happened since has vitiated that sad prediction. A previous meeting was a further step in the way. An important question on the reorganization of the police had to be sent upwards to the Control Council[32] because it couldn't be decided in the Kommandatura, and it couldn't be decided in the Kommandatura because the Russians took a very stubborn stand. They just wouldn't tolerate the reorganization and they objected to its being handled on a sectoral basis.

Berlin, Political Adviser to the British Deputy Director, William Robert Norris Hinde (see Doc. 28, fn. 11).

26 See Doc. 27, fn. 26.

27 Ina Delahaye (1906–1972), Russian-British actress and singer, married to Colonel J. V. Delahaye (died 1955).

28 See minutes of the 11th meeting of the Commandants on April 12, 1946, BKC/M (46) 11, English version, in: LAB, B Rep. 036-01 (Office of Military Government, Berlin Sector [OMGBS]), 11/148-1/10.

29 See Doc. 20, fn. 10.

30 See Doc. 35.

31 See Doc. 29, fn. 14.

32 See Doc. 14, fn. 5.

Yesterday's meeting lasted from ten in the morning until after seven at night with a short break for lunch. The largest meeting of the Kommandatura yet. Only the last meeting was somewhat shorter. The initial question to be discussed was how soon elections could be held in Berlin. Remember the Russians had agreed at the last meeting to come to this meeting prepared to announce the earliest possible date at which they would be willing to hold elections. But they simply refused to carry out this promise and to name a date. The British and the French named their dates as they had promised, around the 1st of August. But the Russians – the new Russian Commandant is Kotikov[33], launched into terrific arguments to show that no date could be specified. Instead they proposed a long series of investigations which would have to be made before a date could be agreed upon, and took by and large an unpleasantly stubborn attitude. It is clear, that after the elections which have been held in Europe (Austria![34] and the local elections in the American zone[35]) the Russians are going to take no further chances. They will not consent to our election in so important a place as Berlin, until they are sure that it will go, if not entirely their way, at least in a way that is not altogether unfavorable. That is what this party maneuvering here is all about. Their arguments were absolutely stinking from any point of view except theirs. They know what Berlin means to Germany, and they want a victory of the new Communist dominated SED when elections are held in Berlin.

After about four hours of wrangling on this subject, it was passed on to the higher authorities, the Control Council. Everyone was tired and annoyed by this time. The next subject was the recognition of the anti-merger SPD's and the new SED – the Socialist Unity Party. I had written out a statement of our policy for the last meeting which was circulated among all the Commandants. It proposed simply that both parties be recognized. The Russians had, evidently, carefully studied this statement, and were impressed by its essential fairness. In fact they kept discussing and quoting it throughout their argument, which of course flattered me. But they were at the same time shrewd. Having blocked at the previous meeting the recognition of the anti-merger SPD's, they were now willing to come around on this point, if only, we would recognize without delay the

33 See Doc. 35, fn. 5.

34 In the election for Austrian National Council on November 25, 1945, the Kommunistische Partei Österreichs had only gained 5.42 percent of valid votes. See *Keesing's Archiv der Gegenwart*, vol. XV (1945), p. 539 E. The election ended "with a bombshell, because the Communists had to settle with extremely bad results." ("mit einem Knalleffekt, da sich die Kommunisten mit einem denkbar schlechten Ergebnis abzufinden hatten.") Richard Hufschmied, "Sonderfall Wien? Die Alliierten und Österreich 1943–1955," in: *Die Vier Mächte in Berlin. Beiträge zur Politik der Alliierten in der besetzten Stadt*, eds. Michael Bienert/Uwe Schaper/Andrea Theissen in collaboration with Werner Breunig (= Schriftenreihe des Landesarchivs Berlin, vol. 9), Berlin 2007, pp. 109–129, here p. 114.

35 The KPD had achieved disappointing results in the local elections that had taken place in January 1946 in the smaller municipalities of the American zone of Germany. See *Keesing's Archiv der Gegenwart*, vol. XVI (1946), p. 628 D; Conrad F. Latour/Thilo Vogelsang, *Okkupation und Wiederaufbau. Die Tätigkeit der Militärregierung in der amerikanischen Besatzungszone Deutschlands 1944–1947* (Studien zur Zeitgeschichte), Stuttgart 1973, pp. 110f.

SEP which they have been promoting. In all justice these were not entitled to this. They wanted it because there is to be a 1 May celebration here, and they wanted to have their party recognized for this celebration, and to show how quickly they could manage to gain this recognition. I was for going along with the Russians on this proposition. It meant sacrificing a bit but not very much, and we should have acquired a reputation on this issue at least, of meaning what we said. At it was General Barker, at the moment when it came to making a decision was physically exhausted. I believe I have told you what a heroic stand he takes in simply going through a day's work.[36] Moreover the British took an unexpected stand, one that contradicted their previous decision. They wanted recognition for the SPD, but as for the SED, they wanted this decision passed upwards. The French too took a strangely contradictory stand. Usually they are clear, precise and logical. This was an unexpected reverse. They would recognize the SPD but as for the SED, they would have to go upwards. At the moment of decision I was not called upon by General Barker for advice. I had briefed him the day before and we had agreed that under no considerations was the question to go upwards. This was a matter for the Kommandatura to decide. We were striving in fact to have the K[ommandatura] establish methods of controlling Berlin politics. But instead of going along with the Russians as he should have, and making clear that we meant what we said when we proposed that both SPD + SED should be recognized under similar conditions, he faltered, and essentially broke his word, and went along with the British and French, with whom his sympathies naturally lie, and supported, contrary to our agreement of the evening before, sending up the matter to the Control Council. I do not know what the Russians thought but I know what I should have thought. Simply that the Americans make a proposition and do not keep their word. He missed a great chance in not going with the Soviets against the British and the French. It now goes up to General Clay[37], for whom I am going to prepare a memorandum on the subject. I was desolate about the outcome. My suggestions had been good. They had struck a responsive chord with the Russians and then we renigged. How can General Kotikov trust us henceforth. Two major questions which the Kommandatura could really have decided among themselves now go to higher authority. The reputation of the competency of the Kommandatura is now discredited. What we wanted, namely the right to manage our own affairs, is now discredited by the thought that maybe we are not capable of managing our own affairs. And the international machinery of Berlin is thus made to appear unworkable. I am laboring under the impression of immediate effects. These iron themselves out in the long run. But they iron themselves out better when there are not so many stubborn wrinkles and creases to flatten out. It is all very fascinating in a way. The important decisions depend upon so many factors that the historian cannot ever hope to get at from the documents. The fundamental explanation of all this is poor General Barker's spine[38]. That hole in his

36 See Doc. 33.

37 See Doc. 2, fn. 6.

38 Barker had back problems. Frank L. Howley (see Doc. 20, fn. 18) writes: "Because of a bad back, he sat at meetings in a padded chair, with a big green pillow behind him, but always started to squirm in acute discomfort after the first half hour." Frank Howley, *Berlin Command*, New York 1950, p. 109.

spine which will make him a cripple if he doesn't go home soon. He is a hero in spite of this disaster. In the long run he will be borne out.

I must stop now. I'll write again tomorrow and get to the precious details of these letters which really interest me more than all this. I love you, much more than all Berlin, than all Germany, than all Europe, than all the world. A sweet good-night to my beloved Em[ily]. Edgar

Doc. 41
Letter to His Wife
Berlin, April 30, 1946

Dearest Emily –

I came home to the Club[1] tonight to find a photograph of General Barker[2] with a rewarding and cordial inscription, and a gracious note.[3] He has abandoned his job to General Keating[4] and will take off on Thursday[5].[6] He has been a fine person to come to know, and I regret very much his going. The new general is quite unpolitical, though not, I take it, without intelligence. I am told he is something of a hot headed Irishman.

I was going to say something about the details of the weekend. You will say I am being spoiled and demoralized, – a continuation of the corruption that OSS[7] started when they gave Paul[8] and me the blue Buick[9]. On Saturday[10] afternoon, for example, I took a little time out to go sailing with Captain Americus Mitchell[11], in the red sailboat we used the week before. It is a nice one, and, as the

1 Refers to the Wannsee Hotel/Wannsee Officers' Club, Am Sandwerder 17/19. See Doc. 25, fn. 9.
2 See Doc. 20, fn. 10.
3 This photo is neither among the Edgar N. Johnson Papers (UChicago Library, Special Collections Research Center), nor among the documents from the estate of Edgar N. Johnson, private collection of Candice E. and Thomas R. Johnson, Denver, Colorado, USA.
4 See Doc. 39, fn. 6.
5 May 2, 1946.
6 "Maj. Gen. R. W. Barker, Commanding General of Berlin District was transferred yesterday to Washington, D. C. He was replaced by Maj. Gen. Frank A. Keating who has had nine months occupation duty in Bavaria. Gen. Keating came overseas in 1944 with the 102nd Infantry Division." "Barker Leaves," in: *OMGUS Observer* from May 3, 1946, p. 3.
7 Office of Strategic Services. See Doc. 1, fn. 9.
8 Probably refers to Paul R. Sweet. See Doc. 2, fn. 28.
9 American car brand.
10 April 27, 1946.
11 Probably Americus Mitchell (1916–2003), Captain, 1935–1939 Vanderbilt University (1944 BA), physics instructor, as of 1942 US Army Air Corps, towards the end of the Second World War assigned to the US Strategic Bombing Survey (Europe), Headquarters Company Berlin District, October 1946 relieved from active duty, 1955 JD, George Washington University Law School, 1976 MM (Finance), Northwestern University Graduate School, patent attorney. "He did love sailing," writes Mitchell's granddaughter Mary E. Bonk in an email to Werner Breunig from December 20, 2017. As Mitchell's daughter, Miriam-Ellen Bonk, writes in an email to Werner Breu-

afternoon was somewhat breezy, we sped back and forth across the lake, with no helping to manage the craft at some intervals. I thought of our being at a lake somewhere, where we could have a sailboat, and go off with our boys for an afternoon. This is honest-to-God, conspicuous consumption.

When I came back I found an invitation from Ambassador Murphy[12] for dinner. Well I figured out that this was to be a colloquy on the paper I had written on the Jurr[13] and Kammermeier[14] case – (the two Communists whom we recently arrested and sentenced to five years)[15].[16] But it was nothing of the sort. I was by no means flattered to have it turn out to be a dinner given for a meandering Congressman (McGeehie[17] of Mississippi[18]) and his party, which included the consul of Zurich[19], one Sam Brown[20]. There were some Frenchmen there (a Professor Siegfried[21] who teaches geography) and others. The Congressman I found a little bit colorful, but on the whole utterly obnoxious. He was a violent anti-New-Dealer,[22] and a representative of all the fine chivalry and potent prejudices of the deep South – about as sad a man to represent America to Europeans as I can imagine. And from the political point of view, certainly an utterly incomprehensible person. The quite personal and petty details which he described as governing Washington politics reveal how far removed any academic treatment of this subject is. There is hardly a principle involved that is not false and showy. Truman[23], he assured us all, was at heart a conservative. He knew him well from

nig from December 28, 2017, it was during his stay in Germany that "he met my mother Christl Liebold, who grew up near Erfurt."

12 See Doc. 8, fn. 13.

13 Gerhard Jurr (1905–1971), German party secretary (KPD), trained plumber, 1929 KPD, 1934/1935 attended International Lenin School of the Comintern, Moscow, 1936 arrested and sentenced by the Volksgerichtshof to 15 years in prison, until 1945 in the penitentiary of Brandenburg, then district administration of Berlin-Schöneberg, secretary of the Schöneberg district KPD.

14 Wilhelm Kammermeier (1889–1954), German administration employee, head of the Zentralbüro für die Unterbezirksverwaltungen in Berlin-Schöneberg and head of the KPD Betriebsgruppe in the Schöneberg Bezirksamt.

15 See Doc. 33.

16 Murphy led a commission that was formed on April 8, 1946, in order to review the verdicts against Jurr and Kammermeier. See Harold Hurwitz, *Die Eintracht der Siegermächte und die Orientierungsnot der Deutschen 1945–1946* (= Demokratie und Antikommunismus in Berlin nach 1945, vol. III), Cologne 1984, p. 216.

17 Daniel (Dan) R. McGehee (1883–1962), American lawyer and politician (Democratic Party), 1924–1928 and 1932–1934 member of Mississippi State Senate, 1928–1932 Mississippi State House of Representatives, 1935–1947 member of Congress.

18 US state.

19 City in Switzerland.

20 Refers to Sam E. Woods (1892–1953), American diplomat, BS, Mississippi State Teachers College, as of 1929 Foreign Service, 1937–1941 Commercial Attaché, Berlin, 1942–1947 Consul General, Zurich and Vaduz, 1947–1952 Consul General, Munich.

21 André Siegfried (1875–1959), French economic geographer, as of 1933 Professor, Collège de France, as of 1944 member of the Académie Française.

22 McGehee was "a New Deal critic in congress and an opponent of the fair employment practice act and anti-poll tax measures." "War Hero Wins Congress Seat in Mississippi," in: *Chicago Daily Tribune* from August 28, 1946, p. 6.

23 See Doc. 5, fn. 19.

prolonged poker games. The Congressman was pot-bellied and drank a little too much. He and his party are off on a 12 day jaunt (arranged by Judge Rosenman[24]) between sessions of Congress. I questioned Brown (a staunch admirer of Wallace[25] – who is a professional gardener) about bringing families to Switzerland. He said that Geneva[26] was the best place, but that Zurich was also possible and offered his services. Do you want to come to Switzerland?

On Sunday[27] there was a reception for General Barker and General Keating, the departing and arriving generals of Berlin District. All people of importance were invited, and appeared for awhile. Murphy, General Millburn[28], Clay[29]. (I enclose a snap of Keating and myself taken by Americus.[30] I don't know who the other officer is. Also one of the grounds in front of the Club[31]). Drinks, food, and music by an orchestra led by a female violinist called Ingeborg[32], who seems to be a favorite in Berlin. General Barker invited me to have a ride with him and his staff in his launch after the reception. And I went.[33]

The interesting thing about the reception to me was that Keating gave me the first indication that he wanted me to continue for him in the same capacity in which I have been acting for Barker. As I was sitting talking with him and Clay he mentioned to Clay that he would like to have me perform the rôle of an ambassador to him, such as Clay had in Murphy. He subsequently mentioned to me

24 Samuel I. Rosenman (1896–1973), American lawyer, 1919 LLB, University of Columbia, 1932–1943 Justice New York Supreme Court, 1943–1945 Special Counsel to President Roosevelt, 1945/1946 to President Truman.

25 Henry A. Wallace (1888–1965), American politician (Republican Party, then Democratic Party, and lastly Progressive Party), 1933–1940 US Secretary of Agriculture, 1941–1945 Vice President of the United States, 1945/1946 US Secretary of Commerce.

26 City in Switzerland.

27 April 28, 1946.

28 Bryan L. Milburn. See Doc. 15, fn. 20.

29 See Doc. 2, fn. 6.

30 Probably refers to the photo reproduced in Appendix of Illustrations as ill. 28.

31 Probably refers to the photo reproduced in Appendix of Illustrations as ill. 44. It was taken at the entrance to the Wannsee Hotel/Wannsee Officers' Club (see Doc. 25, fn. 9).

32 Ingeborg von Streletzky (1916–2011), violinist and orchestra leader. "The Americans were also delighted. Ingeborg conquered the American clubs, she played in front of General Clay and General [Maxwell D.] Taylor, 'received dazzling offers to go over there,'" ("Auch die Amerikaner waren begeistert. Ingeborg eroberte die amerikanischen Clubs, sie spielte vor General Clay und General [Maxwell D.] Taylor, 'erhielt glänzende Angebote nach drüben,'") writes Gregor Eisenhauer in his obituary. "Ingeborg von Streletzky. Geb. 1916. Es war keine gütige Fee, es war harte Arbeit und unbarmherzige Dressur," in: *Der Tagesspiegel* from November 25, 2011, p. 12. "But she stayed in Berlin. What kept her? 'The affection of so many people here, who write me wonderful letters, and my most thankful and dearest audience, those blinded in the war.'" ("Aber sie blieb in Berlin. Was sie hielt? 'Die Zuneigung so vieler Menschen hier, die mir wunderschöne Briefe schreiben, und meine dankbarsten und liebsten Zuhörer, die Kriegsblinden.'") Ibid.

33 Photos of the boat ride on Wannsee in Appendix of Illustrations, ill. 29, ill. 30, and ill. 31.

moving over from the present quarters in Berlin District[34] to his headquarters in the Telefunken Building[35]. Clay answered with the reminder that I was only loaned to B[erlin] D[istrict] on a temporary basis, and that I was subsequently to take on the job of Regional Military Governor[36] (this is the Stuttgart[37] job after Pollock[38] goes). I have scarcely been in my office across from Murphy in the Directors' Building at Omgus[39], although I have been told that there are piles of stuff coming through that office for me. To move over from B[erlin] D[istrict] to Keating would mean that I had three offices, which is rather impossible.

The point of all this is that Clay has evidently forgotten that he promised that I could return in the Fall, and is counting on me to take over Pollock's job when he returns to the states in August. I want to know what you really think. What I have said to you on this subject so far I have really meant, namely that I am not too much interested. I am perfectly ready to return to Nebraska in the Fall. At the same time there are considerations which I suppose we are obliged to think about. The two issues in my mind are 1. being with you and the boys; 2. security for you and the boys. There is also in the back of my mind – Dad[40]. If I am to stay on here, you should come nearer as soon as possible. How interested are you in some European experience? I don't know how long this occupation is to last. Certainly for several years. By staying here, I could have a 10,000 dollar job for this period. As a result of this experience I don't suppose I really have to worry about a job in the future. If I stayed another year, this would involve tearing up roots in Nebraska, unless Henry[41] were willing to say, one year more – Yes – but no further consideration. If we kept the house in Lincoln[42] we should always have some place to return to. Out of a salary of 10,000 for a few years we should be able to save enough to keep us going until we found a suitable job. How does this affect the boys? How does it affect Dad? Do we want to be adventurous enough to tear up roots at Nebraska and trust to our luck? If we saved enough we could live on our savings for awhile and I could do some writing which in itself might guarantee any security for the future, without too much of worry about teaching or any other kind of job. The question of serving your country is now – at this stage of the game – out. You would be serving your country but the pressure on this score, I now feel is over. I came back here honestly with this in mind and what I came back for is not now available. We have to think about ourselves, now, for a bit.

Have you any desires? any ideas? I'll go on with this again but we should be sketching out the future.

34 Refers to Johnson's quarters at OMGBD. See Doc. 25, fn. 13.

35 US Headquarters Berlin District was located in the Telefunken Building on Goerzallee, Berlin-Lichterfelde.

36 Refers to the leadership of RGCO. See Doc. 2, fn. 11.

37 Capital of the state of Württemberg-Baden in the American zone of Germany.

38 See Doc. 15, fn. 12.

39 See Doc. 17, fn. 45.

40 Frank E. Johnson. See Doc. 3, fn. 12.

41 Charles Henry Oldfather. See Doc. 2, fn. 19.

42 Capital of the US state of Nebraska, where Johnson lived with his family and taught at the university.

I love you my Sweetheart, and I don't want to miss the chance of our having in the years to come the best that can be arranged. Please tell the boys about me, and I send you my fondest and most tender caresses. I only want the finest for us all. Edgar

Doc. 42
Letter to His Wife
Berlin, May 1, 1946

Dearest and Sweetest –

When I came in my office this morning there was a bouquet of tulips on my desk. I discovered they had been brought by my German driver[1], who told me his wife had gotten them for me. I have been sending some of my PX[2] rations home with him. And on the commode which contains coats and hats was a bouquet of apple blossoms brought by my German secretary[3] for whom I have done nothing. She is a Frau but about her family life I haven't inquired. This I think is the simple way to get along with the Germans – be so nice to them that they really want to bring you flowers.

I also went to the May day celebration today in the so-called Lustgarten[4].[5] I wanted any generals to go but at the last moment they turned me down – mistakenly I think. It was a celebration the organization of which I resent. We had tried to insist that it should be an unpolitical affair open to all workers' groups who wished to participate. General Barker[6] even went to see General Kotikov[7] on this point and he gave his assurances. It wasn't a blatant celebration of the new SED but it was clearly under their auspices. Efforts to get other speakers from other parties failed and only speakers representing the right point of view were permitted to hold the platform.[8] They were more moderate than they have been but I don't like these methods. There were some 200,000 to 300,000 Germans on the square – workers who had marched from the suburbs into the center of the city. They were an awfully depressing sight to see. These Germans are thoroughly knocked out. They looked physically exhausted

1 Artur Sanow. See Doc. 40, fn. 13.

2 Post Exchange, retail store on US Army posts.

3 Possibly Frau Donneck. See Doc. 80.

4 The Lustgarten, originally part of the Berlin City Palace, is on the northern side of the Spree Island in the administrative district of Mitte.

5 An FDGB rally took place in the Lustgarten on May Day, focused on the merger of the KPD and SPD into the SED. See B. K., "Die Kundgebung der 500 000 im Lustgarten. Berlins Bekenntnis zur Einheit der Arbeiterklasse und zur Demokratie," in: *Berliner Zeitung* from May 3, 1946, [p. 2]; "Lustgarten im Zeichen der 'Einheit,'" in: *Der Tagesspiegel* from May 3, 1946, p. 4.

6 See Doc. 20, fn. 10.

7 See Doc. 35, fn. 5.

8 Speeches were held by both Chairmen of the SED, Otto Grotewohl (see Doc. 30, fn. 8) and Wilhelm Pieck (see Doc. 30, fn. 9), the 1st Chairman of the FDGB Executive Committee, Hans Jendretzky (see Doc. 83, fn. 113), SED, and the head of the Berlin Women's Committee, Katharina Kern (1900–1985), SED.

and they were dressed in all manner of old clothes. These were workers, metropolitan workers, who have no means to take care of themselves on the black market[9] or out in the country – and in Berlin it is hard to get out into the country, which is Russian country. They were so tired by the time they had marched into the city's center that they were not much interested in the speeches. The speakers, fresh and vigorous because they have better ration cards and receive extra supplements from the Russians were unable to awaken any enthusiasm. There were loud speakers about, but most of the people I could see were clapping because other people were clapping. They began to go home before the speeches were over. Maybe my driver is right. They have begun this political movement too early in Germany. People have to have more time to make up their minds. It seemed impossible to imagine that these were, not long ago, a part of the Herrenvolk. They came out in such numbers, I think, primarily because there had been nothing like this for such a long time. There is, after all, so little excitement for them in Germany.

Two letters from you today (April 22, April 26th!)[10] make me horribly lonesome. I am easily precipitated into this state. The one contained John's[11] very touching letter to the Easter Rabbit (how can this faith be translated into something real without in the meantime undergoing disillusion?) and the other your confession of your own loneliness. The passing remarks in this letter really contain the answer to all the questions I put in a letter of yesterday if only we could resolve ourselves not to discuss alternate answers. "These months are gone forever." "And sometimes I do wonder if it is all worth it." "To be released, oh when?" "I hope September, my darling." As you know I am ready to state September in Lincoln[12], rather than September here. It is September in either case. And it is September wherever you decide it to be. Or if you do not wish to decide, then it is September in Lincoln. Or to put it otherwise if you don't wish to come here then it is September in Lincoln. I don't really believe that when this episode is over it will have been worth it. To be with you for one day and night is worth more than all this. To have been there over Easter is worth more than this. The money is all very tempting but we can't be led astray by this, and the kind of life which one leads over here is not the kind of life we are used to – I mean the quiet, scholarly kind. Here one does no reading, outside of the professional reading he is obliged to do. The patriotic motive diminishes when it is no longer a question of saving human lives of our own people at the moment. And I can work to stave off the coming war as well at home as here. Perhaps better there. In any case, I think, I shall retreat into our home, and nestle into your bosom, and not come out much again. Life is after all to be lived mostly for the moment, and not too much for the future, I shall not be completely satisfied teaching in Nebraska but neither, I think, should we be completely satisfied here. (The first

9 See Doc. 21, fn. 11.

10 Letters in: Documents from the estate of Edgar N. Johnson, private collection of Candice E. and Thomas R. Johnson, Denver, Colorado, USA.

11 Johnson's son John. See Doc. 2, fn. 15.

12 Capital of the US state of Nebraska, where Johnson lived with his family and taught at the university.

batch of wives has arrived here.[13] I met a colonel's wife tonight. They occupy a beautiful mansion overlooking Wannsee[14]. This is hard for me to take.)

I want to be with you, my dearest, that is all, and that is enough. I don't want you overburdened in the way that you now are. I want to come back to a home where you are. I want to see your lovely face and your lovely body. I want to run my hands through your hair and kiss your eyes and lips and cheeks. I want to hold you close to me for a very long time. I want our naked bodies lovingly to be in touch. I want my hands and lips to be where you want them to be. I want to be able to come to you over and over again, and to be the boy you call me. We are blessed with a love that knows only how to grow. I want to give myself up to you, to share in the bliss which we can have. Oh my dear I want to come into you, and to stay there forever. I love you my darling Emily, and there is no comfort except that the days do pass and that there will be a release. Edgar

Doc. 43
Letter to His Wife
Berlin, May 5, 1946[1]

Dearest Emily –

I have thought of a compromise solution to the question of our future which I would like to put to you, and also to Henry[2] when I next write. I just received a nice letter from him.

It is this: I decide to return to the University of Nebraska[3] in the Fall of 1947. This is irrevocable. Meanwhile I make arrangements to bring you and the boys over here as soon as possible. I tell Clay[4] that I will take the Stuttgart[5] job[6] when Pollock[7] goes in August and you and the boys will join me there. We shall stay there together until next June. The following summer we shall spend in Europe, or in England, or both, vacationing, seeing things. We shall return home to Lincoln[8] together in the Fall.

13 The first wives and children of members of the American occupation forces had arrived in Berlin on April 30, 1946; a train from Bremerhaven had brought them to the city after a ten-day sea voyage. See Kathleen McLaughlin, "First U. S. Families Arrive in Berlin. Wives and Children Hailed in Poignant Reunions – Amazed at Beauty of Country," in: *The New York Times* from May 1, 1946, p. 4; Lyn Davis, "'Operation Dependency …' Families' Arrival Has Rousing Climax," in: *OMGUS Observer* from May 3, 1946, pp. 1 and 4f.

14 Probably refers to Großer Wannsee, a bight of the Havel (see Doc. 74, fn. 24) in southwest Berlin.

1 In the heading it says: "Sunday, 6 May 1946." In 1946 May 5 was a Sunday, not May 6.

2 Charles Henry Oldfather. See Doc. 2, fn. 19.

3 University founded in 1869 in Lincoln, Nebraska.

4 See Doc. 2, fn. 6.

5 Capital of the state of Württemberg-Baden in the American zone of Germany.

6 Leadership of RGCO in Stuttgart. See Doc. 2, fn. 11.

7 See Doc. 15, fn. 12.

This plan leaves Dad[9] unprovided for, and depends upon a satisfactory solution of this question for adoption.

Its advantages are:

1. That it brings us together in this European experience and offers the opportunity for a little European travel, which, indeed, might never come again.

2. It gives us the advantage of this 10,000 salary for another year. Henry said in his letter that he has recommended me this Spring for 4200, the minimum salary of a full professor. This, of course, is more than twice that. By careful living here we should be able to save a great deal of it, even more perhaps than would be necessary to spend the next summer travelling. I really think of England in this connection, which you would love, and so would I. Something of the continent could be seen in between.

3. This would fill out my experience here. As it is my experience will be limited to Berlin. The Stuttgart job takes care of our whole zone, and puts me in touch with the leading people there, as well as with those in Omgus[10]. Although I am not any longer much moved by the patriotic motive, there is no doubt that staying here another year would be helpful to the USA. I would come to have a pretty good grip of the German problem as it appears to be a couple years after military defeat of Germany.

4. While I should be obliged to return to Nebraska for a few years, this prolonged experience might lead to something which would better suit our hearts' desire than permanently staying there.

The real point of this is whether you would like some European experience with the difficulties that are involved of having it with young children. I long to share the days' experience with you. That, together with being a part of you, is what I miss most. The Wannsee[11] is only a lake with boats on it to look at. This plan does not abandon our security at Nebraska, it does not abandon our lovely home there, it has the advantage of compromising with the advantages of my position here and the advantages of being there. It depends, of course, upon Henry's decision. If he says that they can't wait for another year, then my decision I think is clear. I come home. We are not of the adventurous sort. At least, I am not.

What do you think? Would you like to see something of Europe now, under these unfortunate circumstances? Would you like to guide me in my work from day to day. Or would you prefer to have me come back to Lincoln to you rather than to come to Stuttgart to me?

I am writing a report on the SED for the Branch[12].[13] If you were here it would be much better.

I love you, oh my dearest, and my boys. Edgar

8 Capital of the US state of Nebraska, where Johnson lived with his family and taught at the university.

9 Frank E. Johnson. See Doc. 3, fn. 12.

10 See Doc. 17, fn. 45.

11 Refers to Großer Wannsee, a bight of the Havel (see Doc. 74, fn. 24) in southwest Berlin.

12 Civil Administration Branch, OMGBD. See Doc. 28, fn. 5.

13 Probably refers to the report on the SED in the Special Report of Civil Administration Branch, OMGBD, from May 6, 1946: Berlin Summary. May Day, Political Parties, Elections, SED review, in: BArch, Koblenz, Germany, Z 45 F, 17/258-3/2.

Doc. 44
Letter to His Wife
Berlin, May 6, 1946

Sweet and dear Emily –

The best thing about the day was the gift from you – the watch came in perfect condition.[1] I put it on immediately, and it has run perfectly ever since, and I do not expect there will be any trouble with it. I am sorry you had to pay so much for it for I don't suppose we have any right really to afford so expensive a watch for me. But it is neat and handsome, just the right size so as not to make it conspicuous, and the black leather strap fits perfectly without an extra hole. I think I told you that I had a chance to buy a watch from a German – through my driver[2] – soldier who got it in the army. He wants two cartons of cigarettes for it. I thought it would be nice to get for John[3] who would be delighted to have a real watch. I can't pay for it with the cigarettes I get from the PX[4] for this is illegal but if you could send me a few cartons from Dalton's[5] I could get it for John. Certainly it is worth from our point of view 2 cartons of cigarettes. These cigarettes however cost on the German black market[6] 1400 marks a carton which is no less than $ 140 dollars a carton (140 marks – $ 14, a package).[7] But you can hardly figure this way. My new watch, with a second hand even, and if I read correctly 17 jewels! I shall treasure too as a memento of you always in sight. I have a ring from you on the same hand.

On the way home tonight my driver took out of his pocket a purple velvet case with silver earings containing large brilliants. Some German had asked him to try to sell them for him. They belong to his aunt. He wanted ten cartons of cigarettes or in marks equivalent $ 1400 dollars (= 15 dollars in cigarettes). I was not interested. This is what is happening here, people getting rid of things in order to buy food that they need on the black market. Sanow[8] said that ten cartons of cigarettes would buy about 35 pounds of butter which is of course what people need most.

On the way down to work this morning Sanow told me his wife had cancer. She is 36 and he spoke of her in loving terms. She has had radium treatments, which burnt her somewhat badly, and these have helped keep it down I guess. But radium treatments are not available here now since the Russians are supposed to have taken it all and sent it back to Russia. He is now going to try to get her radium bath treatments, which I can't imagine will do much good. It is beginning to pain her. The doctor says she needs radium treatment. She told him that she wouldn't live long. Not a very nice way to begin the day. There is

1 See Doc. 27.
2 Artur Sanow. See Doc. 40, fn. 13.
3 Johnson's son John. See Doc. 2, fn. 15.
4 Post Exchange, retail store on US Army posts.
5 Department store in Lincoln, Nebraska.
6 See Doc. 21, fn. 11.
7 See Doc. 27, fn. 10.
8 See Doc. 40, fn. 13.

of course a general shortage of medicines here.[9] Even alcohol is hard to get and one does not know how much suffering is caused by this alone. I'd like to get Sanow's wife a radium treatment but I don't know whether we have any radium here or whether it is available to Germans if we have. There must be many cases like this.

Two Social Democrats came into my office today. They live in the Russian Sector and have refused to follow the Russian and Communist line and go in for the new party. One of them has been advised by his friends to get out of the Russian sector for fear that something might happen to him. These friends have been summoned to the headquarters of the local Russian Commandant and asked many questions about the man. What are his political opinions? What meetings has he recently attended? How does he conduct himself. The man has in his possession papers which he feels will incriminate others if they are taken. He now sleeps different places from night to night for fear of being found. The other man has a family. He is an independent Social Democrat. He has been summoned before the local Russian Commandant and told that his political views and activity are anti-Russian. He tried to explain that his political views and activity had nothing to do with being anti-Russian. They were just his political views. But the Russians professed not to understand. They both want to move into our Sector, and I shall try to do what I can. They live in terror, and under a terror which is not very different from the Nazi system. This makes you sick. Why do the Russians have to deal in terror methods. That they come to us is a great tribute. That is, in a sense, what America stands for. But we can't take in all the Germans who want to move from the Russian into the American Sector. Nor does this make for good American-Russian relations. The Russians will now say, if we take those men over, that they are being used by us as agents to spy on the Russians. God knows how many Russian agents are in our Sector, or even in our offices. What would you do, take them in or not?

It is the same with the Liberal Democratic Party[10] here in Berlin – one of the two conservative parties[11]. They are being hamstrung by the Russians in their zone, and in the city. They want to move over into our sector for the freedom that it brings.[12] This is again what we stand for. We shall probably let them come over. But the Russians will use this to paint us as the supporters of reaction. They have already done this enough in the course of the merger struggle, and if the independent Social Democrats are the representatives of reaction you can imagine what

9 See *Die Sitzungsprotokolle des Magistrats der Stadt Berlin 1945/46*, part II, *1946*, edited and introduced by Dieter Hanauske (= Schriftenreihe des Landesarchivs Berlin, vol. 2/II), Berlin 1999, Doc. 96, fn. 59.

10 The Liberal-Demokratische Partei Deutschlands (LDP) went public with a call for foundation on July 5, 1945. See *Berlin. Quellen und Dokumente 1945–1951*, edited on behalf of the Senate of Berlin, eds. Hans J. Reichhardt/Hanns U. Treutler/Albrecht Lampe (= Schriftenreihe zur Berliner Zeitgeschichte, vol. 4/half-vol. 1), Berlin 1964, no. 472.

11 The CDU, which understood itself as an interconfessional Christian bourgeois union, was permitted along with the bourgeois-liberal LDP. See Doc. 21, fn. 29.

12 The office of the Berlin regional association was located at Taubenstraße 48/49 in the administrative district of Mitte (Soviet sector).

the Liberal Democratic Party can be painted to be. It is likely that what the Russians are aiming at is something like a one party system. They hope, through the instrumentality of the new unity party to liquidate the Social Democrats. Having done that the other two conservative parties will be easy to liquidate.

Is all this worth fighting a war about if it should come to this? I must say I am not very hopeful tonight. When I read the press reports of the Council of Foreign Ministers in Paris[13] I am even less hopeful. They have returned the South Tyrol to Italy.[14] This is a decision which may not of course cause trouble enough to help bring on a war. But it is based on a kind of justice that I do not understand. Of course Austria is a defeated nation and Italy managed to scramble out of the war. The area in dispute is of course indisputably Austrian. It is given to Italy to help with her economic recovery. But the Italians, under Mussolini[15], used dastardly methods to Italianize the area to which they really have no right. The talk about Trieste[16] and Venetia Giulia[17] also frightens me. There I am on the other side. Trieste is an Italian city. This even Molotov[18] admits but he thinks it should go to Jugo-Slavia which, it's going to Jugo-Slavia puts Russia at the head of the Adriatic. I don't see how this Conference is to come to any common conclusions, or if it does that they are going to be any good. But I certainly should not like to be in Byrnes'[19] place. If Berlin is a tough job, Paris is a God-awful job.

13 The first session of the Paris conference of the Council of Foreign Ministers took place from April 25–May 15, 1946, second session from June 15–July 12, 1946. See Oliver Jäkel, "Außenministerkonferenz Paris (25. 4.–15. 5. und 15. 6.–12. 7.1946)," in: *Deutschland unter alliierter Besatzung 1945–1949/55*, ed. Wolfgang Benz, Berlin 1999, p. 219.

14 In the Treaty of Saint-Germain-en-Laye from September 10, 1919, Austria had to cede German-speaking South Tyrol to Italy. In 1943 the country was occupied by German troops. After the Second World War, Austria sought restitution of South Tyrol. On May 1, 1946, the four victorious powers conclusively refused Austria's request for a popular referendum in South Tyrol. See Rolf Steininger, *Südtirol im 20. Jahrhundert. Vom Leben und Überleben einer Minderheit*, Innsbruck and Vienna 1997; Hans Heiss/Gustav Pfeifer (eds.), *Südtirol – Stunde Null? Kriegsende 1945–1946* (= Veröffentlichungen des Südtiroler Landesarchivs, vol. 10), Innsbruck, Vienna, and Munich 2000; Rudolf Lill, *Südtirol in der Zeit des Nationalismus*, Constance 2002.

15 Benito Mussolini (1883–1945), Italian politician, 1922–1943 fascist dictator of Italy, 1943–1945 leader of the Italian Social Republic.

16 In the Treaty of Saint-Germain-en-Laye, Austria had to cede the city of Trieste, which had been part of its territory since 1382, to Italy. Occupation by German troops followed in 1943, and in 1945 the city as well as its northern and western environs (Zone A) were occupied by Anglo-American troops, southern environs (Zone B) by Yugoslavian troops. In the Paris Peace Treaty of February 10, 1947, Trieste became a Free Territory under responsibility of the UN. Based on the London Memorandum of October 5, 1954, the city and Zone A were restored to Italy, while extended Zone B remained under Yugoslavia.

17 Italy had to cede Istria to Yugoslavia in the Paris Peace Treaty.

18 Vyacheslav Mikhailovich Molotov, originally Skryabin (1890–1986), Soviet politician, 1926–1956 member of the Politburo of the CPSU, 1930–1941 Chairman of the Council of People's Commissars, 1939–1949 and 1953–1956 Foreign Minister of the Soviet Union.

19 See Doc. 5, fn. 17.

I don't know why I wrote you my yesterday's proposal.[20] It was, I suppose, in part the aftermath of a meeting with Social Democrats during the previous week, and I thought that such people ought to be helped. But I don't know that I am very convinced of what I said. If I go down to Stuttgart[21] there won't be many Social Democrats to support although I suppose there are other decent people to support. There are of course some points in my proposal worth considering on their own, I suppose. At the moment I think perhaps I ought to come home right away. I am not actually necessary to the Berlin operation. I am sort of kept there by Clay[22] because he thinks I may go to Stuttgart later. If I don't this is of course a waste of the tax payer's money, though of course, having brought me over here they are obligated to keep me employed for the time I promised to come over. After all they kept me unemployed for some time at the beginning of this year. But the situation is really – the German situation I mean – so hopeless. Nothing much can be done under present circumstances. And you get tired working up your anti-Russian feelings which point to no good end. There is really not much hope for Europe and I wonder if we want to fight to keep it out of the Russian orbit! This is the kind of spirit Russian toughness creates! It is what the Nazis thrived on! I think it used to be called appeasement.

I think you were right about that second-hand piano at S + M[23].[24] I am terrified at the rise in price of the piano we wanted to buy. We, of course, don't have to buy a Steinway[25]. There are other good pianos: the Mason and Hamlin[26] and the Baldwin[27]. But their prices will also be up. I hope we can get a piano out of this sacrifice but we may have to decide on a smaller one. If you have time you might inquire elsewhere. I don't have any desire to trade with American Nazis.

O. K., let's paint the house ourselves. I ought to come home in time enough to do it.

I don't understand the notice you got about the allotment.[28] My salary began with February 8th. By May 8th you should have 1800 dollars coming to you, and I should have the residue of this three months' pay.[29] May be it will be this way. I have had no salary check here as yet. Please let me know.[30]

20 See Doc. 43.

21 Capital of the state of Württemberg-Baden in the American zone of Germany.

22 See Doc. 2, fn. 6.

23 Schmoller & Mueller Music Store.

24 Emily L. Johnson had written on April 27, 1946: "Schmoller + Mueller had a Style B second hand Steinway advertised and I was in yesterday to see it. Old and somewhat shabby looking." Letter in: Documents from the estate of Edgar N. Johnson, private collection of Candice E. and Thomas R. Johnson, Denver, Colorado, USA.

25 See Doc. 4, fn. 25.

26 The company Mason and Hamlin was founded in 1854 by Henry Mason (1831–1890) and Emmons Hamlin (1821–1885) in Boston, Massachusetts.

27 Company founder was Dwight H. Baldwin (1821–1899).

28 See communication regarding the monthly allotment of 600 dollars to Emily L. Johnson in Appendix of Illustrations, ill. 19.

29 See Doc. 15.

30 Emily L. Johnson in her letter from May 10/13, 1946: "The only money I've received from your new job was 600 on May 10th or thereabouts. It was marked 'for April.' You'd better enquire about Febr. 8–April 1." Letter in: Documents from the estate of

Tomorrow is the 7th of May. I have been away from you three months and here two months. Three months more will be August 8th. And a month after that I should be pretty close to you if I am not already with you. That is really my only comfort. Goodnight my sweet beloved. I take all those caresses which my imagination conjures up, and I send you all of me. I love you, dearest, and I wonder why I am away from you. Kiss the boys for me. Edgar

Doc. 45
Letter to His Wife
Berlin, May 8, 1946

To my dearest and sweetest one:

Today is a holiday here – the first anniversary of V-E day[1]. As a day it is a brilliant one. Bright warm sun – fresh breeze. The lake[2] is rough and the sail boats are having a wonderful time. I ought to be out sailing with my Captain Americus Mitchell[3] in his red boat. A year ago – on the first V-E day I was in Caserta[4]. I still of course remember the great relief of that day. It was finally over. I remember the delicious quality of the Italian spring day. OSS[5] gave a party in the garden of the hunting lodge belonging to the present crown prince of Italy[6]. I shall always remember this garden for the lovely wisteria which hung from the iron railing. It was at this party that a student of mine turned up. This boy who helped to plaster our house and who had been bombing Vienna and other Austrian cities. I remember also that General McNarney[7] was at the party – the general who is now running Germany. It did not seem to me then that this was the way to celebrate V-E day. To-day, in so far as I know, there is no official celebration except that people are taking the day off – going sailing, playing golf. The Allies are not even celebrating the day together – the British are to be sure taking the day off. But the Russians are celebrating tomorrow with some kind of a parade.[8] We, I guess, are making some kind of a taken contribution to their celebration.

Edgar N. Johnson, private collection of Candice E. and Thomas R. Johnson, Denver, Colorado, USA.

1 V-E day stands for "Victory-in-Europe day" and designates May 8, 1945, when the Second World War ended in Europe.

2 Refers to Großer Wannsee, a bight of the Havel (see Doc. 74, fn. 24) in southwest Berlin.

3 See Doc. 41, fn. 11.

4 City in the Italian region of Campania. See Doc. 37, fn. 8.

5 Office of Strategic Services. See Doc. 1, fn. 9.

6 Umberto (1904–1983), May/June 1946 King of Italy as Umberto II.

7 See Doc. 17, fn. 41.

8 On May 9, 1946, a parade took place on Charlottenburger Chaussee in the administrative district of Tiergarten, in front of the Soviet memorial. Soviet, American, British, and French troops took part. See *Berliner Zeitung* from May 10, 1946 [p. 1].

It is natural to ask what has been accomplished in this year, and to answer it fairly one would have to balance what was possible with what has really been done. Of course you know my general point of view. On the international level – in Austria and Germany – I take it that as much has been done as could be done. The machinery is still standing and it functions in the solution of minor problems. Some major problems of a negative sort (level of industry for a future Germany) have also been settled. This is something even though there is no possibility yet of making peace with Austria let alone Germany. And peace is even far off yet in re Italy, the Balkans and Finland. In our own sphere of action, that is in our zones, I think much more could have been done if we had begun to collaborate immediately with those Germans and Austrians whom we could trust. It took us a long time to get around to this. In Berlin we have not really done it yet in our sector. At lunch today (with Mr. Muccio[9] State Department, Don Heath[10], ditto, and a Mr. Chase[11], ditto) there was still talk of the de-Nazification problem. This cannot be settled in a short time, and certainly we have made much progress, but we could have made much more by acting in this manner from the beginning, by taking, that is, the proper people in our confidence. To be sure other important things have been done – the German armed forces have in large part been demobilized and sent home. The displaced persons,[12] have for the most part been taken care of. The people have been kept alive and sufficiently well treated to avoid any disorder. But it would not be correct to say that much of a positive nature has been done. I suppose it is too much to expect that one can act negatively and positively at the same time, though that is what has to be done here. I suppose that what we have done positively compares none too well with what the Russians have done positively in their zone. But we could not have done what they did – our economic stage at home forbids it. And what we have done has been done with methods which are infinitely preferable – and one can hope that they will ultimately get the kind of results which we want for Germany.

I will give you an example, however, of the difficulties under which we labor. There is being held in Hannover[13], tomorrow and Friday[14], a meeting of Social Democrats of the western zones, S[ocial] D[emocrat]s who are maintainig a position of independence over and against the KPD[15].[16] The leaders of the group

9 See Doc. 20, fn. 21.

10 Donald R. Heath. See Doc. 8, fn. 15.

11 Warren M. Chase (1905–1994), American diplomat, 1925 BA, Amherst College, as of 1929 Department of State, 1937–1939 Hamburg, 1945–1948 Foreign Service Officer, Staff of US Political Adviser on German Affairs.

12 Civilians of non-German citizenship who were displaced from their homes into the territory of the German Reich by the German occupation authorities during the Second World War. See Juliane Wetzel, "Displaced Persons (DPs)," in: *Deutschland unter alliierter Besatzung 1945–1949/55*, ed. Wolfgang Benz, Berlin 1999, pp. 338–342.

13 City in the British zone of Germany, as of November 1, 1946, capital of the state of Lower Saxony.

14 May 10, 1946.

15 See Doc. 20, fn. 12.

16 From May 9–11, 1946, the party conference of the SPD for the three Western zones took place in Hannover. The official refoundation of the party was implemented, and Kurt Schumacher (see Doc. 39, fn. 15) was elected as Party Chairman.

of S[ocial] D[emocrat]s here who have fought the unity party wanted to attend this convention. The British managed to transport about 12 of them today in the personal plane, I believe, of Sir William Strang[17], Ambassador Murphy's[18] counterpart. The question arose of whether we could get a plane for the rest of them to go. It was the State Department people who took up this possibility and showed sympathy but at the last moment this morning, Ambassador Murphy took the view that the getting of a plane was an operational matter with which he had nothing to do. So Don Heath threw the matter into my lap at noon. The leaders have been kept waiting all day today in the hope that a plane might be made available. I have been in touch with two generals – my General Keating[19], and General Harper[20], the head of the armed forces division here. I have still to receive an answer from Harper but it seems that it is too late. The general was afraid that if it became known in the states that we were transporting German Civilian Social Democrats to a convention by plane, when we were saying at the same time that we did not have enough planes to fly our own soldiers, that there would be trouble. He is going to call Don Heath and let me know. I think I shall try an admiral before giving up, since I understand there is an admiral here with a plane of his own. But it is sickening. The situation is of course that the State Department doesn't want to take the responsibility. They want to pass the [responsibility] back to me. I don't believe there is much point to this political neutrality. How in the hell can you be neutral unless you don't give a damn. And what is the point of trying to go ahead and formally giving the appearance of supporting the S[ocial] D[emocrat]s when in a pinch you can't really support them. May be I'll go on see Murphy and ask him. If the S[ocial] D[emocrat]s don't receive some support from us their best men will go where they can get support – our Russian friends. And that support will be at the price of joining the unity party.

I love you my Sweetheart – there is no neutrality about that. Col. Glaser[21] has left for a two weeks motor trip in England. When he mentioned it I could only think of our doing a motor trip in England next summer – and I guess that is, in substance – my chief reason for being willing to consider, staying over here for another year. Kiss my dear boys – and my dear beloved one let me take you very closely to me – Edgar

P. S. I just had a call from the General who could have arranged the air trip. He talked to Don Heath and when put to it Don Heath backed down in face of certain reasonable objections of the General – particularly the lateness of the request. So Don Heath is another Murphy when it comes to the test. This is the

17 Sir William Strang (1893–1978), British diplomat, as of 1919 Foreign Office, 1943–1945 representative of Great Britain on the European Advisory Commission, 1945–1947 Political Adviser to the Commander-in-Chief of the British occupation troups in Germany, 1947–1949 Undersecretary, Foreign Office, head of the Germany division.

18 See Doc. 8, fn. 13.

19 See Doc. 39, fn. 6.

20 Robert W. Harper (1900–1982), Major General, 1945–1947 Director, Armed Forces Division, OMGUS.

21 See Doc. 28, fn. 4.

sort of thing which makes me want to come home. How can you defend political neutrality. It is clear that under the present circumstances to defend our political democracy is to defend the Social Democrats, but we really aren't ready to do it. It would be so easy to become cynical. E[dgar]

Doc. 46
Letter to His Wife
Berlin, May 9, 1946

Dearest –

A lovely letter today written on the first.[1] It makes me rather lonesome for the good things I am missing. The things that after all are everything to me. It is your sweet self that writes the letter and tells me these things. You who are tending this garden and taking care of these wonderful children. There is a garden here tended by a professor. There are still tulips, wonderful blues, especially a deep purple stock, and thousands of pansies, and vigorous delphinium on the malls. But I can't react to them. I am becoming quite insensitive to the natural world about me. There is a nightingale about here, and a cuckoo and I do hear them. But it is a world I cannot absorb. It is you and your garden, – it is really yours now – that I should like to see, and this I think could open me up. Our "big and fat and dimpled Hi Timmy[2]" I have really never come to know and what you say of him does not make it easy to go on not knowing him. Our sweet John going out with his May baskets, playing his Sonatina before the judges as you say we have come to expect he would play it and then going out to the recital on Sunday[3], this boy's growing life I am not experiencing. And what I am doing here has really no great importance, and will not have. I sometimes feel myself caught in the web of very ambitious people like Col. Glaser[4] even, and Col. Howley[5], who are out to make this show a pleasure and an adventure for themselves.

You say you have written Mrs. Zumwinkel[6]. It is just possible that she may have something for us, let us say for the month before school starts again. I hope so. I am ready to stop talking about staying over here, unless your reaction to my recent proposal is stronger than I think it is going to be. We might as well stop being tempted by a 10,000 dollar salary which we really don't believe in anyway, and to which we should never be proud of succumbing. The presence of so many

1 Emily L. Johnson's letter from May 1, 1946, in: Documents from the estate of Edgar N. Johnson, private collection of Candice E. and Thomas R. Johnson, Denver, Colorado, USA.

2 Johnson's son Thomas. See Doc. 2, fn. 16. Emily L. Johnson had written: "When he sees you, he says 'Hi, Timmy.'"

3 May 5, 1946.

4 See Doc. 28, fn. 4.

5 See Doc. 20, fn. 18.

6 Essie Zumwinkel (1892–1981), renter of vacation houses in the Rocky Mountains in the US state of Colorado.

wives over here does not help my present mood but I doubt if you would strike up much intimacy with them, and I sometimes doubt very much the quality of people who are staying over here. I suppose it is really no place for John and Hi-Timmy, and there would not be for you as there is not for me any pleasure in living in the midst of these poor people. The papers are already beginning to speak of a winter next year harder than the one which these people have gone through. So why should we continue to speculate and threaten to be adventurous. Why don't I say that I'll be home on or about September first. Tell me why.

I had a rather hurried and cool letter from Norman[7] today saying that Dad[8] had gotten a job repairing pianos in a music store and couldn't possibly be gotten away from Milwaukee[9] at the moment. He seems to be happy in his work and would not even take off a day to go with them to La Porte[10]. La Porte I guess is too painful for him now. He did go to Chicago recently to visit Auntie[11] and Mildred[12], but especially to go out to the cemetery[13] – the poor sweet man. How utterly lonesome he must be.

I love you my sweet and need you very very much – need you to share the days and nights, and to keep my zeal burning. I love you, my heart very tenderly. Edgar

Doc. 47
Letter to His Wife
Berlin, Wannsee Hotel[1], Am Sandwerder 17/19, May 11, 1946

Dear Sweetheart –

I am very lonely and really am not able to take this very well. It is not only the wives, but now there are children. I believe a second boat-load has arrived.[2] Tonight at dinner, a little American lady, a little older than Hi-Timmy[3] did not

7 Norman D. Johnson. See Doc. 3, fn. 13.
8 Frank E. Johnson. See Doc. 3, fn. 12.
9 City in the US state of Wisconsin.
10 City in the US state of Indiana, where Edgar N. Johnson went to high school and where his parents spent a large part of their lives.
11 Hannah Walstrom. See Doc. 4, fn. 14.
12 Mildred H. Williams. See Doc. 4, fn. 12.
13 To the grave of his wife, Mabel A. Johnson, née Walstrom (1876–1944), Edgar N. Johnson's mother, born in Chicago, Illinois, daughter of parents who immigrated from Sweden in 1868, married in 1895, died on December 29, 1944, in Chicago, where she was also buried.

1 See Doc. 25, fn. 9.
2 The first wives and children of members of the American occupation forces had arrived in Berlin on April 30, 1946. See Doc. 42, fn. 13. More relatives arrived on May 10, 1946. See "More U. S. Families Come to OMGUS," in: *OMGUS Observer* from May 17, 1946, p. 4.
3 Johnson's son Thomas, who was 22 months old at the time. See Doc. 2, fn. 16, and Doc. 46, fn. 2.

appreciate the splendor of the Wannsee Hotel in Berlin. She protested so violently that her Mother had to carry her out – to the embarrassment of papa who was left alone at the table with his coffee. I leave you to imagine what was going through my mind during all this. I have perhaps made a fatal mistake in not insisting that I should stay over long enough this time to bring you along. Without that decision I can't bring you here, although I understand that it is possible to make application for your coming over just in case it should be possible later on. This, I think, I had better do.

I went down to sit on the pier a bit after my solitary meal in order to get rid of my melancholy. On the way back to the house I chatted a bit with the gardener[4] of this place. He has been here for 25 years. He first worked for an Englishman who was a member of the Reparations Commission after the last war[5].[6] The next inhabitant was a Jewish banker (Anholt[7]) for whom he worked for sixteen years until 1938,[8] when the Nazis caught up with the Jewish banker and he had to flee to Holland.[9] It was at that moment that Herr Funk[10], the innocent Herr Funk of Nürnberg[11] took over the place.[12] Viewing the garden, however, did not help my mood much. I did not realize that the spinach we

4 Albert Redmann (1891–1978).

5 The Allied Reparations Commission established the German obligations for reparations after the First World War.

6 The member of the Allied Reparations Commission in Berlin was the Belgian-British botanist and geographer Dr. Marcel Hardy (1876–ca. 1944/1945), "who was selected to organize the Agricultural Section of the Commission." "News and Notes," in: *The American Journal of Sociology*, vol. 26, no. 4 (January 1921), pp. 519–523, here p. 520. His daughter Miette (1899–1996) recollects: "[…] Father was nominated as one of the five representatives of the Reparations Commission started in early 1920. Father went first and looked for a house for the family, as well as being briefed in what he was supposed to do in the Commission. And that was how we came to Berlin, Germany, in time to spend our first Christmas there, in a large well-appointed house in Wansee whose garden led right up the lake, where we were able to learn to skate in the winter and sail in the summer." Seven Chapters of Miette Dernbach's (née Hardy) Family Biography, p. 37, in: University of Strathclyde Archives, Glasgow, Great Britain, T-MIN/31. Miette writes that her father worked for the Reparations Commission until 1923. See ibid., pp. 38f. In Berlin Miette met the architect Eckart Muthesius (1904–1989), and later married him. See ibid., pp. 37f. and 42. She had a second marriage with the sculptor, painter, and craftsman Joseph Dernbach-Mayen (1908–1990).

7 Hans Arnhold (1888–1966), German-American banker, as of 1911 representative and as of 1918 branch manager of the Gebr. Arnhold bank, Dresden, in Berlin, 1921 conversion to Gebr. Arnhold, Dresden-Berlin, as of 1931 syndicate with the Berlin bank S. Bleichröder, emigration to the USA, senior partner of the bank Arnhold & S. Bleichroeder, Inc.

8 In the Berlin directory Hans Arnhold is listed for the last time in 1938. See *Berliner Adreßbuch*, 1938: Arnhold, Hans.

9 Arnhold emigrated to the USA, possibly via Holland.

10 See Doc. 25, fn. 10.

11 Nuremberg, city in the state of Bavaria in the American zone of Germany.

12 In the Berlin directory the Reich Ministry of Economics is listed as owner as of 1940, and Funk as resident. See *Berliner Adreßbuch*, 1940–1943: Nikolassee, Am Sandwerder 17.19.

have been eating came from his garden. He has everything coming. There is much to learn from him. He has for example berry bushes – gooseberries and currants in the form of little trees, which could be easily strewn throughout our garden without interfering with the sun on the vegetables. And cherry trees which grow alongside of a wall – a modification of the ones we saw at Mount Vernon[13]. His gardening has brought him through the crises all right – Englishman – Jew – Nazi – Americans, and he goes on growing his flowers and his vegetables.

I learned today that a new job may be offered me. I went up to my office in the Director's Building[14] today to look over the stuff which, I had been told was coming into my office there. I had consented recently to its being occupied by a certain Col. Oppenheimer[15], who is a personal assistant to Clay[16] on matters of De-Nazification. When I saw him I recognized him as a man with whom I had had something to do in London. He was then working with a Special Legal Unit which was dealing with Austrian affairs.[17] He recognized me also and we had some talk, and then had lunch together in the Snack Bar next to the Director's Building. He is going home around May 20th and is looking for someone to take his place. In fact he told me that he had recommended to Clay that either Dorn[18] or I should take his place.[19]

He is the author of the plan to turn over the whole question of De-Nazification to the Germans in our zone. As you perhaps know from the press after long and rather extreme measures of our own to solve the De-Nazification problem – the matter was turned over to the Germans. This man is the author of the law which was finally worked out with the Germans, and accepted in our zone as the law for the final solution of the Nazi problem.[20] It is now in the

13 Former plantation of the first President of the United States, George Washington (1732–1799), in the US state of Virginia.

14 On the grounds of the OMGUS headquarters. See Doc. 17, fn. 45.

15 Fritz E. Oppenheimer (1898–1968), German-American lawyer, Lieutenant Colonel, born in Berlin, Germany, 1922 Dr. jur., University of Breslau, as of 1925 lawyer for international law, Berlin, 1936 emigration to Great Britain, 1940 USA, 1943–1946 US Army, 1945/1946 Special Assistant, OMGUS, responsible for denazification, German legal reform and reform of the courts, worked on the development of the laws issued by OMGUS and the Allied Control Authority, 1946–1948 Special Assistant for German-Austrian Affairs, Department of State.

16 See Doc. 2, fn. 6.

17 At the joint headquarters of the American and British Expeditionary Forces (Supreme Headquarters, Allied Expeditionary Forces [SHAEF]), Oppenheimer had worked for the Special Legal Unit – Germany/Austria (SLUGA), Civil Affairs Section (G-5).

18 See Doc. 2, fn. 10.

19 In June 1946 Dorn was appointed as Clay's Personal Adviser on Denazification, while retaining his previous duties. See Josef Henke/Klaus Oldenhage, "Office of Military Government for Germany (U. S.)," in: *OMGUS-Handbuch. Die amerikanische Militärregierung in Deutschland 1945–1949*, ed. Christoph Weisz (= Quellen und Darstellungen zur Zeitgeschichte, vol. 35), Munich 1994, pp. 1–142, here pp. 45f.

20 Refers to the Gesetz zur Befreiung von Nationalsozialismus und Militarismus vom 5. März 1946 (Law for Liberation from National Socialism and Militarism from March 5, 1946), reproduced in: *Sammlung der Länderratsgesetze (LRGS)*, n. p. and n. d.,

process of being executed. All the Nazis in the zone have been registered, and they are to be tried in special tribunals and prosecuted by special prosecutors. In Bavaria[21] many of these tribunals have been set up, the prosecuting offices have been set up and things are ready to go. In Baden-Wurttemburg[22], and in Hesse[23] things are going a little bit more slowly. It would be my job, as a special assistant of Clay to see that the Germans push through this program successfully, to be responsible for any improvements in the system, to report on the progress made, and to be responsible for reporting on the political implications of the process. Oppenheimer thinks that if the machinery gets properly set up and is able to function, the De-Nazification of our zone ought to be carried through in about 9 months. It is of course a challenge of a kind. There have been many who have insisted that this task should never have been turned over to the Germans, and that they are bound to fail. It involves keeping in close touch with the De-Nazification machinery in the zone, with the Military Government officials with the German officials responsible, and coordinating the whole matter with the proper people here in Omgus[24]. It involves also attending the meetings of the De-Nazification Committee of the Länderrat[25] in Stuttgart[26]. I saw Oppenheimer's memorandum to Clay outlining the organization he would like to leave behind him and proposing my name, along with Dorn's, as his successor. How he came across my name, I don't know. He didn't identify me until today.

I don't know, of course, what decision Clay and Adcock[27] will make. But if the job comes to me I am inclined to take it. I have always been interested in the problem. I have always thought that it should be done with the help of the Germans. It is a job that has to be accomplished before much that is positive can go ahead. It involves the whole question of the Church and of Youth. In the case of the Church the un-de-Nazified condition of the clergy is simply scandalous. The job with Berlin District has lost a bit of its spice – now that General Barker[28] has gone. I think that Col. Glaser[29] would be only too glad to get rid of me, since my position as political advisor to the Commanding General sort of cramps his style. He is moreover a jealous and ambitious person, an advertising man, who takes, I think a certain amount of pleasure in shoving people about. This job involves acting on one's own. It gets me out of this island in the Soviet Zone Berlin, and in close touch with our own work in the zone. And what we do in our own zone in this respect may have something to do with the way in

pp. 95–112. The law transferred practical implementation of denazification to German authorities. On denazification, see Angelika Königseder, "Entnazifizierung," in: *Deutschland unter alliierter Besatzung 1945–1949/55*, ed. Wolfgang Benz, Berlin 1999, pp. 114–117.

21 State in the American zone of Germany.

22 Refers to the state of Württemberg-Baden in the American zone of Germany.

23 Refers to the state of Greater Hesse in the American zone of Germany.

24 See Doc. 17, fn. 45.

25 See Doc. 15, fn. 10.

26 Capital of the state of Württemberg-Baden in the American zone of Germany.

27 See Doc. 14, fn. 9.

28 See Doc. 20, fn. 10.

29 See Doc. 28, fn. 4.

which the problem is handled in the rest of Germany. It might be nice to be able to say that you saw the De-Nazification policy through in Germany.

But it brings up again the question of our future together and this I shall not be able to let go unsolved for very much longer. The Berlin District job does not make it desirable that I should stay here any longer than next Fall. My staying here, from the standpoint of a job, depends upon either the Stuttgart or this de-Nazification job.[30] If the plan for a central administration for Germany goes through in the near future, the bottom is knocked out of the Stuttgart job, since, with a central administration for Germany, the Länderrat is no longer necessary. Besides, the Länderrat job is, as I have come to conceive of it, primarily a high-powered administrative job and as you will know I am not the best administrator in the world. Staying on here for the Stuttgart job is primarily to stay on for the 10,000 dollars and the possibility that we might do some traveling together next summer.

The de-Nazification job, however, aside from the 10,000 dollars and the same prospect of doing some traveling together next summer does bring a little more to the fore the motive of helping your government complete a job which it has more or less bungled heretofore and upon which it has now got a secure footing. I would promise, if Henry[31] agreed to let me go for another year, and you would agree to come over here with the boys, to see this thing through – since it could been seen through by the summer of next year.

I wonder if you could help me make this decision, or to get ready to make it. You must decide whether you would prefer to have me home by next Fall, or whether you would be willing to go to the trouble of bringing yourself and the boys over here by next Fall. There is still the advantage of a 10,000 salary for another year, and the opportunity of doing some travel, I think it ought to be in England, next summer.

If you decided that you wanted to come here, I should do my best to arrange for excellent quarters for you and the boys to live in. For our headquarters would be in Berlin. Moreover, you would be free, here, of responsibility for everything except management. It is easy and cheap enough to provide for cooks, maids, and even nurses for the children. I believe that most of this would be at government expense. If we made such a decision it would be, as I suggested in my previous letter, only for another year. We should then return to Nebraska. Sometimes I think we should take this chance. Suppose, for example, we never got back to Europe. I should do a much better job with you and the boys at my side, because then life would be full each day.

I've got to have you by my side either here or in Lincoln[32]. I am not trying to pass the buck to you, but in a sense it is really your decision. Do you want me

30 "The Stuttgart job appears from here the most important," wrote Franz L. Neumann (see Doc. 1, fn. 8) a few days later from Washington, D. C., to Johnson. "That does not mean that the De-Nazification job is not important. It merely means that there ought to be more Edgar Johnsons in Germany." Letter from May 17, 1946, in: UChicago Library, Special Collections Research Center, Edgar N. Johnson Papers.

31 Charles Henry Oldfather. See Doc. 2, fn. 19.

32 Capital of the US state of Nebraska, where Johnson lived with his family and taught at the university.

there or do you want to come here? If you think of coming here you might sound out Henry on the possibility of another year without any tergiversation at the end of this period. There is something to be said for this war experience culminating in an experience which we really share on the spot. Here we could have some of the experience of a metropolitan existence – there is much opera and music here which I have no desire to go in for alone. There would also be a good music teacher for John[33] here. Personally I have no great desire for more European experience as such unless it be with you. I can't stand being alone. It is not good for me. These wives and children here make life unbearable and this hotel is obviously a place where they congregate.

I love you my darling and I want you close to me all the time. If you don't want to come here, I shall be in Lincoln in the Fall. I love you, my Emily. Edgar

Doc. 48
Letter to His Wife
Berlin, May 14, 1946

Dear Sweet Ones:

I shan't have a decent chance to write a good letter until Thursday[1] but I must write a little note tonight, after the departure of guests, to say how much contentment recent letters[2] have brought, and the things which they contained. I was mad to come back here without my lovely pictures.[3] The snaps have done my heart wonderfully good. The ones of you my dearest are the best thing I have seen since I left you. I love you, my sweet heart. The ones of the boys are simply grand. These precious and fine human beings. Then another letter contained John's[4] recital program[5] and another a description of his magisterial commencement of the program.[6] I resent not being there to see him bring them to order, and to hear him play, and I'm glad for John's and Herbert's[7] sake that

33 Johnson's son John. See Doc. 2, fn. 15.

1 May 16, 1946.
2 Letters in: Documents from the estate of Edgar N. Johnson, private collection of Candice E. and Thomas R. Johnson, Denver, Colorado, USA.
3 See Doc. 33 and Doc. 33, fn. 58.
4 Johnson's son John. See Doc. 2, fn. 15.
5 The youngest participant, John had taken part in a recital for young students at the Lincoln Music Teachers' Association on May 5, 1946, with a piano piece – Rondo in F by the Italian composer Muzio Clementi (1752–1832). Program in: Documents from the estate of Edgar N. Johnson, private collection of Candice E. and Thomas R. Johnson, Denver, Colorado, USA. See Appendix of Illustrations, ill. 18.
6 Emily L. Johnson in her letter from May 6, 1946: "[…] your little boy played at his recital. Herbert [Schmidt; see Doc. 29, fn. 12] termed it an 'auspicious beginning.' Poor dear, he was the only 6 year old, and he had to play first. It was a very noisy audience, and John just sat and calmly looked at them waiting for silence, which he finally got! He played very well indeed."
7 Herbert Schmidt. See Doc. 29, fn. 12.

it was an auspicious beginning (Eugene List[8] has been hanging around here the last few days and I have longed to talk with him about John but there has been no chance)[9]. You also mention the first columbine, an experience of such intense delight that we seem to have shared similarly.[10] And then you tell me that you are reading some papers for Ray Franz[11].[12] You are quite wonderful. You of course have nothing to do – but this temptation is too great. When I get back to you that is one thing I shall never neglect again – sharing a rich intellectual life with you. You must let me. I can't say either that I was not pleased to be put on the Council of the Mediaeval Academy[13].[14] These things, combined with your comments on coming over here, lead to one conclusion which I think you know. I love my sweet ones very much, and I feel rather close to them tonight. I wish I really were. Such treasures, Edgar

8 Eugene List (1918–1985), American pianist.

9 Eugene List and his wife, the violinist Carroll Glenn List, née Glenn (1918–1983), had given a joint concert on May 11, 1946, in the Titania-Palast on Schloßstraße in the Berlin administrative district of Steglitz, "for an audience of U. S. and Allied Troops. […] After their Berlin engagement List and his wife will go to Prague, Czechoslovakia, where they will represent the U. S. in the forthcoming Prague International Music Festival. Before their return to the U. S., this couple will give concerts in Paris, Budapest, Vienna and Rome." "Lists to Give Joint Recital At Titania," in: *OMGUS Observer* from May 10, 1946, p. 2. See Barbara E. Scott Fisher, "Carroll and Eugene List Carry Musical Language of Good Will Overseas. Young Artists Share Careers In Work, Play," in: *The Christian Science Monitor* from May 8, 1946, p. 13; "List, Pianist, Returns From Tour Of Europe," in: *The New York Times* from June 19, 1946, p. 17.

10 Emily L. Johnson in her letter from May 6, 1946: "Do you remember our *first* sight of a columbine, on the path up among the rocks behind the Gasses [see Doc. 63, fn. 29] cabin at Evergreen [see Doc. 63, fn. 31]? I'll never forget it. You just can't believe such a flower is possible."

11 Ray W. Frantz. See Doc. 11, fn. 15.

12 Emily L. Johnson in her letter from May 6, 1946: "Ray Frantz called me tonight and asked if I'd read his exam papers and a few English 21 papers he now has on hand. His reader has gone to the hospital all of a sudden + he's left in a pinch – I shouldn't do it, but I'm terribly flattered that anyone should think after 10 years that I've brains enough to read English papers." In June 1935 she had earned a Bachelor of Arts in English and history at the University of Nebraska.

13 The Mediaeval Academy of America, founded in 1925. See http://www.medievalacademy.org/ (accessed March 2, 2018).

14 At the 21st Annual Meeting of the Corporation of the Mediaeval Academy of America on April 27, 1946, in Cambridge, Massachusetts, Johnson had been elected member of the council (Councillor). See "Historical News," in: *The American Historical Review*, vol. 51, no. 4 (July 1946), pp. 788–804, here pp. 794f.; "The Mediaeval Academy of America. Proceedings of the Twenty-first Annual Meeting of the Corporation 1946," in: *Speculum*, vol. 21, no. 3 (July 1946), pp. 362–375, here p. 362. Johnson remained a member of the council until 1949.

Doc. 49
Letter to His Wife
Berlin, Wannsee Officers' Club[1], Am Sandwerder 17/19, May 19, 1946

My beloved Emily –

I am a bit lonesome this morning after what has been a rather strenuous week. I feel a great need of talking to you. I have read your recent letters[2] over again and they have comforted me, and of course, now, I have always the new snaps[3] in front of me. These are fine likenesses of my dear ones in that batch.

On Monday[4] evening I had dinner with the Colonel in Military Government, Berlin District,[5] who has charge of labor. It is Colonel Abe Kramer[6] who has had a tremendous amount of experience with the National Labor Relations Board[7]. He had just come back from the Leipzig[8] Fair[9]. The Russians put themselves out to arrange a good show in Leipzig (I should have gone perhaps). There was much on display but absolutely nothing to sell, and of course no raw materials to make anything with. All the Americans who went had the experience of being stopped many times by Germans and asked when the Russians were leaving, and when we were coming back (we had Leipzig to begin with you remember[10]). But the Germans are only doing what the Austrians were doing when we came in there. I am sick of this kind of talk, and incidentally, sick of the Germans as well. But I suppose there is no helping the fact that after 12 years of anti-Russian talk, of the war, and of experience with the Russians they should feel this way. And they know very well of course that quadripartite relations do not run very smoothly. But their attitude, in that it contributes to hostility is no good. If it leads, or helps to lead to war they are the chief sufferers. And I don't like to have them deliberately try to stimulate the differences. An

1 See Doc. 25, fn. 9.

2 Letters in: Documents from the estate of Edgar N. Johnson, private collection of Candice E. and Thomas R. Johnson, Denver, Colorado, USA.

3 Refers to photos of his wife and sons. See Doc. 48.

4 May 13, 1946.

5 See Doc. 25, fn. 13.

6 Abe Kramer (1908–1968), Major, 1941/1942 Field Examiner, National Labor Relations Board, 1942–1947 US Army, 1946/1947 Chief, Manpower Branch, OMGBD/OMGBS, 1947–1949 Deputy Manpower Adviser, OMGBY.

7 The National Labor Relations Board, founded in 1935, organizes elections for the admission of unions as representatives in companies and investigates unfair labor conditions.

8 City in the state of Saxony in the Soviet zone of Germany.

9 Oldest and most significant trade fair in Germany. The first postwar Leipzig Trade Fair had taken place from May 8–12, 1946. Exhibitors from all four occupation zones and the Soviet Union were represented. "In the 2,750 exhibits were household items, stoves, refrigerators, dresses and furs, jewelry, textile goods, and all the other sundry articles formerly turned out by the nation's industry." "Leipzig Fair," in: *OMGUS Observer* from May 17, 1946, p. 5.

10 In April 1945, Leipzig had been occupied by American troops. After withdrawal into the occupation zone allocated to them by the London Protocol (see Doc. 83, fn. 88), the city came under Soviet control.

assistant Burger-meister of Kreuzberg[11] told my driver[12] the other day that he was sure that the U. S. and Britain would soon present an ultimatum to the Russians telling them to get out of Germany. Kramer is a leftist and labor union man, and he went through the history of this fight to get them into some kind of line. The unions are organized into one large federation here and it is largely under the control of the Communists, many of them trained in Russia.[13] It is supposed to be unpolitical, but as a matter of fact it has gone over strongly to the new SED party. In its organizational steps it has thumbed its nose pretty consistently at the Allies and gone its own way, and it threatens to do so again with new elections which it is planning to hold in the various industrial branches of the union. The Russians permit no employers' associations (we do) and consequently in their zone the unions have a pretty strong hand, and they are making strong demands to share in the complete management of the plants. But there is going to be more and more unemployment here since stocks of raw materials are dwindling. Kramer was a comfort. There are few men so capable and so energetic here, and I am glad he is planning to stay on. But he has only one or two people help him control the labor activities of a huge city, and of the American sector of it.

On Tuesday[14] I had dinner with Rodnick[15] and his wife[16]. Do you remember my talking about Rodnick, a cultural anthropologist who uses the word culture

11 First Deputy Mayor of the Berlin administrative district of Kreuzberg was Georg Henschel (1912–1981), SPD, Second Deputy Mayor was Karl Krüger, no party affiliation.

12 Artur Sanow. See Doc. 40, fn. 13.

13 On the Freier Deutscher Gewerkschaftsbund (FDGB), founded in February 1946 in Berlin for the entire Soviet zone, see Werner Müller, "Freier Deutscher Gewerkschaftsbund (FDGB)," in: *SBZ-Handbuch. Staatliche Verwaltungen, Parteien, gesellschaftliche Organisationen und ihre Führungskräfte in der Sowjetischen Besatzungszone Deutschlands 1945–1949*, on behalf of the Arbeitsbereich Geschichte und Politik der DDR at the University of Mannheim and the Institut für Zeitgeschichte Munich, eds. Martin Broszat/Hermann Weber, Munich 1990, pp. 626–664; Michael Fichter, "Gewerkschaften," in: *Deutschland unter alliierter Besatzung 1945–1949/55*, ed. Wolfgang Benz, Berlin 1999, pp. 129–134.

14 May 14, 1946.

15 David Rodnick (1908–1980), American sociologist and anthropologist, 1936 PhD, University of Pennsylvania, worked for OSS during the Second World War, 1947–1951 Adviser, Columbia University, project in contemporary cultures, 1955–1959 Assistant Director, Institute for International Social Research, Princeton, New Jersey, 1959–1961 Professor, Interamerican University, Puerto Rico, 1961–1963 Professor of Sociology and Anthropology, Iowa Wesleyan College, 1963–1965 Senior Sociologist, Operations Research, Inc., Washington, D. C., 1965–1975 Professor of Sociology and Anthropology, Texas Technological University, 1975–1977 Visiting Professor, University of Hamburg. "Following World War II, he began cultural analysis of European countries and cultures including posts at the Office of Military Government in occupied Germany, the Paris office of Air University, the University of Oslo, Columbia University, and Princeton University. In the 1950s he became a professor at Inter-American University, San German, Puerto Rico, before moving to Iowa Wesleyan College and then Texas Technological University (1965–1975)." https://legacy.lib.utexas.edu/taro/utcah/02351/cah-02351.html (accessed March 2, 2018).

16 Elizabeth A. Rodnick, née Amis (1911–1999), worked for OSS during the Second World War.

and pattern so many times in every five minutes as to make you sick. They did an interesting thing while working for the Information Control Services branch here.[17] They went to a little town in Hesse, Eschwege[18], close to the Russian and the French borders[19] and sat down there for a period of about six months to find out what was going on. They got to know most of the people of the town and had occasion to watch the detailed activity of military government there. It was a sad picture they paint both of the Germans and of military government, so sad that I was utterly in despair when they left and wondered whether there was actually any hope in the Germans, or indeed in us, and whether, if this was the general situation prevailing in our zone, we should not simply get out of here and not bother with a job for which we are not fitted either by experience or interest. This was worse than Upper Austria[20], and Rodnick evidently had some of the spirit in him that we had when in Austria. Walter Dorn[21] says his report was not fair. Dorn had to go down and fire the Military Government officer. Well – it was not so much that there was anything happening in Eschwege that we have not heard about but that it was all lumped together in one little place, having an altogether disastrous effect on the Germans. Much drunkenness, for example. Officers starting to drink around noon, then going out and trying to play ball with German kids, unable to do so and falling down and having to be picked up. Mistresses – the Rodnicks claim they were put up in a house where four M[ilitary] G[overnment] officers were openly living with Fräuleins – indeed one of the bedrooms was always open and the blue silk night dress of one of the ladies always draped over the bed in proud display. Black Market[22]. The PX[23] supplies coming into town for a small contingent of M[ilitary] G[overnment] officers were originally sent for a whole company which had as a matter of fact gone but the supplies continued to come in the same amount. The Rodnicks were offered 48 chocolate bars each for one week. This in addition to all the rest including cameras and radios. You know where most of this went. They told me the story of 2 GI's[24] who took 2 cartons of cigarettes from the bed of a captain and arranged between them that one was to sell it to a black market dealer and the other was to hi-jack the dealer on the way home. The cigarettes were accordingly returned to the bed of the captain who was annoyed, not because of their dishonesty but because they had not informed him they were tak-

17 David Rodnick later writes in the introduction to his book *Postwar Germans. An Anthropologist's Account*: "The book is based on five months of intensive anthropological field work in central and northeastern Hesse, carried on with the assistance of my wife, Elizabeth Amis Rodnick, between December, 1945, and June, 1946, as part of our duties with the Information Control Division of the Office of Military Government." David Rodnick, *Postwar Germans. An Anthropologist's Account*, New Haven, Connecticut, 1948, p. IX.

18 Small town in the northeast of the state of Greater Hesse in the American zone of Germany.

19 Eschwege was near the Soviet zone of Germany, but not near the French zone.

20 Upper Austria bordered on former Czechoslovakia and Germany.

21 See Doc. 2, fn. 10.

22 See Doc. 21, fn. 11.

23 Post Exchange, retail store on US Army posts.

24 Government Issues, slang for American soldiers.

ing the cigarettes away. The situation in the local government is bad if not worse than what we found in Upper Austria. The Nazis in and the anti-Nazis out or in very unimportant positions, and this because the M[ilitary] Governor thought that the Nazis were the right people to turn over things to. They were the kind of people he would deal with at home, whereas the anti-Nazis were riff-raff-no-account. All this was accompanied by a perfectly cold-blooded attitude to the whole situation. The Rodnicks were told by officers that they knew of course that at home they would have to occupy a very small and unimportant position in life. But here they were cock of the walks – they ran the government and the people as they never could do at home, and by God they were going to stay here just as long as they could. In fact one of them said he was going to stay at least until he had made 20,000 dollars. I only hope Eschwege is not typical. Walter Dorn says that it is not but he has concern about the growing resentment of the Germans in the zone to us. Here people say we are Bolshevists with creased trousers. What the Rodnicks had to say about the Germans themselves was not encouraging. They visited schools and youth groups, political meetings and they like and had nothing to report of initiative, vitality, or ideas. This of course can't be expected. But you have got to have some groups upon which you can depend. May be these people are really hopeless.

Wednesday[25] night I had dinner with a British Major Hayes[26] who is Chairman of the Local Government Committee in the Kommandatura[27], and who is leaving. His place is being taken by a Major Ashton[28], a merchant from Liverpool[29] who has dealt with cotton in Texas[30].[31] The dinner was in a British Mess and it was put on in considerable style. The French and Russians were invited but the Russians as usual did not show up. The Frenchman had been in the banking business. At the conclusion of the dinner there was a toast to the king. I almost made the mistake of smoking before it but I was warned by Ashton that it was not done. Nobody smokes before the toast. The table is cleared of

25 May 15, 1946.

26 Harold Hays (1896–1980), Major, Administration and Local Government Section, Military Government British Troops Berlin (MGBTB), British representative on the Local Government Committee, Allied Kommandatura Berlin. Photos with Hays in Appendix of Illustrations, ill. 68 and ill. 77.

27 See Doc. 29, fn. 14.

28 John Pennington Ashton (1891–1978), Major, 1953/1954 Mayor of Wallasey (a town near Liverpool in England).

29 City on the northwest coast of England.

30 US state.

31 Ashton filled in for Hays as representative for Great Britain on the Local Government Committee and as Chairman in the meetings on May 17, 23, and 31, 1946. See minutes of the 18th meeting of the Local Government Committee, Allied Kommandatura Berlin, on May 17, 1946, LG/M (46) 18, English version, in: TNA, Allied Kommandatura: Directives, Minutes and Papers, FO 1112/378; minutes of the 19th meeting of the Local Government Committee, Allied Kommandatura Berlin, on May 23, 1946, LG/M (46) 19, English version, in: ibid.; minutes of the 20th meeting of the Local Government Committee, Allied Kommandatura Berlin, on May 31, 1946, LG/M (46) 20, English version, in: ibid.; minutes of the 21st meeting of the Local Government Committee, Allied Kommandatura Berlin, on May 31, 1946, LG/M (46) 21, English version, in: ibid.

everything except one glass of wine per person. The person presiding stands. All stand. Then he says, "Mr. *Vice* – (this is the person at the other end of the table) I give you the King." And Mr. Vice says "To the King." And they all drink, and that is that. The Major Ashton is proud to belong to a regiment whose history stretches back to the Revolution[32], and he was afraid that the Labor Government might break up these old regiments and these fine traditions. I don't see that they do any harm. I heard from Major Hayes much criticism of English Military Government. I don't suppose they really make much more of an impression than we. But they are much more willing to impose their way upon the Germans than we are. It was the same in Austria. They have had a much larger time to get used to doing things in a certain way, and it seems therefore natural to them but that others should do it in the same way. They annoy the Russians, I am afraid, very very much. Yet they are comparatively easy to get along with, and you don't have to be afraid of trickery at least where they are concerned.

Thursday[33] I should have written you but I was completely worn out and went to bed. On Friday[34] Robert Eisenberg[35] (OSS[36] Washington) invited me over to dinner with three Germans, one Herr Mommsen[37], grandson of the famous classical historian[38] and a friend of Felix Gilbert's[39], a Herr Haas[40] who is the trea-

32 Refers to the Glorious Revolution of 1688, when the Stuart King James II (1633–1701) was deposed and his daughter ascended to the throne as Queen Mary II (1662–1694) with her husband, William III of Orange (1650–1702).

33 May 16, 1946.

34 May 17, 1946.

35 Robert Eisenberg (1908–1987), American lawyer, born in Waidhofen, Lower Austria, 1931 Dr. jur., German University in Prague, 1939 emigration to Italy and France, 1941 USA, 1943 US citizenship, 1943–1945 US Army (OSS), 1945–1968 Department of State.

36 Office of Strategic Services. See Doc. 1, fn. 9. Refers here to a successor agency of OSS.

37 Konrad Mommsen (1896–1973), German businessman, sentenced to six months in prison during the Nazi period for supporting Jews living in hiding, after 1945 adviser to the American military government.

38 Theodor Mommsen (1817–1903), German classical historian, honored with the Nobel Prize for Literature in 1902 for his monumental work *Römische Geschichte* (*History of Rome*).

39 Felix Gilbert (see Doc. 1, fn. 11), like Konrad Mommsen's brother Theodor Ernst Mommsen (1905–1958), was an historian from Germany. Both had been students of Friedrich Meinecke (see Doc. 1, fn. 11), and both had emigrated to the USA in the 1930s.

40 Friedrich Haas (1896–1988), German lawyer and politician (CDU), studies in science, economics, and law, University of Freiburg im Breisgau and University of Munich, 1922 doctorate as Dr. oec. publ., 1925–1928 assistant judge for occupation damages in the Reichswirtschaftsgericht, Berlin, 1929–1931 employment as Magistratsrat in the district administration of Charlottenburg, as of 1931 in the central administration of the city of Berlin, (as of 1937 as Obermagistratsrat, as of 1938 as Stadtdirektor), until 1933 Deutsche Zentrumspartei, 1945 CDU, October–December 1945 Deputy Director of the Rechtsamt, as of December 1945 Deputy Director of the Finance Department of the Magistrat, in this position from March–December 1946 Acting Director of the Finance Department (Department A), December 1946–1951 Director of the Department of Finance (City Treasurer), 1951–1958 Senator for Finance, at the same

surer of the city of Berlin, and a Willi Brandt[41], a Marxist professor at the Russian controlled University of Berlin[42]. It was an interesting evening, a good deal of it being spent on the Nurnberg[43] trials[44] in condemnation of Schacht[45] and in

time 1953–1955 Senator for Federal Affairs, 1958–1961 President of the Berlin Oberverwaltungsgericht. Photo of Haas in Appendix of Illustrations, ill. 83.

41 Refers to the German lawyer Dr. Günter Brandt (1894–1968), "an independent leftist on the Berlin intellectual scene of 1945–48 forgotten today." Wolfgang Schivelbusch, *In a Cold Crater. Cultural and Intellectual Life in Berlin, 1945–1948*, trans. Kelly Barry (= Weimar and Now. German Cultural Criticism, 18), Berkeley and Los Angeles, California, and London 1998, p. 175. Along with Konrad Mommsen and Arno Scholz (see Doc. 40, fn. 10), Günter Brandt had applied to the British military government for the licensing of the newspaper *Telegraf* (see Doc. 40, fn. 10). Only Scholz appeared as licensee, while Mommsen had backed out, "because Scholz had refused to work with Brandt, a Communist." ("weil Scholz sich geweigert hatte, mit Brandt, einem Kommunisten, zusammenzuarbeiten.") Peter Köpf, *Die Mommsens. Von 1848 bis heute – die Geschichte einer Familie ist die Geschichte der Deutschen*, Hamburg, Leipzig, and Vienna 2004, p. 85. Brandt became Editor-in-Chief of *Sonntag,* the weekly newspaper published by the Kulturbund zur demokratischen Erneuerung Deutschlands, which first appeared in July 1946. In addition he regularly wrote for *Die Weltbühne*. Brandt was a professor with a lectureship for civil law at the University of Berlin, and as of 1950 he taught at the Freie Universität Berlin.

42 University founded in 1810, ceremoniously reopened on January 29, 1946. To assure Soviet influence on the university, according to Reimer Hansen, "Neuer Name in historischer Tradition. Von der Friedrich-Wilhelms- zur Humboldt-Universität 1945–1949," in: *Berlin in Geschichte und Gegenwart. Jahrbuch des Landesarchivs Berlin 2009*, pp. 349–375, here p. 373: "According to the Germany policies of the 'Big Three' negotiated at the conferences in Yalta and Potsdam, Berlin was not supposed to belong to any of the occupation zones, and it was to be administrated by the Allied Kommandatura and the Berlin Magistrat. However, with conspiratorial approval of the Soviet military administration, the German Central Administration for National Education usurped responsibility for the university. The university was thus illegally subordinated to the Communist Soviet military and German civil administration of the Soviet zone." ("Nach der auf den Kriegskonferenzen in Jalta und Potsdam vereinbarten Deutschlandpolitik der 'Großen Drei' sollte Berlin keiner der Besatzungszonen angehören und von der Alliierten Kommandantur und dem Berliner Magistrat verwaltet werden. Die Deutsche Zentralverwaltung für Volksbildung riss jedoch mit konspirativer Billigung der Sowjetischen Militäradministration die Zuständigkeit für die Universität an sich. Hiermit war die Universität widerrechtlich der kommunistischen sowjetischen Militär- und deutschen Zivilverwaltung der sowjetischen Besatzungszone unterstellt worden.")

43 Nuremberg, city in the state of Bavaria in the American zone of Germany.

44 Nuremberg trial against 22 major war criminals and six organizations indicted as criminal. The trial took place before a specifically established ad hoc tribunal, the International Military Tribunal. The trial lasted from November 20, 1945–October 1, 1946. See Heinz Boberach, "Strafrechtliche Verfolgung von NS-Verbrechen," in: *Deutschland unter alliierter Besatzung 1945–1949/55*, ed. Wolfgang Benz, Berlin 1999, pp. 181–186; Manfred Görtemaker, "Rache der Sieger oder Suche nach Gerechtigkeit? Der Nürnberger Hauptkriegsverbrecherprozess 1945/46," in: *Die Vier Mächte in Berlin. Beiträge zur Politik der Alliierten in der besetzten Stadt*, eds. Michael Bienert/Uwe Schaper/Andrea Theissen in collaboration with Werner Breunig (= Schriftenreihe des Landesarchivs Berlin, vol. 9), Berlin 2007, pp. 133–145.

45 Hjalmar Schacht (1877–1970), German banker and politician, 1923–1930 Reich Currency Commissioner and Reichsbank President, 1933–1939 once again Reichsbank

ridicule of Raeder[46]. But I was discouraged about the way these Germans talk about each other. They were quite insistent, and this was a sound note, that the Germans should pursue an internationalist line rather than their present nationalist one. But they called the Germans simply political idiots who could not now be trusted with the management of their own affairs. Brandt told the story of being at a movie where shots were displayed of the Nurnberg and Dachau[47] trials[48], at the latter of which the Mauthausen[49] boys[50] were being tried, that ugly bunch which I saw in their cells when I was there. When Jackson[51] appeared on the screen, the lady next to him leaned over to him and said that he looked like a war criminal, and when the criminals themselves were shown she commented on what fine looking Germans they were. Brandt said nothing. When the Mauthausen murderers were shown she broke out again with the remark that they were such fine looking men. He then had to silence her with the remark, "Were you ever in Mauthausen." She just took it for granted that any German in the audience would share her point of view. I am afraid this has to be a very long occupation, and that we have to make very long range plans. These people have literally to be re-educated over a long period by themselves but under our direction. I think now we should go very slowly in letting them resume responsibility for themselves over anything like a centralized state.

Last night I had dinner or rather an after dinner talk with this Mrs. Delahaye[52], whom I have mentioned.[53] I waited for 45 minutes for my driver to come and get me but he didn't show up. On the way home from here in the afternoon, he had been picked up by the MP's[54] for speeding – they are terribly strict here because of the numerous accidents – and kept waiting until about 11:30 last night in the MP police station. He called me about mid-night and was

President and 1934–1937 also Reich Economics Minister, 1935–1937 Reich Plenipotentiary for War Economy, 1937–1943 Reich Minister without Portfolio, 1944/1945 concentration camp, indicted and acquitted by the International Military Tribunal in Nuremberg.

46 Erich Raeder (1876–1960), German naval officer, 1928 promotion to Admiral, 1928–1935 head of naval command, 1935–1943 Commander-in-Chief of the Kriegsmarine, 1939 promotion to Grand Admiral, sentenced by the International Military Tribunal in Nuremberg to life imprisonment, released in 1955 for health reasons.

47 City northwest of Munich in the state of Bavaria in the American zone of Germany.

48 The Dachau trials were military court trials by the US Army against defendents who were accused of war crimes and crimes against humanity. They took place from 1945–1948 in the Dachau internment camp, site of the Dachau concentration camp until the end of April 1945.

49 Refers to the Mauthausen concentration camp in Upper Austria, in which more than 200,000 people were imprisoned between 1938 and 1945, approximately half of whom were murdered.

50 Refers to the camp personnel of the Mauthausen concentration camp, on trial from March 29–May 13, 1946, in the Mauthausen trial, second Dachau trial.

51 Robert H. Jackson (1892–1954), American lawyer, 1940/1941 US Attorney General, 1941–1954 Associate Justice, US Supreme Court, 1945/1946 US Chief Prosecutor, International Military Tribunal, Nuremberg.

52 Johnson's German teacher. See Doc. 40, fn. 27.

53 See Doc. 40.

54 Military Police officers.

rather furious, I gathered. I had to rescue him once before from the MP's for leaving his car open while he was in his house. He was doubtful last night if they would continue him in his job, but said he could get other work. He insisted they would not let him call me. I shall intervene for him if I can but I was certainly at a loss last night. When I got to Harnack house[55] this Russian lady has already begun to eat. Afterwards our conversation was a bit trivial and she left early. I had a difficult time in getting back to the hotel. Our car got lost and never arrived, but I finally got another from the Berlin District Motor Pool. There was drinking and dancing at Harnack house. I noticed they are now selling wine with meals and most people had bottles. When I went home there was a very unpleasant drunken scene in front of the house. A belligerent officer whom they couldn't get into a cab. I am afraid there is far too much drinking here, by the wrong kind of people. I don't like the looks of many I see about me. We just aren't a colonial people, and for many this is just another racket.

There have been many meetings during the week. I took Col. Glaser's[56] place at a meeting of the Local Government Committee[57].[58] We were supposed to talk about future elections in Berlin but the Russians don't want to talk about elections in Berlin. They stalled unmercifully at the last meeting and at this meeting the Russian Major Feldman[59], a rather nice chap, wasted one hour and a half quarrelling over the minutes. He resents the English particularly, resented something Major Hayes had inserted into the minutes, and because his own translation was inaccurate there was a long fuss. In fact the whole afternoon was wasted. There was also a Kommandatura[60] meeting in the morning at which

55 See Doc. 15, fn. 16.

56 See Doc. 28, fn. 4. Glaser was on a trip to England. See Doc. 45.

57 See Doc. 29, fn. 14.

58 See minutes of the 18th meeting of the Local Government Committee, Allied Kommandatura Berlin, on May 17, 1946, LG/M (46) 18, English version, in: TNA, Allied Kommandatura: Directives, Minutes and Papers, FO 1112/378.

59 Iosif Moiseyevich Feldman (born 1905), Soviet Major, 1927–1937 and again as of 1939 Red Army, 1930 graduate of the Military Technical Aviation School, 1941 graduate of the Leningrad Institute of Languages, 1945 Deputy Editor-in-Chief of the *Berliner Zeitung*, SMAG censor, 1946–1949 Deputy Editor-in-Chief of the *Tägliche Rundschau*, Editor-in-Chief of the *Nacht-Expreß*, 1949 arrested under suspicion of espionage as an employee of the Information Administration of SMAG and brought to the Soviet Union. Wolfgang Schivelbusch writes: "As Eugenia Kazeva, a colleague of his in the SMAD, recalls, Feldmann was one of the Jewish intellectuals from Leningrad so numerous in the intelligence division, a 'small, round, mobile, and very clever man.'" Wolfgang Schivelbusch, *In a Cold Crater. Cultural and Intellectual Life in Berlin, 1945–1948*, trans. Kelly Barry (= Weimar and Now. German Cultural Criticism, 18), Berkeley and Los Angeles, California, and London 1998, p. 168. The British representative on the Local Government Committee, Harold Hays (see fn. 26), later remembered Feldman: "[…] Feldman was trained in law and had been educated at the university at Kiev. He was a Ukrainian Jew," and: "Feldman was not only uncompromising and unhelpful, but at times plainly insolent." Memoirs of Harold Hays, chapter 10: Berlin Constitution 1946, p. 147, in: Imperial War Museum (IWM) Duxford, Cambridgeshire, Great Britain, Lieutenant Colonel Harold Hays MBE Collection. Photo with Feldman in Appendix of Illustrations, ill. 68.

60 See Doc. 20, fn. 11.

nothing important happened.[61] But things will soon begin to happen there again. The pro-merger SPD people have written what I think is an intolerably fresh letter to the Kommandatura.[62] Yesterday[63] I went to a meeting of the Political Directorate[64] (Don Heath[65] + opposites) at which the question of the recognition of SPD + SED came up, and went through this far. Don called me to his side in the course of the discussion. The tone of this meeting was very different. Quick, rapid-fire negotiation unlike anything I have ever seen. The Russian, Ivanov[66], about the smoothest Russian I have seen here. He made slighting remarks about Commandants. It was so quick it was difficult for me to follow. For this kind of exchange you have to be very skilled and very experienced. There was no translation of French because everybody knew it.

The Military Government people in Berlin District come to me more and more with their problems. There is too much to do.

Kathleen McLaughlin[67] called on me the other day. She seems a very quiet, modest and capable person. She said she might be in again.

Your letters make it quite clear that you don't want to bring the boys over here. I certainly am not the one to say that this is not wise. They make clear also that you do not feel able to make a decision for yourself on over there or over here. I take it my recent letter on this subject will bring the same response. This I think leads in only one direction, the direction you speak of when you say that you guess I might decide to return to Nebraska. I have never thought that if I returned to Nebraska I should not be happy there. You underestimate your importance to me when you say "I don't think that you can necessarily be happy wherever I am." I expect that there will be some necessary readjustment to my work, but I think that will not take a long time. Once having made the decision

61 Refers to the 14th meeting of the Commandants on May 17, 1946. See minutes of this meeting, BKC/M (46) 14, English version, in: LAB, B Rep. 036-01 (Office of Military Government, Berlin Sector [OMGBS]), 11/148-1/10.

62 In the minutes of the 14th meeting of the Commandants, BKC/M (46) 14-142, it says: "The Meeting had before it a letter from the Pro-Fusion Committee of the SPD asking for clarification upon its status vis à vis the Allies." This may refer to a letter from the former Central Committee of the SPD from May 9, 1946, which requests a decision on the distribution of the property and assets of the former SPD. See BK/O (46) 261 from June 13, 1946, in: LAB, F Rep. 280 (Quellensammlung zur Berliner Zeitgeschichte [LAZ-Sammlung]), no. 12601.

63 May 18, 1946.

64 See minutes of the 36th meeting of the Political Directorate, Allied Control Authority, on May 18 and May 20, 1946, DPOL/M (46) 19, French version, in: Archives de l'Occupation Française (AOF) en Allemagne et en Autriche, Ministère des Affaires Etrangères, Colmar, France, Services Français à Berlin, Groupe Français du Conseil de Contrôle (GFCC), Bureau des Archives, caisse 1140, paquet 51.

65 Donald R. Heath (see Doc. 8, fn. 15) was the American representative in the Political Directorate, Allied Control Authority.

66 Nikolai Vasilyevich Ivanov (1905–1996), Soviet diplomat, 1938/1939 First Secretary of the Soviet Embassy in Berlin, 1944/1945 adviser to the Soviet delegation on the European Advisory Commission, London, 1945–1947 head of the Political Department in the Administration of the Political Adviser, SMAG, and Deputy of the Political Adviser for general questions.

67 See Doc. 33, fn. 43.

to come back, I shan't be out looking for trouble. From what I gather from your letters, and what I read and what I learn from others who are returning from home no serious person can be completely happy with the present situation at home. Nor at Nebraska will things be any better. But there is much to do at home to try to get the country into some shape for assuming its responsibilities in the world and to try to clean house at home (the one-party system in the South struck me as a phrase the other day). I have also still to educate myself. I don't think, therefore, I'll bring up the subject again unless something unusual happens. When shall I plan to be there. I should say somewhere in the neighborhood of Sept. 1st. May be you will have secured some kind of an answer from Mrs. Zumwinkel[68]. I need you all so very very much. I am no good alone. The prospect and the definite decision will help. Keep the phlox blooming until I get there, my own sweet beloved Emily.

In this connection Henry[69] has written saying that they lost Paul Sweet[70] but got a young instructor[71].[72] They certainly did not offer Paul very much.[73] Henry says also that he plans to give up the chairmanship and plans to support a system of election of a chairman within the department and appointment by the chancellor. I suppose Glenn[74] ought to have it.[75] Well he also told me that he recommended to Boucher[76] that I be raised from my present level 3980 to 4200 the minimum salary of a full professor. He did the same for Jim[77] and others. Boucher sliced all these recommendations but in the case of Jim and me he sliced them 200 dollars apiece, giving us a raise of twenty dollars apiece. This is nothing less than a deliberate affront. I am going to write him and tell him so

68 See Doc. 46, fn. 6.

69 Charles Henry Oldfather. See Doc. 2, fn. 19.

70 See Doc. 2, fn. 28.

71 Refers to David L. Dowd (1918–1968), American historian, 1946 PhD, University of California, 1946–1949 Instructor, University of Nebraska, then taught at the University of Florida, and lastly at the University of Kentucky.

72 See Doc. 2 and Doc. 11.

73 Emily L. Johnson had written about this in her letter from May 10/13, 1946: "In answer to my query about Paul S[weet], Jim Sellers [see fn. 77] yesterday said he'd taken a job at Chicago at 4500. Henry had offered him 3600." Letter in: Documents from the estate of Edgar N. Johnson, private collection of Candice E. and Thomas R. Johnson, Denver, Colorado, USA.

74 Glenn W. Gray (1900–1979), American historian, 1928 PhD, Cornell University, taught from 1924–1926 at Cornell University, as of 1926 at the University of Nebraska, Professor.

75 In the autumn of 1946, after his return to the University of Nebraska, Johnson became temporary Chairman of the Department of History.

76 Chauncey S. Boucher (1886–1955), American historian, 1914 PhD, University of Michigan, taught at the University of Michigan, Washington University, Ohio State University, University of Texas, and University of Wisconsin, as of 1923 University of Chicago, 1926–1935 Dean, College of Arts, Literature, and Science, University of Chicago, 1935–1938 President, West Virginia University, 1938–1946 Chancellor, University of Nebraska, taught from 1947–1952 at Knox College.

77 James L. Sellers (1891–1966), American historian, 1922 PhD, University of Wisconsin, 1922–1930 Instructor, University of Wisconsin, 1930–1959 Professor, University of Nebraska.

and refuse to accept the twenty dollars, the effrontery.[78] If he were going to be the chancellor next year certainly I should hesitate to come back.[79]

You will have to send the lawn-mower downtown to get it sharpened. They do it at the sporting goods store I think.

Did you ever get any money from the government? Did you ever receive a package I sent from Washington containing papers? Have you ever received similar packages from Washington, sent by Coburn Kidd[80].

Bye-bye Sweetheart. I'll try not to wait so long next time. I love you and the boys with all my heart. Kiss and hold them closely for me. It would be so wonderful if I could be with you for only a little while. Bye-bye Sweet, my lovely Emily. Edgar

Doc. 50
Letter to His Wife
Berlin, Wannsee Officers' Club[1], Am Sandwerder 17/19, May 20, 1946

Dear Sweetheart –

Let me try to summarize a busy day in order to prove to you that there are things to do over here.

I must say I overslept a bit this morning after being up a bit late at Walter Dorn's[2] last night. Walter Lichtenstein[3] was there and a Professor Gewehr[4], who was responsible for getting Gene Anderson[5] away from us when we first tried to get him for Nebraska.[6] Walter D[orn] has been down to Bavaria[7] for a

78 Alison G. Murie (see Doc. 68, fn. 5) writes in an email to Werner Breunig from January 10, 2010: "[…] there was a story that Chancellor Boucher wrote to him offering him a derisory salary raise if he would come back, and Edgar refused it with contempt. This was naturally applauded among his friends."

79 "Boucher was replaced the following year, to general relief among my parents' friends," writes Alison G. Murie (see Doc. 68, fn. 5) in an email to Werner Breunig from January 15, 2010. Boucher remained in office until August 31, 1946; his successor was the biochemist Reuben G. Gustavson (1892–1974), who held the office till 1953.

80 Coburn B. Kidd (1909–1981), 1935 PhD, University of St. Andrews, Scotland, 1937–1940 Assistant Archivist, National Archives, 1939 LLB, Georgetown University, 1943–1945 US Army, as of 1946 Department of State (1946/1947 Research Analyst).

1 See Doc. 25, fn. 9.

2 See Doc. 2, fn. 10.

3 See Doc. 20, fn. 39.

4 Wesley M. Gewehr (1888–1961), American historian, 1922 PhD, University of Chicago, taught 1919–1922 at Morningside College, 1922–1929 at Denison University, 1924/1925 Exchange Professor, Tsing Hua College, Beijing, 1929–1940 American University, 1940–1958 University of Maryland, 1945/1946 Head of History, Army University, Shrivenham, Great Britain, Professor in US Army University, Biarritz, France, attached to Army Lecture Bureau, Germany.

5 Eugene N. Anderson. See Doc. 1, fn. 1.

6 In 1936 Anderson had been appointed as Professor at American University in Washington, D. C., where Gewehr had been teaching since 1929, and did not come to the University of Nebraska.

couple of weeks and he is filled with somewhat the same ideas as those I referred to in my yesterday's letter[8]. He is concerned with the growing resentment against us in our zone. He is concerned, not so much with the prevalence of a Nazi type of mind, but with the persistence of the imperialist-nationalist old German type of mind, which regards the war and Hitlerism as a passing incident, and takes for granted that Germany will be permitted to revert to its old practices but Europe can't get along without Germany's coal and steel and Germany's industry and skill. Walter seems to be convinced at the moment also that our most important effort should be an educational one and that it should be planned over a long period. He speaks of having to stay here for at least ten years. All these things I tend to share also.

Not long after I got to the office Col. Abe Kramer[9] came in to give me the latest dope on the trade unions. They have decided, in a kind of way, to ask for permission to hold elections in their industrial branches – this is a bit of a victory for him. But I learned later in the day that his efforts to get additional personnel for his section[10] have been turned down, and I imagine that, as the result of this, he will simply pack up and go home – a great loss to Military Government here.

My driver[11] was furious this morning at the way he was treated yesterday.[12] The motor pool operator let him sit for 8 hours in the M. P. station without trying to get him out. "He is no friend of the Germans," Artur remarked, and then added by way of trying to understand: "Perhaps he lost a friend of relative in the war." But he couldn't forgive this treatment. I reminded him that he had been driving a little bit too fast, and that in Vienna, we arrested Chancellors of the Republic as well as drivers. He referred to the fact that the Oberburgermeister of Berlin, Werner[13], was also arrested recently and kept sitting in the MP station for hours. He admired this lack of distinction made in arrests. But still he wore sore. I can never forget that he has a young wife who will soon die with cancer, the poor devil. He says she has a great craving for lemonade. Could you get ahold of some lemon powder, and possibly orange powder also with which they might make some beverages? I keep giving him stuff for her. I think I told you there is no radium here for her to be treated with. She speaks now constantly of death.

At 10:30 I went to another meeting of the Political Directorate[14] in the Allied Control Authority Building[15] which was to discuss the question of a date for elections in Berlin.[16] Ivannov[17], the Russian delegate was quite compromising.

7 State in the American zone of Germany.

8 See Doc. 49.

9 See Doc. 49, fn. 6.

10 Manpower Branch, OMGBD.

11 Artur Sanow. See Doc. 40, fn. 13.

12 See Doc. 49.

13 See Doc. 27, fn. 30, and Doc. 39, fn. 23.

14 See minutes of the 36th meeting of the Political Directorate, Allied Control Authority, on May 18 and May 20, 1946, DPOL/M (46) 19, French version, in: AOF, Services Français à Berlin, GFCC, Bureau des Archives, caisse 1140, paquet 51.

15 Building of the Kammergericht. See Doc. 19, fn. 9.

16 See Doc. 49.

17 Nikolai Vasilyevich Ivanov. See Doc. 49, fn. 66.

The British began by quoting the Potsdam agreement[18] on the necessity for holding early elections,[19] and Ivanov[20] countered by asking when the British were going to hold elections in their zone.[21] Since the British have had no elections they were not in a very good position to argue for early elections in Berlin, although they tried to argue that Berlin was not the British zone. The Russians excepted us in their attack because they admitted that we had held elections comparable to those in Berlin and were in a position to advocate early elections. They then proposed that elections be held in Berlin comparable to those held in the zones outside of the American and indeed proposed the month of October. This was indeed a couple months earlier than had been proposed in the Kommandatura[22]. The British, French and ourselves proposed August. October is a kind of compromise between August and December. But the Russians proposed also holding elections in only what corresponds to the wards in Berlin, and not for the city as a whole. Since this seemed to be an unnecessary waste we wanted to think this over for a week, and as it was decided. It is nice to see the questions which we initiated in the Kommandatura get some kind of push in higher quarters. Indeed the Russians seem, on the whole, to be in a more conciliatory mood.

I had lunch with Roger Wells[23] who also attended the Directorate meeting.

After lunch I had to undertake a fight with the Control and Personnel offices of Omgus[24] over the classification of a couple positions in our newly established

18 The Potsdam Agreement designates the results of the Potsdam Conference from July 17–August 2, 1945, at the Cecilenhof Palace in Potsdam. It regulated treatment of Germany after the unconditional surrender. Participants in this conference were the heads of state and government of the three victorious powers, USA, Great Britain, and the Soviet Union, and their foreign ministers. See Manfred Görtemaker, "Potsdamer Konferenz (17.7.–2.8.1945)," in: *Deutschland unter alliierter Besatzung 1945–1949/55*, ed. Wolfgang Benz, Berlin 1999, pp. 214–218.

19 In the Potsdam Agreement of August 2, 1945, it says under III. Germany, A. Political Principles: "9. The administration of affairs in Germany should be directed towards the decentralization of the political structure and the development of local responsibility. To this end: I. local self-government shall be restored throughout Germany on democratic principles and in particular through elective councils as rapidly as is consistent with military security and the purposes of military occupation; II. all democratic political parties with rights of assembly and of public discussion shall be allowed and encouraged throughout Germany; III. representative and elective principles shall be introduced into regional, provincial and state (Land) administration as rapidly as may be justified by the successful application of these principles in local selfgovernment; [...]." *Berlin. Quellen und Dokumente 1945–1951*, edited on behalf of the Senate of Berlin, eds. Hans J. Reichhardt/Hanns U. Treutler/Albrecht Lampe (= Schriftenreihe zur Berliner Zeitgeschichte, vol. 4/half-vol. 1), Berlin 1964, no. 54, p. 86.

20 See Doc. 49, fn. 66.

21 Gemeinde elections were not held in the states of the British zone of Germany until September 15, 1946. See *Keesing's Archiv der Gegenwart*, vol. XVI (1946), p. 868 A. Landkreis and Stadtkreis elections, Bürgerschaft elections in Bremen and Hamburg, followed on October 13, 1946. See ibid., pp. 895 G and 896 A.

22 See Doc. 20, fn. 11.

23 See Doc. 19, fn. 17.

24 See Doc. 17, fn. 45.

branch[25]. They had cut the classifications down from what we had expected. This was fighting for large salaries for Col. Glaser[26] and Capt. Biel[27]. I think the salaries given them are really large enough. But they, apparently, don't and rather than see them refuse the jobs and the section go to smash I am willing to take up the battle. I urged people to reconsider the classification and they promised to, but what will come out of it finally I don't know. But I'm not going to fight their battles any more.

Then I had conferences with Roger Wells again and Don Heath[28] over the proposal to be made to the Russians next Friday[29] on the question of Berlin elections. These went on until about 5:30 and I got back to Berlin District about six.

Tomorrow is lunch with Walter Dorn. Tomorrow is dinner out. And Wednesday[30] is dinner out with Herr Grotewohl[31] the leader of the new SED party here. This ought to be interesting but it looks like another strenuous week.

At dinner I talked with Col. Babcock[32] about making a protest in the Kommandatura about political and religious impartiality in appointments to public office. Those Communists! And so it goes.

I long for a bit of peace. No time to think about anything. I long for you too and for the boys. Maybe I will get a letter tomorrow. I love you my sweetheart, my dearest one. Goodnight. Edgar

Doc. 51
Letter to His Wife
Berlin, May 23, 1946

Dearest –

I'm dreadfully tired tonight and am going straight to bed. Last night Brewster Morris[1] had Grotewohl[2] (the head of the pro-merger Social Democrats and member of the Executive Committee of SED) to dinner, and I was there. It lasted too late. I am no good after this kind of a late evening the next day. This was after a night out the night before. And I sat from two until seven today on a meeting of the Local Government Committee of the Kommandatura[3], dis-

25 Refers to the Civil Administration Branch, OMGBD. See Doc. 28, fn. 5.
26 See Doc. 28, fn. 4.
27 See Doc. 20, fn. 31.
28 Donald R. Heath. See Doc. 8, fn. 15.
29 May 24, 1946.
30 May 22, 1946.
31 See Doc. 30, fn. 8.
32 William T. Babcock (1898–1950), Lieutenant Colonel, 1946 Chief, Public Safety Branch, OMGBD, 1946–1949 Deputy Director, OMGBD/OMGBS, 1947–1949 US Deputy Commandant, Allied Kommandatura Berlin, 1949 Director, OMGBS, 1949/1950 Deputy Commissioner, HICOG, Berlin Element.

1 See Doc. 31, fn. 13.
2 See Doc. 30, fn. 8.
3 See Doc. 29, fn. 14.

cussing a new constitution for Berlin and electoral procedure.[4] Since I am going to a meeting of the Political Directorate[5] tomorrow I've got to be fresh since they work like a whirl-wind. I'll tell you about Grotewohl later.[6]

Just now I want to say a sweet hello and to confirm, after another letter from you on the subject, what I said in a recent letter about coming home. Let us consider the matter closed. I am coming home. Nothing could keep me from you and the boys any longer than next fall. And although you are willing to come over here if I want to stay for the Stuttgart job[7], I haven't the slightest intention of asking you to do so. First of all I am not sufficiently interested in it. And secondly, it is quite clear that you don't care much about coming here simply for the sake of coming here or going any place else in Europe. And I think your reactions are healthy and sound. This is not a good place for introverts and people with sensibilities to be. I believe the atmosphere is becoming more corrupt – corrupt in the sense of creating a privileged conqueror-class which is interested in nothing much more than what they can get out of it. That is most of them. Walter Dorn[8] admitted to me the other day that he found himself thinking things which under normal circumstances he never would consider – his sensibilities being corrupted. The decision gives me comfort. I now have this to look forward to. But I shall be desperately lonely until I can see you. If you can get something in the mountains for a little while I should like it very much. At the same time I agree on painting the house ourselves – I should say myself. If I start to paint a house it will take a very very long time.

I checked on my pay recently. I haven't been getting any money because nobody has ever turned in a time sheet. It is taken care of now and I shall be paid full salary until April when your first allotment was paid.[9] I'll send this to you and suggest seriously that you use it to buy a new car, if you can get one. You need this in your present desperate plight.

I send you all my love – my dearest Emily. Edgar

4 See minutes of the 19th meeting of the Local Government Committee, Allied Kommandatura Berlin, on May 23, 1946, LG/M (46) 19, English version, in: TNA, Allied Kommandatura: Directives, Minutes and Papers, FO 1112/378; Appendix of Illustrations, ill. 66 and ill. 67.

5 Political Directorate, Allied Control Authority.

6 See Doc. 52.

7 Refers to the leadership of RGCO. See Doc. 2, fn. 11.

8 See Doc. 2, fn. 10.

9 See Doc. 44.

Doc. 52
Letter to His Wife
Berlin, Wannsee[1], May 25, 1946[2]

Dear Sweetheart –

Another week gone – I must say they go quickly enough and I don't seem to accomplish much in the course of them. But the passing is now beginning to have real significance for me since I know that the date for leaving here is thus approaching. I know I shall never regret not staying on, and once having made the decision will quickly find my way back into American life – such as it happens to. From here everything seems to be chaotic there. Of course I see no American papers except the awful Stars and Stripes[3] and the almost as awful Paris edition of the Herald Tribune[4].[5] I try to keep up mostly with the German newspapers, and except for those under American and British and French license they keep me in pretty constant turmoil. Censorship is an ugly thing and under Russian auspices very unpleasant. Everything possible is done to put us in a bad light and to make the Russians seem the guiding angels of the world. There is always, however, something to put us in a bad light. Even our strikes are held against us. You would think that there would be at least enough fairness to recognize that here are workmen trying and succeeding in improving their standard of living. Instead it is always to illustrate the chaotic nature of our economy and incidentally to intimidate workers here. In Russia there are no such things as strikes. I prefer to have strikes. There are strikes taking place here now – "sit-down strikes" to force upon employers the acceptance of the right of co-management on the part of the workers – the sort of thing which the CIO[6] attempted with General Motors[7] when I was home.

I attended Clay's[8] staff meeting[9] this morning, the first I have been able to attend for a couple of weeks. It is not encouraging to attend one because so lit-

1 Refers either to Großer Wannsee, a bight of the Havel (see Doc. 74, fn. 24) in southwest Berlin, or Berlin-Wannsee, an area in the administrative district of Zehlendorf.

2 The letter is dated March 25, 1946; as indicated by the content, however, it was written on May 25, 1946.

3 American military newspaper.

4 *New York Herald Tribune*, American daily newspaper, Republican orientation.

5 "'Stars and Stripes' – the unofficial paper of the US Armed Forces in the European theater. Printed in Germany with international coverage. Distributed by subscription. 'New York Herald Tribune' – Printed in Paris and distributed by subscription. Will be sold also at Post Exchange news stands." *US Sector of Berlin. Information for New Arrivals*, published by Headquarters, Berlin District, 25 April 1946/15 July 1946, p. 19, http://www.berlinbrats.org/pdfs/46Guide.pdf (accessed March 2, 2018).

6 Congress of Industrial Organizations, 1935–1955 federation of trade unions that primarily organized unskilled industrial workers in the USA and Canada.

7 American car company founded in 1908, headquarters in Detroit, in the US state of Michigan.

8 See Doc. 2, fn. 6.

9 See minutes of the OMGUS staff conference on May 25, 1946, in: Archiv des IfZ, OMGUS – Staff Conferences (copies of minutes), Fg 12/4.

tle that is actually important is happening to put Germany on its feet. It is not sure that the new denazification law[10] which the Germans put into effect is really going to work out well. There is much dissatisfaction with it, especially on the part of the church, which doesn't want to get rid of its Nazi clergy, and has protested to Clay who rejected their complaints. Incidently I am not to have the de-Nazification job I referred to.[11] Walter Dorn[12] is going to take it over. I suppose they haven't quite enough for him to do, and in any case he is better qualified for it from some points of view. De-Nazification is already a joke among the Germans when it is not a tragedy. Grotewohl[13] told the story the other night[14] of the man working at cleaning away debris in the streets. He was approached ruefully by a passerby who said he wished he had a job like that. He used to have he said. "And why did you lose it?" "Oh, I was a Nazi and was fired." "Well," replied the other, "I am a Nazi too and that's why they put me on this job." There is also going around the statement that "In the Russian zone you see three smoke-stacks on every factory going, in the British zone two, but in the American zone the only activity you see is wasps chasing Nazis." It came out in Clay's meeting this morning that the camps for civilian internees (these are mostly Nazis put away for safe keeping) are much better fed than the ordinary German civilian. So if you don't mind your loss of freedom you can be better fed. The Germans are of course irritable over the loss of houses to American families. Some 362 houses are now occupied by American families in Berlin, and 51 more have to be taken over to accommodate those on the spot. Of course there is such a shortage of proper houses in our sector that practically anything that is available has to be taken over, irrespective of who has it. This is just a situation which has to be faced. If there are not enough Nazi houses available others have to be taken. And of course the Germans believe that we are going out of our way to keep the Nazis in their houses and drive the others out. It is true that concentration camp people have had to get out to make room for the conquerors.

I had a good little example yesterday of the danger inherent in not having a little understanding of the situation one is dealing with. There suddenly appeared in my office three officers with my driver[15]. They said they had seen him give the Nazi salute in the courtyard and that the other drivers had received it with laughter. They wanted to arrest him and have him tried. I just couldn't believe that Sanow had seriously given the Nazi salute[16] or that it had been received in a mocking spirit. He was not a member of the party[17], is a good anti-Merger Social Democrat[18] and a typical Berliner who likes a joke, and is gen-

10 See Doc. 47, fn. 20.

11 See Doc. 47.

12 See Doc. 2, fn. 10.

13 See Doc. 30, fn. 8.

14 See Doc. 51.

15 Artur Sanow. See Doc. 40, fn. 13.

16 For the Nazi salute, banned after 1945, the right arm was raised diagonally upward to eye level with a flat palm. See Tilman Allert, *Der deutsche Gruß. Geschichte einer unheilvollen Geste*, Frankfurt am Main 2005.

17 Refers to the NSDAP.

18 A Social Democrat who opposed the merger of the SPD and KPD.

erally speaking, when not thinking of his poor wife[19], in good humor. He said he had done it as a joke and that it had been received as a joke by the drivers. This seemed to me, from what I knew of him to be the truth. I think that I might even give the Hitler salute in a jovial mood. But I had a hard time convincing these officers that this was so. They were about to go home to the USA, and wanted to arrest him before going. They had fought the war to keep things like this from happening. I finally told them I would have Sanow call together the drivers and given them a serious talk on the possibility of such action being misunderstood when done on US property + observed by those who did not know what was going on. They were then persuaded to let him go. Sanow called together the drivers. The atmosphere between Germans and many Americans is not pleasant. The barriers of misunderstanding are very high and wide.

Sunday morning [26. Mai 1946].

I thought this morning that it was now four months since I have seen you and that if I stay on through August there will be only three more to go – more than half the time, at least is gone. In a sense I have promised to stay on here until the fall. I have thought that a convenient terminus date would be Sept. 8. That would be seven months. And I take it my services are terminated where they began – in Omaha[20]. When does school begin in September? If however you manage to get a place in the mountains for August and September (you speak of putting the Sellers[21] on the look out)[22] I should be tempted to leave earlier, even though I suppose we should have this extra month of salary for the months that are ahead. Moving out to the mountains after Labor Day[23] seems a little strenuous if we are to be there for only a week or so. If I paint the house (where are we going to get the equipment) that will take plenty of time, and there are undoubtedly plenty of other things to do. What, by the way, did you ever do about those chairs that I left on your hands? Are they still where I left them. I should be content to stay at home with you and the kids and getting robes and things together in preparation for the beginning of school. In any case it is downhill again for the next two or three months with some little steep up-hill grades on the way.

The bow-hairs, by the way, did come and I delivered them.[24] Mr. Baldner[25] said I was an angel. Thanks for getting them. I have not seen him since. I am a little beware of Germans for whom I have done favors, because they have always more for you to do, and after a while you get fed up.

19 His wife was suffering from cancer. See Doc. 44 and Doc. 50.

20 City in the US state of Nebraska, northeast of Johnson's home in Lincoln.

21 James L. Sellers (see Doc. 49, fn. 77) and his wife, Nell K. Sellers, née Kennedy (died 1946).

22 See Emily L. Johnson's letter from May 10/13, 1946, in: Documents from the estate of Edgar N. Johnson, private collection of Candice E. and Thomas R. Johnson, Denver, Colorado, USA.

23 US national holiday since 1894, always observed on the first Monday in September.

24 Refers to the bow hairs that Johnson had gotten sent from the USA for the cellist Max Baldner (see Doc. 21, fn. 18). See Doc. 25 and Doc. 38.

25 See Doc. 21, fn. 18.

It was here a less strenuous week than last but not much less. I had to go out on Tuesday[26] to an evening prepared by a member of the staff in the office. Then on Wednesday[27] came Mr. Grotewohl's evening at Brewster Morris's[28].[29] It was an interesting one because we were in the presence of a shrewd politician who had for the moment compromised his best principles in order to roll with what he thinks is the wave of the future – the unity party here. It was clear, however, that if the wave recedes, he will try to get back into the fold which he left. I hope they reject him if he does. He has moved into the Russian Sector and is, of course, provided with all the things he needs. I didn't like the look in his eye nor react to his proposition that now that the dirt was over we should forget it, establish peace, and work together for the future. Things are not quite so simple. He has a vigorous mind, speaks by way of reference to Communist orators, of "epileptic politicians who foam at the mouth," and makes easy comparisons between "the Germany of Goethe[30] and the Germany of Göring[31]." We put him through a rather hard evening, and he took it well. But he was hardly a man in whom you could really put your trust.[32]

Friday[33] I went with Walter Dorn to the theatre – my first here. It was Sternheim's[34] "The Snob"[35] in Max Reinhardt's[36] "Deutsches Theatre."[37, 38] But I couldn't take very well the way in which the play was worked out – since the

26 May 21, 1946.
27 May 22, 1946.
28 See Doc. 31, fn. 13.
29 See Doc. 51.
30 Johann Wolfgang von Goethe (1749–1832), German writer.
31 See Doc. 22, fn. 24.
32 In a report after the evening with Grotewohl, Brewster H. Morris expressed the opinion that the SED Chairman "is still at heart a democrat and is therefore well worth keeping contact with." Cited in Anjana Buckow, *Zwischen Propaganda und Realpolitik. Die USA und der sowjetisch besetzte Teil Deutschlands 1945–1955* (= USA-Studien, vol. 13), Stuttgart 2003, p. 77.
33 May 24, 1946.
34 Carl Sternheim (1878–1942), German writer.
35 Comedy in three acts, first performance in 1914 in the Kammerspiele of the Deutsches Theater in Berlin, part of Sternheim's comedy cycle *Aus dem bürgerlichen Heldenleben* (From the Heroic Life of the Bourgeoisie).
36 Max Reinhardt (1873–1943), Austrian actor, director, and theater manager, managed the Deutsches Theater in Berlin from 1905–1930, founded the Kammerspiele in the adjacent building in 1906.
37 Deutsches Theater, Schumannstraße 13a, Berlin-Mitte. The Friedrich-Wilhelmstädtisches Theater, opened in 1850, had been given the name "Deutsches Theater" in 1883.
38 The performance began at 6 p. m. See *Berliner Zeitung* from May 24, 1946, [p. 4]. The premiere had taken place on May 3, 1946. See Walther Karsch, "Sternheims und Gründgens' Wiederkehr. 'Der Snob' in Max Reinhardts Deutschem Theater," in: *Der Tagesspiegel* from May 5, 1946, p. 3 (supplement); Paul Rilla, "Carl Sternheim: 'Der Snob.' Gustaf Gründgens im Deutschen Theater," in: *Berliner Zeitung* from May 5, 1946, [p. 3]; Georg Zivier, "Ein Grosser kehrt wieder. Carl Sternheim: 'Der Snob' im Deutschen Theater," in: *Telegraf* from May 5, 1946, p. 5. See also "Ein Gespräch mit Gustaf Gründgens. 'Was ich schon immer spielen wollte …' – Wie es zur Aufführung des 'Snob' kam," in: *Telegraf* from May 1, 1946, p. 6.

snob won out, and pushed everyone aside. The leading man Grundjens[39] was a Nazi. We OK'd him before we knew too much about him, and then tried to un-O. K. him. But the Russians objected to this. The Theatre is in their Sector, and so he goes on. He certainly looked like a good Nazi. I went to Walter's big house on the Kleiner Wannsee[40] afterwards, and we talked mostly about what is going on here. Walter is not fundamentally more hopeful than I. I think he is going home at the end of the summer but he is much more flattered by his position here than I should be under similar circumstances. He is after all a German trained to be respectful of his superiors. Nevertheless men like him are needed here.

I went to two meetings of the Political Directorate during the week.[41] The question of the recognition of the parties[42] is stalled on account of the French who do not know whether they can recognize the new Socialist Unity Party and have sent home for instructions. It is of course a vital matter with them. A strong Socialist-Communist Party here would be a strong impetus to a similar one in France which could then take over the government. The last elections[43] however moved from the left to the right, and it's a question whether the French Gov[ernmen]t[44] wants, before the next elections[45], to encourage in even the slightest way, the

39 The role of Christian Maske was played by Gustaf Gründgens (1899–1963), German actor, director, and theater manager, in the Nazi period general director of the Preußisches Staatstheater, started acting again in 1946 after return from a Soviet internment camp.

40 See Doc. 33, fn. 10.

41 Refers to the meetings of the Political Directorate, Allied Control Authority, on May 20 and 24, 1946. See minutes of the 36th meeting of the Political Directorate, Allied Control Authority, on May 18 and May 20, 1946, DPOL/M (46) 19, French version, in: AOF, Services Français à Berlin, GFCC, Bureau des Archives, caisse 1140, paquet 51; minutes of the 37th meeting of the Political Directorate, Allied Control Authority, on May 24, 1946, DPOL/M (46) 20, French version, in: ibid.

42 Refers to recognition of the SED and the newly organized SPD in Berlin.

43 Refers to the popular referendum from May 5, 1946, with which the draft constitution that had been passed by the votes of the Communist-Socialist majority in the National Constituent Assembly was rejected. See *Keesing's Archiv der Gegenwart*, vol. XVI (1946), p. 741 D. A feature article of the French-licensed newspaper *Der Kurier* said that the result of the referendum "clearly proves that the majority in the National Assembly no longer speaks for the majority in the country. […] In the last elections on October 21, the Socialists and Communists had received ten million votes as opposed to nine million for all of the remaining parties. The popular referendum shows that this ratio has been reversed. This time the extreme left received only nine million votes, while opponents of the constitution collected ten and a half million, for 53.9 percent to 46.1 percent." ("beweist eindeutig, daß die Mehrheit in der Nationalversammlung nicht mehr der Mehrheit im Lande entspricht. […] Die Sozialisten und Kommunisten hatten bei den letzten Wahlen am 21. Oktober zehn Millionen Stimmen erhalten gegen neun Millionen sämtlicher übrigen Parteien. Die Volksabstimmung zeigt, daß sich dieses Verhältnis umgekehrt hat. Diesmal hat die äußerste Linke nur neun Millionen Stimmen erreicht, während die Gegner der Verfassung zehneinhalb Millionen zusammengebracht haben, das macht 53,9 gegen 46,1 Prozent.") "Liberale gegen autoritäre Demokratie," in: *Der Kurier* from May 6, 1946, pp. 1f., here p. 1.

44 Provisional Government of the French Republic, coalition government made up of Communists (Parti Communiste Français [PCF]), Christian Democrats (Mouvement

French forces of the left. They might wait therefore until after the elections before making up their minds. At the second meeting the handsome, clever and reasonably conciliatory Russian representative, Mr. Ivanov[46], annoyed and disappointed over this postponement, said, that although he was willing privately to have elections held in Berlin in October, he could not discuss the question officially until the matter of recognition had been settled, which was a perfectly fair proposition. And so the stalemate will go on for some time. It seems to be the case with all important questions. It is difficult to arrive at a common basis in a hurry. Take the fundamental question of the Potsdam agreement[47] providing for central agencies in certain fields.[48] It has been held up by the French for months, and there is no prospect that it will be settled for many months to come.[49] As long as Germany is not treated as an economic unit things will stagnate. It is clear that the Russians do not wish to share their zone with the rest. The only club we have here is to refuse reparations to them from the west for so long as they refuse to carry out the Potsdam agreement as a whole. This I think we are ready to do but it will take a long time to implement.

It is rather fun representing your government in even the smallest negotiations. I sat on the Local Gov[ernmen]t Committee[50] for a couple of sessions in discussions on the future constitution of Berlin, and some progress was made.[51]

Républicain Populaire [MRP]), and Socialists (Section Française de l'Internationale Ouvrière [SFIO]). The Socialist Félix Gouin (1884–1977) was President of the Provisional Government (January–June 1946).

45 On June 2, 1946, a new National Constituent Assembly was elected. See *Keesing's Archiv der Gegenwart*, vol. XVI (1946), p. 771 D; "Schwergewicht verlagert," in: *Der Kurier* from June 3, 1946, p. 1.

46 See Doc. 49, fn. 66.

47 See Doc. 50, fn. 18.

48 The Potsdam Agreement provided for the establishment of "certain essential central German administrative departments, headed by State Secretaries, [...] particularly in the fields of finance, transport, communications, foreign trade and industry. Such departments will act under the direction of the Control Council." *Berlin. Quellen und Dokumente 1945–1951*, edited on behalf of the Senate of Berlin, eds. Hans J. Reichhardt/Hanns U. Treutler/Albrecht Lampe (= Schriftenreihe zur Berliner Zeitgeschichte, vol. 4/half-vol. 1), Berlin 1964, no. 54, p. 86.

49 France had major reservations about the establishment of central German administrative departments. Through decentralized political and economic structures, it wanted to inhibit a revitalization of Germany. See Elisabeth Kraus, *Ministerien für das ganze Deutschland? Der Alliierte Kontrollrat und die Frage gesamtdeutscher Zentralverwaltungen* (= Studien zur Zeitgeschichte, vol. 37), Munich 1990; Gunther Mai, *Der Alliierte Kontrollrat in Deutschland 1945–1948. Alliierte Einheit – deutsche Teilung?* (= Quellen und Darstellungen zur Zeitgeschichte, vol. 37), Munich 1995, pp. 83–92.

50 See Doc. 29, fn. 14.

51 See minutes of the 17th meeting of the Local Government Committee, Allied Kommandatura Berlin, on May 10, 1946, LG/M (46) 17, English version, in: TNA, Allied Kommandatura: Directives, Minutes and Papers, FO 1112/378; minutes of the 18th meeting of the Local Government Committee, Allied Kommandatura Berlin, on May 17, 1946, LG/M (46) 18, English version, in: ibid.; minutes of the 19th meeting of the Local Government Committee, Allied Kommandatura Berlin, on May 23, 1946, LG/M (46) 19, English version, in: ibid.

Whether I shall continue I do not know. Col. Glaser[52] is back and may want to take over.[53] Since he knows no German he is hardly the person to take over these negotiations.

It is interesting to see how many little things are thrown on to you. A small group of students from the U[niversity] of Berlin[54] were sent to me by the education people[55] to help arrange a program of lecture discussions on America. I shall be able to help a little and will probably talk a little myself on one occasion. A publisher[56] who is going to put out an edition of Franklin's[57] Autobiography[58] and Bowers'[59] Jefferson and Hamilton[60] wants Forewords by Americans and he has been sent to me.[61] I may try the one on Franklin whose Autobiography I am just now reading it so happens. The people in Military Government of Berlin come to me. The director of public safety[62] wants to know whether it is wise to forbid police to join political parties (this is directed against the Communists who are trying desperately to control the police). I said No. This is

52 See Doc. 28, fn. 4.

53 Glaser, who did not take part in the meetings of the Local Government Committee on May 10, 17, and 23, 1946, had returned from his trip to England. See Doc. 45.

54 See Doc. 20, fn. 44.

55 Refers to representatives of the American military government tasked with educational matters.

56 Refers to the Berlin publisher Karl Heinz Henssel (1917–2014). His press, Karl H. Henssel Verlag (office: Rheinstraße 46, Berlin-Friedenau), a press for fiction and books in the humanties, had been licensed by the American military government in December 1945. See "Publishers licensed by the U. S. authorities," notification of the Information Services Control Section, U. S. Headquarters Berlin District, Publications Sub-Section, from December 13, 1945, in: LAB, B Rep. 036-01 (Office of Military Government, Berlin Sector [OMGBS]), 4/17-1/33. A business card that Johnson received from Henssel can be found in: Documents from the estate of Edgar N. Johnson, private collection of Candice E. and Thomas R. Johnson, Denver, Colorado, USA.

57 Benjamin Franklin (1706–1790), American politician, scientist, and writer, one of the Founding Fathers of the United States of America.

58 Franklin's unfinished autobiography, published posthumously. "Towards the end of his life, he endeavored to write an autobiography for the benefit of his son, yet he could not complete it under the pressure of his various affairs." ("Gegen das Ende seines Lebens unternahm er es, zu Nutz und Frommen seines Sohnes eine Autobiographie zu schreiben, die er jedoch im Drange seiner vielfältigen Geschäfte nicht beenden konnte.") "Benjamin Franklin. Auszug aus der Autobiographie," in: *Die Neue Zeitung* from April 26, 1946, feuilleton and arts supplement.

59 Claude G. Bowers (1878–1958), American writer and diplomat.

60 The book *Jefferson and Hamilton. The Struggle for Democracy in America* was first published in 1925.

61 *Benjamin Franklin. Sein Leben von ihm selbst erzählt* was published in 1946 by Karl H. Henssel Verlag, Berlin, with a foreword by Edgar N. Johnson; this was a revised reproduction of the 1875 translation by Berthold Auerbach. See the book cover in Appendix of Illustrations, ill. 65. *Jefferson und Hamilton* by Claude G. Bowers followed in 1948 (German translation by Grete Rambach, née Lorch).

62 William T. Babcock. See Doc. 50, fn. 32.

63 Albert W. Paddock, Major, January–June 1946 Chief, Public Welfare Branch, OMGBD.

more than we ask at home. The Director of Welfare[63] wants to do somewhat the same with Welfare Workers (the Communists control them too). Local personnel officers in our Sector refuse jobs to qualified applicants because they do not belong to the party or are too religious. "We don't want pious people around who pray all day." The Food people come to me wanting to know what to do about the Main Food Office[64] which is still full of Nazis as well as Communists and there is much food being lost, and stolen and wasted, etc., etc.

There are not enough qualified people here to do the job.

I love you my dearest Emily, my sweet wife and I long for you. I hope those damn English papers are through.[65] Kiss my sweet boys for me and I send you every tender caress. The time when we shall really be close to each other again is at least in sight. I love her very very dearly. Edgar

Doc. 53
Letter to His Wife
Berlin, Wannsee Officers' Club[1], Am Sandwerder 17/19, May 27, 1946

My own sweet Emily –

One of the nicest things you ever said about me was in a recent letter[2] when you were commenting on Mary Lancaster's[3] imminent marriage. You said simply that you wished that we had met long before we did meet and had been married thereupon.[4] I do not like to think of what we actually have missed by that's not having occurred. But it is so much the more reason for my hastening back to you.

As you know by now the decision about my coming home is made, not to be reconsidered or to be discussed except in terms of anticipation. I have written Jim[5] to that effect and yesterday I wrote a long letter to Henry[6] to that effect, telling him incidently some of the things I expected from the University upon

64 Refers to the Magistrat Department of Nutrition.

65 Emily L. Johnson was reading exam papers for Ray W. Frantz (see Doc. 11, fn. 15). See Doc. 48, fn. 12.

1 See Doc. 25, fn. 9.

2 Emily L. Johnson's letter from May 15, 1946, in: Documents from the estate of Edgar N. Johnson, private collection of Candice E. and Thomas R. Johnson, Denver, Colorado, USA.

3 Mary Lancaster, later married Hopkins, daughter of Mary B. Lancaster, née Brown (ca. 1892–1948) and Lane W. Lancaster (1892–1962), American political scientist, 1923 PhD, University of Pennsylvania, 1930–1960 Professor, University of Nebraska. Mary Lancaster married Robert E. Hopkins on May 28, 1946. See Emily L. Johnson's letter from May 28, 1946, in: Documents from the estate of Edgar N. Johnson, private collection of Candice E. and Thomas R. Johnson, Denver, Colorado, USA.

4 Emily L. Johnson had written: "I wish we had met and been married long before we did."

5 James L. Sellers. See Doc. 49, fn. 77.

6 Charles Henry Oldfather. See Doc. 2, fn. 19.

my return in order that the full hope and promise of academic life might be in some measure realized at Nebraska. I hope he will understand the letter. Because I went out of my way to say some nice things to him and I do not want it considered as flattery. For, after all, if Henry were not there, in some position of authority, it would not be so easy to come back to the Univ[ersity] of Nebraska. Whatever may be his odd decisions at the moment, he is an honest and decent human, and there are few like him.

My present mood is indeed to return immediately and abandon the petty men about me and the corrupting atmosphere, and to return to the strength and comfort of your bosom and the delicacy of your spirit. It is perhaps better that I should not abandon the scene quite so easily. General Keating[7] is quite innocent of politics. He has some trust in me, and I'd rather have him in my hands in what is to come in the next few months, than in the hands of a comparatively ignorant, grasping, envious and ambitious advertising man such as Colonel Glaser[8], even though I have to suffer a little at Glaser's hands. It is quite clear in my mind that Glaser would like nothing better than for me to abandon the field to him. And since he doesn't know a word of German this is not quite what I propose to do. Four months have now passed and there are at the most only three left. I'd better leave what imprint I can before I leave, and if it is nothing else, it must be that of one who can put the interests of his country a little bit above those of himself. This sounds awfully bombastic and stuff-shirted but it really is not. I do not say that my motives are of the purest but I do say that the guiding ones are not concerned with the guarantee of my present position or the jealous exclusion of any one who threatens it. Anyone can have my position who can crowd me out of it. But he will have to be worth it. And I refuse to be bothered with the petty annoyances set in my way by men who have influence to bear in petty affairs but who are incapable of rising to any greater consideration than their own little empire in the months or days that are to come.

I don't think they will put pressure on me to stay. Oh! Clay[9] may say some nice things about the need for my taking Pollock's[10] place[11] but he is quite sufficient to his task, and there are always others. I shall ask, before I go, for the privilege of taking a round of our zone, so that I may come home pretty well informed about what Americans are doing here. This I think will be granted me. I'll write a final report for Clay, and then come home to you and John[12] and Timmy[13]. I have the feeling that I shall remain secluded from all but your and mine and our boys' and my student world for a long time to come. The values of this world are so clear and indisputable, they can be so easily destroyed again (I mean only the possibility of enjoying them) that it would be folly to do much else than to cultivate them to the last refinement.

7 See Doc. 39, fn. 6.
8 See Doc. 28, fn. 4.
9 See Doc. 2, fn. 10.
10 See Doc. 15, fn. 12.
11 Refers to the leadership of RGCO. See Doc. 2, fn. 11.
12 Johnson's son John. See Doc. 2, fn. 15.
13 Johnson's son Thomas. See Doc. 2, fn. 16.

So from the world of affairs, such as I have been able to touch it, I shall return to your most precious self, with no greater desire than to cultivate you in so far as in me lies, and to realize those potentialities of our love and life together that we are aware of but have not really probed. Aside from being the companion and husband that you most desire, I shall be there to order to be a proper associate for our fine boys. I am very conscious of this responsibility. And after this will come my students. And after this the world. You are always, and so correctly insistent upon this "Time which does not tarry." Let us resolve, my own sweet darling, when once we are together again in each other's arms, that all our moments together shall be calculated to achieve the dream of an almost perfect happiness that we are capable of. Only its realization, in the few years that are ahead of us, will justify this wanton abandonment of you, especially this last one, that I have been guilty of. I love you my sweet and lovely Emily, with you, and in your constant presence I can hope to be what I am capable of being. That will not be bad for you or John or Timmy. And that can only be where we are all together. Goodnight, my dearest, my beloved. Edgar

Doc. 54
Letter to His Wife
Berlin, Wannsee Officers' Club[1], Am Sandwerder 17/19, May 28, 1946

Dear Sweetheart –

I went to my first meeting of the Coordinating Committee[2] today.[3] This is the Committee just below the Control Council[4] itself. Clay[5] represents us, General Robertson[6] the British, General Koeltz[7] the French and General Dratvin[8] the Russians. I got to go because they were discussing the recognition of the SPD and the SED. This was being held up because the French had to consult their government. It passed easily enough this afternoon after the French had received word that they could recognize the two parties. This gives a chance for the Political Directorate tomorrow to discuss the question of elections.[9] I am

1 See Doc. 25, fn. 9.

2 See Doc. 15, fn. 21.

3 See minutes of the 57th meeting of the Coordinating Committee, Allied Control Authority, on May 28, 1946, CORC/M (46) 28, French version, in: AOF, Services Français à Berlin, GFCC, Bureau des Archives, caisse 1133, paquet 7.

4 See Doc. 16, fn. 11.

5 See Doc. 2, fn. 6.

6 Sir Brian Hubert Robertson (1896–1974), Lieutenant General, 1945–1947 Deputy Military Governor, Germany (UK), 1947–1949 Military Governor, Germany (UK), and Commander-in-Chief of British Forces of Occupation in Germany, 1949/1950 High Commissioner (UK), Allied High Commission, Germany.

7 Louis Marie Koeltz (1884–1970), Général de Corps d'Armée, 1945–June 1946 head of the Groupe Français du Conseil de Contrôle.

8 Mikhail Ivanovich Dratvin (1897–1953), Soviet Lieutenant General, 1945–1947 Chief of Staff, SMAG, 1947–1949 First Deputy of the Supreme Chief of SMAG.

9 See minutes of the 38th meeting of the Political Directorate, Allied Control Authority, on May 29, 1946, DPOL/M (46) 21-192, French version, in: AOF, Services Français à Berlin, GFCC, Bureau des Archives, caisse 1140, paquet 51.

going to that also with the consent of Don Heath[10]. Since I am here I want to follow up these questions through the hierarchy. With the setting of a date for elections and the recognition of the two parties the stage is set for an election campaign here during the summer. The election will probably be in October, after I have left. It will be the same here as it was in Austria. All the excitement without waiting for the event. But I can think of something much more exciting than an election in Berlin, and I don't have to tell you what it is.

General Robertson presided in a rather austere manner, as the British are inclined to do, showing evident displeasure at some of the attitudes struck by the Russians. Across from him sat Dratvin, even more formidable and unpleasant. To Robertson's right was Koeltz, agreeable and civilized, and on his left our capable General Clay.

It started out unpleasantly with the consideration of a quadripartite Commission to investigate in all the four zones the disarmament of Germany. The Russians had rejected the proposal on the previous meeting on the ground that in so far as the western zones were concerned there was no disarmament that had taken place in the economic field and therefore nothing to investigate. What is clear of course is that the Russians don't want a Commission monkeying around in their zone investigating what has happened to the industry in their zone. The Russians did not change their tune at this meeting. Then Robertson wanted an agreement on a text of a Communique to the press stating that the Soviets opposed a disarmament commission. The Russians would not agree to consider such a Communique and wanted it postponed until the next meeting. Clay and Robertson said they felt free to communicate themselves to their respective presses. The Russians objected to this. It was agreed to the disgust of everyone except the Russians to put the Communique off until the next meeting.

There was not much else that happened. Clay made a plan for national trade unions in connection with a paper on trade unions. And Koeltz ended the meeting with a plea that more coal from the Saar[11] be delivered to France and less to the Germans. I don't believe there will be much left of Germany when everybody gets through taking what he wants, and of course there is much justice in this. After fighting together they all went into a neighboring room for what Robertson called tea, which was indeed a very high tea. I went in for a moment to see what it was like. The principals all sat around one big table and the lesser lights sat around in the corners.

I want to go to one meeting of the Control Council itself in order to get a complete picture of the international machinery.

I have just finished Franklin's[12] Autobiography[13].[14] It is by far too episodic but it makes you long for the comparative simplicity of 18th century America.

10 Donald R. Heath (see Doc. 8, fn. 15) was the American representative in the Political Directorate, Allied Control Authority.

11 Refers to the territory of today's Saarland, which was initially part of the French zone of Germany, then removed from responsibility of the Allied Control Authority to become a French protectorate.

12 See Doc. 52, fn. 57.

13 See Doc. 52, fn. 58.

14 See Doc. 52.

I love you my sweet heart and my boys and give you a tender good-night. I am very tired and shall go straight to bed. I hope those papers are over.[15] Goodnight my sweet ones – Edgar

Doc. 55
Letter to His Wife
Berlin, Wannsee Officers' Club[1], Am Sandwerder 17/19, May 31, 1946

Dear Sweetheart –

If today is any example of how the world is run or can be run under quadripartite leadership, then I fear for the world. I have sat at quadripartite meetings from 10 this morning until six this evening with almost nothing accomplished. For most of the day it was the local government committee[2] trying to come to some agreements about electoral procedure for the forthcoming elections in Berlin (October) and about a provisional constitution for the city of Berlin.[3] We had decided to hold a special meeting this morning in order to make up for lost time. To begin with the French representative, a clear headed French lawyer by the name of Ziegelmaier[4] (all Frenchmen of importance here seem to have German names – the commanding General is Koeltz[5]) made a suggestion which I made three weeks ago but was then put aside, that we ask the Germans to frame the text of an electoral procedure and then base our discussions upon this text. This was now accepted by everyone, and the Committee sat down to draft a letter. This took until 1 o'clock. We then went along to have lunch at the English Blue and White Club. After lunch we got into a discussion of how this letter was to get to the proper Berlin authorities. A terrific argument developed, led by the Soviet representative (a Major Feldman[6] – a young boy who has been able to make no sense out this business of electoral procedure and constitutions and who does not therefore want to reveal his insecurity by going in for a discussion of them). In order to settle our difficulties we had to drag down the English and Soviet representatives of the

15 Emily L. Johnson was reading exam papers for Ray W. Frantz (see Doc. 11, fn. 15). See Doc. 48, fn. 12.

1 See Doc. 25, fn. 9.

2 See Doc. 29, fn. 14.

3 See minutes of the 20th meeting of the Local Government Committee, Allied Kommandatura Berlin, on May 31, 1946, LG/M (46) 20, English version, in: TNA, Allied Kommandatura: Directives, Minutes and Papers, FO 1112/378; minutes of the 21st meeting of the Local Government Committee, Allied Kommandatura Berlin, on May 31, 1946, LG/M (46) 21, English version, in: ibid.

4 Jean Victor Ziegelmeyer (1911–1987), Capitaine, French lawyer, Section Juridique du Gouvernement Militaire Français du Grand-Berlin, then French Liaison Officer at the Berlin Magistrat, later founded and headed a Société d'électronique in France. Photos with Ziegelmeyer in Appendix of Illustrations, ill. 68 and ill. 77.

5 See Doc. 54, fn. 7.

6 See Doc. 49, fn. 59.

Allied Secretariat of the Kommandatura[7], and they only muddled the waters. It was finally agreed at about 4:30 that the text of the letter we had drawn up should be turned over to the Secretariat and gotten to the proper Berlin authorities in some way or another. The British chairman was really insufferable also. I may have mentioned him,[8] a Major Ashton[9] who is a former cotton importer from Liverpool[10] (whom the English Labor government is now liquidating because they intend to take over the cotton importing business) and who is leading member of the Conservative Party in the City Council at Liverpool[11]. He was simply terrible, so terrible in fact, that I deliberately refused to go out tonight to any English mess where I should have had to spend the evening with him and another of his kind a Major Hayes[12]. They are fine people, all right. You can't help liking them in their way. But these two certainly don't know how to get along with other people. They just antagonize everybody by their insistence that there is only one way to do a thing and that is the English way. Well after the letter was finally gotten off we started off on our regular meeting which was supposed to discuss the Berlin Constitution. Before a meeting can go ahead the minutes of the last meeting have to be approved. The Russians usually stall a great deal on the actual text of the minutes, and this time was nothing new. Then Major Feldman was at it again. Captain Ziegelmaier also had some objections to make and by the time we got through approving three sets of minutes, it was time to go home. And so as the result of a day's discussion we got a letter and some minutes approved but no headway made on the Berlin elections or the Berlin constitution. It reminded me of Fling's[13] course on the Paris Peace Conference[14].[15]

7 See Doc. 20, fn. 11.
8 See Doc. 49.
9 See Doc. 49, fn. 28.
10 City on the northwest coast of England.
11 Ashton was active in local politics in Wallasey near Liverpool, member of the Wallasey Council since 1935.
12 Harold Hays. See Doc. 49, fn. 26.
13 Fred M. Fling (1860–1934), American historian, 1883 BA, Bowdoin College, 1890 Dr. phil., University of Leipzig, taught as of 1891 at the University of Nebraska, Professor of European History.
14 Refers to the Paris Peace Conference in 1919/1920, at which a total of 32 states discussed the peace terms that should be set for the German Reich and its wartime allies.
15 Representing the Historical Branch of the General Staff, Fling had gathered material during the Paris Peace Conference for a history of the conference. "[…] Fling has sailed to France with the group who accompanied President Wilson, to represent at Paris, during the period of the peace conference, the interests of the Historical Branch of the General Staff and to accumulate materials for that portion of its history of which he has charge, the portion relating to the diplomatic history of the war and the peace." "Historical News," in: *The American Historical Review*, vol. 24, no. 2 (January 1919), pp. 308–348, here p. 311. "[…] his proposed account of the 1919 Versailles Peace Conference, which he attended as a research historian, never appeared." Robert E. Knoll, *Prairie University. A History of the University of Nebraska*, Lincoln, Nebraska, 1995, p. 65. Fling was known for his commitment "to precision, completeness, and detail." Ibid.

In the course of the meeting, I was called into the Commandants' meeting[16], where upon my initiative, final recognition was made of the SPD and SED throughout Berlin.[17] May be that's enough for a day. But there was an unpleasant fight about a Youth Celebration which the Youth Committee of the Magistrat[18] wants to hold in Berlin on 5 June. We opposed it and held to our guns because the Russians had been holding up discussions on the problem of youth organizations in the Education Committee[19]. This seems to be the only way you can get along with them.[20]

Yesterday was Memorial Day[21] and I worked all day. At eleven I saw a young German publisher[22] who wants me to write a little foreword for a translation of Franklin's[23] autobiography[24] which he is putting out.[25] This I think I'll do since I have just read it. In the late afternoon, after working all day on Berlin elections and constitution which came to nothing today I took Col. Glaser[26] over to General Keating's[27] to discuss the recognition of the parties at today's Commandants' meeting. I was made melancholy by General Keating's informing us that he had broken three strikes during the war (a coal strike in West Virginia, a street car strike in Philadelphia, and an air-plant strike in California). He also thinks that because of the labor difficulties we are now having in America, we are about to go Socialist or Communist in the USA. A person like this you have to stick with in order to get things properly done. Afterwards I went to one of the nicest evenings I have had in Berlin. You remember my cellist friend Baldner[28]. Well two of his younger children[29] were confirmed yesterday[30]. A table in

16 See minutes of the 15th meeting of the Commandants on May 31, 1946, BKC/M (46) 15, English version, in: LAB, B Rep. 036-01 (Office of Military Government, Berlin Sector [OMGBS]), 11/148-1/10.

17 See BK/O (46) 247 from May 31, 1946, in: LAB, C Rep. 901 (Landesleitung Berlin der SED), no. 517; BK/O (46) 248 from May 31, 1946, in: LAB, F Rep. 280 (Quellensammlung zur Berliner Zeitgeschichte [LAZ-Sammlung]), no. 4865.

18 See Hermann Weber, "Freie Deutsche Jugend (FDJ)," in: *SBZ-Handbuch. Staatliche Verwaltungen, Parteien, gesellschaftliche Organisationen und ihre Führungskräfte in der Sowjetischen Besatzungszone Deutschlands 1945–1949*, on behalf of the Arbeitsbereich Geschichte und Politik der DDR at the University of Mannheim and the Institut für Zeitgeschichte Munich, eds. Martin Broszat/Hermann Weber, Munich 1990, pp. 665–690, here p. 667.

19 Committee of the Allied Kommandatura Berlin.

20 In the end the event was approved and took place on June 18, 1946. See *Berlin. Kampf um Freiheit und Selbstverwaltung 1945–1946*, edited on behalf of the Senate of Berlin (= Schriftenreihe zur Berliner Zeitgeschichte, vol. 1), revised and supplemented second edition, Berlin 1961, p. 461, no. 38.

21 American holiday in honor of those who have died serving in the US military. See "Memorial Day – 1946," in: *OMGUS Observer* from May 31, 1946, p. 1.

22 Refers to the Berlin publisher Karl Heinz Henssel. See Doc. 52, fn. 56.

23 See Doc. 52, fn. 57.

24 See Doc. 52, fn. 58.

25 See Doc. 52 and Doc. 54.

26 See Doc. 28, fn. 4.

27 See Doc. 39, fn. 6.

28 See Doc. 21, fn. 18.

29 Refers to the twins Angelika and Lutz Baldner. See Doc. 21, fn. 24.

30 Ascension Day, May 30, 1946.

the living room was covered with confirmation presents, two of which were drawings, handsome drawings which Baldner himself had made as gifts for his kids. One was a view of a small town in Silesia[31] whither they had gone during the war to escape bombing,[32] and the other of a head of the crucified Christ which he had seen once in a church in Perpignan[33]. He is an extraordinary person. His quartet[34] played a lovely Mozart[35] quartet, the only one I was told that Mozart wrote in a minor key, and a Terzett of Dvorak[36] which I had never heard before. They also played the theme and variations movement from the Death and the Maiden Quartet[37]. We sat out on a terrace of a bombed-out house[38] while the music came from an inside room. The children sat in the inside room and were in audible rapture during most of the music. There were a lot of people there – both Americans and Germans including my old friend of steamer days, Dr. Max Rheinstein[39].

The evening before was taken up also. I had to go to a cocktail party of General Keating's at which I talked to Chinese, Brazilians and Danes and also considerably with General Clay[40] about the KPD and the future of America in Germany. He has a terribly good head. Thereupon I had to go to a party at the Lakeside Club[41], which is now housed in what was formerly General Eisenhower's[42] house on an island[43] in the Wannsee[44]. This was given by Col. Tay-

31 Territory in the southeast of the state of Prussia, under Polish administration after the Second World War.

32 To escape the bombing, in 1943 the Baldner family had retreated to the Lower Silesian property of the resistance fighter Paul Graf Yorck von Wartenburg (1902–2002), where they stayed in the forester's lodge near Niehmen. They returned to Berlin after July 20, 1944. Information from Thomas Baldner (see Doc. 21, fn. 24) in a telephone conversation with Werner Breunig on April 29, 2009.

33 City in Southern France.

34 Refers to the Zernick Quartet (see Doc. 38, fn. 3). Max Baldner played with this quartet from 1945 until his death in 1946.

35 Wolfgang Amadeus Mozart (1756–1791), Austrian composer.

36 See Doc. 34, fn. 7.

37 String Quartet No. 14 *Der Tod und das Mädchen* (Death and the Maiden) by Franz Schubert (see Doc. 38, fn. 2).

38 Podbielskiallee 57. See Doc. 21, fn. 25. According to Thomas Baldner in an email to Werner Breunig from September 20, 2010, in the house "there were gatherings of the great minds of Berlin and American friends, which was due to my father's outstanding personality. It almost goes without saying that there […] was a lot of music, in which I frequently took part as a very young student, accompanying my father and other musicians." ("fanden Zusammenkünfte der großen Geister Berlins mit den amerikanischen Freunden statt, was wohl auf der überragenden Persönlichkeit meines Vaters fußte. Es versteht sich fast von selbst, dass da […] viel Musik gemacht wurde, an der ich als blutjunger Student als Begleiter meines Vaters und anderer Musiker auch immer wieder teilnahm.")

39 See Doc. 11, fn. 22.

40 See Doc. 2, fn. 6.

41 See Doc. 17 and Doc. 18. The Lakeside Club was initially housed at Am Großen Wannsee 2/4. See Doc. 18, fn. 20.

42 See Doc. 18, fn. 25.

43 Inselstraße 16 on Schwanenwerder Island (see Doc. 17, fn. 13 and 14). This is where General Eisenhower had taken up quarters in August 1945. As of 1938 the owner had been chemical industrialist Maximilian Baginski (1891–1964). See Rüdiger Reitmeier, "Sonnenwenden – Geschichte, Glanz und Parties," in: Burkhardt Sonnenstuhl

lor[45] and his wife[46]. I ran into a certain Olsen[47] there who was active in Nebraska doing rehabilitation work with farmers. He complained of how little help he could get from the University. It was a large party with people walking about on the terraces looking down on the lake. The Heaths[48] were there, and at Keating's party. I had had lunch with them before going to the Political Directorate[49] to hear the discussion about Berlin elections. At the Directorate the Russian delegate (Ivanov[50]) called upon me to help with the discussion. Feldman in today's Committee meetings referred to this. The Soviets have their eyes open as to persons. Sometimes I think I could negotiate with them.

Doesn't this sound perfectly rotten – all this party talk. I am sick of it. It's got to the point now where there has to be one huge party after the other to pay debts. I can't stand this pace. It's one reason why I don't want to stay here, and I don't think you would like it either.

I thought the Civil Service money might amount to a little more. If you are sure there is going to be more and considerable inflation in the USA it is better to convert this money into something other than the equivalent of money, unless we hold the bond until the dollar gets stabilized again. A thousand dollars bond, if we had to cash it, might only buy 500 dollars worth of stuff when we had to cash it. If we just forgot it however – that's something else. To spend it on reducing the balance on the house, on a car, on a piano would hardly be a mistake. Perhaps we should save it to spend on the boys in the right manner.

(ed.), *Prominente in Berlin-Wannsee und ihre Geschichten*, Berlin 2006, pp. 17–67, here p. 44; Harry Balkow-Gölitzer, "Dwight D. Eisenhower," in: ibid., pp. 130–132, here p. 132; Georg Schertz, "Schwanenwerder. Eine Insel im Spiegelbild der Geschichte," in: *Berlin in Geschichte und Gegenwart. Jahrbuch des Landesarchivs Berlin 2005*, pp. 209–223, here pp. 218–220; Lothar Uebel, "Neue Hoffnung nach Verfall und Stagnation?", in: Janin Reif/Horst Schumacher/Lothar Uebel, *Schwanenwerder. Ein Inselparadies in Berlin*, Berlin 2000, pp. 129–138, here p. 129; registration cards Max Baginski, in: LAB, B Rep. 021 (Einwohnermeldeamt Berlin). Photo of the house in Appendix of Illustrations, ill. 60.

44 Refers to Großer Wannsee, a bight of the Havel (see Doc. 74, fn. 24) in southwest Berlin.

45 See Doc. 17, fn. 26.

46 Katherine W. Taylor, née Wright.

47 C. Arild Olsen (1898–1990), 1920 Candidate Theology, Grand View College Seminary, 1927 MA, University of Chicago, 1925–1930 taught history and social sciences, Grand View College, 1932–1938 President, Grand View College, 1939–1945 Farm Security Administration, Lincoln, Nebraska/Washington, D. C., as of 1945 OMGUS, 1947 Chief, Office of Religious Affairs, Education and Religious Affairs Branch, Internal Affairs and Communications Division, OMGUS, 1948/1949 Chief, Religious Affairs Branch, Education and Cultural Relations Division, OMGUS, then Office High Commissioner Germany, as of 1951 National Council of the Churches of Christ in the USA, 1952 honorary doctorate from Augustana College.

48 Donald R. Heath (see Doc. 8, fn. 15) and Louise B. Heath, née Bell (1895–1981).

49 See minutes of the 38th meeting of the Political Directorate, Allied Control Authority, on May 29, 1946, DPOL/M (46) 21, French version, in: AOF, Services Français à Berlin, GFCC, Bureau des Archives, caisse 1140, paquet 51.

50 See Doc. 49, fn. 66.

I hope John[51] gets to learn how to swim. May be there would be a camp available for him somewhere near Lincoln[52]. I am terribly anxious to hear him read. Give him a big tight hug from me. And Timmy[53] too. What you say about him is alarming (milk and glass) and ingratiating.[54] I hope those terrible papers are through, honey.[55] Don't take any more in this summer. If you are willing they will always come to you for there is no better. Good night, my lovely Emily. I love you with all my heart, and send you the tenderest caresses I know. Edgar

Doc. 56
Letter to His Wife
Berlin, Wannsee Officers' Club[1], Am Sandwerder 17/19, June 2, 1946

Dearest Emily –

You have been in my mind almost all the day. I cannot tell you in how many ways. In very very intimate and tender ways. In one's imagination, many many thousands of miles away from the object of his love, one contemplates how he would act were he to have his love beside him, in a fashion somewhat different from what he actually would do were he really to have his love beside him. That is, I suppose, because he cannot quite imagine what his love would do. She has left him on one occasion to accept the most delicate caresses of which his imagination was capable. Sometimes these are infinite. They have been infinite today. When I should have had my mind on other things I have been able only to consider, how would it be to be with my love, today and tonight, for many days and many nights. Could we find new ways to tell each other how much we loved each other? I think so.

As it is I must go on with the account of my social engagements. You will be interested at least to know that in General Clay's[2] staff meeting[3] of yesterday, General Keating[4] complained of the number of parties that were being held at the expense of the Berlin commissary. You will be interested to know also that General Clay himself joined in with Keating's complaint, and suggested that

51 Johnson's son John. See Doc. 2, fn. 15.
52 Capital of the US state of Nebraska, where Johnson lived with his family and taught at the university.
53 Johnson's son Thomas. See Doc. 2, fn. 16.
54 See Emily L. Johnson's letter to her husband from May 23, 1946, in: Documents from the estate of Edgar N. Johnson, private collection of Candice E. and Thomas R. Johnson, Denver, Colorado, USA.
55 Emily L. Johnson was reading exam papers for Ray W. Frantz (see Doc. 11, fn. 15). See Doc. 48, fn. 12.

1 See Doc. 25, fn. 9.
2 See Doc. 2, fn. 6.
3 See minutes of the OMGUS staff conference on June 1, 1946, in: Archiv des IfZ, OMGUS – Staff Conferences (copies of minutes), Fg 12/4.
4 See Doc. 39, fn. 6.

some steps ought to be taken to diminish the lavish display of food that is made at some buffet parties. He said that it was a bit anomalous that the Americans over here should be eating better than the Americans at home. General Clay is usually on the right side, but I have learned enough to know that it takes a long while before orders from the top get down to where they are really effective. Clay went out of his way to recommend that at least, on the mess tables, here we could do as much as was being done at home, we could take off the bread, and we could put signs about urging people to be careful with food. I don't know what the Germans think when they see such lavishness. It hardly fits the picture. There are still to be seen in our PX's[5] what I hoped, soon after my arrival here would be the case, huge boxes in which could be deposited, the surplus supplies which no one would ever use. It is a little embarrassing, when in the PX, to have a GI[6] ahead of you determined to buy everything that is possible to buy. For you know very well that he isn't going to use all this stuff. He just buys it in order to make money on the Black Market[7]. We are much too generous with all these things. It is simply the pressure of people back home to have things sold over here. After all, as Lt. Fromson[8] remarked to me in Austria, you can't expect American business men to let a market as big as this one get away from them. The Germans have to use the Black Market. My new driver (Sanow[9] has been suspended a week for exceeding the speed limit) frankly declares that it is necessary for him to patronize the B[lack] M[arket] if he is to get enough of the proper food to support his wife, a 4 ½ y[ea]r old daughter, and his Mother. Where his Father is he does not know. The Poles took his Father away last summer, and he has not been heard of since.

At Clay's staff meeting it was also announced that an American officer who was motoring through the countryside with his wife and child was shot at.[10] This is the only example of this kind of action that I have heard of.

The number of automobile accidents here continues to be shocking. At least one death a day. And the number of attacks upon American soldiers, and the number of attacks of American soldiers upon Germans, does not abate. The % of colored soldiers participating in these attacks is high. In many cases it is sim-

5 Post Exchanges, retail stores on US Army posts.

6 Government Issue, slang for American soldier.

7 See Doc. 21, fn. 11.

8 Howard A. Fromson (born 1921), American economics expert, 1943 BA, Harvard University, 1943–1945 OSS employee, Economic Intelligence Officer in North Africa, Italy, and Austria, 1958 founded the Anocoil Corporation, Rockville, Connecticut.

9 See Doc. 40, fn. 13.

10 In the minutes of the OMGUS staff conference on June 1, 1946, pp. 11f., in: Archiv des IfZ, OMGUS – Staff Conferences (copies of minutes), Fg 12/4, it says: "During the period twenty-one incidents involving attacks on US personnel were reported. This past week saw fifteen such incidents and six were shown the previous week. In the majority of cases, US soldiers were beaten up by groups of young Germans, altho in six cases the attacks were made with firearms. In Ebersbach a captain driving with his newly arrived wife and child was fired at and the bullet passed thru the windshield and rear window of the car without, however, injuring any of the occupants. The Mannheim area showed the greatest concentration of such incidents and this particular city for months has been the scene of incidents of all categories."

ply the result of their attempting to get their prostitute friends out of jail where they have been put awaiting physical examinations. It is a long way from the lofty decisions of General Clay, and the activities of political parties in Berlin, the colored GI's spending the nights with German prostitutes. I don't suppose that any historian, or other person can quite comprehend it all.

Keating admitted to me at the staff meeting that the number of incidents involving Germans + GI's is still alarming. At the same time it must not be forgotten that daily there are being held court martials involving such cases, and that every day American officers are sending GI's to jail for years on end because they have been guilty of assaulting Germans. But the court martials do not get into the press. Indeed they hardly get around to anybody except those who participate in the court martials. My friend, Captain Americus Mitchel[11], is now sitting on a court martial, and he participates daily in trials which result in penning up American soldiers for unwarranted assaults upon Germans. So we try to do right.

Yesterday I went sailing with Americus in our red boat. It was a good day. And I was glad for the release since after the difficulties on Friday[12].[13] I could not quite combat the lull on Saturday[14], and wondered whether it was not my duty to save the American tax payers the large salary they are paying me and come home. In the course of our sail we had thrust upon us a German Fraulein who was being carried about in a launch of the Major who supervises the sailing upon the Wannsee[15]. She wanted a ride in a sail-boat. She was a pretty piece but an apparent phony because when once cast in our midst she tried to impress us with how, in Hamburg[16], she used to spend the summers in her brother's yacht sailing around Copenhagen[17]. Actually I don't think she had ever been in a sail-boat before. And I could not help but think of the many American girls who are working here who would have enjoyed being in our sail-boat, rather than this pretty and shapely little German bitch.

Today I actually did a bit of studying. I worked on my foreword to the German translation of Franklin's[18] autobiography[19].[20] I am re-reading it, taking notes as I go. But I must confess this Franklin is just a little bit too American for me. He had his eyes a little too securely fixed upon the dollar work or upon its colonial equivalent, and if anything, I shall have to soft-pedal this in my foreword. I wonder what a Soviet historian would do with this piece of Benjamin's. Do you remember the lady he came across in London who was living the life of a nun, because she could find no nunnery to enter in England. What impressed

11 Americus Mitchell. See Doc. 41, fn. 11.
12 May 31, 1946.
13 See Doc. 55.
14 June 1, 1946.
15 Refers to Großer Wannsee, a bight of the Havel (see Doc. 74, fn. 24) in southwest Berlin.
16 City in the British zone of Germany.
17 Capital of Denmark.
18 See Doc. 52, fn. 57.
19 See Doc. 52, fn. 58.
20 See Doc. 52, Doc. 54, and Doc. 55.

Franklin was not the general austerity of her life and the sacrificial quality of it. He learned that she lived on cold oatmeal water and nothing else. Therefore he felt inclined to warn his son that it was possible to live on only a penny or so a day – as much as it would take to supply enough oat-meal water to keep one alive.

I saw Otto Suhr[21] this afternoon and brought him a package that Franz[22] sent. He is a very able fellow, and I only wish he were the actual leader of the Social Democrats rather than the temporary General Secretary.[23] After this I went to a cocktail party given by General Millbourne[24] who treated me very warmly (General Clay's Chief of Staff). I spent most of the time talking to Joe Keenan[25], Clay's labor adviser, a hard boiled, close to the earth, Irish Catholic, Federation of Labor, Trade Union man who wants to send some Jesuit priests and American nuns over here to teach the Germans democracy. How confused we are getting.

I love you my sweet and must return to my imaginings as I go to sleep. It is now June, and the weeks go by. Ultimately I shall be in your arms. Good-night my beloved, my dearest Em[ily]. Edgar

Doc. 57
Letter to His Wife
Berlin, June 3, 1946

Dear lovely one –

You are a difficult person. When once I think I have a question decided, and write all around that I have it decided, behold a letter[1] comes from you throwing the whole question open again. I had the impression that you didn't want to

21 See Doc. 40, fn. 7.

22 Franz L. Neumann. See Doc. 1, fn. 8.

23 Suhr was initially Acting Secretary General of the newly organized Berlin SPD. See Doc. 40, fn. 7. Franz Neumann (see Doc. 37, fn. 26), one of the three SPD Chairmen, had convinced him "that, with his organizational talent, he was the right person for the post of Acting Party Secretary." ("daß er mit seinem Organisationstalent der richtige für den Posten des geschäftsführenden Parteisekretärs sei.") Gunter Lange, *Otto Suhr. Im Schatten von Ernst Reuter und Willy Brandt. Eine Biographie* (Reihe Praktische Demokratie), Bonn 1994, p. 125. Suhr was then elected Secretary General at the party conference of the Berlin SPD on August 17/18, 1946. See *Telegraf* from August 20, 1946, p. 4.

24 Bryan L. Milburn. See Doc. 15, fn. 20.

25 Joseph D. Keenan (1896–1984), American union official, as of 1937 Secretary, Chicago Federation of Labor, 1943–1945 Vice Chairman for Labor, War Production Board, 1945–1947 Labor Adviser to Lucius D. Clay (see Doc. 2, fn. 6), 1954–1976 International Secretary, International Brotherhood of Electrical Workers. Clay and Keenan had already worked together on the War Production Board. See John H. Backer, *Die deutschen Jahre des Generals Clay. Der Weg zur Bundesrepublik 1945–1949*, Munich 1983, p. 294.

1 Refers to Emily L. Johnson's letter from May 28, 1946, in: Documents from the estate of Edgar N. Johnson, private collection of Candice E. and Thomas R. Johnson, Denver, Colorado, USA.

2 Refers to sons John and Thomas. See Doc. 2, fn. 15 and 16.

come to Europe, that you didn't want to bring the boys[2] to Europe. Now you say, after an evening with Ola and Orin[3] during which they tried to persuade you to come over here for a year "for the things it would give us together" that "I am not unaware of this aspect of it and if *you* want to stay on another year, I'd *most happily* join you." You never said this before, that is the *most happily* part of it and I have gone on the theory that you really didn't want to come over, and to suffer the responsibility of bringing the kids over. Well I'm not switching over immediately to the other point of view but it does put a little different light on it. I think that what I'd better do is to go and see Clay[4] and make sure that the job is mine if I want it. Then I'd better make sure that there will be such a job for the time that we might want to stay here. We are getting a little tough on the Russians and are refusing to dismantle any more plants in our zone until Russia consents to treat Germany as an economic unit. Treating Germany as an economic unit involves setting up some central administrative agencies. Central administrative agencies spell the doom of our set-up at Stuttgart[5].[6] I don't want to be without a job again. But if he says definitely I can have the job, and it seems likely that the job will last until next summer then I shall reconsider this matter. The thing to do then is to decide it in a hurry so as to get you over here as soon as possible if case we stay, or to get me back in Lincoln[7]. I just won't live without you at my side any longer than I have to, and the end of when I have to is in sight. Of course I love you very much for all the indecision. I love you very much for consenting to read those papers[8] at my expense. But I hope you won't do it again. Tomorrow I'll answer your wonderful letter of today more in detail. Goodnight my adorable one. I send you all of me. Edgar

Doc. 58
Letter to His Wife
Berlin, June 5, 1946

Dear Sweetheart:

They called another holiday today – D day.[1] If only we had a few more Allies here we shouldn't have to work there would be so many holidays. I have spent

3 Olga F. Stepanek (1906–1998), née Folda, 1930 MA (English), University of Chicago, and her husband, Orin Stepanek (1888–1955), American modern language philologist, 1914 MA, Harvard University, taught as of 1920 at the University of Nebraska, as of 1930 as Associate Professor of English and Slavonic Languages.

4 See Doc. 2, fn. 6.

5 Capital of the state of Württemberg-Baden in the American zone of Germany.

6 Means that central German administrative agencies would make the Länderrat of the American zone of Germany and the RGCO in Stuttgart unnecessary. See Doc. 2, fn. 11.

7 Capital of the US state of Nebraska, where Johnson lived with his family and taught at the university.

8 Refers to the exam papers that Emily L. Johnson was correcting for Ray W. Frantz (see Doc. 11, fn. 15). See Doc. 48, fn. 12.

1 Refers to the second anniversary of D-Day, the beginning of the landing of Allied troops in Normandy on June 6, 1944. "The second anniversary of D-Day, when Unit-

the day so far rereading Franklin's[2] Autobiography[3] by way of getting ready to open this Foreword over the week-end.[4] Tonight I have to go to Brewster Morris's[5] to meet Pieck[6] the former Communist leader, and now one of the Chairmen of the Executive Committee of the SED. The SED is showing itself a little more conciliatory. They have evidently received orders to cooperate. The other night Ullbricht[7], another of their Russian trained Communists came to our office[8] and talked a long time.[9] They are like the Nazis now and want to forget the past. But it is to be feared that this calm is only the preliminary to another offensive and where it will land no one knows. You remember when I came here I said that our relations with the Soviets were gradually getting worse. They have continued to go in that direction so that now it is a matter of official comment and are all urged to keep up good personal relations while the official relations are not good. I think I mentioned the last meeting of the Coordinating Committee[10] I attended, the one which continued to fight over a Disarmament Commission to view the extent to which disarmament had gone in the four zones.[11] The Russians do not want investigation into economic disarmament. I hope they are not making munitions. In any case with their usual wearing down tactics they succeeded in getting the question held up for another meeting. There was unusually frank talk to them by Robertson[12] and Clay[13] both of whom complained of the utter futility to which the Russians were reducing the Committee. Robertson told them plainly that what was in the document upon which they were trying to agree was the plain truth but that the Soviet Delegation was not interested in having the plain truth go into the record. But Robertson, at the same time, is very lofty and a bit supercilious in his approach. Somebody said to me the other day that they wished the war would come so we could get it over in a hurry while we have the atom bomb[14]. This is vile talk and

ed States and British troops breached the continental defense of Germany, will be observed as a holiday throughout the E[uropean] T[heater]," General Joseph T. McNarney (see Doc. 17, fn. 41) had announced. "2nd Anniversary of D-Day Is ET Holiday Tomorrow," in: *The Stars and Stripes*, European Edition, from June 5, 1946, p. 1. See "D-Day Anniversary," in: *OMGUS Observer* from June 7, 1946, p. 3.

2 See Doc. 52, fn. 57.

3 See Doc. 52, fn. 58.

4 See Doc. 52, Doc. 54, Doc. 55, and Doc. 56.

5 See Doc. 31, fn. 13.

6 See Doc. 30, fn. 9.

7 Walter Ulbricht. See Doc. 39, fn. 24.

8 Office of the Civil Administration Branch, OMGBD.

9 See Special Report of Civil Administration Branch, OMGBD, from June 10, 1946: Berlin Elections. Political Opinion and Summary, pp. 2–6, in: BArch, Koblenz, Germany, Z 45 F, 17/258-3/2.

10 See Doc. 15, fn. 21.

11 See Doc. 54.

12 See Doc. 54, fn. 6.

13 See Doc. 2, fn. 6.

14 The American nuclear project had been started as a counterweight to the suspected German project. On August 6 and 9, 1945, the first air attacks with atomic bombs were launched in the war against Japan, on the cities of Hiroshima and Nagasaki. The Americans initially had a monopoly on nuclear weapons, broken in 1949 by the successful explosion of a Soviet atomic bomb.

I don't believe it will necessarily come to this but it is hard to see what the compromise is going to be. Perhaps we are lucky in having the UNO[15] in existence in case these normal methods of reaching decisions do not work. It would all be a little better if we could give everybody a chance to express himself. But as long as all of eastern Europe, with the exception of Czecho-Slovakia[16] and possibly Austria[17] is kept under minority governments who use terroristic methods there is nothing they cannot do. The Russian controlled press here,[18] and radio[19] are horrible to me. Our press is bad enough but it's wonderful compared to this. Elections for city governments were carried out in our zone a week ago Sunday[20].[21] They were not mentioned in the Berlin radio. Instead the municipal elections in Turkey were being talked about.[22] They were not mentioned in the overt Russian newspaper here. And the way they distort all the news to point the guilty finger at the USA is maddening. I wonder what the people at home would really think if they knew just how they were being treated by the Russian licensed newspapers here. I hope the ice will be broken at Paris.[23] If not there can only be a further deterioration in relationships. It is not easy to see the outcome.

Two years ago I was on the high seas abandoning you, it has seemed, forever.[24] I shall of course never forget the early morning of this day aboard the New Amsterdam[25] when we were ordered through the first boat drill and then told

15 United Nations Organization, association of states founded in 1945, most important tasks: securing world peace, compliance with international law, protection of human rights, and promotion of international cooperation.

16 The Czechoslovak Republic became Communist in 1948, when the Communists seized complete power with a coup.

17 Austria was rebuilt separately and independently from Germany; like Germany, it was divided into occupation zones.

18 This included daily newspapers like the *Berliner Zeitung* and the *Tägliche Rundschau.*

19 Refers to the Berliner Rundfunk, which was controlled by Soviet occupation forces. At the end of the war, the Soviets had taken over the Haus des Rundfunks on Masurenallee in the district of Charlottenburg, and they retained control even after Western forces had arrived and the British had taken over the district.

20 May 26, 1946.

21 Municipal elections for the Stadtkreise in Bavaria, Greater Hesse, and Württemberg-Baden. See *Keesing's Archiv der Gegenwart*, vol. XVI (1946), p. 763 A; "Das Ergebnis der Städtewahlen. Hohe Wahlbeteiligung – CSU und SPD als stärkste Parteien," in: *Die Neue Zeitung* from May 31, 1946, p. 3; Conrad F. Latour/Thilo Vogelsang, *Okkupation und Wiederaufbau. Die Tätigkeit der Militärregierung in der amerikanischen Besatzungszone Deutschlands 1944–1947* (Studien zur Zeitgeschichte), Stuttgart 1973, p. 111.

22 Municipal elections were held in Turkey on May 26, 1946. See *Der Tagesspiegel* from May 30, 1946, [p. 1] ("Spiegel des Erdballs").

23 Refers to the Paris conference of the Council of Foreign Ministers. See Doc. 44, fn. 13.

24 In June 1944, Johnson had been on the way to London as an employee of the Research and Analysis Branch, OSS.

25 In 1938 the transatlantic liner *Nieuw Amsterdam* was launched as the flagship of the Holland-Amerika Lijn, and the biggest ship up to that point under the Dutch flag. It was used for troop transport in the Second World War, "completing 44 wartime voyages carrying nearly 400,000 passengers, mostly troops." https://www.hollandamerica.

that the invasion of France had been launched.[26] Nor of course the first day of arrival in London when we were greeted by the first V-1[27]. That was not an easy summer and fall for any of us. The world is at least freed for the moment of such terrors, though the terrors it has are serious enough.

When I think over these two years and try to relate it to the prospect of staying on here it seems now that I have had enough. I have not been to Clay as I suggested in my last note to you, and I don't know when I shall go.[28] I thought today that perhaps I should ask to go to Stuttgart[29] and look over the job[30] in some detail but I don't know as I shall. If we should go there we would be contented enough, I suppose, as contented as it is possible to be under these circumstances. Somebody mentioned the other day that Pollock[31] does an awful lot of entertaining of various people there, and I don't look forward to a lot of entertaining. I have had enough of these parties and can't really keep up the pace. It is for the professional diplomats. We should see some parts of Europe while we were here but it would be difficult to see them properly with the boys as young as they are, and there is a great deal to be said for waiting until Europe revives a bit and the boys are a bit older before going on sight-seeing tours. I sometimes feel moreover that if I stay over here another year I shall be quite spoiled for the scholarly life. Maybe I am already. Jim[32] said in a recent letter that "you can hardly imagine what an attractive home and family you are denying yourself." Without more enthusiasm from you I don't imagine I shall be able to work up enough enthusiasm to stay on. I suppose this is very unadventurous.

I had the finance office here send you a check for 1600 dollars which brings up my salary to June 1st.[33] I kept out $ 148.51 to keep me going here for awhile since I was running rather low, having had no check since my arrival.[34] I don't know how you want to use this. I have suggested a car for your needs there which goodness knows are heavy enough.[35] There is the piano for John[36] than which there is nothing more important. We also have to keep some reserve for taxes. If I stay until Sept. 1 you will get 1800 dollars more in allotments. What I get here will be a little more than I need for expenses, and we can count on about 275 from retirement at some later date. Nor do I think that I shall take

com/blog/topics/news/next-signature-class-ship-to-be-named-ms-nieuw-amsterdam/ (accessed March 2, 2018). See http://www.gallagherstory.com/ww2/chapter11.html (accessed March 2, 2018).

26 On June 6, 1944, the landing of Allied troops at Normandy had begun. See fn. 1.

27 Fieseler Fi 103, also known as V-1 (Vergeltungswaffe 1), a rocket-propelled flying bomb used by the German Luftwaffe as of June 1944 against English cities, especially London.

28 See Doc. 57.

29 Capital of the state of Württemberg-Baden in the American zone of Germany.

30 Refers to the leadership of RGCO. See Doc. 2, fn. 11.

31 See Doc. 15, fn. 12.

32 James L. Sellers. See Doc. 49, fn. 77.

33 See Doc. 44 and Doc. 51.

34 See Doc. 51.

35 See Doc. 51 and Doc. 55.

36 Johnson's son John. See Doc. 2, fn. 15.

any leave since that will give us another half months salary. May be we can squeeze both the car and the piano out of this.

I'm so happy that Mrs. Brown[37] has returned.[38] Congratulate my dear John on his going to the lesson alone.[39]

I should like to have seen you in your black dress with the beads, daisies in your hair, white gloves.[40] Also your new hat. Your mention of our wedding day with what went on before and what has gone on since stirs up more than usual, and I think about you pretty constantly wonderful memories and emotions. I wonder if this is the place to continue the honeymoon. I must have some gray hairs also to match yours. I can't believe they are very important – You will always be very lovely to me. If there are lovely ladies here I have not noticed them to the extent that I have been tempted to seek them out. I love you very much, my darling, and I long for you and wish only for the swift passing of the months. Edgar

Doc. 59
Letter to His Wife
Berlin, June 9, 1946

Dear Sweetheart –

The Germans and English are celebrating a Whitsuntide holiday today and tomorrow but the Americans go on irreligiously with their affairs. It happens to be a rather rainy day and the boats on the lake[1] are turning in with their wet sails. There was a handsome vase with lovely delphinium in it in the window at breakfast this morning. I have noticed that the flowers here bloom at about the same time as at home, possibly a bit later.

At breakfast there was a colonel who is stationed at Frankfurt[2] and is up here on some kind of a furlough. He is from Mississippi[3] though he now lives in Texas[4]. His plans for bringing his family over are, I imagine, typical of those who are making similar plans. He has two daughters, one 11 and one 17. They are coming too. For the 17 year old he is going to try to find a University in Switzerland or France if she can come home once a month. Otherwise he is going to

37 See Doc. 33, fn. 50.

38 See Emily L. Johnson's letter from May 28, 1946, in: Documents from the estate of Edgar N. Johnson, private collection of Candice E. and Thomas R. Johnson, Denver, Colorado, USA.

39 See ibid.

40 Emily L. Johnson had written about Mary Lancaster's wedding, and her husband is referring to this. See Doc. 53, fn. 3.

1 Refers to Großer Wannsee, a bight of the Havel (see Doc. 74, fn. 24) in southwest Berlin.

2 Frankfurt am Main, city in the state of Greater Hesse in the American zone of Germany.

3 US state.

4 US state.

keep her home. She is studying painting (the best southern tradition) and he will get a private tutor in painting for her, and a language tutor. The eleven year old will also have a language tutor (German and French) and will study the piano. He hopes that while they are here they can do a lot of traveling in western Europe, and indeed in Germany which he admits is very very beautiful. Col. Glaser[5] is going to bring over an 18 year old son[6] if he is released from the Marines, and is seeking a University for him in Europe which will not require a knowledge of German.[7] I met a wife at a party last night. Mrs. Clay[8] was at the opera with Don Heath[9]. I saw Col. Rosengren[10] going through the halls with his six year old son[11] in the Internal Affairs and Administration building[12].

From your note of May 31 I gather that your earlier reactions to my staying here and your coming over with the boys correspond to your real wishes, and that the "most happily" has to do chiefly with your conforming to a decision I would make.[13] At least in this present note you seem to have no regrets about my coming home around the first of September rather than staying here. I have found it difficult to reopen in my mind the question of staying here since we seem to have been agreed that it was, on the whole, best that I should come home. I shall have to give Clay[14] my decision soon since he may wish to arrange for giving someone else the Pollock[15] job[16], and also be of the opinion that if I am not going to Stuttgart[17] it is a waste of government money for me to stay here.

5 See Doc. 28, fn. 4.

6 Anthony J. Glaser (born 1927), 1944/1945 studied engineering at Tufts College (since 1954: Tufts University), 1945/1946 Marine Corps, 1946–1948 residence in Berlin, attended American University of Berlin, 1951 graduated from the College of Engineering, Syracuse University, 1951–1953 Air Force, 1953–1993 Industrial Engineer.

7 In an email to Werner Breunig from August 22, 2009, Anthony J. Glaser writes: "My mother, Marguerite [see Doc. 40, fn. 22], joined my father in late summer, 1946 and I followed shortly thereafter – probably in October – after being discharged from the US Marine Corps where I had served since March, 1945 when I became 18. I was 19 and a half when I arrived in Berlin and 21 and a half when I left two years later (9/48) during the Soviet blockade of Berlin." Further: "I had completed one year of engineering before joining the Marines. I considered continuing my education at a university, but instead I attended a few courses at the American University of Berlin (a United States Armed Forces Institute – USAFI school)."

8 Marjorie McK. Clay, née McKeown (1898–1992), wife of Lucius D. Clay (see Doc. 2, fn. 6).

9 Donald R. Heath. See Doc. 8, fn. 15.

10 See Doc. 19, fn. 18.

11 Erik L. Rosengren (born 1939).

12 Roswell P. Rosengren worked for the Civil Service Branch of the Civil Administration Division at that time.

13 Johnson is referring to Emily L. Johnson's letters from May 28 and May 31, 1946, in: Documents from the estate of Edgar N. Johnson, private collection of Candice E. and Thomas R. Johnson, Denver, Colorado, USA. See Doc. 57.

14 See Doc. 2, fn. 6.

15 See Doc. 15, fn. 12.

16 Pollock was intending to give up his post as Director, RGCO, OMGUS, and return to the USA.

17 Capital of the state of Württemberg-Baden in the American zone of Germany.

I had a fine long letter from Harold Vedeler[18], the first one, really, I have had, since I saw him in Washington.[19] He has come to the conclusion, and I gather that this is the conclusion of those he works with in the state department that it is useless to continue to maintain the present pretense of international solidarity since it is only too clear that the Soviets are interested in achieving their particular aims (an international Communist world) at the expense of all cooperation if necessary. He thinks we must organize the so-called western world in accordance with new international institutions and that when once that is accomplished it will be so strong that the Russians will have to deal with it on a full reciprocal basis. Only after the western world has been organized as a unit strong enough to bargain collectively with the Soviets (not weakly separated into national fragments) will the Russians see that they cannot take advantage (as the Nazis did) of a divided western world, and will be obliged to modify their aims. Only after this can there be some accommodation of East and West into a one world, and that can only come after a long development. I think he is right. It is a dangerous policy but it is less dangerous than making constant concessions to the Russians, and failing to organize ourselves.

I went to Mozart's[20] "Abduction from the Seraglio" which was put on for the first time at the Staatsoper yesterday afternoon.[21] I had seen it only once before at Munich[22] and had forgotten what a wonderfully rich opera it was. Afterwards Col. Glaser gave a party for some of the leading members of the cast and other guests – the tenor Peter Anders[23] (whom I had met previously), the leading soprano, Erna Berger[24], a quiet, modest person and an excellent musician, her understudy, an Elizabeth Streik[25] (21 years) old, with a slight but beautifully trained coloratura voice. There were others there, a grand baritone named Greindl[26], a powerful mezzo-soprano, Frau Bose[27], and the director of the opera, one

18 See Doc. 2, fn. 12. Vedeler's letter from May 30, 1946, is available in: UChicago Library, Special Collections Research Center, Edgar N. Johnson Papers.

19 See Doc. 2 and Doc. 4.

20 See Doc. 55, fn. 35.

21 The premiere of the opera *Die Entführung aus dem Serail* (The Abduction from the Seraglio) by Wolfgang Amadeus Mozart took place on June 8, 1946, at 5 p. m. at the Deutsche Staatsoper, Admiralspalast, in the district of Mitte, Friedrichstraße 101/102. Karl Schmidt (1895–1950) was the conductor, and the director was Karl August Neumann (1897–1947). See Kurt Westphal, "'Die Entführung aus dem Serail.' Neuinszenierung in der Staatsoper," in: *Berliner Zeitung* from June 12, 1946, [p. 3]; Lina Jung, "Die Entführung aus dem Serail. Mozart in der Staatsoper," in: *Der Tagesspiegel* from June 13, 1946, supplement. The Staatsoper had resumed performance at the Admiralspalast on August 23, 1945, after the destruction of their Unter den Linden venue.

22 Capital of the state of Bavaria in the America zone of Germany.

23 Peter Anders (1908–1954), German tenor (Belmonte in *The Abduction from the Seraglio*).

24 Erna Berger (1900–1990), German soprano (Konstanze in *The Abduction from the Seraglio*).

25 Refers to Rita Streich (1920–1987), German coloratura soprano (Blonde in *The Abduction from the Seraglio*).

26 Josef Greindl (1912–1993), German bass-baritone.

27 Refers to Petronella Boser, née Hofmann (1910–1994), German mezzo-soprano.

Legal[28]. Unfortunately Legal and Greindl have a more or less Nazi past. Col. Glaser had some of them sing at his party. Greindl sang some Wagner[29], (Wotan's farewell[30]), Anders some Schubert[31] and Schuman[32] songs, and Bose, an aria from Samson and Delilah[33]). This was all very wonderful singing. But somehow the affair left me cold because it was so patently arranged. Col. Glaser, as I have told you, is a publicity man and he naturally sees things from the point of view of public relations. So all the right people were there, right from the point of view of his position, and there were some Germans there who would be nice to have in order that the right people could talk to them. He invited a Social Democrat who might be the future mayor of Berlin[34] because somebody else wanted to talk about politics and he wanted to be in contact with anyone who might be a future mayor of Berlin. I suppose this is only proper. But instead of being a group of people who came to hear and talk about music and associate with German artists it was rather a miscellaneous assortment of Americans for whom the Germans were performing. Social Democrats, Communists, Nazis. The Col. said he had no objection using a Nazi singer for his party.

I am glad the papers[35] are finished for I expect to profit a little from it and I know that you are relieved. I hope you will use the money for a new dress or at least something to adorn your person. Ray[36] ought to be very grateful. I hope that the late hours you complain of have not contributed to the arthritis you complain of. This has me worried. You know I have always in the back of my

28 Ernst Legal (1881–1955), German actor, director, and theater manager, training as a bookseller, afterwards Großherzogliche Musik- und Theaterschule Weimar, 1933–1936 director of the Theater in der Saarlandstraße, Berlin, then senior director at the Berlin Schiller-Theater, 1945–1952 head of the former Preußisches Staatstheater and theater manager of the Deutsche Staatsoper, Berlin.

29 Richard Wagner (1813–1883), German composer.

30 Wotan's aria "Leb' wohl, du kühnes, herrliches Kind!" (Wotan's farewell to Brünnhilde) from the third act, third scene of the opera *Die Walküre* (The Valkyrie).

31 See Doc. 38, fn. 2.

32 Robert Schumann (1810–1856), German composer.

33 Opera by the French composer Camille Saint-Saëns (1835–1921).

34 It is unclear which Social Democrat is meant. After the municipal elections on October 20, 1946, the Berlin SPD had two candidates for nomination for the Oberbürgermeister election: former Prussian Finance Minister Hermann Lüdemann (1880–1959), 1947–1949 Minister-President of Schleswig-Holstein, and District Mayor of Berlin-Wilmersdorf, Otto Ostrowski (1883–1963). Ostrowski was nominated on October 29, 1946, and then elected as Oberbürgermeister by the Stadtverordnetenversammlung of Greater Berlin on December 5, 1946. See Wolfgang Ribbe, "Otto Ostrowski," in: *Stadtoberhäupter. Biographien Berliner Bürgermeister im 19. und 20. Jahrhundert*, ed. Wolfgang Ribbe (= Berlinische Lebensbilder, vol. 7), Berlin 1992, pp. 357–371, here pp. 357 and 365. The SPD politician Ernst Reuter (1889–1953) returned to Berlin from Turkish exile in the middle of December 1946, too late to be considered as a possible Oberbürgermeister. Reuter was elected Oberbürgermeister in June 1947 after Ostowski's resignation, but not confirmed by the Allied Kommandatura as a result of Soviet objections. See Daniel Koerfer, "Ernst Reuter," in: ibid., pp. 419–442, here pp. 429–431.

35 Refers to the exam papers that Emily L. Johnson was correcting for Ray W. Frantz (see Doc. 11, fn. 15). See Doc. 48, fn. 12.

36 Ray W. Frantz. See Doc. 11, fn. 15.

mind the prepossession that someday you are going to pay with your health for the manner in which you do not take care of yourself. When you speak of arthritis I can conjure up dreadful pictures of people (the wife of our former graduate dean) who have suffered painfully and chronically from this ailment. So please go to the doctor, and take it easy for awhile. I love my sweet Emily very much. I know how sensitive she is to any pain and the prospect of her suffering from anything like chronic arthritis is unbearable. Please take care of yourself, honey. I have a hunch I'll get a letter from you tomorrow and that will start the week off well. I love you my sweet one. Hug the boys for me and take my fondest embraces. Edgar

Doc. 60
Postcard to His Sons[1]
Berlin, June 9, 1946

Dear Sweet Kid:

These are still Vienna cards.[2]

Mother wrote me about how you went to your music lesson all alone, and I wanted to tell you how proud that makes me. But I'm kind of sorry too because now I can't take you to your music lessons any more, and we had good times doing that. I love my Bre'r Rabbit[3]. Father Bear

Doc. 61
Letter to His Wife
Berlin, June 13, 1946

Dearest –

I have felt somewhat better today. Because, for one, I did go to bed early last night, and escaped, as you would say, from this baffled immediate world. I therefore felt somewhat refreshed this morning. But, for two, I have succeeded

1 John and Thomas. See Doc. 2, fn. 15 and 16. While the card is addressed to both sons, Johnson only addresses John in the text.

2 Johnson wrote on a postcard that he still had from Vienna.

3 "Brother Rabbit," the main character in the Uncle Remus serial stories by Joel Chandler Harris (1848–1908), which first appeared in 1879 in the newspaper *The Atlanta Constitution* and quickly became popular after the official end of racial segregation due to their optimistic portrayal of American race relations. "Brother Rabbit" always prevails against stronger adversaries by means of his cunning.

1 See minutes of the 16th meeting of the Commandants on June 14, 1946, BKC/M (46) 16, English version, in: LAB, B Rep. 036-01 (Office of Military Government, Berlin Sector [OMGBS]), 11/148-1/10.

2 See Doc. 39, fn. 6.

3 See Doc. 35, fn. 5.

in justifying my existence a bit by participating in getting something done. Tomorrow at the meeting of the Commandants,[1] General Keating[2] under the item of the Agenda called unfinished business, will say to the Soviet Commandant, General Kotikov[3], "General, it has come to my attention, through several of my officers, that the judges in my (American Sector) sector have been interrogated by the president of the Kammergericht[4] (a Russian appointee of the highest court in Berlin) as to their political affiliations. Such an interrogation is contrary to the best principles of American administration. We do not believe that judges have any political interests to serve. They have only justice to serve. This interrogation, according to our information was upon orders of the Russian Kommandatura. I have ordered my officers to conduct an investigation through the instrumentality of the Legal Committee, but meanwhile I wonder if you know anything about the order, and if you do, whether you could tell us something about it, or arrange to tell us something about it at our next meeting."[5] This I helped to arrange through a personal conference with Keating this afternoon, attended also by Colonel Glaser[6], and a Colonel McNeil[7]. The German judges in our sector are particularly sensitive to political intimidation. They are sensitive to it not only because under the Nazis judges had to be political, and interpret the will of the people but because it so happens that since our arrival here, four of our judges (i. e. in the American sector) have simply disappeared, and have never been heard of since. Everyone knows that the Russians have carried them off but how and where and why nobody seems to be able to find out, even after prolonged quadripartite negotiations. Accordingly when judges in our sector are asked by their superiors to indicate their present political affiliations (the recent political history of Berlin is behind this) they fear that this is the prelude to their being carried off in some mysterious manner and disappearing behind what is beginning to be called the Soviet iron curtain[8].

4 President of the Kammergericht was Georg Strucksberg (1884–1965), German lawyer, Dr. jur., 1945–January 1946 Vice President and February 1946–1951 President of the Kammergericht in Berlin (as of 1949 West Berlin). The Kammergericht was re-established by the Allied Kommandatura as the highest judicial body in Berlin, instead of the Stadtgericht established immediately after the end of the war. The Kammergericht had been granted a building in the Soviet sector on Neue Friedrichstraße (today: Littenstraße).

5 See the memorandum (Subject: Representations to be made at Allied Kommandatura Meeting in Connection with Intimidation of Judges) from Louis Glaser to Frank A. Keating from June 13, 1946, in: LAB, B Rep. 036-01 (Office of Military Government, Berlin Sector [OMGBS]), 4/136-1/9.

6 See Doc. 28, fn. 4.

7 John P. MacNeill, Lieutenant Colonel, Chief, German Courts Section, Legal Branch, OMGBD.

8 The British politician Winston Churchill (1874–1965), 1940–1945 and 1951–1955 Prime Minister, had first spoken of an "iron curtain" on May 12, 1945, in a telegram to US President Harry S. Truman (see Doc. 5, fn. 19), then in his speech on March 5, 1946, in Fulton, Missouri: "From Stettin in the Baltic to Trieste in the Adriatic, an iron curtain has descended across the Continent." https://www.winstonchurchill.org/resources/speeches/1946-1963-elder-statesman/the-sinews-of-peace/ (accessed March 2, 2018).

This came to my attention this afternoon after Col. Glaser consulted me as to what to do about the matter. Judges who had thus been intimidated came to our officers in some fright. Consider how impudent this is, the Russian Kommandatura orders an interrogation of the political affiliation of the judges in the American sector of Berlin! The matter was first brought to the attention of one Col. Pape[9] who was disinclined to do anything about it, disclined because orders have come out to the effect that our relations with the Russians are so bad that everything must be done to avoid any unpleasantness. This, of course, because of the conference of the ambassadors and foreign ministers which is to open in Paris on Saturday[10].[11] But the information came to us independently, and we learned, moreover, from one of the judges who is a legal consultant of ours, that among the highest judges of the Kammergericht, the same interrogation was being made upon the behest of the Soviet authorities. What Col. Pape was unwilling to do we were willing to do. Col. Glaser wanted to draft a memorandum suggesting to Keating that he take up the matter. I dislike this paper way of getting things done and suggested that we go to see Keating immediately about the matter. The general, for all his political innocence, has never yet refused to do the correct thing, and when once he sensed the situation agreed that a protest should be made in the Kommandatura[12]. Accordingly, it will be made. The Soviet authorities will at least be informed that we know what they are up to, and do not like it.

While we were with Keating he proceeded to tell us some of the difficulties he is having with the Russians during what it supposed to be a quiescent period. There are almost a million people in our sector.[13] There is constant difficulty because Soviet soldiers come over and rape, steal and plunder. Keating has had to protest 27 such cases in recent weeks. It so happens that this is something our soldiers do not do. If they want to rape and plunder and loot they do it in our sector and do not go over to the Russian sector. But we are very stringent when it comes to traffic regulations, because there have been so many accidents with untoward fatalities in our sector. And when it comes to traffic regulations a Russian soldier or officer is treated no differently than anyone else. All our drivers are terrified at the sight of an M. P. The Russians are reckless drivers, and rather than come under military arrest they drive hell bent for election through all traffic lights into all parts of the city. Our M. P.'s are armed and some of them are a little nervous at the trigger. Consequently there have been not only wild chases of M. P.'s after Russian soldiers and officers but shooting matches in which Russians have been wounded and killed. It is all very nasty and unpleasant business.

9 Wesley F. Pape (1893–1967), Colonel, American lawyer, 1918 and 1940–1946 US Army, 1922 LLB, Southeastern University, 1924 MPL, National University, 1945–June 1946 Deputy Chief, Legal Branch, OMGBD, July 1946–1949 Chief, Legal Branch, OMGBD/OMGBS, then Chief, Legal Affairs Division, HICOG, Berlin Element.

10 June 15, 1946.

11 The second session of the Paris conference of the Council of Foreign Ministers took place from June 15 to July 12, 1946. See Doc. 44, fn. 13.

12 See Doc. 20, fn. 11.

13 On October 29, 1946, the American sector had a population of 979,846 residents. See *Berlin in Zahlen 1947. Taschenbuch*, ed. Hauptamt für Statistik, Berlin 1949, p. 76.

But I guess it is inevitable when thousands of soldiers of different nationalities are placed beside each other within rather narrow confines.

I had lunch with Walter Dorn[14] today and he is quite pessimistic over what can be done to speed up the German handling of the de-Nazification question.[15] You remember that he now has this responsibility.[16] A main part of the difficulty is that the Germans who can handle the problem are so poorly fed that they haven't the energy to carry on with the problem. German officials faint in their offices continuously for lack of strength. Nor is there much by way of salary to encourage them. You remember what I said earlier about the moral courage to fight the battle, our battle. When that is present there has to be food to nourish it. Pieck[17], the Communist leader here, is a pot-bellied leader of the workers. The Russians keep him, and all of their supporters well fed.

I visited the quarters I may have to move into today. They are quite nice. The ground floor of a house close to the Schlachtensee[18] which is surrounded by a pinewood. There is a piano and there is a housekeeper who says she loves to cook. I think I am permitted to buy a certain amount of supplies from the commissary.

I waited for a letter today but I know you have much to do. Anyway I feel a little better and I love you and our fine boys and I kiss and hug you all very closely. Edgar

Doc. 62
Letter to His Wife
Berlin, June 15, 1946

Dearest Emily –

I have felt a little abandoned by you this week. For some reason or other I have longed intensely for a word from you, more intensely than usual, and nothing has come since Monday[1].[2] Don't think I am blaming you. I have some understanding of what you have on your hands, and after the experiences you have been through since I left I can well imagine that some other untoward thing has turned up to drive you frantic. And I guess I put too much hope on your completion of those papers[3] for Ray[4], and believed that it would be possible to have the benefit of your gracious and facile pen in somewhat greater

14 See Doc. 2, fn. 10.
15 See Doc. 47 and Doc. 52.
16 See Doc. 52.
17 See Doc. 30, fn. 9.
18 Lake in the district of Zehlendorf, part of the American sector.

1 June 10, 1946.
2 Probably refers to Emily L. Johnson's letter from June 4, 1946, in: Documents from the estate of Edgar N. Johnson, private collection of Candice E. and Thomas R. Johnson, Denver, Colorado, USA.
3 Refers to the exam papers that Emily L. Johnson was correcting. See Doc. 48, fn. 12.
4 Ray W. Frantz. See Doc. 11, fn. 15.

abundance after they were through. I shall be rewarded in any case next week, perhaps even on Monday[5]. Soon this kind of dependence upon the mail will be over. Today is the 15th of June and within two months or close to thereabouts I should be starting back to you. That seems, all in all a short time if we consider how long I really have been away. For I have been able to work out in my own mind no good reasons for prolonging my stay here let alone whipping up enthusiasm to take the place of reasons. I do not look forward to returning to America. Though I am anxious to return to certain people there.

My desire to return is not fortified by the news in today's press. I refer to the defeat of Griswold[6] by Butler[7].[8] This happens to come at a moment when it makes a great impression upon my mind. Yesterday I sat for hours again in the local government committee of the Commandatura[9].[10] We had finally got to the point of deciding which draft of the constitution of Berlin we would discuss, the constitution of 1920[11], or the draft recently prepared by the present municipal government[12]. Since the present municipal government is largely Soviet appointed[13] Major Feldmann[14], the Soviet delegate will consider no other draft as the basis for discussion. Major Hayes[15], however, the British delegate, after consulting German constitutional experts and what appears to be veritable legions of English constitutional lawyers has come to the conclusion that the Magistrat's (the present city administration's) draft is an impossible one and that it would be a waste of time to discuss it. We who have consulted no German experts, and have no constitutional lawyers available, have stood with the Soviets, since it was agreed earlier that this was the draft that would be discussed, and since we feel

5 June 17, 1946.

6 Dwight P. Griswold (1893–1954), American politician (Republican Party), 1941–1947 Governor of Nebraska, 1946 unsuccessful in his bid for nomination as Republican candidate for the US Senate, 1947 Director, Internal Affairs and Communications Division, OMGUS, 1947/1948 Chief, American Mission for Aid to Greece, 1953/1954 Nebraska Senator.

7 Hugh A. Butler (1878–1954), American politician (Republican Party), 1941–1954 Nebraska Senator.

8 In the primary elections of the Republican Party in Nebraska on June 11, 1946, the isolationist Butler had been nominated as candidate for US Senate, prevailing against the internationalist Griswold. See Warren Moscow, "Griswold Beaten in Nebraska Vote. Candidate Backed by Stassen Loses in Primary Linked to 1948 White House Race," in: *The New York Times* from June 12, 1946, p. 1.

9 See Doc. 29, fn. 14.

10 See minutes of the 23rd meeting of the Local Government Committee, Allied Kommandatura Berlin, on June 14, 1946, LG/M (46) 23, French version, in: TNA, Allied Kommandatura: Directives, Minutes and Papers, FO 1112/378; English version in: TNA, Control Commission for Germany (British Element), CCG (BE), FO 1012/246.

11 Gesetz über die Bildung einer neuen Stadtgemeinde Berlin vom 27. April 1920 (Law on the Formation of a New City Municipality of Berlin from April 27, 1920), in: *Preußische Gesetzsammlung*, 1920, pp. 123–150.

12 Draft of the Magistrat from April 29, 1946, in: *Vorläufige Verfassung von Groß-Berlin*, annotated by Dr. Haas, Treasurer of Greater Berlin, revised fourth edition, Berlin 1947, pp. 115–126.

13 See Doc. 27, fn. 30.

14 Iosif Moiseyevich Feldman. See Doc. 49, fn. 59.

15 Harold Hays. See Doc. 49, fn. 26.

that it doesn't make much difference which draft we discuss if we get down to discussing some draft. The constitution is due 15 July[16] and we have it all to discuss at the moment. The Soviet delegate became perfectly enraged at the lecturing of Major Hayes, a little superior and a little patronizing. At one moment, in utter disgust he took out a Russian newspaper and began to read it while the Britisher was talking. Since the French chairman[17] was not adamant on the point, though as a lawyer he was inclined to be sympathetic to the English proposal, we soon had Major Hayes out on a limb, and when confronted with a proposal to report to the Commandants that the Committee could not agree and that a new one should be appointed, he capitulated, after insisting that a statement of his point of view be incorporated into the minutes[18] – when once we got down to discussing actual terms of the constitution we got along better. But I shall always remember that at a moment when Allied relations are at their worst since the conclusion of the war, and at a moment when we are told that at the present meeting of the foreign ministers[19] the split is likely to come between east and west the relations between the Soviets and ourselves in the local government committee were friendly. Maybe Major Feldman will remember that too as we get ready to fight the next war (which I really don't believe).

I am glad too that at this crucial point I was able to go to the Russian political adviser of General Kotikov[20], a certain Mr. Panim[21] and pay my respects. I had been made known to him by Colonel Kramer[22], our labor officer, who gets along with him. I suggested that it might be possible to have dinner sometime and he responded that that would be very agreeable. May be I'll have a chance to talk heart to heart with a Russian yet, before leaving this theatre. It would be a great event for me.

I think I made reference to the incident of the Russians calling for the political affiliations of the judges in our sector.[23] Well General Keating[24] made the protest at the Kommandatura[25] meeting on Friday[26].[27] It was a desultory meet-

16 Time was ticking with respect to the election date. Concerned about implementation of the October elections, the Commandants had instructed the Local Government Committee, "to hasten its work and to submit a draft of the constitution by the 15th July." Minutes of the 16th meeting of the Commandants on June 14, 1946, BKC/M (46) 16-157, English version, in: LAB, B Rep. 036-01 (Office of Military Government, Berlin Sector [OMGBS]), 11/148-1/10.

17 Jean Victor Ziegelmeyer. See Doc. 55, fn. 4.

18 See Statement by the British Member from June 17, 1946, in: TNA, Allied Kommandatura: Directives, Minutes and Papers, FO 1112/378.

19 On the Paris conference of the Council of Foreign Ministers, see Doc. 44, fn. 13.

20 See Doc. 35, fn. 5.

21 Alexei Vasilyevich Panin (born 1911), Soviet Major, as of 1945 representative of the Political Adviser, Administration of the Military Commandant of the Soviet sector of the city of Berlin.

22 See Doc. 49, fn. 6.

23 See Doc. 61.

24 See Doc. 39, fn. 6.

25 See Doc. 20, fn. 11.

26 June 14, 1946.

27 See minutes of the 16th meeting of the Commandants on June 14, 1946, BKC/M (46) 16-158, English version, in: LAB, B Rep. 036-01 (Office of Military Government, Berlin Sector [OMGBS]), 11/148-1/10.

ing. General Kotikov seemed weary of trying to combat the French-Anglo-American agreement on most questions. In fact the Russians in the Kommandatura have been trying to reduce the number of meetings that are held. They want to reduce the number of committee meetings, the number of meetings of the deputy commandants, and the number of meetings of the commandants themselves. In Omgus[28] too they are trying to reduce the number of occasions when it is necessary to talk things over across the table. This may be the prelude to the break which is to come at Paris[29], a preliminary announcement that the Russians are withdrawing to their own sphere and to hell with the consequences. General Keating got a strong reaction to his protest. Kotikov said he knew nothing about it and had given no such orders, that this was just an attempt of the Germans to sow discord among the Allies and that he would conduct a thoroughgoing investigation. We also investigated and found out that whether or not Kotikov had knowledge of it, the fact was that some Russian had ordered it, and the order was conveyed to the president of the supreme court by a vice-president[30] who was a member of the SED. When we tried to contact the president of the Kammergericht (a Dr. Strucksberg[31]) he had already been summoned to Russian headquarters, and told to cancel the order inasmuch as it had been misunderstood. What the Russians wanted was not the present political affiliation of judges but their political affiliation as of 1 January and 1 May 1945 which indeed makes absolutely no sense whatever. In any case our protest, based on the correct premises, resulted in a Russian cancellation of their order, and this is a little victory. At the same time that we can be friendly with the Russians, we can also make protests, and all this we can do by adhering to a simple American creed which has no anti- or pro-Soviet bias but only is attempting to carry out what we as a nation represent.

At this moment comes the news from Nebraska[32]. Walter Lippmann[33] has an article on the result in the New York Herald Tribune[34] (Paris edition) in which he opines that it is a confirmation of the American trend towards isolationism.[35] The other papers are full of it. It is given especial significances because of Stassen's[36]

28 See Doc. 17, fn. 45.

29 On the Paris conference of the Council of Foreign Ministers, see Doc. 44, fn. 13.

30 Refers to Richard Hartmann (1902–1965), German lawyer, 1923 Dr. jur., 1945–February 1946 Amtsgerichtsrat, Amtsgericht Berlin-Treptow/Amtsgericht Berlin-Köpenick, March 1946–1949 Vice President of the Kammergericht in Berlin, subseqently lawyer and notary, Berlin (East). Hartmann was a member of the SED and came from the KPD, to which he had belonged since July 1, 1945.

31 See Doc. 61, fn. 4.

32 US state.

33 Walter Lippmann (1889–1974), American journalist, political commentator, and writer, 1909 BA, Harvard University, as of 1931 his newspaper column "Today and Tomorrow" appeared in the *New York Herald Tribune*.

34 American daily newspaper, Republican orientation.

35 Lippmann had written the article "Portent From Nebraska" for his column "Today and Tomorrow." See *New York Herald Tribune*, European Edition, from June 13, 1946, p. 4.

36 Harold E. Stassen (1907–2001), American lawyer and politician (Republican Party), 1939–1943 Minnesota Governor, 1948–1953 President, University of Pennsylvania, between 1948 and 1992 defeated nine times in nomination of the presidential candidate of the Republican Party.

support of Griswold. I wonder if the Nebraskans realize the extent to which this is world news, and how much the Europeans will seek in it a confirmation of their notion that we are certain to abandon them again. There is no point in going over the details. But I resolved upon reading the news today what when I got home I should try to arrange for a speaking tour throughout Nebraska, may be you could go with me, in the course of which I should try to chide them in correct fashion for this one thing only their abandonment of their responsibility and this return to their hay-like gorging on their own corn. I think I could prepare an effective speech and at least raise some questions. May be the University could arrange this tour, or perhaps I should do it on behalf of the democratic candidate who is opposing Mr. Butler. I should rather like, I think, campaigning against Mr. Butler. That's carrying on the battle at home, if one can't carry it on in Berlin.

Good night my blessed one, and my dear boys. I shall end on the note I began with. Today is the 15 June and in eight weeks or so I shall be setting forth from here on the way back to you. This time it is for good. No more prolonged interruptions of our life together, a life which I shall try to live to the very full, devoted to the most intimate cultivation of one another. Good night my beloved. I love you as no other person or thing, and I long for you. Edgar

Doc. 63
Letter to His Wife
Berlin, June 17, 1946

Dearest –

I was rewarded today with two fine letters from you.[1] Another from Paul Sweet[2],[3] and another from Henry[4].[5] Henry's letter refers to his bringing over Dowd[6] to meet you and to see the house. "Nobody was there. But we walked around the yard and certainly every prospect was one to please. I could wish that the Oldfathers[7] had such an attractive home. And you are blest in your family. No doubting that." Undoubtedly a good deal of tragedy back of Henry's remarks in so far as it concerns the Oldfathers. And much tribute to you. I can imagine how well everything looks.

1 Emily L. Johnson's letters from June 10 and 11/12, 1946, in: Documents from the estate of Edgar N. Johnson, private collection of Candice E. and Thomas R. Johnson, Denver, Colorado, USA.

2 See Doc. 2, fn. 28.

3 Sweet's letter from June 10, 1946, is available in: UChicago Library, Special Collections Research Center, Edgar N. Johnson Papers.

4 Charles Henry Oldfather. See Doc. 2, fn. 19.

5 Oldfather's letter from June 13, 1946, is available in: Documents from the estate of Edgar N. Johnson, private collection of Candice E. and Thomas R. Johnson, Denver, Colorado, USA.

6 See Doc. 49, fn. 71.

7 The family of Charles Henry Oldfather and his wife, Margaret K. Oldfather, née McLelland (1887–1956).

You are aware by this time that aside from the first reaction of mine to your "most happily" joining me, I have understood it pretty well, and come to a pretty final conclusion about my fate here. I have not been to General Clay[8] about staying on, nor do I think that I shall go to him. In fact I have begun to compose in my own mind the letter which I shall soon have to submit to him, telling him that I have decided to return to the University, and asking for the privilege of doing a little bit of travel in the zone[9] before returning. There is every patriotic reason to stay on here. There is every patriotic motive to return home. They both are of a piece. Paul wrote that had he to do it over again he would stay with the government until he got the academic job of his choosing. He has, in fact, accepted the Chicago job.[10] If under present circumstances I have decided not to stay here, I do not see what could, in the way of a job, persuade me to change my mind. But I come back in the expectation of rejoining you and the boys and not of being especially happy with the University, Nebraska[11], or the USA.

The Knabe[12] sounds like a real compromise if it is at all in any kind of shape. It is a well made piano though not in the Steinway[13] or Mason and Hamlin[14] class. May be we just can't afford the latter right now. Would it be possible to get Mr. Heller[15] to investigate the mechanism of the thing, and to get Herbert[16] to try it out? I like the size of it. The Stein[17], I think, is a kind of neither here nor there piano. The Knabe could be turned in for something later if we could afford a new piano, or if Gretchen[18] decided some day that she wanted to sell her Steinway. I don't think the age necessarily means anything. I am in favor of getting some kind of a decent piano for John[19], out of all this. Otherwise we shall find our little accumulation slipping away from us as the inflation gets worse. Buy the Knabe if it will last until the day when John really has to have a first class instrument. It must be better than that up-right Steinway of the Sellers[20]. I even think dear John's ear is to be trusted in this matter.

8 See Doc. 2, fn. 6.
9 Refers to the American zone of Germany.
10 See Doc. 49, fn. 73. Sweet taught in 1946/1947 at the University of Chicago. See Doc. 2, fn. 28.
11 US state.
12 Refers to a piano from the Knabe Piano Company, founded in 1837 in Baltimore, Maryland.
13 See Doc. 4, fn. 25.
14 See Doc. 44, fn. 26.
15 Probably William F. Heller, piano tuner and repairman.
16 Herbert Schmidt. See Doc. 29, fn. 12.
17 Piano from the Charles Frederick Stein Piano Company.
18 May refer to Margarete (Gretchen) H. Rogers, née Hochdoerfer, as of 1960 married Carstensen (1886–1969), American linguist, 1909 MA, University of Illinois, 1929 PhD, University of Chicago, also studied in Germany (at the University of Marburg and University of Berlin), taught at the University of Nebraska as Professor of Germanic Languages until her marriage to George H. Rogers in 1937.
19 Johnson's son John. See Doc. 2, fn. 15.
20 James L. Sellers (see Doc. 49, fn. 77) and his wife, Nell K. Sellers, née Kennedy (see Doc. 52, fn. 21).

You are so evidently in need of a rest and a complete one. Can't something be arranged for a few weeks in September in the mountains? What we should have is a hotel arrangement so that you would be quite free from cooking, etc. How about the Meeker Lodge[21]? That, as I remember it was a pleasant and comparatively inexpensive place. Or may be just something on a Minnesota[22] or an Iowa[23] lake. I could take care of the kids[24] most of the time. It would be a great treat after all this separation. If we take a cottage or cabin someplace, it will be very hard work for you. If we stay at home, I shall be tempted to get into notes and be thinking about lectures. Away from Lincoln[25] there would be no such opportunity. Or may be the Ozarks[26]. Or may be something in the Black Hills[27]. Your descriptions of these unbearable Nebraska days with the bad withering winds is discouraging. Early September can be bad too. The Hamiltons[28] know Minnesota places. If you can escape to someplace by September first, I could join you in that place. How about that wonderful Lodge we ran into the day after we arrived in the Gass'[29] cottage in Bear Creek Canyon[30].[31] What lake was it on?

There is an unpleasant intensity about Berlin, these days, as the immediate future of the world is being decided at Paris.[32] Most ugly rumors are going about with respect to Russian intentions. I talked with somebody yesterday who ought to know, if anybody, what is going on and he speaks of five Russian armies being concentrated in the Russian zone from the Czech border to Stettin[33], so powerful that, if anything were to happen they could sweep the rest of

21 Vacation house in Meeker Park, near Allenspark, Colorado.

22 US state, northeast of Nebraska.

23 US state, east of Nebraska.

24 Refers to sons John and Thomas. See Doc. 2, fn. 15 and 16.

25 Capital of the US state of Nebraska, where Johnson lived with his family and taught at the university.

26 The Ozarks is a highland region that takes up most of the southern part of the US state of Missouri.

27 A mountain range in the west of the US state of South Dakota that reaches into northeast Wyoming.

28 Probably refers to the family of Cliff S. Hamilton (1889–1975), 1922 PhD, Northwestern University, 1923–1927 and 1929–1957 Professor of Chemistry (1939–1956 Chairman of Department of Chemistry and Chemical Engineering), University of Nebraska.

29 Refers to the family of Sherlock B. Gass (1878–1945), 1904 PhB, University of Chicago, as of 1905 University of Nebraska, Professor of English.

30 In the US state of Colorado, west of Denver.

31 Geoffrey A. Gass, son of Sherlock B. Gass, in an email to Werner Breunig from December 30, 2009: "The cottage was located just outside the little town of Evergreen, about 20 miles WSW of Denver. I'm not sure of the name of the little creek across the road from the cabin. We spent summers there until 1936 when my father's first heart attack precluded his going to any high-altitude locations. The cabin there was built by my father and his brothers probably back in the 1920's. It was sold […] around 1940."

32 On the Paris conference of the Council of Foreign Ministers, see Doc. 44, fn. 13.

33 Until 1945 capital of the Prussian province of Pomerania, afterwards under Polish administration.

the western powers out of Germany and not be stopped until they reached the Atlantic and the Spanish border. It is quite possible that it is Franco's[34] armies which are preserving him in Western eyes. General Keating[35] let me attend his staff meeting this morning and he is taking the normal precautions of a military leader who must protect the most important installations under his command, the Tempelhof airfield[36], for example. And the troops are being provided with extra ammunition. You must be very very cautious in your mention of these things. They can be exaggerated way beyond their real significance. I am not an alarmist. But it is interesting to see what happens when a political situation gets tense. I wonder if this place, at least, is a good one for you and the boys to be.

Your baby and boy (there are appellations which I am only too willing to take from you) was dumped into the lake[37] yesterday. Walter Dorn[38] and I were out getting a little exercise paddling and withdrew into a boathouse to escape a bad rain. In getting out of the house, our sensitive craft quite unexpectedly turned over and we were thrown into the water and the boat got nicely filled. So it was a mess bailing the water out and getting back home. My watch is indeed waterproof.[39]

I went to the General[40] today about staying in my nice quarters[41], and he said I was to stay here.[42] This is really more convenient even if I don't have a piano.

I love you, my sweet Emily. 4 ½ months are gone. There are 2 ½ left. Then we shall be together for a very long time. Goodnight, my blessed one, my dearest.
Edgar

Doc. 64
Letter to His Wife
Berlin, June 18, 1946

My darling –

I am sending you, under separate cover, a carbon copy of the Foreword I prepared for this German translation of Franklin's[1] Autobiography[2].[3] If you will pardon, I shall say that I don't think it's bad. Indeed I think that it is perhaps the

[34] Francisco Franco (1892–1975), Spanish General and dictator, ruled over Spain from 1939 until his death.
[35] See Doc. 39, fn. 6.
[36] Berlin Tempelhof airport, which had started regular service in 1923.
[37] Probably refers to Großer or Kleiner Wannsee.
[38] See Doc. 2, fn. 10.
[39] See Doc. 44.
[40] Probably Frank A. Keating. See Doc. 39, fn. 6.
[41] Am Sandwerder 17/19. See Doc. 25, fn. 9.
[42] Johnson had written about a possible move to accommodations near Schlachtensee in his letter from June 13, 1946 (Doc. 61).

[1] See Doc. 52, fn. 57.
[2] See Doc. 52, fn. 58.
[3] See Doc. 52, Doc. 54, Doc. 55, Doc. 56, and Doc. 58.

best thing I have ever written. Properly understood there is much of myself in it, the meaning of the war for me, the experience in Austria, and especially the experience here, which I think, the intelligent German can catch, all these things rising up through Franklin's text and catching hold of certain phrases and sentences which seem to have particular meaning for this sad Berlin of June 1946. I shall be anxious to hear what you think. If you think it good enough I wish you would give it to Orin[4] to read, and if he thinks it's good enough, ask him to give it to Wimberly[5] for publication in the Prairie Schooner[6]. If it is possible I should like to have some off-prints of it there. One says continuously that the Germans need talking to. After Butler's[7] victory[8] I am sure the Nebraskans[9] need talking to. I am not sure they are in a position to understand Franklin, but if you agree, I shouldn't mind giving this Foreword a little publicity.[10]

I have got a momentary political bug. It is the one I mentioned to you in a recent letter.[11] The nomination of Butler et al. is an enormous disgrace and cannot represent the real convictions of simple Nebraskans who have been properly instructed as to what is going on over here. I propose to offer my services to the Democratic Party of Nebraska to campaign against Butler for as much as they want to use me. I can't believe that the new Chancellor[12] would object, and if he did I should do it anyway. If I felt that I was having any kind of influence upon Nebraska audiences, and sometimes I think I could let go my academic reserve and get down to basic sentiments which might have a popular emotional appeal. The Democrats might think I were worth trying for a candidacy for Congress[13].

4 Orin Stepanek. See Doc. 57, fn. 3.

5 Lowry C. Wimberly (1890–1959), American modern language philologist, 1925 PhD, University of Nebraska, until 1956 Professor of English, University of Nebraska.

6 Literary magazine that Wimberly had founded in 1926 at the University of Nebraska; he was its first editor until 1956.

7 See Doc. 62, fn. 7.

8 See Doc. 62, fn. 8.

9 Residents of the US state of Nebraska.

10 In her review of the 1946 book (see Doc. 52, fn. 61), Ursula Seyffarth also addresses Johnson's foreword: "The foreword by Edgar N. Johnson establishes the connection between this work from a past century and our world of today. Humanely above any bias or pharisaic desire to educate, it assumes a German task between East and West as immanent, seeing Franklin's ethos as a matter of importance for all of today's humanity." ("Das Vorwort von Edgar N. Johnson stellt die Verbindung zwischen diesem Dokument eines vergangenen Jahrhunderts und unserer heutigen Welt her, indem es, menschenwürdig erhaben über jegliche Parteilichkeit oder pharisäisches Erziehenwollen, eine deutsche Aufgabe zwischen Ost und West als immanent annimmt und das Franklin'sche Ethos als Anliegen der ganzen heutigen Menschheit sieht.") *Welt und Wort. Literarische Monatsschrift*, November 1946, p. 188. The foreword was also excerpted in *Horizont. Halbmonatsschrift für junge Menschen*. See "Benjamin Franklin und die deutsche Jugend," in: *Horizont*, vol. 1, no. 20 (September 1, 1946), p. 19.

11 See Doc. 62.

12 Refers to the future Chancellor of the University of Nebraska. The office was to be held by the biochemist Reuben G. Gustavson (see Doc. 49, fn. 79) as of September 1946.

13 Congress, the legislature of the USA, is composed of the Senate and the House of Representatives.

In any case I wish you would give me Paul Good's[14] address. He is one of the leading Democrats in the state, and I should like to write him about it. He would know whether or not it is a foolhardy idea. My general outlook, and recent experience are such as should, if properly expressed evoke some kind of response. In any case I should like to give it a try. There would then be some kind of life to balance the sedentary academic existence, and I could raise, in our backward state some pertinent and awkward questions.

By the way, Paul Sweet[15] mentioned in a recent letter that some part of my medieval text was quoted on the editorial page of a recent issue of the Christian Science Monitor[16].[17] Have you heard anything about it?

The tale of John's[18] urinating on the floor of the porch off the dining room was indeed a strange one.[19] The way in which you handled it was, I think, quite extraordinary. If he really could not explain why he did it then there is, I believe, little point in punishing him – punishing him, that is, for something he himself could not understand. Such punishment would seem to him quite unforgivable.

I have been working on the new Constitution for Berlin all day. A draft is due for the Commandants on 15 July 1946.[20] After that there will be the matter of electoral procedure to decide upon and that will have to be ready about 1 August.[21] After that I think my job will be about done here. I can't wait until the elections are held,[22] and the electoral campaign itself won't be worth prolonging my stay here. If Clay[23] lets me do a little trip through the zone I should be ready to start for home, perhaps, sometime shortly after the middle of August, and perhaps get there around the first of September rather than around the 8th.

14 Paul F. Good (1893–1971), American lawyer and politician (Democratic Party), 1921 MA, Oxford University, England, 1933–1935 Nebraska State Attorney General, 1936–1956 Chancellor, Diocese of Nebraska, Protestant Episcopal Church.

15 See Doc. 2, fn. 28.

16 Publication of the American Christian Science Publishing Society.

17 See Doc. 63, fn. 3. Text passages from James Westfall Thompson/Edgar Nathaniel Johnson, *An Introduction to Medieval Europe, 300–1500*, New York 1937, chapter 19 ("The Revival of Trade and Industry"), pp. 566–568, were reproduced under the heading "The Weavers of the Thirteenth Century," in *The Christian Science Monitor* from June 7, 1946, p. 14.

18 Johnson's son John. See Doc. 2, fn. 15.

19 Johnson is referring to a letter from Emily L. Johnson from June 11/12, 1946, in: Documents from the estate of Edgar N. Johnson, private collection of Candice E. and Thomas R. Johnson, Denver, Colorado, USA.

20 See Doc. 62, fn. 16.

21 On July 4, 1946, the Local Government Committee, Allied Kommandatura Berlin, received the draft of an electoral procedure from the Magistrat. "[…] the Committee will give this document immediate consideration." LOC GOV/R (46) 30 from July 5, 1946, Appendix A, English version, in: TNA, Allied Kommandatura: Directives, Minutes and Papers, FO 1112/377.

22 On June 3, 1946, the Coordinating Committee of the Allied Control Authority (see Doc. 15, fn. 21) had decided to let elections be held in Berlin in October 1946. See Werner Breunig, *Verfassunggebung in Berlin 1945–1950* (= Beiträge zur Politischen Wissenschaft, vol. 58), Berlin 1990, p. 183.

23 See Doc. 2, fn. 6.

We shall need the extra week together. I found two good experts at Omgus[24] today who will help with some of the technical side of the Constitution, with proportional representation, for example, about which I hardly understand anything. I must say though, I find it a little amusing to be working on the Constitution of Berlin, though it is no less amusing than some of the other things I have been into in recent years. Colonel Glaser[25] is quite helpless with this since he knows no word of German, and the draft of the Constitution as submitted by the City Government[26] is of course not in English. There is an English translation but it is pretty frightful and no one could make much sense of it. This is a good example of what could happen if there were no-one around who could handle the German in some fashion.

So I shall be busy until this is done and that is some comfort. Then I shall have the great excitement of preparing to go home. I have the impression that many of the best people are not staying on another year. The stalemate reached on the quadripartite level has a bad effect on morale. Americans like to get some place.

I love you my darling. Kiss the sweet boys for me, and let's plan on a little get-away before school takes up. My own sweet girl, good-night. Edgar

Doc. 65
Letter to His Wife
Berlin, June 19, 1946

Dearest –

A letter from you today telling me of the farewell dinner with the Marshalls[1].[2] I don't understand how they have been mistreated. He was hired for a year and the department has not re-hired him. It is quite accurate to say that we don't want another man in English history.[3] If we are to emphasize anything it is hardly English history. None of us would want that – certainly not Glenn[4] who may be somewhat terrified at the thought of two volumes on Manchester[5].[6] I'm a lit-

24 See Doc. 17, fn. 45.

25 See Doc. 28, fn. 4.

26 Draft of the Magistrat from April 29, 1946. See Doc. 62, fn. 12.

1 Family of Leon S. Marshall (1904–1989), American historian, 1928 MA, University of Colorado, taught as of 1930 at Westminster College, New Wilmington, Pennsylvania, 1937 PhD, University of Pittsburgh, 1945/1946 Visiting Professor of European History, University of Nebraska, September 1946–1970 Kent State University (as of 1948 Full Professor).

2 Emily L. Johnson's letter from June 13, 1946, in: Documents from the estate of Edgar N. Johnson, private collection of Candice E. and Thomas R. Johnson, Denver, Colorado, USA.

3 Glenn W. Gray (see Doc. 49, fn. 74) already worked on English history in the Department of History of the University of Nebraska.

4 Glenn W. Gray. See Doc. 49, fn. 74.

5 City in England.

6 Emily L. Johnson in her letter from June 13, 1946: "The great point is, I am convinced, that he [Leon S. Marshall] has one book on *Manchester* now on the press +

tle terrified myself – Manchester – the cultural patterns of Manchester. I don't see that his age has anything to do with it. It is understandable that you don't like to tell a man to his face that you don't think his teaching was good enough to warrant what would then have been a permanent appointment at the University. Marshall must have had some idea of why he wasn't being re engaged, and why he couldn't be told the whole truth. I don't think it is necessary to accuse Glenn of some kind of conspiracy. Of course it is very hard not to have made good, but in this case I don't see that the department is to blame for this.

As for Glenn's being chairman I don't know as I am in favor of that either.[7] Henry[8] suggested in a recent letter that we ought to elect a chairman among ourselves and then have the chancellor make the appointment.[9] I don't know as I favor that either in so small a department voting against each other might cause unforgivable resentments. Henry would never vote for Jim[10], and Alden[11] I should suspect would feel obliged to vote for him. Since Glenn has never published anything except the two chapters in my book[12] which nobody has liked I don't think he is entitled to the distinction, no matter how excellent an administrator he might be or how much he knows. Nor with Jim's awkwardness does he make a likely chairman. I think the chancellor better make the appointment or that we should have it together – one a year. Jim has never published very much either. I don't think Glenn wants me to have it. He said something about my not being burdened with it when I was home. I am not anxious for it since it would be only extra administrative and personal problems pain, having to do with raises and promotions. Should Glenn get a full professorship without ever having to publish anything, etc. But should I refuse it, if it comes my way?[13] Ben Franklin[14] said he would never ask for, never refuse, and never resign from an office.[15]

another nearly finished, and Glenn just can't take it." Leon S. Marshall's book *The Development of Public Opinion in Manchester, 1780–1820* was published in 1946 in Syracuse, New York. This was also the title of his 1937 dissertation.

7 Emily L. Johnson: "*I* am against Glenn as chairman of the department. He is lazy, selfish, and willing to cut off an other's head if it's in his interest. Very sweet, to be sure, but not sweet to those who get in his way."

8 Charles Henry Oldfather. See Doc. 2, fn. 19.

9 See Doc. 49.

10 James L. Sellers. See Doc. 49, fn. 77.

11 John R. Alden (1908–1991), American historian, 1939 PhD, University of Michigan, taught at Michigan State Normal College, at Bowling Green State University, as of 1945 at the University of Nebraska (1946 as Assistant Professor), and 1955–1976 at Duke University.

12 James Westfall Thompson/Edgar Nathaniel Johnson, *An Introduction to Medieval Europe, 300–1500*, New York 1937. Glenn W. Gray had written chapter 15 ("The Development of the English State [1066–1272]"), pp. 432–462, and chapter 25 ("The Development of the English State [1272–1485]"), pp. 833–862. Johnson included these two chapters on England in order to cover all fields.

13 Johnson became temporary Chairman in the autumn of 1946. See Doc. 49, fn. 75.

14 Benjamin Franklin. See Doc. 52, fn. 57.

15 "[…] I had read or heard of some Public Man, who made it a Rule never to ask for an Office, and never to refuse one when offer'd to him. I approve, says I, of his Rule, and will practise it with a small Addition; I shall never *ask*, never *refuse*, nor ever *resign* an Office." Benjamin Franklin, *The Autobiography*, with an introduction by Daniel Aaron, New York 1990, p. 109.

In some ways I hate to enter this small world again, and I think perhaps I shouldn't. You will be interested to know that I wrote the first draft of my letter to Clay[16] today – saying that I wanted to be home on or about the first of September.[17] I think when I get there I shall want, despite all my talk about trying to get into politics[18] to do nothing much more than stay at home and tend to my classes. Staying at home will mean cultivating you, cultivating the boys, and I suppose the garden. We have lost over two years, and you are always rightly reminding me of how really little time there is left. It is rather futile to think that I shall ever be able to do anything much outside of the rôle of teacher, and there is much still that I have to make up for. May be the time is coming with the boys getting a little older when you will get a better break, and when we can share more fully than we have ever shared, and cultivate more than we have ever cultivated a larger intellectual life. I have always in mind too being adequate for the boys. All this is enough without worrying about others promotions and salaries.

Tomorrow will be a full day at the Kommandatura[19,20] talking about the Constitution of Berlin – whether the councilmen of Berlin shall have free rides on the trolleys or not.[21] But that is an easy one. I say no.

Goodnight my sweet one. In ten more days June will have gone. I love you very much. I think may be you have some idea how much. This is really an impossible existence here. Goodnight, sweetheart. Edgar

16 See Doc. 2, fn. 6.

17 See Doc. 63.

18 See Doc. 62 and Doc. 64.

19 See Doc. 20, fn. 11.

20 Johnson is referring to the meeting of the Local Government Committee, Allied Kommandatura Berlin, that was set for June 20, 1946.

21 Article 11 of the Magistrat's draft from April 29, 1946, reads: "The members of the Abgeordnetenversammlung shall have the right to free travel within Berlin on public transportation, attendance fees, and reimbursement of wages lost as a result of meetings." ("Die Mitglieder der Abgeordnetenversammlung erhalten das Recht zur freien Fahrt innerhalb von Berlin auf den öffentlichen Verkehrsmitteln, Sitzungsgeld und Erstattung des durch die Sitzungen entstandenen Lohnausfalls.") *Vorläufige Verfassung von Groß-Berlin*, annotated by Dr. Haas, Treasurer of Greater Berlin, revised fourth edition, Berlin 1947, p. 119. Article 8 of the Provisional Constitution of Greater Berlin issued by the Allies on August 13, 1946, reads: "The members of the Stadtverordnetenversammlung shall have the right to free travel within Greater Berlin on public transportation along with attendance fees and reimbursement of wages lost as the result of a meeting." ("Die Mitglieder der Stadtverordnetenversammlung erhalten das Recht zur freien Fahrt innerhalb von Groß-Berlin auf den öffentlichen Verkehrsmitteln nebst Sitzungsgeld und Erstattung des durch die Sitzung entstandenen Lohnausfalles.") Ibid., p. 9.

Doc. 66
Letter to His Wife
Berlin, June 23, 1946

Dearest –

I have not written for a couple days. The evenings have been taken up for the last three days. Wednesday[1] the French threw an orchestra concert at which some French woman with a very complicated name[2] played the Tschaikowsky[3] second piano concerto[4], I think it was, and the Berlin Philharmonic Orchestra[5], conducted by a Roumanian (Cellibidache)[6] played the Beethoven 5th[7].[8] I went with Colonel Glaser[9] after a very unsatisfactory meeting of the Local Government Committee[10].[11] It was the first time I had heard the Philharmonic. It is not a bad orchestra at present and the conducter is above average. The orchestra was obliged to play, to begin with, the four national anthems of the Allies. This must be a little painful to do. This puts them in their places right away. They are a kind of slave labor. But they must feel a little rewarded when their efforts at playing German music (the 5th) are heavily applauded by the Allies, and this in a manner to indicate that they are not being applauded simply as slaves who have done good work. In a sense therefore the Germans had the victory, and I wonder whether in the longer sense they might not get it again by having us leave here sooner than we should. Sometimes I feel very insecure about this – feel indeed that they may be running us. I had the feeling tonight, for example, when I discovered, at the mess in Harnack house[12], that the two girls seated at our table were not Americans but Germans. Now German girls are not permit-

1 Correct: Thursday. Refers to June 20, 1946.

2 Monique de la Bruchollerie (1915–1972), French pianist.

3 Peter Ilich Tchaikovsky (1840–1893), Russian composer.

4 Correct: first piano concerto (Piano Concerto No. 1 in B-flat Minor, Op. 23).

5 The Berliner Philharmonisches Orchester was founded in 1882. Its first concert after the Second World War was held on May 26, 1945, at the Titania-Palast on Schloßstraße in the Berlin administrative district of Steglitz. The old Philharmonie on Bernburger Straße in the administrative district of Tiergarten had been destroyed, and Titania-Palast became the orchestra's permanent venue.

6 Sergiu Celibidache (1912–1996), German director of Romanian origin, led the Berliner Philharmoniker ad interim from 1945–1952.

7 Symphony No. 5 in C Minor, Op. 67, by Ludwig van Beethoven (see Doc. 37, fn. 29).

8 The concert took place on June 20, 1946, at 9 p. m. at the Deutsche Staatsoper in the Admiralspalast, district of Mitte, Friedrichstraße 101/102. See *Der Tagesspiegel* from June 20, 1946, supplement; roi, "Französische Pianistin in Berlin," in: *Telegraf* from June 21, 1946, p. 5; Erwin Kroll, "Philharmonisches Konzert. Solistin: Monique de la Bruchollerie," in: *Der Tagesspiegel* from June 22, 1946, supplement; Fritz Brust, "Schwer erkämpftes Musikerlebnis. Am Flügel Monique de la Bruchollerie," in: *Telegraf* from June 22, 1946, p. 5.

9 See Doc. 28, fn. 4.

10 See Doc. 29, fn. 14.

11 See minutes of the 24th meeting of the Local Government Committee, Allied Kommandatura Berlin, on June 20, 1946, LG/M (46) 24, French version, in: TNA, Allied Kommandatura: Directives, Minutes and Papers, FO 1112/378.

12 See Doc. 15, fn. 16.

ted in this mess. These tried to put on a good show by talking broken English but when we began to question them, they got up and left hastily. Evidently two German girls, who, of course, may be in our employ, but who evidently had crashed this mess. If they can do this, there are other things they can do.

Last night Don Heath[13] gave a musicale, and afterwards supper. He had a German trio (viola, clarinet, piano), an unusually beautiful combination which I had not heard before, play a lovely Schumann[14] and a Mozart[15] trio. Then he had Erna Bergner[16], whom I believe I have mentioned to you in another connection,[17] sing a Mozart aria, and a wonderful Schubert[18] song with clarinet and piano accompaniment. It was all very nice and intimate, a small group and the proper music. I talked with the clarinetist some. He knew all about Benny Goodman[19], and would like to come to America. A great majority of Germans, I think, would now like to emigrate, if only they had some place to go. Having ruined their own country they would now like to escape the consequences of that ruin.

I spent this morning talking with a German professor (Drum[20]) about the Constitution of Berlin.[21] He is now a consultant for Omgus[22].[23] His wife's[24] un-

13 Donald R. Heath. See Doc. 8, fn. 15.

14 See Doc. 59, fn. 32.

15 See Doc. 55, fn. 35.

16 Erna Berger. See Doc. 59, fn. 24.

17 See Doc. 59.

18 See Doc. 38, fn. 2.

19 Benny Goodman (1909–1986), American jazz musician (clarinetist) and bandleader.

20 Refers to Friedrich Glum (1891–1974), German lawyer, 1920 Dr. jur., University of Tübingen, 1920–1937 Secretary General/General Director of the Kaiser-Wilhelm-Gesellschaft zur Förderung der Wissenschaften, 1923 Habilitation, University of Berlin, 1923–1937 Privatdozent/außerordentlicher Professor of Constitutional and Administrative Law, University of Berlin, as of 1939 real estate and financial broker, 1945–July 1946 adviser to the American military government in Berlin on constitutional and administrative matters, as of August 1946 Ministerialdirigent in the Bavarian State Chancellery, 1948 CSU, as of 1949 Adjunct Lecturer, University of Munich.

21 Glum was hired by the American military government at the end of 1945 to contribute to the creation of a provisional constitution for Berlin. Friedrich Glum writes in *Zwischen Wissenschaft, Wirtschaft und Politik. Erlebtes und Erdachtes in vier Reichen*, Bonn 1964, p. 561: "Richmond, who was the Americans' political officer for Berlin, wanted my help mainly in order for me to draw up a draft for a new city constitution of Berlin. […] I was supposed to draft the future constitution of Greater Berlin for Richmond. We gathered material and I produced a draft with which Richmond was highly satisfied. It was not difficult for me, as I had already worked on the Greater Berlin Act in 1919 and 1920." ("Richmond, der der politische Offizier der Amerikaner für Berlin war, wollte meine Hilfe hauptsächlich haben, um einen Entwurf für eine neue Stadtverfassung von Berlin von mir ausgearbeitet zu erhalten. […] Ich sollte also Richmond die künftige Verfassung für Groß-Berlin entwerfen. Wir sammelten dafür Material, und ich machte einen Entwurf, von dem Richmond hochbefriedigt war. Es fiel mir dies ja auch nicht schwer, hatte ich doch schon an dem Gesetz für Groß-Berlin 1919 und 1920 mitgearbeitet.") Richmond was Legal Officer Clarence Richmond (1896–1989), Lieutenant Colonel, American lawyer, 1917 graduate of Boston University Law School, took part in the First World War, in the 1920s and 1930s City Solicitor, Welfare Commissioner, Alderman, library trustee, and school committee member, 1941–1946 US Army's Judge Advocate Corps, 1945/1946

cle was a famous Bavarian sculptor, Hildebrand[25], who did a lot of Munich's public fountains[26]. His house[27] was full of his stuff some of which he would like to sell. Do you want me to bring home a Hildebrand's St. Cecilia[28].[29] It is rather nice but I don't know where we would put it. One of his sons is a painter[30] and

Chief, Local Government and Administration Sub-Section, Political Affairs Sub-Section, Legal Section, A1A1 Military Government Detachment, G-5 Section, US Headquarters Berlin District/OMGBD, worked as a lawyer until 1982.

22 See Doc. 17, fn. 45.

23 Glum was adviser to the American military government in Berlin from December 1, 1945, to July 31, 1946. See BArch, Koblenz, Germany, Nachlass Friedrich Glum, N 1457/2.

24 Elisabeth Glum, née Hildebrand (1896–1984); father: Otto Hildebrand (1858–1927), as of 1904 ordentlicher Professor of Surgery at the University of Berlin and Director of the Charité surgical university clinic, Geheimer Medizinalrat; mother: Frieda Hildebrand, née Freiin von Seebach (1868–1940).

25 Adolf von Hildebrand (1847–1921), German sculptor, in his time Germany's leading sculptor in monument and fountain art.

26 In Munich there are three major city fountains by Adolf von Hildebrand: the Wittelsbacher Brunnen, the Hubertusbrunnen, and the Reinhardbrunnen. See Sigrid Esche-Braunfels, *Adolf von Hildebrand (1847–1921)*, Berlin 1993, especially pp. 210–225, 228–243, and 261–285; Sigrid Braunfels, *Skulptur und Architektur des Wasserspiels. Die Brunnen Adolf von Hildebrands*, Munich and Berlin 2005, especially pp. 9–79.

27 Glum lived at Kirchweg 28, Berlin-Nikolassee. See Jörg Riedel, "Friedrich Glum," in: Burkhardt Sonnenstuhl (ed.), *Prominente in Berlin-Wannsee und ihre Geschichten*, Berlin 2006, pp. 143–146, here p. 144 (ill.: "Kirchweg 28 heute").

28 Saint Cecilia, said to have lived in the 3rd century AD in Rome, martyr, patron of church music.

29 Johnson probably saw a terracotta relief that today belongs to the Museum für Kunst und Kulturgeschichte at the Philipps-Universität Marburg. This is the second version of a relief that Adolf von Hildebrand made after the death of the pianist and music patron Elisabeth von Herzogenberg, née von Stockhausen (1847–1892), wife of the composer Heinrich von Herzogenberg (1843–1900). Made for a tomb of white majolica, it represented the deceased as St. Cecilia playing the organ. The tomb is located in the old cemetery of the Italian spa town San Remo. See Sigrid Esche-Braunfels, *Adolf von Hildebrand (1847–1921)*, Berlin 1993, pp. 181–183 and 370–372. As the Marburg University Museum shared with Werner Breunig in an email from May 29, 2009, the second version of the relief was indeed temporarily owned by the Glums. On the museum's inventory card, the 79-cm high (rounded on the top) and 44-cm wide relief is described as follows: "Beneath a groined vault sits a woman (half-length portrait), turned to the left, both hands on the keys of an organ cut off by the left edge of the image. A halo hovers over her head, with hair partially pulled back at the neck, partially falling freely." ("Unter einem Kreuzgratgewölbe sitzt, nach links gewendet, eine Frau (Kniestück), deren beide Hände auf der Tastatur einer vom linken Bildrand überschnittenen Orgel liegen. Über dem Kopf mit teils im Nacken zusammengefaßten, teils frei herabfallendem Haar schwebt ein Heiligenschein.") The inventory card additionally offers the information that Adolf von Hildebrand had made the terracotta relief in 1897 for Heinrich von Herzogenberg, and after the latter's death (1900) it was returned to the Hildebrand family. The museum acquired it in 1979 from the gallery Arnoldi-Livie, Munich.

30 Peter Glum (born 1920), "a person of thoroughly artistic nature" ("eine durch und durch künstlerische Natur"), according to Friedrich Glum, *Zwischen Wissenschaft, Wirtschaft und Politik. Erlebtes und Erdachtes in vier Reichen*, Bonn 1964, p. 528.

the house was full of modern paintings. He has four other children[31] and they all play musical instruments. His wife is a pianist,[32] and he a very elegant professor with a neat moustache and a sleek grey beard. I don't understand it. All this city elegance and the Nazis. Of course he is horrified with the Russians.

The rest of the day I spent with Harold Trevors[33], a colleague of Harold Vedeler's[34] in the state department who is doing the rounds after a mission to London. I think he was amazed at the luxury of this place. We took a ride through the ruins of Berlin – a horribly depressing ride. My driver[35] says the Berliners could rebuild the city in five years.

Good-night my sweetheart. I love you. June is soon over. I think I'll hear from you tomorrow. Edgar

Doc. 67
Letter to His Wife
Berlin, Wannsee Officers' Club[1], Am Sandwerder 17/19, June 26, 1946

Dearest, my own dearest:

It is amazing what company one falls into. Tonight I had dinner with a group of officers who are in charge of court martial and military police work here. The man in charge is a Colonel Karl Frank[2] who invited me after hearing me talk before the officers of Berlin District. He used to teach Military Science at the University of Kansas[3] and there is from his point of view a mid-western bond. At the table were a colonel, a couple of majors, a couple of captains, and a civil-

31 Hildebrand (1922–2010), Ursula (1923–2018), Michael (1925–2012), and Christine (born 1928).

32 Friedrich Glum, *Zwischen Wissenschaft, Wirtschaft und Politik. Erlebtes und Erdachtes in vier Reichen*, Bonn 1964, p. 164: "All three daughters of my father-in-law were musical and had received very good training, […] the oldest, my bride, was trained as a pianist by Edwin Fischer." ("Alle drei Töchter meines Schwiegervaters waren musikalisch und hatten eine sehr gute Ausbildung erhalten, […] die älteste, meine Braut, als Pianistin bei Edwin Fischer.") Edwin Fischer (1886–1960) was a Swiss pianist, director, and music teacher, who worked for a long time in Berlin.

33 Refers to Howard Trivers (1909–1987), American diplomat, 1932 MA, Harvard University, 1932/1933 University of Heidelberg, 1934/1935 Teaching Assistant, Harvard University, 1935–1938 University of Freiburg im Breisgau, 1941 PhD, Harvard University, 1941–1969 Department of State, lastly as Consul General in Zurich.

34 Like Howard Trivers, Harold C. Vedeler (see Doc. 2, fn. 12) was Foreign Affairs Specialist, Division of Central European Affairs, Department of State, beginning in April 1946.

35 Artur Sanow. See Doc. 40, fn. 13.

1 See Doc. 25, fn. 9.

2 Karl C. Frank (1899–1993), Lieutenant Colonel, 1935–1940 Assistant Professor of Military Science and Tactics, Kansas State College of Agriculture and Applied Science (since 1959: Kansas State University), 1952–1954 taught military science and tactics at Utah State Agricultural College (since 1957: Utah State University).

3 University founded in 1865 in Lawrence, Kansas.

ian. The colonel looks forward to nothing but bringing his wife and children here, and installing them in a beautiful house at Heidelberg[4], overlooking the Neckar-valley[5]. One of the majors was (and is) a stalwart and intelligent organizer of military police. The other major and the two captains are hard-boiled first sergeants (formerly) who have acquired commissions. One, an Irishman, who loves to tell stories about Catholic priests, conducts the local rifle range. The two others, one a Mainer[6] + the other from the south, run the stockade in which over two hundred and fifty criminal GI's[7] are kept. The civilian[8] grew up in gangster politics in New Jersey[9] (Mayor Hague[10]).[11] (The Colonel from Kansas told me this). He is an Italian who has just had imported from the States some records of Caruso[12], Scipa[13] and Gigli[14]. He speaks the hard-boiled language of the American tough and he is head of CID here, i. e., Criminal Investigation Department. He directs all investigations against GI's and officers who violate military regulations, and against Germans who do the same. Many cases were being discussed at the table including that of a chaplain who was such a notorious thief that he was ordered by General Barker[15] to get out of the theater. I go to General Clay's[16] Staff Meetings[17] every week and I hear about the incidents committed by American GI's against German civilians. These are the boys who investigate these incidents, that for instance of the GI who entered an apartment of a German and raped his twelve-year old daughter. My imagination is not quite rich enough to take this all in. Your's would be. I ought to have a private secretary on hand to whom I would dictate every evening. Or I ought to have the imagination and capacity of a novelist who has the ability to put this rich detail in dramatic setting. As it is I am keeping no journal, no diary. Only my letters to you contain a chronicle of what is happening to me. These omit so much rich detail that a large part of this experience will have been lost, except as it cuts certain grooves in the cranial convolutions.

4 University city in the state of Württemberg-Baden in the American zone of Germany, survived the Second World War with hardly any damage.

5 Romantic river valley.

6 From the US state of Maine.

7 Government Issues, slang for American soldiers.

8 Refers to Orazio R. Carlucci (1910–1985), 1st Lieutenant, 1946–1949 Director, Criminal Investigation Division, US Army, Berlin.

9 US state.

10 Frank Hague (1876–1956), American politician (Democratic Party), 1917–1947 Mayor of Jersey City, New Jersey, 1924–1949 Vice Chairman, Democratic National Committee. "His name is synonymous with that early 20th century urban American blend of political favoritism and social welfare known as bossism." http://www.cityofjerseycity.org/hague/index.shtml (accessed March 2, 2018).

11 Information on Carlucci's past in: LAB, B Rep. 036-01 (Office of Military Government, Berlin Sector [OMGBS]), 4/137-3/7.

12 Enrico Caruso (1873–1921), Italian tenor.

13 Tito Schipa (1888–1965), Italian tenor.

14 Beniamino Gigli (1890–1957), Italian tenor.

15 See Doc. 20, fn. 10.

16 See Doc. 2, fn. 6.

17 See Doc. 16, fn. 10.

Monday[18], Tuesday[19], and today have been hard. 5 hours of Monday was spent arguing the constitution of Berlin with the Russians,[20] and little Major Feldmann[21] succeeded in keeping anything at all from being done, after we thought that at last the stage was set for smooth running. We were so depressed and even outraged at the outcome that we decided that General Keating[22] ought to make a strong protest to the Commandants at the Kommandatura[23] on Tuesday. My advertising colonel[24] and I worked until midnight on Monday (I writing and he, for the most part typing) preparing statements for Keating to make to the Commandants on Tuesday. We saw him early yesterday morning, and thought that we had him well briefed. But in spite of our (my) well prepared statements, the General muffed the ball at the meeting of the Commandants[25] and supported an utterly illogical and impossible position. We missed out again taking a stand which would make the Russians feel good, feel that they were supporting us and we them. Today I have sat in Committee[26] Meeting for 8 hours.[27] Major Feldmann, having, together with the English, blocked all progress to date had over him today a Colonel[28] who did all the talking, and things went better. At least we got through a few articles of the new constitution. The fact that the obstructionist, Major Hayes[29], was supplanted by an Englishman who knows Russian,[30] and who moreover is conciliatory, helped a great deal. But an 8 hour session is a long session in three languages and I was

18 June 24, 1946.

19 June 25, 1946.

20 See minutes of the 25th meeting of the Local Government Committee, Allied Kommandatura Berlin, on June 24, 1946, LG/M (46) 25, French version, in: TNA, Allied Kommandatura: Directives, Minutes and Papers, FO 1112/378.

21 Iosif Moiseyevich Feldman. See Doc. 49, fn. 59.

22 See Doc. 39, fn. 6.

23 See Doc. 20, fn. 11.

24 Refers to Louis Glaser. See Doc. 28, fn. 4.

25 See minutes of the 17th meeting of the Commandants on June 25, 1946, BKC/M (46) 17-162, English version, in: LAB, B Rep. 036-01 (Office of Military Government, Berlin Sector [OMGBS]), 11/148-1/10.

26 Local Government Committee, Allied Kommandatura Berlin. See Doc. 29, fn. 14.

27 See minutes of the 26th meeting of the Local Government Committee, Allied Kommandatura Berlin, on June 26, 1946, LG/M (46) 26, French version, in: TNA, Allied Kommandatura: Directives, Minutes and Papers, FO 1112/378.

28 Refers to Alexander Mikhailovich Zozulya (born 1910), Soviet Lieutenant Colonel, as of 1945 aide for domestic policy in the Administration of the Political Adviser, SMAG, then Political Adviser to the Soviet Commandant, October 1946–1947 Soviet Chief of Staff of the Allied Kommandatura Berlin. Louis Glaser says of Zozulya: "a Soviet political officer evidently with considerable discretionary power and a skillful debater." Glaser's report from August 26, 1946, on the creation of the Provisional Constitution of Greater Berlin, in: Archiv des IfZ, OMGUS-Akten (microfiche reproduction), 1945–46/10/5. Jean Victor Ziegelmeyer (see Doc. 55, fn. 4) on Zozulya: "un jeune et sémillant officier de l'Armée Rouge," "ancien professeur d'histoire à l'Université d'Odessa." Jacques Robichon/J. V. Ziegelmeyer, *L'affaire de Berlin 1945–1959* (L'air du temps), ninth edition, Paris 1959, p. 88.

29 Harold Hays. See Doc. 49, fn. 26.

30 Probably refers to Kenneth Angus Spencer (see Doc. 40, fn. 25), Political Adviser to the Deputy British Commandant (see Doc. 28, fn. 11), who had Russian language

worn out at the end of it. I was slightly amused also (no more than that) to have the Colonel (my advertising colonel) leave the meeting for a few hours (I being therefore responsible while he was gone) in order to go to a press conference at which there were to be such important people as representatives of the NAM[31], officers of the National City Bank of New York City, etc., etc.[32] When he came back he announced that he had made an impromptu speech before them. Well OK. It is good for Glaser's[33] business when he gets back home. It would not contribute to my business, though I leave you to deduce who should have made the speech. I also noticed with similar amusement that the stationery which the Colonel, my advertising colonel, chose for typing the statements which the

skills and took part in meetings of the Local Government Committee. In his memoirs Spencer writes: "Though without any formal training, my fluent German and French, and useful knowledge of Russian, and in particular my background interest in politics for the previous 20 years and understanding of political processes, enabled me to carry out my duties with reasonable efficiency." K. A. Spencer, *Flycatcher. Memoirs of an amateur entomologist*, The Hague 1992, p. 20. "During my time in Berlin, my knowledge of Russian, limited as it was, proved invaluable. It also greatly improved through contacts with Red Army officers and particularly by attendance at the four-power meetings of the Allied Kommandatura. Everything said in English was translated into French and Russian, everything said in French into English and Russian, and everything said in Russian into English and French. Each meeting thus provided a three-hour Russian lesson." Ibid., p. 24. "In Berlin from 1945 to 1947 my knowledge of Russian, although imperfect, was nevertheless invaluable and greatly helped establish friendly relations with the numerous Red Army officers with whom I had frequent official contact." Ibid., p. 26. Spencer took part in meetings of the Local Government Committee, Allied Kommandatura Berlin, while the provisional Berlin constitution was under discussion. See Louis Glaser's report from August 26, 1946, on the creation of the Provisional Constitution of Greater Berlin, in: Archiv des IfZ, OMGUS-Akten (microfiche reproduction), 1945–46/10/5.

31 National Association of Manufacturers, American manufacturer organization.

32 Six American business executives were staying in Berlin as guests of the American military government in order to learn about the German economic situation. "The men who flew here from Paris where they had attended sessions of the council of the International Chamber of Commerce, were Philip D. Reed, chairman of the General Electric Company and chairman of the United States section of the International Chamber of Commerce; Robert R. Wason, president of the National Association of Manufacturers; Robert Gaylord, chairman of the Executive Committee of the National Association of Manufacturers; John Abbink, chairman of the National Foreign Trade Council; Randolph Burgess, vice chairman of the National City Bank of New York and chairman of the International Chamber of Commerce's committee on monetary relations, and Benjamin H. Beckhart, economist of the Chase National Bank of New York." "U. S. Executives in Berlin. Six Business Leaders Plan Study of Economic Conditions," in: *The New York Times* from June 23, 1946, p. 21. See "Positive Aktionen notwendig," in: *Der Tagesspiegel* from June 26, 1946, [p. 3]; "Want Curbs Eased on German Market. Six American Business Chiefs on Visit There Call for Move to Develop Foreign Trade. Task Thus Far Negative. Burgess, Reed Hold Time Ripe for Positive Action to Spur Two-Way Commerce," in: *The New York Times* from June 26, 1946, p. 33; "Deutschlands Exportaussichten. USA-Industrielle über die deutsche Wirtschafts- und Finanzlage," in: *Die Neue Zeitung* from June 28, 1946, p. 4.

33 See Doc. 28, fn. 4.

General was to make to the Commandants on Tuesday, was stationery which contained the information that there was such a thing as the Civil Administration Branch[34], and that Col. Glaser was its chief. General Barker told me when I came to him that it was just as well that I should get along with the colonel, and that perhaps I ought to retain him in the section. I only say these things to illustrate.

Your letters of the last couple days (two of them) are both depressing and exciting.[35] For one who is encouraging me to come back to Nebraska[36] this fall, you do not do a very good job of telling me that except for my family, there is much to return to, except the most despicable of climates, and a pretty sorry lot of human beings. You go so far as to say that those persons with whom I shall be most intimately associated, are indeed people whom you now loathe, and I take it this means only Glenn[37], Jimmy[38] Henry[39] and Alden[40]. Harold Trevors[41] told me yesterday (I mentioned him in a previous letter[42]) that he thought it very strange and absurd that I should be abandoning my position here, which was of considerable importance, to return to the academic life of Nebraska. Here I would be associated with the making of history rather than the teaching of it. He insisted that if I stayed on here for a few more years, I could accumulate enough money to carry us over an interim period until I could get an academic position which would be worthy of my experience in the past few years. Sometimes I think, particularly after the receipt of Henry's last letter[43], that the boys whom you now loathe, are resentful of what I have been engaged in for the last couple of years and that they take particular pleasure in bringing me back, in reducing the 10,000 to 4,000, and in subjecting me to petty academic routine and to petty university politics and to provincial isolationism of our backward mid-west. You yourself indicate that you want to get out. I say to you, my sweetest, let us pick the place we want to be, whether the Pacific NW or New England[44], whether the glorious SW or a choice spot in the south. If I abandon this life (and I do not desire to preserve it) it is only because I want with you and the boys, to engage upon a manner of living which will do justice to our capacities to live well. We shall seek out our place no matter where it is. We could get it.

[34] Civil Administration Branch, OMGBD. See Doc. 28, fn. 5.

[35] Letters in: Documents from the estate of Edgar N. Johnson, private collection of Candice E. and Thomas R. Johnson, Denver, Colorado, USA.

[36] US state.

[37] Glenn W. Gray. See Doc. 49, fn. 74.

[38] James L. Sellers. See Doc. 49, fn. 77.

[39] Henry Charles Oldfather. See Doc. 2, fn. 19.

[40] See Doc. 65, fn. 11.

[41] Howard Trivers. See Doc. 66, fn. 33.

[42] See Doc. 66.

[43] Probably refers to Charles Henry Oldfather's letter from June 13, 1946, in: Documents from the estate of Edgar N. Johnson, private collection of Candice E. and Thomas R. Johnson, Denver, Colorado, USA.

[44] New England is a region in the northeast of the USA, after Virginia the first English settlement in North America. The region of New England includes the states of Connecticut, Maine, Massachusetts, New Hampshire, Rhode Island, and Vermont.

The news about the possibility, no the certainty, of getting back our old cottage is too good to be true.[45] I have not submitted my letter to General Clay,[46] but when I do I think I shall change the date upon which I said I should like to be in Lincoln[47] (i. e. Sept. 1) to August 21. I am so glad you seized upon the opportunity of taking the place at the moment it was presented. Papa will join you as soon as he can. He will try to arrange to be there before you set off for Colorado[48] (in this instance, I think, money is no consideration) but he may not be able to make it. You go ahead and make your own plans. If I am there in time, O. K., if not then I shall join you at the cottage. And we shall ask Henry and the boys to announce that I shall be back for classes after the preliminary monkey business is over. I am not sure you are wise about the car (how are we to get to the High Drive[49] for example?) but I am willing to submit to your decision in this regard.[50] (Did you get my 1600 dollars?).[51] It will be no inconvenience for me to be in Lincoln without a car. I only ask that on one of these days in Colorado you will arrange that the boys will be taken care of, and that you and I will start off in the early morning on a hike which will take us to the highest peak in Colorado[52] (we have been there before), and that this shall be the inauguration, if not before, (I should say continuation), of the sweetest and most intimate life that two people have ever lived together. Then no matter what our life, as associated with the University, will turn out to be, together with our sweet kids, it will be such as no untoward exterior circumstances can disturb. If we miss this wonderful chance, we shall have only ourselves to blame. I love you my darling. I have only one chance to make my life somewhat complete, and that is through you. I take you into my arms and hold you very close. I love you. We must try to realize this. Kiss sweet John and Timmy. Your "darling boy," Edgar

45 Emily L. Johnson in her letter from June 17, 1946: "I am also happy – vaguely – because I had a note from Mrs. Zumwinkel [see Doc. 46, fn. 6] saying we could have a cabin – our old one – on Aug. 22, for as long as we want it." Letter in: Documents from the estate of Edgar N. Johnson, private collection of Candice E. and Thomas R. Johnson, Denver, Colorado, USA.

46 See Doc. 63 and Doc. 65.

47 Capital of the US state of Nebraska, where Johnson lived with his family and taught at the university.

48 US state.

49 A scenic drive in the Rocky Mountains, Colorado.

50 Emily L. Johnson in her letter from June 17, 1946: "About a car: I am against getting one now, even if I could. The inconveniences of not having one are many, but we do get along, and 'think of the money we save.'" Letter in: Documents from the estate of Edgar N. Johnson, private collection of Candice E. and Thomas R. Johnson, Denver, Colorado, USA. See Doc. 51.

51 See Doc. 58.

52 Probably refers to the highest point in Rocky Mountain National Park, Longs Peak, over 4,300 m or almost 14,300 ft. high, beloved by mountain climbers.

Doc. 68
Letter to His Wife
Berlin, Wannsee Officers' Club[1], Am Sandwerder 17/19, June 29, 1946

My sweet one:

It is a lovely day, and the Americans, I take it, are making the most of it. I shall not conceal that I am very lonesome for you and the boys. But the end of this comes suddenly into view. It seems silly not to try to get home by the 21st of August in order to go out with you and the boys to Colorado[2]. I, of course, may not make it by that date in which case I shall have to join you in Meeker Park[3]. In any case I think you should try to take someone along. Not only to help you until I get there in case I don't make it in Lincoln[4], but it might be nice to have someone stay with the children in case we wanted to go out for a hike alone on some of these days. You would appear to be lucky if you could get Alison[5] to go along.

I have not done anything more with my letter to Clay[6].[7] He announced this morning at the staff conference[8] that he was going to Paris[9] on Tuesday[10], where, I suppose, the German problem will be taken up. I imagine, however, that he will be back at the end of the week, and I shall try to get a letter to him by that time. In it I shall ask for the privilege of going to the zone for a couple of weeks. I do not know whether it will be possible for me to fly home. I rather doubt it inasmuch as it has been announced that flying facilities have been much curtailed, and I do not intend to spend money on paying for my own transportation home by air.

If it is to be by boat then I suppose I should be leaving here around the first of August. That might get me to New York around the 15th. I don't know whether I have to go to Washington or not. In case I don't have to, I don't think I

1 See Doc. 25, fn. 9.

2 US state.

3 Vacation area near Allenspark, Colorado.

4 Capital of the US state of Nebraska, where Johnson lived with his family and taught at the university.

5 Alison E. Gass, later married Murie (1931–2013), daughter of Sherlock B. Gass (see Doc. 63, fn. 29), babysitter for the children of Emily L. and Edgar N. Johnson. In an email to Werner Breunig from January 10, 2010, she writes: "[…] I remember the Johnsons very well. They were dear friends of my parents. Given the times & manners of the day, my relationship with them was somewhat more formal. I knew Emily better, since the kids were largely her province. They had a nice record player and an interesting collection of records. I discovered a taste for Schubert's [see Doc. 38, fn. 2] string quintets there (after putting the kids to bed). […] My mother and I left Lincoln permanently in 1947, and I don't believe I ever saw the Johnsons after that, though my mother would have kept in touch with them by mail."

6 See Doc. 2, fn. 6.

7 See Doc. 63, Doc. 65, and Doc. 67.

8 See minutes of the OMGUS staff conference on June 29, 1946, in: Archiv des IfZ, OMGUS – Staff Conferences (copies of minutes), Fg 12/4.

9 On the conference of the Council of Foreign Ministers see Doc. 44, fn. 13.

10 June 25, 1946.

shall even though it would be nice to see Polly[11] and Gene[12], and Marguerite[13] and Harold[14], and perhaps wise to call on some people in the State Department. I could then go on straight to Chicago where I must see Aunt Hannah[15], and Mildred[16] and David[17], and go up to Milwaukee[18] to see Dad[19] (whom I have very shamefully neglected) and inevitably Norman[20] and Lucille[21]. Then to Omaha[22], where I take it, a final cutting off of relations with the War Department could be made, and then to you in Lincoln, or if not in Lincoln then in Colorado. If this is the way it is to be and I am to have the privilege of going to the zone for a couple of weeks. I should not be in Berlin longer than about two weeks more which seems incredible. As a matter of fact I suppose I should really leave here for good and go to Le Havre[23], from which port I suppose one sails, via Frankfurt[24]. I left there for you in November of last year, and got back very quickly by air.

But by the 15 July at least my main task in Berlin will have been done,[25] I think. We are supposed to have the constitution of Berlin, together with an electoral procedure ready for the Commandants by their next meeting which is the 9th of July.[26] I don't know whether we shall quite be able to make this, but at the present moment it looks as if we might, and in that event, as long as I am not going to stay here, there is not much point in my staying much longer. When they sent me down here there were two big problems to be solved, the problem of the merger[27] (you remember letters on that subject) and the problem of elections in Berlin. By the time the constitution and electoral procedure are completed these two problems will have been settled. The plan of the electoral campaign will have been begun, and there is not much point in my getting started on that.

11 Pauline R. Anderson. See Doc. 2, fn. 2.
12 Eugene N. Anderson. See Doc. 1, fn. 1.
13 Marguerite D. Vedeler. See Doc. 2, fn. 13.
14 Harold C. Vedeler. See Doc. 2, fn. 12.
15 Hannah Walstrom. See Doc. 4, fn. 14.
16 Mildred H. Williams. See Doc. 4, fn. 12.
17 David G. Williams. See Doc. 4, fn. 17.
18 City in the US state of Wisconsin.
19 Frank E. Johnson. See Doc. 3, fn. 12.
20 Norman D. Johnson. See Doc. 3, fn. 13.
21 Lucille Johnson. See Doc. 3, fn. 17.
22 City in the US state of Nebraska, northeast of Johnson's home in Lincoln.
23 French seaport city on the Atlantic coast.
24 Frankfurt am Main, city in the state of Greater Hesse in the American zone of Germany.
25 See Doc. 62, and Doc. 62, fn. 16; Doc. 64.
26 The Commandants had decided in their meeting on June 25, 1946, "to instruct the Local Government Committee to continue its work on the draft constitution and electoral procedure without delay and to submit to the Meeting of the Commandants on 9th July (i) A draft of the constitution (ii) a recommendation on electoral procedure taking into account, in particular, the four points submitted by the British representative (para 350 of BKD/M (46) 28)." Minutes of the 17th meeting of the Commandants on June 25, 1946, BKC/M (46) 17-162, English version, in: LAB, B Rep. 036-01 (Office of Military Government, Berlin Sector [OMGBS]), 11/148-1/10.
27 Refers to the merger of the KPD and SPD into the SED.

This morning at nine o'clock I saw Mrs. Heath[28], the wife of Don Heath[29] who is Murphy's[30] second here and head of the division of political affairs. She is the vice-president or something of the sort of the wives' organization[31] here (there are now about 170 of them[32]) and she has to organize a program for the club which these wives are forming. She wanted me to talk over the possible program for such a club, and it turned out also that she wanted me to open up the program by a speech to the ladies. I did not consent to do it immediately but I am to give her an answer by tomorrow, and although it involves a lot of extra work, I think I'll do it. My notion would be that the ladies should undertake something positive in Berlin, that they should not sit back and enjoy their luxurious houses, and their retinues of servants, and organize the social life of a military post, a university campus, or a missionary compound but that they should get busy and associate themselves with the elements in Berlin life which are working towards the same goals as we are. Insofar as I can gather they are much dominated by military hierarchy, and want to get back to bridge and possibly lectures on German porcelain, which they hope to acquire while here. I will suggest associating themselves with forward-looking elements in German life, and acting as a liaison with American women at home who have to be led into the notion of seeing this thing through. I have too good a notion of what happens at dinner-tables not to know that such a talk would not have repercussions in, let us say, the best circles. I know something about the power of women. And I know how I shall begin my little speech. I hope it will be psychologically correct. I shall say, "There is only one person whom I should like to be added to the members of this organization (I mean only present in the audience) but I am not sure, that if she were here, she would bother to come out and listen to her husband talk." This interview kept me from attending General Keating's[33] staff meeting and he did not like it. At least there was a summons for me at 35 Grunewaldstrasse[34] to attend. But since Mrs. Heath kept me I did not wish to interrupt the meeting and the General took it all right. As a matter of fact I had lost interest because after last week's meeting at which certain problems were discussed, Colonel Howley[35] demanded (he is director of MGBD[36]) that General Keating should be presented not with the failures of

28 See Doc. 55, fn. 48.

29 Donald R. Heath. See Doc. 8, fn. 15.

30 See Doc. 8, fn. 13.

31 Refers to the American Women's Club of Berlin, which came together for its first official meeting on June 25, 1946, in Harnack House (see Doc. 15, fn. 16). For the first three months Marjorie McK. Clay (see Doc. 59, fn. 8) was appointed as President, Louise B. Heath as Vice President and General Program Chairman. See "U. S. Wives Form Club," in: *OMGUS Observer* from May 31, 1946, p. 2; "Women's Club Members Adopt Constitution," in: *OMGUS Observer* from June 28, 1946, p. 2.

32 Refers to the wives of members of the American occupation forces who had recently arrived in Berlin.

33 See Doc. 39, fn. 6.

34 Grunewaldstraße 35 in the district of Steglitz, OMGBD headquarters. See Doc. 25, fn. 13.

35 See Doc. 20, fn. 18.

36 Military Government, Berlin District. See Doc. 25, fn. 13.

M[ilitary] G[overnment], but with their accomplishments. In other words we are doing an impeccable job. And I was disappointed to hear from General Keating that the meeting went much better this morning. Then I went to Clay's staff meeting[37]. It was announced there that on next Tuesday[38], American officials would proclaim an amnesty (from all de-Nazification laws) for anybody born after July 1, 1919.[39] This means all these kids who were 14 at the time when Hitler[40] came to power would be exempted from any de-Nazification process if they were not in the worst categories of Nazis[41]. This would include people who are now 27 years of age. Clay admitted this was dangerous, and for the first time, I heard from him a statement to the effect that its success would depend upon a successful positive program for the youth of this age – such as we have not had yet and such as – I wonder – we are not likely to get from the people who are here responsible. It is meant to suggest however our great trust in the German youth, our faith that they are not a lost generation and can therefore be brought around. But at this same meeting it was announced that the attacks by bands of German youth upon American personnel (including women) were increasing noticeably and that stringest measures are now necessary in those communities where these attacks are most numerous. These attacks, however, bear a certain relationship to the attacks of American soldiers upon German civilians. These things should not be overemphasized, but they do take place.

The work on the Constitution has been going along more smoothly. These were two full day meetings this week, Wednesday[42] and Friday[43].[44] The Russians have made a complete turn-about (vide Molotov[45] at Paris[46]) and the En-

37 See fn. 8.

38 July 2, 1946.

39 On July 2, 1946, at the 10th convention of the Länderrat (see Doc. 15, fn. 10), the Director of RGCO, James K. Pollock (see Doc. 15, fn. 12), read a message from the Deputy Military Governor Lucius D. Clay, in which Clay expressed the readiness of the American military government to accept an application by the Länderrat for general amnesty for German youth. See "10. Tagung des Länderrates des amerikanischen Besatzungsgebietes in Stuttgart, 2. Juli 1946," in: *Akten zur Vorgeschichte der Bundesrepublik Deutschland 1945–1949*, vol. 1, *September 1945–Dezember 1946*, eds. Walter Vogel/Christoph Weisz, Munich and Vienna 1976, no. 24, pp. 572f.; "Amnestie für die Jugend. Milderung im Schicksal der Evakuierten? – Botschaft General Clays," in: *Die Neue Zeitung* from July 5, 1946, p. 3; *Keesing's Archiv der Gegenwart*, vol. XVI (1946), p. 799 E.

40 See Doc. 22, fn. 19.

41 Groups I and II (War Criminals and Activists) of the Gesetz zur Befreiung von Nationalsozialismus und Militarismus vom 5. März 1946 (Law for Liberation from National Socialism and Militarism from March 5, 1946) (see Doc. 47, fn. 20).

42 June 26, 1946.

43 June 28, 1946.

44 See minutes of the 26th meeting of the Local Government Committee, Allied Kommandatura Berlin, on June 26, 1946, LG/M (46) 26, French version, in: TNA, Allied Kommandatura: Directives, Minutes and Papers, FO 1112/378; minutes of the 27th meeting of the Local Government Committee, Allied Kommandatura Berlin, on June 28, 1946, LG/M (46) 27, French version, in: ibid.

45 See Doc. 44, fn. 18.

46 On the Paris conference of the Council of Foreign Ministers see Doc. 44, fn. 13.

glish have been not quite so sticky. The little Russian major[47] has been virtually supplanted by a Russian colonel[48], who has evidently been instructed to get work done, and the understanding we achieved in fighting the British on a previous occasion has now developed into a kind of friendship. Since the Russians know that I attend meetings of the Commandatura[49], Political Directorate[50] and Coordinating Committee[51] they listen to me, and since I am reasonable are quite willing to get along. I was amazed yesterday to have a proposition (and an important one) accepted by them, almost without debate. I am enclosing a menu of the luncheon held in the Kommandatura after our Wednesday meeting.[52] This month is French chairmanship and the menu is typically French – that is mediatory.[53] To a great extent these negotiations depend upon persons – persons who are not stubborn and in re the Soviets not positively anti-Russian. Liberal Americans have a great rôle to play in diplomatic negotiations but there are not many of them here.

Thursday[54] evening I spent with a group of University of Berlin[55] students who are interested in the USA. I brought them a handsome American lady who spoke on Social Welfare in the USA (Miss Beklin[56] who has worked in

47 Refers to Major Iosif Moiseyevich Feldman. See Doc. 49, fn. 59.

48 Refers to Lieutenant Colonel Alexander Mikhailovich Zozulya. See Doc. 67, fn. 28.

49 See Doc. 20, fn. 11.

50 Political Directorate, Allied Control Authority.

51 See Doc. 15, fn. 21.

52 See Appendix of Illustrations, ill. 38.

53 The menu, which consisted among other things of "Potage Windsor," "Salade Russe," and "Pommes Anglaises," reflected the role of balance and mediation that the French tried to play among the Allies. See Wolfgang Benz, "Vorwort," in: Dorothea Führe, *Die französische Besatzungspolitik in Berlin von 1945 bis 1949. Déprussianisation und Décentralisation*, Berlin 2001, pp. VII–IX, here p. VIII. The occuaption forces acting as chair were also responsible for catering. See Kenneth Angus Spencer (see Doc. 40, fn. 25): "Chairmanship of the meetings at all levels rotated monthly, with the duty country being responsible not only for arranging the agenda of the meetings but also for providing the lunches, which played an important part in the day's work. Without being jingoistic I can fairly claim that the British month produced the best work, with more problems being solved under British chairmanship than was achieved by any of the other Allies. However, by general consensus the meals provided by the British were by far the most inferior. During the Russian month the reverse applied. Few effective decisions were reached but the Russian food was magnificent, with ample vodka, wines and champagne from the Crimea. After such lunches little was achieved. One aspect of the American months was interesting. They daily flew in from Copenhagen supplies of fresh dairy produce for the large American colony in Berlin. At their lunches, no alcohol was provided but merely fresh cold milk. It was amusing to watch the vodka-swilling Russians having to be content with milk. At least everyone kept awake after these lunches!" K. A. Spencer, *Flycatcher. Memoirs of an amateur entomologist*, The Hague 1992, pp. 21f.

54 June 27, 1946.

55 University founded in 1810, ceremoniously reopened on January 29, 1946.

56 Mildred L. C. Biklen, later Mildred B. Smith (1903–1993), American social worker, 1928 BA, University of Iowa, graduate work, University of Chicago and University of Nebraska, 1934/1935 Case Work Supervisor and Director of Lancaster County Relief Bureau, 1935/1936 Supervisor of Employment District 3 Works Progress Admin-

Nebraska). There was president of Columbia Teacher's College[57] guy (Alexander[58]) who is a prohibitionist and a North Carolinian[59].[60] We need some very alive people in this field of Education and Religion.

I love you, my sweetheart, and it won't be long now. Edgar

Doc. 69
Letter to His Father[1]
Berlin, Wannsee Officers' Club[2], Am Sandwerder 17/19, June 29, 1946

Dear Dad –

I am ashamed for not having written you long before this. When I left you in February I thought you would be going out to Lincoln[3] soon but Norman[4] has written me to the effect that you have gotten a job with a music store in Milwaukee[5] repairing pianos, and that you did not feel that you could go.[6] I can understand this very well. A chance to go back to the kind of work you used to

istration, Associate Director of Works Progress Administration for Nebraska, as of 1936 Supervisor of Assistance, Nebraska State Assistance and Child Welfare Department, January–June 1946 Deputy Chief, Public Welfare Branch, OMGBD, June 1946/1947 Chief, Public Welfare Branch, OMGBD/OMGBS, 1947/1948 Chief, Public Welfare Branch, Internal Affairs and Communications Division, OMGUS, 1948/1949 Chief, Public Welfare Branch, Civil Administration Division, OMGUS.

57 Teachers College, Columbia University, New York City, founded in 1887.

58 Richard T. Alexander (1887–1971), American educationalist, 1910/1911 taught at Robert College, Turkey, 1911/1912 first stay in Germany, 1914–1924 taught at George Peabody College for Teachers, 1918 PhD, Columbia University, 1924–1951 Teachers College, Columbia University, Professor of Education, 1946/1947 Education and Religious Affairs Branch, Internal Affairs and Communications Division, OMGUS, 1947/1948 Chief, Education and Religious Affairs Branch, Internal Affairs and Communications Division, OMGUS, 1948 Chief, Education Branch, Education and Cultural Relations Division, OMGUS. John W. Taylor (see Doc. 17, fn. 26), his former student, had asked him to come to Germany as an employee of the military government. "[…] John had contacted or had revised and made arrangements for the state department to talk to my dad," recalls Richard T. Alexander's son, Richard T. Alexander Jr. (1917–2017). http://volweb.utk.edu/~wpcsws/wp-content/uploads/2013/04/2004-Alexander-Richard-Part-II.pdf (accessed March 3, 2018).

59 Residents of the US state of North Carolina.

60 Richard T. Alexander was close friends with the head of Teachers College (1927–1949 Dean, 1949–1954 President), William F. Russell (1890–1956). See http://www.culturedandcompetentteacher.com/nashville-and-peabody-1914-1924.html (accessed March 3, 2018).

1 Frank E. Johnson. See Doc. 3, fn. 12.

2 See Doc. 25, fn. 9.

3 Capital of the US state of Nebraska, where Johnson lived with his family and taught at the university.

4 Norman D. Johnson. See Doc. 3, fn. 13.

5 City in the US state of Wisconsin.

6 See Doc. 46.

do, you couldn't very well afford to pass up, and I know how important keeping busy is to you as it is to every one.

I have been a little disappointed in coming back here. As Norman may have told you, the job I thought I was going to get wasn't ready for me when I came because of the long time it took for me to get back here. Consequently I was sent down to Berlin to become the political adviser of the Commanding General of the troops in the Berlin area. This work has been interesting and important enough, and I have not felt that my time was wasted. During the first part of it there was a nasty political fight going on here between the Communists and the Socialists. The Communists, with the support of Russia, wanted the Socialists to join with them in a united workers' party, and the Socialists wanted to retain their independence. The Socialists lost out in the Russian zone, but in Berlin, with the help of the British, French, and ourselves they managed to preserve their independence. I had something to do with this and for this I am glad. Since that time we have been busy trying to get ready for elections in Berlin in October. This has meant preparing a constitution for the city and preparing for the machinery of elections. In another week or so this work should be done.

Then I think I am coming home. It is something of a temptation to stay on here but Emily does not want to come over with the children, and I am not sure that I want to abandon the university for work of this kind inasmuch as there is really no guarantee of how long it will last. I shall have to take a huge salary cut, which, with the inflation imminent in America will make things a bit difficult but I have made up my mind. I couldn't stay over here another year in any case without my family. On my way out to Lincoln from New York or Washington I shall stop off in Chicago and come up to Milwaukee to see you. According to my present plans this should be somewhere between the 15th and 21st of August. Emily is going out to Colorado[7] with the boys around the 21st of August, and I shall try to join her either in Lincoln or in Colorado.

So it won't be too long before I shall be seeing you and we can then have another chance at talking things over. I am glad you have been well, and that you have got something like your old work back again. I have some idea of how hard things are for you. I love you very much, my fine Father, and I shall be very happy to see you again. Your son, Edgar

Doc. 70
Letter to His Wife
Berlin, July 2, 1946[1]

Dearest –

Just a note. I shall have to neglect you a bit until the Constitution for Berlin is finished and until my speech for the ladies[2] is through. But I just wanted to

7 US state.

1 See the letter and corresponding envelope in Appendix of Illustrations, ill. 13 and ill. 14.

2 Refers to the planned lecture for the American Women's Club of Berlin. See Doc. 68 and Doc. 68, fn. 31.

say tonight that I have completed letters to Generals Clay[3] and Keating[4] saying that I wished to be returned to the USA in time for arrival in Lincoln[5] Nebraska, on or before 21 August 1946.[6] I also asked General Clay for the privilege of spending a couple of weeks in the zone[7] previous to my departure. This I think he will grant me. If so I shall be in Berlin for only a couple of weeks more.

Yesterday's meeting at the Kommandatura[8] was rather successful.[9] As a result of a Russian lunch (they are chairmen this month), which included much vodka and wine, it all got rather friendly. Major Feldman[10] remarked to me that the Soviets had found a way of speaking with the Americans that they couldn't find with the British. And I took occasion to ask a Russian what they meant by accusing us of atomic diplomacy. I didn't get a good answer but I did get a promise to come and talk it over some time. This I hope I can arrange before I leave. I was with the Berlin students[11] against last night. Bob Schmidt[12] sang with guitar accompaniment some folk songs for them.

Two years ago you were about to give birth to our sweet Timmy.[13] Not long after we shall have been married 10 years.[14] I love you my blessed darling. Edgar

Doc. 71
Letter to His Wife
Berlin, Wannsee Officers' Club[1], Am Sandwerder 17/19, July 7, 1946

My beloved:

I walked down to the lake[2] after dinner, and while there I suddenly smiled. I thought that today was the 7 July. In six weeks then we should be on our way to Colorado[3] together. I haven't received an answer from my letter to Clay[4].[5] He

3 See Doc. 2, fn. 6.
4 See Doc. 39, fn. 6.
5 Capital of the US state of Nebraska, where Johnson lived with his family and taught at the university.
6 See Doc. 63, Doc. 65, Doc. 67, and Doc. 68.
7 Refers to the American zone of Germany.
8 See Doc. 20, fn. 11.
9 See minutes of the 28th meeting of the Local Government Committee, Allied Kommandatura Berlin, on July 1, 1946, LG/M (46) 28, Russian version, in: TNA, Allied Kommandatura: Directives, Minutes and Papers, FO 1112/378.
10 See Doc. 49, fn. 59.
11 See Doc. 68.
12 Possibly one of the students.
13 Son Thomas (see Doc. 2, fn. 16) was born on July 8, 1944.
14 Edgar N. and Emily L. Johnson had been married since July 14, 1936.

1 See Doc. 25, fn. 9.
2 Refers to Großer Wannsee, a bight of the Havel (see Doc. 74, fn. 24) in southwest Berlin.
3 US state.
4 See Doc. 2, fn. 6.
5 See Doc. 63, Doc. 65, Doc. 67, Doc. 68, and Doc. 70.

has been in Paris.[6] He returned yesterday afternoon to Berlin, and is leaving again tonight for Paris. As yet the matter of Germany has not come up before the Foreign Ministers of Paris and Clay is supposed to be in a bad frame of mind. Supposedly it will come up before the Ministers during the early part of the next week, and he is supposed to be back in a few days. I doubt if my letter has been put in his hands during the brief interval of his return from Paris. It will have to wait accordingly until the end of the week. I understand that Pollock[7] is going back to Michigan[8] even though Clay does not wish him to go. Clay will be losing, accordingly his three chief professional assistants, Pollock, Dorn[9], and myself and that is, I believe, a thing which he cannot take very lightly. I understood also that the return is now made to the U. S. from Bremen[10] instead of Le Havre[11] on the many ships which bring supplies here. A boat is supposed to leave almost every day. Therefore I imagine that I shall be leaving from there somewhere in the neighborhood of the first of August. Henry[12] wrote recently that they had not been able to get a man of professorial rank for Harold's[13] place, and that instead they would try to get another instructor.[14] And from what you continue to report of the academic atmosphere in Nebraska, I wonder, indeed, to what I am returning in the University. Am I returning to Glenn[15], Jim[16], Alden[17] and a couple of young instructors. This I must confess is not returning to very very much. But I am not really returning to the University. I am returning to you and to the boys, and to our establishment. It will not be easy to give up a sense of being a small part of what is really going on in the world and I shall be tempted to continue a little along this line. I don't imagine, however, that it will last long. I imagine that except for the classroom I shall soon abandon all these plans for participating in public life and return only too willingly to you, the boys and what houses us there, to books, to writing and to the perfection of our little way of life. I might even return a little to the piano.[18]

6 Clay took part in the Paris conference of the Council of Foreign Ministers. See Doc. 44, fn. 13.
7 See Doc. 15, fn. 12.
8 US state. Pollock taught at the University of Michigan as Professor of Political Science.
9 See Doc. 2, fn. 10.
10 Bremen/Bremerhaven was an American exclave in the coastal region of the British zone. See Andreas Röpcke, "Office of Military Government for Bremen," in: *OMGUS-Handbuch. Die amerikanische Militärregierung in Deutschland 1945–1949*, ed. Christoph Weisz (= Quellen und Darstellungen zur Zeitgeschichte, vol. 35), Munich 1994, pp. 597–670, here pp. 599–637.
11 French seaport city on the Atlantic coast.
12 Charles Henry Oldfather. See Doc. 2, fn. 19.
13 Harold C. Vedeler. See Doc. 2, fn. 12.
14 Along with David L. Dowd (see Doc. 49, fn. 71), Albin T. Anderson was hired as Instructor. Albin T. Anderson (1911–1996), 1933 MA and 1947 PhD, University of California, Berkeley, until 1979 Professor, University of Nebraska, 1984/1985 President, Institute for Continued Learning, University of California, San Diego.
15 Glenn W. Gray. See Doc. 49, fn. 74.
16 James L. Sellers. See Doc. 49, fn. 77.
17 See Doc. 65, fn. 11.
18 Johnson was an accomplished piano player. See Doc. 21, fn. 6.

You seem to have been very sensible about this piano business. I'm glad, after what you have said about it, that you turned down this Knabe instrument which, from all you say would have been just another piano.[19] There is no point in having just another piano. It must be something different, fine, brilliant, mellow and definitely exciting to play. And if you are in any doubt about these things don't buy. We should be eternally dissatisfied with it and John[20] would never feel the thrill of having a wonderful instrument to go to. I know what I am talking about. I used to go from our good upright at home to practice on Mr. Sooter's[21] piano and it was always an exciting experience. The reason why I want a larger piano is just because of this experience – the little ones don't have the difference. If I could buy that big one of our friend in Washington (we certainly, as you say, missed out on that deal)[22] for somewhere near 1,000 dollars, I'd go to Washington to buy. Your experience shows however, that there are plenty of pianos about, people trying to take advantage of the scarcity. I wouldn't therefore rush it if you aren't sure. I rather go in debt some and get a proper new one than to buy a doubtful old one. In fact the only one you can really be sure about is a new one.

It has been an interesting day. I got up early to go to a meeting of SPD functionaries and trade union leaders.[23] They were meeting to protest the kind of elections which have been held earlier in the industrial branches by the present unitary (SED controlled) Federation of Free German Trade Unions[24]. It was encouraging to me because I hear and see so few Germans who are really democratic. In this meeting, however, a simple young woman got up, who works in a factory in the Russian sector which makes telephones. She has never been active in trade union activities or politics before but she has had enough of dictation and espionage and has revolted in a most courageous manner and speaks out her mind. It so happens that the women in this factory outnumber the men about 70 to 30, and she has got the women under her leadership, and is in a position to control the factory. She was bitter against the Russians, in a most undiplomatic fashion. I don't know whether there were any Russian officers present or not. I didn't see any. She condemned the way she is being spied upon by the SED (Communist) people in the factory who watch her every movement

19 See Doc. 63.

20 Johnson's son John. See Doc. 2, fn. 15.

21 Apparently an acquaintance in the USA with whom he shared his passion for playing the piano.

22 See Emily L. Johnson's letter from June 26/28, 1946, in: Documents from the estate of Edgar N. Johnson, private collection of Candice E. and Thomas R. Johnson, Denver, Colorado, USA.

23 The functionary conference on the topic of "Gewerkschaften und Betriebsratswahlen" (unions and works council elections) took place on July 7, 1946, in Kliems Festsälen at Hasenheide 10 in the Berlin administrative district of Kreuzberg. See "Die Unsicherheit in Berlin. Die verschwundenen SPD-Funktionäre – Kampf um Betriebsdemokratie," in: *Der Sozialdemokrat* from July 8, 1946, p. 2; "'Keine zweite Arbeitsfront.' Konferenz sozialdemokratischer Betriebsfunktionäre," in: *Telegraf* from July 9, 1946, p. 3; "Kritische Aeusserungen," in: *Der Kurier* from July 8, 1946, p. 2; pr., "SPD und Betriebsratswahlen," in: *Der Tagesspiegel* from July 9, 1946, [p. 2].

24 On the Freier Deutscher Gewerkschaftsbund (FDGB), see Doc. 49, fn. 13.

and listen to her every telephone call. The Russians recently sent a delegation of their Trade Union people here and they visited this factory. But the Communists didn't permit her to speak. It is very clear to these SPD people that the Communists are no different from the Nazis. She also speaks out boldly to the Russian officers with whom she comes into contact. I had a chance to say "gut" to her after her speech. She may disappear any day. A couple of SPD leaders have recently disappeared.[25] She doesn't care. She is in this business to speak out her mind and to act accordingly. This is the kind of person we ought to seek out and support. There are so few of them. We have haven't got sense enough, however, to make this selection. I ran into a man who came to me for protection from the Russians lately and whom, I thought, might have disappeared.[26] But he has moved into the American sector.

After the meeting I went to a concert of the Philharmonic.[27] They played the Prokofieff Classical Symphony[28], which I think as delightful as ever. Erna Berger[29], whom I mentioned before,[30] and whom I met going into the hall sang a Concerto for Soprano and Orchestra written by Glière[31]. The first movement was one of the most beautiful things of its kind I have ever heard. The program ended with Shostakovich's 5th Symphony.[32] It is in some instances heavy handed as the Russians are often apt to be, and in other passage there is long dull

25 Those who had disappeared were Hermann Löwenthal (1900–1947), head of the SPD operational group in the Berlin Magistrat, and Julius Scherff (1886–1947), member of the Executive Committee of the Berlin SPD. They were arrested at the end of June 1946 by Soviet occupation forces and died in 1947 in prison. See Harold Hurwitz in collaboration with Ursula Böhme/Andreas Malycha, *Die Stalinisierung der SED. Zum Verlust von Freiräumen und sozialdemokratischer Identität in den Vorständen 1946–1949* (= Schriften des Zentralinstituts für sozialwissenschaftliche Forschung der Freien Universität Berlin, vol. 79), Opladen 1997, pp. 54 and 157f.; Günter Fippel, *Demokratische Gegner und Willküropfer von Besatzungsmacht und SED in Sachsenhausen (1946 bis 1950). Das sowjetische Speziallager Sachsenhausen – Teil des Stalinschen Lagerimperiums*, in collaboration with Paul Radicke, with an introductory essay by Klaus-Dieter Müller, eds. Klaus-Dieter Müller/Mike Schmeitzner, Leipzig 2008, p. 122.

26 Possibly refers to one of the two Social Democrats who had come to him on May 6, 1946, because they felt threatened as opponents of the merger in the Soviet sector and wanted to move to the American sector. See Doc. 44.

27 Symphony concert of the Berliner Philharmonisches Orchester under the direction of Sergiu Celibidache (see Doc. 66, fn. 6) at 11 a. m. at the Deutsche Staatsoper in the Admiralspalast in the district of Mitte, Friedrichstraße 101/102. On the program were works by renowned Russian composers of the time. See bog., "Die fünfte Symphonie von Schostakowitsch. Symphonie-Konzert der Berliner Philharmoniker," in: *Berliner Zeitung* from July 9, 1946, [p. 3]; Erwin Kroll, "Russische Symphonik," in: *Der Tagesspiegel* from July 9, 1946, [p. 6].

28 Symphony No. 1 (*Symphonie classique*) by Sergei Sergeyevich Prokofiev (1891–1953), Russian composer.

29 See Doc. 59, fn. 24.

30 See Doc. 59 and Doc. 66.

31 Concerto for Coloratura Soprano and Orchestra by Reinhold Glière (1875–1956), Russian composer of Belgian descent.

32 Symphony No. 5 of the Russian composer Dmitri Dmitriyevich Shostakovich (1906–1975). This was the German premiere.

33 Symphony No. 7, known as the *Leningrad* Symphony.

34 Donald R. Heath. See Doc. 8, fn. 15.

Communist argument. But there is also much that is stunning, and some that is beautiful. I'd like to know it better. It seemed to me a far different work from the 7th[33], a long winded speech that bored me very much in Vienna.

I then went to Don Heath's[34] for lunch after which I read to Mrs. Heath[35] the speech I have written for the women on Tuesday[36].[37] She liked this very much, thank God, so I don't have to think about recasting it. But after my experience with the little trade union leader today I shall have to add some things. Their son[38] is arriving here tomorrow, and they are especially excited. He is an 18 year old who has just graduated from the Salisbury school[39] at Salisbury Connecticut[40], and going to Hamilton College[41] (Erhardt's[42] College) this fall. Someday we shall have a couple of 18 year olds going off to college.

Then I went to Col. Glaser's[43] to talk about briefing General Keating[44] for the session on the Constitution of Berlin for the Commandants on Tuesday[45].[46] He begged me before I left to urge General Keating not to get another political adviser when I left but to content himself with Col. Lou[is] Glaser as political adviser. He is afraid of being pushed out of the picture. All very human enough. Nobody likes being pushed out of the picture.

There is much that I have omitted during the last few days but I'll keep it until we see each other which won't be very long. Good-night, my sweet and dearly beloved. Tell John to have the Bach[47] Invention[48] ready for me[49] and tell Timmy about Father. I love you, my sweetheart. Edgar

35 See Doc. 55, fn. 48.

36 July 9, 1946.

37 See Doc. 68 and Doc. 70. Under the heading "Women's Club Meets Tuesday," the *OMGUS Observer* from July 5, 1946, p. 2, writes among other things: "The second meeting of the Women's Club of Berlin will take place at Harnack House [see Doc. 15, fn. 16] this Tuesday, July 9, at 3 p. m. A short business meeting will be held, followed by a talk given by Dr. E. N. Johnson, Special Assistant to the Commanding General, Headquarters Berlin District. His topic is to be 'The Relationship of Dependents to Occupation.' A special invitation is extended to all women who have just arrived in Berlin as well as to those who have not attended the previous meeting."

38 Donald R. Heath Jr. (born 1928).

39 College-preparatory school founded in 1901.

40 City in the US state of Connecticut.

41 College in Clinton, New York, founded in 1793 as Hamilton-Oneida Academy, 1812 as Hamilton College.

42 See Doc. 20, fn. 30.

43 See Doc. 28, fn. 4.

44 See Doc. 39, fn. 6.

45 July 9, 1946.

46 See Doc. 68. The Local Government Committee, Allied Kommandatura Berlin, had completed its deliberations on July 5, 1946. See LOC GOV/R (46) 30 from July 5, 1946, English and Russian version, in: TNA, Allied Kommandatura: Directives, Minutes and Papers, FO 1112/377; Appendix of Illustrations, ill. 70. Photo of Johnson during a break of the Local Government Committee on July 5, 1946, in Appendix of Illustrations, ill. 69.

47 See Doc. 13, fn. 20.

48 Bach's Inventions are conceived as exercises in playing and composition.

49 Emily L. Johnson in her letter from June 29, 1946: "John has a Bach invention for his lesson – hard, but beautiful." Letter in: Documents from the estate of Edgar N. Johnson, private collection of Candice E. and Thomas R. Johnson, Denver, Colorado, USA.

Doc. 72
Letter to His Wife
Berlin, Wannsee Officers' Club[1], Am Sandwerder 17/19, July 9, 1946

My beloved –

It was very exciting to come back after my talk to the American wives[2] and find two letters from my lady – those of July 3 + 4th[3]. The one contains the account of the acquisition of the Steinway[4], and the other the account of the 4th of July with the Basoco's[5]. I am very very excited!!!! too over the acquisition of the piano, but I am sorry you had to get sick over it. It seems to me you have been very wise, very careful and have got what sounds like an excellent instrument. It is everything that we wanted. It is beyond the ordinary baby grand size. It is a Steinway of some vintage. You have paid less for it than we were willing to pay for a new one. It seems to be in very excellent condition

1 See Doc. 25, fn. 9.

2 Refers to the lecture that Johnson gave at the second meeting of the American Women's Club of Berlin on July 9, 1946, at Harnack House (see Doc. 15, fn. 16). See Doc. 68, Doc. 70, Doc. 71, and Doc. 71, fn. 37. Under the heading "'Shun Nazis', Wives Told At Women's Club Meeting," the *OMGUS Observer* writes on July 12, 1946, p. 2: "American families should have no toleration for Nazi-Germans, no matter how cultured or charming they seem to be, stated Dr. E. N. Johnson, Special Assistant to the Commanding General, Headquarters, B[erlin] D[istrict] at the second meeting of the American Women's Club of Berlin, Tuesday, when he discussed the responsibilities of American women in occupation. 'But Germans who conspicuously fought and resisted the influence of distorted Nazi minds should be fought and resisted the influence of [sic!] build their country along democratic lines,' he pointed out. 'The American women should reach out to German women like Helen Weber who are now trying to organize healthy political parties in a wholesome German government, or to persons like Gunther Weisenborn, who after imprisonment in concentration camps for underground activities against the Nazis, is still trying to direct the people away from the hypnotic influence of Nazism.' As Berlin is the nerve center of the world, Dr. Johnson said that what happened here would have lasting influence on the world of tomorrow. Therefore it is up to American women, who other women of the world are closely watching, to study international situations and keep abreast of world problems, particularly those to which they are so close. As the American families are apt to lose their sense of value and timing because of their comfortable communities, he advised them not to isolate themselves from the German people and their problems. 'The coming of American wives and families to Europe,' Dr. Johnson said, 'is but a further extension of America into Europe, a further representation of the best that America stands for in a Germany which has sore need for it. Your coming, in fact, amounts to the introduction into Germany of another American institution, the American home.'" See Appendix of Illustrations, ill. 64.

3 Letters in: Documents from the estate of Edgar N. Johnson, private collection of Candice E. and Thomas R. Johnson, Denver, Colorado, USA.

4 See Doc. 4, fn. 25.

5 Doris Basoco (1910–2000) and Miguel A. Basoco (1900–1981), American mathematician, 1929 PhD, California Institute of Technology, taught as of 1930 at the University of Nebraska, 1944/1945 Acting Director and 1947–1954 Director of the Mathematical Institute.

and to have been little played on. If Byler[6] was willing to buy it, and Herbert[7] was willing to buy it, being as you say enthusiastic over it, and John[8] loved it, I don't see what better checking you could have. And you did check on the sounding board, and hammers, and keys. It is all too good to be true. I'm so glad you didn't pick up the indifferent Knabe.[9] If I have done nothing else in the war, I have made it possible for you to get a piano for our lovely John. It is one of the best things we have done, and we shall never regret it. Your suggestion that I take a lesson a week strikes a warm note in my heart, and I think I'll take it up. I suppose it would be a certain stimulus for John, and it would be good for me. Maybe I can get learn how to play nicely some things. It would be a bond with our dear boy too. Can you stand so much practicing around the house. John will thank us some day for this. I'll remember to keep the secret. You are superb.

The day with the Basoco's was one I would not covet. I am reminded again of how well you have done again with the boys. As I remember it there is nothing John does not like except peanuts, and there is something organic about that. And Timmy likewise. I am so anxious to see you and them.

And it won't be long now. General Clay[10] did see my letter while he was here.[11] I had a call from Colonel (formerly General) Millburn[12], saying that he had approved of my trip to the zone, and that I should come to his office at any time and make arrangements. General Keating[13] also wrote me a very nice letter, saying he hoped I would get the trip to the zone, and that he did not know how he would have gotten along without me here.[14] That is saying too much but I am glad he feels that I have not been utterly useless. I was trying to figure out a time schedule last night which would make it possible for me to get to Lincoln[15] by 21 August, and I think I should leave here on or about the first of August. If I take two full weeks in the zone, which I should do that means actually leaving here in a few days. But this, I think, I cannot do. The constitution

6 May refer to Arthur W. Byler, American pianist and professor, 1919–1925 studies at Bethany College, Lindsborg, Kansas, taught as of 1927 at Doane College, Professor of Piano and Theory, Chairman, Department of Music.

7 Herbert Schmidt. See Doc. 29, fn. 12.

8 Johnson's son John. See Doc. 2, fn. 15.

9 See Doc. 63 and Doc. 71.

10 See Doc. 2, fn. 6.

11 See Doc. 63, Doc. 65, Doc. 67, Doc. 68, Doc. 70, and Doc. 71.

12 Bryan L. Milburn. See Doc. 15, fn. 20.

13 See Doc. 39, fn. 6.

14 In the letter from July 5, 1946, in: Documents from the estate of Edgar N. Johnson, private collection of Candice E. and Thomas R. Johnson, Denver, Colorado, USA, it says among other things: "It is hoped that your request for release, as well as a tour of the zone for two weeks, will be approved. You deserve anything that may be granted. It has been a genuine pleasure to work with you, and in leaving, you will take back the heartfelt gratitude of my office for the magnificent assistance you rendered in your present capacity. I do not know what I would have done without your help." See Appendix of Illustrations, ill. 75.

15 Capital of the US state of Nebraska, where Johnson lived with his family and taught at the university.

and electoral procedure will not actually be finished until the 19th of August, when they come before the Commandants for final approval.[16] I could leave for Frankfurt[17] on the evening of that day, have twelve days in the zone, and plan to get back here by 1 August and off to Bremen[18] that night. That would be about 12 days. I suppose I ought to try to go to Vienna again, and catch up with the situation there. Maybe I could get some material for writing. But that would take time off from the zone. In any case my days here are numbered – 10 more at the most. It seems almost incredible. These departures come suddenly. Then I shall be off to you and the boys, and we shall be off to the mountains. There was an article in the Stars and Stripes[19] about the polio epidemic in Colorado[20].[21] May be we have no business to take this chance. Most of the cases seem to be concentrated in Denver[22] which we should try to avoid. Isn't there someplace else we can get off by taking a slower train perhaps, and make our way to Meeker lodge[23]. Or else can arrangements be made in advance to meet us at the train and away we go. Couldn't Mrs. Zumwinckel[24] make arrangements with a local driver at Meeker to come to Denver and meet the train, so that there would be no delay whatsoever in getting out of the city. You'd better get good accommodations. At the worst you could sleep with Timmy in a lower berth and John and I could sleep in an upper. He would think that this is fun.

The Constitution was presented to the Commandants this morning.[25] Keating used statements I had drawn up to present the American case. The generals were quite amazed that we presented an agreed upon report[26], and

16 Refers to July 19, 1946. In their meeting on July 9, 1946, the Commandants approved the draft constitution of the Local Government Committee in principle, but returned it to the Committee to clarify individual questions. The final version was supposed to be ready for the Commandants on July 19, 1946. See minutes of the 18th meeting of the Commandants on July 9, 1946, BKC/M (46) 18-170, English version, in: LAB, B Rep. 036-01 (Office of Military Government, Berlin Sector [OMGBS]), 4/132-3/11.

17 Frankfurt am Main, city in the state of Greater Hesse in the American zone of Germany.

18 See Doc. 71, fn. 10.

19 American military newspaper.

20 US state.

21 Under the heading "Polio Cases Spread In Colorado Area" *The Stars and Stripes*, European Edition, reports on July 9, 1946, p. 5: "Infantile paralysis was nearing epidemic proportions in Colorado today as the state was given emergency status by the National Foundation for Infantile Paralysis. Dr. Roy Cleere, executive secretary for the state board of health, announced that 99 cases of poliomielitis had been reported recently in Colorado, with 56 of them in the metropolitan Denver area. Eight victims have died. All public pools and beaches have been closed in Denver in an effort to halt the disease."

22 Capital of the US state of Colorado, at the eastern foot of the Rocky Mountains.

23 See Doc. 63, fn. 21.

24 Essie Zumwinkel. See Doc. 46, fn. 6.

25 See minutes of the 18th meeting of the Commandants on July 9, 1946, BKC/M (46) 18-170, English version, in: LAB, B Rep. 036-01 (Office of Military Government, Berlin Sector [OMGBS]), 4/132-3/11.

26 See LOC GOV/R (46) 30 from July 5, 1946, Russian and English version, in: TNA, Allied Kommandatura: Directives, Minutes and Papers, FO 1112/377; Appendix of Illustrations, ill. 70.

Kotikov[27] had prepared a special statement of commendation which was to go into the minutes. I understand also that Keating is going to make some kind of a citation for Glaser[28] and me for our work on the Committee[29].[30] It will all seem rather petty some weeks hence but it has been fun doing. These last meetings have been strenuous under Russian chairmanship what with their terrible luncheons. But the Russians are going all out to be friendly these days. At the end of the meeting yesterday,[31] they gave a tea with all their drinks accompanying. You know you have to drink bottoms up with the Russians. At the end of the Commandants meeting today Kotikov invited the crowd to lunch as a kind of celebration. I had another engagement but in any case I couldn't have taken it. Col. Zozulya[32], with whom I have got rather friendly was very disappointed. The Russians are sensitive on this score.

The ladies seemed to like the speech and asked for copies.[33] I referred to you at the beginning and at the end. Soon I shall be leaving here for you. I love you my blessed one, oh so much. There are wonderful days ahead of us. Kiss the sweet boys. I love you. Edgar

Doc. 73
Letter to His Wife
Berlin, Wannsee Officers' Club[1], Am Sandwerder 17/19, July 12, 1946

Dearest:

I am aware that on Sunday[2] we shall have been married for ten years.[3] I have thought I would call you by long distance telephone on that date but in view of the excessive cost (4 dollars a minute), and of the fact that we really wouldn't

27 See Doc. 35, fn. 5.

28 See Doc. 28, fn. 4.

29 Local Government Committee, Allied Kommandatura Berlin.

30 See Doc. 80. Glaser was awarded a "Certificate of Commendation": "For meritorious service during the period 1 January 1946 to 1 July 1946 while serving as Chief of Civil Administration Branch for Military Government distinguished himself by outstanding performance of duty. The capability and resourcefulness displayed in addition to his untiring energy and loyal devotion to duty reflect great credit upon himself and the military service. Lieutenant Colonel GLASER is hereby authorized to wear the Army Commendation Ribbon by direction of the Secretary of War." Certificate of Commendation from July 30, 1946, in: Documents from the estate of Louis Glaser, private collection of Anthony J. Glaser, Bethesda, Maryland, USA. See Appendix of Illustrations, ill. 34.

31 See minutes of the 32nd meeting of the Local Government Committee, Allied Kommandatura Berlin, on July 8, 1946, LG/M (46) 32, Russian version, in: TNA, Allied Kommandatura: Directives, Minutes and Papers, FO 1112/378.

32 See Doc. 67, fn. 28.

33 See above.

1 See Doc. 25, fn. 9.

2 July 14, 1946.

3 Edgar N. and Emily L. Johnson had been married since July 14, 1936.

get anything said to each other, I have decided to save the money. I think may be you will approve. I have talked with some who have done it and they find it quite unsatisfactory. Since we can't be together on that date we shall have to postpone our festivity until we see each other. The details of that day are precious and fresh in my mind and I have to go over them. I think I have gone over them in many letters to you since we have been apart I am going over them now. I love you very much sweetheart. The days of that summer which followed, and indeed most of the days, I meant almost every one of them, and almost every hour of every one of them that has since gone have only served to make clear how great a misfortune it is that we were not married at least ten years earlier. They have been the only years of my life which really count. What we have lost it is impossible to retrieve, but it can heighten an awareness of the necessity to live out our remaining years to the full. We shall have to remind each other in the morning, or in the evening that the day which is to come or which has just gone will be one less or is one less among the few which are still allotted to us. Until the great separation we shall have none such as we have had for the past two years and more. I shall try to be worthy of your presence in the days that are to come. I love you, my darling and my sweetheart.

I actually took some steps to get back to you today by the 21st[4]. I went to General Clay's[5] administrative officer, a Mr. Baird and told him I was leaving between 1 August and 5 August, and that he should be getting orders ready. He says it will be quite necessary to leave by that time if I hope to make it. I guess it is possible to terminate one's services with the War Department in New York. Accordingly it will not be necessary to go to Washington, and since I am really not looking for a job, I don't think I'll go unless there is an abundance of time. I care to see there only Gene[6] and Polly[7] and Harold[8] and Marguerite[9]. It is more important that I spend a little time with Dad[10], and Mildred[11] and Aunt Hannah[12]. I think I should like to go to the cemetery also,[13] then come out straight to you. I also made some preliminary arrangements for trips to the zone. I'll leave here for that trip after the Commandants meeting on next Friday[14], or on Saturday[15] next. I asked for the privilege of going to Vienna but I don't know whether it will be granted, or if I really have time to go. I'd like to catch up on the situation there because it is, for the moment, so very tense. But I have put Stuttgart[16] on the list. I at least ought to get a glimpse of the job I was to have, and I have

4 August 21, 1946.
5 See Doc. 2, fn. 6.
6 Eugene N. Anderson. See Doc. 1, fn. 1.
7 Pauline R. Anderson. See Doc. 2, fn. 2.
8 Harold C. Vedeler. See Doc. 2, fn. 12.
9 Marguerite D. Vedeler. See Doc. 2, fn. 13.
10 Frank E. Johnson. See Doc. 3, fn. 12.
11 Mildred H. Williams. See Doc. 4, fn. 12.
12 Hannah Walstrom. See Doc. 4, fn. 14.
13 To his mother's grave in Chicago, Illinois. See Doc. 46, fn. 13.
14 July 19, 1946.
15 July 20, 1946.
16 Capital of the state of Württemberg-Baden in the American zone of Germany.

put Heidelberg[17] on the list too. I'll try to get as much done as I can, but evidently I am going to be rushed. I'll come back here for only a day or so, and then off to Bremen[18] where, I understand, I shall be delayed for a couple of days.

I shall leave here with regret because there is much to do but I have never thought that my decision to leave is unwise. We do not have the resources to go adventuring here. Many of the important people here who are staying on, have, I imagine, independent means. Anyway I am coming back to you, my sweetheart, for a very very long time and first of all for a wonderful re-experiencing of our last Colorado[19] experience. I love you, my Emily, and boys. It is hardly more than five weeks now. I kiss you all. Edgar

Doc. 74
Letter to His Wife
Berlin, Wannsee Officers' Club[1], Am Sandwerder 17/19, July 14, 1946

My sweet Emily –

This is the day 10 years ago.[2] 10 full and precious years. And 5 weeks from today I should be there. And five weeks from tonight we should be starting off together on a holiday in the mountains in our old cabin. This all turns out very beautifully. I imagine you have arranged to take Alison[3] or Tascha[4] along so that we may have some hiking together.[5] You were after all a very determined climber and I can't imagine that you will be very contented to remain confined to the environment of the cabin for any great length of time. I can't wait to share John's[6] excitement about it all.

This then is, I suppose, my last Sunday in Berlin. It is a lovely Sunday. The sporting Americans have just made their appearance on the lake[7] in what amounts almost to a fleet of sail-boats. I can hear the shouts of the children over at the Wannsee beach[8] which is not so far from here. It is a pleasant sound –

17 University city in the state of Württemberg-Baden in the American zone of Germany.
18 See Doc. 71, fn. 10.
19 US state.

1 See Doc. 25, fn. 9.
2 Refers to the tenth wedding anniversary; Edgar N. and Emily L. Johnson had been married since July 14, 1936. See Doc. 73.
3 Alison E. Gass. See Doc. 68, fn. 5.
4 Natasha (Tasha) Stepanek (born 1933), daughter of Olga F. and Orin Stepanek (see Doc. 57, fn. 3).
5 Emily L. Johnson in her letter from July 3, 1946: "I am still toying with the idea of taking Alison Gass or Tasha Stepanek along as a babysitter so we can be free to go on a few points together." Letter in: Documents from the estate of Edgar N. Johnson, private collection of Candice E. and Thomas R. Johnson, Denver, Colorado, USA.
6 Johnson's son John. See Doc. 2, fn. 15.
7 Refers to Großer Wannsee, a bight of the Havel (see Doc. 74, fn. 24) in southwest Berlin.
8 Refers to Strandbad Wannsee, a public beach on the eastern shore of Großer Wannsee.

the kind of sound that you don't often hear in Berlin – shouts of delight over the release from the dingy houses and rubble of the city and over the chance to frolic in the sunshine. Artur[9] is coming at about one o'clock and I am going out for an hour or so and take some pictures of this forlorn city so that you can see something of what has happened to it.[10] I shall work here in the afternoon. Tonight I have been invited to go to Suhr's[11] to meet some of the Social Democrats. I have to go because he postponed a gathering from last-night to tonight in order that I might come. I suppose it is the last time I shall see the Social Democrats – those people who put up such a good fight when I first came here, but who have since lost a good deal of this drive, and are now quibbling about very small things.

Yesterday I suppose was the last staff meeting of General Keating[12] and Colonel Howley[13] that I shall attend. They had a sign at my chair this time. "Political Advisor." Then I went to Clay's[14] Staff meeting[15]. He had not returned as yet from Paris[16], and I imagine he will return a rather disappointed man since the German matter has really been postponed until November,[17] and not much further progress can be expected here until fundamental decisions have been taken. These meetings have in fact been rather dull for several weeks. Except for keeping the machinery going not much is happening. I discovered that a

9 Artur Sanow. See Doc. 40, fn. 13.

10 Photos that Johnson may have taken on this day in Appendix of Illustrations, ill. 50 and ill. 51.

11 Otto Suhr. See Doc. 40, fn. 7.

12 See Doc. 39, fn. 6.

13 See Doc. 20, fn. 18.

14 See Doc. 2, fn. 6.

15 See minutes of the OMGUS staff conference on July 13, 1946, in: Archiv des IfZ, OMGUS – Staff Conferences (copies of minutes), Fg 12/5.

16 Clay had taken part in the Paris conference of the Council of Foreign Ministers that was being held until July 12, 1946. See Doc. 44, fn. 13.

17 As the press reported after the end of the Paris conference, the Foreign Ministers were supposed to hold a special conference on Germany in the autumn of 1946. "The Foreign Ministers agreed to hold *a special conference on the German question in the autumn* – after the adjournment of the United Nations General Assembly beginning in September. The exact date of this conference has not yet been set. According to reports of the French news agency 'AFP,' the Foreign Ministers have agreed on *November*." ("Die Außenminister kamen überein, *im Herbst* – nach der Vertagung der im September beginnenden Vollversammlung der Vereinten Nationen – *eine Sonderkonferenz über die deutsche Frage* abzuhalten. Der genaue Zeitpunkt dieser Konferenz wurde noch nicht festgelegt. Nach Mitteilung der französischen Nachrichtenagentur 'AFP' sollen sich die Außenminister auf den *November* geeinigt haben.") "Deutschland-Konferenz im November. Die Grundsätze der amerikanischen Politik in Deutschland," in: *Der Tagesspiegel* from July 13, 1946, supplement. "[...] the German question will remain in limbo into November, until the day when, according to the Paris agreement, the Ministers will come together to make conclusive decisions regarding the future face of Germany." ("[...] die deutsche Frage wird bis in den November hinein in der Schwebe bleiben, bis zu dem Tage, da nach der Pariser Absprache die Minister zusammentreffen wollen, um sich endgültig über das zukünftige Gesicht Deutschlands klar zu werden.") "Die Ergebnisse von Paris," in: *Der Tagesspiegel* from July 14, 1946, [p. 1].

sign had been put at my chair for these meetings also. "Adviser to the Deputy Military Governor." Walter Dorn[18] told me yesterday that Clay feels that he has been at this job long enough, and that a civilian should take over. I wonder who that civilian is going to be if and when. There seems to be a general feeling about here that we are not going to stay here very long – a very horrible mistake, I think. The Germans think this also. I had lunch with Walter Dorn and he was wrapped up in his de-Nazification problems, which are, indeed, serious enough. The church, for example, that church which I once thought was going to be such a great help in bringing back Germany to its feet, while it has, to be sure, dismissed some of its Nazi adherents, is now taking the stand that preachers who are punished by the De-Nazification law[19] in our zone we can't force it to keep from the pulpit because only the church can say who may preach the word of God, and for us to say that preachers may not preach, is an unwarranted interference by us (the state) in the affairs of the church. They may have to take this interference.

After lunch I went back to the office for awhile and then took off to a French fête given in honor of a certain famous speech which De Gaulle[20] made at London on 18 June 1940 when he said that France may have lost a battle, but it had not lost the war,[21] and in honor too of today – Bastille Day[22]; yet De Gaulle overshadows the Bastille. It was in the nature of an aquatic and athletic display at one of Berlin's outing places, Tegelort[23] on the Havel[24].[25] I could only stay a few minutes because I had an appointment with Dr. Haas[26] and his wife[27] to go to the opera.

18 See Doc. 2, fn. 10.

19 Gesetz zur Befreiung von Nationalsozialismus und Militarismus vom 5. März 1946 (Law for Liberation from National Socialism and Militarism from March 5, 1946). See Doc. 47, fn. 20.

20 Charles de Gaulle (1890–1970), French General and politician, 1943/1944 President of the Comité Français de la Liberation Nationale, 1944–1946 head of two successive provisional governments, January 1946 resignation, 1947–1953 founder and Chairman of the Rassemblement Populaire Français, 1958/1959 President of the Council of Ministers, 1959–1969 President of the French Republic.

21 In his speech on June 18, 1940, from exile in London, de Gaulle had called on the French to continue the war against the Axis Powers alongside Great Britain, from the colonies. Afterwards he became the leader of the French resistance against German occupation forces and the Vichy regime.

22 French national holiday since 1880. The storming of the Bastille occurred on July 14, 1789, and the Fête de la Fédération took place on July 14, 1790.

23 A location in the area of Konradshöhe in the Berlin administrative district of Reinickendorf (French sector of Berlin).

24 River that runs through Berlin, about 30 km in length.

25 Celebration of the French national holiday commenced with the event in Tegelort on July 13, 1946. "The three-day holiday celebration began Saturday afternoon with a combination regatta and fair at the French Nautique Sport Club of Tegelort. Sailing, rowing and swimming races were followed by dancing and a water carnival with decorated floats which ended in a burst of fireworks." "Bastille Day Observed By French Here," in: *OMGUS Observer* from July 19, 1946, p. 3.

26 See Doc. 49, fn. 40.

Dr. Haas is a member of the Magistrat[28] who wrote the first draft of the constitution of Berlin upon which we have been working.[29] He is trying desperately to correct some of the mistakes which we have had to make but I don't know whether I shall be able to get them out or not. He is a practising Catholic, a southern German[30], who has been in the city government since 1939[31], a simple modest unambitious and principled man who tries first of all to do his duty. He may leave Berlin to become the mayor of Heidelberg[32],[33] though he feels that he would be missing the international show here if he went down there. Yesterday was his 50th birthday.[34] He married late,[35] a very simple woman, and they have no children. He showed me the flowers and inscription which the 8000 people who work for him in the Finance section presented him.[36] He showed me a bottle of champagne which the Communist Vice-Mayor (Maron[37] – trained in Russia) gave to him. I noticed it was the same as the Russians serve at the Kommandatura[38]. Germans to Russians to a Communist Vice-Mayor to

27 Charlotte Haas, née Wegener (1905–1963).

28 Haas had provisionally taken over the affairs of the finance department in March 1946.

29 On April 9, 1946, Haas had submitted a draft constitution to the Magistrat for discussion. It was edited and then presented to the Allied Kommandatura, for discussion in the Local Government Committee. See *Vorläufige Verfassung von Groß-Berlin*, annotated by Dr. Haas, Treasurer of Greater Berlin, revised fourth edition, Berlin 1947, pp. 26f. Haas had presented a very first draft constitution to the Magistrat on November 8, 1945. See ibid., pp. 25f.

30 Born in Untereggingen/Kreis Waldshut in Baden.

31 Beginning in 1929 Haas had been Magistratsrat in the Charlottenburg district administration.

32 University city in the state of Württemberg-Baden in the American zone of Germany.

33 On July 27, 1946, the Heidelberg Stadtrat elected CDU candidate Dr. Hugo Swart (1885–1952) as Oberbürgermeister. See "Oberbürgermeisterwahl in Heidelberg," in: *Rhein-Neckar-Zeitung* from July 30, 1946, p. 1; Gerhard Hinz, "Ernst Walz †," in: *Ruperto-Carola. Zeitschrift der Vereinigung der Freunde der Studentenschaft der Universität Heidelberg e. V.*, June 1967, pp. 46f., here p. 46. Despite kind support from the Stadtarchiv Heidelberg it was not possible to prove whether Haas made himself available to the Heidelberg CDU as a candidate for the office of Oberbürgermeister.

34 Haas was born on July 13, 1896.

35 Haas had been married since 1936.

36 The central administration of the Magistrat had 9,000 employees in May 1946. See *Das erste Jahr. Berlin im Neuaufbau. Ein Rechenschaftsbericht des Magistrats der Stadt Berlin*, edited on behalf of the Magistrat of the City of Berlin, Berlin 1946, p. 26. Presumably there were around 800 people employed in the finance department (not 8,000).

37 Karl Maron (1903–1975), German politician (KPD/SED), 1925 KPD, 1934 emigration to Denmark and 1935 to the Soviet Union, as of 1943 Deputy Editor-in-Chief of *Freies Deutschland* (newspaper of the National Committee "Freies Deutschland"), 1945 return to Berlin as a member of the "Ulbricht Group," 1945–December 1946 First Deputy of the Oberbürgermeister of the City of Berlin, 1946 SED, November 1946–1948 member of the Stadtverordnetenversammlung of Greater Berlin, 1954–1975 member of the Central Committee of the SED, 1955–1963 Interior Minister of the GDR and head of the German Volkspolizei.

38 See Doc. 20, fn. 11.

a Catholic German city treasurer. The Ober-Burgermeister[39] wrote him a flowery letter. A subordinate in our sector gave him a bottle of schnaps. There were other flowers and the city porcelain factory[40] gave him one of its pieces. The little satisfactions go on underneath the tragic covering. The opera was Butterfly[41] and it was not very well done – nothing like the performances in Vienna. I brought them out here for dinner and they stayed until after twelve – the first Germans, I imagine, who have been entertained in this expensive club[42]. It is an event which I suppose he will long remember and he is the kind of German upon whom Germany will have to rebuild. He is going to introduce me to Cardinal Preysing[43] before I go, and I shall try to get Preysing to introduce me to Faulhaber[44] whom I shall try to see in Munich[45]. Since I once was interested in the Church I ought to try to see a few of these people before I leave.[46]

Were we going to stay here for a very long time it would be fun to devote oneself's to the rebirth of Germany. But I believe that, at the moment, I have other things to devote myself to. You know what I mean. I love my sweet wife and my very sweet boys. A kiss for them. Edgar

Doc. 75
Letter to His Wife
Berlin, Wannsee Officers' Club[1], Am Sandwerder 17/19, July 15, 1946

My sweet and only one:

After a rather long and difficult meeting of the local government committee[2] on yesterday I came back to find two lovely letters from you awaiting me. One

39 Arthur Werner. See Doc. 27, fn. 30, and Doc. 39, fn. 23.

40 Former state porcelain factory that was maintained as the Berlin porcelain factory, supervised by the finance department of the Magistrat. See *Die Sitzungsprotokolle des Magistrats der Stadt Berlin 1945/46*, part I, *1945*, edited and introduced by Dieter Hanauske (= Schriftenreihe des Landesarchivs Berlin, vol. 2/I), Berlin 1995, Doc. 52, pp. 699f.

41 *Madame Butterfly*, opera by Giacomo Puccini (1858–1924), performance of the Deutsche Staatsoper in the Admiralspalast in the district of Mitte, Friedrichstraße 101/102, on July 13, 1946, 6 p. m. Premiere: January 26, 1946. See Kurt Westphal, "Puccini und seine 'Butterfly.' Zur Neuinszenierung in der Staatsoper," in: *Berliner Zeitung* from January 29, 1946, [p. 3].

42 Refers to the Wannsee Hotel/Wannsee Officers' Club. See Doc. 25, fn. 9.

43 Cardinal Konrad Graf von Preysing-Lichtenegg-Moos (1880–1950), German bishop, 1932–1935 Bishop of Eichstätt, as of 1935 Bishop of Berlin, leader in the Catholic Church's resistance against National Socialist church politics, 1946 appointed as Cardinal, founded numerous aid organizations for the rebuilding of Berlin.

44 See Doc. 11, fn. 26.

45 Munich, capital of the state of Bavaria in the American zone of Germany.

46 See Doc. 21, fn. 35.

1 See Doc. 25, fn. 9.

2 See Doc. 29, fn. 14; minutes of the 34th meeting of the Local Government Committee, Allied Kommandatura Berlin, on July 15, 1946, LG/M (46) 34, Russian version, in: TNA, Allied Kommandatura: Directives, Minutes and Papers, FO 1112/378.

was a letter that had gone somewhat astray, since it dated back to the 3 July.[3] The other was as recent as the 9th of July.[4] The first reminded me of how far I am from the kids what with a young son who has to be reprimanded and punished for saying Yipe and Jeez too frequently, and another who learns phrases upon their mere mention to him. "That's all right." "You are two years old." The second was an account of Timmy's birthday party[5] (wherein the imaginative aptitude of my sweet Emily came into play. I am thinking of Pooh[6]!) and of the chairs which we now have of our new piano, and of Gretchen's[7] piano. Your characterization of the two pianos strikes home with me. I don't know our new one except from your descriptions of your experiences with pianos. But I do remember Gretchen's piano from having played on it and your description is as I experienced it. The difference consists of the contrast between your adjective "brilliant" from which I deduce a clear, volatile treble and a rather resounding bass, and your adjective "sweet" which implies no especial contrast but rather a satisfactory tone throughout treble and bass. You are right. The ordinary pianist prefers the brilliance which means the contrast rather than the sweetness, which is all right for Christmas carols but hardly for a Chopin[8] Étude. John[9] I am sure will come to prefer the brilliance to the sweetness for without brilliance there is no pianism. I think indeed that through your perspicacity we have been saved from a piano which is only sweet.

Things have begun to hum a bit today in preparation for my trip to the zone. It is very convenient to have generals on the tip of your tongue. It looks at present as if I shall take my driver, Sanow[10], and my car along with me. They are, at least, on my orders at present, and I am seeing Keating[11] tomorrow morning to get his consent. I saw the Education and Religion people[12] this morning and made arrangements to see some of the so-called church heroes about which I wrote while I was in R + A, OSS[13].[14] They do not happen to be at the moment, the heroes I thought they were going to be. I have an appointment for Thursday[15]

3 See letter from July 2, 1946 (postmark from July 3, 1946), in: Documents from the estate of Edgar N. Johnson, private collection of Candice E. and Thomas R. Johnson, Denver, Colorado, USA.

4 See letter from July 8, 1946 (postmark from July 9, 1946), in: Documents from the estate of Edgar N. Johnson, private collection of Candice E. and Thomas R. Johnson, Denver, Colorado, USA.

5 Johnson's son Thomas (see Doc. 2, fn. 16) had turned two on July 8, 1946.

6 May refer to Winnie-the-Pooh, a children's book character from Alan A. Milne (1882–1956).

7 See Doc. 63, fn. 18.

8 Frédéric Chopin (1810–1849), Polish composer and pianist, 1831 moved to France, where his father came from.

9 Johnson's son John. See Doc. 2, fn. 15.

10 See Doc. 40, fn. 13.

11 See Doc. 39, fn. 6.

12 Refers to employees of the Education and Religious Affairs Branch, Internal Affairs and Communications Division, OMGUS.

13 Research and Analysis Branch, Office of Strategic Services. See Doc. 1, fn. 9.

14 See Doc. 21, fn. 35.

15 July 18, 1946.

morning to meet Cardinal Preysing[16], the prelate of Berlin, one of the Catholic heroes, and I am going to try to get him to give me a letter of introduction to Cardinal Faulhaber[17] of Munich[18], one of the heroes of southern Germany. I made arrangements this morning to see the important political people in the zone, and also to attend a meeting of the Nurnberg[19] trial[20] in case I should get to Nurnberg, which I think I should try to do. I'd like to get a look at Göring[21] and at Funk[22] whose bathroom I happen now to be using. Vienna is also on my orders, or at least I think it is going to be by tomorrow, and I shall therefore have the chance to talk with my friends there, and bring my Vienna experience up to date. I dropped in to see Don Heath[23] this morning, whom I have often mentioned. He expressed regret at my leaving and said quite sincerely that if I found the life of the University to be a little too much to take, I should write him here at Berlin with the idea of coming into the service of the State Department here. I think he meant it. And I am glad that I spoke for his wife[24] before the wives here.[25] Your suggestion that I should perhaps make it a point to go to Washington, just in case, I think I may follow. It will be good to see Gene[26] and Harold[27] again. Gene will perhaps be coming over here later on.[28] And I could speak to General Hilldring[29] also who is the big man on occupation matters now. You may be interested to know that the Education people would be glad to take me on for an important job if I wished to come back here.

16 See Doc. 74, fn. 43.

17 See Doc. 11, fn. 26.

18 Munich, capital of the state of Bavaria in the American zone of Germany.

19 Nuremberg, city in the state of Bavaria in the American zone of Germany.

20 See Doc. 49, fn. 44.

21 See Doc. 22, fn. 24.

22 See Doc. 25, fn. 10.

23 Donald R. Heath. See Doc. 8, fn. 15.

24 Louise B. Heath. See Doc. 55, fn. 48.

25 Johnson is referring to the lecture that he had given on July 9, 1946, for the American Women's Club of Berlin. See Doc. 72, fn. 2.

26 Eugene N. Anderson. See Doc. 1, fn. 1.

27 Harold C. Vedeler. See Doc. 2, fn. 12.

28 Anderson was supposed to travel as a representative of the Department of State, Occupied Areas Division, with the United States Education Mission to Germany. "Gene plans to come over in August + hopes to get permission from Clay [see Doc. 2, fn. 6] to travel a bit – some educational group," Emily had written to her husband on June 10, 1946. Letter in: Documents from the estate of Edgar N. Johnson, private collection of Candice E. and Thomas R. Johnson, Denver, Colorado, USA. Tasked with reporting on the state of education in the American zone and developing a program for necessary reforms, the delegation arrived in Berlin on August 24, 1946. There they held discussions with members of the American military government, and subsequently the delegation traveled through the states of the US zone. After just a month of activity they concluded their work. See *Die Neue Zeitung* from August 23, 1946, p. 1, from August 30, 1946, p. 1, from September 6, 1946, p. 2, from September 23, 1946, p. 2, and from October 18, 1946, p. 2; "Educators Tour American Zone To See Schools," in: *OMGUS Observer* from August 30, 1946, p. 4; James F. Tent, *Mission on the Rhine. Reeducation and Denazification in American-Occupied Germany*, Chicago and London 1982, pp. 114f.

29 See Doc. 2, fn. 4.

It may be a little difficult, with all this, to get back to you by the 20th or the 21st[30]. This is however my aim. I shall get in touch with you upon my arrival in New York. I don't see why you could not wait for me in case I were a day or two late, although I am perfectly willing to admit that there is no reason why you should wait for me. A day or two extra in the mountains, is a day or two extra in the mountains. I think, however, that with the chance to do a good job in the zone, and with the chance to go to Vienna, I should do both. The itinerary I worked out today brings me to Bremen[31] about the 5th of August. I understand I lose a couple of days there, and that one must count on at least ten days on the Atlantic. This may leave me little enough time to get from New York to you, or I may have luck and have some extra days to spare. In any case I shall do my best.

Letters may be a little sporadic from now on, and I may not be able to write very regularly. Yet I shall be gathering up experience to relate to you when I see you. This is, I think, a good way to end it all. I shall wait to see General Clay[32] and other important ones until I return from the zone. I shall get in touch with you soon after my arrival in New York to learn from you what I should really do next.

Goodnight, my love, a sweet kiss for you and for the boys. Tell John there is much fun in store for us in the mountains and forever afterwards. Get the fishing rod ready if you can find it. I love you all very very much. My sweet ones to whom I am returning. Edgar

Doc. 76
Letter to His Wife
Butzbach[1], Greater Hesse, Officers' Club – formerly Deutsches Haus[2], July 21, 1946

Dearest –

According to our plans I was to be with you a month from today in Colorado[3]. Considering what has happened today and yesterday it is unlikely that I

30 August 1946.

31 See Doc. 71, fn. 10.

32 See Doc. 2, fn. 6.

1 City in the state of Greater Hesse in the American zone of Germany, at the northeast passage from the Taunus to the Wetterau.

2 During the Nazi period the best hotel in the city along with Hessischer Hof. After the American invasion it became the Officers' Club, "that is, the American officers lived here. In addition the Officer's Club was visited by numerous 'young ladies' who had boyfriends there (customary of the time)." ("d. h. hier wohnten die amerikanischen Offiziere. Außerdem wurde der Offiziersclub auch von zahlreichen 'Fräuleins' besucht, die hier ihre Freunde hatten [zeitüblich].") Email from Dieter Wolf, head of the Museum and Stadtarchiv of the City of Butzbach, to Werner Breunig from July 12, 2007.

3 US state.

shall ever get there. For my trip to the zone[4] has had a very inauspicious start. I started out with what I thought was a car in very good condition – neither the driver[5] nor the motor pool ever led me to believe otherwise. We started yesterday morning, after I had spent a whole day (except for a meeting of the Kommandatura[6] at which the constitution was finally adopted[7]) trying to get papers for my driver to come along.[8] The papers worked very well – nobody made any trouble and we were on our way. Outside of Kassel[9] we got a flat tire but had an extra one with us so that was no trouble. In Kassel I delivered to Mrs. Moore's[10] sister[11] the things which I took with me from Lincoln[12].[13] I had a most unpleasant time there, not with Mrs. Moore's sister, who seems to be pleasant enough but with her husband, a retired bureaucrat who occupied a low civil service position who told me right away in the usual fashion the usual German story and what was wrong with the occupation. The chief complaint was of course that he had lost his house to the Americans, and was now forced to live in a couple of rooms. Kassel is one of the worst bombed out places in all Germany,[14] and he is lucky to have these rooms. Besides they have a garden. I reminded him that many places in London were wiped out by German bombing[15] and that there were serious housing shortages in all the places where Germans had been in any form. This made no impression upon him. He didn't think the bombing of London was serious. The officers who now live in his house have mistresses, and the mistresses take the fruit and the vegetables from the garden which he has there too. I heard about our favoring victims of the concentration camps in public office (he means Social Democrats and Communists) to the exclusion, I think he meant, of people like himself. He even said they were worse than the Nazis which made me very angry and I asked him please not to say that to me. He then complained violently about our de-Nazifi-

4 Refers to the American zone of Germany.

5 Artur Sanow. See Doc. 40, fn. 13.

6 See Doc. 20, fn. 11.

7 On July 19, 1946, the Commandants approved the constitution. See minutes of the 19th meeting of the Commandants on July 19, 1946, BKC/M (46) 19-175, English version, in: LAB, B Rep. 036-01 (Office of Military Government, Berlin Sector [OMGBS]), 5/36-1/5.

8 See Headquarters Berlin District, United States Army, Subject: Orders, July 19, 1946, in: Documents from the estate of Edgar N. Johnson, private collection of Candice E. and Thomas R. Johnson, Denver, Colorado, USA.

9 City in Greater Hesse in the American zone of Germany.

10 See Doc. 33, fn. 60.

11 Rosalie Eberle. See Doc. 33, fn. 63.

12 Capital of the US state of Nebraska, where Johnson lived with his family and taught at the university.

13 See Doc. 33.

14 Kassel had experienced the heaviest bombardment on October 22, 1943; approximately 10,000 people died. See Werner Dettmar, *Die Zerstörung Kassels im Oktober 1943. Eine Dokumentation*, Fuldabrück 1983.

15 "From 7 September 1940 until 11 May 1941, an estimated 18,800 tons of explosive were dropped on London by German bombers. According to conservative estimates, over 15,000 people were killed and 3.5 million homes damaged during the attacks,

cation program, and indicated that he was a witness for what he considered local and harmless Nazis in the tribunals which are now being set up by the Germans to try the Nazis. I replied that until the Germans had enough moral strength to deal with this problem vigorously they would not win the respect of the world. Everything he said annoyed me. He expects us to bring a paradise to the Germans, as their right, immediately, utterly unmindful of anything the Germans may have brought to the world in the last few years. I didn't stay any longer than I had to, and was not very nice I think. But I found myself asking myself afterwards, just why am I over here trying to help the Germans in the face of this attitude. It is well to let them stew in their own juice or to turn them over to the Russians. Of course I don't really believe this.

Incidently Mrs. Moore's sister remarked that when she was in Lincoln she met the Werkmeister's[16] and upon her arrival at the house, Werkmeister hauled out a recent picture of Hitler[17] which he expected her to admire. I guess there is no doubt he was a good Nazi supporter. We ought to de-nazify our own faculty.

But to get back to my own woes. On the way from Kassel to Frankfurt[18], the motor developed a bad clanky sound which made it impossible to proceed. I hitched a ride to the nearest service station on the autobahn, and made arrangements to have the car towed in. Then Sanow[19] and I were sent to this town of Butzbach to stay for the night, I in the Officers' Club and he in a PW[20] work camp[21]. On the way here (and it was about a 25 mile trip) the lights of the jeep

which became known as the Blitz (from the German Blitzkrieg, meaning 'lightning war'). Some historians suggest that the number of deaths was closer to 30,000." "Blitz," in: Kenneth J. Panton, *Historical Dictionary of London* (= Historical Dictionaries of Cities of the World, no. 11), Lanham, Maryland, and London 2001, pp. 60f. It is possible to trace exactly where German bombs fell in London during the Second World War on an interactive map: http://bombsight.org/#15/51.5050/-0.0900 (accessed March 4, 2018).

16 Lucyle T. Werkmeister, née Thomas (1908–1999) and her husband, William H. Werkmeister (1901–1993), American philosophy professor, born in Asendorf, Germany, first studied at the University of Münster and University of Frankfurt am Main, emigrated to the USA in the 1920s, became an American citizen, 1927 PhD, University of Nebraska, taught until 1953 at the University of Nebraska, in the winter semester 1936/1937 Visiting Professor at the University of Berlin, Englisches Seminar, Amerika-Abteilung, 1953–1966 University of Southern California, Director of the School of Philosophy, lastly Distinguished Professor at Florida State University.

17 See Doc. 22, fn. 19.

18 Frankfurt am Main, city in the state of Greater Hesse in the American zone of Germany.

19 See Doc. 40, fn. 13.

20 Prisoner of War.

21 Dieter Wolf, head of the Museum and Stadtarchiv of the City of Butzbach, finds it plausible that Johnson's driver was assigned a place to sleep in the stables of the castle barracks, which were used as Wehrmacht barracks until the end of March 1945. Wolf had "occasionally been told by contemporary German witnesses that they had sometimes worked in the stables of the castle barracks, where a camp for prisoners of war had been set up for a time." ("gelegentlich von deutschen Zeitzeugen erzählt bekommen, sie hätten zeitweise im Marstallgebäude der Schlosskaserne, wo ein Kriegsgefangenenlager zeitweise eingerichtet worden war, gearbeitet.") Email from Dieter Wolf to Werner Breunig from December 9, 2011.

22 See Doc. 63, fn. 30.

went out and we had to travel most of the way over pretty terrible roads in a pretty black night. Previously we had done some pretty wild chasing over fields. It reminded me of our introduction to Bear Creek Canyon[22]. When I got here the local officers were having a dance with their fräuleins. It is the center of an Ordnance Depot[23] and an Engineering school[24]. I was exhausted and went to bed. Today the car was hauled from the Service Station to the workshop here. The engine has developed bad defects and new parts are needed which are practically impossible to get. We have called both Frankfurt and Stuttgart[25]. Accordingly I shall have to send the car and Sanow back to Berlin tomorrow, and go on my own way, depending upon local transportation. By the time I get out of here I shall have lost 2 ½ days of my trip which is just a little bit tough. I almost feel like returning to Berlin with Sanow and the car.

If my conversation here with the subordinate officers and civilians is any evidence, the situation here is pretty rotten. The top officers, a Major Stephens[26], and a Captain Rosendale[27] are OK. But the others, outside of duty cannot make a very good impression upon the local population. I think they do their own particular jobs here all right but the place is overridden with mistresses. I saw them at the party last night, and they were in the Club this morning waiting for their men. In fact Sgt. Herman told me that the men have been with their fräuleins so long that when they have a party it is like husbands and wives being together. His fraulein has a three year old daughter to whom he is devoted and gives all his rations. After the party they all go home with their frauleins and sleep with them for awhile. I don't suppose there is any point in getting exciting about this. These men would all have families at home. The sergeant at the Service Station said that he had been fornicating all night. And if you believe the local officers (there is no military government here) the town is still Nazi and is running by Nazis or Nazi sympathizers. The attitude of the major officers is defeatist. We should just get out of here. An occupation can do no good. It reminds me of Eschwege[28],[29] and I suppose it is like this everywhere.

Bye-bye my sweet one, whom I shall soon see. Edgar

23 The Butzbach Ordnance Depot "was the central US repair facility for military vehicles for all of southern Germany" ("war der zentrale US-Ausbesserungsbetrieb für Militärfahrzeuge für ganz Süddeutschland"), according to Dieter Wolf, head of the Museum and Stadtarchiv of the City of Butzbach, in an email to Werner Breunig from July 12, 2007.

24 In April 1946 the US Army Engineer Training Center had moved to Butzbach from Epernay in France. See http://www.usarmygermany.com/School_Comd/USAREUR_SchoolCommand.htm (accessed March 4, 2018).

25 Capital of the state of Württemberg-Baden in the American zone of Germany.

26 Thomas M. Stephens, Major, 1945–November 1946 Commanding Officer, Butzbach Ordnance Depot.

27 David Rosendale (1906–2009), Captain, born in Dokkum, Netherlands, 1934 US citizenship, University of Denver, 1942–1948 US Army, Executive Officer, 47th Ordnance Battalion, 1948/1949 Deputy Chief, Liaison and Security Control Division, OMGHE, as of 1949 Foreign Service Staff Officer, Field Operations Division, Office of Land Commissioner for Hesse (OLCH).

28 Small town in the northeast of the state of Greater Hesse in the American zone of Germany.

29 See Doc. 49.

Doc. 77
Letter to His Wife
Stuttgart[1], July 26, 1946

Dearest –

A note to tell you of the progress of the journey. I left Wiesbaden[2] at about 9 this morning and came on here mostly via the Autobahn. The one interesting stop was at Darmstadt[3] where I visited an internment camp[4] where 17,000 Nazis considered dangerous enough to be put away are kept. In some ways it was an amazing institution. They have organized a university within the camp and there are all sorts of workshops, and artists' ateliers busy doing things, I am afraid, for American officers. There is a theatre and an orchestra. Indeed they played the Egmont Overture[5] for me. But I hardly know what to think. I learned that these people were being fed 1700 calories a day which is a good deal more than the average German gets. And one man at a machine who was doing especially hard work was getting a ration of 2500 calories which is more than the heavy workers ration in Germany. A German guard outside the camp, a PW[6], told Sanow[7] that he would gladly enter the camp, and the driver himself can't understand this treatment. I had only a casual glimpse of something more than an hour but they were a hard looking crew. I got a view of Darmstadt which has been almost destroyed by a 20 minute raid in November 1943[8] I think it was.[9]

1 Capital of the state of Württemberg-Baden in the American zone of Germany.
2 Capital of the state of Greater Hesse in the American zone of Germany.
3 City in the state of Greater Hesse in the American zone of Germany.
4 Refers to the American internment camp "Civil Internment Enclosure 91" (CI Camp 91) in Darmstadt, Rheinstraße, in which up to 25,000 internees were held. See http://www.digam.net/index.php?page=10&lput=632 (accessed March 4, 2018); Dieter Emig/Alfred G. Frei, "Office of Military Government for Hesse," in: *OMGUS-Handbuch. Die amerikanische Militärregierung in Deutschland 1945–1949*, ed. Christoph Weisz (= Quellen und Darstellungen zur Zeitgeschichte, vol. 35), Munich 1994, pp. 317–453, here pp. 428f.
5 By Ludwig van Beethoven (see Doc. 37, fn. 29).
6 Prisoner of War.
7 See Doc. 40, fn. 13.
8 In the night from September 11 to 12, 1944, Darmstadt was largely destroyed by a major attack of the Royal Air Force with subsequent firestorm. See Klaus Schmidt, *Die Brandnacht. Dokumente von der Zerstörung Darmstadts am 11. September 1944*, third edition, Darmstadt 1964.
9 Johnson does not mention the visit that he paid to the District President in Darmstadt, Ludwig Bergsträsser (1883–1960), with Major William R. Sheehan on July 26, 1946. Bergsträsser writes in his diary: "Around noon Sheehan came with Professor Edgar N. Johnson, who will soon return to the States to work there, also in the public, against the illusionists and for the development of German conditions. For three weeks now he is visiting the American zone to inform himself about the particulars. Long, very interesting conversation. He asked all kinds of questions and was amazed when I said to him that it is a great stupidity that books cannot be sent to us from over there. Ultimately I don't see the reason why we are only allowed to send letters with private content. If, for example, I wish to write about political things to send over there, I have to ask Sheehan to pass it along, I can't do it directly. He also asked about the possibility of further democratic development and many other things. I

This trip is going to be somewhat unsatisfactory because it is so rushed. I have been late in getting started, as you know, and it seems foolish, having made the effort, not to do it as well as I can. I think I'll cut out Vienna, however, since that will make me too late but I hate to cut out a visit to the Nuremberg[10] trials[11]. I will get back to Berlin, according to my present schedule, a little late, but I won't delay. I understand also that there is a jam on transportation home from Bremen[12]. It looks therefore as if I shall not be able to make it home by the 20th or 21st[13]. I won't know very definitely, of course, until I see when I get away from Bremen, and I can cable you, en voyage, or telephone you immediately upon arrival in New York.

I got to talk with some of the important Germans in Wiesbaden but not as many as I hoped because they are off on vacation. The trip to Marburg[14] was

emphasized economic necessity, also resources coming in for our export, and pointed to Offenbach industry. He worked in the International Kommandatura in Berlin and talked about how laborious it is, because of the language alone. They argued for two hours just about the question of the oath and the word 'unparteiisch' [impartial], which the Russians desperately wanted to construe as 'unpolitical.' He very much agreed with my opinion that there should be large-scale exchange of professors and students, and also teachers. When I said during our conversation that I have never been in the States, he said it must be arranged for me to come over someday soon. He strongly emphasized the significance of denazification for public opinion in the USA." ("Gegen Mittag kam Sheehan mit Professor Edgar N. Johnson, der bald in die Staaten zurückkehrt und dort gegen die Illusionisten und für die Entwicklung der deutschen Zustände auch in der Öffentlichkeit wirken will. Er besucht jetzt drei Wochen die amerikanische Zone, um sich im einzelnen zu informieren. Langes, sehr interessantes Gespräch. Er stellte vielerlei Fragen und war erstaunt, wie ich ihm sagte, es sei doch eine Dummheit, daß uns nicht von drüben Bücher geschickt werden dürften. Schließlich sähe ich den Grund nicht ein, warum wir nur Briefe privaten Inhalts hinüberschicken dürften. Wenn ich z. B. über politische Dinge nach drüben schreiben wolle, müsse ich Sheehan bitten, diese weiterzugeben, und könne das nicht direkt tun. Er fragte auch nach den Möglichkeiten der demokratischen Weiterentwicklung und vielen anderen Dingen. Ich betonte die wirtschaftliche Notwendigkeit, auch das Hereinkommen von Rohstoffen für unseren Export, verwies auf die Offenbacher Industrie. Er hat in der Internationalen Kommandantur in Berlin gearbeitet und erzählte, wie umständlich es sei, schon der Sprache wegen. Sie hätten allein über die Frage des Eides und das Wort 'unparteiisch', das die Russen krampfhaft als 'unpolitisch' auffassen wollten, zwei Stunden diskutiert. Meiner Meinung, daß Austausch von Professoren und Studenten, auch Lehrern im großen Maßstab geschehen müsse, stimmte er sehr zu. Als ich im Gespräch sagte, ich wäre noch nie in den Staaten gewesen, sagte er, das müsse arrangiert werden, daß ich bald einmal hinüberkomme. Er betonte sehr stark die Bedeutung der Denazifizierung für die öffentliche Meinung in USA.") Ludwig Bergsträsser, *Befreiung, Besatzung, Neubeginn. Tagebuch des Darmstädter Regierungspräsidenten 1945–1948*, ed. Walter Mühlhausen (= Biographische Quellen zur deutschen Geschichte nach 1945, vol. 5), Munich 1987, pp. 149f. A business card that Johnson received from Bergsträsser can be found in: Documents from the estate of Edgar N. Johnson, private collection of Candice E. and Thomas R. Johnson, Denver, Colorado, USA.

10 City in the state of Bavaria in the American zone of Germany.

11 See Doc. 49, fn. 44.

12 See Doc. 71, fn. 10.

13 August 1946.

14 University city in the state of Greater Hesse in the American zone of Germany.

interesting to see how we work through the Universities, and to see how American life goes on in this kind of a town. I think you might enjoy life in a smaller German town in the zone. The trip is however in many respects anti-climactical. My work is really over and the uncertainty of our future in Germany makes it seems pointless to consider how much positive good we can do here. The Germans, I am sure, are itching for us to leave in order to get control themselves.

I love you my darling and it won't be many weeks now before I shall see you and the lovely boys. A sweet kiss and a tight squeeze. Goodnight, my darling. Edgar

Doc. 78
Letter to His Wife
Stuttgart[1], July 28, 1946

My dearest –

Col. Dawson[2], the director of the M[ilitary] G[overnment] set up in Baden-Wurttemberg[3] has let me stay in his villa here, as Col. Newman[4], the director of M[ilitary] G[overnment] in Greater Hesse let me stay with him in Wiesbaden[5]. They are both academic people. Newman was a superintendent of schools in Long Island[6] some place, and Dawson is a Professor of Law at Western Reserve[7] in Cleveland[8]. An executive officer of Dawson's (Col. Winning[9]) is on the faculty of the Business School of New York University[10]. At Wiesbaden, the head of the Civil Administration Branch was a friend of Glenn's[11] at Cor-

1 Capital of the state of Württemberg-Baden in the American zone of Germany.

2 William W. Dawson (1892–1947), Colonel, American lawyer, taught as of 1927 at the School of Law, Western Reserve University, Professor, 1945/1946 Director, OMGWB, as of August 1946 Director, RGCO, OMGUS.

3 Correct: Württemberg-Baden, state in the American zone of Germany.

4 James R. Newman (1902–1964), Colonel, American educationalist, 1930 MA and 1940 EdD, Teachers College, Columbia University, schoolteacher, Supervising Principal for the 16th District Schools of Long Island, as of 1941 US Army, 1945–1949 Director, OMGGH/OMGHE, 1949–1952 Land Commissioner for Hesse. Photo with Newman in Appendix of Illustrations, ill. 21.

5 Capital of the state of Greater Hesse in the American zone of Germany.

6 Island belonging to the US state of New York.

7 Western Reserve University (since 1967: Case Western Reserve University).

8 City in the US state of Ohio.

9 Charles D. Winning (1894–1988), Colonel, American literary scholar, 1932 PhD, New York University, Professor of General Literature, School of Commerce, Accounts and Finance, New York University, 1945–March 1946 Deputy Director, OMGWB, June 1946–1947 Director, Government Group/Government Affairs Office, OMGWB, 1947/1948 Director, RGCO, OMGUS, 1948/1949 Director, Education and Cultural Relations Division, OMGBY, then Chief, Public Affairs Division, Office of Land Commissioner for Bavaria (OLCB).

10 School of Commerce, Accounts and Finance (today Leonard N. Stern School of Business), New York University, New York City.

11 Glenn W. Gray. See Doc. 49, fn. 74.

nell[12] (Landin[13]), and here in Civil Administration there is a pupil of Shumate's[14] at Minnesota[15] (Scammon[16]). So there are plenty of academic people scattered about this show. Dawson and Winning were home recently and decided to come back for at least another year. They are bringing their wives[17]. Everyone feels some insecurity about the future of M[ilitary] G[overnment] here and there are bets being made on the chance that M[ilitary] G[overnment] will not be here a year from now. Aside from all other questions, it is, I think, just as well that I am coming home now. It is unlikely that the M[ilitary] G[overnment] character of the occupation will last so long that there is much of a chance, were there even the desire, to pursue a long range policy here. And there are those on the spot who feel that because of the conduct of our troops, and the impression this makes on the Germans, it is just as well that we withdraw our troops as soon as possible. There seems to be much greater trust of the Germans here in the zone where, of course, the relationship is first hand, and not removed, as it is in Berlin.

This is a lovely spot, and it would have been pleasant to be here. I think possibly, if it had worked out that way, that you would have been reasonably contented here, but not for the short space of a year. Somebody mentioned at breakfast that 5000 dependents are arriving in August and 4000 in September, and that already in Frankfurt[18], the shipment of dependents has had to be curtailed because of the shortage of housing. This will be a more serious than ever problem because the Germans are already considerably annoyed at the situation.[19] Maybe you and the boys couldn't have come over in any case, which, if I

12 Cornell University, Ithaca, New York. Glenn W. Gray had received his PhD from Cornell University in 1928.

13 Harold W. Landin (1903–1991), Major, American historian, 1928 PhD, Cornell University, taught until 1942 at Smith College and at Ohio State University, 1945–1947 Director, Civil Administration Division, OMGGH/OMGHE, as of 1947 Chief, Democratization Branch, Civil Administration Division, OMGUS.

14 Roger V. Shumate (1900–1954), American political scientist, 1933 PhD, University of Minnesota, taught from 1929–1931 at the University of Cincinnati, 1931–1933 University of Minnesota, 1933–1937 University of Pittsburgh, as of 1937 University of Nebraska, Professor of Political Science, Director of Research, Legislative Council of the US state of Nebraska.

15 University of Minnesota, Minneapolis and Saint Paul, Minnesota.

16 Richard M. Scammon (1915–2001), First Lieutenant, American political scientist, 1935 BA, University of Minnesota, 1938 MA, University of Michigan, 1939–1941 Research Secretary, Radio Office, University of Chicago, 1941–1946 US Army, 1945/1946 Administration and Local Government Officer, OMGWB, 1946–1948 Chief, Election Affairs Branch/Election and Political Parties Branch/Political Activities Branch, Civil Administration Division, OMGUS, 1948–1955 Department of State (Chief, Division of Research for Western Europe), 1961–1965 Director, Bureau of the Census, Department of Commerce.

17 Marguerite Dawson; Freda G. Winning, née Gerwin (1901–1978), PhD, New York University, Professor of Education, Chairman, Home Economics Department, School of Education, New York University, 1975–1978 President, Cleveland Branch, American Association of University Women.

18 Frankfurt am Main, city in the state of Greater Hesse in the American zone of Germany.

19 On March 23, 1946, Johnson wrote about the planned evacuation of the Sonnenberg housing development in the south of Stuttgart. See Doc. 26 and Doc. 26, fn. 8 and 9.

had stayed, would have made it intolerable for me. I visited Pollock[20] at the Länderrat[21] quarters yesterday morning (quarters of the former Gauleiter[22]).[23] He has the most palatial and colonial office I have yet seen in Germany. I can see that he is a very difficult person – capable, to be sure, but a little of a stuffed shirt. At least he treated me rather coldly and off-hand, leaving me to be impressed with his importance. Yet at the same time he was polite, has invited me to dinner today, and I am to have a chance to see the Länderrat at work tomorrow and Tuesday[24] by attending a couple of Committee meetings.

I took a pleasure ride yesterday into the French zone and visited a wonderful Cistercian abbey (Bebenhausen)[25] which I saw during my first stay here[26].

I am going to drive to Heidelberg[27] this afternoon to see some of the professors there.

According to my present schedule I shall arrive in Bremen[28], the evening of 8 August. When I get out of there is a question. I am very lonesome for you, feel very far away from you and the boys. But it will be less than a month now. I love you my darling, and shall never leave you again. Edgar

Doc. 79
Letter to His Wife
Munich[1], August 1, 1946

Dearest –

I am very lonesome for you and am in a mood to cut this trip short + go back to Berlin. The chief cause of this is that I came here last night, on from Nurnberg[2], hoping to get started on a little talking here today, only to find that it is a holiday here: "Air Corps Day"[3] and that there is no one around. I shall try to do

20 See Doc. 15, fn. 12.
21 See Doc. 15, fn. 10.
22 Wilhelm Murr (1888–1945), NS politician, 1928–1945 Gauleiter of the NSDAP in Württemberg-Hohenzollern, 1930–1932 and 1933–1945 member of the Reichstag, 1932/1933 member of the Landtag of Württemberg, 1933–1945 Reich Governor in Württemberg and Hohenzollern.
23 The Länderrat and the RGCO had their headquarters in the Villa Reitzenstein, today office of the Minister-President of Baden-Württemberg.
24 July 30, 1946.
25 Bebenhausen Abbey, a former Cistercian monastery in Bebenhausen near Tübingen. As of November 22, 1946, the Beratende Landesversammlung (advisory state assembly) of the state of Württemberg-Hohenzollern, part of the French zone of Germany, convened here, and as of June 3, 1947, so did the Landtag.
26 May refer to Johnson's study trip to Germany in 1927/1928.
27 University city in the state of Württemberg-Baden in the American zone of Germany.
28 See Doc. 71, fn. 10.

1 Capital of the state of Bavaria in the American zone of Germany.
2 Nuremberg, city in the state of Bavaria in the American zone of Germany.
3 On August 1, 1907, the Aeronautical Division, US Signal Corps, was established, the first predecessor of today's United States Air Force.

something this afternoon by way of seeing UNRRA[4] people in Pasing[5] and perhaps arranging to see some of their camps[6] this afternoon. The brass is also down from Berlin, General Clay[7] and General Adcock[8] to witness the opening of some kind of an industrial exhibition here.[9] I suppose actually there is no point in getting back to Berlin, inasmuch as I should arrive there over the weekend, and could accordingly get nothing done but get ahold of some letters from you that will be there.

I perhaps labor under the spell of the Nurnberg trial[10] yesterday, which I could have attended in the afternoon as well as the morning had I known there was a holiday here.[11] It is hardly what you would call a spectacle since the court room is none too large.[12] The 22 prisoners are crowded into 2 rows of benches. These were not all there yesterday. Hess[13] wasn't there. Nor Ribbenthrop[14] nor Raeder[15] but the rest were, and except for one or two, they are a horrible looking bunch. Göring[16] looks like a violent degenerate. Streicher[17] the Jew barker

4 United Nations Relief and Rehabilitation Administration, aid organization of the United Nations for groups of people in need, especially refugees and displaced persons in the Allied occupied territories. See Gioia-Olivia Karnagel, "United Nations Relief and Rehabilitation Administration (UNRRA)," in: *Deutschland unter alliierter Besatzung 1945–1949/55*, ed. Wolfgang Benz, Berlin 1999, pp. 310f.

5 District of Munich since 1938. The headquarters of UNRRA for the American zone of Germany were located in Munich-Pasing. See *UNRRA. The History of the United Nations Relief and Rehabilitation Administration*, prepared by a special staff under the direction of George Woodbridge, vol. I, New York 1950, p. 193 (chart VII: Field organization chart, Displaced Persons operations, Germany).

6 Camps managed by the UNRRA for the temporary accommodation of displaced persons.

7 See Doc. 2, fn. 6.

8 See Doc. 14, fn. 9.

9 On August 3, 1946, the *Exportschau, Leistungsschau der Bayerischen Wirtschaft* (Export Show, Exhibition of Bavarian Industry) opened in the Haus der Kunst in Munich. See *Die Neue Zeitung* from August 2, 1946, p. 8, and from August 5, 1946, pp. 1f. and 8.

10 See Doc. 49, fn. 44.

11 Johnson was a trial observer on July 30, 1946, and in the morning session on July 31, 1946.

12 The trial took place in Courtroom 600 of the Nuremberg Palace of Justice.

13 Rudolf Heß (1894–1987), NS politician, as of 1933 Reich Minister without Portfolio, appointed by Adolf Hitler (see Doc. 22, fn. 19) as his Deputy in the NSDAP, flew to Scotland in 1941 to negotiate peace with Douglas Douglas-Hamilton, 14th Duke of Hamilton (1903–1973), captured by the British as a prisoner of war, sentenced by the International Military Tribunal as a major war criminal to life imprisonment, served in the Spandau Prison until his death.

14 Joachim von Ribbentrop (1893–1946), NS politician, 1936–1938 German Ambassador to Great Britain, 1938–1945 Reich Foreign Minister, sentenced by the International Military Tribunal as a major war criminal to death and executed.

15 See Doc. 49, fn. 46.

16 See Doc. 22, fn. 24.

17 Julius Streicher (1885–1946), NS politician, as of 1923 publisher of the antisemitic weekly paper *Der Stürmer*, 1924–1932 member of the Landtag of Bavaria, 1925–1939 Gauleiter of the NSDAP in Middle Franconia/Franconia, 1932–1945 member of the Reichstag, sentenced by the International Military Tribunal as a major war criminal to death and executed.

an Unter-Mensch if there ever was one. Von Papen[18] looks like a monkey, and so indeed does Frick[19], the Minister of the interior. Schacht[20] too is a very inferior looking person. Except for a few they seemed to be all in a fairly cheerful state of mind, and munched bread during the hearing. Their trial is over, and now the organizations of the Party[21] are being tried. Yesterday they had a Gauleiter (Hoffman[22] from Hamburg[23]), an Ortsgruppenleiter (also Bürgermeister)[24] and Blockleiter[25] on the stand trying to tell the court how harmless all this activity was.[26] The microphone system does not work any too well. It broke down during the proceedings and stalled things for awhile. It might have been a going of ordinary criminals instead of extraordinary criminals.

Last night I went out to see Frau Engelhorn[27] and her daughter[28]. She looks much less well than when I saw here in November[29]. And she has now had the

18 Franz von Papen (1879–1969), German politician (Deutsche Zentrumspartei), 1932 Reich Chancellor, in 1933 paved the way for the seizure of power by Adolf Hitler (see Doc. 22, fn. 19), served in Hitler's government as Vice Chancellor, 1934 resignation as cabinet member and appointment as Special Envoy in the German Embassy in Austria, 1936 Ambassador to Austria, 1939 Ambassador to Turkey, acquitted by the International Military Tribunal but sentenced by a Spruchkammer (denazification court) to eight years of labor camp, 1949 early release.

19 Wilhelm Frick (1877–1946), NS politician, 1930/1931 Interior Minister and Minister of Education in the state of Thuringia, 1933–1943 Reich Minister of the Interior, 1943–1945 Reich Protector of Bohemia and Moravia, sentenced to death by the International Military Tribunal as a major war criminal and executed.

20 See Doc. 49, fn. 45.

21 Nationalsozialistische Deutsche Arbeiterpartei (NSDAP).

22 Karl Kaufmann (1900–1969), NS politician, 1928–1930 member of the Prussian Landtag, 1929–1945 Gauleiter of the NSDAP in Hamburg, 1930–1945 member of the Reichstag, 1933–1945 Reich Governor in Hamburg.

23 City in the British zone of Germany.

24 Hans Wegscheider (born 1885), German master blacksmith and animal healer, 1933–1945 Ortsgruppenleiter of the NSDAP and Mayor of Hirschdorf near St. Lorenz, Kreis Kempten-Land.

25 Dr. Ernst Hirth (born 1896), German Landgerichtsrat, 1942–1945 Blockleiter of the NSDAP in Nuremberg.

26 On July 30 Kaufmann and Willi Meyer-Wendeborn (born 1891), 1934–1945 Kreisleiter of the NSDAP in Cloppenburg (Oldenburg) in Gau Weser-Ems, previously Ortsgruppenleiter of the NSDAP, were on the witness stand, and in the morning session on July 31, Meyer-Wendeborn, Wegscheider, and Hirth. See Internationaler Militärgerichtshof Nürnberg (ed.), *Der Prozeß gegen die Hauptkriegsverbrecher vor dem Internationalen Militärgerichtshof, Nürnberg 14. November 1945–1. Oktober 1946*, vol. XX, *Verhandlungsniederschriften 30. Juli 1946–10. August 1946*, Nuremberg 1948, pp. 7–118.

27 Anna Engelhorn, née Winnecke (1875–1957), born in Strasbourg, Alsace, then part of Germany, daughter of August Winnecke (1835–1897), Professor of Astronomy at the University of Strasbourg and Director of the Observatory, and a German-Russian woman (Hedwig Winnecke, née Dell [1846–1919]), active as a painter and lithographer, lived in Munich after 1919, in 1920 married widowed former bank director Kommerzienrat Karl Engelhorn (1856–1927), as of 1931 member of the Anthroposophical Society. On Anna Winnecke's artistic work, see François Lotz in collaboration with Joseph Fuchs/Léon Kieffer/René Metz, *Artistes-Peintres Alsaciens de jadis et de naguère (1880–1982)*, Kaysersberg 1987, p. 358. For an overview of the artistic

misfortune of having her house[30] and furniture confiscated by the Americans as part of the so-called American Military Communities[31] which are established here in the zone: blocks of barbed-wire surrounded houses. The Germans don't react well to this separation. They don't take well the insistence upon letting houses remain empty in the compound. In Frankfurt[32] they call the American enclosure – the Ghetto of the Pharisees[33]. Frau Engelhorn urged me to stay over here and bring the family. Evidently they don't run into too many congenial Americans. She is, however, still sprightly and full of good humor. They have to use the black market[34]. They had 2 pancakes apiece for supper.

I'll leave here over the weekend for Berlin and get away from there as soon as possible. It is all over anyway, insofar as I can see, and I sometimes ask why, indeed, I ever came down here to the zone. I love you my sweetheart, and the month begins today during which we shall be together again. Kiss the sweet boys for me, and let me hold you very tight. Edgar

work, see also A. Bauer/J. Carpentier, *Répertoire des Artistes d'Alsace des XIXe et XXe siècles. Peintres – Sculpteurs – Graveurs – Dessinateurs, V–Z*, Strasbourg 1991, p. 425. In 1908 Anna Winnecke was represented with a lithograph at the *Große Berliner Kunstausstellung*. See "Verzeichnis der ausgestellten Kunstwerke nach Sälen geordnet," in: *Katalog der Grossen Berliner Kunst-Ausstellung 1908*, Berlin, Stuttgart, and Leipzig 1908, pp. 1–176, here p. 18. In 1927/1928, during his time studying in Munich, Edgar N. Johnson lived in the boarding house that Anna Engelhorn ran at Hohenstaufenstraße 10/II. See *Personenstand der Ludwig-Maximilians-Universität München. Winter-Halbjahr 1927/28*, Munich 1928, p. 116. Photo of Engelhorn in Appendix of Illustrations, ill. 79.

28 Refers to Anna Engelhorn's stepdaughter Hedwig Engelhorn (1893–1968), born in Strasbourg, Alsace, studied law and public economics, doctoral studies at the University of Freiburg im Breisgau. Hedwig Engelhorn lived with Anna Engelhorn.

29 In November 1945, when Johnson traveled through Germany after completion of his duties in Austria, before returning to the USA.

30 Harthauser Straße 90. According to information from the Stadtarchiv Munich from August 4, 2009/March 26, 2010, Anna Engelhorn had lived at Harthauser Straße 90 since 1937, her move to Dr.-Max-Straße 15 in Grünwald was registered on July 8, 1946.

31 On the military communities, see Thomas Leuerer, *Die Stationierung amerikanischer Streitkräfte in Deutschland. Militärgemeinden der U. S. Army in Deutschland seit 1945 als ziviles Element der Stationierungspolitik der Vereinigten Staaten* (= Politik und Gesellschaft. Würzburger Universitätsschriften, vol. 6), Würzburg 1997.

32 Frankfurt am Main, city in the state of Greater Hesse in the American zone of Germany.

33 Hebrew "perushim," the separated ones, members of an ancient Jewish party that strictly observed religious laws, figuratively refers to arrogant, self-righteous hypocrites.

34 See Doc. 21, fn. 11.

Doc. 80
Letter to His Wife
Bremerhaven[1], August 7, 1946

My darling –

I am at last on the way to you, to be with you for a very very long time I hope. I am trying to write this in a huge lounge at this staging area[2]. Five feet away someone is trying to play boogie woogie[3] on the bass of a tin-pan piano[4]. They are getting ready for some kind of a performance. Whether, under these circumstances I can manage to get anything written I don't know.

I don't believe I have written you since I went to Oberammergau[5]. I started something there which I didn't finish and where it is now I don't know – somewhere in the mess of papers I have piled along.[6] After the nice treatment I got in Wiesbaden[7] and Stuttgart[8] I was treated somewhat shabbily in Munich I thought: At least General Müller[9] paid no attention to me, nor any of his henchmen, and the people on his M[ilitary] G[overnment] staff whom I could find in their offices were a little condescending or else a little dead. The nicest thing about the trip was, I guess, the couple visits to Frau Engelhorn[10].[11] I think I mentioned that she had been thrown out of her house to make room for one of those so-called American Communities[12], a compound surrounded by barbed-wire. She doesn't know quite where she is going to land for the winter. She doesn't look as well as when I saw her last November[13] but she still has sharp intelligence, good humor, and is certainly one of the best if not really the best German, I have ever met. I also talked with Högner[14], the S[o-

1 See Doc. 71, fn. 10.

2 Bremerhaven Staging Area.

3 A form of solo piano style that emerged among black musicians in the first decade of the 20th century in the USA.

4 A cheap, out of tune piano.

5 Town in the state of Bavaria in the American zone of Germany, known above all for the Passion Play that has taken place every ten years since 1634.

6 The letter from Oberammergau from August 1, 1946, unsigned and never sent, can be found in: Documents from the estate of Edgar N. Johnson, private collection of Candice E. and Thomas R. Johnson, Denver, Colorado, USA. In this letter, Johnson writes about his detour to Oberammergau, where he stayed in the guesthouse of the European Theater Intelligence School.

7 Capital of the state of Greater Hesse in the American zone of Germany.

8 Capital of the state of Württemberg-Baden in the American zone of Germany.

9 Walter J. Muller (1895–1967), Brigadier General, 1918 graduate of the United States Military Academy, 1945–1947 Director, OMGBY, 1953–1955 member and Chairman of the German-Allied parole board in Bad Godesberg for the review of sentencing of war criminals, an office in the division of the American High Commissioner for Germany. Photo with Muller in Appendix of Illustrations, ill. 21.

10 See Doc. 79, fn. 27.

11 See Doc. 79.

12 See Doc. 79, fn. 31.

13 November 1945, when Johnson traveled through Germany after completion of his duties in Austria, before returning to the USA. See Doc. 79.

14 Wilhelm Hoegner. See Doc. 11, fn. 27.

cial] D[emocrat] Minister President, Baumgartner[15], the CSU[16] Minister of Food and Agriculture, Pfeiffer[17], the Minister of De-Nazification, and Dr. Seifrid[18], the SPD Minister of the Interior. I had a long talk with Dr. Josef Müller[19], the head of the CSU (Christian Social Union) in Bavaria, and with a certain Herr Herwarth[20], a so-called Ambassadorial Adviser, formerly in the foreign service of the Nazis, whom OSS[21] helped a great deal when we were in Salzburg[22], and who is very very grateful for this help. All the big shots from Berlin were down to witness the opening of an export-import expedition[23], a rather elegant but pathetic attempt of the Bavarians to show us how ready they are to go ahead. I had planned to see others – and go elsewhere in Bavaria but when Saturday[24] noon came, and things closed up, I could not make up my mind to stay any longer, nor to try a trip to Austria. Instead Sanow[25] and I decided to go back to Berlin. We had to stop at Stuttgart to get my coat

15 Joseph Baumgartner (1904–1964), German economist and politician, 1929 Dr. oec. publ., University of Munich, 1945 CSU, 1945–1948 Bavarian Minister of Agriculture, 1946 member of the Verfassunggebende Landesversammlung (constituent state assembly) of Bavaria, 1946–1962 member of the Landtag of Bavaria, 1948 Bayernpartei, 1948–1959 Chairman of the Bayernpartei, 1949–1951 member of the Bundestag, 1954–1957 Bavarian Minister of Agriculture and Deputy Minister-President.

16 Christlich-Soziale Union, a Christian conservative party in Bavaria. Founding meeting at the state level on January 8, 1946.

17 Anton Pfeiffer (1888–1957), German politician (CSU), 1913 Dr. phil., University of Munich, modern language philologist, teacher, 1918–1933 Secretary General of the Bayerische Volkspartei, 1928–1933 member of the Landtag of Bavaria, 1945–July 1946 and December 1946–1950 head of the Bavarian State Chancellery, July–December 1946 Bavarian State Minister for Special Tasks (denazification), 1946–1950 member of the Landtag of Bavaria, 1948 coorganizer and head of the Constitutional Convention at Herrenchiemsee, 1948/1949 member of the Parlamentarischer Rat (parliamentary council) in Bonn, Chairman of the CDU/CSU faction, 1950/1951 Consul General in Belgium, 1951–1954 Ambassador to Belgium.

18 Josef Seifried (1892–1962), German politician (SPD), 1928–1933 and 1946–1950 member of the Landtag of Bavaria, 1945–1947 Bavarian State Minister of the Interior, 1946 member of the Verfassunggebende Landesversammlung (constituent state assembly) of Bavaria, 1948 member of the Parlamentarischer Rat (parliamentary council) in Bonn.

19 Josef Müller (1898–1979), German politician (CSU), 1925 Dr. oec. publ., University of Munich, as of 1927 lawyer, 1943–1945 arrest for high treason and imprisonment in Berlin, Buchenwald, Flossenbürg, and Dachau, 1946 member of the Verfassunggebende Landesversammlung (constituent state assembly) of Bavaria, 1946–1949 Chairman of the CSU, 1946–1962 member of the Landtag of Bavaria, 1947–1952 Bavarian Minister of Justice, until 1950 also Deputy Minister-President.

20 Hans-Heinrich Herwarth von Bittenfeld (1904–1999), German diplomat, 1931–1939 Attaché and Legationssekretär, German embassy in Moscow, 1945–1949 Bavarian State Chancellery (1946 Regierungsdirektor), 1955–1961 Ambassador to Great Britain, 1961–1965 State Secretary and head of the Office of the Federal President, 1965–1969 Ambassador to Italy, 1969–1977 President of the Goethe-Institut.

21 Office of Strategic Services. See Doc. 1, fn. 9.

22 City in the American zone of Austria.

23 See Doc. 79, fn. 9.

24 August 3, 1946.

25 See Doc. 40, fn. 13.

which I had absent-mindedly left at Col. Dawson's[26], and at Oberursel[27] to pick up the Mercedes-Benz[28], which you remember went blouie[29] our first day out of Berlin.[30] We had very bad luck on this way back. Small goings – wrong with the motor on two occasions which Sanow fortunately was able to repair, and three flats mind you. We got into Oberursel about 1 a. m. and were met by a very cordial, considerate, and efficient Mr. Henry Bose[31] in charge of the motor pool who turned over to us the repaired Mercedes-Benz, put us up for the night (Sanow too), gave us an elegant breakfast and sandwiches to take along. He is of German descent he said and prefers the Germans who work for him to many of the Americans who do.

There was no more difficulty on the way to Berlin on Sunday[32] and we got in about 7 o'clock. I went to see Col. Glaser[33] in the hope that he had your mail for me but he didn't. In fact his wife[34] was arriving that evening, and he was not particularly interested in me. But he did have a German phrase that he wanted translated. I then tried to find your letters at the office but without luck and went out to Wannsee[35] to go to bed. For on the last days of the trip I developed this stomach trouble which I had in Austria and was in none too vigorous a condition. It is still with me but I think it will be over by the time I get home. I think it is only a question of a good deal of fatigue and will clear up on the boat over.

The letters[36] were in my hand on Monday[37] morning and they bucked me up no end. I will leave the decision about Colorado[38] to you. From what I read here Minnesota[39] is as bad as Colorado.[40]

26 See Doc. 78, fn. 2.

27 City in the state of Greater Hesse in the American zone of Germany.

28 German car brand, created in 1926 with the merger of Daimler-Motoren-Gesellschaft and Benz & Cie.

29 Meant is "went blooey," slang for "broke down."

30 See Doc. 76.

31 Possibly Henry H. Bose (born 1913), Army Serial Number: 32214673 (civilian occupation: semiskilled mechanics and repairmen, motor vehicles).

32 August 4, 1946.

33 See Doc. 28, fn. 4.

34 Marguerite K. Glaser. See Doc. 40, fn. 22.

35 To the Wannsee Officers' Club, Am Sandwerder 17/19. See Doc. 25, fn. 9.

36 In: Documents from the estate of Edgar N. Johnson, private collection of Candice E. and Thomas R. Johnson, Denver, Colorado, USA.

37 August 5, 1946.

38 US state.

39 US state.

40 Here Johnson is referring to the spread of the polio epidemic; he means that a trip with the family to Minnesota (see Doc. 63) would be just as problematic as the planned trip to Colorado. See Doc. 72 and Doc. 72, fn. 21; "Minnesota Reports 86 New Polio Cases," in: *The New York Times* from August 6, 1946, p. 21; "Polio Cases Reach 706 In Minnesota. 46 Added in Day to Year's Total – Woodring Says Curare Cured His Daughter," in: *The New York Times* from August 7, 1946, p. 28; "660 Polio Cases Listed In Minnesota Epidemic," in: *New York Herald Tribune*, European Edition, from August 7, 1946, p. 4.

Monday I cleaned out my desk. Col. Glaser had me to dinner with his wife and with Col. Howley[41] and his wife[42], and the English representative[43] on the Local Gov[ernmen]t Committee[44] who wanted my signature on his specially prepared copy of the Berlin Constitution which he is going to present to the Museum of the 5th Royal Engineers[45] I think it was. It was not an especially encouraging farewell dinner. Col. Glaser has admitted to me that his wife was difficult, and that I could see. Mrs. Howley, much like the Colonel, admitted that she was being utterly spoiled here with so much elegance, and so many servants. I wish we had better people to represent M[ilitary] G[overnment] in Berlin. By better I mean unadvertising and able to get closer to the Germans.

I tried to do good-byes yesterday but didn't have much luck. Frau Donneck, my German secretary had beautiful dahlias on my desk. I saw Mr. Muccio[46] and Brewster Morris[47]. Louis Wiesner[48] was out of town. Lloyd Steere[49] was very cordial and wanted me to stop in Washington and talk with people there. Mr. Murphy[50] was not in town. General Clay[51] was not in town. General Adcock[52] was not in town. Walter Dorn[53] was not in town. I had a very nice talk with General Keating[54] who is definitely on the ball. I also saw Col. Howley again. They were trying desperately to get up some kind of a citation for me, legion of merit, or ribbon of merit, or some such thing but there were some technical difficulties. Instead they are going to write a letter to the new Chancellor[55]

41 See Doc. 20, fn. 18.

42 Edith Howley, née Cadwallader (1910–1985), 1930 BS in Ed, University of Pennsylvania, 1930–1935 teacher, Springfield Township High School, Montgomery County, Pennsylvania, 1962 MLS, Rutgers University, as of 1962 librarian.

43 Probably refers to Harold Hays. See Doc. 49, fn. 26.

44 Local Government Committee, Allied Kommandatura Berlin. See Doc. 29, fn. 14.

45 Probably refers to the Royal Engineers Museum in Gillingham, Kent, Great Britain. According to information from the Royal Engineers Museum from June 24, 2009, the copy of the constitution is not found among the museum's holdings. The copy is also not included in the Lieutenant Colonel Harold Hays MBE Collection, maintained by the IWM Duxford. In an email to Werner Breunig from June 30, 2009, from the IWM Duxford, Department of Documents, archivist Stephen Walton writes that the collection unfortunately does "not include a copy of the Provisional Constitution – in his memoirs Hays writes that 'My colleagues and I [on the Committee] were quite frankly jubilant with the result. This was the greatest individual measure ever agreed by the Allied Kommandatura to date. We gleefully signed copies of the documents for each other as mementos …' – there is, however, no further reference to these signed copies. I am unable to say what might have happened to the copy signed by Johnson."

46 See Doc. 20, fn. 21.

47 See Doc. 31, fn. 13.

48 See Doc. 8, fn. 11.

49 Loyd V. Steere. See Doc. 20, fn. 23.

50 See Doc. 8, fn. 13.

51 See Doc. 2, fn. 6.

52 See Doc. 14, fn. 9.

53 See Doc. 2, fn. 10.

54 See Doc. 39, fn. 6.

55 Reuben G. Gustavson. See Doc. 49, fn. 79.

about me.[56] I guess they are really grateful for what I tried to do. I said goodbye to Sanow who could not be with me the last two days because of more difficulties with the car.

About the middle of the afternoon I went out to the Club[57] to pack, distributed some cigarettes to those who had been kind to me there, left some PX[58] supplies for my driver, and made for the station at 6:00. The train left at 6:32 and we had to sit up all night. I have developed a very bad back (may be its sacro-iliac) which I think will also be over by the time I see you. Conditions are rather crude at this. Staying one-thousands waiting to go home. But not so bad as Camp Home-Run[59].

It is the 7th. It is almost certain that I shall be here three or four days. I think it is equally certain that the boat will take at least ten days to New York. I don't think you'd better wait for me in Lincoln[60]. Get away as soon as possible and I'll join you there[61]. I am longing to be with you, and it will certainly be before the end of the 3 weeks. I love my very sweet ones very much. Kisses to them. Edgar

Doc. 81
Letter to His Wife
Bremerhaven[1], August 9, 1946

Sweetheart –

Still here but things are moving. The processing is complete today with baggage inspection, currency control, and physical examination. We get orders and tickets this afternoon. But I don't suppose we shall actually get on the boat until tomorrow. That is the 10th. Someone remarked here that it takes the boat

56 A letter to Gustavson from August 8, 1946, suggested for General Lucius D. Clay's signature can be found in: LAB, B Rep. 036-01 (Office of Military Government, Berlin Sector [OMGBS]), 4/135-2/14. On July 29, 1946, Keating sent this message to Clay: "1. Dr. Johnson has done a great personal service for me and important work for Military Government in Berlin during his short stay at the Office of Military Government, Berlin District. 2. The Berlin constitution was a difficult, complicated task for which he deserves great credit. In view of the fact that he has been under my command too short a time for the commendation ribbon, it's recommended that he be given this commendation or some other one by your office which he has served for more than six months." LAB, B Rep. 036-01 (Office of Military Government, Berlin Sector [OMGBS]), 4/136-1/9.

57 Refers to the Wannsee Officers' Club, Am Sandwerder 17/19. See Doc. 25, fn. 9.

58 Post Exchange, retail store on US Army posts.

59 In Le Havre. See Doc. 13 and Doc. 13, fn. 8.

60 Capital of the US state of Nebraska, where Johnson lived with his family and taught at the university.

61 Refers to the resort in the Rocky Mountains in the US state of Colorado where Johnson was planning to vacation with his family upon return.

1 See Doc. 71, fn. 10.

eight or nine days to get across. It is a so-called Victory Ship[2]. "Colby-Victory."[3] If she really makes it that quickly there is some chance that I'll make it in time to leave with you on the 21st for Meeker Park[4]. I do not actually have to go to Washington. Lloyd Steere[5] asked me to go in order to talk with Riddleberger[6] and General Hilldring[7] especially. My friend from Austrian days is now in Washington – Joe Gray[8], taking over Erhardt's[9] former job as personnel manager for the State Department. He would be the man to see about a job. I learn that Francis Cunningham, Jr.[10], is taking over the Scandinavian desk in the department, and that my very good friend Charlie Thayer[11] is taking over the Southern European desk. But I don't want to see them. Nor do I think that this is especially the time to go looking about for a job. After all I am committed to go back to the University, and that means, at least, for about a year. If at the end of that time I don't seem to have settled down in the University, and we think I ought to look for something else, I can always go to Washington and inquire. Lloyd wanted me to talk about my impressions of Berlin and Germany but this I can put down in some form of writing. So if there is any chance of getting to you on time I shall just skip Washington. But I've got to stop over in Chicago – possibly to see Biddy[12], certainly to see Auntie[13], Dad[14], Mildred[15], and, if it can be managed, Paul Sweet[16]. I should hope this wouldn't take longer

2 Victory ships were transport ships that had been built in the USA during the Second World War, produced in large numbers within a short time using standardized design. Victory Ships were the further development of Liberty ships (see Doc. 2), outperforming the latter in speed and range.

3 The ship, named after Colby College in Waterville in the US state of Maine, had arrived in Bremerhaven on August 5, 1946. It set sail again on August 11. See vol. 2 of Hafenverkehrsbücher Bremerhaven, Überseehäfen und Columbuskaje – Seeschifffahrt, in: Staatsarchiv Bremen (StAB), Germany, 4,72/2-57. The ship reached New York on August 20, 1946. See "Hospital Ship With 414 Patients To Arrive Today," in: *The Washington Post* from August 21, 1946, p. 3; "Marine and Aviation Reports," in: *The New York Times* from August 19, 1946, p. 39.

4 See Doc. 68, fn. 3.

5 Loyd V. Steere. See Doc. 20, fn. 23.

6 See Doc. 8, fn. 2.

7 See Doc. 2, fn. 4.

8 Cecil W. (Joe) Gray (1898–1983), American diplomat, 1920 BA, Roanoke College, as of 1923 Department of State, 1944–1946 Counselor of Mission, Office of US Political Adviser on Austrian Affairs, Commanding General, US Army Forces, Mediterranean Theater, as of April 1946 Chief, Division of Foreign Service Personnel in the Washington, D. C., department, as of 1948 Consul General, Paris.

9 See Doc. 20, fn. 30.

10 H. Francis Cunningham Jr. (1912–1999) from Lincoln, Nebraska, American diplomat, 1933 BA, University of Nebraska, 1938–1969 Department of State, June 1946–1948 Division of Northern European Affairs, 1957–1959 Consul General, Bonn.

11 Charles W. Thayer. See Doc. 33, fn. 25.

12 Alice D. Bickford, née Dean (born 1864), mother of John D. Bickford (see Doc. 14, fn. 3).

13 Hannah Walstrom. See Doc. 4, fn. 14.

14 Frank E. Johnson. See Doc. 3, fn. 12.

15 Mildred H. Williams. See Doc. 4, fn. 12.

16 See Doc. 2, fn. 28, and Doc. 63, fn. 10.

than a day. In case of severe difficulties I can try to fly some of the way, say from Chicago to Omaha[17] which would some considerable. In any case if it is so close, you might hold over for a day. If for no other reason I think I could be of some help with the kids. The papers here are now full of the Minnesota[18] polio epidemic, as if the Colorado[19] one were dying down.[20] I hope so. It would be more than we can stand to have anything happen to either of the boys because we decided to spend a little time in Colorado.

I am loafing here quite easily. I did read some articles in Life[21] by Dulles[22] concerning what our policy in re Russia should be, and while the first one was good as an analysis of the problem, the second on what we should do about it seemed none too helpful.[23] He suggests making it plain to the Russians that we believe that our democratic principles are of divine origin. I am not so sure this will impress them. If we can't do more than he says then we have already lost to Russia. I have also read here Carl Van Doren's[24] book on Liberal Education[25], a sort of modified Hutchins[26] – Buchanan[27] treatment of the problem.[28] It did put me in the frame of mind of considering students again. His big point is, I think, the one Sherlock[29] made when he read his paper before some club or meeting that we

17 City in the US state of Nebraska, northeast of Johnson's home in Lincoln.

18 US state.

19 US state.

20 See Doc. 80 and Doc. 80, fn. 40; "660 Stricken by Polio In Minnesota Epidemic," in: *The Stars and Stripes*, European Edition, from August 8, 1946, p. 4.

21 American magazine.

22 John Foster Dulles (1888–1959), American lawyer and politician (Republican Party), 1911 LLB, The George Washington University Law School, 1911–1949 member of the New York law firm Sullivan & Cromwell (as of 1926 Senior Partner), 1919 member of the American peace delegation in Paris, 1945 US delegate at the founding conference of the United Nations and at subsequent General Assemblies, 1951 special envoy significantly involved in the signing of the Treaty of Peace with Japan, 1953–1959 US Secretary of State.

23 See John Foster Dulles, "Thoughts on Soviet Foreign Policy and What To Do About It," in: *Life* from June 3, 1946, pp. 112–126 (Part I), and from June 10, 1946, pp. 118–130 (Part II).

24 Refers not to Carl Van Doren (1885–1950), but rather his brother Mark Van Doren (1894–1972), American writer, 1920 PhD, Columbia University, taught from 1920–1959 at Columbia University, as of 1942 as Full Professor of English.

25 *Liberal Education*, New York 1943.

26 Robert M. Hutchins (1899–1977), American lawyer and educator, 1921 BA, Yale University, 1925 LLB, Yale Law School, 1927–1929 Professor of Law, Yale Law School, 1929 LLD, West Virginia University, 1929–1945 President, University of Chicago, 1945–1951 Chancellor, University of Chicago.

27 Scott M. Buchanan (1895–1968), American philosophy professor and educator, founder of the Great Books Program at St. John's College, Annapolis, Maryland (see fn. 32), 1925 PhD, Harvard University, 1929–1936 Professor of Philosophy, University of Virginia, 1936/1937 University of Chicago (appointed by Robert M. Hutchins to help in the creation of a Committee on Liberal Arts), 1937–1946 Dean, St. John's College.

28 See Mary Ann Dzuback, *Robert M. Hutchins. Portrait of an Educator*, Chicago and London 1991.

29 Sherlock B. Gass. See Doc. 63, fn. 29.

attended, (Rosenlof[30] presided you remember + spoke on obituaries) viz., that in American there is no large and common basis of ideas that the teacher or writer can take for granted is present in every cultivated mind. He therefore recommends the St. John's[31] curriculum[32] – the best books notion. I shall have to introduce a little of that in my culture course[33] this year. As a result of the loafing the stomach is better and also the back. I took a little walk yesterday.

My thoughts, however, are really centering upon one thing only – upon you first of all whom I have not seen now for seven months, and upon John, soon to be 7,[34] and upon Thomas, now over 2[35] – and how quickly I can get to you. The world of larger affairs has faded from my mind for the time being – first, because in this kind of a set-up there is no point in it (going through the mill is dreadful on the ego), and second, because it is really behind me this time. At present I'm just anonymous. But I am making for you and the boys. I love you with all my heart and soon hope to be able to demonstrate this with something more than words. Edgar

Doc. 82
Letter to His Wife
Bremerhaven[1], August 9, 1946

Dearest –

It's all very sad here at the present moment. Just as we completed our processing yesterday a notice was put on the bulletin board saying that the War Department had ordered that no civilians in its employ were to travel on Victory Ships[2]. We were scheduled to go off tomorrow on a Victory Ship, and now of course we are not going. Nobody seems to know the reason for this order. Whether, that is, it is because civilians who have gone home on these Victory Ships have complained so much, or whether, as was suggested by a Colonel this morning, it has to do with the cost of transportation home. It is a most extraordinarily arbitrary thing to do. Not only to make it applicable without further notice but to make it retroactive to include those who was already booked for

30 George W. Rosenlof (1891–1974), American educationalist, 1929 PhD, Columbia University, Registrar, University Examiner, and Director of Admissions, Professor of Secondary Education (Secretary of the Faculties and of the University Senate), University of Nebraska.

31 St. John's College in Annapolis, Maryland, since 1964 second campus in Santa Fe, New Mexico, founded in 1696 as a preparatory school, King William's School, since 1784 St. John's College.

32 Since 1937, St. John's College follows an unusual curriculum, the Great Books Program, based on works of Western philosophy and literature.

33 Refers to a course at the University of Nebraska.

34 Son John (see Doc. 2, fn. 15) was born on September 15, 1939.

35 Son Thomas (see Doc. 2, fn. 16) was born on July 8, 1944.

1 See Doc. 71, fn. 10.

2 See Doc. 81, fn. 2.

passage. Just another horrible example of the danger of inconsiderate bureaucracy. Well I went to see the Commanding Officer of this Port, a nice Colonel Pirtle[3], who called in another Colonel. They tried to get an exemption made in Frankfurt[4] for those civilians who were scheduled to go tomorrow but to no avail. It now appears that there is a ship in port that is not a Victory Ship, the Marine Robin[5]. It appears also that civilians may sail on it. But when it is to sail nobody knows whether that is before or after many more victory ships have sailed. These ships can't sail empty, and there are not enough troops here at present to fill them rapidly. The Robin carries some 2000 troops. If Victory Ships go off before she does, they will have to wait before enough troops pile up to fill her before she can go. So I don't know when I am going to get away. The other possibility is to hire passage on a commercial freighter. There is one here that is leaving the 14th, and if the situation doesn't otherwise clear up I may try to get passage on it. It is supposed to make the trip in 10 days but if it is a tramp freighter one doesn't know when it will ever get to America.

If it seems worth it I shall call Clay[6] this afternoon, after consulting more people here.

So don't count on anything. Get off to the mountains on time with some help. I'll come when it is possible to come, and no one knows at the present moment when that will be. It is all very disgusting.

But I love you, my dearest, and my sweet boys. If there is no good chance to get away otherwise, I'll pay my way on this commercial ship. Though so far as the money is concerned, this will be making a present to the government. Edgar

Doc. 83
Report, "Five Months in Berlin"
Typescript, undated

[I]

It had been rather discouraging in Austria the year before. The fine zeal of the Moscow Declaration of November 1943[1] could not undo the essential absurdity

3 James J. Pirtle (1896–1967), Colonel, 1925 BA, Wabash College, Commanding Officer, 3rd Replacement Depot, Bremerhaven Staging Area.

4 Frankfurt am Main, city in the state of Greater Hesse in the American zone of Germany.

5 The American troop ship *Marine Robin* had arrived in Bremerhaven from Shanghai on August 4, 1946. On board the ship were 1,100 Germans who were being returned home after having been interned during the war in China and Singapore. See *Die Neue Zeitung* from August 9, 1946, p. 1 ("Bilder vom Tage"). The ship set sail again on August 15, 1946. See vol. 2 of Hafenverkehrsbücher Bremerhaven, Überseehäfen und Columbuskaje – Seeschifffahrt, in: StAB, 4,72/2-57.

6 See Doc. 2, fn. 6.

1 Moscow Declaration on Austria, signed on November 1, 1943, by the Foreign Ministers of the USA, Soviet Union, and Great Britain. Austria was designated therein as

of imposing upon this little country a quadripartite occupation[2]. For as long as this lasted Austria would necessarily remain a sacrifice to the international rivalry which no clumsy occupational machinery could conceal. The starving and dead at Mauthausen[3], however, had demonstrated that there was much to be done in the country, no matter what the obstacles. The sentences of the Moscow Declaration had been re-inforced by encouraging directives in handbooks of military government, and papers of the State Department. There were some people in positions of authority who took these directives seriously and were impatient to carry them out. In general, however, moral fervor in the support of the simple democratic principles we were supposed to represent, was, in the early days of the occupation, weak. The nasty question always remained, "Did we really, under the circumstances, have anything positive to offer this people?"

When the government of the United States so mutilated the Office of Strategic Services[4] as to render it essentially innocuous, there was nothing to do but to return to the University. It did not seem quite right. There were still voices making themselves heard in American public circles who were talking about winning the peace. The peace was not actually being won in Austria. It might be won elsewhere; perhaps in Germany. At the moment a promising experiment was being inaugurated in the American zone: Bavaria, Baden-Wurttemberg and Greater-Hesse.[5] This was the Länderrat[6], the Council of States, located at Stuttgart[7]. Those in authority in Germany suggested a return to help with this Council. The gluttonous and somewhat gaudy America of the early winter of 1945–46 was a little difficult to absorb. The petty and long-suffering complacency of important elements in a mid-western college community was a little alien to the bleak ruins of Cologne[8] and Kassel[9]. Yet if those in authority in

the first free country to have fallen victim to Adolf Hitler's (see Doc. 22, fn. 19) policy of aggression. The "Anschluss" of Austria into the German Reich from March 1938 was declared null and void. See Richard Hufschmied, "Sonderfall Wien? Die Alliierten und Österreich 1943–1955," in: *Die Vier Mächte in Berlin. Beiträge zur Politik der Alliierten in der besetzten Stadt*, eds. Michael Bienert/Uwe Schaper/Andrea Theissen in collaboration with Werner Breunig (= Schriftenreihe des Landesarchivs Berlin, vol. 9), Berlin 2007, pp. 109–129, here pp. 109f.

2 Due to the absence of an exile government, the Allies had decided to occupy Austria for the time being and to establish a common control system. The Agreement on Control Machinery in Austria (First Control Agreement) from July 4, 1945, passed by the European Advisory Commission in London, provided for the establishment of the Allied Commission for Austria. See ibid., pp. 114f.

3 See Doc. 49, fn. 49.

4 See Doc. 1, fn. 9.

5 In the American zone, the three Länder designated as states, Bavaria, Greater Hesse, and Württemberg-Baden, were formed by Military Government Proclamation No. 2 from September 19, 1945. See *Keesing's Archiv der Gegenwart*, vol. XV (1945), p. 440 A. Text reprint: *Der Länderrat des amerikanischen Besatzungsgebietes*, edited on behalf of the Minister-Presidents of Bavaria, Hesse, Württemberg-Baden and the President of the Senate of the Free Hanseatic City of Bremen by the Directorate of the Länderrat, compiled by Lia Härtel, former Länderrat archivist, Stuttgart and Cologne 1951, pp. 201f.

6 See Doc. 15, fn. 10.

7 Capital of the state of Württemberg-Baden in the American zone of Germany.

8 City in the British zone of Germany.

Germany wished help, those in authority in the War Department at Washington did not know how, in time, to get it where it was needed. At the moment of the return to Germany it had long been necessary to send someone else to Stuttgart. The generals were, I am afraid, a little puzzled over what to do with me when I arrived.

It was to have been via plane. It was explained, however, at the last moment that demobilization had so crippled the ground forces that it was impossible to maintain sufficient planes in the air. Accordingly it must be via the George W. Goethals[10]. There had been talk of hunger and starvation in Europe. I knew indeed that I had detected starvation on the ashen faces of the Viennese. Except for its small contingent of civilians, however, and for the supply of baby equipment which was to administer to the comfort and necessity of returning French brides, the boat was empty.

These civilians were the people who were going to Germany to assist in winning the peace.[11] There were those who were high-minded and earnest, aware of the difficulties of the problem and of the awful import of its outcome. A few of these were Germans who had taken refuge with us from the land they were now hoping to rescue.[12] Many of those in a similar category, whom one met or later heard of in Germany, did their rescue work in a fashion contrary to the principles and methods of the America of their adoption, embarrassing their country and making more difficult its occupational task. The professor of administrative law at the University of Chicago[13] was not one of these.[14] He was to be responsible on the American side for the elimination of Nazism from German law. The amount of additional good he did in eliminating from German minds unfortunate prejudices about Americans, it would be difficult to measure. There were American academics on board who had not yet had their opportunity of participating very actively in the cause of their country. The very roly-poly professor of economics[15] in a California women's college[16], for example, who was as suspicious as one of his good nature could be of the ultimate feasibility of the occupation of Germany. There were specialist civil servants summoned from Washington for their expert opinion on particular phases of the occupation. The New York road builder[17] who had to inspect the bridges and roads of our zone, and who, when he was through, foretold disaster for efficient military transportation if material for surfacing these roads were not imported from the United States in great abundance. The specialist in administration of whom all empire builders had to beware before they could staff their

9 City in the state of Greater Hesse in the American zone of Germany.

10 USAT *George W. Goethals*. See Doc. 7, fn. 18.

11 Refers to civil employees of the American military government in Germany.

12 Refers to Germans who had found refuge in the USA during the Nazi period, who were returning to Germany as employees and advisers of the American military government.

13 University in Chicago, Illinois, founded in 1890.

14 Refers to the emigrant Max Rheinstein (see Doc. 11, fn. 22), who was on board.

15 Glenn E. Hoover. See Doc. 9, fn. 10.

16 Mills College in Oakland, California.

17 William J. Anderson. See Doc. 9, fn. 8.

branches and divisions with the improper number of high civil service ratings. There were also the opportunists and adventurers, the gravy lappers, who were concerned with leaves, how long they would have to work, and how much they would get paid for overtime, husky-throated, hard-faced women among them. Some of these had been well instructed in the possibilities of the black market[18] abroad, and came well supplied with the articles they knew would sell for handsome prices. I saw one of these again in Paris.[19] He was flushed with his first successful deal on the black market. I saw him the day after he arrived in Berlin. He displayed to me the first fruits of his operations on the Berlin black market. It was jewelry which some poor German had felt obliged to exchange for his cigarettes or his chocolate.[20] These Germans, ruined middle class families or old retired heads of families deprived of their pensions, assembled in such numbers about places where Americans congregated that special guards were established to drive them off. These were not exactly, in spite of the excellence of a few, the best Americans who could have been chosen to assist in winning the peace. The best Americans, it appeared, were not that interested in winning the peace.

If Mauthausen had been an incentive to work in Austria, the German scientist aboard the Goethals was a similar incentive to work in Germany. He was a young man whom, together with many of his kind, we had picked up after the close of hostilities and sent to work on rockets and remote control projectiles in Maryland[21]. He was not indeed the worst kind of a Nazi scientist. He said he had never joined the Party[22] despite all the pressure to which he had been subjected. He held indeed the reassuring opinion, which I had always held, that it was actually never necessary for anyone to join the Party. Yet he was that worst kind of a scientist who, with perfect amorality, was willing to prostitute his talents for any political cause. He had worked on V-1 and V-2[23]. He was a leader in the research at Peenemünde[24]. He could talk exultantly about the great "progress" made when V-2 supplanted V-1. His imagination leaped into the future. There was not reason why, in a few years, rockets should not be carrying passengers across the Atlantic in forty minutes. They would, in fact, soon be able to circle the earth in continuous rounds. He had had, however, to pay his

18 See Doc. 21, fn. 11.

19 See Doc. 21.

20 See Doc. 27, fn. 10.

21 US state. The Naval Ordnance Laboratory was located in White Oak, Maryland.

22 Refers to the Nationalsozialistische Deutsche Arbeiterpartei (NSDAP).

23 Vergeltungswaffe 1 and Vergeltungswaffe 2, weapon systems that were developed during the Second World War in National Socialist Germany for "Vergeltung" (vengeance) against Allied air strikes on German cities. The V-1 cruise missile was first fired at London in June 1944, and the liquid-feuled ballistic missile V-2 was used beginning in September 1944. See Walter Dornberger, *Peenemünde. Die Geschichte der V-Waffen*, with a preface by Eberhard Rees, Huntsville/Alabama, Eßlingen 1981.

24 Municipality on the Baltic Sea island of Usedom. In 1936 an army research center ("Peenemünde-Ost") was established here, expanded in 1938 with the Luftwaffe test site, "Peenemünde-West." While the liquid-feuled ballistic missile V-2 was being developed in Peenemünde-Ost, the Luftwaffe was testing the cruise missile V-1 in Peenemünde-West. See ibid.

price with personal tragedy. His wife was awaiting him for burial in the cold darkness of a mortuary. She had contracted pneumonia on a voyage from the British zone to Frankfurt[25] to learn why, after his removal to the States, she had never heard from him. In the Germany he had really helped to destroy he would have to begin anew, and find a place for his two children. There is no doubt that he will be able to do so. Scientists of his training are at a premium with the occupiers. Scientists, too, of his training would be used not only by the kind of Germany which would arise if the peace were won, but also by the kind of Germany which could arise if the peace were lost.

When the Goethals tumbled its civilians into the capacious lap of OMGUS (Office of Military Government U. S.)[26] in Berlin, this headquarters was about to gather into its bosom a child it had never learned quite how to control, the headquarters for the military government of the American zone[27] at Frankfurt. While the advantages of consolidation could be seen, it was not so easy to understand why the consolidation should not have been made at Frankfurt rather than Berlin. To be sure there was necessary quadripartite business to be done at Berlin, but to control the military government of the American zone more effectively, moving into, rather than away from the zone might seem more satisfactory. Those who were actually directing the military government of the zone from the local capitals might welcome this remote control, regard it even as an enhancement of the efficiency of military government itself. The distance from Berlin, however, made it easier for officials to remain isolated there, and to feel the necessity for an old Carolingian institution, the missi dominici[28].

Yet the amalgamation in Berlin enlarged the American family which gathered for work each morning the building clustering around Kronprinzenallee[29] and Saargemünderstrasse[30].[31] This community, situated pleasantly in the midst of its tulip beds was fast taking on the nature of a university campus, an army post, or a missionary compound. Removed from the actualities of the zone, this little region in Dahlem[32] was almost as far removed from the actualities of Berlin, the Tiergarten transformed into a vegetable garden,[33] the dead streets from which nobody had ever yet tried to extricate the dead, the millions of shabby and hungry Berliners, who, somehow, still managed to make the city their habitation. Nobody could say that these Americans were not being well

25 Frankfurt am Main, city in the state of Greater Hesse in the American zone of Germany.

26 See Doc. 17, fn. 45.

27 Refers to OMGUSZ in Frankfurt am Main, which had the task of carrying out policies determined by OMGUS in the American zone. When OMGUSZ was dissolved, these tasks were transferred to OMGUS, with minor exceptions. See Doc. 15, fn. 32.

28 See Doc. 24, fn. 17.

29 In Berlin-Dahlem. Since 1949 the street has been called Clayallee.

30 Saargemünder Straße, Berlin-Dahlem.

31 Refers to the grounds in Berlin-Dahlem where OMGUS had its offices. See Doc. 17, fn. 45.

32 Area in the Berlin administrative district of Zehlendorf.

33 The largest park in Berlin, located in the district of the same name, was used by the hungry population to grow vegetables.

taken care of. It cannot be assumed that, except for a few in very responsible positions, they were over-worked. American food was abundantly available in attractive messing centers. It was not necessary to eat without the accompaniment of a German orchestra, or without the stimulation of preparatory cocktails, served, as in the Harnack House[34], in the atmosphere of a sophisticated metropolitan cocktail lounge. For awhile all Americans seemed to be going around with bottles under their arms. There were few forms of entertainment in which one could not indulge. There was the Russian directed opera and orchestra,[35] the lively theatre, the art exhibits and the night clubs. There were horses to canter through the Grunewald[36]. The Wannsee[37] on week-ends was gaily covered with a great variety of sailing and motor craft, confiscated from the Germans who were now confined to bathing on a portion of the Strandbad[38], and serviced by the various yacht clubs.

Nobody from the lowliest to the high could complain about quarters. We had simply taken over the best available, and could not be bothered much about the political histories of those we obliged to get out. The professor of administrative law[39] on the boat found himself sharing a house[40] which belonged to a distinguished German cellist[41], who because of his Jewish wife[42], had been harassed by the Nazis.[43] With his five children[44] he had moved into an adjoining bombed-out house[45] where he had been offered American supplies at black market prices by the very American officer who was responsible for his withdrawal. The professor invited him back, not to re-occupy his house but to participate in social gatherings at which Americans and Germans were present. And this distinguished cellist (Max Baldner of the Klinger Quartet[46]) brought his Stradivarius[47] and played for his American expropriators in his own house, in order, as he hoped, to help bridge the chasm between Germans and Americans.

34 See Doc. 15, fn. 16.
35 Refers to the Deutsche Staatsoper and its orchestra. Because the Staatsoper's building on Unter den Linden was destroyed, the Admiralspalast, Friedrichstraße 101/102 in the district of Mitte, became the permanent venue in August 1945.
36 A woodland area of around 3,000 hectares that encompasses large areas of the districts of Wilmersdorf (British sector) and Zehlendorf (American sector), as well as a small part of Charlottenburg (British sector), east of the lower Havel (see Doc. 74, fn. 24).
37 Refers to Großer Wannsee, a bight of the Havel (see Doc. 74, fn. 24) in southwest Berlin.
38 Strandbad Wannsee, a public beach on the eastern shore of Großer Wannsee.
39 Max Rheinstein. See Doc. 11, fn. 22.
40 Podbielskiallee 65. See Doc. 21, fn. 17.
41 Max Baldner. See Doc. 21, fn. 18.
42 Charlotte Baldner, née Lindemann. See Doc. 21, fn. 21.
43 See Doc. 21, fn. 22.
44 Max Baldner had four children. See Doc. 21, fn. 24. The fifth child was not a member of the family. See Doc. 25, fn. 44.
45 Podbielskiallee 57. See Doc. 21, fn. 25.
46 Klingler Quartet. See Doc. 21, fn. 19.
47 See Doc. 38, fn. 15.

The very important people lived in the houses of the very important people of the preceding era in a atmosphere of what would have to be described as elegant luxury. The large electrically operated plate glass windows which opened the living rooms into the gardens were a sign of rank. The Wannsee region was among the most select. I was permitted to occupy quarters in the Wannsee Officers' Club[48], operated for the officers of Berlin District. It had formerly been the abode of the Nazi Minister of Economics, Mr. Funk[49], who now occupies quarters of an entirely different character at Nürnberg[50]. Mr. Funk, the gardener[51] explained, and gardeners like bureaucrats have a nice ability to survive all regimes, had acquired it from a Jewish banker[52] now in Holland[53], who, in turn, after the last war[54], had acquired it from a British member[55] of the Reparations Commission[56]. If its architecture was insignificant, it did afford commodious and even opulent services. "This," asserted the officer in charge, a genial yachting enthusiast, "is the best mess in Berlin." I never had any reason to doubt it. Elegant food served by a corps of professional waiters from some of Berlin's best hotels. You could have German and French champagne with dinner, served in the proper ice-containers. The grounds were beautifully landscaped, and the flower gardens supplied gorgeous blooms, plucked and arranged by a special member of the staff. The exotic lavender rhododendrons were followed by tall spikes of blue delphinium, these in turn by the roses and the snapdragons. Over the air-raid shelter the gardener grew his lettuce, his spinach and his beans. In the garden, not far to the right of the swimming pool on the front lawn, he grew his fruit. The lawn itself, kept carefully groomed, sloped down to the lake. Of a late evening you could find fishing from the pier, to which came every afternoon a motor launch for the use of the guests of the club, the melancholy pastry cook who had once had his own shops in Sofia[57] and Constantinople[58]. On this pier one could sit, suffering the humiliation of being bitten by German mosquitoes, gazing into the western skies across the lake as a usually magnificent sun descended, thinking about winning the peace and the formation of a new group of American colonial governors.

Into this bountiful life the dependents were coming.[59] At the Officers' Club the shrieks of a young daughter, protesting so violently against the unaccus-

48 Am Sandwerder 17/19 in the Berlin administrative district of Zehlendorf, Wannsee area. See Doc. 25, fn. 9.

49 See Doc. 25, fn. 10.

50 Nuremberg, city in the state of Bavaria in the American zone of Germany. Funk and other defendants in the trial of major war criminals were being held in the prison of the Nuremberg Palace of Justice.

51 Albert Redmann. See Doc. 47, fn. 4.

52 Hans Arnhold. See Doc. 47, fn. 7.

53 See Doc. 47, fn. 9.

54 Refers to the First World War (1914–1918).

55 Marcel Hardy. See Doc. 47, fn. 6.

56 The Allied Reparations Commission had dealt with the assessment and supervision of reparations to be paid by the German Reich.

57 Capital of Bulgaria.

58 Former name for Istanbul, Turkish city on the Bosphorus.

59 On April 30, 1946, the first wives and children of members of the American occupation forces arrived in Berlin. See Doc. 42, fn. 13.

tomed elegance of her surroundings that her embarrassed mother had to carry her from the room, broke upon the calm of the diners. It was, however, now no more difficult for them than it had been previously for their husbands. Indeed they were frank to admit that it was much less difficult than it had been at home. High ranking officers gave purpose to their lives in organizing the forces and equipment necessary to do over quarters for the family that was about to arrive. In some instances the stuffy furniture of an old mansion had to be replaced with its stream-lined equivalent even if the continent had to be scoured to do it. In others, the plan of a too militaristically conceived formal garden had to be modified along more democratic lines. In spite of the efforts of some wives to create one, there was no servant problem. There were more cooks and maids, more chauffeurs and gardeners, and of course more governesses than had ever been made available to these people before. They admitted and liked it. It was something of a relief to come from a troubled environment where there were such things as strikes, to the serenity of Dahlem, Zehlendorf or Wannsee[60]. If it was to continue like this they would be prepared to stay a long time. Some women were worried about their figures under such an easy routine. Others felt the danger of being completely spoiled with such complete staffs. Yet the organization of the Berlin Women's Club[61], with departments calculated to fit any interest from bridge to porcelain, promised to relieve whatever boredom might be in store with so much leisure time, even if it did not bring the women into any closer contact with German Berlin. Indeed this closer contact was at the moment not encouraged. In the American zone the American Military Communities[62] were protected from the Germans by fences and forbidding rolls of barbed wire.[63] Some Germans were sensitive about this. Some, whose empty houses stood within, were bitter. In Frankfurt, the American compound behind its barbed-wire was even called, 'the Ghetto of the Pharisees'[64].

II

Beyond this pleasant American world was Berlin. There could be no doubt that this city was still the most important in Germany even if the French were considerably annoyed when a local newspaper, for reasons other than the fact, adopted as part of its masthead the phrase *Zeitung der Hauptstadt Deutschlands*.[65] From the point of view of what was going on here, it was even the most important city in Europe. From the point of view of the struggle between East and West it was one of the most fascinating, if discouraging, focal points in the world. It was still the capital of Germany in the minds not only of the Berliners,

60 Areas in the Berlin administrative district of Zehlendorf.

61 Refers to the American Women's Club of Berlin. See Doc. 68, fn. 31.

62 See Doc. 79, fn. 31.

63 See Doc. 79.

64 See Doc. 79, fn. 33.

65 The daily newspaper published by the Berlin district committee of the SED, *Vorwärts. Berliner Volksblatt*, had as its second subtitle *Das Abendblatt der Hauptstadt Deutschlands*.

but of those outside of Berlin who suffered from the isolation imposed by the four zones. The political parties organized here[66] did not regard themselves as anything other than parts of the national parties. No political convention was limited to members from Berlin, or to members from Berlin and the enveloping Russian Zone. 'Guests' from all the zones were invited and came whenever it was possible. It was clear to an outsider who attended such conventions that the chief joy of the German participants was to feel reunited again in an assembly consisting of Germans from all over the Reich. If in such an assembly a capable orator spoke movingly of the sufferings and tragedy of the fatherland, he could easily reduce his audience to tears. If, in such a gathering, the guest from Bavaria, a roughly-hewn native son (Josef Müller[67], the leader of the Christian Social Union[68]) spoke of the desirability of Berlin and Bavaria's acting together, he called forth a dramatic response not necessarily to be expected from a Berlin audience for a Bavarian.[69] With Germany so obviously and variously atomized, the exhibition of any kind of a partial unity was the occasion for unwonted excitement.

If Berlin was still in the German mind the capital of the Reich, it was even more interesting to speculate whether Berlin was actually to become again the capital of the Russian zone. As it was Berlin was an international island in the Russian sea, or if you would believe some Germans, an international oasis in the Russian desert. Before the inauguration of the quadripartite government of the city, the Kommandatura[70], Berlin had actually been the capital of the Russian Zone.[71] In abandoning Berlin as a military objective to pursue the Wehrmacht[72] elsewhere,[73] we had permitted the Russians to execute the plans for the government of the city that they had long worked out with the Free Germany Committee[74]. The leading

66 The parties initially permitted in Berlin were the KPD, SPD, CDU, and LDP. See Doc. 20, fn. 12 and 13, Doc. 21, fn. 29, and Doc. 44, fn. 10. After the merger of the KPD and SPD into the SED, the SED as well as the SPD newly constituted by opponents of the merger were recognized in Berlin.

67 See Doc. 80, fn. 19.

68 See Doc. 80, fn. 16.

69 Müller had taken part as a guest in the party conference of the CDU for the Soviet zone and Berlin, which took place in Berlin from June 15–17, 1946. See *Berlin. Kampf um Freiheit und Selbstverwaltung 1945–1946*, edited on behalf of the Senate of Berlin (= Schriftenreihe zur Berliner Zeitgeschichte, vol. 1), revised and supplemented second edition, Berlin 1961, p. 459, no. 31. It cannot be determined from Johnson's letters whether he attended the party conference.

70 See Doc. 20, fn. 11.

71 After the end of the war, Berlin had been under the exclusive control of Soviet occupation forces for two months, until the arrival of the Western powers. During this time the city effectively belonged to the Soviet zone of Germany.

72 The armed forces of Nazi Germany.

73 Towards the end of the war, the Americans had decided to leave the conquest of Berlin to Soviet armed foces; Anglo-American armed forces were to defeat remaining German forces south of Berlin and join the Soviets near Dresden. See Jean E. Smith, *Der Weg ins Dilemma. Preisgabe und Verteidigung der Stadt Berlin*, Berlin 1965, pp. 42–59.

74 Founded in 1943, the National Committee "Freies Deutschland" was an organization of German prisoners of war and Communist emigrants, supported by the Soviet gov-

officials in this government, trained in Russia, were ready at hand when the conquest of the city was complete.[75] When, accordingly, the Magistrate was set up[76] it contained such men as Bürgermeister Maron[77], who was to do the actual governing of the city while Oberbürgermeister Werner[78], whom everybody know to be a kind of nincompoop, made the speeches and stopped to bow in deferential acknowledgement whenever he was applauded. The president of the police, Marquard[79], was also a Russian trained Communist. The head of the department of personnel[80] was the son of Wilhelm Pieck[81], the venerable if somewhat empty-headed Communist leader who had spent his last years of exile in Russia. To-

ernment. Its task was to win over German soldiers on the front for the fight against the NS regime, and also to deploy captured soldiers and officers in the Soviet Union for propaganda purposes. After 1945 many members of the National Committee received key positions in the Soviet zone and in the future GDR. See Bodo Scheurig, *Verräter oder Patrioten. Das Nationalkomitee "Freies Deutschland" und der Bund Deutscher Offiziere in der Sowjetunion 1943–1945*, Berlin and Frankfurt am Main 1993; *Das Nationalkomitee "Freies Deutschland" und der Bund Deutscher Offiziere*, ed. Gerd R. Ueberschär (Die Zeit des Nationalsozialismus. Eine Buchreihe), Frankfurt am Main 1995.

75 The three most important posts in the Magistrat were occupied by Communists who had been trained in the Soviet Union: Karl Maron (see Doc. 74, fn. 37), First Deputy of the Oberbürgermeister, Arthur Pieck (1899–1970), head of the Department of Personnel and Administration, Otto Winzer (1902–1975), head of the Department of Education. Maron and Winzer had returned from Moscow with the "Ulbricht Group." Maron, KPD member since 1925, had lived in the Soviet Union since 1935 and worked as an employee of the press department of the Comintern, and as of 1943 as Deputy Editor-in-Chief of the newspaper of the National Committee "Freies Deutschland." Pieck, who had been a KPD member since 1919, had worked for the press department of the Comintern after his emigration to the Soviet Union, among other jobs; he had become a Soviet citizen in 1938 and acted as an officer in the Political Administration of the Red Army after the German invasion of the Soviet Union. Winzer, who had joined the Kommunistischer Jugendverband Deutschlands in 1919 and the KPD in 1925, had worked until 1935 as an editor and publishing director for Communist newspapers and magazines in Germany and other European countries; he then went to the Soviet Union, where he worked for the Comintern, Foreign Languages Publishing House, Deutscher Volkssender, and as a teacher at an Antifa school.

76 The first postwar Berlin Magistrat, put together by the "Ulbricht Group" and subsequently confirmed by the Soviet Commandant, Colonel General Nikolai Erastovich Berzarin (1904–1945), and by the Commander-in-Chief of the Group of Soviet Occupation Forces in Germany, Marshal of the Soviet Union Georgy Konstantinovich Zhukov (see fn. 155), was publically introduced and officially activated on May 19, 1945. On the establishment of the Magistrat, see *Die Sitzungsprotokolle des Magistrats der Stadt Berlin 1945/46*, part I, *1945*, edited and introduced by Dieter Hanauske (= Schriftenreihe des Landesarchivs Berlin, vol. 2/I), Berlin 1995, pp. 31–48; Werner Breunig, "Berlin 1945/46. Vom Kriegsende bis zum parlamentarischen Neubeginn," in: *"Berlin kommt wieder." Die Nachkriegsjahre 1945/46* (= Ausstellungskataloge des Landesarchivs Berlin, 16), Berlin 2005, pp. 7–43, here pp. 12–17.

77 See Doc. 74, fn. 37.

78 See Doc. 27, fn. 30, and Doc. 39, fn. 23.

79 Paul Markgraf. See Doc. 27, fn. 29.

80 Arthur Pieck. See fn. 75.

81 See Doc. 30, fn. 9.

gether with him came Walter Ulbricht[82], whose German long residence in the Soviet Union[83] had given a slightly Russian accent, trying desperately to look like Lenin[84],[85] an unscrupulous and clever demagogue. So, in a capital city which the Russians had captured, there was installed a central government dominated by men who can be considered as the agents of Russian policy. In the administration appointed to assist them in the central departments and in the districts of the city, it was inevitable that the Communists received a larger percentage of the jobs than their actual strength in the electorate warranted.

When the western Allies were finally admitted into Berlin,[86] and when in accordance with the terms worked out in the European Advisory Commission[87] in London, the Kommandatura was put to work,[88] the character of the Berlin *Magistrat* remained unchanged. The Red Army[89], understandable, would have considered it an unnecessary affront to have suggested that the government of the city would now have to be modified. In point of fact, except for its essentially undemocratic character, it was, as a temporary expedient, hardly as bad as that. In this spirit, and in the desire to get on with the new international control of the city, the western Allies went so far as to approve all that this Berlin gov-

82 See Doc. 39, fn. 24.

83 Ulbricht had lived in the Soviet Union since 1938.

84 See Doc. 39, fn. 25.

85 See Doc. 39, fn. 26.

86 After the withdrawal of Allied troops to their assigned occupation zones had begun on July 1, 1945, the occupation of Berlin's Western sectors by the troops of the Western forces could follow. See Wolfgang Ribbe, *Berlin 1945–2000. Grundzüge der Stadtgeschichte* (= Kleine Schriftenreihe der Historischen Kommission zu Berlin, no. 6), Berlin 2002, pp. 28–30.

87 See Doc. 34, fn. 15.

88 The basis for the common administration of Berlin by the Allies was established by the so-called London Protocol, agreed upon by the European Advisory Commission on September 12, 1944, and supplemented on November 14, 1944, and the so-called London Agreement of November 14, 1944. See "Protokoll zwischen den Vereinigten Staaten, Großbritannien und der Sowjetunion vom 12. September 1944 über die Besatzungszonen in Deutschland und die Verwaltung von Groß-Berlin," in: *Dokumente zur Berlin-Frage 1944–1966*, with a foreword by the Governing Mayor of Berlin, ed. Forschungsinstitut der Deutschen Gesellschaft für Auswärtige Politik e. V., Bonn, in collaboration with the Senate of Berlin (= Schriften des Forschungsinstituts der Deutschen Gesellschaft für Auswärtige Politik e. V., Bonn, Reihe: Internationale Politik und Wirtschaft, vol. 52/I), fourth edition, Munich 1987, Doc. 1; "Abkommen zwischen den Vereinigten Staaten, Großbritannien und der Sowjetunion vom 14. November 1944 über Ergänzungen zu dem Protokoll vom 12. September 1944 über die Besatzungszonen von Deutschland und die Verwaltung von Groß-Berlin" (excerpt), in: ibid., Doc. 2; "Londoner Abkommen vom 14. November 1944 über die Kontrolleinrichtungen in Deutschland in der durch das Ergänzungsabkommen vom 1. Mai 1945 über den Beitritt der Französischen Republik abgeänderten Fassung" (excerpt), in: ibid., Doc. 3. The London Protocol already provided for the establishment of an inter-Allied administrative authority for Berlin (Kommandatura). In the London Agreement it was determined that the Kommandatura would work under the general leadership of the Control Council for Germany (see Doc. 14, fn. 5), and would receive commands from the Coordinating Committee (see Doc. 15, fn. 21).

89 Official designation for the armed forces of the Soviet Union until 1946.

ernment had previously done.[90] It may be questioned whether they knew quite of what they were approving. When they came to understand it in part they were not satisfied with what they had approved. Yet it was difficult, if not impossible, to secure any very fundamental modifications by way of negotiation in the Kommandatura.[91] The only recourse left open to them was to keep close watch on the functioning of the central administration and, if necessary, to place obstacles in its way in their own national sectors of the city. At the moment that these avenues of action became open, the American reduction of the personnel engaged in military government in Berlin was so drastic that it was neither possible to keep close watch on the *Magistrat*, or to keep in close enough contact with what was going on in the American sector of Berlin, a sector whose population is approximately a million[92]. We had one liaison officer at the *Magistrat*[93], and four liaison officers in our six *Verwaltungsbezirke*[94]. What, moreover, had once been approved was somewhat sacred to the Soviet authorities. It was accordingly always a delicate matter to introduce local changes in the districts. It was, too, always a question of how far it was wise to go in breaking up the unity of a politically partial and none too efficient administration of the city. It was always embarrassing to have to admit that the international administration of a city meant it gradual separation into four parts. Yet this meant that the government remained the government which the Russians had set up, and that Berlin, instead of a fifth zone, was still a kind of capital of the Russian zone.

The city was always subject to the pressure of events in the Russian zone. All the central organizations for that zone were still located there.[95] It was no dis-

90 With Order No. 1 from July 11, 1945, the Allied Kommandatura decreed: "Until special notice, all existing regulations and ordinances issued by the Commander of the Soviet Army Garrison and Military Commandant of the City of Berlin, and by the German administration under Allied Control, regulating the order and conduct of the population of Berlin, and also the liability of the population for the violation of such regulations and ordinances, or for unlawful acts against Allied occupation troops, shall remain in force." *Berlin. Kampf um Freiheit und Selbstverwaltung 1945–1946*, edited on behalf of the Senate of Berlin (= Schriftenreihe zur Berliner Zeitgeschichte, vol. 1), revised and supplemented second edition, Berlin 1961, p. 617. The Western forces thus acknowledged structures that originated from the phase of exclusive Soviet occupation.

91 Decisions at all levels of the Allied administration of Berlin could only be made unanimously.

92 See Doc. 61, fn. 13.

93 The Liaison Officer at the Magistrat was Joseph C. Joublanc (1894–1965), Lieutenant Colonel. See Roster of Officers assigned to OMG BD, June 25, 1946, p. 1, in: LAB, B Rep. 036-01 (Office of Military Government, Berlin Sector [OMGBS]), 4/136-1/9.

94 Refers to the Berlin administrative districts (Verwaltungsbezirke) of Steglitz (VBK 1), Zehlendorf (VBK 2), Kreuzberg (VBK 3), Tempelhof (VBK 4), Schöneberg (VBK 5), and Neukölln (VBK 6). In June 1946 the Liaison Officers were Lee H. Burnham, Major (Steglitz), Matthew J. Kasprzycki (1915–1984), Captain (Tempelhof and Neukölln), George F. Pawling, Major (Kreuzberg and Schöneberg), and John A. Sabo, Major (Zehlendorf). See Roster of Officers assigned to OMG BD, June 25, 1946, pp. 1f., in: LAB, B Rep. 036-01 (Office of Military Government, Berlin Sector [OMGBS]), 4/136-1/9.

95 The central administrative offices in the Soviet zone, established on the basis of Order No. 17 of the Supreme Chief of the Soviet Military Administration in Germany

tance at all to the Russian headquarters at Karlshorst[96],[97] and it was no secret that Communist leaders, in and out of the *Magistrat*, went there for instructions. The political parties which had been organized for the Russian zone were identical with those of Berlin.[98] Indeed the leaders of these parties regarded themselves as national and not local leaders. Membership on national, zonal or purely Berlin executive boards was interchangeable. What was done in the Russian zone it was always felt had to be done in Berlin in order to complete or at least to restore the former unity. The zonal organization of the trade unions,[99] with a common governing board for Berlin, always took it for granted that what happened in the zone automatically happened in Berlin as it had before the introduction of quadripartite control. The zonal organization of youth,[100] wedged into the city in the Russian sector, took for granted its final assumption of the leadership of the Berlin youth. The whole press of the city, except finally for the Social Democratic press under English and French license,[101] and the American

from July 27, 1945, were located in the Soviet sector of Berlin. See *Um ein antifaschistisch-demokratisches Deutschland. Dokumente aus den Jahren 1945–1949*, eds. Ministerium für Auswärtige Angelegenheiten der DDR/Ministerium für Auswärtige Angelegenheiten der UdSSR, Berlin 1968, Doc. 32; Wolfgang Ribbe, *Berlin 1945–2000. Grundzüge der Stadtgeschichte* (= Kleine Schriftenreihe der Historischen Kommission zu Berlin, no. 6), Berlin 2002, p. 31.

96 Area in the Berlin district of Lichtenberg.

97 In Order No. 1 of the Supreme Chief of the Soviet Military Administration in Germany from June 9, 1945, it says among other things: "The location of the Soviet Military Administration is the city of Berlin." ("Der Standort der Sowjetischen Militärverwaltung ist die Stadt Berlin.") *Befehle des Obersten Chefs der Sowjetischen Militärverwaltung in Deutschland. Aus dem Stab der Sowjetischen Militärverwaltung in Deutschland*, Sammelheft 1, *1945*, Berlin 1946, p. 9.

98 On June 10, 1945, the Soviets had already allowed the formation and activity of antifascist political parties in their occupation area, the Soviet zone and Berlin. See "Befehl Nr. 2 des Obersten Chefs der Sowjetischen Militärverwaltung in Deutschland vom 10. Juni 1945," in: ibid., pp. 9f.

99 On the Freier Deutscher Gewerkschaftsbund (FDGB), see Doc. 49, fn. 13.

100 On the Freie Deutsche Jugend (FDJ), which emerged from the antifascist youth committees, see Hermann Weber, "Freie Deutsche Jugend (FDJ)," in: *SBZ-Handbuch. Staatliche Verwaltungen, Parteien, gesellschaftliche Organisationen und ihre Führungskräfte in der Sowjetischen Besatzungszone Deutschlands 1945–1949*, on behalf of the Arbeitsbereich Geschichte und Politik der DDR at the University of Mannheim and the Institut für Zeitgeschichte Munich, eds. Martin Broszat/Hermann Weber, Munich 1990, pp. 665–690; Katharina Lange, "Freie Deutsche Jugend (FDJ)," in: *Deutschland unter alliierter Besatzung 1945–1949/55*, ed. Wolfgang Benz, Berlin 1999, pp. 264f.

101 The *Spandauer Volksblatt* was published beginning on March 5, 1946, with the first British newspaper license in Berlin. *Telegraf*, a newspaper licensed by the British military administration and linked to the SPD, was published beginning on March 22, 1946. The Berlin SPD published the daily newspaper *Der Sozialdemokrat* beginning on June 3, 1946, likewise with authorization from the British. *Der Kurier*, an evening paper published beginning on November 12, 1945, had a French license. See *Berlin. Kampf um Freiheit und Selbstverwaltung 1945–1946*, edited on behalf of the Senate of Berlin (= Schriftenreihe zur Berliner Zeitgeschichte, vol. 1), revised and supplemented second edition, Berlin 1961, p. 259, no. 32, p. 378, no. 13, p. 393, no. 71, and p. 452, no. 7.

licensed *Tagesspiegel*[102] was under rigid Russian censorship. Nobody had been able to do anything effective about the Berlin radio[103]. It had always been a matter of astonishment to some observers that after the initiation of quadripartite government this radio remained what it was and where it was. It remained an essentially Russian station whose programs were subject to a kind of censorship which made German artists often furious when they were not more amused. This when Goethe[104] lyrics were interrupted and forbidden as fascist or militaristic. It remained in the *Rundfunkhaus*[105] in the British sector where it had always been, and why, without any change in status or character the British permitted it to remain there, nobody quite understood. It was always the Russian theory that this was a radio originally set up for the Russian zone, and that quadripartite control of the city made no difference.

Thus one had in Berlin the European situation in miniature. In the Russian zone about the city, into which no ordinary mortal thought of trespassing, the Soviet authorities were carrying out long prepared plans for introducing as much of the Soviet system as they could, or preparing by gradual stages for its introduction. There was no doubt about this. My Russian friend told me when I accused him of it that he was not one of those Russians who was so absurd as to think it could be done. The pattern, however, was unmistakable, and the methods, to Germans and western Allies alike, so repugnantly familiar. It was difficult to feel that our Soviet ally, in spite of all her protestations, was much concerned with what happened to Germans or to Germany. It had been the same in Austria where Americans were inclined to take the Moscow Declaration[106] seriously. It was easy from the past to understand this point of view, but to one who had hopes of cultivating a better future, this cynical, one is almost tempted to say unscrupulous realism, was disheartening. If, however, they were not seriously concerned with the German future, they would have the German people believe that they were the only power who was so concerned. Certainly any German future in which they would be interested would have to be within the Russian orbit, and as close to the Communist order as possible. The Germans must be convinced of the necessity, the superiority, and the inevitability of this outcome by the use of every kind of persuasion. The German peasant and working man, the future social foundations of whatever German state there might be, must be weaned from the attraction of American capitalism and English socialism, both associated with certain democratic liberties. In the Russian controlled papers in Berlin, Communist or otherwise, little was left undone to discredit these powers for what they were doing in Germany, at home, or elsewhere in the world. No American who read the Berlin daily press (and there were not enough of them) but who was regularly antagonized by the cynical distortion of the news, and by the abject following of the Russian lead by the German Communists and the Berlin radio.

102 *Der Tagesspiegel* was first published on September 27, 1945. See ibid., p. 202, no. 85.

103 The Berliner Rundfunk, controlled by Soviet occupation forces. See Doc. 58, fn. 19.

104 See Doc. 52, fn. 30.

105 Haus des Rundfunks. See Doc. 58, fn. 19.

106 See fn. 1.

At the same time that in the Russian zone society was being remodeled by the agrarian reform[107], by the dismantling of German industry[108], and by the socialization of remaining industries, formerly belonging to Nazis or war profiteers or those whom local committees decided to expropriate,[109] the attack on the inert, weary, and hungry German mind and body began. The watchword was always unity – *Einheit.* The word that had done more than any one thing to ruin the German people[110] was now dinned into their ears again with such sickening frequency and such hollow mockery that it drove many to seek security in the far removed centuries of the worst feudal anarchy. These wondrously patriotic perorations, these touching appeals to human brotherhood were made to beaten, broken, bent, and bewildered Germans by stooges who were kept fat and sleek by the special gift packages and extra rations of their Soviet paymasters. The belly of Pieck lost none of its bulk, the goatee of Ulbricht none of its trim, the voice of Fechner[111] none of its bark, and the gleam of Grotewohl's[112] eyes nothing but its trustworthiness, as they beat the tom-tom for the Germans to go through their paces.

It was first the unity of unpolitical trade unions preached by a shrewd, exasperating and Communist Jendretsky[113], who preferred to thumb his nose at

107 The agrarian reform improvised in September 1945 under the slogan "Junkerland in Bauernhand" (Junker land into farmer's hands) disempowerd a traditional social and political elite through the expropriation without compensation of private landholdings of more than 100 hectares, fundamentally changing rural property structure and social structure. See Günter J. Trittel, "Bodenreform," in: *Deutschland unter alliierter Besatzung 1945–1949/55*, ed. Wolfgang Benz, Berlin 1999, pp. 105–108.

108 On dismantlement by the Soviet Union in the Soviet zone and Berlin, see Werner Bührer, "Reparationen," in: ibid., pp. 161–167.

109 See Elke Scherstjanoi, "Sowjetische Besatzungspolitik," in: ibid., pp. 73–89, here p. 86; "Befehl Nr. 124 des Obersten Chefs der Sowjetischen Militärverwaltung in Deutschland vom 30. Oktober 1945," in: *Befehle des Obersten Chefs der Sowjetischen Militärverwaltung in Deutschland. Aus dem Stab der Sowjetischen Militärverwaltung in Deutschland*, Sammelheft 1, *1945*, Berlin 1946, pp. 20–22; "Befehl Nr. 126 des Obersten Chefs der Sowjetischen Militärverwaltung in Deutschland vom 31. Oktober 1945," in: *Um ein antifaschistisch-demokratisches Deutschland. Dokumente aus den Jahren 1945–1949*, eds. Ministerium für Auswärtige Angelegenheiten der DDR/ Ministerium für Auswärtige Angelegenheiten der UdSSR, Berlin 1968, Doc. 72; "Befehl Nr. 97 des Obersten Chefs der Sowjetischen Militärverwaltung in Deutschland vom 29. März 1946," in: ibid., Doc. 96.

110 Johnson is apparently thinking of the Gesetz zur Sicherung der Einheit von Partei und Staat vom 1. Dezember 1933 (Law to Safeguard the Unity of Party and State from December 1, 1933) (in: *Reichsgesetzblatt*, Teil I, 1933, p. 1016), with which the National Socialist single-party state was legally entrenched.

111 See Doc. 39, fn. 29.

112 See Doc. 30, fn. 8.

113 Hans Jendretzky (1897–1992), German politician (KPD/SED), 1919 USPD, 1920 KPD, 1928–1932 member of the Prussian Landtag, 1945/1946 head of the Magistrat Department of Employment/Labor, cosigner of the appeal by the preparatory trade union committee for Greater Berlin from June 15, 1945, until the beginning of February 1946 provisional First Chairman of the Berlin FDGB, February 1946–1948 First Chairman of the FDGB Bundesvorstand, 1946 SED, 1948–1953 First Secretary of the Landesleitung/Bezirksleitung Greater Berlin of the SED, 1950–1954 and 1958–1990 member of the Volkskammer of the GDR, 1990 PDS.

American military government rather than to work with it. There followed the political unity of the working classes.[114] The great love of the Communists for their Social Democratic comrades, so plain to the careful student of the history of the German working class, was now to find its fulfillment in the great effacement. The Communist party would simply disappear. The Social Democratic party would do likewise. Out of this mutual and magical disappearance would come a new mystic fusion, – the Socialist Unity Party of Germany (Sozialistische Einheitspartei Deutschlands – SED). The gates to a new paradise, the paradise being established in the Russian zone, would now be opened.

It was then the unity of unpolitical youth. The wasteful competition of rival political and religious youth movements was to yield to a cooperative movement, properly guided and disciplined by Communists from above. It was finally the unity of the German women.[115] One trade union, one political party, one youth movement, one women's organization, it all had a familiar ring. It would have been more exciting had it been more spontaneous. Still the awful and frightening thing was the pressure, real and threatened, yes, even the terror. These unities were what one of the occupying powers wanted, was determined to have, knew how to get. There were privileges for those who knew how to comply and penalties for those who refused. The NKVD[116] was active. People disappeared and things happened to them. One knew about specific cases. People were watched. They were questioned. They came pleading for protection. This was the system that was crowding in on quadripartite Berlin from the Russian zone and the Russian sector. Could it be stopped? Could it be modified? Could East and West really come together in the city?

III

My orientation along the highways and by-ways of OMGUS was interrupted when it was suggested that I go to help with the situation in Berlin by acting as

114 Refers to the merger of the KPD and SPD into the SED.

115 Initially women had joined together in antifascist women's committees. Soviet occupation forces sought to found a single women's association, and in March 1947 the Demokratischer Frauenbund Deutschlands was founded in Berlin. See Gerda Weber, "Demokratischer Frauenbund Deutschlands (DFD)," in: *SBZ-Handbuch. Staatliche Verwaltungen, Parteien, gesellschaftliche Organisationen und ihre Führungskräfte in der Sowjetischen Besatzungszone Deutschlands 1945–1949*, on behalf of the Arbeitsbereich Geschichte und Politik der DDR at the University of Mannheim and the Institut für Zeitgeschichte Munich, eds. Martin Broszat/Hermann Weber, Munich 1990, pp. 691–713; Katrin Wehry, "Demokratischer Frauenbund Deutschlands (DFD)," in: *Deutschland unter alliierter Besatzung 1945–1949/55*, ed. Wolfgang Benz, Berlin 1999, pp. 244f.

116 Narodnyy Komissariat Vnutrennikh Del, People's Commissariat of Internal Affairs, Soviet ministry formed in 1934. The functions of the OGPU (Obyedinyonnoye Gosudarstvennoye Politicheskoye Upravleniye, Joint State Political Directorate, the secret police organization) were transferred to the NKVD, which is known for its role in political repression and for carrying out the Great Purge (1935–1939).

a political adviser to the commanding general[117]. It was late March. The political atmosphere of the city was tense. To be sure the Christian Democratic Union[118] and the Liberal Democratic Party[119] were safely hamstrung by the limitations put upon their activity by the Soviet authorities. In the political camp of the workers, however, revolt was in the air. The drive conducted by the Soviet authorities for the unification of the Communist and the Social Democratic parties into the new Socialist Unity Party was reaching its climax.[120] The Soviet authorities had evidently decided that the union must be completed by May first, and every step was being taken to meet this schedule. The pressure in the Russian zone was so great that the Social Democrats there had been completely intimidated. Under no circumstances had it been necessary to intimidate the Communists, whose prospects with the new party were so fair, whose power so enlarged, and whose rewards so great, that, except possibly for a very few, they needed no prodding from their Russian overlords. The international occupation of Berlin, however, made it possible for the Social Democrats there to resist the pressure of the Soviets upon their party leaders. They were quite willing to prove false the assumption that what could be done in the Russian zone could be done also in Berlin. A principle of party organization was at stake. Could a party executive irrespective of the wishes of its members, determine the future of the party? Could it alone decide that the party was no longer to exist? The independents said no. At a meeting of party functionaries on the first of March[121] they decided upon the simple democratic expedient of taking a vote of all members of the Social Democratic Party (they called it an *Urabstimmung*) on whether they desired an immediate amalgamation with the Communist Party. The vote was to be taken on the thirty-first of March.

The official policy of the United States Government in all internal German political struggles was neutrality. This was a policy which some Americans could not understand. It was rather obvious to them that there was no such thing as political neutrality. To the extent that this meant political indifference it was undesirable. If it means, as it meant to many military government officers when they were first called upon to establish German or Austrian governments, reliance upon officials who claimed to adhere to no political party, this was only to put into power political amorality which in practice usually meant

117 Commanding General, US Headquarters Berlin District, was Ray W. Barker. See Doc. 20, fn. 10.

118 On the CDU, see Doc. 21, fn. 29, and Doc. 44, fn. 11.

119 On the LDP, see Doc. 44, fn. 10.

120 Massive pressure for the unification was put on the SPD; repressive measures by Soviet occupation forces against Social Democratic opponents of a merger of the SPD and KPD into the SED included arrests. See Doc. 30.

121 Functionary conference of the Berlin SPD on March 1, 1946, at the Admiralspalast in the district of Mitte, Friedrichstraße 101/102. See *Berlin. Kampf um Freiheit und Selbstverwaltung 1945–1946*, edited on behalf of the Senate of Berlin (= Schriftenreihe zur Berliner Zeitgeschichte, vol. 1), revised and supplemented second edition, Berlin 1961, pp. 374f., no. 5; Harold Hurwitz in cooperation with Andreas Büning/Johannes-Berthold Hohmann/Klaus Sühl/Ingolore Mensch-Khan, *Die Anfänge des Widerstands*, part 2, *Zwischen Selbsttäuschung und Zivilcourage: Der Fusionskampf* (= Demokratie und Antikommunismus in Berlin nach 1945, vol. IV), Cologne 1990, pp. 1022–1030.

political reaction. If a policy of political neutrality meant that the American government did not care which party came to control Germany, this view was short sighted. In the present situation, however, the doctrine of political neutrality conflicted with the democratic doctrine we were also called upon to uphold. It conflicted as well with the program of international cooperation. It was clear that in this Berlin struggle the Communists, and the pro-merger Social Democrats who had gone over to them, were using methods which under no circumstances could be called democratic. The idea of an *Urabstimmung* corresponded altogether too simply to our notions of democratic procedure to call forth any kind of a protest. Therefore in supporting the right of the Social Democrats to take this vote, we had to oppose the Communists and their Social Democratic hangers-on, who were denying it. In so doing we were opposing our Soviet ally, who wanted nothing more anxiously than to see this merger carried through speedily and without opposition. There had always been, of course, the academic question of the respective nature of democracy as used by the Soviets and ourselves. It was instructive, therefore, to observe that in supporting what we felt instinctively to be democratic we were running head on into the Russians. There was more, however, in the struggle than supporting what we felt to be democratic. We were supporting also what we felt to be a little heroic. Elsewhere the Social Democrats had lacked the courage to fight this superimposed unity. In Berlin, at considerable risk to themselves, this courage was not lacking. Men like Otto Suhr[122], the present General Secretary of the Berlin Social Democrats, gave up their jobs with the Russian zonal administration in order to take up the fight.[123] These were the kind of Germans we wanted to support, the kind in whose hands a future Germany ought to be. They seemed to have learned something from the abdication of the Social Democrats in 1933.[124]

Mr. Grotewohl, and the members of his purged Executive Committee[125], unwilling to trust the results of a referendum, tried to thwart it. They did not succeed. When it showed that they had been repudiated they tried to misinterpret it. This only showed to what lengths they were willing to go. The fact that the referendum was not held in the Russian sector of Berlin only made the fundamental issue clearer. In Berlin the Social Democratic Party continued to exist. In Berlin the Russian plans had for the moment been halted. They had been halted by a vote.

This snag in the program of a speedy amalgamation brought a change in the person of the Russian commander-in-chief for Berlin. General Smirnov[126]

122 See Doc. 40, fn. 7.

123 Otto Suhr was senior department head in the German Central Administration of Industry in the Soviet zone until March 1946, and Secretary General of the Berlin SPD after its reconstitution.

124 The SPD had been banned on June 22, 1933. Beforehand it had adopted a course of adaptation without managing to prevent the party ban. See Ossip K. Flechtheim, "Die Anpassung der SPD: 1914, 1933 und 1959," in: *Politologie und Soziologie. Otto Stammer zum 65. Geburtstag*, ed. Jürgen Fijalkowski, Cologne and Opladen 1965, pp. 182–202.

125 SPD Central Committee, executive committee of the SPD responsible for the Soviet zone and Berlin, from which opponents of the merger had separated themselves.

126 See Doc. 25, fn. 23.

brought along with him in early April General Kotikov[127],[128] who, it was understood, had successfully managed the merger in Saxony[129].[130] The new general was tall and good-looking, if somewhat flabby. His white hair was streaked with yellow. His face was usually weary and troubled, and it seemed anxious for the occasion when it could break into a smile. Obviously he was a hard worker and a hard fighter. When the Social Democrats, reorganized after their democratic revolt, repudiated their old and elected new leaders, and proposed to the Kommandatura the recognition of their efforts,[131] the General, with a certain amount of scornful indifference, would not hear of it. These new leaders were, he said, unknown to him. Although he must have known that he could hardly be believed, he asserted that he was unfamiliar with the political situation in Berlin and that he was not able to discuss the question. He preferred evidently to await developments. Yet he must also have realized that if the new and as yet unrecognized Socialist Unity Party wished to organize throughout Berlin the same privilege would have to be accorded to the reorganized Social Democratic Party. One couldn't encourage a revolt and still permit it to be crushed.

Accordingly, until the SED was officially recognized, it was not permitted to organize in the western sectors of the city, while, at the same time, the new leadership of the Social Democrats was permitted to take over the old organization in these sectors. The Soviet authorities soon recognized the situation. In order to facilitate the organization of the SED in all Berlin they were soon anxious to accord recognition to the Social Democrats they had hoped to obliterate. The empty formalities of conventions completing the merger in both the Russian zone and Berlin were nevertheless carried out. At the final meeting[132] Mr. Pieck and Mr. Grotewohl staged the dramatic scene of standing with clasped hands while the audience rose.[133] General Kotikov was sitting in the royal box.

When recognition for both parties finally came,[134] it turned out to be but the beginning of another phase of the struggle. The Soviet authorities were not will-

127 See Doc. 35, fn. 5.

128 On April 2, 1946, at the meeting of the Allied Commandants, Lieutenant General Smirnov introduced Major General Kotikov as his successor. See "Die 32. (10. im Jahre 1946) Sitzung der Alliierten Kommandantur der Stadt Berlin. Generalmajor A. G. Kotikow – neuer Kommandant des sowjetischen Sektors der Stadt Berlin. Kommuniqué," in: *Tägliche Rundschau* from April 3, 1946, p. 1.

129 Province of Saxony(-Anhalt).

130 Kotikov was head of administration for the Soviet Military Administration in the Province of Saxony(-Anhalt) in Halle from 1945–March 1946.

131 On April 7, 1946, opponents of the merger organized a party conference at the Zehlendorf Zinnowwaldschule, during which they voted on their own district committee. On April 8 this committee applied to the Allied Kommandatura for licensing of the newly constituted Berlin SPD. See *Die Sitzungsprotokolle des Magistrats der Stadt Berlin 1945/46*, part II, *1946*, edited and introduced by Dieter Hanauske (= Schriftenreihe des Landesarchivs Berlin, vol. 2/II), Berlin 1999, p. 6.

132 Refers to the party unification conference of the KPD and SPD on April 21/22, 1946, in the former venue of the Deutsche Staatsoper, at the Admiralspalast in the Berlin administrative district of Mitte, Friedrichstraße 101/102. See Doc. 39, fn. 19.

133 "The orchestra played the *Fidelio* Overture by Ludwig van Beethoven [see Doc. 37, fn. 29]. A few minutes later Wilhelm Pieck and Otto Grotewohl came onto the stage from different sides, met in the middle, and shook hands to a storm of applause lasting several minutes." ("Das Orchester spielte die Fidelio-Ouvertüre von Ludwig van

ing to permit the Social Democrats to organize in the Russian sector in quite the same way as the SED was being permitted to organize in other sectors of the city. If the Social Democrats could not be prohibited they could be controlled. Some Social Democrats disappeared.[135] The newly elected leaders of the Party in the various districts in the Russian sector were not recognized if they had displayed an attitude called 'anti-Soviet' or 'anti-Red Army'. The essential test of this attitude was whether the elected leaders had been for or against the merger. The Social Democrats were faced with a nice dilemma: how could a party which had been born out of opposition to the fusion choose leaders which had not opposed the fusion. At the same moment a larger issue was raised. The SED leaders, with the consent of the western Allies, were beginning their invasion of the western zones. I heard them shouting in the ruined market place of Nürnberg and wondered if the event were symbolic. Social Democrats there were amazed. The Soviets had destroyed the Social Democrats in their zone. There was no question of western Social Democrats going into the Russian zone to reorganize the fold. Even if invited they would have been afraid to go and run the risk of simply disappearing. It was suggested, therefore, that the Soviet authorities might again see the point if no SED activity were permitted in the West for as long as no Social Democratic activity were permitted in the East. Yet something had been done in Berlin to relieve the pressure from the East, and it had been done finally with the reluctant consent of the East. The iron grip of unity, uniformity and unanimity had been loosened, and this because there were four powers instead of one.

IV

In the course of the battle over the merger the question of elections for Berlin had arisen. It was clearly recognized by the American authorities uninterested in preserving for an unnecessarily long period the regime of the existing *Magistrat*, that the simplest way to undo this regime was to prepare for elections for a new municipal government. It was a program which the Americans could pursue with propriety inasmuch as they had already instituted the series of elec-

Beethoven. Einige Minuten später kamen Wilhelm Pieck und Otto Grotewohl von verschiedenen Seiten auf die Bühne, trafen sich in der Mitte und reichten sich unter minutenlangem stürmischem Beifall die Hände.") Thus the description by Wolfgang Leonhard, *Die Revolution entläßt ihre Kinder*, eighth edition, Munich 1985, p. 386. The handshake between Pieck and Grotewohl symbolically sealed the merger of the KPD and SPD. As an emblem, the entwined hands became the party badge of the SED.

134 Because no agreement could be reached by the Allied Kommandatura regarding the admission applications of the SED and newly constituted SPD, the matter was presented to the Coordinating Committee of the Allied Control Authority. There, on May 28, 1946, representatives of the four powers agreed to permit the SED and SPD in all of Berlin. Correspondingly, the Allied Kommandatura approved the admission and activity of both parties in all four sectors. See BK/O (46) 248 from May 31, 1946, in: LAB, F Rep. 280 (Quellensammlung zur Berliner Zeitgeschichte [LAZ-Sammlung]), no. 4865.

135 Hermann Löwenthal and Julius Scherff disappeared, for example. See Doc. 71, fn. 25.

tions in their zone which aimed at creating popular governments.[136] Although the British and French were not to hold elections in their zones until the autumn,[137] they were willing to see earlier elections in Berlin. The Soviet authorities, however, for as long as the political situation remained unclarified, were unwilling to touch the question of elections, and prepared a most elaborate and irrelevant defence against them. When, it was settled that the SED was to be permitted to spread throughout Berlin, and the date for their own municipal elections in their zone had been decided upon,[138] they came quickly and easily to an agreement on an election date. It was later than the western Allies had wanted, but it was earlier than had first been suggested by Soviet officials.

If there were to be elections in October,[139] then the Local Government Committee of the Kommandatura[140] would have to rouse itself from its lethargy to produce a constitution for Berlin, and an electoral ordinance in accordance with which such elections might be held. This Committee had been standing still for months. It had been standing still because the Soviet authorities had not decided upon the main lines of their policy on these matters. It was the Russian representative's job to keep the Committee inert until these decisions were made. Everybody liked the Russian Major[141]. He was short, stocky and black-haired. His studies in the law had been interrupted by the war in which he had

136 Local elections had taken place in the smaller municipalities of the American zone of Germany in January 1946 (see Doc. 40, fn. 35), elections for the Kreistage followed, as in the larger municipalities, and for the Stadtkreise (see Doc. 58, fn. 21). See Conrad F. Latour/Thilo Vogelsang, *Okkupation und Wiederaufbau. Die Tätigkeit der Militärregierung in der amerikanischen Besatzungszone Deutschlands 1944–1947* (Studien zur Zeitgeschichte), Stuttgart 1973, pp. 109–111; Wolfram Werner, "Wahlen," in: *Deutschland unter alliierter Besatzung 1945–1949/55*, ed. Wolfgang Benz, Berlin 1999, pp. 194–200.

137 On September 15, 1946, Gemeinde elections took place in the states of the British (see Doc. 50, fn. 21) and French zones in Germany. See *Keesing's Archiv der Gegenwart*, vol. XVI (1946), p. 868 A and C. On October 13, 1946, Landkreis and Stadtkreis elections, Bürgerschaft elections in Bremen and Hamburg, took place in the British zone, and elections for the Kreisversammlungen in the French zone. See ibid., p. 895 G and H as well as p. 896 A. In the French zone on November 17, 1946, members of the Kreistage and representatives of the municipal councils from cities of over 7,000 inhabitents elected the beratende Landesversammlungen (advisory state assemblies) of the three states, which were at the same time constituent assemblies. See ibid., pp. 927f. E.

138 Gemeinde elections in the Soviet zone of Germany took place on September 1, 1946, in Saxony, on September 8 in Saxony-Anhalt and Thuringia, and on September 15 in Brandenburg and Mecklenburg. See *Keesing's Archiv der Gegenwart*, vol. XVI (1946), pp. 859 C, 863 G, and 868 B.

139 On May 29, 1946, the members of the Political Directorate, Allied Control Authority, had agreed to let elections be held in October 1946. See minutes of the 38th meeting of the Political Directorate, Allied Control Authority, on May 29, 1946, DPOL/M (46) 21-192, French version, in: AOF, Services Français à Berlin, GFCC, Bureau des Archives, caisse 1140, paquet 51; Werner Breunig, *Verfassunggebung in Berlin 1945–1950* (= Beiträge zur Politischen Wissenschaft, vol. 58), Berlin 1990, p. 182.

140 See Doc. 29, fn. 14.

141 Iosif Moiseyevich Feldman. See Doc. 49, fn. 59.

covered himself with glory. His chest bore an impressive array of Soviet decorations. His superiors, however, did not give him much latitude in the conduct of the negotiations in the Committee. It was clear too that the little, and at times somewhat belligerent Major was terrified of his superiors. It was rumored at least that his predecessor on the Committee[142] had been given other work to do because he was unnecessarily conciliatory. The combination of legal logic and Marxist logic served well to cover up what some members of the Committee felt were purely dilatory tactics. In any case the Major could waste more time in correcting the minutes of the previous meeting than probably any other person in Berlin. If, in the preparation of any document or report there was more than a word or a comma to insert, his efforts to get the decision postponed until the next meeting were often clumsy and obvious. Yet those of us who had no such superiors, who were left comparatively free to come to agreements, were sympathetic with the Major's plight, even though at times, the lack of agility of his mind seemed to explain the circumspection of his superiors. At any rate if a constitution were to be produced in a hurry he would have to have help. At the last moment this was supplied in the person of an academic colonel[143]. The new colonel was the principal of a little school in the Caucasus. His graduate studies had been interrupted at the moment when he was about to take his doctorate. His thesis on some phase of the history of the Caucasus region was waiting to be published. He was an atheist and a Communist, the son of a working man, and proud of what the Soviet state had done for him and for simple people like him. His superiors evidently trusted his ability for it was clear upon his first appearance that he had been given instructions to agree upon a constitution for Berlin. In the subsequent sessions the little Major was little more than a secretary. The Colonel carried on the argument, made the speeches and the concessions.

It was, nevertheless, somewhat anomalous that this Committee should presume to act as a constitutional assembly for the city of Berlin. Except for the French representative[144], none of the regular members of the Committee know very much German,[145] nor were they any too conversant with the constitutional history of the city. They had passed off the preliminary work to the *Magistrat* with an order that it was to prepare, on the basis of the constitutional laws be-

142 His predecessor was Captain Kasatkin. See *Die Entstehung der Verfassung von Berlin. Eine Dokumentation*, vol. I, on behalf of the President of the Abgeordnetenhaus of Berlin, ed. Hans J. Reichhardt in collaboration with Werner Breunig/Josephine Gabler, Berlin and New York 1990, Doc. 37, p. 242, Doc. 44, p. 255, and Doc. 45, p. 256. The British representative on the Local Government Committee, Harold Hays (see Doc. 49, fn. 26), later recalled Kasatkin: "[...] a geologist with little or no knowledge of constitutional matters. He was a very charming man, quiet, tactful, and helpful, but was obviously working strictly according to instructions." Memoirs of Harold Hays, chapter 10: Berlin Constitution 1946, p. 145, in: IWM Duxford, Lieutenant Colonel Harold Hays MBE Collection.

143 Refers to Alexander Mikhailovich Zozulya. See Doc. 67, fn. 28.

144 Jean Victor Ziegelmeyer. See Doc. 55, fn. 4.

145 The French representative on the Committee was a man from Alsace who came from an old Colmar family.

fore 1933, the draft of a temporary constitution for the city.[146] This meant that after some preliminary discussions as to what the constitution was to contain, the actual drafting was left to the only technically competent member of this body, the very busy acting treasurer of the city, Dr. Friedrich Haas[147], who, it can be easily understood, in spite of his preliminary work upon the question, was obliged to prepare this draft somewhat hurriedly.[148] To the Soviet representatives it was a draft prepared by their Magistrat. To the British representatives, when once they learned how quickly it had been drafted,[149] it was an impossible text. They proposed instead that the texts of the Municipal Ordinance of 1857[150], the Constitution of 1920[151], and the amendments of 1931[152], be used as the basis of discussion. This last proposal was clearly impossible if a constitution were to be produced at all. The British representative was finally beaten down by the other members of the Committee. He withdrew his proposal upon the threat that a report be made to the Commandants that the Committee could not agree on how to begin to discuss a constitution for Berlin.

The draft constitution of Berlin began to be discussed paragraph by paragraph. It was not easy. The interpreters were not so expert that they could always reproduce in another tongue the very precise meaning of the original language. One therefore often had the feeling that he was agreeing to what he

146 The Magistrat's first draft of a provisional constitution, which was delivered to the Allied Kommandatura for approval on January 16, 1946, had been rejected by the Local Government Committee on February 8, 1946. With BK/O (46) 144 from March 28, 1946, the Magistrat was directed to prepare a new draft constitution by May 1, 1946, which was to be based on the Gesetz über die Bildung einer neuen Stadtgemeinde Berlin vom 27. April 1920 (Law on the Formation of a New City Municipality of Berlin from April 27, 1920) (in: *Preußische Gesetzsammlung*, 1920, pp. 123–150), and the Gesetz über die vorläufige Regelung verschiedener Punkte des Gemeindeverfassungsrechts für die Hauptstadt Berlin vom 30. März 1931 (Law for the Preliminary Regulation of Different Points of Municipal Constitutional Law for the Capital Berlin from March 30, 1931) (in: *Preußische Gesetzsammlung*, 1931, pp. 39–44), to the extent that the 1931 regulation corresponded with democratic principles. See Werner Breunig, *Verfassunggebung in Berlin 1945–1950* (= Beiträge zur Politischen Wissenschaft, vol. 58), Berlin 1990, pp. 154–169.

147 See Doc. 49, fn. 40.

148 See Doc. 74, fn. 29.

149 Only one month was provided for the preparation of the new draft constitution. See Werner Breunig, *Verfassunggebung in Berlin 1945–1950* (= Beiträge zur Politischen Wissenschaft, vol. 58), Berlin 1990, p. 169.

150 Refers to the Städte-Ordnung für die sechs östlichen Provinzen der Preußischen Monarchie vom 30. Mai 1853 (Cities Ordinance for the Six Eastern Provinces of the Prussian Monarchy from May 30, 1853), in: *Gesetz-Sammlung für die Königlichen Preußischen Staaten*, 1853, pp. 261–290.

151 Refers to the Gesetz über die Bildung einer neuen Stadtgemeinde Berlin vom 27. April 1920 (Law on the Formation of a New City Municipality of Berlin from April 27, 1920). See fn. 146.

152 Refers to the Gesetz über die vorläufige Regelung verschiedener Punkte des Gemeindeverfassungsrechts für die Hauptstadt Berlin vom 30. März 1931 (Law for the Preliminary Regulation of Different Points of Municipal Constitutional Law for the Capital Berlin from March 30, 1931). See fn. 146.

thought he understood. It was, of course, not enough to understand and agree with each other in three different languages. It was necessary also to agree upon the wording of the German text and this involved the use of additional interpreters. This produced at moments almost inextricable crises. The Soviet delegates at one point discovered that they had agreed to a clause providing that the members of the newly elected *Magistrat* were to take on oath to administer their offices impartially. The German word was *unparteiisch*. The Russian colonel understood this German word to mean unpolitically. He could not understand therefore how a member of the *Magistrat*, elected from a political party, could be expected to administer his office unpolitically. When, after prolonged discussion, he was convinced that *unparteiisch* meant impartial at the same time.[153] For those who fret over the seeming lack of speed in the conduct of international negotiations it is to reflect whether it is not remarkable that they can be conducted at all.

The necessity for meeting in long sessions at frequent intervals soon broke down whatever official character there was to these meetings. The members of the Committee became friends. As meeting after meeting passed and every difficulty was settled, it became clear that no difficulty was to be too great; the Committee would come out with an agreed report. It was not only necessary to work and argue and discuss together. It was also necessary to eat and drink together, now at one mess and now at another. During the last month[154] the Russians were in the chair, and their luncheons at the Kommandatura became notoriously strenuous. The Russians liked late luncheons. The tables were heavy with bottles. Vodka made from the best German potatoes, vermouth, and General Zhukov's[155] beer, reputed to be 12 %. This, when mixed with caviar, smoked salmon, borsch, and sour cream dressing, broke down the staid character of the conversation and relaxed the negotiations for what was left of the afternoon's work. "What did the Russian papers mean when they accused America of atomic diplomacy?"[156] If the Soviet representatives were hungry for all views on contemporary events why didn't they simply subscribe to the London[157] or the New York Times[158]? Would our Russian friends ever come to see us in America or we them in Russia? Was it possible then that there would be another war this time between East and West? If the Local Government Committee had the world in its hands there would be no such war. Back in the Committee room, the question of whether the Germans should be permitted to hold secret sessions of their councils became less serious when the French (represented in

153 See Doc. 77, fn. 9.

154 July 1946.

155 Georgy Konstantinovich Zhukov (1896–1974), Marshal of the Soviet Union, accepted the surrender of the German Wehrmacht on May 8, 1945, as Commander-in-Chief of the First Belorussian Front, 1945–March 1946 Commander-in-Chief of the Group of Soviet Forces in Germany and Supreme Chief of SMAG, 1955–1957 Minister of Defense of the Soviet Union.

156 See Doc. 70.

157 Refers to *The Times*, a British daily newspaper, sometimes referred to as *The London Times* or *The Times of London.*

158 American daily newspaper.

Germany only by Alsatians[159]) explained that in Colmar[160], his home town, the municipal council used to hold secret sessions. His father[161], however, was the mayor of Colmar and after every secret session he reported its discussion and conclusions to his wife[162], and the secrecy was not long maintained. The British were inclined to grow more lyrical about the superiority of their own municipal and governmental institutions. Did we realize what a fine charter the city of Liverpool[163] possessed, and how good it would be for Berlin, it was intimated, if some features of this charter could be imported from England? Was it not just a little bit ordinary to permit the elected chairman of the new city assembly to be called a mere "Vorsitzende"? Now take the example of the Speaker of the House of Commons.[164] He did not speak but on ceremonial occasions he marched before the Prime Minister.

The Constitution for Berlin was in fact becoming less and less German and more and more international. The fact that the existing *Magistrat* was none too popular with some members of the Committee made it seem desirable to limit the independent position which Prussian municipal law granted to this organ. The British and the Soviets were, at the same time, anxious to introduce the parliamentary system into Berlin. Not only were the individual members of the *Magistrat* made subject to recall for cause, but the *Magistrat* as a collective body was made subject, under certain conditions, to dismissal by the city council. This principle was even carried so far as to make the local administrations in the wards, subject, under limitations, to the will of the councils of the wards. There were those in the Committee who felt that as a result of certain legislative powers left to the Magistrat, the unnatural conception of a constitution by four powers had produced an abnormal child. For the rest, however, the Magistrat's draft was repaired as the Allies thought necessary. The gravity of the decisions was tempered somewhat by the provision that this was to be only a temporary constitution, and that the new city assembly itself was to have the opportunity of correcting the mistakes of the Local Government Committee in a new constitution for Berlin. While it was felt that the German specialists need not be deprived of a smile at some of the things the constitution might contain, nobody wanted them to laugh.

The documents were ready for the Commandants at the required date.[165] There was general amazement. This was the first agreed-upon, i. e., unanimous

159 Alsatians were frequently deployed in Germany because of their German language skills.

160 City in Alsace.

161 Joseph Ziegelmeyer (1877–1947), 1935–1940 and 1945 First Deputy of the Mayor, Colmar.

162 Jeanne Ziegelmeyer, née Meyer (1872–1948).

163 City on the northwest coast of England.

164 The House of Commons, lower house of the British Parliament, elects a chair from among its members at the beginning of every legislative period, who presides over the Parliament and is designated as Speaker. While he or she does not give any speeches and does not participate in debates, the Speaker appears before the Monarch as spokesperson of the Parliament, thus the name.

165 The Local Government Committee concluded its discussion on July 5, 1946, and on July 9 the draft constitution was presented to the Commandants in due time. See

report upon a major problem that the Kommandatura had witnessed for months. The question of the reorganization of the police, for example, had long been sent upward by the Commandants, and had been drifting for months in the higher reaches of the Control Council[166].[167] The question of the organization of the Berlin youth had reached nowhere in the Committee on Education[168].[169] Yet the Local Government Committee was saying to the Commandants that after its initial difficulties, there was no word, or phrase, or sentence in this new temporary constitution upon which they did not all agree. This session of the Commandants was necessarily made a little festive.[170] General Kotikov made a very complimentary speech congratulating the Committee on its exemplary accomplishment, and proposed that the other Commandants join him in expressing their commendation.[171] He thereupon invited everyone to another strenuous luncheon, a luncheon to celebrate the institution of a democratic government for post-war Berlin. Except for minor details and approvals the constitution was actually finished.[172] In October elections would be held in accordance with its provisions, an election which would overturn the system of government which the Russians had first set up in the city, and indicate to some

Doc. 71, fn. 46; Werner Breunig, *Verfassunggebung in Berlin 1945–1950* (= Beiträge zur Politischen Wissenschaft, vol. 58), Berlin 1990, p. 199.

166 See Doc. 14, fn. 5.

167 On October 4, 1946, with BK/O (46) 391, the Commandants agreed to a plan by the Allied Control Council for the reorganization of the Berlin police. See *Berlin. Kampf um Freiheit und Selbstverwaltung 1945–1946*, edited on behalf of the Senate of Berlin (= Schriftenreihe zur Berliner Zeitgeschichte, vol. 1), revised and supplemented second edition, Berlin 1961, p. 544, no. 13 a; LAB, F Rep. 280 (Quellensammlung zur Berliner Zeitgeschichte [LAZ-Sammlung]), no. 5504.

168 Education Committee, Allied Kommandatura Berlin.

169 According to Johnson in a letter to his wife from May 31, 1946 (Doc. 55), "[...] the Russians had been holding up discussions on the problem of youth organizations in the Education Committee."

170 Refers to the 18th meeting of the Commandants on July 9, 1946. See minutes of the 18th meeting of the Commandants on July 9, 1946, BKC/M (46) 18, English version, in: LAB, B Rep. 036-01 (Office of Military Government, Berlin Sector [OMGBS]), 5/36-1/5.

171 According to the verbatim minutes, Kotikov said: "I think we ought to express in the minutes of the Commandants today the light of spirit prevalent here today. I would like to read to you the formula which I have prepared for our appreciation for the work of the Local Government Com. The committee of Local Affairs has done its work well and fulfilled its obligations in time, the work it has been ordered to do. In expressing our appreciation we have to keep in mind the fact the draft constitution which has been presented by the Local Government Com. to the Magistrat had to be studied very thoroughly and very deeply. Very many points in the draft submitted by the Magistrat had to be worked and re-studied and re-edited many times. I, therefore, propose for the the various attitudes and for the great amount of work the committee has done, I propose that we express our appreciation of the Local Government Com." Verbatim minutes of the 18th meeting of the Commandants on July 9, 1946, English version, p. 7, in: LAB, B Rep. 036-01 (Office of Military Government, Berlin Sector [OMGBS]), 4/132-3/11.

172 While the Commandants approved the draft constitution in their meeting on July 9, 1946, in principle, they returned it to the Local Government Committee to clarify

degree the choice of the Berliners between East and West. After this election the Communists would certainly lose their predominant position in the municipal government which would then reflect the political opinions of the electorate. Once again the Soviet pressure had been limited. Once again it had been limited, this time with open cordiality, with the aid of the Soviet authorities themselves. Once again this had been done because they were four powers in the city instead of one.

V

Suddenly this world vanished overnight into the rather tawdry environment of the Third Replacement Depot[173] at Bremerhaven[174], where, in conversations punctured with four-letter words it was possible to learn what the occupation was really about. In the miserable quarters which the War Department furnished its soldiers, officers, and civilians returning home aboard the Marine Robin[175], where GI's[176] were asked to think of the steak dinner they would be given at the Separation Centers[177] in order to take their minds off their inadequate rations on board, it was possible to reflect, in the awkward postures which the total absence of chairs made necessary, about the meaning of these months in Berlin.

Certainly this occupation of Germany was one of the most, if not the most, important tasks which the United States had ever undertaken beyond its borders. The main reasons for our being in Germany were still good reasons for our staying there for some time to come. The German war potential was not yet destroyed, and the de-Nazification was, still incomplete in our zone, no matter how much more seriously we had taken this problem than the other powers. The inability to implement the clauses of the Potsdam Agreement[178] on treating Germany as an economic unit was responsible for the former situation, and when all is said and done, our own inadequacy was responsible for the latter. We had not known how, from the very beginning, to work closely enough with the proper Germans in solving speedily the Nazi problem. We had, consequently, been obliged to turn over this problem to the Germans themselves. Nobody could be really sure that, at this late date, they would really be able to see it

individual questions. On July 17 the Committee agreed on the final text, which was approved by the Commandants on July 19 and then delivered to the Allied Control Authority. After discussion in the Coordinating Committee, the Commandants finally examined the text of the constitution on August 9, and it was delivered to the Oberbürgermeister with BK/O (46) 326 from August 13, 1946. See Werner Breunig, *Verfassunggebung in Berlin 1945–1950* (= Beiträge zur Politischen Wissenschaft, vol. 58), Berlin 1990, pp. 199–225.

173 Transit and collection station for American soldiers.

174 See Doc. 71, fn. 10.

175 See Doc. 82, fn. 5.

176 Government Issues, slang for American soldiers.

177 Where soldiers were relieved of active duty.

178 See Doc. 50, fn. 18.

through. Even granted that it would be carried through, it would necessarily be done with a mildness which our war and peace aims did not contemplate. Were it solved to everyone's general satisfaction, there still remained those ultra-conservative, nationalist groups in German society who were waiting once more to take over. Those who understood Bavaria, for example, were worried over how little would have been accomplished when once de-Nazification had been reasonably completed. We had been nicely successful with our program of elections, and with the coordination of the administration of the Länder in the Länderrat at Stuttgart. Yet it was still a question here of whether we had not gone a little bit too fast. No German in a position of responsibility would admit this, inasmuch as the relative independence to be achieved from a government established upon popular support was something to be coveted. One could feel how eager in spite of all their deferential courtesy, the Germans were to get rid of us, provided, of course, that certain others left at the same time. Military Government would find it more difficult to direct democratic governments of the Länder. It too would have to respect the constitutions. It was inevitably a serious question whether in so rapidly depleting our personnel in military government, and entrusting more and more responsibility to the Germans, we were not risking letting the German situation get out of our hands again as it had after the last war[179].[180] Since the main objectives of our war had not yet been achieved, certainly this time we could afford to be a little more cautious in abandoning our controls to the Germans. If we had erred on the wrong side after the last war, we might err on the right side after this one.

Undoubtedly much excellent work was being done in promoting the positive side of a democratic program, but not enough. The careful directives prepared by military government were often enough ignored or violated by parallel occupational military authorities. It was no good to write out a procedure which would make the requisitioning of houses less painful to the Germans, if the Air Corps[181], for example, simply swooped down and evacuated blocks of houses over-night, and made away with all the furniture when they departed. It was confusing to spend millions of dollars to bring in food for the Germans, and then to inform them, by public notices over the door-ways of certain messes in officers' clubs that they would not be permitted to utilize the scraps which fell from our tables. These would have to go into the garbage cans.[182] More serious perhaps was the absence of any feeling that knew exactly what we were trying to do in Germany beyond the vague phrases of the Potsdam Agreement, or how long, for example, we were going to stay. How long would we stay within the confines of so-called political neutrality? Was it not possible to see now what was the democratic political hope of this forlorn country? How long were we going to postpone the implementation of a program of the widest and most generous scope in aid of the really forward-looking groups in German educa-

179 Refers to the First World War (1914–1918).

180 After the First World War the USA had turned away from Europe and commenced with isolationist politics.

181 One of the combat arms of the US Army until 1947.

182 In an email to Werner Breunig from June 26, 2007, Georg Schertz, resident of Schwanenwerder Island and Chief of Police in Berlin from 1987–1992, recalls the Lakeside

tion and in the youth movement? How long were we going to postpone weeding out the undesirable elements, both military and civilian, in the forces of the occupation, those callous, cynical, and adventurous youngsters with high civil-service ratings, those untrained officers looking for sinecures, those officers and troops who didn't know how to represent the best which a great democracy exemplifies? How could we keep in Germany, and how could we summon from America to work in Germany, the best forces that we have, if the opportunity were not given to pursue over a relatively fixed period, a constructive policy which would really guarantee the execution of our war aims and support those Germans whom, by now, we should have learned to trust. How long were we going to postpone a publicity and educational program at home which would attempt to persuade the American people that the peace, having not yet been won, was as vital to win as the war?

This inability to give adequate expression abroad to the best, positive, democratic forces in our nation was a constant embarrassment to Americans abroad, and an embarrassment to all those Germans who sought hope and guidance from us. It put us in a false light with respect to our other, and especially our Soviet Allies, who were only too anxious to find fault with us. Here again the instability of our future in Germany precluded our taking a well-worked out and positive stand. The experience in Berlin had shown that there was no reason on earth why we couldn't work well with the Soviet authorities. To be sure we could not hope to come to complete agreement on all matters. If, however, we knew what we wanted, and if we were willing also to pound the table to get it, we had a better chance to be understood and thus to be met half way. The distrust between East and West could be broken only by the utmost frankness, by our own frankness even when and if the Russians did not feel free to be frank. Suspicions could be removed only by dealings in the simplest human terms among people who had convictions which they were willing to defend, and who were likewise friendly, sympathetic and really anxious to understand the other's point of view and to go out of their way to learn it. The Russians do not and dare not underrate the power of democratic principles. They are not so secure and so venerated that they are able to combat beyond measure the popularity of and basic devotion to, these principles among the peoples of Europe. But for so long as we do not demonstrate our unwavering devotion to these principles both at home and abroad, and with something more than talk, and exhibit tangibly our determination to support them in the future at any cost, we cannot expect aid from the Soviets in making ourselves popular. Certain elements of their program appear

Club, which was housed on Schwanenwerder (see Doc. 55): "For us residents, starving at the end of the war, the 'Lakeside Club' had a disappointing practice – today it is impossible to imagine. Groceries that were not consumed – including the nicest things, even packaged goods – were doused in gasoline and burned in view of residents. The residents' requests to help themselves were harshly refused." ("Für uns bei Kriegsende hungernde Anwohner hatte der 'Lakeside Club' eine – das kann man sich heute nicht mehr vorstellen – enttäuschende Praxis. Nicht verbrauchte Lebensmittel – darunter schönste und sogar verpackte Sachen – wurden vor den Augen der Bewohner mit Benzin übergossen und verbrannt. Die Wünsche der Anwohner, sich da zu bedienen, wurden schroff zurückgewiesen.")

to many Germans whose sincerity cannot be questioned, more fundamentally democratic than anything we have been able to conceive for Germany, in spite of the unpalatable methods used to carry them out.

Without underestimating our accomplishments to date, we can do a still better job in Germany. We are in a position therewith to make a splendid, positive contribution to the pacification of Europe and to the world. To do so, however, the American people through their government will have to display more real interest than hitherto, and put into this critical and peaceful effort their very best and most generous efforts: they must see to it that the great positive task that remains to be done is not cast aside through sheer national indifference and the neglect which accompanies it.

Appendix of Illustrations

Ill. 1 *Edgar N. Johnson, around the end of the 1930s.*
Candice E. and Thomas R. Johnson, Denver, Colorado, USA

Ill. 2 *Edgar N. Johnson*
in front of his house in Lincoln, Nebraska,
probably at the end of 1945 or beginning of 1946.
Candice E. and Thomas R. Johnson, Denver, Colorado, USA

Ill. 3 *Emily L. Johnson with sons John (left) and Thomas, Lincoln, Nebraska, end of 1945 or beginning of 1946.*
Candice E. and Thomas R. Johnson, Denver, Colorado, USA

Ill. 4 *Emily L. and Edgar N. Johnson with son John.*
Candice E. and Thomas R. Johnson, Denver, Colorado, USA

Ill. 5 *Emily L. and Edgar N. Johnson.*
Candice E. and Thomas R. Johnson, Denver, Colorado, USA

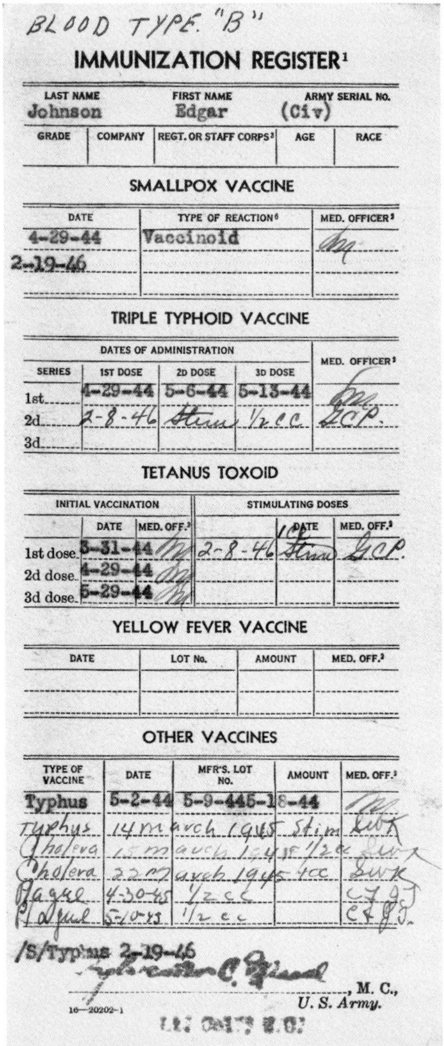

BLOOD TYPE "B"

IMMUNIZATION REGISTER[1]

LAST NAME	FIRST NAME	ARMY SERIAL NO.
Johnson	Edgar	(Civ)

GRADE	COMPANY	REGT. OR STAFF CORPS[2]	AGE	RACE

SMALLPOX VACCINE

DATE	TYPE OF REACTION[6]	MED. OFFICER[3]
4-29-44	Vaccinoid	[illegible]
2-19-46		

TRIPLE TYPHOID VACCINE

SERIES	DATES OF ADMINISTRATION 1ST DOSE	2D DOSE	3D DOSE	MED. OFFICER[3]
1st	4-29-44	5-6-44	5-13-44	[illegible]
2d	2-8-46	Stim	1/2 c.c.	GCP.
3d				

TETANUS TOXOID

	INITIAL VACCINATION DATE	MED. OFF.[3]	STIMULATING DOSES	DATE	MED. OFF.[3]
1st dose	3-31-44	[illegible]	2-8-46	Stim	GCP.
2d dose	4-29-44	[illegible]			
3d dose	5-29-44	[illegible]			

YELLOW FEVER VACCINE

DATE	LOT No.	AMOUNT	MED. OFF.[3]

OTHER VACCINES

TYPE OF VACCINE	DATE	MFR'S. LOT NO.	AMOUNT	MED. OFF.[3]
Typhus	5-2-44	5-9-445-18-44		[illegible]
Typhus	14 march 1945		Stim	[illegible]
Cholera	15 march 1945		1/2 cc	[illegible]
Cholera	22 march 1945		1cc	[illegible]
Plague	4-30-45	1/2 cc		[illegible]
Plague	5-10-45	1/2 cc		[illegible]

/S/Typhus 2-19-46

[illegible], M. C., U. S. Army.

16—20202-1

Ill. 6 *Immunization Register, 1944–1946.*

Candice E. and Thomas R. Johnson, Denver, Colorado, USA

WARNING

This card is issued by the War Department for official use of the authorized holder designated herein. Its use by any other person is unlawful and will make the offender liable to heavy penalty.

The finder of a lost card should promptly place it in the nearest post office or mail box. No envelope or stamp is required.

WAR DEPARTMENT

WASHINGTON, D. C.

CERTIFICATE of Identity of Noncombatant

No. NC 207074

WAR DEPARTMENT
OFFICIAL BUSINESS

PENALTY FOR PRIVATE USE TO AVOID PAYMENT OF POSTAGE, $300

THE ADJUTANT GENERAL
UNITED STATES ARMY
WASHINGTON, D. C.

CERTIFICATE OF IDENTITY OF NONCOMBATANT
(Pars. 76, 94, and 100, FM 27-10)

APO 413, 25 Sept 1944
(Place and date)

The bearer, EDGAR N. JOHNSON, whose signature appears below, is hereby certified to be Civilian attached to the Army of the United States in the European Theater of Operations and, as such, in event of capture by the enemy is entitled to be treated as a prisoner of war, and that he will be given the same treatment and afforded the same privileges as an officer in the Army of the United States of the grade of Major

By order of Theater Commander

(Signature of holder)

SEAL

(Signature of issuing authority)
KERMIT R. COFER, 1st Lt. AGD

IDENTIFYING INFORMATION

Age 43 Weight 141
Height 5 ft. 9½ in.
Color of hair Blonde
Color of eyes Gray

HQ.ETOUSA—14-7-44/5M/50020 (44/5 c2205)

FINGERPRINTS—RIGHT HAND, IF OBTAINABLE

THUMB

Ill. 7 and ill. 8 *Certificate of Identity of Noncombatant, 1944.*
Candice E. and Thomas R. Johnson, Denver, Colorado, USA

Ill. 12 *USAT George W. Goethals, the Army transport ship with which Edgar N. Johnson came to Europe in 1946, photograph from 1945.*
National Archives and Records Administration, College Park, Maryland, USA, photo no. 111-SC-223790

Ill. 13 *Envelope of a letter from Edgar N. Johnson sent to his wife from Berlin, postmark from July 3, 1946.*
The University of Chicago Library, Special Collections Research Center, Chicago, Illinois, USA, Edgar N. Johnson Papers

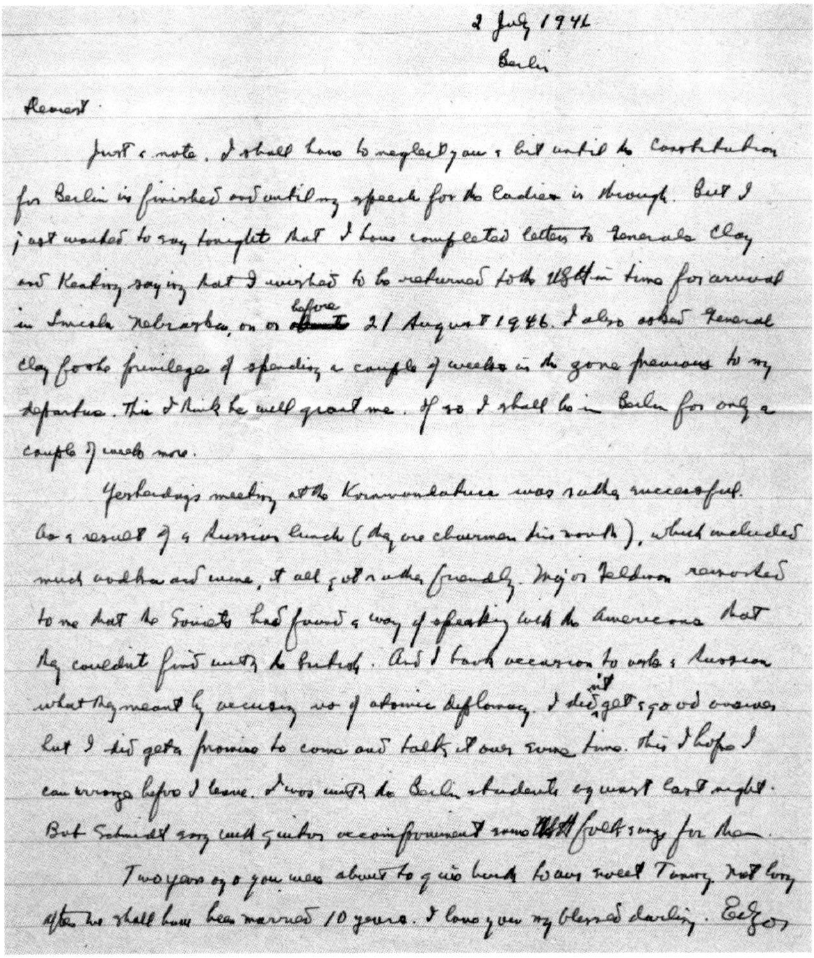

2 July 1946
Berlin

Dearest:

Just a note. I shall have to neglect you a bit until the Constitution for Berlin is finished and until my speech for the Ladies is through. But I just wanted to say tonight that I have completed letters to Generals Clay and Keating saying that I wished to be returned to the US in time for arrival in Lincoln Nebraska, on or ~~about~~ before 21 August 1946. I also asked General Clay for the privilege of spending a couple of weeks in the zone previous to my departure. This I think he will grant me. If so I shall be in Berlin for only a couple of weeks more.

Yesterday's meeting at the Kommandatura was rather successful. As a result of a Russian lunch (they are chairman this month), which included much vodka and wine, it all got rather friendly. Major Feldman remarked to me that the Soviets had found a way of speaking with the Americans that they couldn't find with the British. And I took occasion to ask a Russian what they meant by accusing us of atomic diplomacy. I did not get a good answer but I did get a promise to come and talk it over some time. This I hope I can arrange before I leave. I was with the Berlin students again last night. But Schmidt sang with guitar accompaniment some folk songs for them.

Two years ago you were about to give birth to our sweet Tommy. Not long after we shall have been married 10 years. I love you my blessed darling. Edgar

Ill. 14 *Letter from Edgar N. Johnson sent to his wife from Berlin, July 2, 1946.*
The University of Chicago Library, Special Collections Research Center, Chicago, Illinois, USA, Edgar N. Johnson Papers

Ill. 15 *Envelope of a letter from Emily L. to Edgar N. Johnson, Internal Affairs and Communications Division, OMGUS, postmark from April 12, 1946.*

Candice E. and Thomas R. Johnson, Denver, Colorado, USA

Ill. 16 *Envelope of a letter from Emily L. to Edgar N. Johnson, Civil Administration Branch, OMGBD, postmark from June 12, 1946.*

Candice E. and Thomas R. Johnson, Denver, Colorado, USA

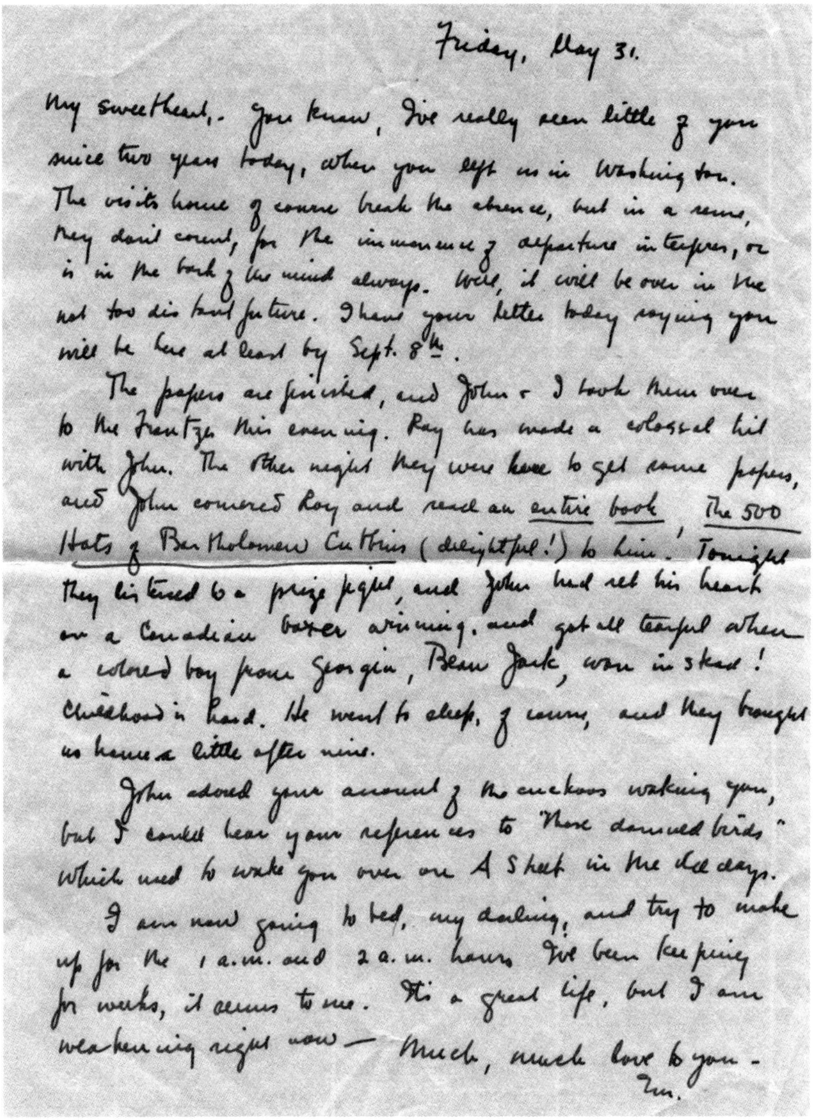

Friday, May 31.

My sweetheart,- You know, I've really seen little of you since two years today, when you left us in Washington. The visits have of course broken the absence, but in a sense, they don't count, for the imminence of departure interferes, or is in the back of the mind always. Well, it will be over in the not too distant future. I have your letter today saying you will be here at least by Sept. 8th.

The papers are finished, and John & I took them over to the Frantzes this evening. Ray has made a colossal hit with John. The other night they were here to get some papers, and John cornered Ray and read an entire book, The 500 Hats of Bartholomew Cubbins (delightful!) to him. Tonight they listened to a prize fight, and John had set his heart on a Canadian boxer winning, and got all tearful when a colored boy from Georgia, Beau Jack, won in [illegible]! [illegible] in hand. He went to sleep, of course, and they brought us home a little after nine.

John adored your account of the cuckoos waking you, but I could hear your references to "those damned birds" which used to wake you over on A Street in the old days.

I am now going to bed, my darling, and try to make up for the 1 a.m. and 2 a.m. hours I've been keeping for weeks, it seems to me. It's a great life, but I am weakening right now — Much, much love to you -

Em.

Ill. 17 *Letter from Emily L. to Edgar N. Johnson, May 31, 1946.*

Candice E. and Thomas R. Johnson, Denver, Colorado, USA

"High Scholarship" Program

JUVENILE STUDENTS

Rondo in F . . . . *Clementi*
John Johnson, age 6

Minuet from Divertimento . . . . *Mozart*
Janet Danielson, age 8

The Coucou . . . . *Daquin*
Priscilla Lowe, age 8

Valse Chromatique . . . . *Godard*
Walter Carlson, age 9

Impromptu, Op. 90 . . . . *Schubert*
Carolyn Hewes, age 9

Melody . . . . *Massenet*
Richard Cole, age 9

Ill. 18 *Program (excerpt) from the Lincoln Music Teachers' Association, piano recital of son John, May 5, 1946.*
Candice E. and Thomas R. Johnson, Denver, Colorado, USA

ALLOTTER'S LAST NAME	FIRST M. I.	ARMY SERIAL NUMBER
JOHNSON	EDGAR N	Z-9952
GRADE OR RANK	MONTHLY AMOUNT	BEGINNING 1ST DAY OF
CIV	$ 600.00	4/46
CREDIT OF (IF ALLOTTEE IS BANK)		ACKNOWLEDGMENT DATE
		18 APR 46

IMPORTANT—THE FIRST PAYMENT ON THIS ALLOTMENT WILL BE MADE ON OR ABOUT:
15 MAY 46
SUBSEQUENT PAYMENTS WILL BE MADE AS THEY FALL DUE SHORTLY AFTER THE BEGINNING OF EACH SUCCEEDING MONTH.

ALLOTTEE:
MRS EMILY L JOHNSON
3268 SO 31ST ST
LINCOLN 2 NEBRASKA

ADDRESS OF ALLOTTER:

ASF ODB FORM NO. 271-471-E305 VDG
REV. JAN 1945
Mail To This Address
PLEASE READ REVERSE SIDE
UARCO—CLEVELAND

Ill. 19 *Monthly allotment of 600 dollars to Emily L. Johnson.*
Candice E. and Thomas R. Johnson, Denver, Colorado, USA

Ill. 20 *James K. Pollock, 1945–August 1946 head of the Regional Government Coordinating Office, OMGUS, at his desk in Stuttgart.*
University of Michigan, Bentley Historical Library, Ann Arbor, Michigan, USA, James K. Pollock Papers, Box 84, Folder OMGUS

Ill. 21 *Representatives of the American occupation forces, Stuttgart, May 17, 1946, from left: James K. Pollock, General Lucius D. Clay, 1945–1947 Deputy Military Governor, Germany (US), General Walter J. Muller, 1945–1947 Director, Office of Military Government, Bavaria, and Colonel James R. Newman, 1945–1949 Director, Office of Military Government, Greater Hesse/Hesse.*
ullstein bild, Berlin, Germany/dpa

Ill. 22 *Robert D. Murphy, 1944–1949 Ambassador, Political Adviser for Germany, at his desk in Berlin, photograph from 1946.*
Stanford University, Hoover Institution Archives, Stanford, California, USA, Robert D. Murphy Papers, Envelope X

Ill. 23 *Walter L. Dorn, 1946/1947 Special Adviser for German Civil Administration and Personal Adviser on Denazification for General Lucius D. Clay, photograph from 1940.*
Columbia University in the City of New York, USA, Rare Book & Manuscript Library, Walter L. Dorn Papers, Box 2

Ill. 24 *General Lucius D. Clay (left) and General Charles K. Gailey Jr., 1945–April 1946 Chief, Civil Administration Branch, Internal Affairs and Communications Division, OMGUS, photograph from ca. 1946, personal dedication from Clay to Gailey in the upper right corner: "To Charlie Gailey The honor was mine. Lucius D. Clay."*
US Army, kindly provided by
Charles K. Gailey III, Springfield, Virginia, USA

Ill. 25 *General Ray W. Barker, 1945–May 1946 US Commandant, Allied Kommandatura Berlin.*
US Army, kindly provided by the
Dwight D. Eisenhower Library, Abilene, Kansas, USA

Ill. 26 *General Ray W. Barker taking the salute on Army Day, US Headquarters Berlin District, Berlin-Lichterfelde, April 6, 1946, behind Barker in the first row to the left: General Eric Paytherus Nares, British Commandant, in the first row from the right: General Alexander Georgievich Kotikov, Soviet Commandant, and General Charles J. M. Lançon, French Commandant.*
Rights holder unknown, kindly provided by the Archiv der sozialen Demokratie der Friedrich-Ebert-Stiftung, Bonn-Bad Godesberg, Germany

Ill. 27 *General Frank A. Keating, May 1946–1947 US Commandant, Allied Kommandatura Berlin, photograph from 1947.*
Archiv der sozialen Demokratie der Friedrich-Ebert-Stiftung, Bonn-Bad Godesberg, Germany

Ill. 28 *Reception for departing American Commandant, General Ray W. Barker, and his successor, General Frank A. Keating (second from left), second from right: Edgar N. Johnson, Wannsee Hotel/Wannsee Officers' Club, Berlin-Wannsee, April 28, 1946.*
The University of Chicago Library, Special Collections Research Center, Chicago, Illinois, USA, Edgar N. Johnson Papers

Ill. 29 *Boating on Wannsee, April 28, 1946, back left: Edgar N. Johnson, back right: General Ray W. Barker, middle left: Major Robert A. Holzman, middle right: Colonel Elmer E. Barnes, at the helm: Colonel John C. MacDonald.*
The University of Chicago Library, Special Collections Research Center, Chicago, Illinois, USA, Edgar N. Johnson Papers

Ill. 30 *Boating on Wannsee,*
April 28, 1946.
The University of Chicago Library, Special Collections Research Center, Chicago, Illinois, USA, Edgar N. Johnson Papers

Ill. 31 *Edgar N. Johnson (back left) in conversation with*
General Ray W. Barker,
April 28, 1946.
The University of Chicago Library, Special Collections Research Center, Chicago, Illinois, USA, Edgar N. Johnson Papers

Ill. 32 *Colonel Frank L. Howley, 1945–1949 Director, OMGBD/OMGBS, photograph from 1949.*
US Army, kindly provided by the Archiv der sozialen Demokratie der Friedrich-Ebert-Stiftung, Bonn-Bad Godesberg, Germany

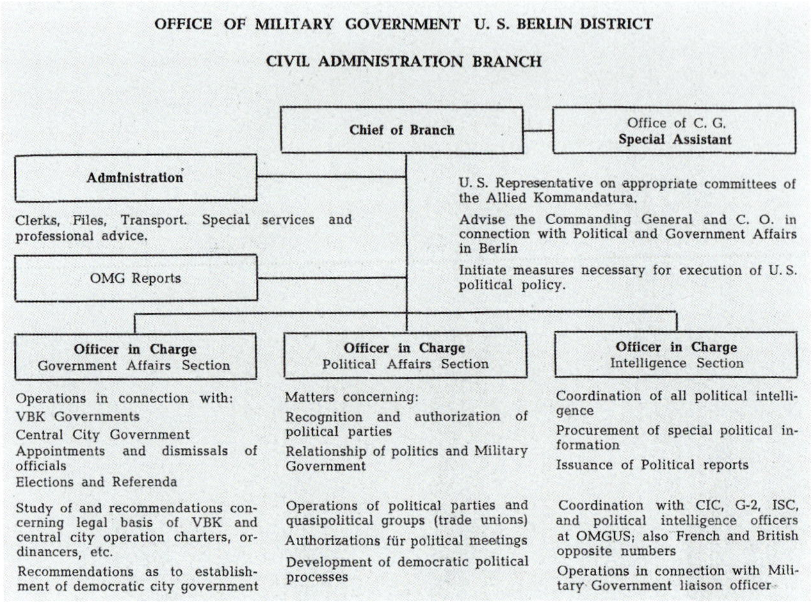

Ill. 33 *Civil Administration Branch, OMGBD, Chief of Branch: Lieutenant Colonel Louis Glaser, Special Assistant: Edgar N. Johnson.*
Office of Military Government U. S. Berlin District (ed.),
Six Months Report, 4 January–3 July 1946, Berlin 1946, p. 40

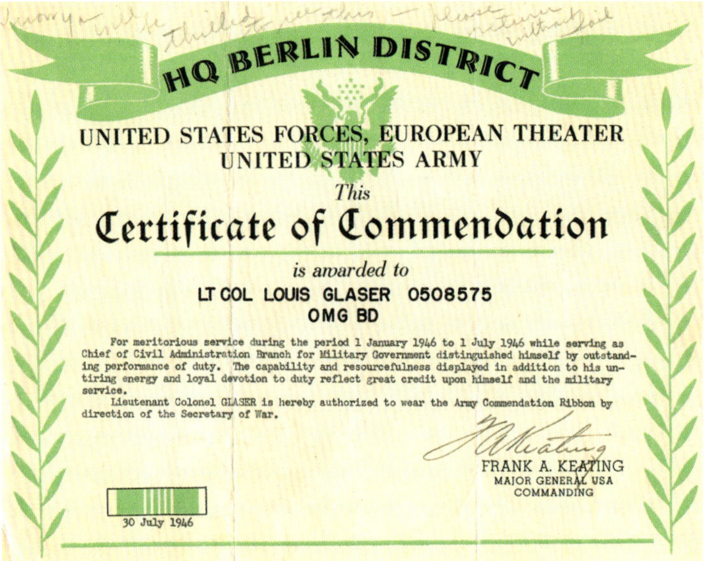

HQ BERLIN DISTRICT

UNITED STATES FORCES, EUROPEAN THEATER
UNITED STATES ARMY

This

Certificate of Commendation

is awarded to

LT COL LOUIS GLASER 0508575
OMG BD

For meritorious service during the period 1 January 1946 to 1 July 1946 while serving as Chief of Civil Administration Branch for Military Government distinguished himself by outstanding performance of duty. The capability and resourcefulness displayed in addition to his untiring energy and loyal devotion to duty reflect great credit upon himself and the military service.

Lieutenant Colonel GLASER is hereby authorized to wear the Army Commendation Ribbon by direction of the Secretary of War.

FRANK A. KEATING
MAJOR GENERAL USA
COMMANDING

30 July 1946

Ill. 34 *Certificate of Commendation for Lieutenant Colonel Louis Glaser, July 30, 1946.*
Anthony J. Glaser, Bethesda, Maryland, USA

Ill. 35 *Louis Glaser,*
January 1946–1948 Chief, Civil Administration Branch/
Civil Administration and Political Affairs Branch, OMGBD/OMGBS,
photograph from ca. 1947.
Rights holder unknown, kindly provided by the
Harry S. Truman Library, Independence, Missouri, USA

Ill. 36 *Allied Control Authority for Germany, at Kleistpark, Berlin-Schöneberg.*
Views and Facts of Berlin. As seen through the eyes of the American soldier and intended for the folks and friends at home, n. p. and n. d.

Ill. 37 *Allied Kommandatura Berlin, Kaiserswerther Straße 16/18, Berlin-Dahlem.*
Views and Facts of Berlin. As seen through the eyes of the American soldier and intended for the folks and friends at home, n. p. and n. d.

Ill. 38 *Menu card, Allied Kommandatura Berlin, June 26, 1946.*
Candice E. and Thomas R. Johnson, Denver, Colorado, USA

Ill. 39 *OMGUS,*
Kronprinzenallee (today Clayallee), Berlin-Dahlem.
Berlinische Galerie. Landesmuseum für Moderne Kunst, Fotografie und Architektur, Berlin, Germany/Henry Ries

Ill. 40 *OMGBD,*
Grunewaldstraße 35, Berlin-Steglitz.
Office of Military Government U. S. Sector, Berlin (ed.),
A Four Year Report, July 1, 1945–September 1, 1949, Berlin 1949, p. 125

Ill. 41 *Harnack House,*
including officers' mess,
Ihnestraße 16, Berlin-Dahlem, garden view.
Archiv der Max-Planck-Gesellschaft, Berlin, Germany

Ill. 42 *Edgar N. Johnson's first residence in Berlin: then Ihnestraße 14, today Brümmerstraße 74, Berlin-Dahlem, photograph from 2009.*
Landesarchiv Berlin, Germany/Barbara Esch-Marowski

Ill. 43 *Edgar N. Johnson's second residence in Berlin: Am Sandwerder 17/19, Berlin-Wannsee, then Wannsee Hotel/Wannsee Officers' Club, today American Academy in Berlin, Hans Arnhold Center, photograph from 2009.*
Landesarchiv Berlin, Germany/Barbara Esch-Marowski

Ill. 44 *Edgar N. Johnson and his chauffeur, Artur Sanow, at the entrance of the Wannsee Hotel/Wannsee Officers' Club, 1946.* The University of Chicago Library, Special Collections Research Center, Chicago, Illinois, USA, Edgar N. Johnson Papers

Ill. 45 *Artur Sanow, Wannsee Hotel/Wannsee Officers' Club, 1946.* The University of Chicago Library, Special Collections Research Center, Chicago, Illinois, USA, Edgar N. Johnson Papers

Ill. 46 *Am Sandwerder 17/19, garden view, photograph from 2009.*
Landesarchiv Berlin, Germany/Barbara Esch-Marowski

Ill. 47 *Am Sandwerder 17/19, view of Großer Wannsee from the terrace, photograph from 2012.*
Candice E. and Thomas R. Johnson, Denver, Colorado, USA

Ill. 48 *Soviet tank memorial in the American sector of Berlin, 1946.*
The University of Chicago Library, Special Collections Research Center,
Chicago, Illinois, USA, Edgar N. Johnson Papers

Ill. 49 *Artur Sanow, 1946.*
The University of Chicago Library, Special Collections Research Center,
Chicago, Illinois, USA, Edgar N. Johnson Papers

Ill. 50 *View of the destroyed Kaiser-Wilhelm-Gedächtniskirche, Berlin-Charlottenburg, 1946.*
The University of Chicago Library, Special Collections Research Center, Chicago, Illinois, USA, Edgar N. Johnson Papers

Ill. 51 *Landscape of ruins with sign in three languages: "YOU ARE LEAVING THE AMERICAN SECTOR," 1946.*
The University of Chicago Library, Special Collections Research Center, Chicago, Illinois, USA, Edgar N. Johnson Papers

Ill. 52 *Am Sandwerder 27, Berlin-Wannsee, 1945–May 1946 residence of General Ray W. Barker, photograph probably from the second half of the 1930s.*
Hedda Dutilh-von Schmidt Seidlitz, Aerdenhout, Netherlands

Ill. 53 *Edgar N. Johnson (left) and Lieutenant Colonel Louis Glaser at the entrance of the residence, April 21, 1946.*
The University of Chicago Library, Special Collections Research Center, Chicago, Illinois, USA, Edgar N. Johnson Papers

Ill. 54 *Am Sandwerder 27, garden view, photograph from 2009.*
Landesarchiv Berlin, Germany/Barbara Esch-Marowski

Ill. 55 *Gelfertstraße 32/34, Berlin-Dahlem, as of 1945 residence of Colonel Frank L. Howley, photograph from 2011.*
Landesarchiv Berlin, Germany/Thomas Platow

Ill. 56 *Podbielskiallee 65, Berlin-Dahlem, former villa of the cellist Max Baldner, requisitioned by American occupation forces in 1945, photograph from 2009.*
Landesarchiv Berlin, Germany/Barbara Esch-Marowski

Ill. 57 *Max Baldner, 1942.*
Thomas Baldner, Bloomington, Indiana, USA

Ill. 58 *The cellist Max Baldner, oil painting by Ewald Vetter, 1946.*
Art postcard, kindly provided by
Helmut Hoffmann, Berlin, Germany

Ill. 59 *Am Großen Wannsee 2/4, Berlin-Wannsee, former villa of the movie actress Brigitte Helm, 1946 Lakeside Club for high-ranking American officers, photograph from 2011.*
Landesarchiv Berlin, Germany/Thomas Platow

Ill. 60 *Inselstraße 16 on Schwanenwerder Island, Berlin-Wannsee, as of 1946 Lakeside Club, photograph from 1953.*
Landesarchiv Berlin, Germany/Gert Schütz, F Rep. 290 (Allgemeine Fotosammlung), no. 29956

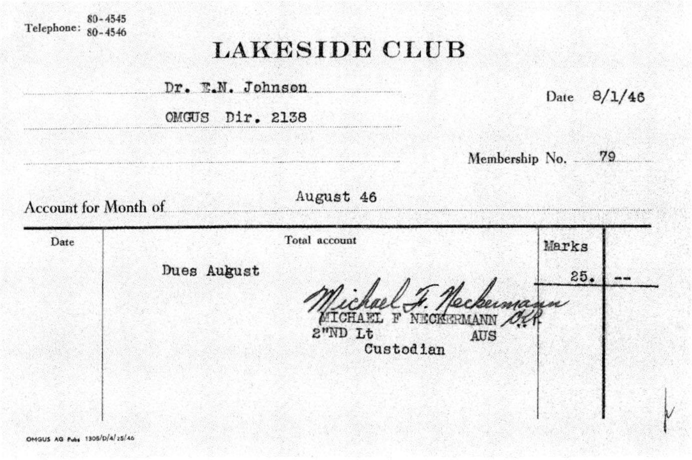

Telephone: 80-4545 80-4546

LAKESIDE CLUB

Dr. E.N. Johnson
OMGUS Dir. 2138

Date 8/1/46

Membership No. 79

Account for Month of August 46

Date	Total account	Marks	
	Dues August	25.	--

Michael F. Neckermann
MICHAEL F NECKERMANN
2"ND Lt AUS
Custodian

OMGUS AG Pubs 1308/D/4/25/46

Ill. 61 *Receipt for Edgar N. Johnson, August 1, 1946.*
Candice E. and Thomas R. Johnson, Denver, Colorado, USA

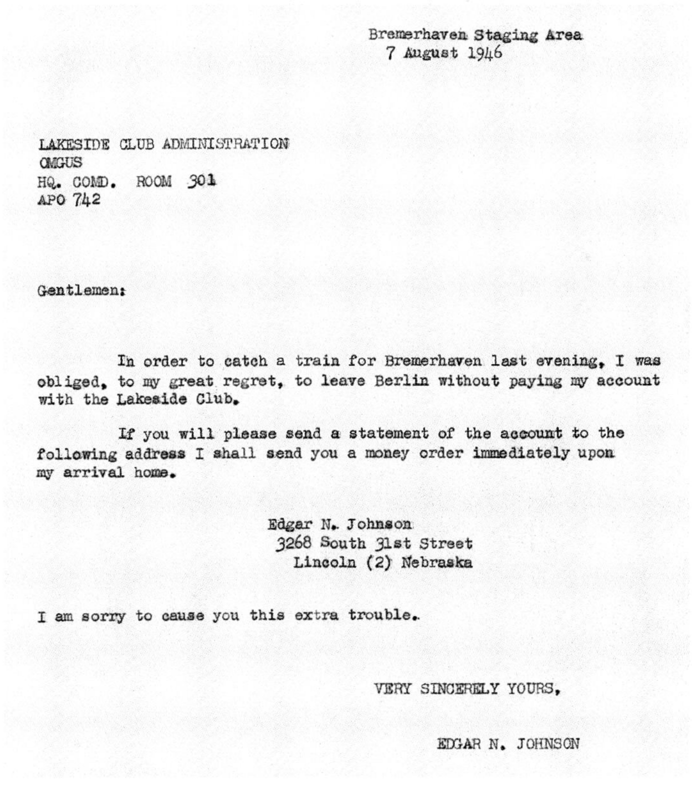

Bremerhaven Staging Area
7 August 1946

LAKESIDE CLUB ADMINISTRATION
OMGUS
HQ. COMD. ROOM 301
APO 742

Gentlemen:

In order to catch a train for Bremerhaven last evening, I was obliged, to my great regret, to leave Berlin without paying my account with the Lakeside Club.

If you will please send a statement of the account to the following address I shall send you a money order immediately upon my arrival home.

Edgar N. Johnson
3268 South 31st Street
Lincoln (2) Nebraska

I am sorry to cause you this extra trouble.

VERY SINCERELY YOURS,

EDGAR N. JOHNSON

Ill. 62 *Letter from Edgar N. Johnson sent to the Lakeside Club Administration from Bremerhaven, August 7, 1946.*
Candice E. and Thomas R. Johnson, Denver, Colorado, USA

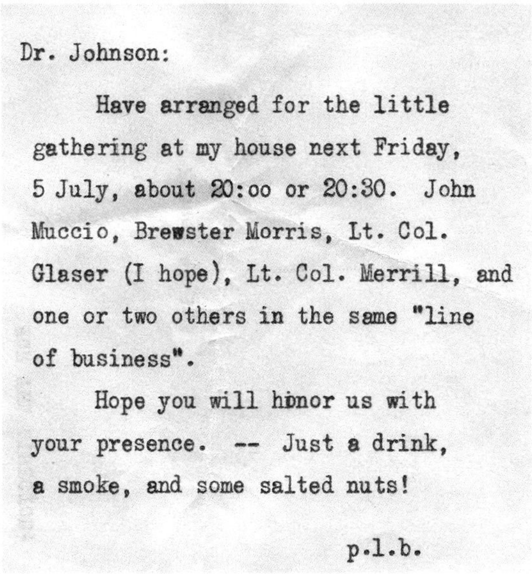

Dr. Johnson:

Have arranged for the little gathering at my house next Friday, 5 July, about 20:oo or 20:30. John Muccio, Brewster Morris, Lt. Col. Glaser (I hope), Lt. Col. Merrill, and one or two others in the same "line of business".

Hope you will honor us with your presence. -- Just a drink, a smoke, and some salted nuts!

p.l.b.

Ill. 63 *Invitation to a gathering on July 5, 1946, p. l. b.: possibly the initials of Philip L. Barbour, Civil Administration Branch, OMGBD.*
Candice E. and Thomas R. Johnson, Denver, Colorado, USA

"Shun Nazis", Wives Told At Women's Club Meeting

American families should have no toleration for Nazi-Germans, no matter how cultured or charming they seem to be, stated Dr. E. N. Johnson, Special Assistant to the Commanding General, Headquarters, B. D. at the second meeting of the American Women's Club of Berlin, Tuesday, when he discussed the responsibilities of American women in occupation.

Ill. 64 *Newspaper article (excerpt) about Edgar N. Johnson's lecture on July 9, 1946, for the American Women's Club of Berlin.*
OMGUS Observer from July 12, 1946, p. 2

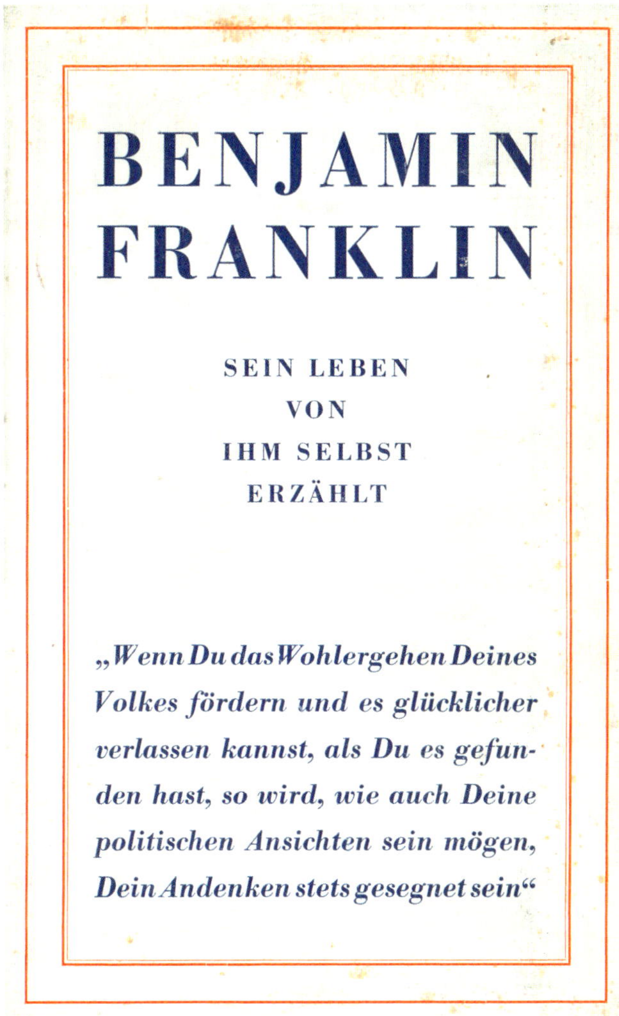

BENJAMIN FRANKLIN

SEIN LEBEN
VON
IHM SELBST
ERZÄHLT

„Wenn Du das Wohlergehen Deines Volkes fördern und es glücklicher verlassen kannst, als Du es gefunden hast, so wird, wie auch Deine politischen Ansichten sein mögen, Dein Andenken stets gesegnet sein“

Ill. 65 *German edition of Benjamin Franklin's autobiography, published in 1946 by Karl H. Henssel Verlag, Berlin, with a foreword by Edgar N. Johnson.*
Kindly provided by
Candice E. and Thomas R. Johnson, Denver, Colorado, USA

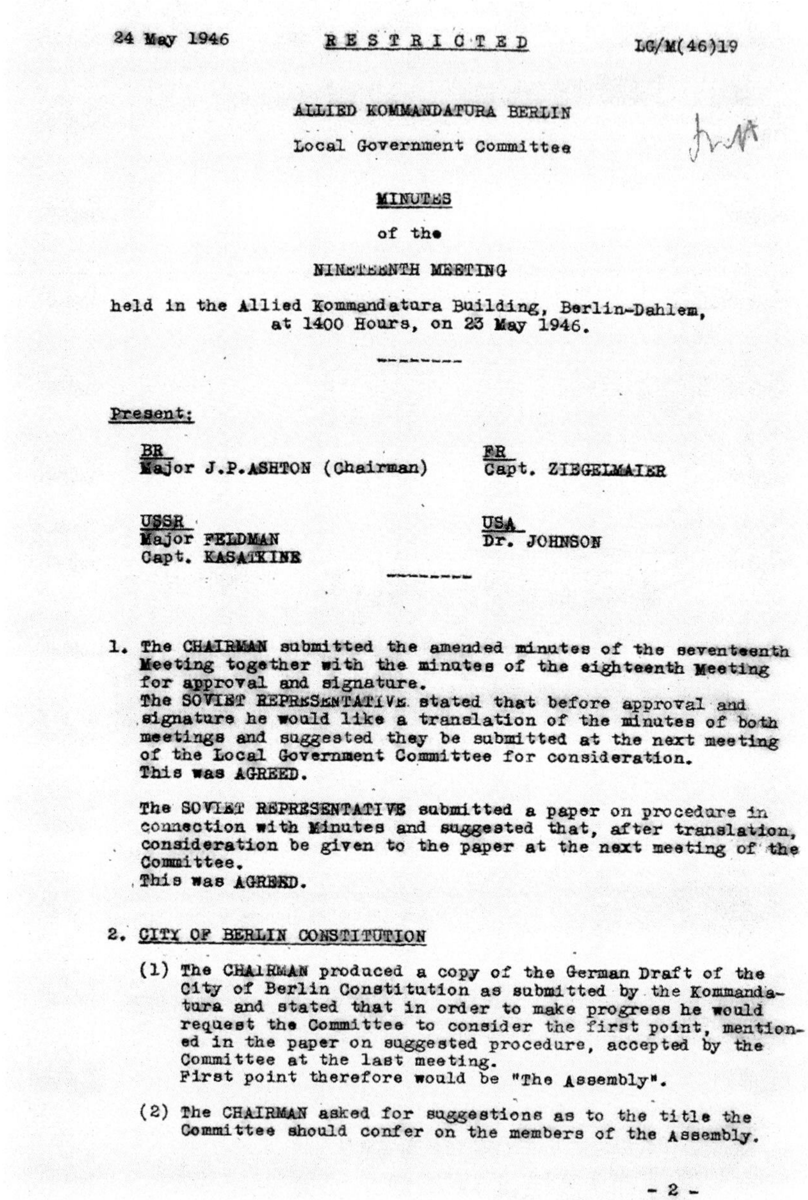

24 May 1946 RESTRICTED LG/M(46)19

ALLIED KOMMANDATURA BERLIN

Local Government Committee

MINUTES

of the

NINETEENTH MEETING

held in the Allied Kommandatura Building, Berlin-Dahlem, at 1400 Hours, on 23 May 1946.

Present:

BR
Major J.P.ASHTON (Chairman)

FR
Capt. ZIEGELMAIER

USSR
Major FELDMAN
Capt. KASATKINE

USA
Dr. JOHNSON

1. The CHAIRMAN submitted the amended minutes of the seventeenth Meeting together with the minutes of the eighteenth Meeting for approval and signature.
The SOVIET REPRESENTATIVE stated that before approval and signature he would like a translation of the minutes of both meetings and suggested they be submitted at the next meeting of the Local Government Committee for consideration.
This was AGREED.

The SOVIET REPRESENTATIVE submitted a paper on procedure in connection with Minutes and suggested that, after translation, consideration be given to the paper at the next meeting of the Committee.
This was AGREED.

2. CITY OF BERLIN CONSTITUTION

(1) The CHAIRMAN produced a copy of the German Draft of the City of Berlin Constitution as submitted by the Kommandatura and stated that in order to make progress he would request the Committee to consider the first point, mentioned in the paper on suggested procedure, accepted by the Committee at the last meeting.
First point therefore would be "The Assembly".

(2) The CHAIRMAN asked for suggestions as to the title the Committee should confer on the members of the Assembly.

- 2 -

Ill. 66 and ill. 67 *First and last page of the protocol from a meeting of the Local Government Committee, Allied Kommandatura Berlin, on May 23, 1946, signed by (from left): Major John Pennington Ashton (Great Britain), Capitaine Jean Victor Ziegelmeyer (France), Major Iosif Moiseyevich Feldman (Soviet Union), and Edgar N. Johnson (USA).*
The National Archives, Kew, Richmond, Surrey, Great Britain, Allied Kommandatura: Directives, Minutes and Papers, FO 1112/378

RESTRICTED

- 5 -

The CHAIRMAN also stated that the Magistrat had undertaken to prepare the Electoral Machinery within three months after a decision is made upon the following points:-

(1) What are we going to elect?
(2) How are we going to elect them?
(3) Who shall vote?

First point concerns the Constitution.

Questions arising on the second point were:-

(1) On Basis of Proportional Representation
(2) On a direct vote of each person
(3) A combination of the two (alternative vote).

To initiate a discussion, the CHAIRMAN suggested that two thirds be elected by direct vote and one third from a modified form of Proportional Representation.

The US REPRESENTATIVE suggested that instead of going ahead with this question to-day, an extraordinary meeting be called of the Local Government Committee to discuss Electoral Procedure.

4. After some discussion, it was

AGREED to hold an extraordinary meeting of the Local Government Committee on Friday 31 May 1946, at 1000 Hours for the purpose of discussing Electoral Procedure, and the Electoral Roll.

5. NEXT ORDINARY MEETING

It was

AGREED that the next ordinary meeting of the Local Government Committee be held on Friday 31 May 1946, at 1400 Hours.

GR BR	FR	USSR	USA

Ill. 68 *Meeting of the Local Government Committee, Allied Kommandatura Berlin, beginning of June 1946, from left, clockwise: the British delegation (secretary, interpreter [Russian], observer from the Control Commission, Major Harold Hays, and interpreter [French]), the French delegation (secretary and Capitaine Jean Victor Ziegelmeyer [Chairman]), the American representative (Lieutenant Colonel Louis Glaser), and the Russian delegation (interpreter [French], Lieutenant Colonel Alexander Mikhailovich Zozulya, and Major Iosif Moiseyevich Feldman).*
Rights holder unknown, kindly provided by Anthony J. Glaser, Bethesda, Maryland, USA

Ill. 69 *Edgar N. Johnson during a break of the Local Government Committee, Allied Kommandatura Berlin, July 5, 1946.*
The University of Chicago Library, Special Collections Research Center, Chicago, Illinois, USA, Edgar N. Johnson Papers

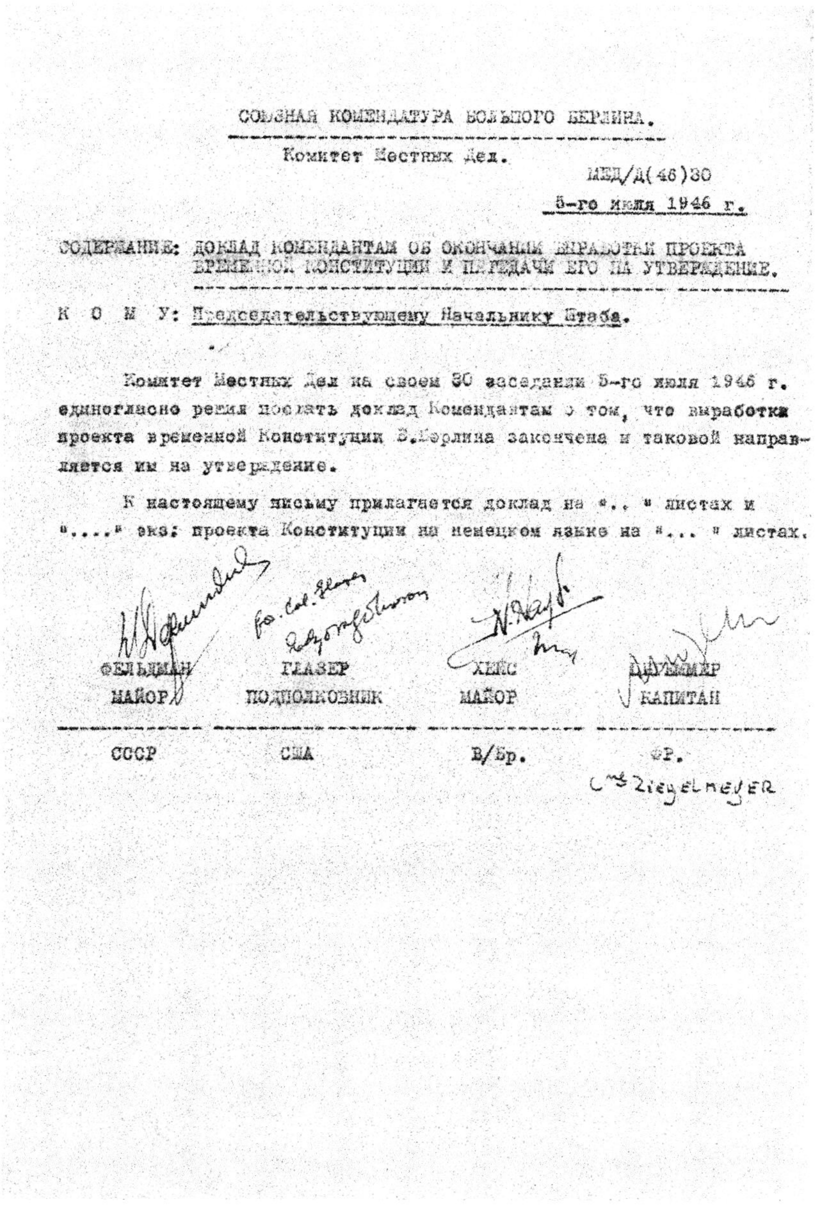

СОЮЗНАЯ КОМЕНДАТУРА БОЛЬШОГО БЕРЛИНА.

Комитет Местных Дел.

МЕД/Д(46)30

5-го июля 1946 г.

СОДЕРЖАНИЕ: ДОКЛАД КОМЕНДАНТАМ ОБ ОКОНЧАНИИ ВЫРАБОТКИ ПРОЕКТА ВРЕМЕННОЙ КОНСТИТУЦИИ И ПЕРЕДАЧИ ЕГО НА УТВЕРЖДЕНИЕ.

К О М У: Председательствующему Начальнику Штаба.

Комитет Местных Дел на своем 30 заседании 5-го июля 1946 г. единогласно решил послать доклад Комендантам о том, что выработка проекта временной Конституции Б.Берлина закончена и таковой направляется им на утверждение.

К настоящему письму прилагается доклад на «.. » листах и «....» экз: проекта Конституции на немецком языке на «... » листах.

ФЕЛЬДМАН МАЙОР	ГЛАЗЕР ПОДПОЛКОВНИК	ХЕЙС МАЙОР	ЦИГЕЛЬМЕЙЕР КАПИТАН
СССР	США	В/Бр.	Фр.

Ill. 70 *Report of the Local Government Committee, Allied Kommandatura Berlin, regarding the draft of a provisional Berlin constitution, July 5, 1946, signed by (from left): Major Iosif Moiseyevich Feldman (Soviet Union), Edgar N. Johnson for Lieutenant Colonel Louis Glaser (USA), Major Harold Hays (Great Britain), and Capitaine Jean Victor Ziegelmeyer (France).*

The National Archives, Kew, Richmond, Surrey, Great Britain, Allied Kommandatura: Directives, Minutes and Papers, FO 1112/377

TEMPORARY CONSTITUTION OF BERLIN

To provide for the situation arising after the collapse of the national-socialist regime, and the occupation by the Allied Powers, and in continuation of the constitutional right, according to the City Statutes of 30 May, 1853, to the Law on the formation of a new Municipality Berlin of 27 April, 1920, and the Law on the preliminary regulation of various problems of the municipal constitutional right of the City of Berlin of 30 March, 1931, Berlin receives the following

CONSTITUTION

Chapter I: GENERAL PROVISIONS

Article 1

(1) Greater Berlin is the exclusively established Public Territorial Corporation for the Territory of the Municipality of Berlin.

(2) Greater Berlin has to fulfil all the public duties in its district in accordance with this Constitution.

(3) Greater Berlin bears the Arms and Flag with the Bear. Particulars hereof will be laid down in a special Order.

Article 2

(1) The whole of the German citizens of Greater Berlin express their will through their elected representative bodies.

(2) All citizens of Greater Berlin are, within the framework of the effective laws, of equal status independent of Race, Sex, Confession and extent of Property owned.

(3) The representative bodies are the Stadtverordnetenversammlung and the Magistrat.

Article 3

(1) The Stadtverordnetenversammlung is constituted on ground of general, equal, direct, and secret election by the inhabitants of Berlin, who are entitled to vote according to the principles of proportional representation.

(2) The members of the Magistrat will be elected by the Stadtverordnetenversammlung for the period of the election term. All political parties composing the Stadtverordnetenversammlung

11

Ill. 71 *Provisional Constitution of Greater Berlin (Temporary Constitution of Berlin) from August 13, 1946, English version, first page of the text from a brochure printed by Printing and Stationery Service, Control Commission for Germany (BE), Berlin.*
Kindly provided by
Anthony J. Glaser, Bethesda, Maryland, USA

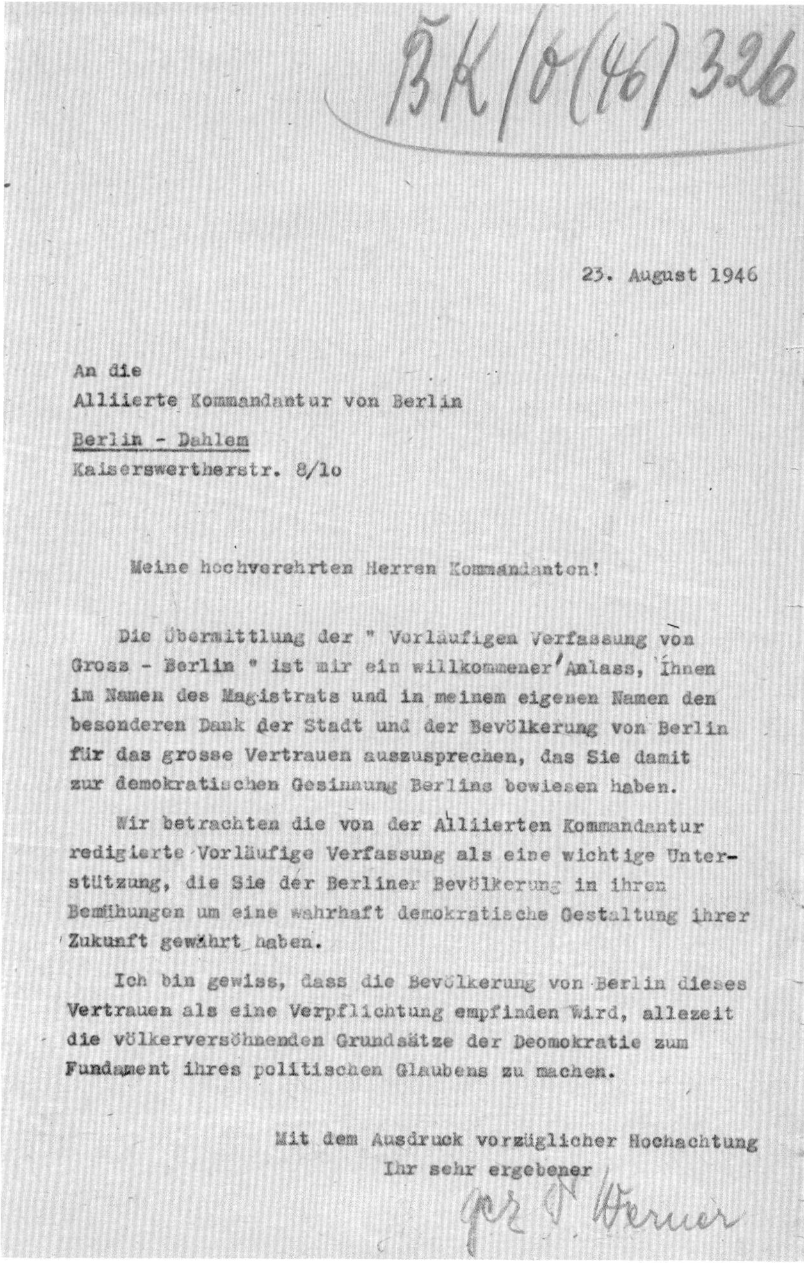

BK/O (46) 326

23. August 1946

An die
Alliierte Kommandantur von Berlin

Berlin - Dahlem
Kaiserswertherstr. 8/10

Meine hochverehrten Herren Kommandanten!

Die Übermittlung der " Vorläufigen Verfassung von Gross - Berlin " ist mir ein willkommener Anlass, Ihnen im Namen des Magistrats und in meinem eigenen Namen den besonderen Dank der Stadt und der Bevölkerung von Berlin für das grosse Vertrauen auszusprechen, das Sie damit zur demokratischen Gesinnung Berlins bewiesen haben.

Wir betrachten die von der Alliierten Kommandantur redigierte Vorläufige Verfassung als eine wichtige Unterstützung, die Sie der Berliner Bevölkerung in ihren Bemühungen um eine wahrhaft demokratische Gestaltung ihrer Zukunft gewährt haben.

Ich bin gewiss, dass die Bevölkerung von Berlin dieses Vertrauen als eine Verpflichtung empfinden wird, allezeit die völkerversöhnenden Grundsätze der Deomokratie zum Fundament ihres politischen Glaubens zu machen.

Mit dem Ausdruck vorzüglicher Hochachtung
Ihr sehr ergebener
gez. Dr. Werner

Ill. 72 *After delivery of the Provisional Constitution of Greater Berlin with BK/O (46) 326: letter of thanks from Oberbürgermeister Arthur Werner to the Commandants, August 23, 1946.*
Landesarchiv Berlin, Germany,
C Rep. 101 (Magistrat von Berlin, Oberbürgermeister), no. 65

ALLIED KOMMANDATURA BERLIN
16-18, Kaiserswerther Str.

31 August 1946

SUBJECT: Letter of Commendation

TO : Local Government Committee,
Allied Kommandatura Berlin:

US Lt. Colonel Louis Glaser
Dr. E. N. Johnson
Mr. P. G. Artzrouni

BR Commander Athelstane Doelberg
Major Harold Hays
Mr. Bernard Francis Emmerson
Capt. John Archibald Robert
Miss Emma Grace Gibson

FR Capt. Jean Victor Ziegelmayer
Lt. Claude Ampoulange
Lt. Georges Dmitrieff
Lt. Antoine Gaspcercic

USSR Lt. Colonel Alexander Zozulya
Major Feldman
Lt. Yurovsky
Lt. Rojko

The Commandants of the Allied Kommandatura Berlin are aware of the long, arduous hours that the Local Government Committee has labored in formulating and drafting the Constitution of the City of Berlin and the instructions to the Magistrat concerning the "Electoral Procedure of Berlin". The members of the Local Government Committee have given unstintingly of their time, and have drawn deeply upon their professional knowledge and experience to complete this important and difficult task assigned them by the Commandants. The completed document on the "Electoral Procedure of Berlin" is a testimonial to the patience and devotion to duty shown by all members of this Committee in reconciling divergent points of view and thereby producing a sound document.

Ill. 73 and ill. 74 *Letter of thanks from the Commandants to the Local Government Committee, Allied Kommandatura Berlin, August 31, 1946.*
Anthony J. Glaser, Bethesda, Maryland, USA

The superior and practical work of the Local Government Committee in producing this document affords an example that all other Committees of the Allied Kommandatura Berlin may well emulate.

The Commandants commend the members of the Local Government Committee individually and collectively for their work in the successful completion of this highly important task.

C. E. RYAN	E. P. NARES	Charles LANCON	A. G. KOTIKOV
Brig. General	Maj.Gen.CBE MC	Gen. de Brig.	Maj. General
US Commandant	BR Commandant	FR Commandant	USSR Commandant

- 2 -

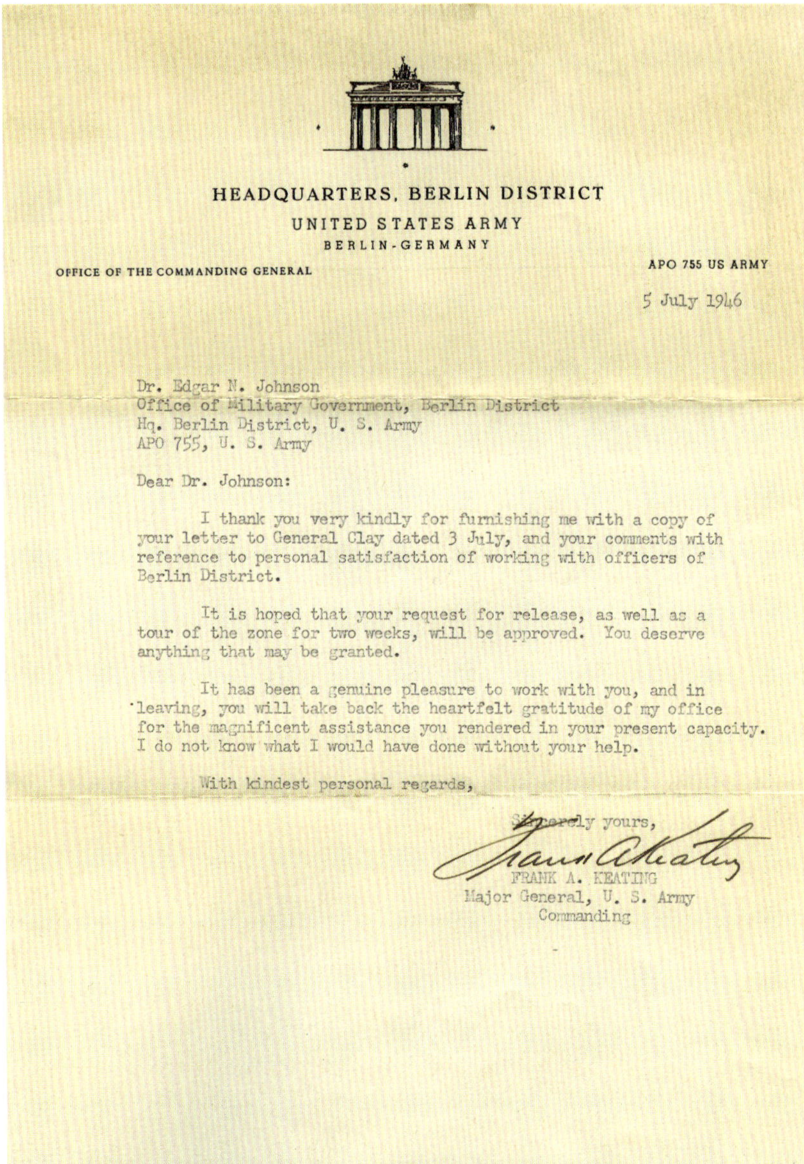

HEADQUARTERS, BERLIN DISTRICT
UNITED STATES ARMY
BERLIN-GERMANY

OFFICE OF THE COMMANDING GENERAL

APO 755 US ARMY

5 July 1946

Dr. Edgar N. Johnson
Office of Military Government, Berlin District
Hq. Berlin District, U. S. Army
APO 755, U. S. Army

Dear Dr. Johnson:

I thank you very kindly for furnishing me with a copy of your letter to General Clay dated 3 July, and your comments with reference to personal satisfaction of working with officers of Berlin District.

It is hoped that your request for release, as well as a tour of the zone for two weeks, will be approved. You deserve anything that may be granted.

It has been a genuine pleasure to work with you, and in leaving, you will take back the heartfelt gratitude of my office for the magnificent assistance you rendered in your present capacity. I do not know what I would have done without your help.

With kindest personal regards,

Sincerely yours,

Frank A. Keating

FRANK A. KEATING
Major General, U. S. Army
Commanding

Ill. 75 *Letter of thanks from General Frank A. Keating to Edgar N. Johnson, July 5, 1946.*

Candice E. and Thomas R. Johnson, Denver, Colorado, USA

OFFICE OF MILITARY GOVERNMENT FOR GERMANY (U. S.)
Office of the Deputy Military Governor
APO 742

12 September 1946

Dear Dr. Johnson:

I too regretted that I did not get to say goodbye to you personally and to express my appreciation for the help you gave to Military Government.

It was unfortunate that delays over which we had no control brought you back to Germany too late for the assignment with the Landerrat. However, it did make you available as the adviser to Berlin Military Government at a time when the political structure of the city was in grave difficulty. Your contribution can be measured by the fact that prior to your departure, the four Allied Governments had agreed on a democratic city charter and a free election.

I shall ever be grateful to you for the spirit in which you undertook a changed assignment and to your insistence on a liberal and democratic philosophy of city government which will mean even more to Berlin and Germany in the future.

We miss you at our staff meetings. However, we also hope you will have an occasional pang of regret that you are not still with us.

In any event, if liberalism can become a reality in Germany, it will grow from the foundation which you helped so much to place.

Sincerely yours,

LUCIUS D. CLAY
Lieutenant General, U. S. Army
Deputy Military Governor

Dr. Edgar N. Johnson
3268 South 31st Street
Lincoln 2, Nebraska

Ill. 76 *Letter of thanks from General Lucius D. Clay to Edgar N. Johnson, September 12, 1946.*
The University of Chicago Library, Special Collections Research Center, Chicago, Illinois, USA, Edgar N. Johnson Papers

Ill. 77 *First postwar elections in Berlin, the members of the Local Government Committee, Allied Kommandatura Berlin, leaving a polling location, October 20, 1946, from left: Colonel Louis Glaser (USA), Major Harold Hays (Great Britain), Capitaine Jean Victor Ziegelmeyer (France), and Major Vladimir Mikhailovich Demidov (Soviet Union).*
Presse Bild Zscheile, Berlin-Schlachtensee, Germany, kindly provided by Anthony J. Glaser, Bethesda, Maryland, USA

Ill. 78 *Ballot for the election of city council members on October 20, 1946.*
Landesarchiv Berlin, Germany, C Rep. 102 (Magistrat von Berlin, Abteilung Verwaltung und Personalpolitik), no. 163

Ill. 79 *Anna Engelhorn,*
Edgar N. Johnson's boarding-house hostess in Munich in 1927/1928,
photograph from the 1920s.
Dieter Loew, Basel, Switzerland

Ill. 80 *Otto Suhr,*
August 1946–1947 Secretary General (previously Acting Secretary General)
of the newly organized Berlin SPD,
photograph from 1946.
Archiv der sozialen Demokratie der Friedrich-Ebert-Stiftung,
Bonn-Bad Godesberg, Germany

Ill. 81 *Franz Neumann,*
April 1946–1958 Chairman of the Berlin SPD,
photograph from 1946.
Pressebildagentur Schirner/Deutsches Historisches Museum, Berlin, Germany

Ill. 82 *Party unification conference of the KPD and SPD at the Admiralspalast, Friedrichstraße 101/102, Berlin-Mitte, April 21, 1946, front row from left: Max Fechner, Wilhelm Pieck, Otto Grotewohl, and Walter Ulbricht.*
Landesarchiv Berlin, Germany, F Rep. 290 (Allgemeine Fotosammlung), no. 74142

Ill. 83 *Friedrich Haas, March–December 1946 Acting City Treasurer, photograph from 1946.*
Landesarchiv Berlin, Germany/Alois Bankhardt, F Rep. 290 (Allgemeine Fotosammlung), no. 88477

Dr. Friedrich H a a s
Mitglied des Magistrats und
Kämmerer von Groß-Berlin
\- - -

Berlin C 2,den 30.Dez.1946.
Neues Stadthaus,Parochialstr. 1-3
Privatanschrift: Bln.-Dahlem, Löhleinstr.27

Lieber Herr J o h n s o n !

Herzlichen Dank für Ihre werten Zeilen, die ich im Oktober erhalten habe. Mit Hilfe von Mr.Biel bin ich bereits zweimal in Süddeutschland gewesen. Das letzte Mal nahm ich an einer interzonalen Tagung von Finanzfachleuten in der französischen Zone teil.

Die Arbeit ist hier vor wie nach den Wahlen in steigendem Tempo weitergegangen. Die Schwierigkeiten haben nicht abgenommen. Die vorläufige Verfassung, an der Sie so großen Anteil hatten, ist am 13.August 1946 veröffentlicht und am Wahltag, am 20.Oktober, in Kraft getreten. Inzwischen ist der neue Magistrat gewählt und hat zum größten Teil seine Tätigkeit aufgenommen. Der Wechsel vom alten, von den Besatzungsmächten eingesetzten, zum neuen, von den Bürgern gewählten, war nicht einfach. Wir befinden uns zur Zeit noch im Übergangsstadium.

Ich selbst wurde im Dezember zum Mitglied des neuen Magistrats, und zwar als Leiter der Rechts- und Verfassungsabteilung gewählt und auch von den Besatzungsmächten bestätigt. Da jedoch für meinen Nachfolger in der Finanzabteilung Schwierigkeiten eintraten, mußte ich am 19.Dezember wieder die Leitung der Finanzabteilung übernehmen. Ich bin nunmehr

<u>also</u>

Ill. 84 and ill. 85 *Letter from Friedrich Haas to Edgar N. Johnson, December 30, 1946.*
The University of Chicago Library, Special Collections Research Center, Chicago, Illinois, USA, Edgar N. Johnson Papers

also der auch in der vorläufigen Verfassung erwähnte Kämmerer von Groß-Berlin und daher gezwungen, die verfassungsrechtlichen Fragen nur noch nebenbei behandeln zu können. Augenblicklich benutze ich die Tage um Weihnachten und Neujahr, um den Ihnen angekündigten Kommentar zur vorläufigen Verfassung zu schreiben. Ich hoffe, mit dem Entwurf Mitte Januar fertig zu seih. Sobald er gedruckt ist, werde ich Ihnen ein Stück zugehen lassen. Daß ich bei der Erläuterung der vorläufigen Verfassung beinahe bei jedem Wort an unsere freundliche und offene Aussprache denke, brauche ich wohl nicht besonders zu betonen. Die Stunden und Tage unseres Kennenlernens und Zusammenarbeitens für eine größere, in die Zukunft weisende gemeinsame Sache bleiben mir unvergessen.

In der Hoffnung, Ihnen bald den Kommentar übermitteln zu können, verbleibt mit den ergebensten Grüßen für ein erfolgreiches Jahr 1947 auch an Ihre werte Frau

Ihr

Ill. 86 *Edgar N. Johnson's "study cabin" in the Rocky Mountains in Colorado, where the letters to his wife were found, photograph from 2012.*
Candice E. and Thomas R. Johnson, Denver, Colorado, USA

List of Abbreviations

AB	Artium Baccalaureus (Bachelor of Arts)
ACA	Allied Control Authority
ACDP	Archiv für Christlich-Demokratische Politik
ACSP	Archiv für Christlich-Soziale Politik
AFP	Agence France-Presse
AG	Aktiengesellschaft
AGO	Adjutant General's Office
a. m.	ante meridiem
AMG	American Military Government
AOF	Archives de l'Occupation Française
APO	Army Post Office
Aug.	August
BA	Bachelor of Arts
BAB	Branchen-Adreßbücher
BArch	Bundesarchiv
BASC	Berlin Air Safety Center
BC	Before Christ
BCS	Bachelor of Commercial Science
BD	Bachelor of Divinity; Berlin District
BE	Bachelor of Engineering; British Element
BICO	Bipartite Control Office
BKC/M	Berlin Kommandatura Commandants/ Minutes of meeting
BKD/M	Berlin Kommandatura Deputy Commandants/ Minutes of meeting
BK/O; BK/Ord.	Berlin Kommandatura/Order
BMus	Bachelor of Music
BS; BSc	Bachelor of Science
BS in Ed	Bachelor of Science in Education
BVG	Berliner Verkehrsbetriebe
BWV	Bachwerkeverzeichnis
ca.	circa
CAF	Clerical, Administrative, and Fiscal Service
Capt.	Captain
C. A. R.	Children of the American Revolution
CARE	Cooperative for American Remittances to Europe
CC	Control Council
C-C	Coca-Cola
CCG (BE)	Control Commission for Germany (British Element)
CDU	Christlich-Demokratische Union
cf.	confer
CI	Civil Internment
CIA; C. I. A.	Central Intelligence Agency

CID	Criminal Investigation Department
Cie.	Compagnie
CIO	Congress of Industrial Organizations
cm	centimeter
Co.	Compagnie; Company
c/o	care of
col.	column
Col.	Colonel
cols.	columns
Cols.	Colonels
Com.	Committee
Comintern	Communist International
CORC/M	Coordinating Committee/Minutes of meeting
CPSU	Communist Party of the Soviet Union
CSU	Christlich-Soziale Union
D. A. R.	Daughters of the American Revolution
D. C.	District of Columbia
D day; D-day; D-Day	Day day; Day-day; Day-Day
DDR	Deutsche Demokratische Republik
DDr.	Doktor Doktor
DFD	Demokratischer Frauenbund Deutschlands
d. h.	das heißt
DIAC	Directorate of Internal Affairs and Communications
DIAC/CAC/M	Directorate of Internal Affairs and Communications/ Civil Administration Committee/Minutes of meeting
DLitt	Doctor Litterarum (Doctor of Letters)
DMus	Doctor of Music
Doc.	Document
Docs.	Documents
DOMG	Director, Office of Military Government
dpa	Deutsche Presse-Agentur
DPOL/M	Political Directorate/Minutes of meeting
DPs	Displaced Persons
Dr.	Doctor; Doktor
Dr. jur.	Doctor juris (Doktor der Rechtswissenschaft)
Dr. med. h. c.	Doctor medicinae honoris causa (Doktor der Medizin ehrenhalber)
Dr. oec. publ.	Doctor oeconomiae publicae (Doktor der Staatswissenschaften)
Dr. phil.	Doctor philosophiae (Doktor der Philosophie)
Dr. rer. pol.	Doctor rerum politicarum (Doktor der Staatswissenschaften)
Drs.	Doctores
EAC; E. A. C.	European Advisory Commission
ECA	Economic Cooperation Administration

ed.	editor
EdD	Educationis Doctor (Doctor of Education)
eds.	editors
e. g.	exempli gratia
email	electronic mail
ET	European Theater
et al.	et alia; et aliae; et alii
etc.	et cetera
e. V.	eingetragener Verein
f.	and the following
FDGB	Freier Deutscher Gewerkschaftsbund
FDJ	Freie Deutsche Jugend
Febr.	February
Fi	Fieseler
fn.	footnote
FO	Foreign Office
fol.	folio
fols.	folios
ft.	foot
GDR	German Democratic Republic
geb.	geboren; geborene
Gebr.	Gebrüder
gen.	genannt
Gen.	General
Gestapo	Geheime Staatspolizei
GFCC	Groupe Français du Conseil de Contrôle
GI; G. I.	Government Issue
GIs; GI's	Government Issues
GMFB	Gouvernement Militaire Français de Berlin
GStA PK	Geheimes Staatsarchiv Preußischer Kulturbesitz
HA	Hauptabteilung
half-vol.	half-volume
HICOG	High Commissioner for Germany
Hon.	Honourable
IA + C	Internal Affairs and Communications
ibid.	ibidem
ID	Identification
id.	idem
i. e.	id est
IfZ	Institut für Zeitgeschichte
ill.	illustration
Inc.	Incorporated
IWM	Imperial War Museum

JD	Juris Doctor (Doctor of Jurisprudence)
Jr.	Junior
km	kilometer
KPD	Kommunistische Partei Deutschlands
LAB	Landesarchiv Berlin
LAZ	Landesarchiv Berlin, Abteilung Zeitgeschichte
LDP	Liberal-Demokratische Partei Deutschlands
LG/M	Local Government/Minutes of meeting
Lieut. Col.	Lieutenant Colonel
LLB	Legum Baccalaureus (Bachelor of Laws)
LLD	Legum Doctor (Doctor of Laws)
LOC GOV/R	Local Government/Report
LRGS	Sammlung der Länderratsgesetze
Lt.	Lieutenant
Lt. Cols.	Lieutenant Colonels
m	meter
MA	Master of Arts
Maj. Gen.	Major General
MBA	Master of Business Administration
MBE	Member of the Order of the British Empire
MD	Medicinae Doctor (Doctor of Medicine)
MdR	Mitglied des Reichstages
MGBD	Military Government, Berlin District
MGBTB	Military Government British Troops Berlin
Mil. Gov.	Military Government
MLS	Master of Library Science
MM	Master of Management
MoMA	Museum of Modern Art
MP; M. P.	Military Police; Military Police officer
M + P	Miller & Paine
MPL	Master of Patent Law
MP's; M. P.'s	Military Police officers
Mr.	Mister
MRP	Mouvement Républicain Populaire
Mrs.	Mistress
MusD	Musicae Doctor (Doctor of Music)
NAM	National Association of Manufacturers
NARA	National Archives and Records Administration
NATO	North Atlantic Treaty Organization
n. d.	no date
NKVD	Narodnyy Komissariat Vnutrennikh Del
no.; No.	numero; Numero
n. p.	no place
Nr.	Nummer

NS	National Socialist; nationalsozialistisch
NSDAP	Nationalsozialistische Deutsche Arbeiterpartei
NW; N. W.	Northwest
NY; N. Y.	New York
od.	oder
OdF	Opfer des Faschismus
OGPU	Obyedinyonnoye Gosudarstvennoye Politicheskoye Upravleniye
Ok; OK; O. K.	okay
OLCB	Office of Land Commissioner for Bavaria
OLCH	Office of Land Commissioner for Hesse
OMGBD; OMG BD	Office of Military Government, Berlin District
OMGBS	Office of Military Government, Berlin Sector
OMGBY	Office of Military Government, Bavaria
OMGGH	Office of Military Government, Greater Hesse
OMGHE	Office of Military Government, Hesse
Omgus; OMGUS	Office of Military Government for Germany (US)
OMGUSZ	Office of Military Government (US Zone)
OMGWB	Office of Military Government, Württemberg-Baden
Op.	Opus
OSS; O. S. S.	Office of Strategic Services
O. T.	Organisation Todt
p.	page
para	paragraph
PCF	Parti Communiste Français
PDS	Partei des Demokratischen Sozialismus
PhB	Philosophiae Baccalaureus (Bachelor of Philosophy)
PhD; Ph. D.	Philosophiae Doctor (Doctor of Philosophy)
pm; p. m.	post meridiem
PM	Postmaster
POE	Port of Embarkation
POLAD	Political Adviser
POW	Prisoner of War
pp.	pages
Prof.	Professor
P. S.	Post Scriptum
PTA	Parent Teacher Association
PW	Prisoner of War
PW's	Prisoners of War
PX	Post Exchange
PX's	Post Exchanges
R + A	Research and Analysis Branch
Rec	Recreation
Rep.	Repositur
Rev.	Reverend

RG	Record Group
RGCO	Regional Government Coordinating Office
SAPMO-BArch	Stiftung Archiv der Parteien und Massen-organisationen der DDR im Bundesarchiv
SBZ	Sowjetische Besatzungszone
SD's	Social Democrats
s. e.	southeast
SED	Sozialistische Einheitspartei Deutschlands
SEP	Sozialistische Einheitspartei
Sept.	September
SFIO	Section Française de l'Internationale Ouvrière
Sgt.	Sergeant
SHAEF	Supreme Headquarters, Allied Expeditionary Forces
SLUGA	Special Legal Unit – Germany/Austria
S + M	Schmoller & Mueller
SMAD	Sowjetische Militäradministration in Deutschland
SMAG	Soviet Military Administration in Germany
SPD	Sozialdemokratische Partei Deutschlands
Sr.	Senior
SS	Steam Ship
St.	Saint; Sankt
StAB	Staatsarchiv Bremen
SW	Southwest
TNA	The National Archives
T. O.	Table of Organization
trans.	translator
u.	und
UChicago	University of Chicago
UCLA	University of California, Los Angeles
UdSSR	Union der Sozialistischen Sowjetrepubliken
UK	United Kingdom
UN	United Nations
UNESCO	United Nations Educational, Scientific and Cultural Organization
Uni	Universität
UNL	University of Nebraska-Lincoln
UNO	United Nations Organization
UNRRA	United Nations Relief and Rehabilitation Administration
U. of C.	University of Chicago
US; U. S.	United States
USA	United States of America
USAFI	United States Armed Forces Institute
USAMHI	United States Army Military History Institute
USAT	United States Army Transport

USFA	United States Forces Austria
USGCC	United States Group, Control Council
USPD	Unabhängige Sozialdemokratische Partei Deutschlands
USS	United States Ship
USSR	Union of Soviet Socialist Republics
UW-Madison	University of Wisconsin-Madison
V-1	Vergeltungswaffe 1
V-2	Vergeltungswaffe 2
VBK	Verwaltungsbezirk
VdN	Verfolgte des Naziregimes
V-E	Victory-in-Europe
VIP	Very Important Person
VIPs	Very Important Persons
viz.	videlicet
vol.	volume
vols.	volumes
V-Waffen	Vergeltungswaffen
Wac; WAC	Women's Army Corps; member of the Women's Army Corps
Wacs	members of the Women's Army Corps
Waves; WAVES	Women Accepted for Volunteer Emergency Service
WHS	Wisconsin Historical Society
WPA	Works Progress Administration; Works Projects Administration
WSW	West-Southwest
z. B.	zum Beispiel

Bibliography

1. Unprinted Sources

Archival Materials

Archiv des Instituts für Zeitgeschichte (IfZ), Munich, Germany
OMGUS-Akten (microfiche reproduction).
OMGUS – Staff Conferences (copies of minutes), Fg 12/3–5.

Archiv für Christlich-Demokratische Politik (ACDP) der Konrad-Adenauer-Stiftung, Sankt Augustin, Germany
Landesverband Berlin, 03-012-032/1.

Archiv für Christlich-Soziale Politik (ACSP) der Hanns-Seidel-Stiftung, Munich, Germany
Nachlass Josef Müller.

Archives de l'Occupation Française (AOF) en Allemagne et en Autriche, Ministère des Affaires Etrangères, Colmar, France
Services Français à Berlin: Gouvernement Militaire Français de Berlin (GMFB), Groupe Français du Conseil de Contrôle (GFCC).

Bundesarchiv (BArch), Koblenz, Germany
Allied Control Authority, Office of Records and Archives, Z 46.
Länderrat des amerikanischen Besatzungsgebietes, 1945–49, Z 1.
Nachlass Friedrich Glum, N 1457.
Office of Military Government for Germany (U. S.) (OMGUS), 1944–49, Z 45 F.

Geheimes Staatsarchiv Preußischer Kulturbesitz (GStA PK), Berlin, Germany
Personalakte Käthe Bungert, I. HA, Rep. 178 (Generaldirektion der Staatsarchive), no. 1404.
Personalakte Ernst Posner, I. HA, Rep. 178 (Generaldirektion der Staatsarchive), no. 1627.

Imperial War Museum (IWM) Duxford, Cambridgeshire, Great Britain
Lieutenant Colonel Harold Hays MBE Collection.

Landesarchiv Berlin (LAB), Germany
Amtsgericht Charlottenburg – Handelsregister, A Rep. 342-02.
Einwohnermeldeamt Berlin, B Rep. 021.
Hauptausschuss "Opfer des Faschismus" (OdF)/Referat Verfolgte des Naziregimes (VdN), C Rep. 118-01.
Kommunistische Partei Deutschlands (KPD) – Bezirksorganisation Groß-Berlin, C Rep. 900-01.
Landesleitung Berlin der SED, C Rep. 901.
Landesverwaltungsamt Berlin, B Rep. 080.
Magistrat von Berlin, Abteilung Verwaltung und Personalpolitik, C Rep. 102.
Magistrat von Berlin, Abteilung Volksbildung, C Rep. 120.
Nachlass Otto Suhr, E Rep. 200-17.
Nachlass Arthur Werner, E Rep. 300-09.
Office of Military Government, Berlin Sector (OMGBS), B Rep. 036-01.
Quellensammlung zur Berliner Zeitgeschichte (LAZ-Sammlung), F Rep. 280.

Rechtsanwaltskammer Berlin, B Rep. 068.
Sammlung Amerikanische Behörden in Berlin, F Rep. 037.
Sozialdemokratische Partei Deutschlands (SPD) – Bezirksorganisation Berlin (1945/46), C Rep. 900-02.

National Archives and Records Administration (NARA), College Park, Maryland, USA
Records of the Office of Strategic Services, Record Group 226.

Staatsarchiv Bremen (StAB), Germany
Vol. 2 of Hafenverkehrsbücher Bremerhaven, Überseehäfen und Columbuskaje – Seeschifffahrt, 4,72/2-57.

Stiftung Archiv der Parteien und Massenorganisationen der DDR im Bundesarchiv (SAPMO-BArch), Berlin, Germany
Nachlass Otto Grotewohl, NY 4090.

The National Archives (TNA), Kew, Richmond, Surrey, Great Britain
Allied Kommandatura: Directives, Minutes and Papers.
Control Commission for Germany (British Element), CCG (BE).

The University of Chicago (UChicago) Library, Special Collections Research Center, Chicago, Illinois, USA
Edgar N. Johnson Papers.

Union College, Schaffer Library, Special Collections, Schenectady, New York, USA
Documents on William J. Anderson.

University of California, Los Angeles (UCLA), Charles E. Young Research Library, Department of Special Collections, Los Angeles, California, USA
Eugene N. Anderson Papers, Collection 2074.

University of Nebraska-Lincoln (UNL) Libraries, Archives & Special Collections, Lincoln, Nebraska, USA
Biographical File of Edgar N. Johnson, RG/52-01, Box 134.
Bulletins & Catalogs (University, General), RG/00-07.

University of Strathclyde Archives, Glasgow, Great Britain
Seven Chapters of Miette Dernbach's (née Hardy) Family Biography, T-MIN/31.

University of Wisconsin-Madison (UW-Madison) Archives, Madison, Wisconsin, USA
Department of History, Faculty Personnel Files.

US Army Military History Institute (USAMHI), Carlisle, Pennsylvania, USA
Frank L. Howley Papers.

Wisconsin Historical Society (WHS) Archives, Madison, Wisconsin, USA
Roswell P. Rosengren Papers.

Privately Held Materials

Glaser, Anthony J., Bethesda, Maryland, USA
Documents from the estate of Louis Glaser.

Johnson, Candice E. and Thomas R., Denver, Colorado, USA
Documents from the estate of Edgar N. Johnson.

Loew, Dieter, Basel, Switzerland
Memoirs of Marcus Löw-Suter.

Emails and Letters

Alekhina, Elena, Leo Tolstoy Yasnaya Polyana museum-estate, email from January 26, 2018.

Anderson Jr., Eugene N., emails from June 23, 2007, July 3, 2007, July 17, 2007, and July 30, 2007.

Anderson, James E., emails from May 30, 2008, and February 24, 2013.

Baldner, Thomas, emails from September 20, 2010, and September 21, 2010.

Bonk, Mary E., email from December 20, 2017.

Bonk, Miriam-Ellen, email from December 28, 2017.

Cherdel, Jean-Yves, email from December 2, 2013.

Davis, Lisa F., Acting Executive Director, Medieval Academy of America, email from May 29, 2013.

Dutilh-von Schmidt Seidlitz, Hedda, letter from October 19, 2010.

Gailey III, Charles K., emails from October 26, 2009, and November 2, 2009.

Gailey, Christine W., emails from October 25, 2009, and October 26, 2009.

Gailey, Timothy H., email from July 29, 2011.

Gass, Geoffrey A., email from December 30, 2009.

Glaser, Anthony J., emails from August 22, 2009, September 27, 2009, and October 23, 2012.

Grady, Sister Mary Rita, Archivist, Regis College Archives, email from April 25, 2013.

Imperial War Museum Duxford, Department of Documents, email from June 30, 2009.

Johnson, Candice E. and Thomas R., emails from May 4, 2007, December 16, 2007, May 24, 2010, June 1, 2010, April 24, 2013, June 14, 2013, October 18, 2013, and May 31, 2017.

Loomis, Kelly, email from June 14, 2012.

Marburg University Museum, email from May 29, 2009.

McLean, Jack, email from July 16, 2008.

Murie, Alison G., emails from January 10, 2010, and January 15, 2010.

National Archives and Records Administration, letter from December 21, 2010.

Oppenheimer, Wolfgang, letter from January 10, 2012.

Schertz, Georg, email from June 26, 2007.

Schuyler, Philip V. R., emails from February 8, 2008, and March 6, 2008.

Stadtarchiv Munich, letter from August 4, 2009, email from March 26, 2010.

The Royal Engineers Museum, email from June 24, 2009.

Treece, Will, Friends Historical Library Intern, Swarthmore College, email from July 6, 2009.

Wimmer, Ulrich, Kammergericht Judge, email from November 6, 2012.

Wolf, Dieter, Head of the Museum and Stadtarchiv of the City of Butzbach, emails from July 12, 2007, and December 9, 2011.

Wolford, Claire A., Graduate Assistant, New York University Archives, email from April 11, 2013.

Personal Communications

Baldner, Thomas, telephone conversation on April 29, 2009.

Gailey, Timothy H., interview on August 10, 2011, in Berlin.

Heller, Aribert, telephone conversation on January 5, 2010.

Impekoven, Holger, telephone conversation on October 16, 2013.

Johnson, Candice E. and Thomas R., interview on September 13, 2012, in Berlin.

Wepper, Angela, telephone conversation on June 18, 2009.

2. Printed Sources and References

Akten zur Vorgeschichte der Bundesrepublik Deutschland 1945–1949, vol. 1, *September 1945–Dezember 1946*, eds. Walter Vogel/Christoph Weisz, Munich and Vienna 1976.

Allert, Tilman: *Der deutsche Gruß. Geschichte einer unheilvollen Geste*, Frankfurt am Main 2005.

Amtliches Fernsprechbuch für den Bezirk der Reichspostdirektion Berlin, 1941.

Ausstellung Ewald Vetter, Walther-Rathenau-Saal, Rathaus-Wedding (Altbau), Berlin 65, Müllerstraße 146/147, 7.10.–11.11.75, exhibition catalog of the Kunstamt Wedding, Berlin 1975.

BAB Straßenführer durch Berlin mit allen Änderungen nach dem neuesten Stand, vol. 1 (1946).

Backer, John H.: *Die deutschen Jahre des Generals Clay. Der Weg zur Bundesrepublik 1945–1949*, Munich 1983.

Baigorri-Jalón, Jesús: *From Paris to Nuremberg. The Birth of Conference Interpreting*, trans. Holly Mikkelson/Barry Slaughter Olsen (= Benjamins Translation Library, 111), Amsterdam and Philadelphia 2014.

Bajohr, Frank: "Gauleiter in Hamburg. Zur Person und Tätigkeit Karl Kaufmanns," in: *Vierteljahrshefte für Zeitgeschichte*, vol. 43 (1995), pp. 267–295.

Bauer, A./J. Carpentier: *Répertoire des Artistes d'Alsace des XIX*[e] *et XX*[e] *siècles. Peintres – Sculpteurs – Graveurs – Dessinateurs, V–Z*, Strasbourg 1991.

Bavendamm, Gundula (ed.): *Amerikaner in Hessen. Eine besondere Beziehung im Wandel der Zeit*, Hanau 2008.

Becker, Josef/Theo Stammen/Peter Waldmann (eds.): *Vorgeschichte der Bundesrepublik Deutschland. Zwischen Kapitulation und Grundgesetz* (= Uni-Taschenbücher 854), Munich 1979.

Befehle des Obersten Chefs der Sowjetischen Militärverwaltung in Deutschland. Aus dem Stab der Sowjetischen Militärverwaltung in Deutschland, Sammelheft 1, *1945*, Berlin 1946.

Benjamin Franklin. Sein Leben von ihm selbst erzählt, Berlin 1946.

Bergsträsser, Ludwig: *Befreiung, Besatzung, Neubeginn. Tagebuch des Darmstädter Regierungspräsidenten 1945–1948*, ed. Walter Mühlhausen (= Biographische Quellen zur deutschen Geschichte nach 1945, vol. 5), Munich 1987.

Bering, Henrik: *Outpost Berlin. The History of the American Military Forces in Berlin, 1945–1994*, Chicago, Berlin, Tokyo, and Moskow 1995.

Berlin. Kampf um Freiheit und Selbstverwaltung 1945–1946, edited on behalf of the Senate of Berlin (= Schriftenreihe zur Berliner Zeitgeschichte, vol. 1), revised and supplemented second edition, Berlin 1961.

Berlin. Quellen und Dokumente 1945–1951, edited on behalf of the Senate of Berlin, eds. Hans J. Reichhardt/Hanns U. Treutler/Albrecht Lampe (= Schriftenreihe zur Berliner Zeitgeschichte, vol. 4/half-volumes 1 and 2), Berlin 1964.

Berlin Handbuch. Das Lexikon der Bundeshauptstadt, ed. Presse- und Informationsamt des Landes Berlin, Berlin 1992.

Berlin in Zahlen 1947. Taschenbuch, ed. Hauptamt für Statistik, Berlin 1949.

Berlin Observer, 1946.

Berlin und seine Bauten, eds. Architekten-Verein zu Berlin/Vereinigung Berliner Architekten, vol. III, *Privatbauten*, Berlin 1896.

Berliner Adreßbuch, 1920–1943.

Berliner Zeitung, 1946.

Biess, Frank: review of: *Fünf Monate in Berlin. Briefe von Edgar N. Johnson aus dem Jahre 1946*, eds. Werner Breunig/Jürgen Wetzel (= Schriftenreihe des Landesarchivs Berlin, vol. 18), Munich 2014, in: *The Journal of Modern History*, vol. 88, no. 4 (December 2016), pp. 983f.

Biografisches Handbuch der Berliner Stadtverordneten und Abgeordneten 1946–1963, on behalf of the President of the Abgeordnetenhaus of Berlin, eds. Werner Breunig/Andreas Herbst, with an introduction by Siegfried Heimann (= Schriftenreihe des Landesarchivs Berlin, vol. 14), Berlin 2011.

Biographic Register of the Department of State, 1944/1945/1949.

Biographical Register of the Officers and Graduates of the U. S. Military Academy at West Point, New York, 1920–1930/1930–1940/1940–1950.

Biographisches Handbuch der deutschsprachigen Emigration nach 1933/International Biographical Dictionary of Central European Emigrés 1933–1945, eds. Institut für Zeitgeschichte, Munich, and Research Foundation for Jewish Immigration, Inc., New York, under the direction of Werner Röder/Herbert A. Strauss, vols. I–III, Munich, New York, London, and Paris 1980/1983.

Blixen, Tania: *Sieben phantastische Geschichten*, Stuttgart 1979.

Boyens, Armin: "Die Kirchenpolitik der amerikanischen Besatzungsmacht in Deutschland von 1944 bis 1946," in: *Kirchen in der Nachkriegszeit. Vier zeitgeschichtliche Beiträge*, by Armin Boyens/Martin Greschat/Rudolf von Thadden/Paolo Pombeni (= Arbeiten zur kirchlichen Zeitgeschichte, Reihe B: Darstellungen, vol. 8), Göttingen 1979, pp. 7–99.

Brandeis University Bulletin, 1958–1959/1963–1964.

Braunfels, Sigrid: *Skulptur und Architektur des Wasserspiels. Die Brunnen Adolf von Hildebrands*, Munich and Berlin 2005.

Breunig, Werner: *Verfassunggebung in Berlin 1945–1950* (= Beiträge zur Politischen Wissenschaft, vol. 58), Berlin 1990.

Breunig, Werner: "Berlin 1945/46. Vom Kriegsende bis zum parlamentarischen Neubeginn," in: *"Berlin kommt wieder." Die Nachkriegsjahre 1945/46* (= Ausstellungskataloge des Landesarchivs Berlin, 16), Berlin 2005, pp. 7–43.

Breunig, Werner: "'Berlin kommt wieder.' Die Nachkriegsjahre 1945/46," in: *Museums-Journal*, vol. 19, no. III (July 2005), pp. 89f.

Breunig, Werner: "Der parlamentarische Neubeginn. Die Konstituierung der Stadtverordnetenversammlung von Groß-Berlin am 26. November 1946," in: *Berlin in Geschichte und Gegenwart. Jahrbuch des Landesarchivs Berlin 2011*, pp. 213–235.

Buckow, Anjana: *Zwischen Propaganda und Realpolitik. Die USA und der sowjetisch besetzte Teil Deutschlands 1945–1955* (= USA-Studien, vol. 13), Stuttgart 2003.

Chalou, George C. (ed.): *The Secrets War. The Office of Strategic Services in World War II*, Washington, D. C., 1992.

Charles, Roland W.: *Troopships of World War II*, with a foreword by Major General Edmond H. Leavey, Washington, D. C., 1947.

Chicago Daily Tribune, 1946.

Clay, Lucius D.: *Entscheidung in Deutschland*, Frankfurt am Main 1950.

Das erste Jahr. Berlin im Neuaufbau. Ein Rechenschaftsbericht des Magistrats der Stadt Berlin, edited on behalf of the Magistrat of the City of Berlin, Berlin 1946.

Das Jahr 1945 und das Kino, Berlin 1995.

Das Nationalkomitee "Freies Deutschland" und der Bund Deutscher Offiziere, ed. Gerd R. Ueberschär (Die Zeit des Nationalsozialismus. Eine Buchreihe), Frankfurt am Main 1995.

Das Volk, 1946.

Davis, Luckett V.: "Louis, Joe," in: *American National Biography*, vol. 13, New York and Oxford 1999, pp. 942–944.

Der Berliner, 1946.

Der Kurier, 1946.

Der Länderrat des amerikanischen Besatzungsgebietes, edited on behalf of the Minister-Presidents of Bavaria, Hesse, Württemberg-Baden and the President of the Senate of the Free Hanseatic City of Bremen by the Directorate of the Länderrat, compiled by Lia Härtel, former Länderrat archivist, Stuttgart and Cologne 1951.

Der Morgen, 1946.

Der Sozialdemokrat, 1946.

Der Tagesspiegel, 1946.

Dettmar, Werner: *Die Zerstörung Kassels im Oktober 1943. Eine Dokumentation*, Fuldabrück 1983.

Deutschland unter alliierter Besatzung 1945–1949/55, ed. Wolfgang Benz, Berlin 1999.

Die Entstehung der Verfassung von Berlin. Eine Dokumentation, on behalf of the President of the Abgeordnetenhaus of Berlin, ed. Hans J. Reichhardt in collaboration with Werner Breunig/Josephine Gabler, 2 vols., Berlin and New York 1990.

Die Neue Zeitung, 1946/1947.

Die Sitzungsprotokolle des Magistrats der Stadt Berlin 1945/46, part I, *1945*, edited and introduced by Dieter Hanauske (= Schriftenreihe des Landesarchivs Berlin, vol. 2/I), Berlin 1995.

Die Sitzungsprotokolle des Magistrats der Stadt Berlin 1945/46, part II, *1946*, edited and introduced by Dieter Hanauske (= Schriftenreihe des Landesarchivs Berlin, vol. 2/II), Berlin 1999.

Die UdSSR und die deutsche Frage 1941–1948. Dokumente aus dem Archiv für Außenpolitik der Russischen Föderation, eds. Jochen P. Laufer/Georgij P. Kynin in collaboration with Viktor Knoll, vol. 2, *9. Mai 1945 bis 3. Oktober 1946*, Berlin 2004.

Die UdSSR und die deutsche Frage 1941–1948. Dokumente aus dem Archiv für Außenpolitik der Russischen Föderation, eds. Jochen P. Laufer/Georgij P. Kynin in collaboration with Viktor Knoll, vol. 3, *6. Oktober 1946 bis 15. Juni 1948*, Berlin 2004.

Die Vier Mächte in Berlin. Beiträge zur Politik der Alliierten in der besetzten Stadt, eds. Michael Bienert/Uwe Schaper/Andrea Theissen in collaboration with Werner Breunig (= Schriftenreihe des Landesarchivs Berlin, vol. 9), Berlin 2007.

Dinesen, Isak: *Seven Gothic Tales* (Penguin Modern Classics), London et al. 1988.

Dinter, Andreas: *Berlin in Trümmern. Ernährungslage und medizinische Versorgung der Bevölkerung Berlins nach dem II. Weltkrieg* (= Geschichte[n] der Medizin, vol. 1), Berlin 1999.

Dokumente zur Berlin-Frage 1944–1966, with a foreword by the Governing Mayor of Berlin, ed. Forschungsinstitut der Deutschen Gesellschaft für Auswärtige Politik e. V., Bonn, in collaboration with the Senate of Berlin (= Schriften des Forschungsinstituts der Deutschen Gesellschaft für Auswärtige Politik e. V., Bonn, Reihe: Internationale Politik und Wirtschaft, vol. 52/I), fourth edition, Munich 1987.

Dorn, Walter L.: *Inspektionsreisen in der US-Zone. Notizen, Denkschriften und Erinnerungen aus dem Nachlaß*, trans. and ed. Lutz Niethammer (= Schriftenreihe der Vierteljahrshefte für Zeitgeschichte, no. 26), Stuttgart 1973.

Dornberger, Walter: *Peenemünde. Die Geschichte der V-Waffen*, with a preface by Eberhard Rees, Huntsville/Alabama, Eßlingen 1981.

Dülffer, Jost: review of: *Fünf Monate in Berlin. Briefe von Edgar N. Johnson aus dem Jahre 1946*, eds. Werner Breunig/Jürgen Wetzel (= Schriftenreihe des Landesarchivs Berlin, vol. 18), Munich 2014, in: *Zeitschrift für Geschichtswissenschaft*, vol. 63, no. 7/8 (July/August 2015), pp. 709f.

Dulles, John Foster: "Thoughts on Soviet Foreign Policy and What To Do About It," in: *Life* from June 3, 1946, pp. 112–126 (Part I), and from June 10, 1946, pp. 118–130 (Part II).

Dzuback, Mary Ann: *Robert M. Hutchins. Portrait of an Educator*, Chicago and London 1991.

Eakin-Thimme, Gabriela Ann: *Geschichte im Exil. Deutschsprachige Historiker nach* 1933 (= Forum deutsche Geschichte, 8), Munich 2005.

Eisenhauer, Gregor: "Ingeborg von Streletzky. Geb. 1916. Es war keine gütige Fee, es war harte Arbeit und unbarmherzige Dressur," in: *Der Tagesspiegel* from November 25, 2011, p. 12.

Eisenhuth, Stefanie: *Die Schutzmacht. Die Amerikaner in Berlin 1945–1994* (= Geschichte der Gegenwart, vol. 19), Göttingen 2018.

Engel, Helmut: *Villen und Landhäuser*, photographed by Wolfgang Reuss (= Meisterwerke Berliner Baukunst, vol. I), Berlin 2001.

Erd, Rainer (ed.): *Reform und Resignation. Gespräche über Franz L. Neumann* (= edition suhrkamp 1239, Neue Folge vol. 239), Frankfurt am Main 1985.

Esche-Braunfels, Sigrid: *Adolf von Hildebrand (1847–1921)*, Berlin 1993.

Fait, Barbara: "'In einer Atmosphäre von Freiheit.' Die Rolle der Amerikaner bei der Verfassunggebung in den Ländern der US-Zone 1946," in: *Vierteljahrshefte für Zeitgeschichte*, vol. 33 (1985), pp. 420–455.

Fait, Barbara: *Demokratische Erneuerung unter dem Sternenbanner. Amerikanische Kontrolle und Verfassunggebung in Bayern 1946* (= Beiträge zur Geschichte des Parlamentarismus und der politischen Parteien, vol. 114), Düsseldorf 1998.

Fichter, Michael: *Besatzungsmacht und Gewerkschaften. Zur Entwicklung und Anwendung der US-Gewerkschaftspolitik in Deutschland 1944–1948* (= Schriften des Zentralinstituts für sozialwissenschaftliche Forschung der Freien Universität Berlin, vol. 40), Opladen 1982.

Fippel, Günter: *Demokratische Gegner und Willküropfer von Besatzungsmacht und SED in Sachsenhausen (1946 bis 1950). Das sowjetische Speziallager Sachsenhausen – Teil des Stalinschen Lagerimperiums*, in collaboration with Paul Radicke, with an introductory essay by Klaus-Dieter Müller, eds. Klaus-Dieter Müller/Mike Schmeitzner, Leipzig 2008.

Fischer, Rolf: *Hermann Lüdemann und die deutsche Demokratie*, Neumünster 2006.

Flechtheim, Ossip K.: "Die Anpassung der SPD: 1914, 1933 und 1959," in: *Politologie und Soziologie. Otto Stammer zum 65. Geburtstag*, ed. Jürgen Fijalkowski, Cologne and Opladen 1965, pp. 182–202.

Franklin, Benjamin: *The Autobiography*, with an introduction by Daniel Aaron, New York 1990.

Franklin, Benjamin: *Autobiographie*, with an afterword by Klaus Harpprecht (= Beck'sche Reihe, 1510), second edition, Munich 2010.

Führe, Dorothea: *Die französische Besatzungspolitik in Berlin von 1945 bis 1949. Déprussianisation und Décentralisation*, Berlin 2001.

Fünf Monate in Berlin. Briefe von Edgar N. Johnson aus dem Jahre 1946, eds. Werner Breunig/Jürgen Wetzel (= Schriftenreihe des Landesarchivs Berlin, vol. 18), Munich 2014.

Füssl, Karl-Heinz: *Die Umerziehung der Deutschen. Jugend und Schule unter den Siegermächten des Zweiten Weltkriegs 1945–1955* (Sammlung Schöningh zur Geschichte und Gegenwart), second edition, Paderborn, Munich, Vienna, and Zurich 1995.

Gaiba, Francesca: *The Origins of Simultaneous Interpretation. The Nuremberg Trial* (Perspectives on Translation), Ottawa 1998.

Gartendenkmale in Berlin: Privatgärten, ed. Katrin Lesser, with an introduction by Klaus-Henning von Krosigk and contributions by Josef Batzhuber et al. (= Beiträge zur Denkmalpflege in Berlin, 21), Petersberg 2005.

Geheimdienstkrieg gegen Deutschland. Subversion, Propaganda und politische Planungen des amerikanischen Geheimdienstes im Zweiten Weltkrieg, eds. Jürgen Heideking/Christof Mauch (Sammlung Vandenhoeck), Göttingen 1993.

Germer, Karl J.: *Von Grotewohl bis Brandt. Ein dokumentarischer Bericht über die SPD in den ersten Nachkriegsjahren*, Landshut 1974.

Geschichtswissenschaft in Berlin im 19. und 20. Jahrhundert. Persönlichkeiten und Institutionen, eds. Reimer Hansen/Wolfgang Ribbe (= Veröffentlichungen der Historischen Kommission zu Berlin, vol. 82; Publikationen der Sektion für die Geschichte Berlins), Berlin and New York 1992.

Gesetz über die Bildung einer neuen Stadtgemeinde Berlin vom 27. April 1920, in: *Preußische Gesetzsammlung*, 1920, pp. 123–150.

Gesetz über die vorläufige Regelung verschiedener Punkte des Gemeindeverfassungsrechts für die Hauptstadt Berlin vom 30. März 1931, in: *Preußische Gesetzsammlung*, 1931, pp. 39–44.

Giesecke, Dagmar: "Ernst Maximilian Posner. Eine skizzenhafte Biographie," thesis, Fachhochschule Potsdam, Fachbereich Archiv – Bibliothek – Dokumentation, 1996.

Gilbert, Felix: *Lehrjahre im alten Europa. Erinnerungen 1905–1945*, Berlin 1989.

Gimbel, John: *Amerikanische Besatzungspolitik in Deutschland 1945–1949*, Frankfurt am Main 1971.

Glum, Friedrich: *Die Organisation der Riesenstadt. Die Verfassungen von Paris, London, New York, Wien und Berlin. Aus Anlaß des Entwurfs der Staatsregierung über die Bildung einer Stadt Groß-Berlin*, Berlin 1920.

Glum, Friedrich: *Zwischen Wissenschaft, Wirtschaft und Politik. Erlebtes und Erdachtes in vier Reichen*, Bonn 1964.

Gniffke, Erich W.: *Jahre mit Ulbricht*, with a foreword by Herbert Wehner, Cologne 1966 (Reprint 1990).

Graml, Hermann: *Die Alliierten und die Teilung Deutschlands. Konflikte und Entscheidungen 1941–1948*, Frankfurt am Main 1985.

Grathwol, Robert P./Donita M. Moorhus: *American Forces in Berlin. Cold War Outpost, 1945–1994*, Washington, D. C., 1994.

Grathwol, Roger P./Donita M. Moorhus: *Berlin and the American Military. A Cold War Chronicle*, ed. Gareth L. Steen, New York and London 1999.

Grebner, Susanne: *Der Telegraf. Entstehung einer SPD-nahen Lizenzzeitung in Berlin 1946 bis 1950* (= Kommunikationsgeschichte, vol. 13), Münster, Hamburg, and London 2002.

Hanauske, Dieter: "'… als leuchtendes Signal für ganz Deutschland.' Der Berliner Magistrat von 1945/46 als 'antifaschistisch-demokratisches' Musterbeispiel?", in: *Berlin in Geschichte und Gegenwart. Jahrbuch des Landesarchivs Berlin 1999*, pp. 145–183.

Hanauske, Dieter: "'Ein ehrlicher Mann, aber etwas naiv.' Arthur Werner – Berliner Oberbürgermeister von 1945/46," in: *Der Bär von Berlin. Jahrbuch 2002 des Vereins für die Geschichte Berlins*, pp. 131–160.

Hansen, Reimer: "Neuer Name in historischer Tradition. Von der Friedrich-Wilhelms- zur Humboldt-Universität 1945–1949," in: *Berlin in Geschichte und Gegenwart. Jahrbuch des Landesarchivs Berlin 2009*, pp. 349–375.

Heiss, Hans/Gustav Pfeifer (eds.): *Südtirol – Stunde Null? Kriegsende 1945–1946* (= Veröffentlichungen des Südtiroler Landesarchivs, vol. 10), Innsbruck, Vienna, and Munich 2000.

Henke, Klaus-Dietmar: *Die amerikanische Besetzung Deutschlands* (= Quellen und Darstellungen zur Zeitgeschichte, vol. 27), Munich 1995.

Henning, Eckart/Marion Kazemi: *Dahlem – Domäne der Wissenschaft. Ein Spaziergang zu den Berliner Instituten der Kaiser-Wilhelm-/Max-Planck-Gesellschaft im "deutschen Oxford"* (= Veröffentlichungen aus dem Archiv der Max-Planck-Gesellschaft, vol. 16/I), expanded and updated fourth edition, Berlin 2009.

Hinz, Gerhard: "Ernst Walz †," in: *Ruperto-Carola. Zeitschrift der Vereinigung der Freunde der Studentenschaft der Universität Heidelberg e. V.*, June 1967, pp. 46f.

Hirtenbriefe und Ansprachen zu Gesellschaft und Politik 1945–1949, ed. Wolfgang Löhr (= Dokumente deutscher Bischöfe, vol. I), Würzburg 1985.

Horizont, 1946.

Howley, Frank: *Berlin Command*, New York 1950.

Hurwitz, Harold: *Die politische Kultur der Bevölkerung und der Neubeginn konservativer Politik* (= Demokratie und Antikommunismus in Berlin nach 1945, vol. I), Cologne 1983.

Hurwitz, Harold/Klaus Sühl: *Autoritäre Tradierung und Demokratiepotential in der sozialdemokratischen Arbeiterbewegung* (= Demokratie und Antikommunismus in Berlin nach 1945, vol. II), Cologne 1984.

Hurwitz, Harold: *Die Eintracht der Siegermächte und die Orientierungsnot der Deutschen 1945–1946* (= Demokratie und Antikommunismus in Berlin nach 1945, vol. III), Cologne 1984.

Hurwitz, Harold, in collaboration with Andreas Büning/Johannes-Berthold Hohmann/Klaus Sühl/Ingolore Mensch-Khan: *Die Anfänge des Widerstands*, part 1, *Führungsan-*

spruch und Isolation der Sozialdemokraten (= Demokratie und Antikommunismus in Berlin nach 1945, vol. IV), Cologne 1990.

Hurwitz, Harold, in collaboration with Andreas Büning/Johannes-Berthold Hohmann/ Klaus Sühl/Ingolore Mensch-Khan: *Die Anfänge des Widerstands*, part 2, *Zwischen Selbsttäuschung und Zivilcourage: Der Fusionskampf* (= Demokratie und Antikommunismus in Berlin nach 1945, vol. IV), Cologne 1990.

Hurwitz, Harold, in collaboration with Ursula Böhme/Andreas Malycha: *Die Stalinisierung der SED. Zum Verlust von Freiräumen und sozialdemokratischer Identität in den Vorständen 1946–1949* (= Schriften des Zentralinstituts für sozialwissenschaftliche Forschung der Freien Universität Berlin, vol. 79), Opladen 1997.

Impekoven, Holger: *Die Alexander von Humboldt-Stiftung und das Ausländerstudium in Deutschland 1925–1945. Von der "geräuschlosen Propaganda" zur Ausbildung der "geistigen Wehr" des "Neuen Europa"* (= Internationale Beziehungen. Theorie und Geschichte, vol. 9), Göttingen 2013.

Internationaler Militärgerichtshof Nürnberg (ed.): *Der Prozeß gegen die Hauptkriegsverbrecher vor dem Internationalen Militärgerichtshof, Nürnberg 14. November 1945–1. Oktober 1946*, vol. XX, *Verhandlungsniederschriften 30. Juli 1946–10. August 1946*, Nuremberg 1948.

Jeschonnek, Friedrich/Dieter Riedel/William Durie: *Alliierte in Berlin 1945–1994. Ein Handbuch zur Geschichte der militärischen Präsenz der Westmächte*, Berlin 2002.

Johnson, Edgar N.: "The American Occupation of Austria," in: *Nebraska History*, vol. 26 (1945), pp. 201–210.

Johnson, Edgar N./John Dean Bickford: "The Contemplated Anglo-German Alliance: 1890–1901," in: *Political Science Quarterly*, vol. 42, no. 1 (March 1927), pp. 1–57.

Jordan, Karl: review of: Edgar Nathaniel Johnson, *The Secular Activities of the German Episcopate, 919–1024*, Lincoln, Nebraska, 1932, in: *Deutsche Literaturzeitung*, 1933, no. 50, cols. 2378–2380.

Kahn, Arthur D.: *Experiment in Occupation. Witness to the Turnabout. Anti-Nazi War to Cold War, 1944–1946*, University Park, Pennsylvania, 2004.

Katalog der Grossen Berliner Kunst-Ausstellung 1908, Berlin, Stuttgart, and Leipzig 1908.

Katz, Barry M.: *Foreign Intelligence. Research and Analysis in the Office of Strategic Services, 1942–1945*, Cambridge, Massachusetts, and London 1989.

Keesing's Archiv der Gegenwart, vols. XV–XVII, 1945–1947.

Keiderling, Gerhard: "Die Alliierte Kommandantur der Stadt Berlin. Von der EAC 1944/45 bis zum Ende der Viermächteverwaltung 1948," in: *Jahrbuch für Geschichte*, vol. 35 (1987), pp. 565–615.

Kemp, Kathryn W.: *God's Capitalist. Asa Candler of Coca-Cola*, Macon, Georgia, 2002.

Knappen, Marshall: *And call it peace*, Chicago 1947.

Knoll, Robert E.: *Prairie University. A History of the University of Nebraska*, Lincoln, Nebraska, 1995.

Kohl, Ulrike: *Die Präsidenten der Kaiser-Wilhelm-Gesellschaft im Nationalsozialismus. Max Planck, Carl Bosch und Albert Vögler zwischen Wissenschaft und Macht* (= Pallas Athene. Beiträge zur Universitäts- und Wissenschaftsgeschichte, vol. 5), Stuttgart 2002.

Köhler, Henning: "Der Beginn des Kalten Krieges. Fünf Monate wohnte der Geschichtsprofessor Edgar N. Johnson 1946 im 'Wannsee-Hotel.' Er schrieb seiner Frau Briefe nach Nebraska. Die sind jetzt aufgetaucht. Ein Dokument der Nachkriegszeit," in: *Berliner Illustrirte Zeitung. Das Wochenend-Magazin der Berliner Morgenpost* from June 28, 2015, p. 3.

Königseder, Angelika: *Flucht nach Berlin. Jüdische Displaced Persons 1945–1948* (= Reihe Dokumente – Texte – Materialien, veröffentlicht vom Zentrum für Antisemitismusforschung der Technischen Universität Berlin, vol. 27), Berlin 1998.

Koop, Volker: *Besetzt. Französische Besatzungspolitik in Deutschland*, Berlin 2005.
Koop, Volker: *Besetzt. Amerikanische Besatzungspolitik in Deutschland*, Berlin 2006.
Koop, Volker: *Besetzt. Britische Besatzungspolitik in Deutschland*, Berlin 2007.
Koop, Volker: *Besetzt. Sowjetische Besatzungspolitik in Deutschland*, Berlin 2008.
Köpf, Peter: *Die Mommsens. Von 1848 bis heute – die Geschichte einer Familie ist die Geschichte der Deutschen*, Hamburg, Leipzig, and Vienna 2004.
Kraus, Elisabeth: *Ministerien für das ganze Deutschland? Der Alliierte Kontrollrat und die Frage gesamtdeutscher Zentralverwaltungen* (= Studien zur Zeitgeschichte, vol. 37), Munich 1990.
Krause, Scott H.: *Bringing Cold War Democracy to West Berlin. A Shared German-American Project, 1940–1972* (= Routledge Studies in Modern European History, 61), London and New York 2019.
Krieger, Wolfgang: *General Lucius D. Clay und die amerikanische Deutschlandpolitik 1945–1949* (= Forschungen und Quellen zur Zeitgeschichte, vol. 10), Stuttgart 1987.
Krüger, Ingo: *Landhäuser und Villen in Berlin & Potsdam*, no. 3, *Großer Wannsee, Colonie Alsen, Villa Liebermann*, Bremen 2005.
Krumholz, Walter, in collaboration with Wilhelm Lutze/Oskar Kruß/Richard Höpfner et al.: *Berlin-ABC*, Berlin and Munich 1969.

Lange, Gunter: *Otto Suhr. Im Schatten von Ernst Reuter und Willy Brandt. Eine Biographie* (Reihe Praktische Demokratie), Bonn 1994.
Latour, Conrad F./Thilo Vogelsang: *Okkupation und Wiederaufbau. Die Tätigkeit der Militärregierung in der amerikanischen Besatzungszone Deutschlands 1944–1947* (Studien zur Zeitgeschichte), Stuttgart 1973.
Leesch, Wolfgang: *Die deutschen Archivare 1500–1945*, vol. 2, *Biographisches Lexikon*, Munich, London, New York, and Paris 1992.
Lehmann, Bernhard: *Katholische Kirche und Besatzungsmacht in Bayern 1945–1949 im Spiegel der OMGUS-Akten* (= Miscellanea Bavarica Monacensia. Dissertationen zur Bayerischen Landes- und Münchner Stadtgeschichte, vol. 153), Munich 1994.
Leonhard, Wolfgang: *Die Revolution entläßt ihre Kinder*, eighth edition, Munich 1985.
Leonhard, Wolfgang: *Meine Geschichte der DDR*, second edition, Berlin 2007.
Leuerer, Thomas: *Die Stationierung amerikanischer Streitkräfte in Deutschland. Militärgemeinden der U. S. Army in Deutschland seit 1945 als ziviles Element der Stationierungspolitik der Vereinigten Staaten* (= Politik und Gesellschaft. Würzburger Universitätsschriften, vol. 6), Würzburg 1997.
Life, 1946.
Lill, Rudolf: *Südtirol in der Zeit des Nationalismus*, Constance 2002.
Lincoln Nebraska State Journal, 1946.
Lotz, François, in collaboration with Joseph Fuchs/Léon Kieffer/René Metz: *Artistes-Peintres Alsaciens de jadis et de naguère (1880–1982)*, Kaysersberg 1987.
Lüdicke, Lars: "Vom Brennpunkt der Welt. Briefe von Edgar N. Johnson über Berlin im Jahr 1946" (review of: *Fünf Monate in Berlin. Briefe von Edgar N. Johnson aus dem Jahre 1946*, eds. Werner Breunig/Jürgen Wetzel [= Schriftenreihe des Landesarchivs Berlin, vol. 18], Munich 2014), in: *Frankfurter Allgemeine Zeitung* from May 5, 2015, p. 6.
Ludwig-Maximilians-Universität München. Verzeichnis der Vorlesungen Winter-Halbjahr 1927/28, Munich 1927.

Maginnis, John J.: *Military Government Journal. Normandy to Berlin*, ed. Robert A. Hart, Amherst, Massachusetts, 1971.
Mai, Gunther: *Der Alliierte Kontrollrat in Deutschland 1945–1948. Alliierte Einheit – deutsche Teilung?* (= Quellen und Darstellungen zur Zeitgeschichte, vol. 37), Munich 1995.
Marquardt-Bigman, Petra: *Amerikanische Geheimdienstanalysen über Deutschland 1942–1949* (= Studien zur Zeitgeschichte, vol. 45), Munich 1995.

Mauch, Christof: *Schattenkrieg gegen Hitler. Das Dritte Reich im Visier der amerikanischen Geheimdienste 1941–1945*, Stuttgart 1999.

Mitchell, Americus: *Mitchell and Related Families*, Kilmarnock, Virginia, 1984.

Mommsen, Wolfgang A.: "Ernst Posner, Mittler zwischen deutschem und amerikanischem Archivwesen. Zu seinem 75. Geburtstag," in: *Der Archivar*, vol. 20 (1967), no. 3, cols. 217–230.

Müller, Tim B.: "Die gelehrten Krieger und die Rockefeller-Revolution. Intellektuelle zwischen Geheimdienst, Neuer Linken und dem Entwurf einer neuen Ideengeschichte," in: *Geschichte und Gesellschaft*, no. 2007/33,2, pp. 198–227.

Murphy, Robert: *Diplomat among Warriors*, Garden City, New York, 1964.

Neiman, Gilbert: "Lazarus Laughs," in: *Accent. A Quarterly of New Literature*, vol. 6, no. 1 (Fall 1945), pp. 13–22.

Nevada State Journal, 1946.

New York Herald Tribune, European Edition, 1946.

Oberreuter, Heinrich/Jürgen Weber (eds.): *Freundliche Feinde? Die Alliierten und die Demokratiegründung in Deutschland* (= Akademiebeiträge zur politischen Bildung, vol. 29), Munich and Landsberg am Lech 1996.

Office of Military Government U. S. Berlin District (ed.): *Six Months Report, 4 July 1945–3 January 1946*, Berlin 1946.

Office of Military Government U. S. Berlin District (ed.): *Six Months Report, 4 January–3 July 1946*, Berlin 1946.

Office of Military Government Berlin Sector (ed.): *Six Months Report, 4 July 1946 to 1 January 1947*, Berlin 1947.

Office of Military Government U. S. Sector, Berlin (ed.): *A Four Year Report, July 1, 1945–September 1, 1949*, Berlin 1949.

Official Army Register, 1945/1946/1947.

OMGUS-Handbuch. Die amerikanische Militärregierung in Deutschland 1945–1949, ed. Christoph Weisz (= Quellen und Darstellungen zur Zeitgeschichte, vol. 35), Munich 1994.

OMGUS Observer, 1946.

Otto, Martin: "Ulrich Biel (1907–1996) – graue Eminenz der (West-)Berliner Politik. Eine erste biografische Annäherung," in: *Berlin in Geschichte und Gegenwart. Jahrbuch des Landesarchivs Berlin 2011*, pp. 285–304.

Otto, Martin: *"Ein stiller Diplomat." Ulrich E. Biel im Gespräch über die Berliner Nachkriegspolitik* (= Ernst-Reuter-Hefte, no. 8), Berlin 2017.

Padover, S. K./L. F. Gittler/P. R. Sweet: "The Political Situation in Aachen," in: *Propaganda in War and Crisis. Materials for American Policy*, edited with an introduction by Daniel Lerner, New York 1951 (Reprint 1972), pp. 434–456.

Panton, Kenneth J.: *Historical Dictionary of London* (= Historical Dictionaries of Cities of the World, no. 11), Lanham, Maryland, and London 2001.

Personenstand der Ludwig-Maximilians-Universität München. Winter-Halbjahr 1927/28, Munich 1928.

Pfetsch, Frank R.: "Die Verfassungspolitik der westlichen Besatzungsmächte in den Ländern nach 1945. Oktroyierte Systemübertragung oder eigenständiger demokratischer Neubeginn?", in: *Aus Politik und Zeitgeschichte. Beilage zur Wochenzeitung Das Parlament*, 22/1986, pp. 3–17.

Pfetsch, Frank R., in collaboration with Werner Breunig/Wolfgang Kringe: *Ursprünge der Zweiten Republik. Prozesse der Verfassungsgebung in den Westzonen und in der Bundesrepublik*, Opladen 1990.

Pollock, James K.: *Besatzung und Staatsaufbau nach 1945. Occupation Diary and Private Correspondence 1945–1948*, ed. Ingrid Krüger-Bulcke (= Biographische Quellen zur deutschen Geschichte nach 1945, vol. 14), Munich 1994.

Poltorak, Arkadi: *Nürnberger Epilog*, fifth edition, Berlin 1988.

Protokoll des Vereinigungsparteitages der Sozialdemokratischen Partei Deutschlands (SPD) und der Kommunistischen Partei Deutschlands (KPD) am 21. und 22. April 1946 in der Staatsoper "Admiralspalast" in Berlin, Berlin 1946.

Rathkolb, Oliver (ed.): *Gesellschaft und Politik am Beginn der Zweiten Republik. Vertrauliche Berichte der US-Militäradministration aus Österreich 1945 in englischer Originalfassung*, Vienna, Cologne, and Graz 1985.

Register of the Department of State, 1946/1948/1950.

Reichsgesetzblatt, Teil I, 1933.

Reif, Janin/Horst Schumacher/Lothar Uebel: *Schwanenwerder. Ein Inselparadies in Berlin*, Berlin 2000.

Reno Evening Gazette, 1946.

Rhein-Neckar-Zeitung, 1946.

Ribbe, Wolfgang: *Berlin 1945–2000. Grundzüge der Stadtgeschichte* (= Kleine Schriftenreihe der Historischen Kommission zu Berlin, no. 6), Berlin 2002.

Robichon, Jacques/J. V. Ziegelmeyer: *L'affaire de Berlin 1945–1959* (L'air du temps), ninth edition, Paris 1959.

Rodnick, David: *Postwar Germans. An Anthropologist's Account*, New Haven, Connecticut, 1948.

Rupieper, Hermann-Josef: *Die Wurzeln der westdeutschen Nachkriegsdemokratie. Der amerikanische Beitrag 1945–1952*, Opladen 1993.

Sammlung der Länderratsgesetze (LRGS), n. p. and n. d.

SBZ-Handbuch. *Staatliche Verwaltungen, Parteien, gesellschaftliche Organisationen und ihre Führungskräfte in der Sowjetischen Besatzungszone Deutschlands 1945–1949*, on behalf of the Arbeitsbereich Geschichte und Politik der DDR at the University of Mannheim and the Institut für Zeitgeschichte Munich, eds. Martin Broszat/Hermann Weber, Munich 1990.

Schertz, Georg: "Schwanenwerder. Eine Insel im Spiegelbild der Geschichte," in: *Berlin in Geschichte und Gegenwart. Jahrbuch des Landesarchivs Berlin 2005*, pp. 209–223.

Scheurig, Bodo: *Verräter oder Patrioten. Das Nationalkomitee "Freies Deutschland" und der Bund Deutscher Offiziere in der Sowjetunion 1943–1945*, Berlin and Frankfurt am Main 1993.

Schivelbusch, Wolfgang: *Vor dem Vorhang. Das geistige Berlin 1945–1948*, Munich and Vienna 1995.

Schivelbusch, Wolfgang: *In a Cold Crater. Cultural and Intellectual Life in Berlin, 1945–1948*, trans. Kelly Barry (= Weimar and Now. German Cultural Criticism, 18), Berkeley and Los Angeles, California, and London 1998.

Schmidt, Klaus: *Die Brandnacht. Dokumente von der Zerstörung Darmstadts am 11. September 1944*, third edition, Darmstadt 1964.

Schmidt, Wolfgang: *Vom Feind zum Partner. Amerikanische Deutschlandpolitik von 1944 bis 1949*, Bonn 1996.

Schnakenberg, Ulrich: *Democracy-building. Britische Einwirkungen auf die Entstehung der Verfassungen Nordwestdeutschlands 1945–1952* (= Veröffentlichungen der Historischen Kommission für Niedersachsen und Bremen, 237), Hannover 2007.

Scholz, Friedrich: *Berlin und seine Justiz. Die Geschichte des Kammergerichtsbezirks 1945 bis 1980*, Berlin and New York 1982.

Schwarz, Max: *MdR. Biographisches Handbuch der Reichstage*, Hannover 1965.

Semler, Daniel: *Brigitte Helm. Der Vamp des deutschen Films*, Munich 2008.

SMAD-Handbuch. Die Sowjetische Militäradministration in Deutschland 1945–1949, on behalf of the Gemeinsame Kommission zur Erforschung der neuesten Geschichte der deutsch-russischen Beziehungen, eds. Horst Möller/Alexandr O. Tschubarjan in collaboration with Wladimir P. Koslow/Sergei W. Mironienko/Hartmut Weber, Munich 2009.

Smith, Bradley F.: *The Shadow Warriors. O. S. S. and the Origins of the C. I. A.*, New York 1983.

Smith, Jean E.: *Der Weg ins Dilemma. Preisgabe und Verteidigung der Stadt Berlin*, Berlin 1965.

Smith, Jean E.: *Lucius D. Clay. An American Life*, New York 1990.

Sonnenstuhl, Burkhardt (ed.): *Prominente in Berlin-Wannsee und ihre Geschichten*, Berlin 2006.

Spandauer Volksblatt, 1946.

Speculum, 1946.

Spencer, K. A.: *Flycatcher. Memoirs of an amateur entomologist*, The Hague 1992.

Städte-Ordnung für die sechs östlichen Provinzen der Preußischen Monarchie vom 30. Mai 1853, in: *Gesetz-Sammlung für die Königlichen Preußischen Staaten*, 1853, pp. 261–290.

Stadtoberhäupter. Biographien Berliner Bürgermeister im 19. und 20. Jahrhundert, ed. Wolfgang Ribbe (= Berlinische Lebensbilder, vol. 7), Berlin 1992.

Steege, Paul: review of*: Fünf Monate in Berlin. Briefe von Edgar N. Johnson aus dem Jahre 1946*, eds. Werner Breunig/Jürgen Wetzel (= Schriftenreihe des Landesarchivs Berlin, vol. 18), Munich 2014, in: *The English Historical Review*, vol. 131, no. 551 (August 2016), pp. 959–961.

Steger, Bernd: "General Clays Stabskonferenzen und die Organisation der amerikanischen Militärregierung in Deutschland. Die 'Clay-Minutes' als historische Quelle," in: *Vierteljahrshefte für Zeitgeschichte*, vol. 27 (1979), pp. 113–130.

Steininger, Rolf: *Südtirol im 20. Jahrhundert. Vom Leben und Überleben einer Minderheit*, Innsbruck and Vienna 1997.

Stiefel, Ernst C./Frank Mecklenburg: *Deutsche Juristen im amerikanischen Exil (1933–1950)*, Tübingen 1991.

Stivers, William/Donald A. Carter: *The City Becomes a Symbol. The U. S. Army in the Occupation of Berlin, 1945–1949* (= Army Historical Series, CMH Pub 45-4-1), Washington, D. C., 2017.

Sträßner, Matthias: *Der Dirigent, der nicht mitspielte. Leo Borchard 1899–1945* (= Schriften der Gedenkstätte Deutscher Widerstand, Reihe A: Analysen und Darstellungen, vol. 9), Berlin 2017.

Sträßner, Matthias: "Chefdirigent für hundert Tage. Wie das Besatzungslastenamt in Berlin 1952 den Status des erschossenen Philharmoniker-Dirigenten Leo Borchard (1899–1945) zu bewerten versuchte," in: *Berlin in Geschichte und Gegenwart. Jahrbuch des Landesarchivs Berlin 2017*, pp. 211–229.

Stuttgarter Zeitung, 1946.

Suhr, Susanne: "Biographische Einleitung," in: *Otto Suhr. Eine Auswahl aus Reden und Schriften*, with a biographical introduction by Susanne Suhr, preface by Ernst Fraenkel, Tübingen 1967, pp. 3–50.

Tägliche Rundschau, 1946.

Telegraf, 1946.

Tent, James F.: *Mission on the Rhine. Reeducation and Denazification in American-Occupied Germany*, Chicago and London 1982.

The American Historical Review, 1919/1942/1946.

The American Journal of Sociology, 1921.

The Atlanta Constitution, 1923.

The Berlin Sentinel, 1945.

The Christian Science Monitor, 1946.

The Grooper, 1946.

The New York Times, 1919/1922/1923/1924/1943/1945/1946.

The Papers of General Lucius D. Clay. Germany, 1945–1949, vol. 1, ed. Jean Edward Smith, a Publication of the Institute of German Studies at Indiana University supported by the Volkswagen Foundation, Bloomington and London 1974.

The Stars and Stripes, European Edition, 1946.

The Washington Post, 1946/1952/1988.

Thompson, James Westfall/Edgar Nathaniel Johnson: *An Introduction to Medieval Europe, 300–1500*, New York 1937.

25 Jahre Theater in Berlin. Theaterpremieren 1945–1970, with a foreword by Friedrich Luft, edited on behalf of the Senate of Berlin, eds. Hans J. Reichhardt/Joachim Drogmann/Helmut Rosenthal/Hanns U. Treutler (= Schriftenreihe zur Berliner Zeitgeschichte, vol. 7), Berlin 1972.

Uhlitz, Manfred: review of: *Fünf Monate in Berlin. Briefe von Edgar N. Johnson aus dem Jahre 1946*, eds. Werner Breunig/Jürgen Wetzel (= Schriftenreihe des Landesarchivs Berlin, vol. 18), Munich 2014, in: *Mitteilungen des Vereins für die Geschichte Berlins*, vol. 114, no. 4 (October 2018), pp. 359f.

Um ein antifaschistisch-demokratisches Deutschland. Dokumente aus den Jahren 1945–1949, eds. Ministerium für Auswärtige Angelegenheiten der DDR/Ministerium für Auswärtige Angelegenheiten der UdSSR, Berlin 1968.

UNRRA. The History of the United Nations Relief and Rehabilitation Administration, prepared by a special staff under the direction of George Woodbridge, vol. I, New York 1950.

Vazansky, Alexander: review of: *Fünf Monate in Berlin. Briefe von Edgar N. Johnson aus dem Jahre 1946*, eds. Werner Breunig/Jürgen Wetzel (= Schriftenreihe des Landesarchivs Berlin, vol. 18), Munich 2014, in: *Jahrbuch für die Geschichte Mittel- und Ostdeutschlands*, vol. 61 (2015), pp. 468–471.

Views and Facts of Berlin. As seen through the eyes of the American soldier and intended for the folks and friends at home, n. p. and n. d.

Vorläufige Verfassung von Groß-Berlin, annotated by Dr. Haas, Treasurer of Greater Berlin, revised fourth edition, Berlin 1947.

Vorwärts, 1946.

Waibel, Dieter: *Von der wohlwollenden Despotie zur Herrschaft des Rechts. Entwicklungsstufen der amerikanischen Besatzung Deutschlands 1944–1949* (= Beiträge zur Rechtsgeschichte des 20. Jahrhunderts, 15), Tübingen 1996.

Weber, Hermann/Andreas Herbst: *Deutsche Kommunisten. Biographisches Handbuch 1918 bis 1945*, revised and greatly expanded second edition, Berlin 2008.

Welt und Wort. Literarische Monatsschrift, 1946.

Weniger, Kay: *Das große Personenlexikon des Films*, vol. 3, *F–H*, Berlin 2001.

Who's who in CIA. Ein biographisches Nachschlagewerk über 3000 Mitarbeiter der zivilen und militärischen Geheimdienstzweige der USA in 120 Staaten, ed. Julius Mader, Berlin 1968.

Willoughby, John: *Remaking the Conquering Heroes. The Social and Geopolitical Impact of the Post-War American Occupation of Germany*, New York and Basingstoke 2001.

Winks, Robin W.: *Cloak & Gown. Scholars in the Secret War, 1939–1961*, New York 1987.

Wistrich, Robert: *Wer war wer im Dritten Reich. Anhänger, Mitläufer, Gegner aus Politik, Wirtschaft, Militär, Kunst und Wissenschaft*, Munich 1983.

Ziegler, Donald J.: *Prelude to Democracy. A Study of Proportional Representation and the Heritage of Weimar Germany, 1871–1920* (= University of Nebraska Studies, New Series no. 20), Lincoln, Nebraska, 1958.

Ziemke, Earl F.: *The U. S. Army in the Occupation of Germany, 1944–1946* (Army Historical Series), Washington, D. C., 1975.

Zur Archäologie der Demokratie in Deutschland. Analysen politischer Emigranten im amerikanischen Geheimdienst, vol. 1, *1943–1945*, ed. Alfons Söllner, Frankfurt am Main 1982.

Zur Archäologie der Demokratie in Deutschland, vol. 2, *Analysen von politischen Emigranten im amerikanischen Außenministerium 1946–1949*, ed. Alfons Söllner, Frankfurt am Main 1986.

3. Internet

http://bombsight.org/#15/51.5050/-0.0900.

http://campus.usal.es/~alfaqueque/pdf/exponuremberg.pdf.

http://volweb.utk.edu/~wpcsws/wp-content/uploads/2013/04/2004-Alexander-Richard-Part-II.pdf.

http://www.berlinbrats.org/pdfs/46Guide.pdf.

http://www.cityofjerseycity.org/hague/index.shtml.

http://www.culturedandcompetentteacher.com/nashville-and-peabody-1914-1924.html.

http://www.digam.net/index.php?page=10&lput=632.

http://www.fr.de/politik/zeitgeschichte/zeitgeschichte/internierungslager-mit-eigener-zeitung-und-universitaet-a-1199998.

http://www.gallagherstory.com/ww2/chapter11.html.

http://www.medievalacademy.org/.

http://www.norwayheritage.com/p_ship.asp?sh=mont6.

http://www.sehepunkte.de/2015/07/26908.html.

http://www.shipscribe.com/usnaux/ww1/ships/gen-goet.htm.

http://www.skylighters.org/special/cigcamps/.

http://www.sonnenberg-verein.de/.

http://www.theberlinobserver.com/archive/1946V2/V2_N13_Mar_30.pdf.

http://www.usarmygermany.com/School_Comd/USAREUR_SchoolCommand.htm.

https://legacy.lib.utexas.edu/taro/utcah/02351/cah-02351.html.

https://news.harvard.edu/gazette/story/2010/09/angeliki-e-laiou/.

https://vimeo.com/12266425.

https://www.amazon.com/gp/customer-reviews/RC115REABPFUX/ref=cm_cr_arp_d_rvw_ttl?ie=UTF8&ASIN=3486735667.

https://www.culver.org/about/the-culver-story/our-foundation.

https://www.dar.org/national-society/about-dar/dar-history.

https://www.frick.org/.

https://www.history.navy.mil/research/histories/ship-histories/danfs/g/george-w-goethals.html.

https://www.hollandamerica.com/blog/topics/news/next-signature-class-ship-to-be-named-ms-nieuw-amsterdam/.

https://www.hsozkult.de/publicationreview/id/rezbuecher-24187.

https://www.ibdb.com/broadway-production/antigone-1773.

https://www.ibdb.com/broadway-production/hamlet-1751.

https://www.lib.uchicago.edu/e/scrc/findingaids/view.php?eadid=ICU.SPCL.ENJOHNSON.

https://www.moma.org/.

https://www.winstonchurchill.org/resources/speeches/1946-1963-elder-statesman/the-sinews-of-peace/.

https://www2.gwu.edu/~erpapers/myday/displaydoc.cfm?_y=1946&_f=md000267.

Index of Names